THE PUEBLO CHILDREN OF THE EARTH MOTHER

VOLUME I

Thomas E. Mails

MARLOWE & COMPANY
NEW YORK

To my wife, Lisa,
my daughter, Allison,
and my sons, Ryan and Andrew

Published by
Marlowe & Company
841 Broadway, Fourth Floor
New York, NY 10003

DESIGNED BY LAURENCE ALEXANDER

Library of Congress Cataloging-in-Publication Data
Mails, Thomas E.
    Pueblo children of the earth mother / by Thomas E. Mails.
        p.   cm.
    Originally published: Garden City, N.Y. : Doubleday, 1983.
    Includes bibliographical references and index.
    ISBN 1-56924-669-6
    1. Pueblo Indians.   I. Title.
    E99.P9M225   1993
    978.9'004974—dc21   98-27441
                                                      CIP

Acknowledgments

I have many to thank for their help and encouragement in this consuming project. Some who must remain nameless assisted me over several years in accumulating data about the Pueblos, and particularly about their dances. Except on those occasions where photography was permitted, in no instance did I record any information while on a pueblo. The data were compiled from memory after I left the dance and the pueblo, and accordingly they were flawed to some extent. They represent the best I could do under the circumstances. My wife, Lisa, merits particular thanks. She has been enormously helpful in every aspect of preparation, besides giving me constant encouragement and helpful advice.

I wish also to thank Dr. Carl S. Dentzel, former Director, now deceased, and the entire staff of the Southwest Museum, Los Angeles; Dr. Patrick T. Houlihan, Director, and the Heard Museum, Phoenix; Arthur Olivas, Curator of Photographic Collections, Museum of New Mexico, Santa Fe; Byron Harvey, who so graciously permitted me to examine the Harvey Collection while it was still housed at the Grand Canyon; Kathleen Whitaker Bennett, former Head Curator, Museum of Man, San Diego; Dr. Charles DiPeso, Director, the Amerind Foundation, Inc., Dragoon Wells, Arizona; the staff of the library, University of California at Riverside; and the authors of the thousands of books and articles that provided the data needed to compile my own account.

Finally, I thank Paul M. Daniell, of the Regency Gallery, Atlanta, Georgia, for his personal interest in the book, and in the Pueblo art, and for his constant and enthusiastic support. There are also those numerous Pueblo friends who have urged me to produce *The Pueblo Children of the Earth Mother* in the belief that it will make a worthwhile contribution to all those who are anxious to know more fully the story of the Anasazi.

THOMAS E. MAILS
Elsinore, California

Books on Native America by Thomas E. Mails:

THE MYSTIC WARRIORS OF THE PLAINS

THE PEOPLE CALLED APACHE

THE PUEBLO CHILDREN OF THE EARTH MOTHER, VOLUMES 1 AND 2

DOG SOLDIERS, BEAR MEN AND BUFFALO WOMEN

SUNDANCING AT ROSEBUD AND PINE RIDGE

THE CHEROKEE PEOPLE

SECRET NATIVE AMERICAN PATHWAYS

FOOLS CROW

FOOLS CROW, WISDOM AND POWER

HOTEVILLA

CONTENTS

Preface

The Pueblo Indians living in Arizona and New Mexico are a remarkable people. For more than two thousand years they and their ancestors, the Anasazi, have walked the centuries warily, finding peace with the spirits to which they reverently entrust themselves, overcoming incredible hardships, tilling their beloved soil as part of a ritual of life, creating ingenious art and architecture, working hard and venerating tranquillity, and seldom turning to wrath or rebellion. The Pueblos have also retained more of their traditional ways than any native peoples in North America. In both the topographical and human landscapes they have changed the least. Because of this, the Pueblo Indians provide a unique doorway through which an observer can step directly into unbroken history.

My telling of the Anasazi and Pueblo story in words and pictures has required two large and detailed volumes:

Volume I describes the history, customs, and accomplishments of the Neighbors of the Anasazi; the Basketmaker Anasazi; and the Virgin, Chaco Canyon, Kayenta, Mesa Verde, and Little Colorado Region Anasazi.

Volume II describes the history, customs, and accomplishments of the Hopi, Zuñi, Acoma, Laguna, and Rio Grande Pueblo Indians from their beginnings to the present.

Except for studies of a few Anasazi ruins, the color plates are portrayals of present-day Pueblo Indians. My purpose in this is twofold: to provide a constant reminder of the firm connection between the living Pueblos and their Anasazi ancestors, and also to emphasize the brilliant and symbolic color that has attended the culture throughout its history.

List of Color Plates

All color plates and drawings are original works of art by the author.

INTRODUCTION

While it is hard to imagine today, the Spaniards who entered the Southwest in the sixteenth century cared little about the cultures of the native peoples they encountered. Instead they searched for gold, property, and slaves. Explorers came upon great ruins and thriving villages, but thought them worthy of no more than passing mention. The early Mexicans and Americans who followed the Spanish did about the same, being far more concerned with their own precarious future than they were with supposed primitives of little consequence.

Not until the end of the 1800s did views begin to change. Various world conditions and Charles Darwin's theory of evolution combined to bring about a new interest in the story of mankind as a whole, and no more promising area for field research was available than the southwestern part of North America. American explorers, government surveyors, and private citizens entered the region and quickly returned with such glowing reports that U.S. government and private eastern museums sponsored repeated expeditions to the Southwest to gather information and to collect such artifacts as were available.

Their earliest efforts were spent in southern Arizona territory. Then, when the great cliff ruins of Mesa Verde, Colorado, were discovered by Richard Wetherill in 1888, already whetted appetites shifted quickly northward toward the Four Corners area, where the borders of Arizona, Utah, Colorado, and New Mexico meet, and within a few years hundreds of spectacular ruins were being examined.

Unfortunately, the first archaeologists to work there had little concern for recording the locations and relationships of artifacts. Excavations were indiscriminate and findings were poorly tabulated. Artifact collectors in general were quick to loot where they could. It was a misfortune that continued for twenty-five years or more and resulted in endless assortments of artifacts separated from their essential data. By 1915, however, the portentous differences in many of the ruins had become so apparent that far more attention was being paid to the sites and associations of items found, although a coordination and a chronology of findings were still lacking.

Almost by accident, the summer of 1927 brought to pass a key development. The Pecos Ruin in New Mexico was being explored by Alfred Vincent Kidder, and a group of forty or so avid Southwestern archaeologists gathered there to share their experiences and viewpoints. As they talked, it became apparent that the time had come to formulate a chronological classification of findings. Before the conference ended, they had hammered out a time and information structure known as the Pecos Classification, which, although it has been refined, is still in use by archaeologists today.

It seems they were now able to determine that by 300 B.C., at the latest, several major and minor cultures in what is now the southwestern United States had developed to the point where remains they left behind could, with some assurance, be associated with them through archaeological research. They were identifiable peoples, and could be traced through the various stages of their development from their appearance to their disappearance or merger with another culture.

Two of the major cultures, the Hohokam and the Mogollon, faded from sight by A.D. 1400 or 1500. The third, known today as the Anasazi, never vanished and is recognizable in the Pueblo peoples living today in Arizona and New Mexico.

The makeup of the Anasazi was the primary concern of the archaeologists at Pecos. At the time of the 1927 conference they were beginning to wonder about the relationship of what they believed were two successive cultures who had occupied a common homeland in the Four Corners area: a foraging people designated as "Basketmakers," because they left behind an abundance of basket remains, and a later people the Spanish called "Pueblos" because they were sedentary in nature and lived in permanent stone or adobe villages.

At Pecos the two were arranged in a rough chronological order, as follows:

Basketmaker I	400 or 300 B.C. to 100 B.C.
Basketmaker II	100 B.C. to A.D. 500 or 700
Basketmaker III	A.D. 500 to 700 or later
Pueblo I	A.D. 700 to 900
Pueblo II	A.D. 900 to 1100 or 1150
Pueblo III	A.D. 1100 or 1150 to 1200 or 1300
Pueblo IV	A.D. 1300 to 1598
Pueblo V	A.D. 1598 to the present

Subsequent findings and conferences, however, corrected the Pecos impression that the Basketmakers had been succeeded by later pueblo-building arrivals. Careful examinations of cultural affiliations all but proved that the Basketmakers and the Pueblos were, and still are today, the same people going through successive cultural phases.

Thus a more unifying term for the evolving culture became necessary, and by good fortune the Navajo had already provided it. Knowing that the stone ruins in the canyons they came to occupy after A.D. 1500 were not those of their own ancestors, the Navajo called the builders of the stone dwellings "Anasazi," which means something like "enemy ancestors" or "ancient ones." Having no better name at hand, archaeologists adopted the Navajo term.

Other knowledge that subsequently came to light included the ability to posit the times when different architectural, physical, social, clothing, and pottery styles came into being. It was also discovered that not everyone among the Anasazi did everything at the same pace or time; that while one area clung to old ways, another would be adopting a new material culture and social and religious ideas.

A modification of the Pecos Classification, called the Roberts Classification, came into being in 1935, and it is frequently used by professionals as an alternate to the Pecos order. When it is compared to that of Pecos, it can be seen that Roberts's classification is more descriptive. One can follow the chronological developments simply by interpreting the titles of each stage, which are:

Basketmaker	A.D. 1 to 550
Modified Basketmaker	A.D. 550 to 750
Developmental Pueblo	A.D. 750 to 1100
Great Pueblo	A.D. 1100 to 1300
Regressive Pueblo	A.D. 1300 to 1600
Historic Pueblo	A.D. 1600 to present

Helpful as the Pecos and Roberts classifications have been in permitting the assignment of Anasazi developments to specific periods, it remains that data regarding these cultural stages cannot be assembled in neat compartments. As this remarkable people passed from one period into the next, certain changes did take place, and archaeologists employ these changes to identify the transition. For example, they can say a given custom was not practiced before. Yet certain other customs were continued. They might be polished and reshaped, but they were kept and carried over into subsequent phases. So true was this that it is probable the Anasazi were never aware of phases in the sense that the archaeologist is.

In speaking of progressive periods and the changes used to "mark" the junctures between them, Arthur H. Rohn makes a point that must be borne in mind. He states that whenever change did take place, continuity attended it. Wholesale innovations were infrequent, abrupt changes were rare. Styles were far more often adapted than adopted.[1]

Those not acquainted with how archaeological dates are arrived at should know that three main methods are used in the Southwest: stratigraphic sequence; the Douglass tree-ring, called dendrochronology; and carbon 14 (C-14). Besides these, several newer methods deserve mention.

While pottery, stone tools, and other inorganic artifacts cannot be dated by dendrochronology or C-14, the chronology of inorganic items can be arranged with a relative degree of certainty by stratigraphic sequence, that is, by associating inorganic items with the datable organic items with which they are found in the different layers of building and trash mounds. If a pottery type or sequence occurring near the top of one mound is also found near the bottom of another mound, the higher portions of the second mound are assumed to be later in time, and a chronological sequence is established.

Pottery is the most valuable item in stratigraphic dating,[2] and the Anasazi and their neighbors created astonishing quantities of it, all made with such competence that thousands of pots and of pieces called shards, or sherds, have survived the centuries.

Worthy of praise for its artistry alone, historic and prehistoric Pueblo pottery is avidly sought by museums and collectors the world over. But further, where it was when found, and what was associated with it, can provide many clues about those who fashioned it, and about its diffusion. The archaeologist who finds it and records everything about it and its location can determine a great deal about its cultural affiliations and chronologies. He can see the uses to which the vessel was originally put and consider how those activities were related to the lifeways of the people. Foreign influences can be noted, and adaptations are revealed. With every such discovery, something more is known about how cultures and people changed and progressed over the centuries.

While stratigraphic dating can establish relative dates, it cannot tell the archaeologist how much later one mound is than another. No one can tell how long it took for a given mound to develop. In consequence, dendrochronology provided a welcome answer to the problem.

Dendrochronology, the study of tree rings, is a precise method of dating some woods. It was developed by astronomer Dr. Andrew E. Douglass during research, beginning in 1901, into a sunspot and rainfall pattern related to climate in the past. While examining the concentric rings within the trunks of certain trees such as pine and redwood he discovered that each ring, or sheath of new fiber, represents, normally, one year's growth, and the number of rings shows the age of the tree. Thus the tree is a calendar—and more, tree rings vary in width, being narrow in dry years and wide in wet years, and as a result reveal the differences in rainfall over the lifetime of the tree.

Since trees of the same kind in a given region exhibit virtually identical rings, examination of the bands enabled Dr. Douglass to trace the climate over scores of centuries by overlapping and matching the inner rings of a newly felled tree with the outer rings of one that was felled when it was just a sapling. Continuing this procedure backward or forward in time made it possible to tell when any given tree had been cut down. As Dr. Douglass matched rings from a number of trees used for posts or beams in Pueblo buildings, he was able to construct a master chart, which with the efforts of others now ranges back to 53 B.C.; at the same time he could date the individual beams.

Dendrochronology has some limitations: it cannot reveal when a beam was first put to use, and it does not allow for variant tree growth patterns. But, although it would be 1929 before the historic tree-ring method was linked to the prehistoric period, by 1919 Dr. Douglass had already provided archaeologists of the Southwest with the essential calendar needed to date with accuracy their ruins and the cultural changes. Despite some objections, the method has proven strikingly harmonious and consistent over the years.

With the advent of dendrochronology, archaeologists found that most ruins were less ancient than previously supposed, and that some major advances in architecture and pottery had come to pass in decades rather than centuries, as once thought.

Developed in the 1940s, the carbon 14 test provided archaeologists with another and more precise way of dating finds that extended back in time beyond the scope of dendrochronology. C-14 is a radioactive isotope, or form, of carbon that every living thing absorbs at a steady rate throughout its life. At death, the absorption of C-14 ceases and the accumulated supply of carbon in an organism begins to break down at a uniform rate into nonradioactive carbon. By measuring the rays at any point in time with an ion counter, scientists can determine the extent to which this breakdown has progressed and how long ago the death of the organism took place. The age of wood, shell, bone, hair, dung, and antler, for example, can be measured with a fair degree of precision up to the age of 44,000 years. C-14 dates are accurate to within 200 years or so, and the method works best on substances from 5 to 25,000 years old. Thus it is more valuable in the study of ancient rather than more recent cultures.

Despite the value of C-14, so precise and economical is tree-ring dating that Southwestern archaeologists seldom use the more recent dating methods such as C-14, obsidian hydration, and thermoluminescence. The exceptions are when remains are older than the 2,200-year-old Southwestern tree-ring chronology, when suitable pieces of wood are not found, and when things other than wood must be dated.[3]

Among the newer dating techniques, obsidian hydration is based on the fact that obsidian, or volcanic glass, absorbs water from the atmosphere or the ground in which it is buried. This process of absorption, proceeding from the outside of the stone to the interior, forms a progressively advancing weathered layer that is clearly distinct from the unweathered part of the stone. In the past, it had been suggested that this absorption process proceeds continuously at a uniform rate. If the rate of hydration had been constant, one could determine the length of time that had elapsed since weathering began by measuring the thickness of the hydration layer. Now, however, it is known that the process varies with the surrounding temperature, and with the kind of obsidian involved. Since these factors are variable, obsidian dating can at best be used only for establishing regional time scales.

A comparatively new method of dating is now in use at Anasazi sites. It is called archaeomagnetic dating and is based on the fact that clays contain tiny particles of iron. When pieces of clay are heated to 1,100 degrees Fahrenheit or higher, the iron particles become fluid, the electrons begin to move, and finally they line up pointing to the earth's magnetic field. Since the field is not fixed, the direction the particles point to depends upon where and when the clay was heated. Knowing this, and having prepared charts, an archaeomagnetic specialist can determine, by scientific comparisons, within a few years when the clay was last heated. Therefore baked pots, clay-lined firepits, and burned dwellings are the best sources for archaeomagnetic samples.

Palynology, fossil pollen analysis, is employed to determine changes in plant cover that have occurred in the past, thus enabling researchers to draw conclusions about climatic changes. It produces evidence about the cultural adaptations ancient peoples had to make in response to changes in their environment.

Ethnographic analogy is used to make certain analogies about the ancient

Anasazi. Pueblo groups in the Southwest continue to build structures of ancient type, to produce certain timeless material culture objects, and to practice ceremonies undoubtedly similar to ancestral customs. With information obtained from historic ethnographic studies, certain comparisons may be made to tell us what life must have been like in ages past.

Thermoluminescence is an experimental radiochemical technique used to date pottery. When reheated to certain temperatures, ceramics emit light. Scientists are attempting to correlate the intensity of this light with the time elapsed since the clay was originally fired.

Aerial photography made minimal contributions to Southwestern archaeology until the last decade, when the combination of the helicopter and new photosynthesis and infrared sensor techniques has enabled researchers to make startling new discoveries at Chaco Canyon, Mesa Verde, and Black Mesa.

When all these dating methods are considered, it is clear that the skilled and progressive archaeologist of today does more than find and identify objects. Once a site is discovered, he records all its visible features, identifies its period of occupation, and locates it in relation to natural features and nearby sites. Then, to recover every possible bit of information, he employs every modern technique, using anything from heavy earth-moving equipment to small tools and brushes. During excavation, the archaeologist records everything recovered, using written descriptions, maps, drawings, and photographs. Every movable object is subjected to laboratory analysis, cleaned, sometimes restored, then labeled, classified, photographed, and listed in a file. If the potential of a site is not exhausted, it may be covered over to await further excavation or simply the day when more advanced dating and testing devices are invented. Finally the archaeologist seeks to interpret his findings and to relate them to the overall subject he pursues.

No longer does he do this by himself. Every expert in the multifaceted field of anthropology enthusiastically contributes his skill to the work: ethnologist, botanist, ornithologist, gemmophologist, zoologist, geologist, ecologist, and many others do their part. Objects go out in a continual stream to universities all over America for study. Bit by bit the conclusions come back. Finally the evidence is pieced together, and the overall picture is drawn for an eager and enterprising audience. The contribution can be large or small. In either case the evidence grows and learning is increased.

Amazingly enough, although much has been accomplished, the surface of Southwestern archaeology has only been scratched. Splendid new discoveries lie just around the corner. Although more than fifteen thousand sites have been located in the Southwest, fewer than 50 percent of them have been explored. Moreover, new techniques of science being applied to the sites promise to bring us information that could never before have been obtained. Perhaps the most exciting aspect of all is that 90 percent of our total technical and scientific knowledge has come to light within the past few decades, guaranteeing that we will soon know infinitely more about the peoples and ruins of the Southwest.

Nevertheless, our debt to those whose wisdom, enthusiasm, and painstaking dedication have already, without the aid of most of the scientific tools, reconstructed so much of the Anasazi culture is gigantic—especially when we bear in mind that the archaeologist and his peers have accomplished most of this on their own. The ancient Anasazi left no written records. The living Anasazi know surprisingly little about their ancestors, and even about one another. They are satisfied with their mythological accounts of origins. They resent intrusions, and with some exceptions they could not care less about what the white man wishes to know about them. Information concerning the Anasazi-Pueblos is usually gained in spite of and not because of them.

In Volume 17 of *The North American Indian*, Edward Sheriff Curtis refers at some length to the reluctance of the Pueblo Indians to talk about their religious ceremonies. "Most Indians are loath to reveal their religious beliefs, to be sure," he wrote, "yet with tact, patience, and tenacity the student can usually obtain desired information. On the Rio Grande, however, one meets organized opposition to the divulging of information so strong that at Santo Domingo, most refractory of the pueblos, proclamations have been issued against affording information to any white people and at more than one pueblo priestly avengers have in the past executed members who have had the temerity to disregard tribal edicts."[4]

One who was executed was a San Ildefonso man who, about the year 1913, gave Matilda Coxe Stevenson, an ethnological researcher, information about the Tewa snake worship, especially mentioning the subject of human sacrifice. "Mrs. Stevenson published this information in a New Mexico newspaper and her informant was promptly executed."[5] Santo Domingo, described by Curtis as "the hotbed of all the old ceremonies," is said to have furnished the killing committee to take care of any offenders regardless of the village in question. "It was a group of men from Santo Domingo which disposed of the man who told too much to Mrs. Stevenson."[6]

I don't know whether the killing referred to was ever documented. Perhaps it happened, perhaps it did not. In any event, it is not likely that an informant would be treated in the same way today. The federal law is a little too formidable for that. But informants would be subject to severe censure, and probably ostracism from the pueblo. Beyond this, and whether or not it is so, pueblo officials will claim that any information having to do with secret religious practices that finds its way into print is unreliable, that it is either tainted or totally untrue. The point is well taken. If they ever admitted that some or all of it was true, their secret life would not be secret anymore.

Fortunately, since a vast amount of literature on the subject is already available, I have had no need to seek for more. What has come to me has been freely given, and it in no wise compromises the secrecy of pueblo ritual. Insofar as my work is concerned, the Pueblos can rest easy in the knowledge that only they possess the full truth and can make it effective when ceremonies are performed. The rest of us "see in a mirror dimly," never face to face. At most we know only in part. And that is quite enough.

A few words should be said about procedure. First of all, archaeologists classify architecture as the "greater" material culture object, and other creations as "lesser" material culture objects. Secular and ceremonial artifacts are included in the latter category. I adhere to this approach. Second, my aim is to present an overview of the Anasazi culture from its origin to the present. Thus it is essential to describe the material culture of each region in a way that permits comparisons to be made between accomplishments and development rates. Sufficient descriptions of regional culture objects are given to allow the student to enter every aspect of the greater Anasazi world, and in this wise to imagine what ancient life was like. At the same time, it would be redundant to provide in full the manufacturing methods and specific uses of every lesser material culture object as it is encountered in each region. Many of the objects were identical in form and use. Accordingly, I describe in detail only the unusual items, and otherwise give summary lists for all regions save the Mesa Verde, where manufacture and use is extensively considered. Those who are frustrated by my unembellished lists can solve the problem by simply turning ahead to the Mesa Verde chapter.

Third, it should be pointed out that writers, on the basis of what is known about present-day Pueblo religious customs, often impute to the ancient Anasazi the same practices. I admit that the ever-accumulating data support this technique. But so long as the scholars are forced to speculate about when given rituals actually began and when certain religious paraphernalia were created and used, I think it best to make comments as they are helpful, while reserving the broader ceremonial treatment to the historic period when it became known in detail at Hopi and Zuñi. In this wise, individual imaginations are allowed to play as they will up and down the reconstruction scale until the present day is reached.

When I use the word "Pueblo" with a capital, it usually refers to the modern Pueblo people. When the lowercase *p* is used, it refers to a given village or, in the plural, to villages.

In citing dimensions, I have given metric equivalents for architectural features only, not for general distances or artifacts.

In a way, I place myself uneasily "in the middle" as I present my overview. My hope is to contribute something worthwhile to the professional and to the lay person. Yet the minute details I include for the former may at times prove tedious to the latter, and those places where I omit data will surely vex the professional who specializes in one area or another. Limitations are, however, forever inescapable in published material. The mechanics of size and time, as well as the circumscriptions of publishing costs, cannot be ignored. In the end, an author can only hope that the presentation, such as it is, accomplishes its aim. With some exceptions the data I include are not, in any event, new. In this instance I'll not apologize. The professionals themselves are forced to walk the same road. Virtually every present-day writer cites a plethora of earlier authorities who accomplished fieldwork that is no longer possible.

With some exceptions, those professionals who have access to all the books and articles listed in the bibliography will know they can find my data and vastly more, for the quantity of literature is enormous and still growing. For example, I summarize the Pueblo religious material in a few chapters. George A. Dorsey and Henry R. Voth needed 358 pages to describe only three Hopi ceremonies. Alexander M. Stephen contributed 1,400 pages on Hopi ritual life. Elsie Clews Parsons required four volumes and 1,275 pages to sum up Pueblo Indian religion. Obviously, my offering in the religious sphere touches only the high points. That is true also of my architectural material, for several of the authors referred to herein have reported at great length regarding their finds. Yet the truth remains that the average lay reader has neither opportunity, time, nor interest to search out and read such substantial works. The exceptions who do read them quickly find that professional data are often presented in such complex terms that they are not able to grasp them. However, the problem does not often occur today. Most writings I cite are long out of print and available only in university libraries amply endowed with anthropological literature.

I have avoided for the most part a general presentation of regional developments, opting instead for the archaeologists' own approach, which is to consider individual sites in chronological fashion. This is a far better answer for those who want to measure progress and change and to know exactly what was happening where at a given time. It also features Anasazi accomplishments, many of which were so ingenious as to excite the utmost admiration. I think we will agree that while one has no recourse but to speak in terms of inanimate architecture and artifacts until the historic period is reached, it is really the human beings we want most to know about. It is, after all, the people who built the buildings and crafted the artifacts.

It is not my purpose to treat the modern Pueblos in those aspects where they have become Americanized in manner, for there they have gone beyond the purview of my material.

I will not deny that when a lesser culture (economically, politically, and militarily) of great antiquity is overcome and begins to be absorbed by a dominant culture, it is fascinating to see how the lesser culture responds and to speculate about the final result. This, however, is a study unto itself, and some excellent case studies have already been done. More still is under way by professionals who are better equipped than I am in time and expertise to carry out such studies.

Chapter 1

SOUTHWEST BEGINNINGS

NEIGHBORS OF THE ANASAZI— CULTURAL DIFFUSION

Of all the Indian nations whose descendants live on today, the Pueblos of Arizona and New Mexico seem at first glance to be the least influenced by other cultures. Much of the outside interest in them is precisely because of that. It is profoundly moving to see what appears to be the pure and ancient past still present and unaffected. To walk among the Pueblo villages and people, and in particular to watch the dances, evokes the strangest sensations imaginable. As a result, it is common for writers to attribute to the Pueblo Indians enduring qualities of life and wisdom and a purity of race seldom granted to others.

How much of that is valid and how much exists only in the imagination may never be known. This much is certain, whatever the Anasazi ancestors actually were, and whatever the Pueblo descendants are today, they are in some part the product of neighboring cultural influences that have helped shape their way of life. Not from their earliest beginnings have the Anasazi lived in a cultural vacuum, and they can be appreciated fully only when they are studied in that light.

Many specialists support this. Within the Southwestern area itself, grains of early influence carried over from the Hunting and the Cochise peoples. Next, and more important still to the developing Anasazi, were the Hohokam, Mogollon, Sinagua, Salado, and Cohonina.

Moreover, it is reasonably certain that some of the cultures influencing the ancient Anasazi eventually merged with them to produce a new culture that is, as of now, truly the child of them all.

Most anthropologists believe that the present-day Pueblos are a combination in greater part of the Anasazi of the Four Corners area; in a lesser part of the Mogollon, who may have physically merged with the Anasazi in several regions after A.D. 1300; and to a lesser extent still of the Sinagua, who may have merged with the Anasazi about A.D. 1200 to produce the Hopi. A few specialists even speculate that the Mogollon and Sinagua split over an extended period of time into numerous small groups that joined various Anasazi groups, so that descendants of the Mogollon and Sinagua are everywhere present among the Pueblos today.

Beyond this physical alloy lies the influence of cultures that, while they did not, so far as is known, merge physically with the Anasazi, nevertheless had cross-cultural relationships with them, each to some extent influencing and being influenced in return. Accordingly, any proper study of the Anasazi must include an overview of those cultures that played so important a part in their world.

Mesoamerica, and perhaps even Peru, also had their part in molding the Anasazi. In speaking of the Mesoamerican demise at the hands of the Spanish, one authority states: "Spanish invaders would come and lay waste to the native cultures. But long before then, something of the Mesoamerican tradition had filtered to the distant north, into the wilds of the North American Southwest and as far east as the Mississippi Valley and beyond. There, in attenuated form, many of the customs, rituals, handicrafts, and living patterns of preconquest Mexico found a new birth and vitality."[1]

Another authority declares that, in the Pueblo III Period, "the Anasazi now came under the influence of the so-called Meso-American civilizations, either directly or by way of the Hohokam tradition. It is from Meso-America that the people of the great pueblos obtained the custom of making mosaics, copper bells, and, increasingly, the use of life forms in art."[2] Clarifying this, he adds that during the misnamed Regressive Pueblo Period "both the polychrome pottery and mural paintings in the kivas show a number of new life forms, such as birds, mythological beasts, and masked dancers, which Brew (1944, pp. 242–245) attributes to influence from the Tlaloc religion of central Meso-America. He suggests, further, that this is the source of the Katcina cult among the modern Pueblo Indians."[3]

Ellis and Hammack state that "the concepts, personnel, and categories of rites in Pueblo religion certainly make up one of our most marked evidences of continued prehistoric contacts between Mexico and the Southwest . . . comparisons suggest that the traits were strained less through a net of time than regionally determined at their source and regionally modified after reception . . . our living Pueblo people still are perpetuating on this northern periphery their derivative form of basic concepts once common to all Mesoamerica."[4]

Bearing all this in mind, we begin our study of the Anasazi with a brief look at ancient Mesoamerica, Central and South America to review what their best-known cultures are like.

Since dates become important in such a pursuit as this, it should be noted that whenever we turn to archaeological literature a surprising variation in dates for the Mesoamerican and Southwestern nations occurs. Since I could not cite them all, I selected those dates that seem to make an effective chronology. Thus my dates should be taken only for what they are: possible times.

The earliest pottery found to date in the New World comes from the coasts of Ecuador and Colombia and is dated at ca. 3000 B.C., or nearly five thousand years ago. This would seem like a promising place to begin, but it isn't. The ruins and burial places of the four "Lands of Gold" in Central and South America—southern Nicaragua, Costa Rica, Panama, and Colombia—have been completely looted by native treasure hunters, and in consequence it is almost impossible to date anything with precision. In addition, the trade routes linking the higher civilizations of the north and south led directly through the region, and even if artifacts could be found along the route, it would be difficult to say for certain just what did originate in the Lands of Gold and which of their cultural customs came from Mexico and Peru.

The situation is quite different in Mexico and Peru. While not enough is known, sufficient discoveries have been made to allow specialists to envision civilizations and to speculate with qualified assurance about their cultural diffusions. Maize, or corn, is clearly the most important of the discoveries.

In the late 1940s archaeologists working in the debris of Bat Cave, Catron County, New Mexico, discovered tiny ears of cultivated maize, at least 5,500 years old.[5] Questions arose immediately about where they had come from, for this particular corn required a wild ancestor that was capable of reproducing itself. Never in prehistoric times had corn spread north or west of Anasazi territory, so the obvious direction to look for the ancestor was south. Finally, in the 1960s, archaeologist Richard S. MacNeish of the University of Alberta found the elusive ancestor in a Tehuacán Valley cave southeast of Mexico City. Plants discovered there—including tiny ears of wild corn—dated back to between 5200 and 3400 B.C., and in trash layers above the one containing the tiny wild corn were subsequent deposits bearing progressively larger ears of cultivated corn, with the highest level dating between A.D. 500 and 1000, a total time span of as much as six thousand years!

The conclusion was inescapable: people were cultivating corn as early as the dates of the discovered ears, and society was already evolving into a farming complex. The Indian civilizations of Mesoamerica and North America were founded on corn, and corn itself was a native of the New World, a development from wild plants found only in the Americas. By 3000 B.C. corn cultivation was spreading rapidly throughout Mesoamerica and had already made its way in infant form into North America, offering new possibilities for people to sustain themselves and to develop other skills. Wherever it arrived it became the staple crop, and today corn has become the most valuable crop grown in the United States. Along with wheat, rice, and potatoes, it ranks as one of the four most important crops in the world. Its importance as a culture-diffusing item is overwhelming. It was the principal step in mankind's long climb toward civilization in the Americas, a miraculous transforming power that encouraged sedentary cultures to develop, as is quickly seen in an examination of Mesoamerica and South America.

In 1938 laborers in a brickworks in the upper valleys of Mexico excavated the earliest evidences of Mexico's past, several graceful clay figurines called "the pretty ladies of Tlatilco." Their age is estimated at somewhere between 2,500 and 3,000 years—1300–700 B.C. It seems that the ladies were given to the dead to accompany them on their journey to the other world, and were shattered in what is thought to be a ritual death so as to be able to do so. Shattering set the "spirit" within the vessel free. We will find this identical custom being carried out by some of the Southwestern cultures of North America before A.D. 750.

Excavations done in the Tlatilco area in the 1950s by Mexican archaeologists exposed no religious architecture, suggesting that the pervading religion that came to dominate cultures in later years had not yet evolved. But they did reveal that Tlatilco people grew maize, beans, and gourds and ate game and fish. Ceramic vessels found in graves included duck and fish forms—both popular among the Southwestern Mogollon much later. Vessels also exhibited an esteem for women, suggesting that men had not reached the dominant role they would achieve in the warring cultures yet to come.

Also close by Mexico City is the hulking, round pyramid of Cuicuilco, which might date back to 1000 B.C. Its terrace is 59 feet (18 m) high and crowned by an altar. It is the oldest religious structure found so far in Mexico and Central America, and its existence proves that the religious life of the Tlatilco culture was developing by this time. Between 400 and 300 B.C., lava from the Xitli volcano covered the pyramid, so that its exact details and dimensions prior to the eruption can never be known. However, maize, religious architecture, and broken funerary offerings already existed in Mesoamerica—all of which made their way north and were found among the Southwestern and Eastern cultures of North America, influencing them.

A word of caution before moving on. No matter how keenly interested one may be in cultural diffusion, it should be recognized that several distinguished authorities feel the idea must be approached with care.

In their book *Mesoamerica: The Evolution of a Civilization*, William T. Sanders and Barbara J. Price distinguish between "cultural evolution," wherein culture change is a result of factors engendered by internal process, and "diffusion," which is a response to the stimulus of contact with other cultures. In either instance, they insist, new customs must be integrated with the existing culture in such a way that the continued functioning of the whole cultural system is possible. As a result, new customs, whether the product of diffusion or of evolution, undergo a selective process.

"Selective process" is the key here. The authors believe that it argues in favor of diffusion within a single culture area wherein people live in a similar environment, and against diffusion between culture areas, especially those some distance apart. The greater the problem of establishing and maintaining contact, the more unlikely it is that diffusion would take place. They support this contention by arguing that much of the culture of one area would not necessarily be useful in, or adaptable to, another. As to how similarities do occur in widely spaced cultures, Sanders and Price argue strongly for independent invention as a result of exploiting geographic resources in similar fashion; some material culture items are so useful that "the probability of their multiple reinvention would be high." They do grant that a culture would more easily adopt a custom useful to it when doing so would be easier than starting from scratch. Otherwise, the preference would be to go one's own way without the interference of new ideas—especially those requiring major changes. "The core features of a culture," such as civilization and urbanism, "are not traits or com-plexes that can be readily diffused by casual or even prolonged contact be-tween groups."

The contentions of Sanders and Price are well taken. In fact, they suit the Anasazi situation remarkably well. The Anasazi have been, from the begin-ning, an industrious, ingenious people, quite capable of going it alone for the most part, and discerningly selective in what they have adopted from other cultures. The brilliant scholar Paul S. Martin states that although he was once an avid "diffusionist," he later opted for independent invention by the major Southwestern cultures.[6] Yet there is no question that diffusion had a decided effect upon the Anasazi and has to some degree continuously shaped their lives and views from beginning to end. That, I believe, becomes increasingly clear as their culture evolves, and it is fascinating to see how it happens. I see nothing denigrating in such an admission. On the contrary, it reveals their flexibility and their recognition that one lives best when a continuing attempt is made to be in harmony with the whole of evolving creation.

SOUTH AMERICA

PERU
2000 B.C.–A.D. 1530
PEAK PERIOD: A.D. 950–1530

Because they are so well known, whenever we think of Peru we think of the Inca. But the Inca were by no means the first or the only great culture in preconquest Peru. In fact, they were the glorious end product of a long and slow development of civilization as a whole in the valley of Cusco and neigh-boring areas.

In 1961 it was established by archaeologists that human beings had lived in Peru as early as 8500 B.C., and five successive groups occupied camps along the coast over a period of six thousand years. A distinct line of plant cultivation was under way by 4000 B.C., long before Mexican maize was introduced there. The earliest Peruvian temples and ceramics are dated 2000 B.C.

Sometime after 2000 B.C. (the earliest radiocarbon date so far is 1600 B.C.), Indians living in a northern highland valley of the Andes built a stone-walled town called Chavín de Huantar. Expanding from there, they created the first known Peruvian empire, and in time passed on their material culture, art, and religion to all the peoples living on the coastal plain.

Later, another mountain empire made contact with the people of Peru's south coast and influenced them in their crafts and spirituality. That empire was in Bolivia, and its central city was Tiahuanaco. It flourished from 100 B.C. to A.D. 600, continued for another four hundred years, and then collapsed.[7]

About A.D. 1000 at least two other significant civilizations came into being along the coastal area of Peru. On the south coast the people created a center for weaving and heavy clay pottery, remnants of the former being among the best yet discovered by archaeologists. On the north coast the Chimu kingdom developed and blossomed until the Inca conquered it in about A.D. 1463. Chan Chan was its greatest trading center, and roads spread out from it to all parts of the kingdom. It contained great pyramids and introduced the Peruvian period known as City Builders.

Village headman of modern Cusco. The use of the bowl-shaped hat perpetuates an Inca decree that such headgear be worn to designate the place of one's birth.

Almost all the methods of weaving used today were known to the ancient Peruvian world. Peru's weavers have been recognized for more than a thousand years for the quality of their woven feather and woolen work, and for their cotton fabrics. Ancient weaving was done in stylized repeated patterns, with geometric symbols and figures of humans, birds, fish, and animals in soft reds, browns, and blues complemented by black. The symbols are similar in style to the depictions common to the Southwest cultures, but heavier in execution. It is important to recognize that artistic products without religious significance were virtually unknown to the peoples of early America. Even today, before starting a new fabric, Peruvian weavers pray for God's blessing.

Another Peruvian accomplishment was the irrigation system. The coastal areas were wastelands except for the river valleys, and there could have been no population growth had not the earliest inhabitants made the river oasis fruitful by digging extensive irrigation ditches, one of them more than 435 miles long.

The Paracas Necropolis Culture of 500–100 B.C. brought its dead to sacred burial grounds on the Paracas Peninsula, where they were laid away in caverns. Our knowledge of the culture is mainly due to its mantles made for the dead. The eviscerated bodies were wrapped like mummies in the richest kind of cloth, and folded blankets with embroidered designs were often laid on the chests of the dead. The dead, in the Peruvian conception, were intermediaries between the living and the heavenly powers, in somewhat the same way that the Katcinas are for the Pueblo Indians today.

Fertility and death were central concerns of most primitive religions in Mexico and South America, and nowhere more so than in the Nazca Culture of the southern coast of Peru, which flowered from A.D. 250 to 750. The Nazca fertility cult took on special importance, for the people struggled unceasingly for a few precious drops of salt-free water and against an unrelenting summer sun. Only political unions with other and more productive agricultural regions in later times rescued them from an obsessive concern over sources of food and permitted at least part of their religious orientation to turn in other directions. As one might expect, the same fertility traits are found among the prehistoric and historic cultures inhabiting the arid areas of the southwestern United States.

Because of its faithfulness to reality, its skillful craftsmanship, and its peerless execution, the Moche Culture, of A.D. 200–800, has become one of the best known in South America. Its pottery decorations depicted a happy and earthy attitude toward life, with even the priests being made more worldly and accessible than before. Sculptured depictions of people are astonishingly realistic and well done. In metalwork, the Moche made many important innovations, continuing the already known goldsmithing, but working also in silver, copper, and lead and using the lost-wax method of casting. Bronze was still unknown, but a copper alloy of gold was improvised and used.

At Chimu, in the years between A.D. 1200 and 1463, the Peruvians invented balances for weighing gold dust and jewels. Their metalsmiths knew how to cold-hammer, cast, and plate cups, beakers, mirrors, and earrings, using silver, gold, copper, and bronze. At one time as many as six thousand men worked in the mines to obtain the metals. But, like other Indians of the area, the Chimu did not invent the wheel or the plow.

Archaeologists believe the ancestors of the Inca may have lived in Peru as early as 2,000 B.C., since ceramics are associated with the Incas, and the earliest Peruvian ceramics are of that date. But it was nearly A.D. 1200 when the Inca made their first bid for power in Peru, and only after that was the area forged into a cultural, political, and military unit. One legend has it that the Inca migrated to the Andes from forests in the east, calling themselves "the children of the sun." With them they carried a wedge of gold, which, according to the legend, would one day sink into the earth. At the place where it sank they were to build a city that would serve as the Inca capital. The wedge finally sank around A.D. 1200, and at that spot the city was founded. They called it Cusco, meaning "navel," for they thought it marked the center of the earth. Cusco is situated more than 11,000 feet above sea level. This opulent royal city had served as a vast ceremonial center, with palaces, temples, and government buildings whose exterior walls were starkly barren. It had a cult of sun worship and three thousand Virgins of the Sun. A mighty fortress called Sacsahuamán guarded Cusco, and a superb system of roads linked all parts of the empire with the capital, complete with rest stations and suspension bridges. The city surpassed anything the Romans had ever built.

With the help of their powerful military forces and organized officials, the Inca's power spread slowly as various tribes were conquered. By A.D. 1460, their closely controlled empire extended from the Amazon forests to the Pacific Ocean, and from what is now Ecuador into Chile. It included about half of Bolivia and part of northwest Argentina. It was a kingdom 2,500 miles long, with at least 7 million subjects.

The Inca were subdivided into tribal groups ruled over by the Topa (supreme) king. Inca society was divided into four distinct classes: the ruling class, the nobility, the common people, and the slaves—who consisted of persons convicted of treason in local revolts. A citizen's way of life depended on the class to which he or she belonged. Rulers and nobility wore sumptuous robes and resided in elaborate palaces of stone and adobe, surrounded by luxury. The common people had simple possessions and lived in small houses of adobe, stone, or cane.

The Inca religion involved many rituals and ceremonies and was concerned mainly with guaranteeing a good food supply, curing illnesses, and foretelling the future. Priests used magic to diagnose and treat illness, and practiced trephining with remarkable success. Religion emphasized purification rites rather than spirituality. Animal sacrifices of llamas or guinea pigs were practiced. Viracocha was the Creator and source of all divine power, fashioning the various tribes of mankind out of figures of stone and clay that he had made in Tiahuanaco.[8] He was assisted by the Sun, Moon, Stars, Weather, Earth, and the Sea. The Sun God, Inti, was the divine ancestor of the Inca rulers, and he protected and matured all the crops. The Inca also felt that many objects, animate and inanimate, had supernatural power. Public ceremonies included dancing, and drinking a beer named *chicha* to the point of drunkenness was considered a religious ritual.

The Inca continued to use silver, copper, gold, and bronze in the craftworks common to Peruvians. They also practiced irrigation and grew maize, cotton, potatoes, and beans, raised guinea pigs for food and alpacas for wool, and utilized llamas as beasts of burden. Inca farm tools had copper or bronze edges; digging sticks had metal or wood points. Everyone received a fair share of food and clothing, and careful records were kept throughout the empire to ensure this.

Most children did not attend school but learned by helping their parents in daily activities. However, some girls selected at the age of ten attended a special school at Cusco where they were trained to serve in the emperor's palace, or to be the wives of noblemen. Some officials from the provinces were sent to Cusco to study warfare, history, religion, and the Quechua language. The Inca never developed a written language, but they worked out a system of numbers for keeping records. Numbers were also used as memory aids in reciting Inca history or verse.

Machu Picchu was an Inca citadel in the Andes. This last capital of the Inca was in a region sealed off from the rest of the world until archaeologist Hiram Bingham discovered it on July 24, 1911. Machu Picchu was constructed in the fifteenth century A.D. Sitting 8,000 feet high on the saddle of a mountain, it was a marvel of houses, temples, and ingeniously terraced gardens where topsoil was carried in, basket by basket, and fertilization was practiced with dead fish, manure, seaweed, and vegetable matter. Machu Picchu farmers grew maize, potatoes, cassavas, pineapples, gourds, cotton, tomatoes, lima beans, and peanuts. With few if any metal tools, the builders did earthquake-proof stonework that rivals the best in the world. Some of the granite stones stand 15 or more feet (4.5 m) high and weigh many tons. All this was done without mortar, the stones being cut so precisely in places that a knife blade could not fit between them. Spanish conquerors never discovered this last hiding place of the Inca nobles.

In the 1530s the Spaniards invaded the Inca empire, and after bitter fighting they ruthlessly overthrew most of it by 1533, doing the best they could thereafter to wipe out all vestiges of the culture, just as the Europeans would later do in North America. Fortunately, Inca influences were already spreading northward to other cultures, which would continue to pass on certain of them until they reached the North American Southwest. The various surviving Inca groups organized civil wars and sponsored uprisings until 1569, when at last the Spanish completely broke their strength. As slaves of the Spanish, the Inca population dropped by 5 million persons to fewer than 2 million. But today the number of people who speak Quechua, the Inca language, has revived and they are more than 6 million. Most of these people live in the mountains of Ecuador, Peru, and Bolivia. There are also 1.5 million Aymara Indians in Peru and Bolivia whose ancestors were once subjects of the Inca.

MESOAMERICA

OLMECS
1350 B.C.–A.D. 200
PEAK PERIOD: 1200–400 B.C.

While proof exists that other groups preceded them, the Olmec Indians are the oldest recognizable cultural group in middle America, and they played an important role in the early stages of the ancient Mexican civilizations; related cultures appeared in many places in Mexico. Their way of life lasted from as early as 1350 B.C. to as late as A.D. 200, its peak being from 1200 to 400 B.C. Located at the center of a great trade network, the Olmecs adopted cultural advances from those they traded with, and spread even more customs of their own to other places.

The name Olmec means "Rubber People"; it is derived from their place of origin in the rubber-growing region of southeast Mexico. By 900 B.C. they were well established and exerting considerable influence. Whether they accomplished this by military conquest or by means of persuasion is not known. Actually, we are only now beginning to learn about them; they came into full view only a generation ago, thanks to the work of archaeologist Michael D. Coe of Yale. La Venta, situated southwest of the Yucatán Peninsula, was their capital and ceremonial center, and remains recently excavated near there by archaeologists include altars; mosaic masks; ceramics; jade figures; obsidian weapons; colossal basalt heads, weighing as much as eighteen tons, with partially Negroid features; and perfectly ground concave mirrors of hematite.

The Olmecs venerated the were-jaguar, half child and half feline, linked with rain and fertility; devised a scientific calendar; and developed a system of hieroglyphic writing. An inscribed Olmec stone slab called stela "C" is considered by historians to be America's oldest known dated work, variously estimated as from 291 B.C. or 31 B.C. Some scholars believe the Olmecs to be by far the greatest sculptors in early America. Yet metal tools were unknown to them, and they carved the hardest stones—basalt, jadeite, and jade—with nothing more than stone implements. Exactly how they did that, and precisely how they moved gigantic pieces of volcanic basalt to La Venta from the Tuxtla Mountains sixty-five miles to the west remains a mystery to this day, but both were prodigious feats. Another Olmec creation, sculptures of an elderly man with a full beard and an aquiline nose, provokes no end of discussion and reinforces the fact that some Mesoamerican Indians had facial hair.

Olmec. *Top,* sitting male figure with infantile features. Terra-cotta. Pre-Classic. *Bottom,* offering set of sixteen male figures and six axes. Jade. Pre-Classic.

So far as is known, the Olmecs were the first to make a rubber ball.[9] They were excellent architects and engineers, their cities being religious centers with pyramid-temple complexes and dwelling places for priests, architects, and artists. In San Lorenzo there was an extensive system of water control. The homes of the ordinary people were clustered around the religious centers and near the fields where they cultivated maize and other crops.

Findings indicate that it was an Olmec custom to sever the heads of the deceased. One unearthed body was tightly flexed and laid on its side. The head had been cut off and placed face down in a large orange-colored marine shell filled with red paint. A burial site at Cerro de las Mesas yielded fifty-two pottery vessels, each of which held the skull of a young adult whose head had been severed from his body. Every skull had been artificially flattened during the owner's lifetime, and the fifty-two heads may have represented a mass sacrifice.

Around 500 B.C. a segment of the Olmec people moved southeast from La Venta to a place where, influenced by Olmec customs, a group of people living in the rain forest areas of Chiapas and Petén began to build what was to become the remarkable Mayan civilization, which at its height may have numbered 2 million people.

MAYA
500 B.C. OR EARLIER—A.D. 1540
PEAK PERIOD: A.D. 300–900

The ordinary Mayan family lived in a house that had a palm- or grass-thatched roof and two doors, no windows, and walls of saplings daubed with mud. Boys and young men lived in separate quarters until they were of marriageable age. Peasant houses were clustered in small settlements around temple pyramids that were dedicated to Mayan rain gods—the sun, moon, stars, earth, water, and wind. Yum Kax was the God of Harvest. Each of the gods played a role in the passing seasons and in the growing of crops. Mayan cities were centers for religious festivals, markets, and courts of justice. Priests lived in the cities only for short periods before and during great religious ceremonies. Human sacrifice was practiced by the Maya, but never on a scale equal to that of the Aztecs yet to come.

Much of the Mayan homeland was covered with a dense tropical forest and lay only 200 to 600 feet above sea level. It was infested with insects that bit at every exposed part of the body, snakes, and sand fleas that bored into toes until people were hardly able to stand. When, from 1839 to 1842, the English architect Frederick Catherwood explored Maya country to record its art and architecture, he had to draw with his gloves on, and he twice came down with malaria. Yet he was absolutely enthralled with what he found, and his reports were so enthusiastic that for years people thought he was lying—savage Indians could in no wise do what he said they did. But, if anything, his

Maya. *Left,* whistle, representing Ah Kin Koc, the God of Dance. Terra-cotta. *Right,* warrior figure. Terra-cotta.

work was an understatement, and Mayan intellect, architecture, and art have since won fame the world over. The Maya achieved outstanding success in astronomy and arithmetic and were the only Indians in ancient America to develop an advanced form of writing. For most of their existence the Maya remained a relatively peaceful people, who, as far as is known, had no professional military organization.

Over a long period Mayan religion became an elaborate tradition combining the worship of nature's forces with a sublime concept of deified heavenly bodies and the four directions of the universe, each of which was represented by its own color: yellow for the south, black for the west, white for the north, and red for the east. Even time itself was given a godlike quality. Understandably, the need to propitiate all these gods in season became central to the Mayan religion. The earth was conceived to be a great flat disk resting on a colossal crocodile's back. The sky above it was held in place by the gods, and surrounding the earth there were thirteen heavens and nine hells, indicating belief in an afterlife. Whether or not cranial deformation was a religious practice is not known, but babies' heads were strapped between two boards to elongate the skulls. The practice may only have reflected a Mayan concept of physical beauty. Techniques also evolved to induce squinty and crossed eyes. The skulls and eyes can be seen today in Mayan sculptures and paintings.

Certain of the Mayan priests became exceptional astronomers, who devised calendars and were able to predict eclipses of the sun and moon. They could also follow celestial movements, and they invented a brilliant system of mathematics containing all the elements of modern arithmetic. The priests recorded time on large stone shafts, called stelae, and on altars, stairways, doorways, and wall panels. Astronomical and religious information, as well as dates, was also recorded in folding books made of bark-cloth paper. The people benefited, and the needs of the priests were amply provided for by grateful farming communities.

Guided by priests who told them when to do what, Mayan farmers grew cotton, maize, sweet potatoes, beans, squash, pumpkins, chili peppers, and cacao trees, and they kept stingless bees for honey. Grinding was done with a stone mano and metate (a small handstone and flat grinding slab). The people rarely ate meat, and they domesticated only turkeys and dogs. Farmers had few good tools and learned little about metals. They used the same wooden planting sticks to plant their corn that had been used for centuries. This was the case with the tools of builders too, yet talented stonecutters guided by master architects constructed great, spectacular religious buildings. The Maya never learned to span a doorway with a true (keystone) arch, but used corbeled vaulting that resulted in high, narrow, windowless rooms. Nor did they discover that the wheel could be employed as an aid in pottery, construction, agriculture, or transportation. Curiously enough, the Olmecs had already made clay toys with wooden axles and, for wheels, clay disks, but the concept was never broadened and converted to mature use by the Olmecs or any of the Mesoamericans.

Mayan arts in general centered on religion. Low-relief carvings of gods and religious ceremonies decorated Mayan temples, altars, and the stelae, some of which were 25 or more feet (7.5 m) tall. The designs were, for the most part, crowded together to make a busy surface, but carvers were required by tradition to show in formal religious symbols all the characteristics of the gods being depicted. Painters had more freedom than carvers and were permitted to portray everyday life. They painted two-dimensional scenes on pottery and in frescoes on temple walls. Strong outlines, bright colors, and a complete absence of shadow or perspective were characteristic of their work. Loom weaving of textiles was an important art, carried out by women, and some pieces were done with the most imaginative designs possible.

Mayan sculptors produced a great number of superior creations in stone, terra-cotta, stucco, and baked clay. They also did inlaid work with jade and shell, and many of their achievements were used as grave offerings. Off the coast of the Yucatán Peninsula, the arid island of Jaina became a home for the dead. More than 20,000 Mayans were buried there. Most of the bodies were placed in the ground in a crouched position, in the mouth was often placed a bead of jade, and in their hands were placed small painted terra-cotta statuettes, marvelously detailed and perhaps depicting mythological beings or the station of or activity in life of the deceased. Some of these sculptured statues were unique, not mass-produced as were Chimu grave offerings in Peru. Other Jaina offerings were made partially in molds. An assemblage of the statuettes would portray virtually the entire life-style of the Maya.

An item of some consequence to those interested in cultural influences is the Mayan baked-clay painted plate that underwent "ceremonial death," a hole being bored near the center, before it was interred with the corpse. One such dug up at Vaxactún pictured a priest encircled by a hieroglyphic inscription.[10] Similar bowls have been found in grave sites of the Mimbres Mogollon in the southwestern United States.

In their treatment of the cat demons on the Peruvian burial cloths of the Paracas Necropolis, Anton and Dockstader state that these embroideries "lived on for the next three or four centuries as decorations on the pottery of the Nazca culture. Most of that decoration is supercharged with symbolic ornamentation which never gives an exact picture of the person or thing portrayed, and this has led many scholars to suspect that it may have some hieroglyphic meaning."[11] They believe these were prayers to be conveyed by the dead to the demons or gods.

Mayan architecture is characterized by high stone pyramids, some rising 200 feet (60 m) with small temples on top. Ostentatiously clothed priests climbed steep stairways to the temples, while the people stood in a court below. Generally, when a priest died his temple and monument were not allowed to survive him. These were "killed" by mutilation, and a new temple was erected.[12] The Maya also built low, multiroomed palaces that probably served as sleeping quarters for the priests during fasting periods before great ceremonies, and for storage, receptions, and administration. Religion, pervading life at all levels, was the communal bond that held the nation together.

The sons of chiefs and priests went to schools where they studied history, hieroglyphic writing, astronomy, and medicine. They also learned how to foretell the future. All Mayan children were expected to know by heart the chants that told the history and legends of their people.

For recreation, with strangely serious consequences, the Maya built large stone ball courts, which may also have served as auditoriums, where a game like a combination of soccer and basketball was played. Some of these courts are larger than modern football fields. Using elbows, knees, and hips, but not hands, players sought to drive a rubber ball through an 18-inch (45 cm) hole in a stone ring 24 feet (7.3 m) high mounted on the opponents' wall at either end of the court. It was so difficult that the first score ended the game. Tradition says that spectators vanished the moment a score was made by a player, since it made him winner of their clothing and jewelry.

It is also said that ball courts were always oriented toward the northeast and southwest and stood for heaven and the underworld. The ball in flight represented the passage of the sun. The game itself symbolized the struggle between light and darkness, summer and winter, life and death. Ball courts were not solely Mayan. Toltecs, Aztecs, central Gulf Coast cultures, and others played this sacred game. A relief in the ball court at El Tajín shows the leader of a team, how he receives his consecration, and how, when the game is lost, he is offered up as a sacrifice.[13]

A system of stone-surfaced roads, usually 30 feet (9 m) wide, connected the Mayan cities of some areas. It is assumed that their primary use was for religious processions. Traders also traveled over them, but preferred water routes and canoes. People of the lowlands traded jaguar pelts, feathers, shells, copal incense, lime, flint knives, and the edible hearts of palm trees. In return they received the highly prized quetzal feathers and jade of the highlands, and obsidian, which was used for ceremonial knives. Yucatán exported salt and finely brocaded cottons to Honduras for cacao beans, which the people used as money. William R. Cole, an American archaeologist who in 1956 and later directed an intensive study of Tikal, discovered evidence of extensive flint deposits. He believes that Tikal was a manufacturing center of the flint that was basic to Mayan life everywhere.[14] One find in a Mayan city, under a floor where an altar once stood, was a delicate mosaic plaque of turquoise that once had been mounted on a wooden base. Since turquoise is not, to my knowledge, native to Mesoamerica, it can be assumed that the stones came through trade from the southwestern United States.

The Classic Period of the Maya began about A.D. 300 and lasted until A.D. 900. During this time the Maya produced the arts and intellectual achievements that made them famous. The cities of Palenque, Piedras Negras, Tikal, and Uaxactún grew up in northern Guatemala and southern Mexico. Copán flourished in Honduras.

The discovery in 1945 of a certain Mayan city, whose name was unknown at the time, caused a sensation in the world press. It was given the name Bonampak, which in Mayan means "Painted Walls." It was an ancient seat of the gods to which offerings were brought on certain days. Its frescoes are considered the most important mural paintings of the pre-Columbian era in either of the Americas. They were painted with a fine brush of unknown construction on a ground of lime 1 to 2 inches (2.5–5 cm) thick. It appears they were executed by a group of artists under the supervision of a master artist who planned the work and laid in the outlines. Two-dimensional in character and without perspective in design or color, bodies are often shown in frontal position, heads and feet always in profile. Dignitaries in rich costume are depicted, as are ritual dances, warfare, and the presentation of captives and their sacrifice. A few hieroglyphics are included.[15]

Tikal was a Mayan city unsurpassed by any other. Temple buildings were so tall, some reaching 258 feet (79 m) that the first Europeans to see them, overgrown by the rain forest, mistook them for hills. Tikal's architecture was powerful and austere, made for ritual and contemplation; it was a holy city of great mystery.

In the 900s those Maya living in the south began to abandon their great cities one by one. No one knows why. Some have speculated that the people revolted against the priests because the priests' prophecies failed to come true. Others think that by using the slash-and-burn technique the farmers exhausted the shallow topsoil; they had no methods for replenishing it and letting it lie fallow. Still other explanations exist. At any rate, during the tenth century the cities fell into ruin and remained so until excavations began at Tikal in 1956.

Modern Maya woman.

This was not, however, the end of the Maya. By the early 900s and continuing until 1200, the Maya living in the Yucatán Peninsula and the Guatemalan highlands flowered again and developed a fairly high culture with strong Mexican influences. A warrior group called the Itzá enlarged the Mayan city of Chichén Itzá, called the Mayan holy city, and it became the most spendid city in the Mayan area, boasting even a spectacular round observatory. From here the Itzá ruled much of Yucatán. More secularly oriented than the early priest-rulers, they introduced many new ideas, such as militarism and the worship of Kukulcán (Quetzalcóatl). No one is certain where the Itzá came from, but archaeologists have traced many of their innovations to Tula, a Toltec settlement north of Mexico City. It is thought that the Toltec tribe, driven out of Tula, settled at Chichén Itzá, some 745 miles distant, and created a mixed culture that continued until Chichén Itzá was abandoned at the start of the thirteenth century.

About 1200 a warrior named Hunas Ceel led a successful revolt against the Itzá and established a new capital at Mayapán. This city ruled over a large area until 1450, when its rulers were defeated by a coalition of dissatisfied city states. The people of Yucatán then split into several groups, and Mayan art and learning began to decline again.

Spanish conquerors invaded Mayan territory in the early 1500s and subdued most of the people with little difficulty, although some of the Maya in the interior retained their independence for another century. By the 1540s the job was done, including the burning of the bark-cloth books because they "contained nothing but superstitions and the falsehoods of the Devil." Only three books, each called a codex, survived to let us know what we could have learned were all the books available today.

More than 2 million descendants of the Maya still live in the area where their ancestors prospered. They belong to various tribes, speak the Mayan language, and follow some of the old religious practices. Unfortunately, they know little about the great achievements of the ancient Mayan civilization.

TEOTIHUACANS
150 B.C.–A.D. 800

Contemporary with the Maya by 100 B.C. were a central Mesoamerican people, the Teotihuacans, who built a spectacular, well-planned industrial city in central Mexico, which ultimately housed as many as 250,000 people. It was built on a grander scale than ancient Athens or Rome and was a true city in the present-day sense rather than just a ceremonial center.

Its name was Teotihuacán, which means "Place Where the Gods Were Made." It was ruled by priest-kings, whose temples were set on top of immense earth pyramids faced with carved stone. Dominating these were the magnificent temple of Quetzalcóatl, the Plumed Serpent God, and the Pyramid of the Sun, severe and majestic, standing 213 feet (64 m) high and 722 feet (217

m) wide on each of its four sides. A surprising number of excellent wall paintings have survived the destruction of the city. These were done in fresco technique in the classic Italian style—painted directly on a still-damp layer of stucco. The subjects were gods holding scrolls, shells, and fertility symbols. The Rain God was Teotihuacán's most important divinity.

By A.D. 300, the culture of Teotihuacán had prospered and expanded 650 miles south to Guatemala, where Teotihuacáns were building new trade centers. Several hundred years later, it all ended. Sometime around A.D. 800 Teotihuacán was abandoned. The inhabitants may have fled from the rising and warlike Toltec culture, which would, in turn, be replaced by the even more powerful Aztecs.

Teotihuacán. *Top left,* figurine with tablita-like rectangular headdress. Jade. *Top right,* brazier representing Huehueteotl. Volcanic rock. *Bottom,* Pyramid of the Sun.

ZAPOTECS
1500 B.C.—A.D. 1000
PEAK PERIOD: A.D. 500–1000

Not much has been learned about the origins of the Zapotecs, who basked in the Mesoamerican sunshine for more than two thousand years and reached their zenith between A.D. 500 and 1000. The Zapotecs spread out geographically between the two great powers, Teotihuacán to the northwest and Maya to the east. On Monte Albán (White Mountain) the Zapotecs laid out a temple complex that was awesome in its proportions and architecturally innovative. Repeatedly enlarged and added to for more than twenty centuries, this was their religious center.

The first period in Monte Albán's history was influenced by the Olmecs. Zapotec pottery, which dates back to 1500 B.C., has typical Olmec traits, and the Zapotecs were early developing their own calendar. It was not until the tenth century A.D. that Monte Albán was abandoned, along with the surrounding territory. Probably the Mixtecs drove the Zapotecs from their sacred mountain, because after A.D. 900 the Mixtecs were using it as a burial ground for their kings.

Mitla is the best-preserved ruined city of ancient Mexico. Its original name was Mictlan, "Entrance into the Kingdom of Death," and it enshrined the tombs of Zapotec kings and priests. Mitla was the home of their great prophet, a high priest so sacred it was believed that any commoner who looked upon him would certainly die. It is thought that the Zapotecs and Mixtecs intermingled here. Today there are still islets of Mixtec speech within the regions settled by the Zapotecs, and the massive architecture at Mitla reflects the combination of both cultures. Perhaps the Zapotecs controlled it first, the Mixtecs later. Spaniards called it a city prouder and more magnificent than any in Spain.

MIXTECS
A.D. 600–1494

The Mixtecs prepared the way for Aztec art and science. Their pictographic writings painted on buckskin trace the genealogies of the leading ruling families back to A.D. 692. Mixtecs produced colored pottery, goldsmith work, and peerless bone carvings, all of which were eagerly sought after by other nations. In all Mexico nothing surpasses the richly decorated pottery of the Mixtecs. Uniquely characteristic of their work are three-legged cups, and bowls done in glowing colors made brighter by polishing. Gods or historic personages are painted upon them in two-dimensional form reminiscent of the great Anasazi murals at Awatovi in Arizona—all done in the style of Mixtec pictorial writing.

Monte Negro (Black Mountain) was the home of the oldest ruling group of Mixtecs. Its early pottery can be dated back to A.D. 1000, but it reveals Olmec influences. Most pre-Columbian pictographic writing that has survived comes from the Mixtec cultural area. In A.D. 1494, after years of fighting, the Aztecs overcame the Mixtecs and carried their craftsmen away to work in the conquerors' capital.

TOLTECS
A.D. 650–1200
PEAK PERIOD: A.D. 900–1200

The Toltecs were the dominant people in the central Mexican highlands from A.D. 900 to 1200. They strongly influenced the Aztecs who followed them, and also the Maya of Yucatán. Buildings at the Mayan city of Chichén Itzá closely resemble Toltec architecture and may have been built under Toltec leadership. Aztec legends referred to the Toltecs as ancient heroes who brought civilization to Mexico.

A people using the Toltec calendar lived in Guatemala before the fall of Teotihuacán, and Guatemala may have been the original Toltec home. About A.D. 650 the Toltec leader Quetzalcóatl, named after the Plumed Serpent God, founded their capital city of Tula. Tula is a Spanish corruption of Tollán, which means "Place of the Reeds." Its ruins, just north of Mexico City, contain several pyramids surmounted by temples in the usual Mexican fashion.

Records tell us there was a succession of nine Toltec high chiefs, each of which expanded by conquest the borders of the Toltec empire, in what is now known as Mexico. Proud and arrogant, the Toltec war chiefs built palaces as fine as the temples of their gods. The Toltecs were excellent builders in stone, and their name means "Master Builders," yet they never mastered the arch. They are famed for their brilliantly painted walls and for their system of picture symbols, which can be translated into any language. By good fortune, the Mixtec tribe of southwestern Mexico learned the system, and it is through their painted books that we have obtained most of our information about the Toltecs.

Sometime before A.D. 950 civil war erupted over differences between the ninth high chief, who like the first was named Quetzalcóatl, and the war chiefs. Tula was nearly destroyed. Famine and pestilence followed and for a time checked the progress of civilizations in much of Mesoamerica. When the scourge had passed, others were waiting in the wings to come onstage. Nomadic Mexican tribes gradually overran weakened Tula, and the entire Toltec empire collapsed just before the twelfth century came to an end.

Toltec. Pyramid and colossal Atlantean in Tula.

AZTECS
A.D. 1150–1521

The Aztecs probably came too late to influence the Southwestern cultures significantly, but a study of these people—who were themselves a product of diffusion—will help us to see for its comparative value what diffusion does.

The Aztecs, at first a small and ineffectual group of people living north of present-day Mexico City, began to build an empire that came to number 5 million citizens. They belonged to the Chichimec tribes, and much of their culture was borrowed from the Toltecs and the advanced Maya in Yucatán.

According to legend, the first Aztecs had lived peacefully on an island in a lake until their god, Huitzilopochtli, appeared to them in A.D. 1168. At his command they set out on a pilgrimage to find a certain sign, for when they found it, they would become a great nation. So the Aztecs moved from place to place, settling each time for a few years and then moving on as they searched for the sign. Captured and enslaved by the people of Culhuacan, they escaped to a swampy island in what is now called the Lake of Mexico. Here their chiefs saw a rock with a cactus growing on it, and on the cactus was an eagle clutching a snake in its talons. That was the sign they had sought, and on this site they built Tenochtitlán, now Mexico City, which eventually became an enormous metropolis, the "Venice of the New World," with, some say, nearly a million inhabitants living in flat-roofed, one-story adobe-brick houses.

By 1502 Aztec armies held central Mexico and most of the southern and fertile half of Mexico. Montezuma, also known as Moctezuma, was High Chief in 1504, and his armies conquered the remaining towns in the warm south.

By Montezuma's time the Aztecs ruled an empire that stretched from the deserts of northern Mexico to the tropical forests of Guatemala. They based their civilization on an extensive system of laws, one being that each family had land allotted to it annually by the tribal chiefs and had the right to cultivate it. Another principle was that only a few families, of Toltec descent, could choose the four chief Aztec rulers. Three had to be of noble birth. The fourth, the high priest, had to be a commoner. Religion dominated every aspect of life. Tenochtitlán was built around two great groups of temple pyramids rising more than 100 feet (30 m). Believing that constant human bloodshed was the only way to make the sun rise each day, the Aztecs continually sacrificed victims to the gods by cutting out their hearts. Usually these victims were prisoners of war, and their lifeless bodies were sometimes eaten in ritual feasts. The black god Quetzalcóatl—not white at all as he is so often said to be—had a penchant for human sacrifice, and some sources describe a mammoth sacrifice of eighty thousand victims that took place in Tenochtitlán around A.D. 1490.[16]

The average Aztec family lived in a simple house built of adobe or poles, with a thatched roof. The Aztecs were enterprising and gifted craftspeople. Among other things, the men were wood-carvers, workers in precious stones and gold, and weavers who fashioned robes richly decorated with hummingbird feathers. Women made pottery, wove baskets, dyed fine cloth, and wove beautiful blankets. Priests made leather books, which were either rolled into scrolls or folded in accordion pleats. Some books related, in picture symbols, a thousand years of native history. Unfortunately, Cortés and his soldiers destroyed many of these priceless documents, which could have helped us to know the Aztecs better. Only a few of the books have survived. The Aztecs also made excellent maps, and it is a stroke of irony that the arch-destroyer Cortés used one to help him cross the peninsula of Yucatán.

The Aztecs cultivated maize, fruit, sweet potatoes, squash, peppers, avocados, cotton, tobacco, hemp, vanilla, rubber, beans, copal resin for incense, and cacao beans, which were used to make a chocolate drink. Corn tortillas and chili peppers were favorite foods. The Aztecs had no plows, draft animals, or iron tools, yet with digging sticks alone the farmers produced enough food for their own needs and those of the craftsmen and government officials. A creation worthy of special mention was the Aztec floating gardens, which still exist in Mexico City. Dogs and turkeys were their only domesticated animals.

Trade was extremely important to the Aztecs, who were adept at travel by land and water, and their influence was spread as much by commerce as by war. As the empire grew, conquered tribes had to pay an annual tribute of goods. By this means, rubber, feathers, and cacao came from the lowland regions of Mexico, and gold and precious stones came from the far south. Over a long period, tribute brought enormous wealth into the Aztec capital. Aztec soldiers enforced tribute with bows and arrows, and historians believe they were the first Indians to use swords. Warriors wore helmets, had armor made of cane or padded cotton, and carried shields of rawhide.

Aztec. *Top right,* plumed serpent figure. Basalt. *Lower left,* ceremonial brazier representing maize deity. Terra-cotta.

Education was in the realm of the priests. Special schools trained selected boys and girls for official religious duties. Schools for average children, called "Houses of Youth," taught history, Aztec traditions, crafts, and religious observances.

Aztec architecture was less refined than that of the Maya, yet executed on a magnificent scale. Thousands of craftsmen worked continuously at building, decorating, and maintaining endless numbers of temples and palaces. Stone images of the gods and symbolic carvings stood by the score in the temples and on the plazas around them. The most famous sculpture found to date has been the great sun disk that is now in the National Museum in Mexico City. It is 12 feet in diameter and weighs 22 tons. It has the image of the Sun God at its center and contains the Aztec version of world history, myths, and prophecy.

Vying with the sun disk in interest today is a 15-ton carved stone, a ceremonial monolith of Coyolxauhqui, the Aztec Moon Goddess, discovered in

Aztec. *Left,* Xipe-Totec, God of Spring. Basalt. *Right,* head of Eagle Knight. Andesite.

1979 by electrical workers repairing cables beneath Mexico City's streets. Archaeologists hail it as of major importance in understanding Aztec religious customs. Many other items of extreme value surrounded the stone, including a more primitive statue of Coyolxauhqui beneath it, and work is already under way to build a museum next to the site. Coyolxauhqui means "Rattlesnake on the Face," and Aztec mythology suggests she was the daughter of Coatlicue, mother of gods, and the sister of Huitzilopochtli, the war god. The stone is approximately 9 feet 9 inches in diameter and was probably carved between A.D. 1480 and 1490. It depicts the dismembered goddess with the rattlesnake on her cheek, an elaborate headdress, a belt with a skull to show she is dead, and ornaments on her knees, feet, and arms.

Cortés and his army entered the Aztec capital in A.D. 1519 and were at first welcomed by Montezuma. When the High Chief realized his mistake, changed his mind, and turned against Cortés, war ensued and Montezuma was killed. For a time the Aztec warriors prevailed and drove Cortés away. But the destructive Spanish leader returned with reinforcements, including Indians who hated the Aztecs. He conquered the last of the Aztecs in 1521, and the empire collapsed like a punctured balloon.

Descendants of the once powerful nation live today in small villages clustered around Mexico City. They still speak the original language, but Cortés did his job well, for most of their customs and religious practices are of Spanish origin. They know little about their illustrious past.

As we move now to the great Southwest, it will be useful to summarize what might have diffused northward from Mesoamerica and have eventually been adapted by the Anasazi.

Authorities have suggested the following as probable diffusions:

1. Maize and its cultivation.
2. Religious ideas, including the Sun and Earth cult, the Katcina cult, and the Plumed Serpent.
3. Macaw and other parrot feathers.
4. Pottery as a craft and some decorative motifs.
5. Ceremonially "killed" ceramic funerary offerings.
6. Architecture—limited to Chaco Canyon.
7. Roadways—limited to Chaco Canyon.
8. Irrigation techniques.
9. Copper bells.

More questionable as diffused items are the atlatl (spear-throwing implement) and the bow and arrow. Certain other cultural items came as far north as the Hohokam and Mogollon, but either were not adapted by the Anasazi or were little used by them. The stone inlay techniques practiced at Chaco Canyon and elsewhere are thought to have come from the Hohokam, although the

Chacoans may have received these initially from Mesoamerica. Earl H. Morris found a burial at Canyon de Chelly, Arizona, in which a blue bead had been placed in the corpse's mouth. As noted, placing a bead in the mouth of a corpse was a common practice of the Maya at Jaina.

West Coast Culture. *Top,* Chac Mool, God of Rain. Basalt. *Lower left,* water carrier. Terra-cotta. *Lower right,* hunchbacked figure with flute, standing on a fish with two heads. Terra-cotta.

THE SOUTHWEST

BIG GAME HUNTERS
10,000–5000 B.C.

By 10,000 B.C. or earlier in southern Arizona and extending across the greater Southwest, there once were peoples whom anthropologists have chosen to call the Big Game Hunters. Knowledge of them is limited mostly to what little has been found at "kill sites" where mammoths and other game were killed for food. From tools, spearpoints, and charcoal found in the same strata as animal bones, evidence of stripped carcasses, and refuse from the process of tool manufacture, it has been concluded that the people specialized in the hunting of large game, and that when the game was exhausted around 5000 B.C., died off from other causes, or migrated to other areas, the hunters migrated and disappeared too, perhaps moving to the Great Plains.

COCHISE
9000 B.C.–A.D. 100

Before the Big Game Hunters were gone, a creative people appeared who have been named the Cochise, after the town of Cochise, Arizona, and the Apache chief of that name. They used a wider range of resources than hunting. They dwelt in the uplands of what is now Arizona and western New Mexico and were a hunting and gathering people, living in crude shelters in the open and in caves that, luckily for us, protected their remains.

The earliest known period of the Cochise is called the Sulphur Springs Stage, which began anywhere from 9000 to 7000 B.C. Excavated Cochise cave sites from this period reveal small handstones and flat grinding slabs, called, respectively, manos and metates, used to grind seeds; fire drills; and crudely flaked large stone implements employed for other purposes. In the absence of evidence to the contrary, it is assumed the major Cochise food source was wild products, such as nuts, seeds, berries, and fruits. Bones of animals now extinct, such as the dire wolf, camel, mammoth, and horse, are present in the sites, but no projectile points from this stage have been found. It is possible that wooden atlatls (spear-throwing implements) were made but have disintegrated.

During the next cultural period, called the Chiricahua Stage (3500 or 3000 B.C.–about 1500 to 1000 B.C.) the Cochise were manufacturing first-rate grinding stones and slabs, mauls, and flake tools. They lived in shallow pithouses, wove baskets of cactus plant fibers, and made some crude pottery. Site findings include projectile points of the type identified today with atlatls. But although hunting activities increased, the people still gathered seed crops as a main diet. In Arizona, other foods would include grass seeds, pigweed, and cattail roots. Meat would include squirrel, mouse, rabbit, antelope, deer, and mountain sheep.

An event of some moment was the arrival of a cultivable corn in New Mexico and Arizona. As mentioned earlier, archaeologists working in a place called Bat Cave in New Mexico found, under ancient debris, ears of corn less than an inch long. These were dated at 3500 B.C. and were probably the first ears of cultivated corn to be grown in North America. The extent of this cultivation in the fourth century B.C. is not known, but researchers are certain that the Cochise had evolved into the first true farmers north of Mexico before 1000 B.C., growing corn, squash, and beans and devising crude methods of storage for their produce. As time passed, they continued to make baskets and also wove mats and nets from plant fibers, and blankets from the skins of rabbits. The Chiricahua Stage ended about 1000 B.C., when a final agricultural stage, known as the San Pedro, came into being that lasted perhaps six hundred years.

Some anthropologists believe that during this period the Cochise were in the process of merging with a new people, the Hohokam, who had begun to move north from Mexico into southern Arizona by 400 B.C. Paul S. Martin, describing his excavation work at Pine Lawn Valley, New Mexico, speaks of the "Cochise-Mogollon," and claims that the Mogollon culture grew directly out of the older subculture, "called the Cochise." About A.D. 1, when pottery was added to what the Cochise had previously known and made, the Cochise culture ended and the Mogollon culture began. This change, says Martin, was only a transition from one stage of the culture to the next.[17]

HOHOKAM AND SALADO
400 B.C.–A.D. 1500

Archaeologists have divided the Hohokam culture into four cultural periods:

The Pioneer Period	400 B.C.–A.D. 500
The Colonial Period	A.D. 500–900
The Sedentary Period	A.D. 900–1100 or 1200
The Classic Period	A.D. 1150–1300 or 1500

Hohokam, pronounced "ho-ho-kom," is a Pima word meaning "Those Who Have Gone." The Hohokam were ancient inhabitants of the southern Arizona deserts, located south of the Mogollon Rim and east of the Yuma County line, around the confluence of the Gila and Salt rivers, and were once thought to have their roots in the Cochise people. Yet they seem to have borrowed so much from the great cultures of Mesoamerica that more recently some archaeologists have come to believe the Hohokam might have migrated to this area as early as 400 B.C. from far down in western Mexico.[18]

Whatever the case, by A.D. 1 the Hohokam were living in large houses, some as long as 32 feet (9.7 m). Dwellings were rectangular, sometimes square, and, like the Mogollon pithouses, had sunken floors. The untidy walls were constructed of brush and mud and had no windows, and entry was made through a side vestibule. Work, including cooking, was done outside, under a brush-covered structure called a ramada.

The largest Hohokam town was Skoaquick (Snaketown), a sprawling, stable community that, in time, covered about 300 acres. With its first excavations in the 1930s, archaeologists learned that Snaketown was inhabited continuously from 400 B.C. to A.D. 1000 and may have been occupied sporadically after that until as late as A.D. 1500, going through numerous stages of cultural development. At its peak in A.D. 900–1100 it consisted of about one hundred large pithouses, each containing several families, together with several ball courts, pit ovens, storage areas, and various other constructions of unknown use, including some that may have fulfilled religious purposes.

Hohokam. All data concerning Snaketown redrawn with minor revisions or deletions from Haury, 1976. All data concerning Casa Grande from National Park Service photographs. *Left,* map showing maximum range of Hohokam and location of major sites. *Top right,* ball court. *Bottom right,* turquoise inlay and shell beads found under one of the floors of Casa Grande village.

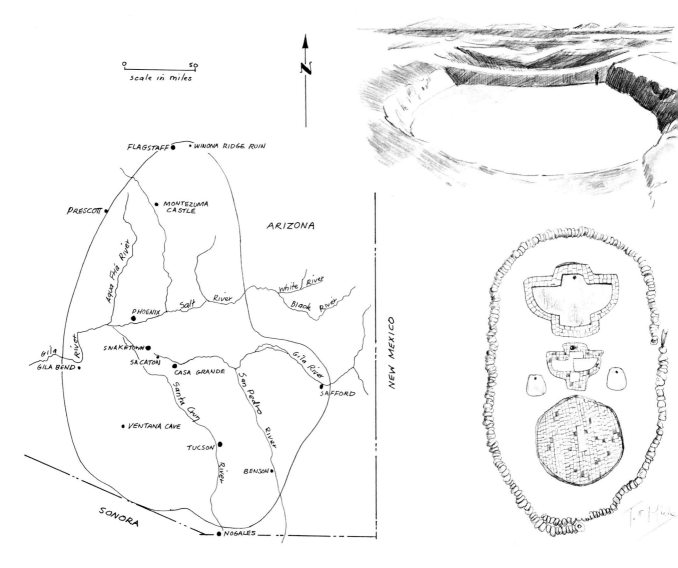

In 1965 archaeologists unearthed at Snaketown the oldest irrigation system known in the United States. According to Dr. Emil W. Haury of the University of Arizona the irrigation system is more than 1,900 years old and bears a striking similarity to systems found in the Tehuacán Valley southeast of Mexico City.

Evidence from excavations further suggests to Dr. Haury that the first migrants from the northwestern Mexican lowlands arrived at the Snaketown area around 400–300 B.C., fully equipped to survive. They were not merely influenced by Mesoamericans; they were Mesoamericans themselves, possibly coastal Mexicans, which explains why their culture in the Southwest flowered quickly rather than over a long period. They had corn, they knew how to irrigate, they had well-formed pottery, stone bowls, and macaws—all without precedent in the Southwest. Add, further, the mounds, ball courts, and copper bells, and the evidence becomes most convincing. If Dr. Haury is right, the next quest will be to determine who the ancestors of the Hohokam were and why they moved north into such an inhospitable country.

The actual length of the Pioneer Period is uncertain, because the perishable mesquite, ironwood, and cottonwood employed in construction by the Hohokam cannot be dated by the tree-ring method. Nevertheless, archaeologists have determined that the Hohokam may at this early time have advanced culturally beyond the Basketmakers who lived to the north. They ate maize and farmed it by river-terrace and flood-plain irrigation methods, augmenting it with mesquite beans, screw bean pods, saguaro cactus fruit, and several others of the wild foods that abound in the desert. Meat consisted of mule deer, jackrabbit, and cottontail. Site findings include projectile points and tools that could have been used to make arrows or atlatl darts. Findings reveal that bison wandered into Hohokam country on rare occasions and were killed, apparently not for food but to obtain the hides and skulls for ceremonial purposes. Also, by A.D. 500 the Hohokam were cultivating cotton in the arid deserts of Arizona, spinning it, and weaving it into cloth. We know that some fish were eaten, since sturgeon bones have been found in Hohokam trash piles. The Hohokam also made wine from the saguaro cactus fruit.

From 400 B.C. to A.D. 100 the Hohokam fashioned brown and gray pottery, thinned by the paddle-and-anvil technique as opposed to the coil-and-scrape method used by the Mogollon culture. (Yet the shapes and designs fashioned by both cultures were similar.) Hohokam vessels were built up with layers of clay coils. Then they were placed bottom up over a small revolving stone or clay anvil shaped like a mushroom. The potter turned the anvil with one hand and used a wooden paddle in the other to flatten and shape the pot. The pot was left to dry, and when it was dry a smooth river pebble dipped in water was used to rub and burnish the surface of the vessel. Finally it was fired in an earth pit and in most cases decorated on the outside, either with incised concentric lines in an ascending spiral or with painted-on red designs. The most common designs were geometric forms, hatched bands and triangles, and impressionistic people, animals, and birds (known as life forms). The same process is used by Yuman and Papago peoples today.[19]

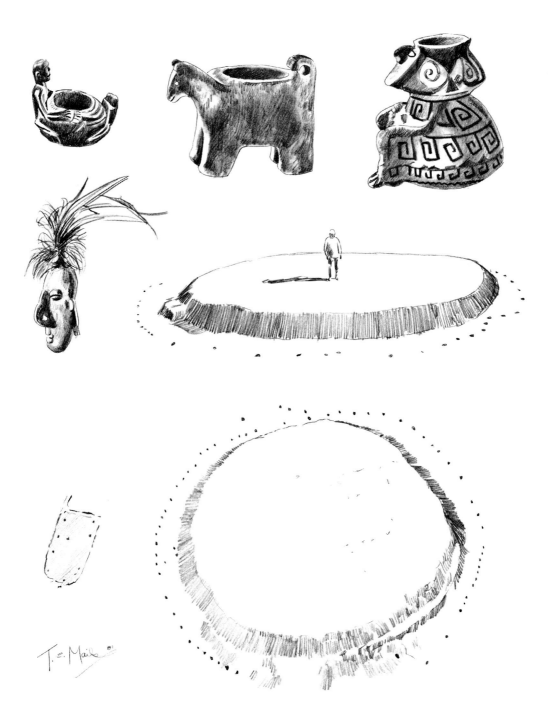

Snaketown and other Hohokam locations. *Top left*, stone censer with paired human figures. *Top middle*, stone effigy censer. *Top right*, human effigy pot, Sacaton Red-on-buff. *Center left*, Santa Cruz Phase clay figure. *Center right*, perspective view of typical mound. *Bottom*, aerial view of mound showing relative scale in comparison to house site at left.

Some Hohokam pottery was heavy-walled, and effigy vessels were shaped that included fired clay snakes, mountain sheep, and human beings, thought to be evidence of Mexican influences. Stone items included bowls, dippers, and palettes of schist on which pigments were ground, also barbed arrow-heads, and hard axes of diorite that were three-quarter-grooved, long-bitted, and with a pronounced collar. Jewelry worn in the Pioneer Period was scarce and plain. Findings include disk-like beads of stone and shell, pendants of turquoise and shell, plain shell bracelets, mosaic work done with turquoise and shell, and incised bone tubes.

The dead were cremated, and their ashes were buried in trenches or pits. Also into the pit with them went many of their ceremonial and personal belongings, and in consequence the extent of the Hohokam's full relationship with Mesoamerica may never be known. Also, while the Hohokam had turkeys, no dog remains have been found in Hohokam sites.

The Hohokam's Colonial Period found them establishing and then enlarging an amazing system of irrigation canals along the Gila and Salt rivers. It became the largest prehistoric irrigation project in North America, requiring great ingenuity, exceptional leadership, and, since there seems to have been no ruling caste, extensive cooperation. It was accomplished with nothing more than baskets, wooden digging sticks, paddles, and stone axes and hoes, yet some of the early canals measured 15 or more feet (4.5 m) wide and 2 feet (1.2 m) deep, had clay-lined walls, and were complete with earthen dams and floodgates of woven mats laid against a fence of poles that crossed the canal.

Colonial Period houses were fashioned like those of the Pioneer Period, and of the same materials, but were smaller and had rounded corners. Walls of poles and brush were set into the floor of the shallow pit, and dirt was backfilled into the space between the walls and the edges of the pit. Fires were built in small but carefully made firepits lined with clay. Entrances were ramped. There is evidence that the Hohokam used outside brush kitchens, called ramadas, much like those used by the modern Pima. At some sites the remains of only a few houses have been found, while other sites contained a hundred or more structures and were occupied for 1,400 years.

During this period what may have been huge ball courts made their appearance among the Hohokam. These were oval depressions as much as 132 feet (40 m) in length, 100 feet (30 m) wide, oriented east and west, and open at both ends. Earthen banks left after the dirt was removed formed side walls 10 or more feet (3 m) high. Three stones seem to have served as markers: one in the middle of the court and one at each end. Hohokam ball courts have been found in the Salt, Gila, and Verde valleys and northeast of Flagstaff at the Wupatki National Monument. They are similar to those seen by the Spaniards who were among the Maya in Mexico, although no positive connection between the Hohokam and Maya has been made. Raw-rubber balls have been found in the Hohokam sites.

Colonial pottery was brown or buff and still painted, in the Pioneer tradition, with red designs using geometric or life elements. Incising was no longer practiced. The design tradition associated with the finest of Hohokam ceramics had begun after A.D. 300 with the production of Snaketown Red-on-buff. Designs employed numerous and repeated human forms and animal forms such as deer, dogs, quail, pelicans, snakes, horned toads, and lizards done in dull red paint on a buff background. The tradition continued through the Gila Butte Red-on-buff phase and reached its peak development in Santa Cruz Red-on-buff and Sacaton Red-on-buff, which are the Hohokam types best known today. The Santa Cruz Phase, from A.D. 700 to 900, revealed a particular fond-

Hohokam. Pottery: *a,* Santa Cruz Red-on-buff plate. *b,* Snaketown Red-on-buff effigy vessel. *c,* Santa Cruz Red-on-buff jar. *d,* Sacaton Red-on-buff shouldered jar. *e,* Salt Red smudged vessel of the Classic Period.

ness for animal designs, particularly mountain sheep effigies. During the Sacaton Phase, from A.D. 900 to 1100, human effigy jars were formed, as well as
many small freestanding clay figurines suggesting Mexican contacts.

The production of effigy vessels by the Hohokam appears to have been
limited, although human effigies are known from the earliest phases and continued to be produced until A.D. 1150. One Sweetwater Red-on-gray jar, dating
from A.D. 100–300 and found at Snaketown, depicted a woman molded in relief
on the side of the vessel.

Hohokam. *Top,* front and back views of clay figurine wearing elaborate Mesoamerican-type
headdress. *Right,* bighorn sheep carving that once was the end of a bone hairpin. *Lower left,*
stone palette and palette holding a censer.

Stone items were carved with desert reptile forms such as lizards and toads, while bone carvings most commonly depicted birds and snakes. Findings from the Colonial Period include carved shell beads and ornaments such as pendants and bracelets. Carved shell rings in the form of snakes have been unearthed as well. The Hohokam also made carefully fitted mosaic mirrors of pyrite crystals and attached them to circular stone bases. The backs of these

Snaketown. Floor plans of a group of Sedentary Period pithouses shown in relationship to common work areas consisting mainly of pits.

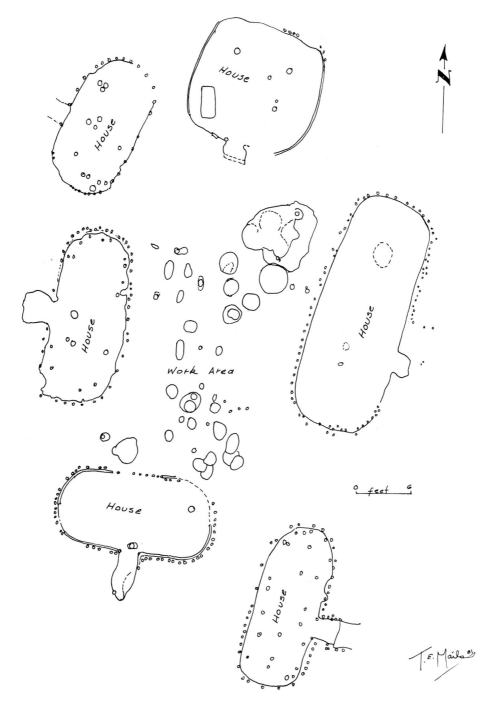

were ornamented with complicated multicolored designs in superimposed layers, some cut away to show the others underneath.

Burial in A.D. 500–900 was still by cremation, and bones, ashes, and offerings were placed in small holes, pits, trenches, and pottery vessels. Dale King states: "One of the most common offerings were palettes of hard rock, carved with a border and often having carved birds, snakes or animals ornamenting

Hohokam—Los Muertos. Plot plans of two compound-type village structures examined by the Hemenway Expedition in the Salt River valley in the vicinity of Phoenix, Arizona, in 1887–88. From Haury, 1945.

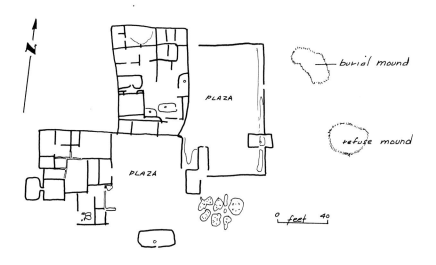

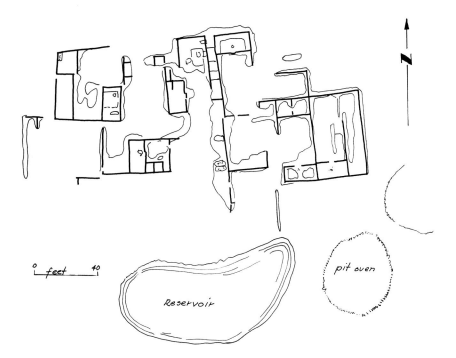

the edges. On the mixing surface of many is a vitreous remnant of a lead mixture. It has been suggested that the lead pigment, possibly a facial or body paint, changed in the heat of the cremation fire from a dull color to a brilliant red with metallic globules, and may have had some ceremonial significance."[20]

The locations of the ball courts, discussed above, indicate the geographic expansion of the Hokokam. From A.D. 500 to 1100 they spread northward to areas east of the Grand Canyon and northeast of the present city of Flagstaff, eastward into southwestern New Mexico, and south into northern Sonora and Chihuahua states in Mexico. They even shared the Sunset Crater area with the Sinagua, Anasazi, and Cohonina. Ruins found over this entire area contain the ball courts, cremations, and pottery common to the Hohokam. After A.D. 1100, it appears that they began to contract back to their earlier locations along the Salt and Gila rivers. There were two distinct groups of Hohokam: the River Hohokam, who occupied the river valleys, and the Desert Hohokam, who inhabited the vast desert region extending south from the Gila River.

During the Sedentary Period, A.D. 900–1100 or 1200, the Hohokam began to concentrate in villages near the Salt and Gila rivers. Their dwellings were shallow pithouses averaging 15 to 27 feet (4.5–8.2 m) in size. Poles supported brush and mud walls and the roof. Corners were rounded, and a 6-inch (15 cm) rim helped to keep out water. Entryways now had steps. It is believed that toward the end of the Sedentary Period some of the Puebloan Salado people moved into the Hohokam area and influenced them to build some (not all) village houses that consisted of several rectangular rooms with combination mud and stone walls, and also settlements enclosed by walls, forming a compound. Ball courts became smaller now, from 70 to 80 feet (21–24 m) long, had closed ends, and unlike earlier courts were oriented north and south.

An unearthed bowl of some consequence pointing to cultural relationships between Southwestern nations is one made by a Hohokam between A.D. 900 and 1100. Its painted designs include Kokopelli, the humpbacked flute player well known as the fertility god of the Anasazi. Because he is represented on this bowl, Kokopelli is thought to have also been the fertility god (or spirit power) of the Hohokam. As the Hohokam evolved, their designs increased in complexity and included representations of animals, masked dancers, and deities. The spiritual ramifications are clear, and we can assume that religion was playing a central role in their lives, just as it had in all the principal cultures of Mesoamerica and South America.

Sedentary Period pottery as a whole became more elaborate, with red-on-buff design panels, negative designs, and interlocking scrolls. Shapes became more varied and included three- and four-legged trays similar to those of the Mixtecs. Huge storage jars were built to hold water and cereals. Pottery figurines had hollow heads, and full-figure effigies in sitting positions were modeled. Findings at digs also indicate a considerable industry in textiles and baskets.

The round mosaic mirrors were still made, but less well than before. This was true also of stone bowls, which were only incised now and no longer had

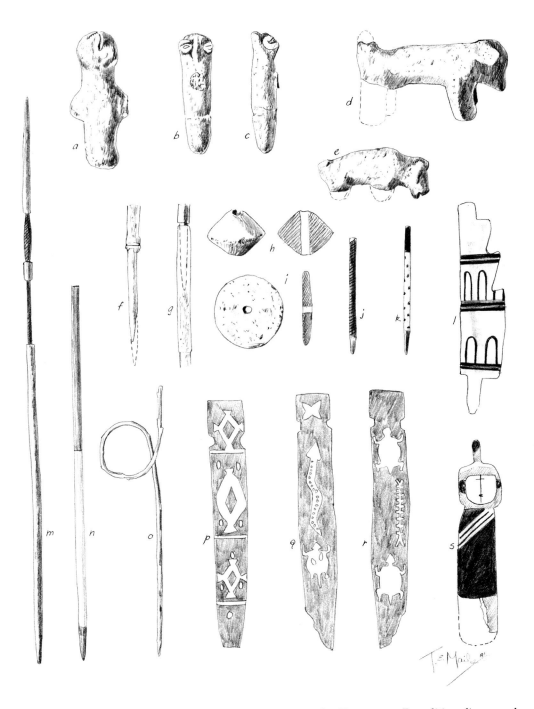

Hohokam. Among its findings in the Salt River valley, the Hemenway Expedition discovered many items, such as those shown here, that show an intriguing similarity to Anasazi artifacts. *a–e*, clay figurines of humans and animals. *f–g*, compound arrow fragments. *h–i*, clay spindle whorls. *j–s*, wooden pahos painted in various colors with symbolic designs. From Haury, 1945.

the carved life figures. The stone metates, mortars, and pestles were well made, and the quality of Hohokam shellwork jewelry reached its peak. Craft workers made pendants, elaborately carved shell bracelets, and disk beads. They did splendid mosaic work by laying tiny pieces of turquoise and shell in a bed of mesquite gum or lac spread over a larger shell obtained through a trade network that extended west to the Pacific Ocean and east to the Gulf Coast. Lac is a plastic gum obtained from the secretions of a small insect that lives on creosote bushes. Etching of shells was also done in this period, perhaps by the use of the fermented juice of saguaro cactus fruit to eat away whatever portions of the design were not covered by lac or plant gum. The shell might be painted to make the etched area stand out. It is probable that a large part of the prehistoric shell ornaments found in the Southwest came from the Hohokam. Since trading was a major industry, we can be certain that many items manufactured by the Hohokam were specifically trade goods.

Remains at sites show that, with the advent of the Classic Hohokam Period in A.D. 1100 or 1150, the Salado people, close cousins of the Anasazi, had moved south into the valleys of east central Arizona and begun to settle near the Hohokam along the Gila and Salt rivers. Salado is Spanish for "salty."

Thanks to the destruction of sites by relic collectors in the past thirty years, relatively little is known about the Salado, and almost no professional excavations have ever been made at Salado sites, yet they seem to have had a pronounced effect upon the other cultures of the Southwest. Some researchers believe they developed from a Mogollon tradition, blending with people from the headwaters of the Little Colorado River in the White Mountain area. By A.D. 900 the Salado culture was recognizable in the Tonto Basin just below the Mogollon Rim and in an area just east of the Sierra Ancha. Apparently the two nations got along well, yet there seems to have been only the slightest intermingling of cultures. No hybrid civilization arose. The Salado kept to their Pueblo-style culture. They were skilled craftsmen in weaving, basketry, wood, and shellwork.

Using the paddle-and-anvil technique, the Salado fashioned first a plain brownware pottery; then Salado Red, which was a Mogollon-like corrugated type; and a Roosevelt Black-on-white which compares to Mogollon Reserve and Tularosa products. After 1200 they produced their best vessels, which were polychromes, and these are known as Pinto, Gila, and Tonto—like those made by the Hohokam during the same period. They were mainly hemispherical bowls, tall-necked jars, and effigy forms, including ducks, dogs, and humans, seemingly influenced by Mexican contacts.

The Salado interred their dead in the ground, and while they built no ceremonial chambers known as kivas, villages that supplanted their pithouses were made up of multistoried stone houses surrounded by walls. Later, possibly because of enemies, they also built cliff dwellings, such as may be seen at Tonto National Monument on the Salt River.

At Tonto the Salado built three large dwelling places of stone and mud: an upper apartment containing about 40 rooms, a lower apartment with 200 rooms, and an annex of 12 rooms. Because it was undisturbed and because of its well-preserved dwellings, it is from Tonto that most of our archaeological evidence about the Salado has come. Excavators have found baskets, mats, sandals, headbands, cradleboards, skirts, cordage, bags, cotton breechclouts, cloaks, blankets, beads, shells, and bone. From these findings, archaeologists have been able to reconstruct a Salado culture based upon hunting, gathering,

Snaketown. *Top right,* plot plan of group of Classic Period houses arranged in walled compound. Surrounding lines show extent of excavated area. *Center,* two views of excavated adobe walls. *Bottom left,* adobe walls with exterior support posts. *Bottom right,* adobe walls reinforced with enclosed posts.

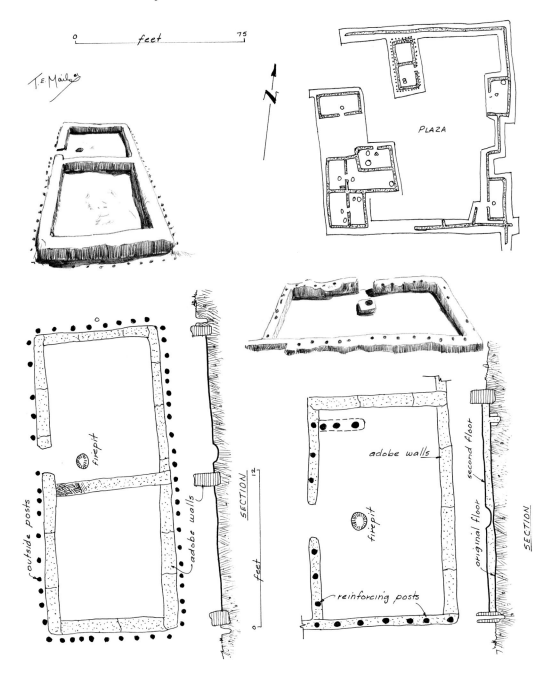

and farming. As many as three hundred kinds of plant were gathered for food, fiber, and medicine. The Salado were unexcelled cotton growers and weavers, their textiles including openwork, diamond twills, and gauze. All were dyed blue, brown, red, or yellow.

Unearthed burials have revealed that Salado women were, on average, five feet tall and men six inches taller. Their heads were slightly flattened in

Salado. Tonto cliff dwelling, Tonto National Monument. *Top,* upper ruin. *Bottom,* lower ruin.

back like those of the Mesa Verde Pueblo people because of hard cradleboards, their faces were small, and their features were delicate. Their teeth—like those of the northern Pueblos—were ground down to nothing by the grit that melded with their black-bean flour when grinding stones were used.[21]

Meanwhile, the Hohokam continued to make their red-on-buff pottery, although in different shapes and with thinner paint. They cremated their dead

Salado. Items found in Tonto cliff ruin. *Top left*, sandal. *Top right*, fragment of woven cotton cloth with a plaid design in brown and white. *Center*, painted pottery. *Bottom left*, large olla or water jar. *Bottom right*, woven breechclout.

and lived as before in their brush and mud houses. They did adopt in part the Salado idea of a village compound, erecting a few clusters of rectangular rooms constructed with vertical poles and adobe walls, grouped within high, thick walls. Yet even substantial parts of these compounds were occupied by large mounds of earth—on top of which it is thought the same old Hohokam brush and mud houses were built—although the mounds could reflect the pyramid-temple constructions of Mesoamerica.

The exception to this typical Hohokam structure may be towering Casa Grande ("Big House"), which was a large watchtower–apartment house complex built about A.D. 1350 and covering eighty acres. Since it is not a typical Hohokam building, some archaeologists believe that Casa Grande's dominating four-story building might have been constructed by the Salado. But if the Hohokam were of Mexican lineage, Casa Grande might be their last attempt, because of changes in area conditions, to return to their most ancient ways.

It is thought that in the classic Hohokam period the Salado must have joined with the Hohokam in working on the irrigation canal system. The size and scope of the ultimate canal development indicates a need for great numbers of workers, since some ditches were dug 7 feet (2 m) deep and 30 feet (9 m) wide, and eventually a total of 500 or more miles of canals were carved out, watering over 200,000 acres and providing for a sea of cornstalks as far as the eye could see.

Theirs was the largest area of land under cultivation in North and South America, and perhaps in the world, at that time. How they did it no archaeologist knows for sure, even now. River water was essential to help them cut the soil, but how did they control the amount of water surging into a ditch 15 or more feet (4.5 m) wide and 2 to 7 feet (0.6–2 m) deep?

It may also have been that the Salado brought in the new stone axes, adzes, picks, and saws that are associated with the Hohokam Classic Period. Stone hoes also became plentiful, although they were only heads with handle extensions or "ears," which indicates the head was held in the hands for digging.

For reasons only guessed at, the Salado seem to have moved westward and vanished from Hohokam country by A.D. 1350, surely no later than 1400. Some ethnologists think traces of them are found among the late pueblos of northern Chihuahua State; others feel the Salado divided and may have merged with the Zuñi, Hopi, Pima, and Papago.

As the Salado slipped away, the Hohokam people themselves began to move. By A.D. 1400–1500 their traceable history ceased, and no one is certain who their descendants are. They may continue to exist today as part of the Arizona Pima and Papago tribes.

The last two hundred years of Hohokam occupancy of the Salt River valley found them pressed by raiding nomadic peoples and the problems common to excessive irrigation. But the Hohokam were a civilized and a peaceful people. In all the excavations done in their country no evidence of war or violence has come to light. Most of the remains found in Hohokam burial sites are those of

Casa Grande. *Top left*, Hohokam pithouse found at Casa Grande. *Top right*, copper bells fashioned from native copper—technique probably learned from the Indians of northern Mexico. *Center left*, a sun hole for telling time. There are three pairs of these in the Casa Grande walls. *Center right*, remains of mixing pits where caliche used in wall construction was mixed. *Bottom*, remains of Casa Grande and its surrounding compound.

Casa Grande. *Top,* Salado pottery taken from Casa Grande ruin. *Center right,* Salado effigy pot, Tonto Polychrome. Heard Museum collection. *Bottom,* items found in a Casa Grande room: *left,* mortar and pestle; *middle,* large storage jar; *right,* mano and metate used for grinding corn.

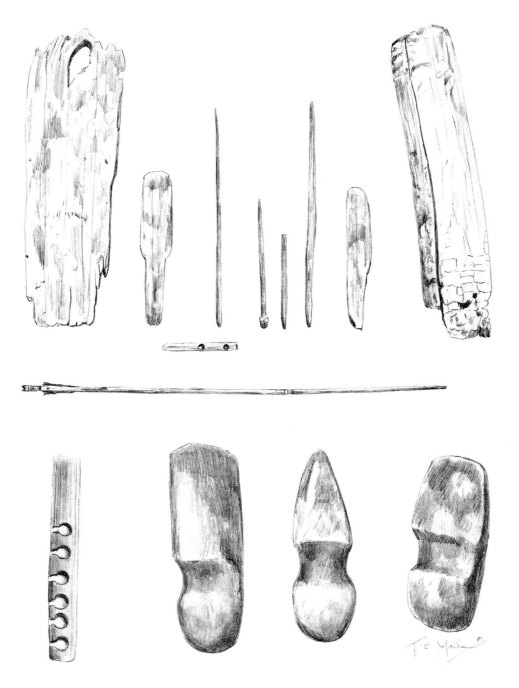

Casa Grande. *Top left*, portion of a flat wood cradleboard. *Top middle and right*, wood paddles, weaving sticks, firedrills. *Center*, arrow. *Bottom left*, enlarged detail of firedrill hearth stick. *Bottom right*, stone axes for cutting timbers.

people who died of natural causes. Moreover, death had occurred at either a very young age or a very old age—showing that death by warfare was not common to them. Their greatest enemy was assuredly not man, until their final days.

Richard Ambler states: "Faced with droughts, flash floods, caliche [a crust of calcium carbonate formed on soils in arid regions] ruining the soil and a breakdown of contact with Mesoamerica due to the collapse of the Tula empire that preceded the Aztecs, the Hohokam gave up their extensive farms and turned to individual gardening, hunting and gathering in the 1400's."[22] With this, he leads them into the transitional period wherein they change from a visible Hohokam culture into whatever they became after that—the Pima or someone else.

An inference here is salient. The idea of their demise being caused by the breakdown of Tula suggests a Hohokam dependence upon, and continuous relationship with, Mesoamerica over an unbroken period of 1,800 years. It takes for granted that they never ceased being Mesoamericans, if Dr. Emil W. Haury is right in his assumption concerning Hohokam origins.

Considering the genius of the Hohokam and their neighbors, it is often asked why they, like the Mesoamericans, failed to develop the wheel and to utilize beasts of burden. Actually, the wheel was not an alien concept to them, for they had stone whorls on their spinning sticks and, as the Olmecs had done centuries earlier, mounted wheels on children's toys. One can only assume that, because beasts of burden were not available until introduced by Europeans in the 1500s, the wheel as a mature instrument must not have seemed useful in the pursuits followed by the desert cultures.

Everyone agrees that the enterprising Hohokam became a prime stimulus to the Anasazi. They provided key ingredients that helped the Anasazi to thrive to the point where they in turn could contribute a great deal to the development of the Hohokam. Cultural diffusions are often like waves. Once set in motion, they come regularly ashore in sizes determined by what has happened at their point of origin. They break on the beach, some quietly, some like thunder, always depositing something, and as they return to the sea they take something else back with them, even if it is only the reshaped matter they left at an earlier time. And the beach itself is never static. Its face changes a little or a lot with every wave.

MOGOLLON
300 B.C.–A.D. 1500

Although the Mogollon (pronounced "muggy-own") culture flourished for 1,800 years, from 300 B.C. or earlier to A.D. 1450–1500, the details are not as well understood as one might hope, perhaps because of the variations in life-style from one population area to another. Named for the high mountains that many of them inhabited along the southern reaches of the New Mexico–Arizona border and extending westward about to the Payson, Arizona, area, the Mogollon created a civilization based upon hunting—first with the atlatl, later with the bow and arrow—gathering nuts and wild edibles, and farming.

They seem to have matured quickly, although in most respects the Mogollon's life-style was never so sophisticated as that of their Hohokam and Anasazi neighbors, perhaps because the semi-isolated villages of the Mogollon were away from the main trade routes and less subject in their formative years to cultural diffusion. Some village sites were occupied for a thousand years.

Pithouses are known the world over, and the Mogollon probably did not invent them, but they did develop and adapt the pithouse, a semi-subterranean dwelling, to where it was especially suited to the climate of their southwestern mountain valleys. The pithouse they built provided excellent insulation against the extremes of mountain temperatures, which could range from a high of 100° F during the day to near-freezing at night.

While some pithouses had partitions, most consisted of a single room, usually round, with a short entrance tunnel appended on the east side. To make the outer walls, a roughly circular excavation about 15 feet (4.5 m) in

Map showing approximate area occupied by the Mogollon, and also showing location of Casas Grandes, an area in what is now northwestern Chihuahua settled by Paquimé people about A.D. 1040. At Casas Grandes the Paquimé organized and directed a sophisticated culture that dominated this portion of the northern frontier for almost three hundred years.

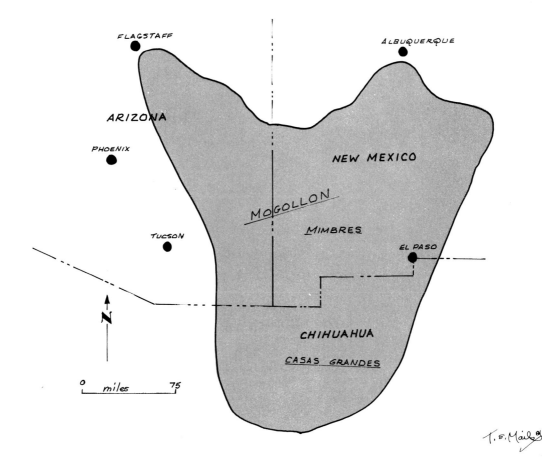

Casas Grandes. *Top,* huge wasp-nest-like granaries made of clay were built in the cliff dwellings not far from Casas Grandes. They were used to store food for times of drought or siege.
Center, decorated pottery from Casas Grandes. *Bottom,* some of the widely scattered ruins of
the Casas Grandes area of northern Chihuahua, Mexico.

diameter and 3 or 4 feet (1–1.2 m) deep was dug. Then twenty or more posts 5 or 6 feet (1.5–1.8 m) long, forked at their upper ends, were set upright into the floor at measured intervals around the perimeter of the pit. A thicker and taller center post was placed in the middle of the house. Small tree limbs were used for wall studs and for ceiling beams to connect the posts, and over these beams were laid tightly woven mats of reed saplings and a final covering of mud plaster 18 inches (45 cm) thick. It is believed that a small hole was left in the roof directly above the hearth for smoke exhaust and light.

When the rest of the house was finished, a floor of compacted gravel and adobe was installed, and small pits were dug in the floor and sidewalls for hearths and storage. Dirt benches and stone-slab storage bins completed the furnishings. We will return to the pithouse when we enter the Basketmaker era; it keeps turning up wherever we go.

Mogollon. *Top,* partial plot plan of SU Site. *Bottom,* map showing location of SU Site. From Martin, 1940.

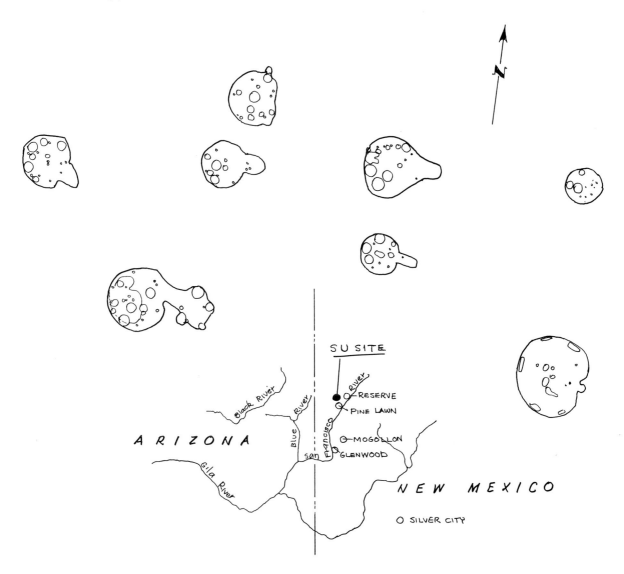

Even at the height of the Mogollon's development in A.D. 1000, their agricultural skills would not permit large settlements. There were seldom more than thirty pithouses in a village, and village populations probably did not exceed two hundred persons. Water was adequate, and corn, squash, beans, and tobacco were grown. Augmenting these crops were honey, various seeds, and wild nuts. Mogollon country was the home of more game than anywhere

Mogollon. Floor plan and perspective view of a typical pithouse.

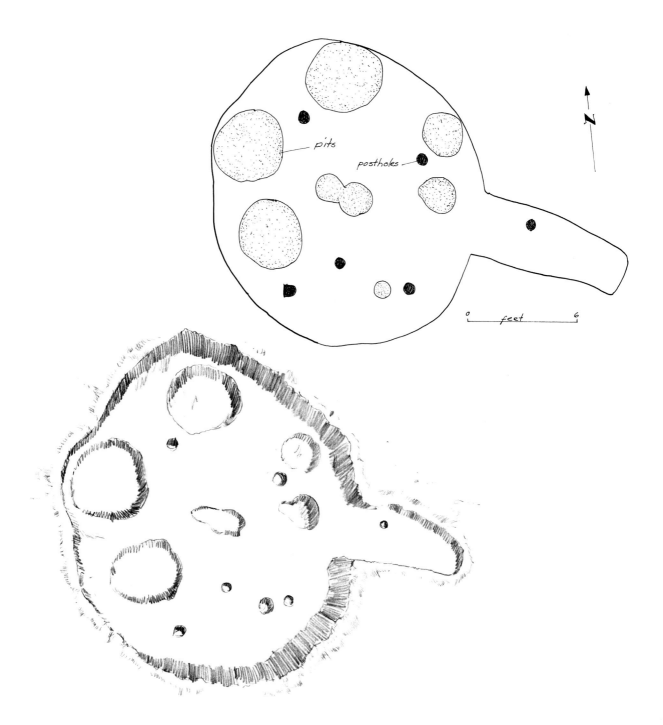

else in the Southwest, and skillful hunters provided ample meat dishes, including turkey, rabbit, deer, and antelope. Dogs were kept as hunting companions and pets.

The Mogollon used large storage pits, some of which were stone-lined and had undercut bell-shaped sides, to store their food. Some experts think pithouses evolved from these, others think it was the other way around. It is

Mogollon. *Top,* floor plan of a pithouse. *Bottom,* section showing structural details and shape of floor. From Martin, 1940.

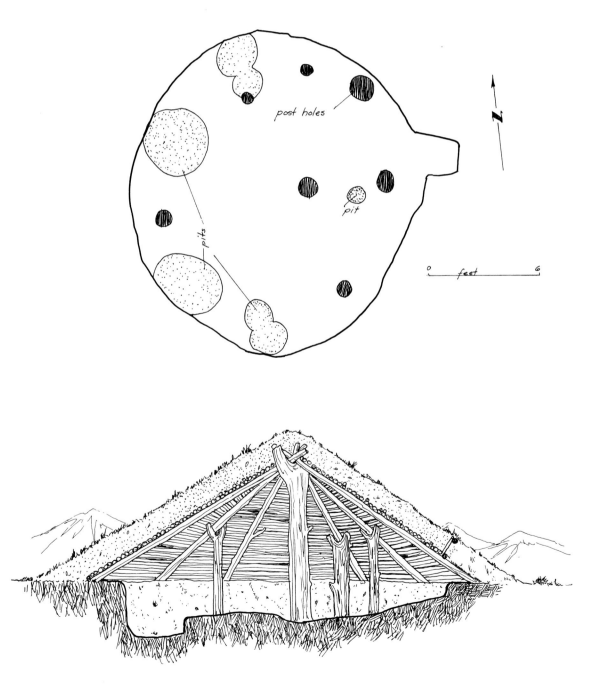

significant that every village included one extra building, a ceremonial house some 30 or 35 feet (9–10.5 m) in diameter—the earliest of the kivas. Constructed after the manner of the pithouse, it was deeper for religious reasons, had a firepit and draft deflector with a ventilation shaft, and apparently was entered from the roof by a ladder. It is quite easy to imagine the priests and people gathering there to perform esoteric ceremonies aimed at keeping them in close harmony with nature and its gods.

Donald Pike claims that throughout the Southwest the Mogollon were "the first with the most" in pottery, in houses, and in armaments. They were imi-

Mogollon. Floor plan and perspective view of an earlier and a later pithouse joined together. From Martin, 1940.

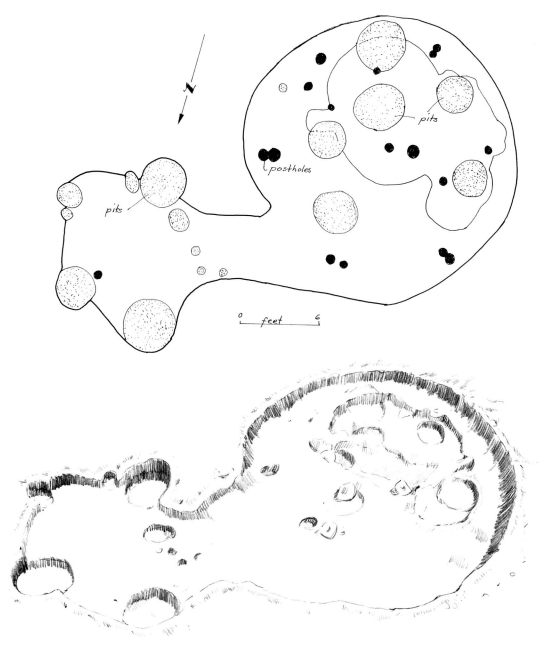

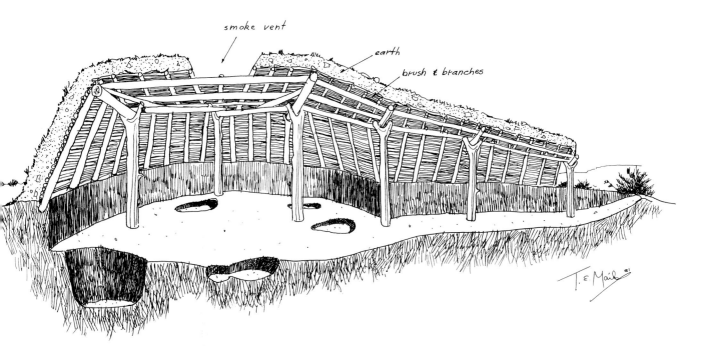

Mogollon. Postulated method of pithouse construction for house with extended entrance. Redrawn with additions from Martin, 1940.

tated everywhere, but they never did more than refine—they never evolved, and archaeologists are not able to establish distinct phases in their culture. In time they were surpassed by the Hohokam and the Anasazi. Then the Mogollon became the imitators, and the Mogollon culture per se ceased to exist.[23]

The Mogollon wove blankets and other garments and fashioned sandals. They also made intricate turquoise-chip jewelry and shell bracelets. Their shells for the bracelets and necklaces resulted from either direct or indirect trade with Pacific Coast Indians. Copper came to them from Mexico in the form of pendants and small bells. The bow and arrow may also have come to them from there, for Mesoamericans had the bow and arrow in pre-Mogollon times. The bow and arrow proved to be a great step forward for the Mogollon, as for any culture, although, being proficient with the atlatl, they did not give it up entirely until well after A.D. 1000.

The Mogollon used the coil-and-scrape technique to manufacture their pottery, and they are remembered today for their thin-walled brownwares and redwares, made throughout most phases of their cultural development. Their first wares were not decorated, and it was only after A.D. 400 that they began to use surface manipulation to decorate a vessel's outside with incised lines and pinched indentations, producing a horizontal corrugated effect. Sometimes the clay coils themselves were left showing and not smoothed. When they

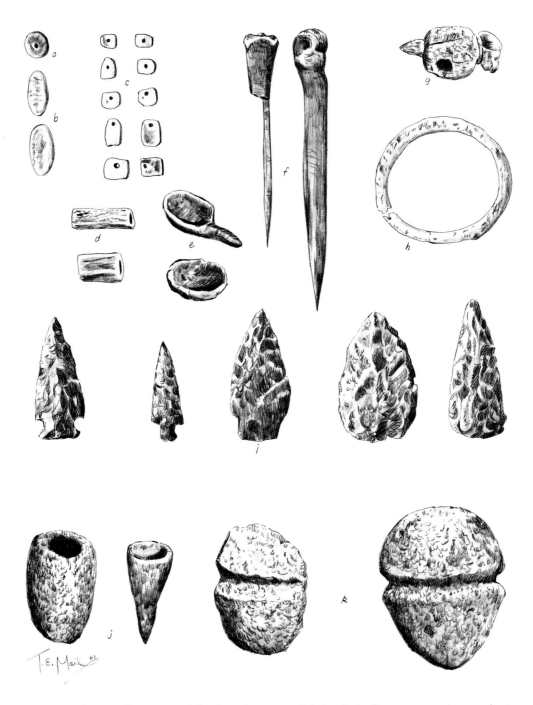

Mogollon. SU Site lesser material culture items: *a*, disk bead. *b*, dice. *c*, turquoise pendants. *d*, tubular bone beads. *e*, miniature vessels. *f*, bone awls. *g*, stone bird effigy. *h*, shell bracelet. *i*, projectile points. *j*, stone pipes. *k*, stone mauls. From Martin, 1940.

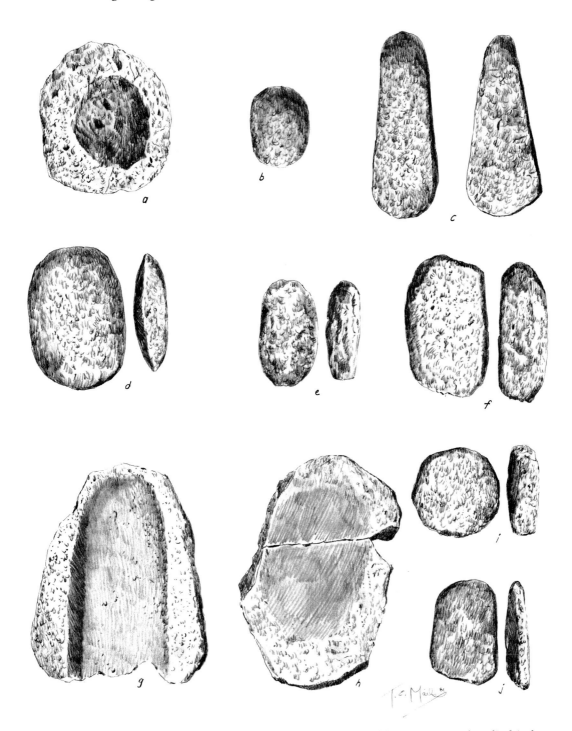

Mogollon. SU Site lesser material culture items of stone: *a*, pebble-type mortar. *b*, cylindrical pestle. *c*, angular pestles. *d*, turtleback mano. *e*, pebble mano. *f*, oblong mano. *g*, trough metate. *h*, basin metate. *i*, disk mano. *j*, wedge-shaped mano. From Martin, 1940.

began to paint their pottery, red paint was used to create a diversity of geometric designs on a brown to pinkish background. Much of this early decorated pottery suggests continual contact and cross-influences between the Mogollon and the Hohokam.

By A.D. 700 bowls were being smudged and vessel exteriors had become more elaborate. Surface manipulation of the clay coils was more complex, while red geometric designs were worked on a white background of imported white clay.

By A.D. 900 or 950 black-on-white types, such as Reserve Black-on-white, had replaced red-on-white pottery. Broad line designs, cross-hatching, and combinations of the two were common. Surface-manipulated brownware exhibited a variety of techniques, in almost every conceivable combination. For example, handles on many small jars and pitchers found at Reserve Period sites were embellished with modeled representations of dog, deer, and other animal forms.

This plethora of surface-decorated pottery continued on into the twelfth century, as did the production of redware and smudged bowls. In the Tularosa and Snowflake black-on-whites the designs were reduced in size and better done, suggesting a more sophisticated Mogollon culture in the making. About A.D. 1200 a McDonald corrugated type appeared that had geometric white designs painted over its corrugated surface. Handles of Tularosa Black-on-white were shaped like animals. Jars and hemispherical bowls were created for specialized purposes, with animal, bird, and abstract forms being used.

For those interested in religious developments, perhaps the most provocative of the ceramic creations produced by prehistoric potters was the effigy vessel, wholly or partly shaped to form a three-dimensional representation of a living object, human, bird, animal, or plant—the bird or duck form being the most commonly employed. With the Anasazi making the greatest number, all three of the major cultural groups in the prehistoric Southwest (Anasazi, Hohokam, and Mogollon) produced effigy pots. Vessel shapes with small openings, such as pitchers, jars, mugs, and canteens, were favored for effigies. Bowls and large jars were almost never used.

As part of their cultural progression, the Mogollon crafted a beautiful pottery called White Mountain Redware, which had a grayware paste coated with an orange to red slip. Designs were similar to those of their black-on-white traditions; Puerco Black-on-red designs, for instance, were simply the Puerco Black-on-white designs executed on red backgrounds. Later types, such as Wingate Black-on-red and St. Johns Polychrome, repeated the designs common to Tularosa and Reserve black-on-whites.

In the 1300s new design elements, such as animal and spirit forms, were introduced, and additional experimentation was done with white paint. White-line designs were drawn on the outside of bowls to create polychrome types, such as Pinedale and Show Low polychromes; Fourmile Polychrome is a superb example of these developments. The appearance among the Mimbres Mogollon of what seem to be Katcina priest-figure and deity designs is especially interesting, since it indicates the existence of a religious system, probably shared by several prehistoric groups, that has continued through the centuries and is found among the modern Pueblo Indians. Vessels with these designs may have been used for ceremonial purposes, since many are mythical, esoteric, or ceremonial subjects, masked and painted, dancing, and making ceremonial gestures.

As the second millennium arrived, Anasazi influence on the Mogollon is so apparent that many of the customs and patterns that had distinguished the latter from their neighbors were altered to a point where some archaeologists prefer to call them, after this time, the "Western Pueblo." It appears that a host of Anasazi moved south into Mogollon country, introducing new architectural techniques, new pottery styles, and new religious ideas. Although the Mogollon pithouse remained in use as a place of ritual and worship, it was abandoned in favor of large masonry pueblos. Some buildings continued to reflect the traditional pithouse, and the Mimbres Mogollon limited their pueblos to single-story structures containing as many as fifty rooms.

The pottery of the late Mogollon period also suggests important cultural changes, in this instance revealing a growing relationship with the Hopi and Zuñi areas and making it likely that the Zuñi and Hopi are, in part, Mogollon descendants.

The Mimbres were a regionally distinctive Mogollon people. Named for their association with the Mimbres River of present-day southwestern New Mexico, but living in both New Mexico and Arizona, they created some of the most refined and imaginative pottery bowls ever made in North America. Since their first discovery in the twentieth century, these creations have delighted collectors and archaeologists and have strongly influenced modern Indian and non-Indian designers in many fields.

The Mogollon as a whole were among the first peoples of the Southwest to fashion pottery, but it was not until A.D. 400, possibly influenced by their Hohokam neighbors, that they began to decorate their vessels with painted designs. Five hundred years went by, and then about A.D. 900 or 950, possibly because of a combination of Maya and Anasazi influences, the Mimbres Mogollon began to fashion a black-on-white ware so splendid and unique that many have thought it was made for specialized uses and played an important role in ceremonial life. Since most Classic Mimbres wares are recovered from graves, one use is quite clear. The Mimbres buried their dead under the floors of their dwellings and covered the face of each corpse with a bowl that was, in contemporary thought, "killed" by carefully punching a hole in its bottom, to make it possible for the bowl to accompany its owner wherever he or she went after death.[24] Some funerary bowls were "killed" by being completely shattered.

In most of my drawings of Mimbres pottery, however, I show the bowls without holes so that the original designs may be appreciated. Bowls were

Mogollon. *a*, Three Circle Neck Corrugated jar. *b*, Alma Plain jar. *c*, section through jar. *d*, Three Circle Neck Corrugated jar. *e*, Alma Plain "seed" jar. *f*, Unpolished Brown globular jar. *g*, Polished Red narrow-mouth jar. *h*, Alma Scored wide-mouth jar.

Mogollon. SU Site lesser material culture items: pottery. *a*, Red Mesa Black-on-white stirrup jar. *b*, painted sherds. *c*, Alma Plain bowl. *d*, San Francisco Red double bowl. *e*, Three Circle Red-on-white bowl. *f*, San Francisco Red double bowl. From Martin, 1940.

Mogollon. Flexed burial with mortuary offerings.

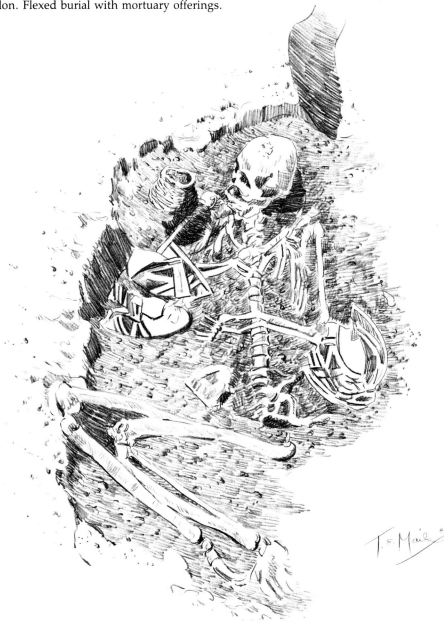

highly individualistic, and as an alternative to the idea of killing the bowl, I've wondered whether some of the portrayals might not have been, even in the case of geometric designs, those of the owners themselves, serving in the way pictographic representations did for Sioux name and life depictions.

The fact that weapons were broken when placed in the Mimbres graves is also provocative.[25] While the comparison may not be apt, Plains Indians did not as a rule break funerary items, taking the position that an exact and useful spirit counterpart would accompany the deceased into the afterlife. If such an idea held for the Mimbres, then breakage of any kind would simply indicate the end of the worldly life of the individual interred, for "spirit" counterparts that were damaged would be of little use.

Hugo Rodeck hints at the possibility of pictographic representation when he states that "it teases the mind to consider that among the geometric devices so often found decorating otherwise realistic Mimbres animal and human figures may be hieroglyphs which in fact 'say' something about the figure on which they are drawn, rather than being mere geometric fancies with no more than decorative significance. To the Mimbres mind some of these may have had a commonly accepted and readily understandable meaning."[26] Earlier, in considering the Maya, I described funerary plates with holes punched or bored in them, and I mention for further consideration Dockstader's supposition that the paintings on them might have had some hieroglyphic meaning.

Still another view regarding the meaning of the painted designs, and perhaps the most plausible one, is that of Ray L. Carlson. He believes that Mimbres painted pottery is related to a cult of the dead, "the same cult of the dead that we know historically as the Kachina (Masked god) cult, the cult of the dead rainmakers."[27] He supports his view by associating the designs with the Zuñi Katcina cult and with the involved creation myth, which is told to initiates, of the beheading of Kaiguani, a youth whose head was cut off because he told cult secrets. At one point in the myth, as the ancestral Zuñi people are crossing the sacred water, some of the children are dropped into it, where they turn into water creatures such as frogs, fish, and turtles, who in time are transformed again into rainmaking Katcinas. In this connection, the painting "in which lines connect men with fish are not depictions of fishing expeditions, but are rainmaking ceremonies which show moisture being drawn from these rain givers."[28] Of course, if Carlson's view is accurate, it is the strongest support yet for the idea that some of the Mogollon, and particularly the Mimbres, merged in time with the Anasazi to become the present-day Zuñi. "Mimbres representational paintings can be interpreted directly in terms of Zuñi myth."[29]

Over the next two or three hundred years, lasting until A.D. 1150, while the Mogollon culture as a whole was beginning to decline, Mimbres potters raised their art to extraordinary levels of sophistication and originality. One can therefore only regret that avid collectors have so despoiled the pot sites that the full significance of the Mimbres culture is seriously obscured.

Mimbres bowls were formed by coiling and scraping. A large chunk of clay was rolled into a long round strip and, beginning at the center of the base, the bowl was built up by braiding strip upon strip until it reached the desired height and shape. Next it was worked inside and out with a scraper and burnished with a smooth stone until remarkably thin and uniform. Then it was dried, covered with a white or pale gray slip, and, after the slip had dried, burnished again until virtually all blemishes were removed.

Mogollon. Examples of designs used by the Mimbres on their pottery.

Mogollon. Examples of designs used by the Mimbres on their pottery.

Painting was done on the bowl interior with either an iron paint or an extract of a dried plant, perhaps mustard, applied with a brush made of yucca leaves shredded at one end to form bristles.[30] The paint varied in its finished effect from deep black to orange-red. With only this limited equipment a Mimbres potter, whether woman or man, could paint parallel lines so thin and firm that fifteen of them could fit within a space less than three quarters of an inch wide, all done so well that it seems it couldn't have been accomplished without a mechanical aid.

As decoration the Mimbres used both naturalistic and geometric designs, similar to elements seen in the monuments and artifacts of ancient Mexico and often combining the two on the same bowl. The geometric patterns are usually quite elaborate and probably are superior to those of any other prehistoric culture. The bold and delicate, the simple and the ornate appear together. Naturalistic designs, although highly stylized and imaginative, are always easy to recognize. Moreover, there seems to have been nothing in the living world around them that the Mimbres artists did not paint. We find flowers, humans, fish, turtles, turkeys, rabbits, bears, insects, mountain lions, antelopes, lizards, rams, and a few artifacts. Nor were the paintings created from common patterns. It is virtually impossible to find two Mimbres bowls that are identical.

So thorough are the depictions, they seem to form a kind of symbolic writing. Daily life and ceremonies are depicted in scenes that can be arranged in chronological order, and the typical life of a Mimbres Mogollon family can be read from beginning to end. Paintings of people performing daily tasks or socializing are abundant on their bowls and offer an unparalleled opportunity to re-create the daily lives and ceremonial activities of the people. Indeed, some of the featured animals and fish might even have been clan symbols.[31] Interestingly, the effigy vessel, except for an occasional bird or duck, was almost totally absent from Mimbres creations.

With the arrival of the Great Drought period in the 1150s the Mimbres Mogollon culture came to an end, and no more of their splendid ceramics were produced. So suddenly were the Mimbres villages abandoned that the least one can say is the ultimate cause was overwhelming; only something like a fierce enemy invasion would explain so abrupt an end to an extraordinary artistic tradition. Touches of the Mimbres design style are evident in kiva murals and on pottery of the Pueblo IV Period, but it is probable they resulted from a continued use of the design style on ceremonial paraphernalia, not that the Mimbres work as such was still being done.

In contrast, the disappearance of the rest of the Mogollon as a distinct cultural entity was probably slow and, to those living at the time, perhaps almost imperceptible. Sometime between the years 1200 and 1400, various village groups migrated north into the desert and mesa country to merge their already Pueblicized culture with that of the natives, and were apparently absorbed into the well-advanced Anasazi society. The Zuñi, as well as other Pueblos of historical and contemporary times, may indeed be in part the descendants of the Mogollon. This much is known: when, in 1540, Coronado passed through the country where they had lived for 1,800 years, on his search for the Seven Cities of Cíbola, the Mogollon culture as an entity was already gone.

COHONINA
A.D. 900–1300?

In an area ranging from the San Francisco Peaks, immediately north of Flagstaff, to the Grand Canyon, lived a people known to archaeologists as the Cohonina. They did some farming and pottery-making, but relied, for all but one period of their life, mostly on hunting for sustenance. Their villages were small, made of perishable materials, and scattered. Little is known about their manner of life or cultural diffusions, but we can assume that they made their contributions to the developing cultures of the Southwest. One evidence is their joining with the Hohokam, Anasazi, and Sinagua for at least part of a two-hundred-year period at a site north of Sunset Crater, Arizona. For a brief time after that, they built some stone towers and dwellings along the south rim of the Grand Canyon, where the ruins can be seen today. As to who their ancestors are, we haven't a hint.

SINAGUA
A.D. 900–1400?

Southeast of the San Francisco Peaks were a people called the Sinagua, meaning "without water." Their earliest homes were pithouses, but by A.D. 1100 they were building masonry surface houses, and before A.D. 1200 large pueblos. An event of great consequence for the Sinagua was the eruption of Sunset Crater about A.D. 1065. The crater continued to erupt for several months, spewing out great quantities of ash, and no doubt caused endless problems for nearby residents. The strong southern winds spread it to the north, east, and west until at last it covered the earth over an 800-square-mile area.

But the ash was to be a blessing in disguise, for it was discovered that the cinders acted as a moisture-holding mulch, and enterprising farmers came with their families from all directions to cultivate the rich fields. The gardens around Sunset Crater became a melting pot of humanity.

Native to the area, the Sinagua arrived first, followed by the Hohokam, the Anasazi, and the Cohonina. For 160 years or more these cultures lived harmoniously together, exchanging some traditions and keeping others. But one day the same strong winds that brought the cinder bonanza began to carry it all away. The farmers did what they could to stem the onslaught, but in the end the winds prevailed. One by one the farmers left for other areas, and by

Sinagua—Wupatki. *a*, stone hoe. *b*, wooden paddle. *c*, squash stems. *d*, 750-year-old corncob. *e*, copper bells. *Top right*, T-shaped doorway. *Bottom*, aerial view of Wupatki ruin and ball court. From National Park Service photographs.

Wupatki. *Top right*, method of framing door lintel. *Top left*, one of many pictographs at Wupatki National Monument. *Bottom*, Lomaki Ruin. From National Park Service photographs.

Wupatki. *Top*, north portion of Wupatki Ruin. *Bottom*, Wupatki ball court.

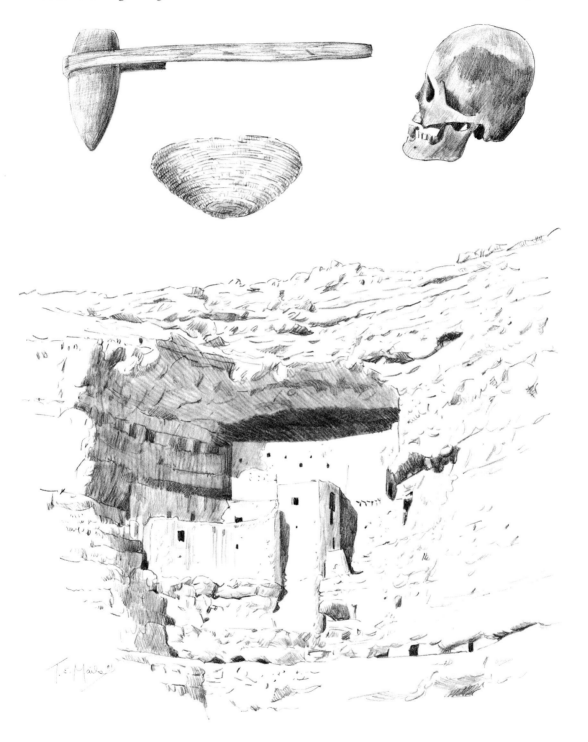

Sinagua. *Bottom*, Montezuma Castle ruin. *Top left*, fully hafted ax found in the largest prehistoric southwestern salt mine, seven miles south. *Top middle*, coiled beargrass basket found inverted over the face of a child. *Top right*, flattened skull of a woman buried in trash dump in front of the castle. From National Park Service photographs.

Sinagua—Walnut Canyon. *Top left*, the common doorway was T-shaped. Some archaeologists think the large part of the opening could be closed with a mat, leaving the small opening for ventilation. The other vent hole at the top of the wall completed the air circulation system. *Top right*, partial remains of rock fortress walls constructed on the high promontories of the canyon. *Bottom*, some of the canyon's 200-odd cliff dwellings.

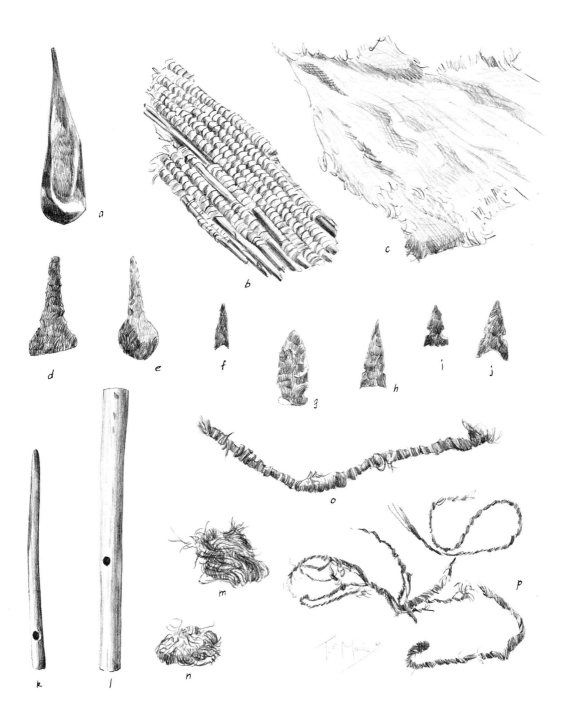

Walnut Canyon. *a*, piece of antler used in flaking arrowheads and knives. *b*, fragment of basketry. *c*, woven cotton cloth. *d–e*, stone drills for making holes in wood, stone, etc. *f–j*, stone projectile points. *k*, bone awl or needle with a broken point. *l*, bone flute. *m–n*, two quids of aqave cactus which the Sinagua cooked and ate. *o*, large string that was part of a turkey feather blanket. *p*, knotted cordage.

Tuzigoot. *Top left,* storage jar. *Top middle,* turquoise inlay (mosaic) ornament. *Top right,* detail of dwelling rooms. *Bottom,* view of Tuzigoot from foot of mesa.

1225 all were gone—leaving behind them more than eight hundred ruins, some of which were spectacular. Wupatki and its ball court is the best known of these, but the ruins are like the displays at a builders' convention: there are multistoried Anasazi-type pueblos, various methods of construction, stone-lined pithouses, and kivas of every sort.

The Sinagua moved from the Sunset Crater area into Walnut Canyon and the Verde River valley to join some of their people already there, into the Tonto Basin, and into other regions where water could be found. By now they were a new culture—themselves, Hohokam, Anasazi, Cohonina, and Mogollon combined.

The best known of the Sinagua pueblo structures is Montezuma Castle, incorrectly so named by area pioneers—the Aztec emperor was never, so far as is known, in Arizona. The castle is a five-story cliff structure with hand-fitted stone walls and foot-thick sycamore ceiling beams, built in a small cave a hundred feet above Beaver Creek. Investigations show that it took three hundred years to complete the nineteen or twenty rooms that make up the castle. In the ruin itself and in the trash heaps below were found heaps of corncobs and evidences of squash, beans, and cotton. These were planted in terraced patches irrigated by well-engineered ditches. Another twenty-two Sinagua dwelling places have been found within a half-mile radius of the castle, and possibly 150 Sinagua occupied the complex at one time.

Sinagua were also located in sprawling Walnut Canyon as early as A.D. 1120. With the water of Walnut Creek readily at hand, flat rim tops for cultivating, and numerous caves available for shelter, over the next century and a half they built more than three hundred small cliff rooms. They tilled their small fields with simple sticks. From juniper, ponderosa pine, piñon, fir, locust, black walnut, aspen, willow, and native plants they fashioned clothing and derived foods. They made cordage of plant fibers and fashioned excellent black-on-white fired ceramics. They hunted with atlatls and spears. By 1270, though, something cataclysmic happened, and suddenly the Sinagua were gone.

Dendrochronology shows that a severe drought devastated the dry-farming areas of the northern Sinagua from A.D. 1215 to 1299, forcing the people to move to the more permanent, spring-fed streams in Arizona's Verde Valley, from which water could be drawn for irrigation. Here they built on the crest of a low hill the stone apartment house called Tuzigoot, which flourished until A.D. 1450.

When scientists excavated Tuzigoot in 1933 and 1934 it turned out to be a treasure chest of artifacts and information. Intricate mosaic and shell jewelry was found, as well as bead necklaces. Pottery sherds were pieced together to restore immense water jars, called ollas. Remains were found of fine basketry woven from grasses, tree barks, and yucca leaves, and of refined cotton textiles produced on an upright loom.

The rooms at Tuzigoot average 12 by 18 feet (3.6–5.5 m). Each has a small entry hatch and an opening for exhausting smoke from cooking and warming fires. By 1299 there were ninety-two such rooms, with children buried beneath the floors of some of them. Adult dead were disposed of with little apparent ceremony. One hundred and seventy burials have been found at Tuzigoot. Seventy-one are of infants and children under eight years of age, and forty bodies range from nine to twenty-one years. Forty-nine of the dead were adults, twenty-one to forty-five years old. Only ten of the people had lived beyond forty-five. It appears that life at Tuzigoot was not easy, nor was it at Montezuma Castle, where the average Sinagua life span was at most thirty-five years.

Map showing approximate area occupied by the Hakataya and their branches about A.D. 600.
After Albert H. Schroeder. The Hakataya were first posited as a culturally distinct group by
Schroeder in 1957. The Hakataya were contemporary prehistoric neighbors of the Anasazi,
Mogollon, Hohokam, Sonoran, Great Basin, and Coastal California cultures. Cultural varia-
tions among Hakatayan groups reflect the variety of environments and the varying influences
of their neighbors. The Hakataya also played an important role in the diffusion of traits into
and through their country over a network of trails linking Arizona and New Mexico with the
California coast.

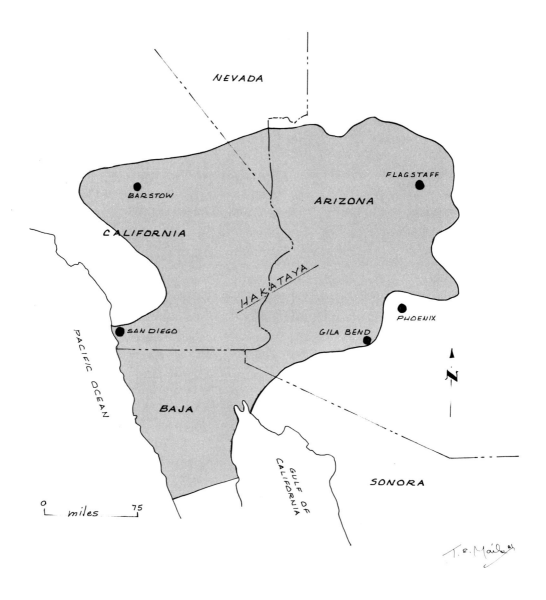

Map showing approximate area occupied by the O'otam. After Charles C. DiPeso. The term O'otam was first introduced by Dr. DiPeso in 1956 as a designation for the prehistoric ancestors of the Piman-speaking groups. This map shows their indigenous areas. Descendants of the Cochise people, the O'otam possessed a culture characterized by open villages made up of shallow pithouses with step or inclined covered passageway entrances, red-on-brown stone polished pottery, a dense brownware, and unsmudged redware. Their tools consisted of block-shaped or basin-shaped metates; triangular, side-notched projectile points; and three-quarter-grooved axes. The intrusion of the Hohokam, in what is generally referred to as the Snaketown Colonial Period, in A.D. 800 brought cotton textiles, changes in ceramics, ball courts, platform mounds, and the long, narrow "gable-roofed house with a covered, bulbous entry." In the years A.D. 1060–1340 a new cultural influence was felt as a result of contacts with the Paquimé people of Casas Grandes. The O'otam accepted such items as contiguous puddled-adobe-surface compounds, road and communications systems, scarlet macaws, new irrigation devices, Casas Grandes potteries, and copper ornaments. The presence of Pueblo stone architecture, slab-lined hearths, courtyards, and both subterranean and surface kivas at ruins such as the Davis Site and the Reeve Ruin indicate the presence of groups of Anasazi among the O'otam sometime around A.D. 1450.

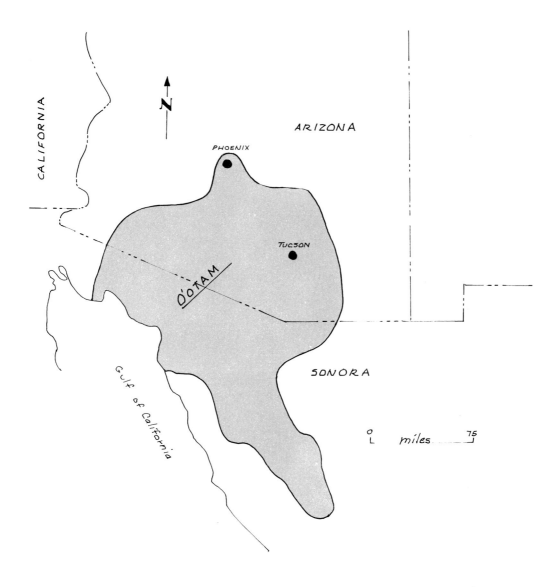

Chapter 2

THE ANASAZI

BASKETMAKER II
ca. 100 B.C.–A.D. 550

ORIGIN

The progenitors of the Anasazi were a Uto-Aztecan people who hunted, gathered, and made baskets as a principal craft, hence the name Basketmakers. It is firmly established that such basketmaking people were settled and active in several locations in North America long before the time of Christ. What is not known is where the Anasazi Basketmakers lived before they moved into the San Juan drainage basin. Some authorities are convinced that the Basketmaker womb was the Great Basin to the west. Many artifacts of the Anasazi Basketmakers of the Four Corners area are identical with those found in Nevada caves and dating from 2000 B.C. Hence it seems logical to conclude that, driven from Nevada by the need for better living conditions and more permanent water sources, the earliest Anasazi migrated eastward and finally settled in the canyons of the San Juan drainage basin, where by A.D. 1 the culture was established and progressing in its new homeland.[1]

Charles Avery Amsden, author of *Prehistoric Southwesterners from Basketmaker to Pueblo*, tends to discount the theory of a Nevada origin. He readily admits that some basketmakers did dwell in upper Nevada, on the northwestern edge of the Southwest, as early as 2000 B.C. But, he argues, they could not have been the ancestors of the Anasazi Basketmaker group. For one thing, they had no agriculture. For another, while they lived much the same kind of life and used similar types of tools and utensils, they did everything a little differently—enough so that archaeologists can distinguish between the two.

Other basketmakers roamed in southwestern Texas, in the area between the Rio Pecos and the Rio Grande. They, too, had the same mode of life, but nothing they achieved evidences the productivity and skill that would mark them as Anasazi forebears. The Texas people did cultivate corn and squash, resembling the Anasazi at least in that important respect. Traces of Basketmaker-like people have been found in northern Mexico, in the states of Coahuila and Chihuahua, and even in southwestern Arkansas. But none of these resemble in any significant way the basketmaking Anasazi, who flowered separately and rapidly into an outstanding culture and accomplished infinitely more in the long run than any of the other known basketmakers. This being the case, at the time of his untimely death in 1941 Amsden still thought it best to keep the progenitor question open until conclusive data came to light.

A latecomer to the list of progenitor candidates is the San Jose Phase of northwestern New Mexico. Here were a hunting and gathering people who lived in small groups and moved according to the season from place to place. It is thought possible they grew corn; but if so, the crop did not play a major role in their diet.[2]

While archaeologists have not yet identified any culture that they would unhesitatingly call Basketmaker I, this much is certain: agriculture, and particularly the cultivation of maize, made the ultimate difference for the Anasazi. It was the fuel that launched them into a new course, for they followed a set and upward path from that time forward. With archaeology as our docent, we pick

Some sites of the Desert Culture. Redrawn from Martin and Plog, 1973.

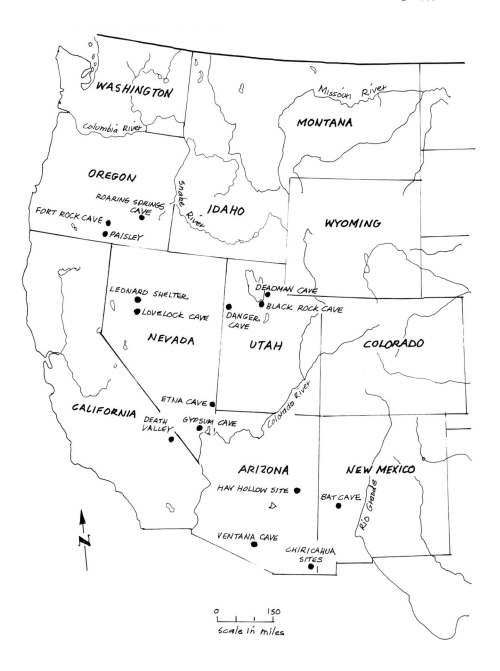

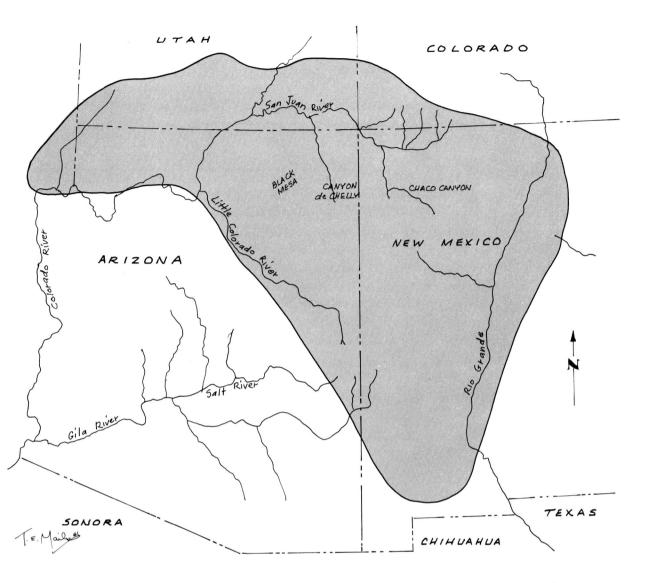

Map showing approximate area occupied by the Anasazi Basketmaker culture prior to the formation of the six major regions. The extension into the southwestern corner of New Mexico must allow for an overlapping and mixture of the Anasazi and Mogollon.

up their story in the Basketmaker II Period, in the San Jose drainage basin, about A.D. 215. The manner of life at that point was mainly nonagricultural, although some agriculture was practiced. Whenever Basketmaker II remains have been found, varying amounts of corncobs, squash rinds, and other agricultural products have been found with them.

Recent discoveries far to the south make it all but positive that the Basketmakers did not develop maize. The queen of crops was being cultivated in Mesoamerica and South America long before the Basketmakers knew of it, and it was already the mainstay of the earlier Mogollon and Hohokam. So reason, with the help of a few hints from archaeology, tells us that corn was brought first to the Southwest to the Hohokam and Mogollon, and was passed by their hands on to several cultures, including the San Juan Basketmakers.[3] Thus it reached the first Anasazi by cultural diffusion, arriving about the time of the birth of Christ. When it did come, it began the slow but dramatic process that would change them inexorably from a seminomadic hunting and gathering culture to a sedentary, agricultural one.

The segment of the Anasazi culture known as Basketmakers flourished in the San Juan drainage basin, popularly known today as the Four Corners area of the United States. Situated north of the Hohokam and Mogollon, these Basketmakers occupied roughly the same country their Pueblo descendants would occupy later. For a long time no one knew Basketmakers had even existed in the southwest plateau country, and we have no population figures for them yet.

During the years of peak discovery in Southwestern archaeology, from the 1880s to 1950, the Anasazi Basketmaker culture, wherever found, was impressively uniform in content at every cultural stage. Findings near Cortez, Colorado, proved to be 78 percent like those of Durango, Colorado, and Kayenta and Canyon del Muerto, Arizona. There were differences in area emphasis.

Southern Paiute woman holding basket tray and carrying conical burden basket, standing in front of a brush shelter of type probably used by the Anasazi. Composite from 1873 photographs by John K. Hillers.

Some locations, such as Tseahatso, in Canyon del Muerto, were primarily burial sites, while Durango sites contained homes evidencing long use. Further, it was learned that the early settlers of the Durango area were of mixed physical strains, all belonging to a genetic stream called Southwestern Plateau, one of the basic breeding stocks that peopled the New World.[4]

The first hint of an earlier people than the pueblo builders came when in 1888 excavations were begun at Mesa Verde, Colorado, and Grand Gulch, Utah. All the pueblo builders practiced the custom of deforming the back of the head by the use of hard cradleboards, and pottery pieces usually accompanied their burials. Yet time after time, while working in lower strata of cave debris than those where bodies buried with pottery offerings had been found, excavators would come upon flexed corpses with large baskets inverted over their heads. The difference between the burial styles was too striking to be ignored. Day by day, year by year, the suspicion grew that the lower corpses represented a different people than the cliff dwellers, earlier in time and, perhaps—although this was an erroneous assumption—having no family relationship with those who came later.

Some authorities give credit for the Basketmaker name to the Wetherill brothers, others to B. T. B. Hyde, who funded some of the early work at the Anasazi dwellings for the American Museum of Natural History in New York City. Whether or not he was the first to invent it, Hyde was using the term "basket makers" by 1894, and soon thereafter everyone working in the field employed it to describe the first of the Anasazi.

DWELLINGS

The earliest Basketmakers lived in caves for part of the year and in flimsy open-air shelters the rest of the time. Evidence concerning their outdoor shelters is scanty. Only a few stone tools were made, since these in large numbers would hinder travel, and what shelters there were, were constructed of perishable materials not able to withstand centuries of exposure to the elements. Circles of stones that are thought to have been part of dwellings have been found in Basketmaker territory, but the stones could as well have been placed there by Utes or Paiutes of a much later time.

Since Utes and Paiutes who followed the old ways were still living in Basketmaker territory in historic times, we can guess, from their open-air dwellings, what those of the earliest Basketmakers must have been like. They were rudely constructed, consisting of a nearly round dome framework of medium-sized tree limbs covered with woven mats or thatched grass. Circles of stones were placed there to brace the structure against the wind. When the weather was good the Paiute built nothing more than a windbreak wall without a roof, and small ramadas, or brush shades, were erected to work under when the hot sunshine demanded. Beds were simply piles of grass and leaves.

A few crude house ruins have been discovered that might have belonged to the earliest Basketmakers; they are somewhat similar to those made by later Basketmakers. At the very least, it is clear that the people did not spend all their time in caves. Cave findings of the earliest Anasazi, such as ashes, fire-pits, bones, and refuse, occur only sparingly in even the largest and best caves yet excavated. This points to the cave as a refuge in stormy or cold weather, rather than a year-round dwelling place.

The ongoing purpose of the Basketmaker cave was to serve as a storage area and a burial ground. Perishable foods and many of the Basketmakers' personal belongings were kept there in cists, and at life's end some of the cists were converted to tombs. Cists were storage pits of ingenious design made with considerable care. They ranged in size from 3 feet (1 m) in diameter and 3 feet (1 m) deep to 8 feet (2.4 m) in diameter and 4 feet (1.2 m) deep—almost big enough to serve as underground houses. Judging by beds of grass, bark, and leaves found in them, some were used as sleeping places.

To make the cist, a hole was dug with wooden scoops in the soft sand-stone floor of the cave, and its edges were lined with the thin slabs of sand-stone that were readily available. The bottom of the pit was sometimes paved with thin slabs; at other times it was given a coating of mud plaster, or a bed of leaves, bark, or grass. Conscientious builders would chink the cracks be-tween lining stones with a combination of small stones, mud, or plant fibers such as shredded juniper bark. Larger pits were sometimes subdivided into bins by slab partitions.

Cist covers were designed to keep animals and debris out. A smaller cist required only a fitted slab of sandstone, but a larger one demanded a more elaborate arrangement. It would be roofed over with a framework of poles and brush, overlaid with bark, grass, and leaves, and sometimes sealed with a layer of clay. An entryway was left in the center, and this was closed by a stone-slab lid. Mud was used either to make a tight seal around the lid or to build a low curb upon which the lid was placed. A few cists had cribbed roofs similar to those used for kivas in pueblo times. (The method of building a cribbed roof will be described when pueblo kiva construction is considered.)

Amsden believed that the simple building practices of the early Basket-makers were to some extent the origin of the terraced cliff houses of later cen-turies. "Pueblo architecture," he says, "was largely, if not entirely, an indige-nous growth, rooted literally enough in the sandy floor of the Basketmaker cave. Here, among the earliest Anasazi of whom we have any knowledge, are such structural features as fitted stone walls mortared and spalled, partitions, contiguous walls, wall recesses forming benches, vaulted roofs, cross-beam roofs with supporting posts to carry their weight, adobe roof coverings, and hatchway entrances. Here is the pueblo in embryo."[5] I doubt that anyone would argue with him, for few archaeologists knew the Basketmakers better than he.

From an archaeologist's point of view, the caves used by the Basketmakers were a godsend. They have preserved a surprising number of structures, arti-

Basketmaker—cave culture. *Top,* perspective view of cave floor covered with cists. *Bottom left,* plot plan of storage cists in Cave II, in the northern wall of Kinboko, Arizona. From Kidder and Guernsey, 1919. *Bottom right,* portion of cists in Basketmaker II cave in Kane County, Utah.

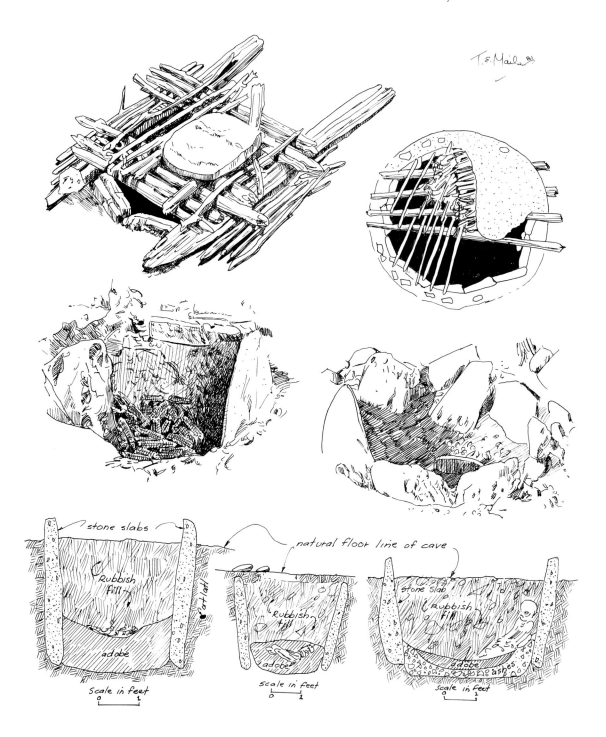

Basketmaker cists. *Top left*, roof of a Basketmaker II cist in Du Pont Cave, Utah. From photograph by Jesse L. Nusbaum. *Top right*, roof of Cist 12, from Kidder and Guernsey, 1919. *Center left*, cist built against cave wall with corn cache, from Kidder and Guernsey. *Center right*, typical cist, from Kidder and Guernsey. *Bottom*, sections through cists used for burials, from Kidder and Guernsey.

facts, and human bodies, all of which have been vital in reconstructing the history of the Basketmakers. Almost all we know of the Basketmakers has been learned from the caves, and it is helpful to have some knowledge of what these were really like.

They were not deep, dark caverns. The typical cave was a relatively shallow and thus well-lighted rock shelter at or near the base of a sandstone cliff. It was formed entirely by nature, and the Basketmakers did nothing to remodel it. Running water in considerable force had, over a long period of time, undercut a portion of the cliff to the point where either the sandstone wore away or the overhanging portion fell, making a stone pocket. Then nature continued to enlarge the pocket, aided in some instances by seepage from within the cliff itself.

The end product was a stone vaulted space of almost any size. Some caves were so small that only a tiny room could be built into them. Others would hold a modern building several stories high. The cave floor was littered with pieces of fallen stone, often in ready sizes to be used by Anasazi builders. Below many a cave was a talus slope created by the largest portions of rock to fall, and these provided even more building material. While a few caves were damp, most were airy and dry, providing shade in summer and protection in winter. Rain would streak the surface of the massive cliff face above a cave, but down below, the greater part of the cave escaped it. A cave might even have a spring of water issuing from the rear of the pocket. Caves were never equal in comfort and quality to modern homes, but they required little preparatory effort, and they worked surprisingly well, costing so little to occupy and maintain that we can only be envious.

APPEARANCE, CLOTHING, ADORNMENT

The bodies of Basketmakers were found in the caves in such good states of preservation that we know today pretty much what they looked like. With some exceptions, they were small by our standards, the women being under five feet, and the men a few inches taller. They were sturdy and strong—the physical labor required to live would guarantee that. Heads were long, narrow, and well proportioned. Basketmakers must have looked much as Pueblo Indians do today, somewhat oriental, with high cheekbones, straight black hair, and an absence of body hair.[6] From what has been learned so far, adults had brown skin and children had lighter skin and finer hair than adults.

The Basketmakers dressed their hair in different ways. Burials in White Dog Cave, Arizona, provided archaeologists with several styles that proved to be similar to burials in other sites. Women usually had their hair hacked off to a length of two or three inches. Since human-hair cordage was frequently made, it is assumed that the women sacrificed their hair for this purpose, although some authorities have wondered whether the hacking might not have been done after death. But considering the multitude of ways in which hair was used, it seems doubtful the people would wait for death to cut a product that kept on growing so beautifully in life. The early Basketmaker men did not make the same sacrifice as the women might have done; they let their hair grow long, wearing it loose on occasion, but more often parted in the center, with a bob at each side and one in the back. The bobs were made by turning a portion of hair back and fastening it in place with string and clay. Alternate styles had the hair tied in the same three places, but hanging loose below the tie. Some men clipped their hair to form an exaggerated part and wore a small queue in addition to the bobs. The queue was formed of slender wisps of hair falling from the crown at the back of the head, wrapped or braided with string. They might have had ritual significance, or else have indicated social rank or occupation.[7] Haircutting seems to have been done with stone knives, and Earl Morris found many caches of hair carefully saved for future use. Small bunches of yucca served as hairbrushes.

Judging by what has been found in grave sites, the men wore nothing or almost nothing when the weather was good—a freedom many people would enjoy today. Burial sites do contain sandals, woven either of coarse splints of yucca leaf, or of cords made by twisting together shredded yucca fiber and Indian hemp. The sandal soles were flat—like a shingle—and had no uppers or heels. They were sometimes rounded at the back, sometimes straight. The toe was always made square. Some heels and toes had fiber fringes. A type of large sandal was woven of coarse fibers for wet-weather wear, and several mud-covered examples have been found. All sandals were held on the foot by two string loops, one large enough to catch a toe or two and the other passing around the front of the ankle and secured at the rear corners of the sandal. One or more strings ran down the front of the foot and connected the two loops.

California and Paiute males of early times wore G-strings and fringe hangings, as would seem to be sensible for a continually climbing people, yet no evidence of a male G-string or breechclout has turned up in a Basketmaker grave. Women wore little more, only sandals and a small apron. The apron was about a foot long and ten inches wide, consisting of loosely hanging yucca strings or cedar fibers in quantities sufficient to cover private areas. It was held up by a waist cord made of the same material. Menstrual pads consisted of long bundles of string or shredded yucca fiber, tucked under a decorated waist cord front and rear.

Aprons and menstrual pads may have been strictly utilitarian, yet this has never been the case with Indians we know more about. Menstruating women have always been a special concern at ceremonial times and were not allowed even to be present at a ground where a ritual was being held. They were banned until the menstrual period ended. I have seen this custom practiced today: by the Sioux at Sun Dances, the Apache at Sunrise Ceremonies for pubescent girls, and the Cherokees at Stomp Dances. Even if a woman is only suspected to be menstruating, the ceremonial arena will be purified, and an announcement will be made to advise any and all guilty parties to leave immediately. There is no point now in examining the reasons, since we do not know the Basketmakers' mind in this regard. But it may well be that this is our first evidence of Basketmaker religion. I doubt that prudishness was in vogue in those days.

The snow and freezing weather that arrived with winter in the Four Corners region called for a body covering. To meet this need, two kinds of wrap-

Basketmaker sandals: *top left,* toe-heel loop sandal tie. *Top right,* toe-heel loop with single cord. *Middle left and bottom right,* sandal-loop tie on foot. *Middle right and lower left,* crisscross tie. From Kidder and Guernsey, 1919, and Mesa Verde Museum.

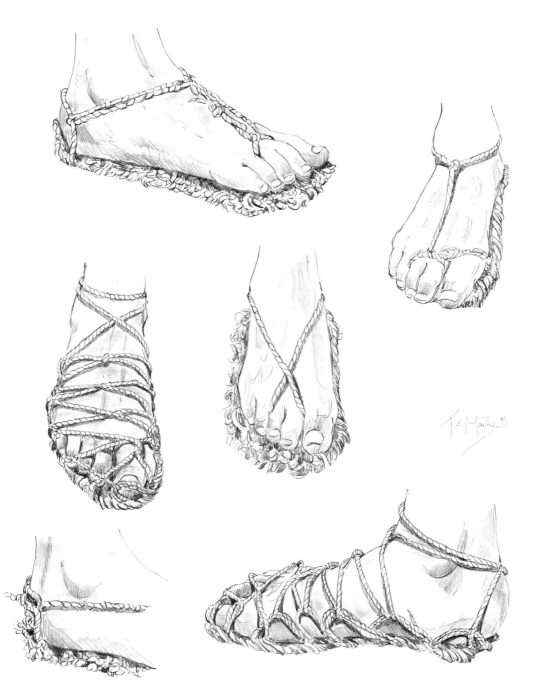

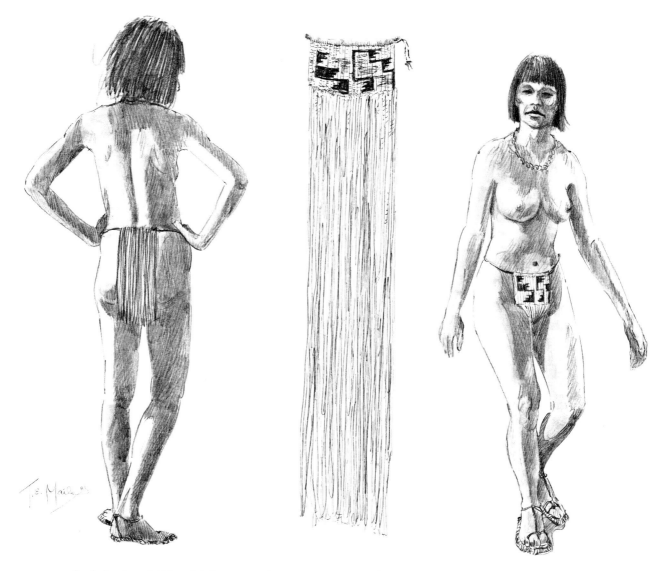

Basketmaker clothing details: woman's apron consisting of small woven band with a four-color design, and 241 yucca-fiber strings. Held in place by a small human-hair rope. The strings were gathered between the legs and looped over the rope at the back. Artifact from Mesa Verde Museum.

arounds were fashioned, serving as robes during the day and blankets at night, and finally as burial wrappings for the deceased. The first kind of wrap-around was a tanned deerskin with thongs attached to fasten it at the chest. The second kind was made by wrapping rabbit-fur strips spirally around yucca cords, placing the finished tubes of fur in parallel rows, and cross-twining these with cordage at intervals of two or three inches. Robes were sometimes ornamented with borders made of cords that had been wrapped with feathered bird-skin strips. The resulting product was quite handsome and warm, and several cultures used the technique. The robes were popular burial wraps.

The Paiute made soft, warm rabbitskin blankets that were wrapped about the shoulders during the day and used as blankets at night. Desert temperatures vary greatly from daytime to nighttime, and in winter the fur robes often spelled the difference between freezing and surviving. The rabbits were taken in November by the drive technique, when the pelts were at their prime, and were skinned in such a way as to keep the pelt intact. First the skin was cut around the paws. Then, beginning with the hind legs, the skin was pulled up and over the rabbit's head. Starting near an eyehole, the skin was cut into a long, thin spiral strip by pulling it skillfully across a sharp knife blade held between the teeth. This formed a strip ten to fifteen feet long. A chain of skins was made by tying the end of one through the eyehole of the next. The skins were twisted by thrusting a stick through the end piece of the chain and then rolling the skin along the thigh—a method also used to make cordage. The skin side was turned in and the fur side was exposed. The skin was then left to dry, after which the rabbit ears were cut off before they could become brittle. To weave a blanket, the chains were looped around a crude loom of willows and twined together with strings of hemp. The coarseness of the weave depended upon taste. An adult's blanket required a hundred rabbit skins; a child's, forty.[8]

A few pieces of plain woven cloth from the early Basketmaker period have been found. However, no loom-weaving equipment has come to light, and so archaeologists can only wonder whether loom weaving accompanied the finger-weaving technique used to make sandals and wrap-arounds.

Jewelry is abundant in grave sites and is always evident in cave paintings. The early Basketmakers were obviously fond of it and created a number of items. Stone beads were ground, polished, and perforated for stringing. Olivella and abalone shells came inland by trade routes, either in the form of beads or as shells to be later worked into beads by the Basketmakers. Native snail shells were turned into beads. Small bones were cut into even lengths and engraved. Seeds such as the juniper berry were strung on cords and made into loops of different lengths, often with pendants hanging from the longer loops. The pendants were cut from shell, abalone being the favored kind, and were also made from polished stone. Necklaces included a choker type similar to that which has always been popular among the Plains Indians. The comparatively simple Basketmaker variety was made of hide or fiber string and had only a pendant or two dangling from it. Amsden, always quick to give credit where credit is due, suggests that the loop and toggle devised by the Basketmakers to fasten the choker may well have been the nifty ancestor of the modern button and buttonhole.[9]

A second religious indication to go along with the menstrual pads and aprons might be the early Basketmakers' use of bird feathers. The feathers of many bird species were used for adornment. Some were attached to robes, others were bound to pins of wood or bone to be worn in the hair. Breathfeather (down) tufts were tied to strings for attachment to other items, just as the Pueblo Indians use them today for pahos (prayer sticks) and for armbands

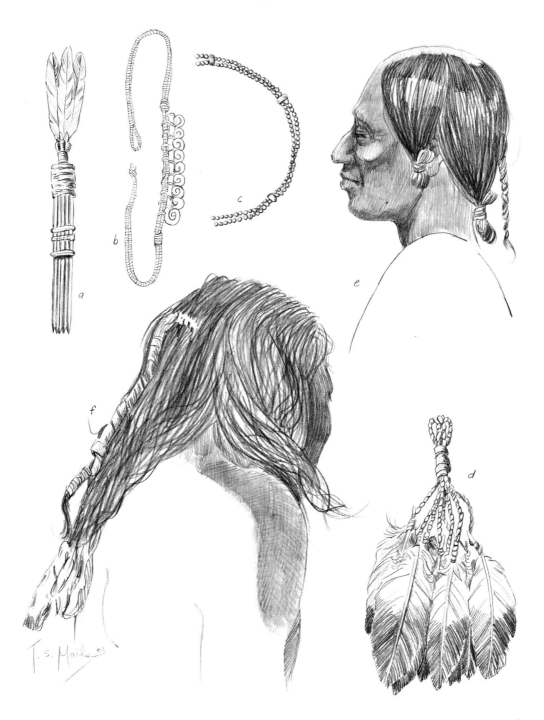

a, Basketmaker II feather ornament probably worn in the hair, White Dog Cave, Arizona. *b,* Basketmaker II shell necklace from Marsh Pass, Arizona. *c,* half of a double-strand necklace of green stone and ephedra seeds from Basketmaker II, Du Pont Cave, Utah (from Jesse L. Nusbaum photograph). *d,* Basketmaker II feather pendant from Marsh Pass. *e–f,* male hairstyles from Basketmaker II and Basketmaker III. From Kidder and Guernsey, 1919.

and hair ties. Finds include bundles of long feathers, each bundle wrapped at the quill to form a handle. These were undoubtedly made for ceremonial purposes. Feathered headbands have also been unearthed. In 1930, at Broken Flute Cave, in Red Rocks Valley, Earl Morris and John Wetherill recovered cylindrical wooden boxes and conical baskets filled with an "unbelievable" assortment of feathers from the golden eagle and other colored feathers.[10]

We can only guess at what the Basketmakers actually believed about birds and their association with spiritual power, but we do know their descendants prize bird feathers for vastly more than their color. Birds are considered intermediary powers between human beings and the spirits above, and are essential in ceremonies. To wear certain feathers is to obtain and set these powers in motion for the good of everything in the universe. It is a way that the higher powers have ordained, and we can reasonably assume the Basketmakers had also come to believe this. They, like all other Indians, could not help pondering the unique attributes and abilities of birds, and how to obtain those abilities for themselves—arriving at the answer still in service today.

Noticeably absent from the cave findings are turquoise and bracelets. A few fragments of relatively crude inlay work have been found, but nothing to suggest the quality or amount of Hohokam products. One pair of lignite ear ornaments has been found. No body painting or tattooing has been observed among the corpses, although pictographic paintings indicate that body painting was done.

RELIGION

Like so many other aspects of their lifeway, the ceremonial practices of the early Basketmakers can only be guessed at and pieced together. An inference is picked up here, another there, until finally some tentative conclusions can be drawn. A reference plane as we do this is the known history of ritual among the Pueblos. When first encountered by Europeans, Pueblo ceremonial life was already developed to the high point of sophistication it maintains today. Interchanges of religious ideas were taking place between the major Pueblo areas—a process that has continued into the present—yet for all but insignificant innovations, such as the Comanche Dance, the adopted and reshaped ideas had already reached maturation with the first Pueblos to use them.

Thus it is entirely possible that by the fifteenth century the growth process was almost done. A few elements were added thereafter to embellish, personalize, and heighten it; although depictions on pottery and in murals became more sublime as familiarity with the concepts grew, the essence of the ceremonials was the same.

It seems reasonable to conclude that religion was the focal point of life and unity for the Anasazi from the beginning, and that, from its embryo form in the early Basketmaker time, religious life developed steadily throughout the cultural changes until it became the esoteric adult it is today.

Living in a land where nature's caprices, water shortages, food supply problems, diseases, and other hazards could often spell the difference between life and death, the Basketmaker Anasazi must surely have done what they could to influence those conditions by ritual practice. A supernatural pantheon, and an attempt to establish regular and fruitful communion with it, was inevitable, just as was the case with the Mesoamerican civilizations whose every aspect of life was influenced by religion.[11]

Although no written record of early Basketmaker religion exists, some determinations regarding their religious progress can be gained from their art, from their artifacts, from their architecture, and from a comparison of these findings with the lifeway of the historic Pueblos.

Since none of the earliest structures seem to have been of a communal nature, it is assumed that the social spirit common to modern Pueblo religion took time to develop. But the nature of burials and even the earliest mortuary offerings show in a persuasive way the progressively strong and broadening flow of the spiritual current. Findings include pipes, feathers, bone whistles, carved wands, stuffed bird heads, bone tubes, fetishes, "killed" baskets, scalps, and, most important, medicine bundles containing lumps of paint pigment, fetish stones, specially worked pieces of wood, feathers, and many other items, similar to those in the bundles of later Plains Indian medicine men, whose use in gaining supernatural aid for divining and curing is well known.[12]

Menstrual customs and the use of bird feathers are further indications of religious attitudes. The placement of a pair of new sandals with each of the dead suggests belief in an afterlife. Dried umbilical cords hung from the sides of infant cradles were probably a prayer for a long and healthy life. Such prayers are offered only by people who believe in higher powers.

In my view, Amsden was fully justified in writing, in his treatise on the Basketmakers: "Ceremonies probably required much of men's time [he could have included women, for they always have an essential role to play], for the Indian's life is a perpetual commingling of practical activity and ritual intended to keep pace with those mystic powers which control the destinies of all life on earth, powers lurking everywhere to bring poverty or plenty, illness or health, to a people who draw no line between the occult and the actual. Ceremonies are a part of the serious business of life, no more to be neglected than hunting or tool-making."[13]

We can easily imagine a father saying to his son, demonstrating religion on the personal level: "Now that you have seen how our atlatl is made and the spear is thrown, you must also know the prayers, chants, and other ritual observances that go with its use—else the game will not come close by, you will be forced to hunt for a long time, and when you find an animal it will run away and you will miss it." Such a statement would, at the very least, emphasize things the Basketmakers had already begun to think. And it would be only a short step from there into the subterranean kiva, which is within and thus closer to the mother of all life and survival: the kiva, in an esoteric sense, is

Mother Earth's womb. And if she protects and preserves the food in the subterranean cists, will she not also protect men who descend into her?

Amsden might also have added that over a period of time some religious information was bound to have come north by diffusion from South America and Mesoamerica, being handed on in turn to the Basketmakers by the Hohokam and Mogollon along with trade items and other customs.

Richard Ambler states flatly that the Anasazi owe much of their culture to Mesoamerica, citing agriculture and pottery and adding that "religious ideas seem to have sprung up in Mesoamerica and spread out like mushrooms." But by the time they reached the Anasazi, he says, they were hardly recognizable as Mesoamerican, and it is mainly by general resemblances that we see the southern influence.[14] Thus he, like most other writers, tends to rule out diffusion by personal contact between the Anasazi and Mesoamericans, an idea I am far from content with. Surely the Anasazi and the Mesoamericans had a few Jack London–like souls who could not rest without first "seeing the world." And surely there were leaders north and south who sent explorers to see just how far realms and trade might be expanded.[15]

Granted that evidence is scant and that diffused ideas were reworked according to personal views and needs, to the point where they could no longer be recognized, bits and pieces continue to reinforce the argument for a diffusion of religious ideas. An example: In describing the Zia Pueblo Snake Order in 1890, Matilda Coxe Stevenson states: "Propitiatory prayers are not offered to the snakes, as, according to the Zia belief, the rattlesnake is a peaceful, and not an angry agent. They know he is friendly, because it is what the old men say, and their father's fathers told them, and they also told them that it was the same with *the snakes in Mexico* [emphasis added]."[16] More support for this comes from Muriel Porter Weaver when in her treatment of Mesoamerican diffusion she writes: "The Puebloan Southwest developed a rich style of its own, which grew out of an infiltration of Mesoamerican ceremonialism with concepts of fire, sun, and a twin war god associated with an early Quetzalcoatl and a basic rain fertility cult."[17]

MALE HUNTING AND CRAFTS

The Basketmakers did not come to the Four Corners country empty-handed. As the hunting and gathering descendants of ancient peoples, they could not have migrated without considerable skills in the survival arts. The seeds of architecture, agriculture, and communal living were already germinating when they arrived.[18] Nevertheless, we should not lose sight of the fact that the Basketmakers were the dawn people of the Anasazi, facing a sometimes hostile wilderness as pioneers with little beyond their own strength, skill, and courage. The odds were not in their favor. Nature was not very bountiful on the semi-arid southwestern plateau. It is true there were large game animals, some small game animals, a few plants that bore edible roots, some wild seeds, and small amounts of fruit. Also, weather conditions were favorable, and the country for the most part was consummately beautiful. But the Basketmakers had no firearms, no metal, no horses, no wheelbarrows, no beasts of burden, only the dog to serve as a friend and pack animal.

Except for items that came to them through trade later on, the first Basketmakers made everything they had from scratch, and they made it very well. Certainly they were a very busy people. On the basis of artifacts found and of later cultures observed, it is assumed that the women, beyond attending to personal hygiene, gathered the food, did the routine housework, cooked, minded the children, and fashioned the textiles and weavings needed for clothing and utensils. Children, like all Indian children, did mostly what they pleased. Men did the hunting and the heavier tasks such as building cists, devising and carving work implements, and fashioning weapons. The way each of these things was done suggests the people were relatively happy. Their handiwork has, without exception, almost an elegant finish. Even their simplest gear was embellished with ingenious details that cost them hours of otherwise needless toil. Unhappy people don't do that. They despair, and leave undone whatever they can.

For hunting, men used weapons and snares. The principal weapon was the atlatl, or spear-thrower, already mentioned as a tool employed by the cultures to the south and, again, thought by some to be a diffused item. The typical Basketmaker version of that slightly curved and tapered throwing stick was a piece of oak about 2 feet long, an inch wide at the broadest end and half an inch thick, with a recessed spur at the upper end to engage the cupped spear or dart butt, and a pair of hide finger loops at the handle end to afford a firm grip. The second and third fingers were passed through the loops, and the other fingers and the thumb grasped the butt of the stick and the spear.

Features that distinguished Basketmaker atlatls from those of most other cultures included the use of the finger loops instead of a wooden cross-pin (some Aztec ceremonial throwers had stone loops),[19] the custom of grooving the throwing stick at the upper end, with the spur at the base of this groove and nearly flush with the surface of the stick, and the addition of a one-ounce carved and polished stone lashed to the back of the stick a few inches above the finger loops. The stone helped to balance the weapon, gave added thrust, and may have served as a hunting fetish to bring good luck. The stones are of different forms, and some seem to be abstract animal effigies—items quite common in historic pueblos.

The spear, or dart, was compound, being made in two parts: a main shaft and a foreshaft. The main shaft was a maximum of 5½ feet long, round, and ½ inch in diameter. A pithy-centered wood was used, such as willow or yucca, both of which have hollow or soft interiors.[20] Its butt end was feathered in the usual fashion of Plains arrows, with three evenly spaced split feathers placed lengthwise, bowed slightly in the middle, and lashed to the shaft at both ends with sinew. Goose and hawk feathers were among those used.[21] A little cup ¼ inch deep was hollowed out in the very end of the spear butt. This fitted onto the spur on the throwing stick and kept it in place during the act of throwing. The foreshaft was a hard stick of oak or mountain mahogany about 6 inches long that was slightly tapered at the butt end and slid snugly into the hollowed-out end of the main shaft. Its front end was notched to receive the 2- or

Atlatl details from Basketmaker I and II periods. *a–b*, method of holding and hurling throwing-stick and dart. *c–e*, stone weights (or fetishes) attached to atlatls. *f*, enlarged detail of spur and cup in throwing stick to hold dart butt. *g–k*, varieties of styles in throwing-sticks. From Kidder and Guernsey, 1919, Campbell Grant, 1978, and other sources.

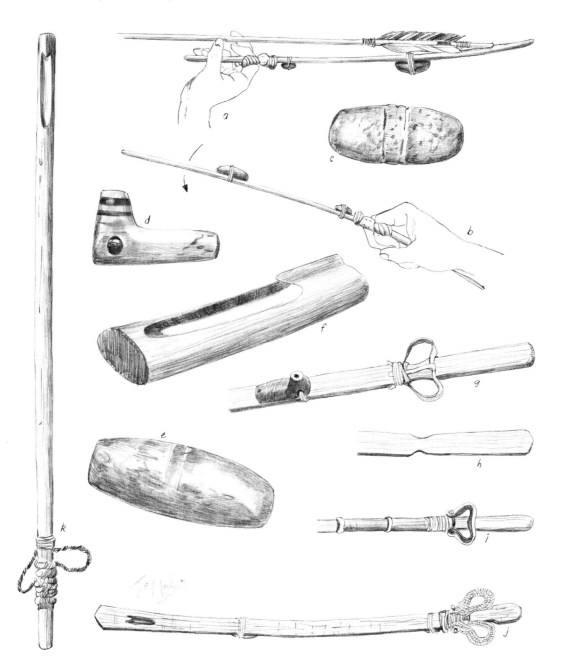

3-inch-long stone spearpoint, which was then secured with sinew lashing, strengthened at times with pitch.

Stewart Peckham notes that the tapered end of the foreshaft was often "rather rough," so that it would fit snugly into the main shaft and not be jarred loose. He also emphasizes that many foreshafts had sharpened, fire-hardened self wooden points—a self point is not added on but is the shaft itself, carved to a point—or else were carved like a top and were blunt.[22] The wooden points were used for birds and small game.

The theory behind the two-part spear is that the separate parts made it possible for the hunter, should the foreshaft and point become lodged, to pull off the main shaft and save it. It is also supposed that the main shaft would fall free from a fleeing animal. Thus the hunter would need to carry with him only a few foreshafts and one or two main shafts. The fact that no quivers have been found in Basketmaker sites makes the theory plausible.

Peckham states that some main shafts were decorated with simple bands or spirals painted in red or black with mineral pigments, soot, or some sort of vegetable dye, and that in other instances the entire main shaft was painted in one color "or may be left unpainted."[23] Shaft painting was a common practice among all Indians, since a marked arrow or spear quickly identified the owner of a disputed kill. Each man had his own set of markings, unique to his spears and arrows, so that no two hunters' shafts were alike. Since the color range was limited, further variations were achieved by the number, width, spacing, and shapes of bands. If more was needed, individual designs would be added.

To throw the spear, the hunter laid it flat on the throwing stick with the cup and spur engaged, and the front of the spear held in position between the knuckles of the two fingers that passed through the loops. He drew his arm upward and then backward as far as possible, took aim at his target, and released the shaft with a long forward sweep of the arm. An expert could cast his spear a hundred yards.

The atlatl had its problems. To throw it effectively for any distance, a hunter was forced to stand, and the moment he moved, so did the quarry. It is assumed, therefore, that some hunting was done from behind piled rocks, so as to be as close as possible to the target.

The bow and arrow, which came to the Basketmakers much later, perhaps as late as A.D. 500,[24] allowed the hunter to shoot more quietly from a hiding place and offered a far greater range than the killing limit of seventy-five yards or so of the atlatl. Nevertheless, it is known that with years of practice the Basketmakers learned to use the atlatl well. Remains attest to this. The skin and bones of deer, antelopes, mountain sheep, mountain lions, and bears have all been found in Basketmaker caves, and even after the bow arrived the atlatl remained in use.

Nets and snares were constructed to catch smaller game such as turkeys, other birds, rabbits, gophers, prairie dogs, badgers, and field mice. Two types of snare have been recovered. The most common type was a slip noose, made of fine string or, usually, human hair and tied to a peg. Other tribes who have made such snares in historical times set them out along pathways frequented by animals or at places where birds came to feed. The unsuspecting victim would get its head caught in the noose and choke itself to death in the attempt to get free. The other type of snare was a larger noose that encircled a net big enough to catch a running rabbit. This was laid over a burrow or set across a runway, and it would close over and entangle any animal pushing against it.

Items used for hunting game: *a*, Basketmaker II grooved rabbit throwing-stick from White Dog Cave, Arizona. *b*, Basketmaker II rabbit net from White Dog Cave. *c*, hinged stick snare. *d*, slip loop or noose snare. *e*, Basketmaker II snare from Du Pont Cave, Utah. From Kidder and Guernsey; Museum of the American Indian, Heye Foundation; and Peabody Museum, Harvard University.

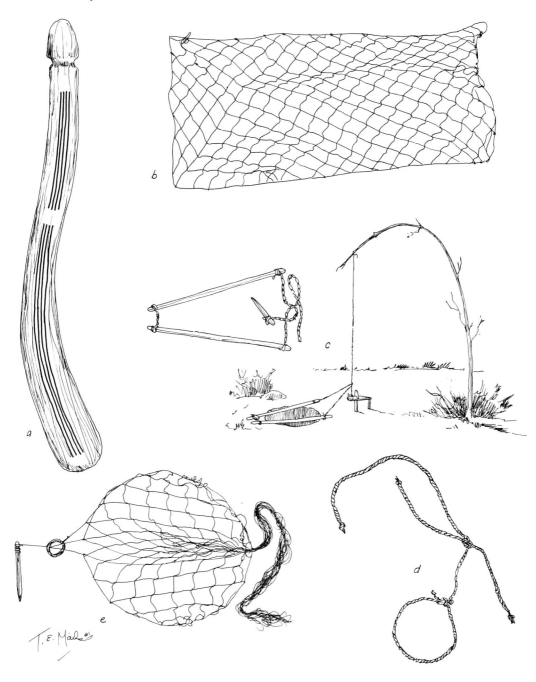

The largest Basketmaker net game trap yet found is 240 feet long and 4 feet wide. It has a 2-inch mesh of five-fiber string and looks like an exceedingly long badminton net. It weighs 2 pounds and has nearly 4 miles of cordage in its meshes. Modern tribes, such as the Paiute, stretched their nets across the neck of a narrow gorge. Men, women, girls, and boys, under the direction of a rabbit hunt captain, then went to the far end of the gorge and began to make their way down it, shouting and beating the brush with sticks, bows, and arrows to drive the game before them. Once the game reached the net and became entangled in it, men stationed there clubbed it to death. It was a gory scene but an effective method, and we can assume it worked as well for the Basketmakers. The night after a successful hunt became a time of celebration for the Paiute, and was an especially good courting time.[25]

Frequently found with the atlatl in burial and storage places is a flat, slightly curved wooden boomerang-like stick about two feet long. The Hopi use such sticks today to knock down small game and call them throwing clubs or rabbit sticks, but Amsden thought the two Basketmaker versions that Kidder and Guernsey found might have been fending sticks employed in battle to turn away enemy weapons. He points out that Mayan and Aztec warriors used virtually identical sticks to knock away enemy missiles, and he adds that the Basketmaker sticks show no evidence of the battering they would have received if thrown by hunters in rocky country. Furthermore, he says, the Basketmaker stick is embellished with a series of grooves on each face, usually four—a sacred number—and the grooves extend nearly from handle to tip. Mayan fending sticks were similarly grooved, although in varying numbers.[26]

The problem with Amsden's idea regarding Basketmaker warfare is that few hints of civil or other warfare are present in Basketmaker sites. Their burials seldom indicate signs of violent death, and no defensive precautions are evident in their living arrangements. A terrible massacre did occur in one of the caves, subsequently called Battle Cave, at Canyon del Muerto, and the remains are those of Basketmakers. Nevertheless, a stone-pointed arrow still in the torso of an old woman proves it was not done by other Basketmakers, for they did not yet have the bow and arrow. All burials were in slab-lined cists, and Morris recorded them as "uncontaminated Basketmaker II."[27]

When men and boys weren't building cists or hunting, they made flint knives and spearpoints by chipping carefully selected flakes with hammerstones and antler tips. They also made new snares, throwers, and spears, and may have shared in the fashioning of nets.

Clay and stone pipe tubes and bowls have also been found in the caves, and each man probably fashioned his own—whether for ceremonial purposes or not is not known. Ambler seems reasonably sure that they were of a religious nature and says that, in later times, similar pipes called "cloud blowers" were often used in ceremonies to create images of clouds to help bring rain. He is quick to add that he feels Basketmaker II men were probably not yet interested in weather control, but rather in acquiring supernatural power to diagnose and cure illnesses.[28]

Pueblo men still plant and care for the cornfields, and perhaps we can assume that early agriculture was also in the capable hands of the Basketmaker males. Planting was done with a pointed but not fire-hardened digging stick, somewhat similar in shape and size to Mesoamerican models.

FEMALE CRAFTS

Whenever a woman had a free moment, she turned to her textile crafts. Basketry, as we have seen, was so widely used that it gave the Basketmaker people their name, and half of the woman's waking hours were devoted to weaving various textile items. Baskets made of yucca and hemp were the pots, pans, bags, and trinket boxes of their homes. They were also needed for food gathering, mortuary offerings, and many other special purposes.

One ingenious form of basket, serving as a water container, was shaped like a large mushroom with the tip cut off, sitting on a cone-like stem. Standing two or three feet high, it held two or three gallons of water. It is an odd-looking specimen, but extremely functional. The inside was coated with piñon pitch to make it waterproof, and two loops of human hair provided for tumpline attachment, permitting support for the container as it was carried, full of water, on the back, while the structural location of the tumpline equalized the inevitable strain on the container. The weight of water would tax both the bearer and the container, if not properly supported.

There were a few small springs in the caves, but larger springs and natural basins were often some distance away, involving some risky climbing with the heavy basket on the woman's back. To reach rainwater in the natural catch basins high in the cliffs, she had to make her way up nearly vertical surfaces, using little more than an occasional ladder, pecked steps, and handholds. At other times she climbed laboriously down the rough talus slopes to reach streams and springs and then, with her basket filled, made the arduous climb back up to the cave. This explains the odd shape of the water-carrying basket. When it was slung on the bearer's back, the flared top rested on the shoulders while the long curve of the lower half fitted itself to the bent back. The bearer's hands were left free to secure handholds. The design of the basket mouth also helped. It was indrawn sharply, to prevent spilling, and a hinged cover, attached with hair loops, prevented the splashing that would otherwise be caused by awkward body motions.

Pitch-coated water bottles have always been popular among many tribes in North America, and the Ute, Paiute, Navajo, Apache, and Pueblo peoples still make them today. The Ozark Bluff-dwellers of Arkansas, who resembled the Basketmakers and lived at about the same time, left pitch-coated water containers behind in their caves. But nothing resembling the early Basketmaker form is known. The usual styles have a narrow neck and fat round bottom. One variation of the Paiute water jar does have a pointed bottom similar to that of the Basketmaker product, but it also has a narrow top and neck. The

Basketmaker water basket was a singular, ingenious invention, another evidence of an intelligent, creative people.

Wide-mouthed, conical baskets were also woven for seed gathering, and the wide mouth made it possible, when a basket was hung on the back from tump straps, for the woman simply to throw the seeds over her shoulder and into the basket. Such baskets can still be seen in use among the Pima, Papago,

a, two digging sticks from Basketmaker II, White Dog Cave, Arizona, after Kidder and Guernsey, 1919. *b,* Basketmaker II digging-stick blade of sheephorn from Tsegi Canyon, Arizona, after Kidder and Guernsey, 1919. *c,* Basketmaker II corn from Du Pont Cave, Utah. *d,* Basketmaker III twilled yucca ring basket from Broken Flute Cave, Arizona, and just above it the pattern and weave used in twilling. *e,* baskets containing foodstuffs from Basketmaker II cists in southeastern Utah.

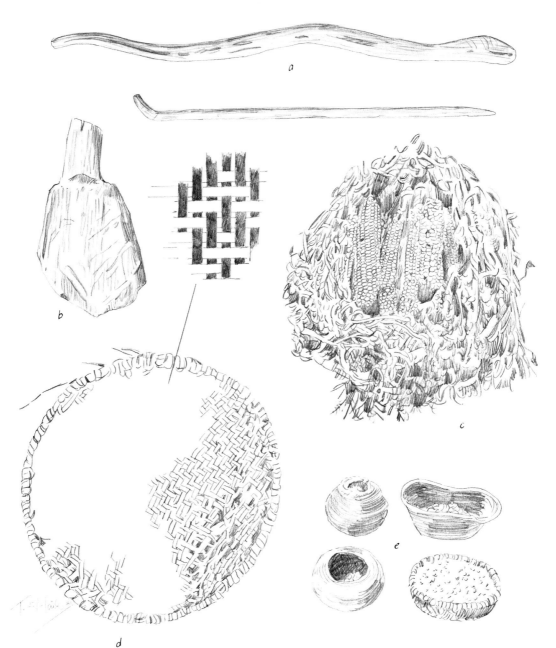

Havasupai, and Paiute. They are a most efficient product and make for little wasted motion.

A second basketry form was the small-mouthed hemispherical bowl. This was a catchall basket designed to hold serving materials, jewelry, and other small items. A third form was the almost flat tray, perhaps used for parching seeds. The fourth and most common form was the bowl shape with a flat

Lesser material culture objects: *a,* Basketmaker III grooved and hafted stone ax from La Plata District, Colorado. *b,* Basketmaker III stone maul from Tsegi Canyon, Arizona. *c–d,* Basketmaker knives consisting of stone blades fixed to wooden handles. *e–o,* stone projectile points. *p,* portions of atlatl darts. From Kidder and Guernsey, 1919, and Earl H. Morris, 1925.

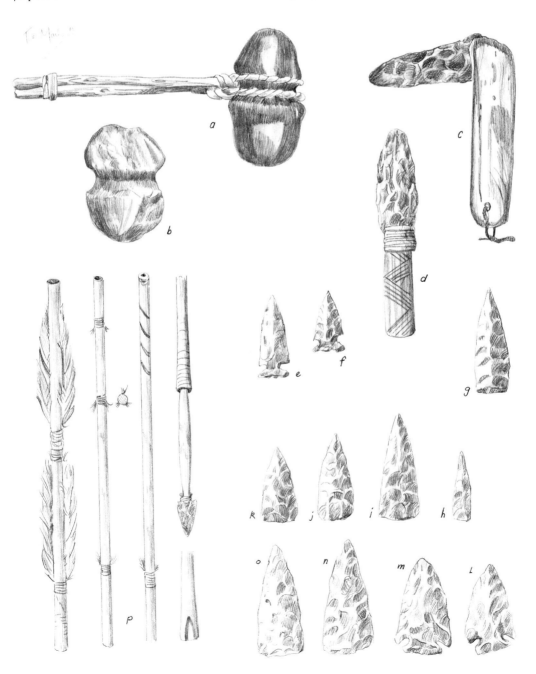

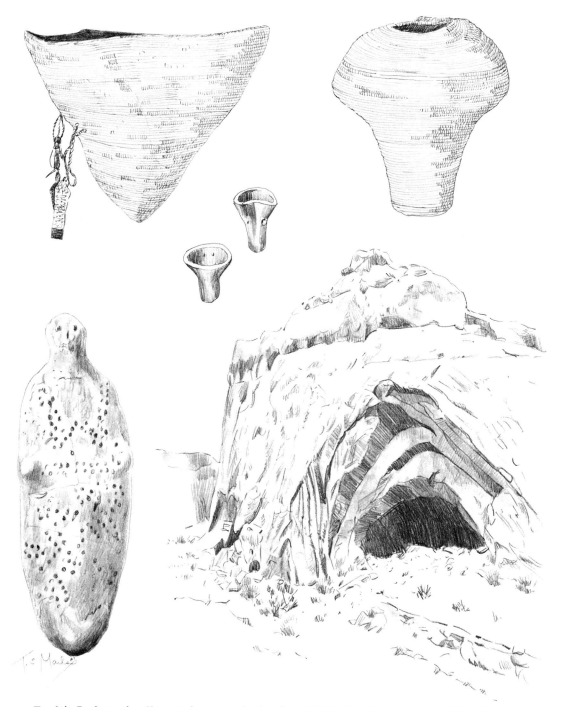

Top left, Basketmaker II conical carrying basket from White Dog Cave, Arizona. From Peabody Museum, Harvard University. *Top right*, Basketmaker II water-carrying basket from Marsh Pass, Arizona. *Center*, Basketmaker III unfired clay cornucopia-like objects from Tsegi Canyon, Arizona. *Bottom left*, Basketmaker III figurine of unfired clay from northeastern Arizona. From Kidder and Guernsey, 1919, and Earl H. Morris, 1925. *Bottom right*, White Dog Cave, where many Basketmaker II remains were found.

bottom and rounded or flaring sides. This provided utility containers, useful for storage and for cooking—although no positive evidence exists for the latter use. Basketry containers smeared with mud and ashes to render them watertight have also been found, along with others that are stained and battered as if from hot-stone boiling, wherein heated stones were dropped into baskets filled with water. This was a form of cooking commonly employed by the Great Plains tribes,[29] and charred wooden sticks, which may have been used in pairs to lift hot rocks, have been found in several Basketmaker sites.[30]

The only technique used for early basketmaking was coiling. This consisted of sewing tightly together with fiber or split twigs a spiraling coil of thin willow rods or bundled fibers, or a combination of both. The Basketmakers nearly always used two slender rods side by side, topped with a thin bundle of fiber, for their foundation coil or base. The sewing stitches were passed by a bone awl through the fiber bundle and around the rods, without interlocking adjacent stitches. The resultant coils were bound together by a flat strip that passed over the top coil and through the next-lower coil. Decoration consisted of geometric and linear designs made by using splints of contrasting color, usually dark red or black, either dyed or natural. Human beings, animals, and birds were not depicted on baskets, but they were applied on a special kind of bag.

An apparently popular type of Basketmaker container, since so many of them were made, was the round woven bag. Bags ranged in length from 2 inches to 2 feet and held from a cupful to a bushel. Their form was that of an egg, and they were perfectly round and seamless.

The method used in weaving the bag was exceedingly clever. Six or more warp strings were bunched at their centers so that the ends radiated out like the ribs of an umbrella. This warp foundation was hung upside down to keep the strings from falling into a tangle, and the weft was intertwined round and round, as the weaver worked outward from the bunched bottom. To broaden the bag at the center more warp strings were added, and to constrict it at the neck the number of strings was reduced. Two weft strands were used together and crisscrossed between wraps in a technique known as double twining.

These bags, whose natural color was a warm yellowish brown, were decorated in one of two ways. The first was the use of strings dyed black, red, or brown as a contrast to the natural golden hue of the weft. These were substituted at chosen points for the undyed weft, making stripes of color. The second way, used to make figures, was either to paint the completed bag or to rub the weft with color. For red, an iron oxide powder was mixed to a paste with water or grease. Browns, blacks, and blues seem to have come from vegetal matter. Yellow was made from yellow ocher (limonite), and white from white clay.

The figures painted on the bags are identical to those the early Basketmakers painted on the red cliff and cave walls: rectangular animals, square-shouldered human figures, and hand prints. (Later on, petroglyphs were pecked in the sandstone, but the early Basketmakers did not do this. They painted. This fact alone has helped many an archaeologist to identify a site as early Basket-maker.)[31]

Skin bags have also been found in Basketmaker sites. Most of these were made from two skins of small animals, such as the prairie dog. H. M. Worm-ington says that the animals were skinned forward from the back legs to the nose. The two skins were then sewed together, the neck of the bag being

Basketmaker weaving: *top left,* tumpline. *Top right,* basketry cap. *Center right,* knitted legging. *Bottom left,* coiled basket and detail of coiled basketry weave. From Kidder and Guernsey, 1919. *Bottom right,* twined woven bag of stripped yucca fiber, without seams, used as container and as burial wrapping. From Earl H. Morris, 1925. Item shown has been ripped down one side.

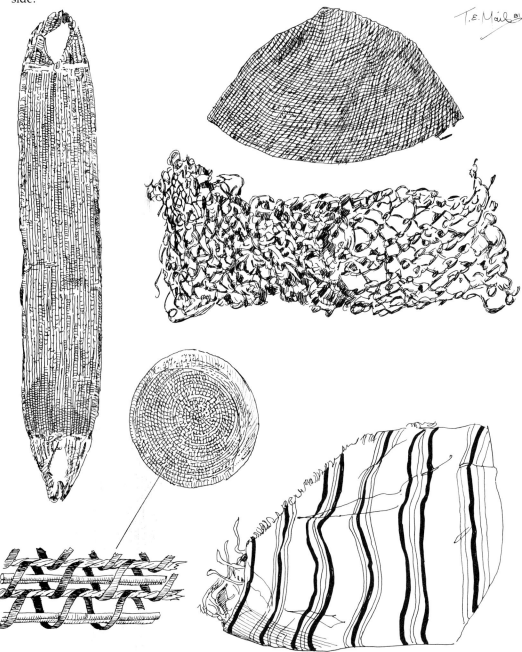

formed by the two heads. "They are usually found to contain oddly-shaped stones or other objects thought to have some ceremonial significance."[32]

It is assumed that the women also made the people's sandals. Typically square-toed, the early sandals were made of the same materials as the bags, and by much the same methods, except that they were woven back and forth rather than round and round. The sole was reinforced by an extra thickness of weft string, to provide a double sole. The only ornamentation was a fringe of deerskin or fiber along the toe and sometimes along the heel. The one exception in decoration is a sandal from Grand Gulch, Utah, that is covered with colored designs.

Sandals were always made with great care. Weaving was tight and the twine was hard and smooth—evidence of the Basketmakers' love of craftsmanship. Findings do include coarser sandals made for muddy days out of loosely intertwined yucca leaves. Archaeologists have come across a few rawhide sandals, but these aren't nearly as handsome as the woven type, and the aesthetically inclined Basketmakers seem to have made very few of them. Besides, skin becomes soggy in wet weather, and unless it is worn until dry it hardens to an uncomfortable degree. This, too, would discourage rawhide production.

Most cast-off sandals found so far are worn out at the heel. Since the people knew about hides and were inventive, it must have occurred to them to add a hide heel to the sole. Apparently, though, heels did not prove to be practical for the terrain the Basketmakers occupied. Still, climbing would seem to be hardest on the sole, not the heel, unless of course the burden bearers scrambled down steep places with their backs to the wall, like sailors down ship's ladders. Heel wear might also be caused by pushing digging sticks into the ground and by considerable running.

Tumplines, the pack straps used for carrying loaded burden baskets and wood, among other things, were another woven and decorated product, as were belts, aprons, and small blankets. Women also made the rabbit-fur robes previously described.

Netmaking was traditionally woman's work. It required countless hours of gathering and pounding the fibers, after which, according to Amsden, they were twisted into smooth cordage with the aid of a string twister.[33]

We do know something of how the Paiute made cordage, and the Basketmakers might have done it the same way. Figuratively speaking, the entire world of these high-desert people was tied together with cords. Bark, sinew, and human hair all played a role. But the best cordage of all was fashioned from Indian hemp or dogbane.

Hemp grows in moist soil along the banks of streams or on land where the water table is high. Each spring new stalks rise up, and during the warm summer they grow shoulder-high, forming thin pods, like milkweed, that scatter when they dry up in the fall. Each stalk has three parts: a thin outer skin, an inner layer of long tough fibers, and a pithy tube that is hollow in the center.

To prepare the hemp, the skin was scraped off. Then the stalk was cracked and split lengthwise by pinching or biting it from the tip to within 6 inches of the base. This 6-inch segment served as a handle. Each half was then bent in small sections until the pith was loosened from the fibers. The pith was scraped off and the fibers were separated by rubbing. A two-ply cord was begun by rolling a few fibers over the leg with the flat of the hand, in a pushing motion. When 2 feet of fibers had been rolled, a second ply was fed in. This procedure was continued until the desired length of cordage was obtained.[34]

The list of female crafts is truly imposing, and the production of textile arts may have required half of the women's time. It is easy to envision them during the winter months, busily at work using up the precious supplies gathered so carefully during the clement summer and fall days. Sewing and repair were done with bone awls or bone needles and either shredded sinew or hair cordage.

The tanning of hides may have been done by both women and men. Lacking better information, we can only assume that tanning was done as the Paiute are known to have done it. The Paiute method required a log about 5 feet long and 8 inches in diameter. The log was stripped of its bark, rounded off at the top, and leaned against a wall. Deer hide was soaked in wet ground until the hair began to loosen. Depending upon the warmth of the weather, this could take from two days to a week.

When it was ready, the wet hide was draped over the log with the head end hooked over the smooth top to keep it in place. With the rib of a deer held horizontally as a scraping tool, the hair was then removed. It came off quite easily, and with luck the matter just under the hair came off at the same time, else this would form a hard membrane when dry. Skill was required to remove the epidermis without cutting the hide. So, if the skin dried out during the scraping process, it was sponged with handfuls of deer hair dipped in water.

The skinning finished, the hide was prepared for tanning with a solution of brains and spinal cords. Deer, antelope, and even rabbit brains and cords were used. The brains were boiled in a container, and the hide was immersed in the solution and left to soak overnight. In the morning it would be bleached and swollen. It was wrung out and again hung on the post to be pulled and stretched continually until dry. Every inch had to be worked, including the edges. Finally a tan color was obtained by hanging the hide, rolled into a cone shape, over a small fire fueled by wood chips.[35]

FOOD GATHERING

As soon as baskets were finished, they were put to use. Food gathering was an essential activity of the women, and the older children, being well suited to it, no doubt assisted. We can envision them setting out as a large, boisterous group early in the morning, women and older girls with cradles and baskets slung on their backs and digging sticks hung over their shoulders by cords, younger girls carrying trays and small baskets to hold smaller items. Mischievous boys not yet old enough to be taken hunting or otherwise aid their fathers still had deft hands to gather seeds and at the same time would be under the eye of their mothers. Youngsters who were weaned but not ready for gathering remained at the village with grandmother and grandfather. The gathering group would seek acorns and piñon nuts, cactus fruit, chokecherries, and the edible portions of various plants and would come home exhausted but laden.

In spring and early summer the Basketmakers gathered wild vegetables: wild onions, lilies, a potato-like plant, or the tender leaves of various plants that could be boiled and eaten like spinach. The edible tubers were rooted out with a digging stick—either one with a sharp point or one with a shovel-like end, many of which have been found in Basketmaker caves.

In late summer the focus shifted to nut and seed gathering, with flat basket trays as well as the burden baskets. Grass and sage grew knee-high and thick on the open mesas, and each tuft of grass held a few dozen seeds in its husks, ripe and ready to fall. Holding a tray in one hand and a stick in the other, a woman bent over each clump in turn and quickly knocked the seeds into the tray. The seeds were then transferred into the larger burden basket, and by day's end an industrious gatherer would have walked several miles and filled her baskets with a bushel or more. We know this is so because caves have yielded bags and baskets still filled with wild mountain rice, grass seeds, and yucca that the occupants never had an opportunity to consume.

Shortly after the long trek home, a happy group of women would pour the seeds into other trays and winnow out the husks. With a softly spoken prayer to the wind to help her, a woman would begin shaking her tray, moving it with a rhythmical, circular sifting motion to drive the chaff over the edges. Then she would hold the tray level with her head and pour the seeds into a large basket on the ground. As they fell, the wind answered her prayer and carried the empty, feather-light husks away. One thousand seven hundred years later, the Pueblo women of the Rio Grande still winnow in this manner, although they first pour the seeds onto a blanket or tarpaulin and from there into large storage containers.

FOOD PREPARATION

Basketmaker methods of food preparation probably varied. Some seeds may have been eaten raw, others cooked. Parching is a favorite method with the Paiute and seemingly was so for the Anasazi, since it gives the seeds a roasted-nut flavor. Parching is done in a flat tray like those used for winnowing. The seeds are scattered over the bottom of the tray, and glowing coals are dropped into their midst with either a wooden-slab shovel or a pair of tongs made by bending a wet branch double. The basket is shaken rapidly, as in winnowing, to mix the coals and seeds and to prevent scorching. After a few moments the coals are skillfully flipped out of the basket and the seeds are tossed to separate them from the ashes. Paiute women are marvels of dexterity at this. Some seed-gathering peoples lined their trays with mud to prevent scorching, and mud vessels seemingly used for parching have been found in Basketmaker caves.[36]

Boiling was another method of cooking. For this the early Basketmaker women used baskets and skin pouches. Cooking baskets were so tightly woven that little water could leak out. Using two sticks as wooden tongs or a forked stick, the women dropped ash-coated, sizzling-hot stones into the water-filled basket to cook mush or meat, and the Basketmakers must have eaten a lot of ashes along with their meal. Sometimes, to provide variety, meat would be roasted over the coals.

Basketmaker-Pueblo woman wearing tumpline and carrying a burden basket.

The usual method of cooking seeds was to grind and crush them into a coarse meal with a stone mano and metate. The mano-metate is probably the most important and familiar of all household implements used by the Indians. Thousands have been found at village and camp sites. Its use, coupled with the development of agriculture, provided the basis for sedentary living and the growth of the New World civilizations of Peru, Mexico, and the Southwest. The name "metate" is a corruption of the Aztec terms *metlapil* and *metlatl* used to describe their stone implements for milling grain. The mano (from the Spanish, meaning "hard") is either a small round river rock or a larger oblong stone, held, depending upon its size and style, in one or both hands. For milling, grain is poured on the metate, and the mano is moved in a rotary grinding motion over the larger metate. This is, when new, simply a flat block of sandstone or porous lava rock, usually rectangular but sometimes oval. A shallow grinding surface is pecked in the block to prepare it for use, and in time the constant grinding results in a deep trough down the center. As cornmeal is ground between the stones, grit from the stones is mixed with the meal and ingested, resulting in badly worn teeth for the consumer. The Basketmaker women molded the ground meal into small cakes and baked them on flat stones that had been heated by the fire.

Wild seeds were the cereal staple of the early Basketmakers, their substitute for our bread. It is probable that Basketmakers used the yucca plant for food as other Southwestern peoples have done. A roasted yucca heart has a sweet flavor and, when chewed, leaves a residue of stringy fibers. Caches of these fibers are abundant in Basketmaker caves. The few wild fruits in the Four Corners area provided other sweets, and it has been suggested that some insect secretions, such as those of aphids, may have provided a wild honey.[37]

Salt is essential to a diet, but no one knows where the Basketmakers obtained theirs. Some would come to them in the form of animal blood, which they, as present-day African tribes do, must have drunk. Another possible source was trade with other cultures, since salt was a popular medium of exchange among the Indians, as were the abalone and olivella shells. Pacific Coast Indians and those along the Gulf of California were potential suppliers of salt. There is a salt lake near Zuñi Pueblo, and the Hopi found salt in the Grand Canyon. Perhaps the Sinagua and Cohonina came upon it there too. Later on, the Basketmaker and Anasazi peoples mined mountain areas in eastern Nevada that were veined with pure rock salt.[38]

CHILDREN AND THEIR EDUCATION

Amsden was convinced by a single piece of archaeological evidence—the baby cradle—that Basketmaker women were "very fond" of their children. The cradle was a carefully finished framework of straight rods tied in a neat crisscross to a stick bent to an oval form. Medium-sized loops attached to the top and bottom of the frame made it possible to hang the cradle like a hammock.

Rough edges at the sides that might scratch the infant were padded with wads of fiber and covered by strips of tanned hide, such as rabbit hide, with the fur left on. There was a removable lining of woven juniper bark, upon which the baby could be lifted out of the cradle. A soft white rabbit-fur blanket was used to wrap the child. It was made in a unique and special way: the lower end was split for half its length to protect it from soiling, and the sides were parted to make room for a finely shredded diaper of juniper bark, held in place by a cord tied horizontally across the cradle.

The baby was held snugly in its cradle by thongs of soft fur cord that passed back and forth through small loops spaced at intervals along the edge of the frame. There was even an umbilical pad to prevent ruptures. This was either a bunch of wadded grass, bark, or cornhusk or a flat piece of pine bark the width of a man's hand. The wad was sewn into a soft, tanned prairie dog skin and tied around the baby's waist with a fur cord. The umbilical cord was severed at birth, and the cut-off piece was dried and hung at the side of the cradle. Amsden says: "It was a part of the baby, a link with the mysterious nether world whence he came, and must not be lost or ill-treated."[39] He also points out that this custom was widespread among primitive folk, but he does not explain the Plains Indian view that to sew the umbilical cord section into a turtle-shaped pouch and attach it to the cradleboard would impart to the child the power for long life. Seemingly, to the Indians, a turtle never died and was extremely hard to kill. A lizard-shaped fetish often accompanied the turtle to turn away those evil powers who might seek to steal the turtle and deprive the child of long life. Of course, we cannot argue that the Basketmakers ever had such thoughts, but the mere act of hanging the dried cord on the cradle does favor it.

Like all Indian versions, the Basketmaker cradle was purely and simply a baby carrier, light and portable and equipped with carrying straps, usually of braided human hair. The import is clear. A baby, whose only source of food was the breast, had to go where the mother went. So the cradle was slung on the back, burden basket style, and taken to wherever work was being done. Strapped in firmly but not too tightly, the secure and contented youngster saw the world, going up and down the hazardous cliff surfaces to new adventures along with everyone else. Indian babies adapted perfectly to this and seemed not to resent in the least being laced, arms and all, into the cradle. I have seen Apache mothers dance all day and all night—except at feeding time—with complaint-free infants lashed in cradleboards hung on their backs.

Arriving at a workplace, a very young infant would be suspended horizontally, hammock style, from any supports that the end loops could be tied to. The cradles of older children would be hung from a tree limb and left to swing in the breeze, or otherwise propped upright against a rock. The early Basketmaker cradle had no hood to shield the child from the sun, but it is assumed that the mother draped a light mat or something similar over the baby's head to keep off sun and insects. The latter were there—dead flies have even been found in cave burials.[40]

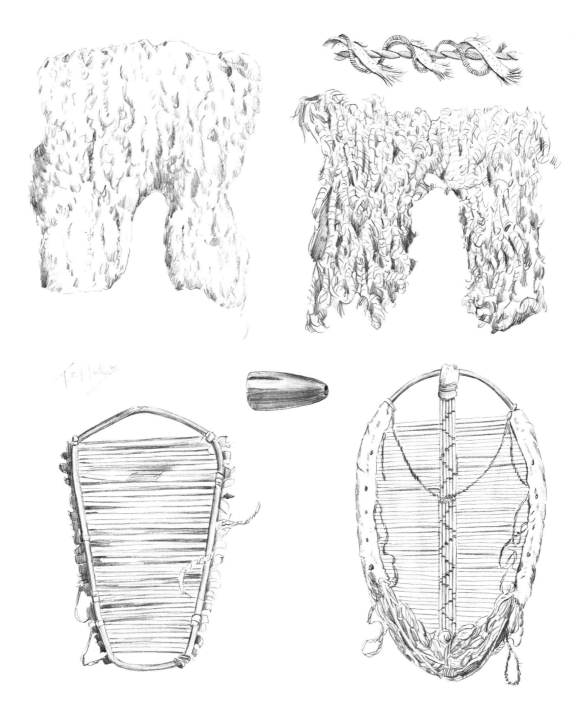

Top left, Basketmaker II rabbit-skin robe found on body of infant, White Dog Cave, Arizona. *Top right*, feather-cloth robe found on same infant, and detail of feather wrapping method. *Center*, Basketmaker II banded slate "cloud-blower" pipe from Du Pont Cave, Utah. *Bottom left and right*, Basketmaker reed cradles from White Dog Cave. From Kidder and Guernsey, 1919.

Judging by historic evidence extending into modern times, Basketmaker children would be nursed for a long time, and children three or four years of age would often run to their mothers for the nourishment intended for the baby. As time passed, though, soft and digestible foods such as gruels and soups would be substituted for the milk, and finally the child would eat the same fare as the adults.

Infant mortality rates have always been painfully high among the Indians, and they remain the highest by far in the United States today. Difficult living conditions, pestilences, and an absence of modern professional care accounted for most Basketmaker infant deaths, just as they did among the early Europeans who settled the West. Surely the doting Basketmaker parents and medicine men did everything they could to prevent such tragedies, but burial sites in most caves reveal that the deaths of very young children outnumbered those of adults. It is ironic that this fact alone has given us all our empirical knowledge about Basketmaker infants. Those that died were lovingly laid away in their cradles and wrappings, thus telling a story that otherwise could never be told.

Children had their own little sandals and robes, but went naked whenever the weather allowed. Pubescent girls put on miniature versions of the tiny aprons all women wore. By nature all children, in play, imitate their parents, yet no imitative toys have been found in burials save one carved wooden image that might have been a doll. However, sticks and rocks and other objects could easily have sufficed for the children of a simple but imaginative people, and the food-gathering and hunting drives would be sources of great fun in themselves. In any event the children would expect little and would be content with less by far than we are; no Basketmaker child ever faced the foibles of luxury as modern generations do.

A child's primary education took place in the field. Girls were always with their mothers, boys with their fathers. Thus the practical and spiritual duties of life were learned by direct participation and under careful supervision. This is still true. Pueblo Indian children have a role to play in everything the people do at feast-day celebrations. Nothing is more charming to us, yet more practical for them, than a group of tiny children dressed in absolutely faithful but miniature costumes bringing up the rear of a long line of Pueblo dancers, lips firmly together, eyes fixed on the ground, spruce boughs and gourd rattles clutched tightly in their hands, and dancing with an intensity that always evokes a white spectator's awe. Whenever the village permits photography, no small amount of film is used up to record the children, for visitors soon realize that an important and impressive training session is under way.

The Basketmaker children learned in other ways too. My old friend Fools Crow, Ceremonial Chief of the Teton Sioux, once told me he never learned so well, as both child and adult, as when sitting around an open fire at night. There is something hushed and special about being there in the flickering light, contemplating the power in the fire and shut off, except for a vision of the stars, by the encompassing blackness from the rest of the world. At no other time are the powers of concentration and the imagination so keen.

Just so the fireplace was the other Basketmaker schoolroom. By the fire the children received their secondary education as they absorbed the unwritten literature of their people. They learned how the world was created, how it is watched over and protected by supernatural forces, how they came to be, and how they came to be living in Basketmaker country. They learned about the birds and the animals, how they became what they are, and what their relationship is to man. Plants and rocks too, they were told, were alive, and must be approached in certain reverent ways. They learned about the heavens, the seasons, and the wind. They were told what daily practices were good and what practices were evil. They learned about the need for harmony among peoples, and they learned about the ritual ceremonies they would one day be adopted into. They learned about death, and they learned that their personal responsibility would be to pass the customs faithfully on to their children, and thus to the generations yet to come. In particular, they learned how to respect their elders, for the elders, after all, were the great sources of learning. Sitting by the fire, the child grew in special and remarkable ways. That is why the Anasazi accomplished what they did. Necessity was their mother of invention, but the wisdom of the elders was the Basketmaker father of necessity.

SOCIAL LIFE

Primitive peoples have had a way of turning most work into near-play. Women were particularly adept at this, and virtually every activity was of a communal nature. Either the tasks were shared or the individual work was done at a community place, such as a plaza prepared for the purpose. Whenever it was possible, one woman would do part of a job, pass it on to the woman sitting next to her for the second stage, and then on to a third woman for the finishing touches. If a certain kind of work could not be divided, the woman would at least do it where she could sit and visit with others.

Amsden was of the opinion that Basketmakers may never have formalized work, just as Indians of today generally do not formalize work, art, or religion. "They weave them into their daily lives so smoothly that no word exists to convey the idea that they may be separated from the whole pattern of living."[41] He wondered whether, even before the blessings of civilization sublimated our animal instincts, there were not human societies in which work and play went hand in hand, "as with happy children out berrying."[42]

If daily life was social in nature, even beyond that would be the social games. Caves have yielded up several pairs of dice, so we know the early Basketmakers were fond of gambling. Some of their dice were made from round sticks, 3 inches long, split through the center in such a way as to make one side flat and the other round. The sticks were grooved to correspond to the dots on modern dice. Other die sets consisted of inch-long pieces of wood or bone rounded on one side and also marked with grooves. Three objects made from round bones, pitch-coated on one side, seem also to have been used for a game of dice. More dice still, these being flat pellets of clay or stone with a flat bead cemented to the rounded top, have been found in sets of seven in several places.

Two wooden balls, about 4 inches in diameter, were found, and they may have been used in a game similar to soccer. Besides these, archaelogists have come across two wooden hoops about 6 inches in diameter, each made by bending a green stick into a circle and tying it with cordage. The hoops suggest a game common to several Southwestern peoples, in which participants seek to throw a dart or arrow through a hoop while it is still rolling.[43]

The Basketmakers did not, as the Hohokam once did, cremate their dead and thus obliterate history. They buried them in the floors and trash heaps of the dry caves. These preserved and mummified the bodies, and to some extent preserved their apparel and wrappings, although objects buried with the bodies often suffered deterioration because of the body moisture and the weight of refuse heaped on top. Not surprisingly, then, most of the Basketmaker finds are not in prime condition. Often, too, the caves suffered from seepage or exposure that resulted in damp spots. Water may be more destructive than fire where artifacts are concerned. Water rots them away, while fire sometimes preserves objects by charring them. Our dating methods can be applied to the artifacts and tell us an amazing amount concerning them.

Thanks to moisture damage, we have only the sketchiest picture of Basketmaker musical instruments, which leaves us wondering whether the Basketmakers had more instruments or were satisfied with very few. The latter may indeed be the case. The Pueblo Indians of today use a remarkably limited range of musical instruments for ceremonies, although any given instrument may be shaped and decorated in a variety of ways. The Pueblos use only drums, bells, flutes, rasps, and rattles, augmented by vocal accompaniments of a most interesting and stirring nature. One has only to hear the muffled "Whoo, whoo" of a line of masked dancers at Hopi and Zuñi to know what I mean.

Basketmaker caves have supplied us with bone and deer hoof rattles. Some are tied to handles of bone or wood, and a few are just strung on a cord and might have been attached, Pueblo style, for ceremonial purposes to an arm or leg band.

Found together with these have been one-stop whistles, made of reeds or hollow bird bones and not more than 5 inches long. The mouth end was left open, the lower end was plugged, and a hole was cut or burned through above the midpoint to provide for a stop valve. Bone whistles are often found in medicine bundles and have always been an integral part of the medicine man's working paraphernalia, being used to "speak" to the spiritual powers and to enlist their aid in curing and in gaining prophetic knowledge. Three whistle specimens have sinew bindings near the hole, and one has what seems to be a tiny bit of reed caught beneath the binding, resembling the reed vibrators in saxophones.

No drum has been found in Basketmaker sites, although this proves little. The Navajo and others pound on the bottom of a basket, and stiff hides are still used as drums by some Indians. Few modern Pueblo dances are done without one drum or several, and we can assume that the drum is inherited and has special significance. A Pueblo drummer will usually purify his hands with a coating of white clay before taking up the drum. This tells us he has a conscious reverence for the power of the drum and for the spiritual sound that it sends out to the people and up to the heavenly powers.

Pipe smoking has always had special religious significance for the Indians. In ancient days pipe smoking was seldom done for purely personal pleasure. The Basketmakers made pipes also, but the purpose of these remains a mystery. The pipes consisted either of tubular shapes or of little cone-shaped heads of stone or fired clay, and usually a short stem of hollow bird bone or of wood was glued into the end of the tube or the pointed tip of the cone. All the pipes found so far have been empty. Wild tobacco, some other leaf, or bark could have served as the pipe mixture, but no one knows for certain what blend was used.

Amsden felt that since pipes of stone and clay are almost imperishable, they should be plentiful in Basketmaker collections if they were in common use. Yet only nine finds are recorded to date: six of stone, three of clay. White Dog Cave, Arizona, the most abundant site discovered so far, had none at all. Thus Amsden concludes, as does Richard Ambler, that smoking was a ritual practice. "Clouds of fragrant smoke," Ambler says, "floating upward to fade into the sky for the purpose of inducing rain, have long been considered a fitting invocation to the heavenly powers."[44]

DEATH AND BURIAL

As it did for other Southwestern Indians, death came for the early Basketmaker adults after an average life-span of thirty-five years. Soon after death and before the body stiffened, it was flexed. To save space, the legs were drawn up until the knees almost touched the chin, and sometimes the feet were bent as well. The arms were doubled up until the hands rested either on the chest or between the drawn-up legs. At times the corpse was bound in this position with cord. Usually a rabbit-fur robe or a large woven bag, split open, was also wrapped around the body, which was then laid on its side in a cist in a cave. Storage cists were sometimes emptied of their contents and converted to graves, or a new cist might be hastily dug for a burial. In an emergency, a shallow hole might be scooped in the soft earth.

A few personal possessions, such as weapons and baskets, were placed with the body as a rule; also food offerings and invariably an unworn pair of sandals—these in particular suggesting a belief in an afterlife, for otherwise a used pair would have sufficed.[45] A large basket was often inverted over the face to protect it. The grave was then filled in with shredded bark and covered with flat stones, branches, and brush, or with earth alone, until the surface was level with the floor of the cave. The centuries would cover the grave with debris and dirt until it was lost from sight, remaining forever so unless a looter or an archaeologist happened by.

Dead children were sometimes buried in large baskets or in large unsplit bags. In Cliff Canyon, Arizona, Earl Morris found a grave containing the skeleton of a child wrapped in a fur-string blanket, covered with a basket, and accompanied by a strand of beads and eight chipped stone blades. As I have said earlier, infants were usually wrapped in fur and laid away in their cradles.

Group burials were common. In one instance nineteen bodies had been jammed "like olives in a jar," into one large pit.[46] Archaeologists feel that this was probably the result of some pestilence, since there were no signs of violent death among the nineteen.

BASKETMAKER III/MODIFIED BASKETMAKERS
A.D. 500–700 OR 750

VILLAGES AND DWELLINGS

Archaeologists believe that the benefits of an agricultural and sedentary life were not immediately apparent to the Basketmakers, and that only over a long span of time, four centuries or more, did they give up their nomadic ways, reluctantly, and settle down. Curiously enough, opting for either manner of life involved a choice between freedoms. The sedentary way would end the freedom to move at will and the freedom to leave nothing behind to worry about. Yet nomads had little they could depend upon when an emergency arose, and they were never free to relax and create so long as each day was dominated by the search for food and shelter. Ultimately, the Basketmakers made their choice. Archaeological findings reveal the unmistakable signs of a firm shift around A.D. 500 from hunting and gathering to farming as a lifeway.

Amsden describes the process of settling down as "a time of crisis in the life history of a primitive group like our Basketmakers."[47] The rewards are great, but the conditions are exacting. Both the material and the spiritual aspects of culture must undergo a profound transformation. New implements must be fabricated, and formerly minor crafts become major. Portable gear is jettisoned, and heavier, serviceable products must be devised. Clay pots must accompany baskets, and even larger storage places have to be built. The settled farmer's "success lies in slow, patient application to the routine toil of gaining a living, year after year, from one small plot of ground. He dare not wander far . . . his world, visible and invisible, bears a very different aspect . . . inevitably his religious and social concepts, like his crafts and day to day customs, reflect this difference."[48]

Farmers need shelter for themselves, their household possessions, and their produce. Villages began to spring up. Small ones occupied the familiar but inconvenient caves where space was at a premium. Larger ones arose in the open country, where the preferred site was a plot of high ground overlooking the farmland below. The Basketmakers recognized that pithouses would not fare well without good drainage and, authorities say, that high ground was more easily defended.

Just whom they would be defending themselves against no one knows. As I have said before, evidences of violence are missing. So it remains an unsolved puzzle why entire Basketmaker villages were commonly put to the torch. Since accidental fires, while common in flammable homes, could hardly

Pithouse village.

have spread so successfully through groups of isolated buildings, enemy presence is suspected.[49] I think it possible, however, that the villagers torched the sites themselves once they decided to move permanently or even decided to abandon their village for a time. Were they not to do so, if they did return they were bound to find new occupants, perhaps human enemies, or every sort of snake, rodent, and vermin infesting their homes, and they would only have to rebuild the wood portions. One suggestion is that the Indians burned a home wherein a person had died. This is a known Indian custom, but it would not account for the destruction of whole villages.

Excavations show that many sites had numerous levels of occupancy. For example, in the La Plata District, New Mexico, Earl Morris found that "on the mesa where we dug, buildings stand on top of buildings of an unknown depth, while under some of the refuse mounds there are fairly well preserved archaic structures of which not a trace would have remained had they not been covered over with a secondary deposit."[50]

Hilltop locations had their disadvantages. Southwestern winds sweeping across crests can be a terror, and wood and stone were more conveniently at hand on the high mesas. Water had to be carried, since most of it was in the valleys or in springs issuing forth from the cliffs. The villagers also had to walk some distance to their fields. Yet all these, apparently, were lesser problems than the drainage and the possible enemies.

The first Basketmaker villages followed no plan. Houses were placed at random in irregular clusters, according to whim, and the villages seem to suggest only the first halting movement toward the close-knit, organized community that came into being later in the period.

When in 1927 Frank H. H. Roberts undertook the excavation of Shabik'-eshchee Village in Chaco Canyon, the first village of pure "Post-Basketmaker" and "Pre-Pueblo" age ever dug, he found eighteen pithouses, a plaza, forty-eight storage bins, and a large kiva. The pithouses were isolated from one another; some were circular and others oval. Some had a ventilated entryway on their southern side, and others were entered via a roof hatchway, the passageway having been abandoned as an entrance and employed solely for fresh air. Pit walls were plastered with adobe.[51] It should be noted that Roberts's remarks concerning the entryway leave open the question of whether the side entry or the ventilator shaft came first.[52]

Also featured at the village was the ramada, a shelter consisting of posts, a bough-covered pole roof, and sometimes a brush wall or two; the ramada was probably used for working and sleeping outdoors on hot summer days and nights, as was the Paiute custom.[53]

Floor features of the Shabik'eshchee homes were identical with those of the houses to the north except for one item: there was a general absence of sipapus.[54] A sipapu is usually a small hole dug in the floor midway between the firepit and the wall. It is about 4 inches (10 cm) in diameter and a few inches deep. Ordinarily it is unlined, but in some kivas the neck of a jar is used to make and retain the opening. As pithouses developed, the sipapu

The ramada, or shade shelter used by Basketmakers and other Southwestern peoples for outdoor work.

became a standard feature, but as protokivas, kivas, and aboveground cere-monial chambers evolved, the sipapu was not always included. All modern Pueblos use the name "sipapu," or a close variation of it, to designate the hole. It symbolizes, in its essence—although broader connotations are given to it— the mythical place of emergence through which the Anasazi ancestors passed in their journey from the inner portions of the earth, where they were created, to the surface of the world upon which they now live.[55] It is also the opening through which the souls of the dead return to the Underworld, where they continue to live much as people do on earth. Some souls become Katcinas, benevolent spirits who come and go through the sipapu as they bless the Pueblo people at specified times in the year.

The absence of the sipapu in some Shabik'eshchee pithouses emphasized the significance of the large kiva in the village, for it signaled a shift from personal to community ritual practice. The kiva was 40 feet (12.2 m) across and 4 feet 2 inches (1.27 m) deep, with a fill suggesting two periods of occupation spaced some time apart. The wooden portion of this kiva had been burned. Roberts believed the kiva represented a beginning of the religious architecture that evolved into the massive kivas found at Chaco Canyon and elsewhere. If so, it meant there were two strains of kiva development. One was the clan-sized kiva that archaeologists think evolved from the cist and pithouse. The other was the Great Kiva, used mainly for community ritual.[56]

At Red Mesa, Colorado, in 1922, Earl Morris uncovered a subterranean house that had several features common to later Pueblo ceremonial chambers, although some traditional elements were still missing. Nevertheless, he called it a "protokiva," and observed that while kivas had been considered an integral part of the Pueblo culture, no one had seriously thought of their being present among the Basketmakers. Yet here they were, and he was excited.[57] The connection between Basketmaker and Pueblo had not yet been established, and now these and other finds, coupled with Roberts's large kiva, were beginning to suggest an unbroken, orderly progression from Basketmaker to Pueblo. It was a factor all but proved and of overwhelming value when the chronology

Top, typical structural system used for walls and ceiling of Basketmaker pithouses. *Bottom*, Basketmaker III protokiva pit with wing walls in La Plata Valley, southwestern Colorado. From Earl H. Morris photograph.

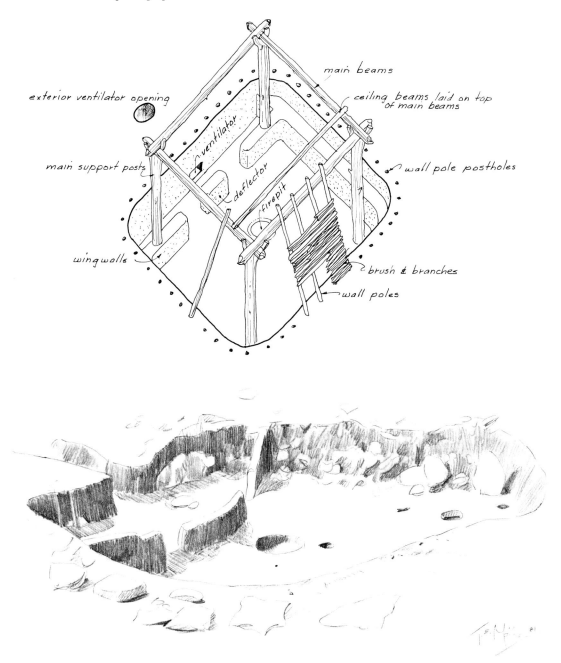

of Anasazi cultural stages was first hammered out at the Pecos Conference in 1927 and polished and augmented during the years immediately following.

The protokiva is an item of great moment in Anasazi culture, and it will be vital to look more closely at it as Basketmaker III and Pueblo I are considered in detail in forthcoming chapters. Fortunately, excavations begun in 1963 at Badger House Community, Mesa Verde National Park, Colorado, give us excellent details of three protokivas as well as of Basketmaker III pithouses, Pueblo Period mesa-top structures, towers, and a Great Kiva. The earliest assigned date for the findings is A.D. 600, and occupancy at Badger House continued for more than six hundred adventurous years.

The protokiva was similar in most details to the pithouse of the same period, and except for wing walls and location one can hardly tell them apart. The protokiva was usually set off by itself, out in front of a row of dwellings. Probably there were other distinguishing features, but we do not know what they were. This holds for kivas today. Unless you know what you are looking for, you cannot separate the aboveground and rectangular kivas in some Rio Grande pueblos and in Zuñi and Acoma from the rest of the structures that enclose them.

Since the Great Kiva is from a later period than the protokiva, we will consider it at the proper chronological time.

The pithouses at Badger House Community include one construction feature that differs considerably from what is found in pithouses elsewhere. Some have an earthen bench lining the walls, and holes in the bench indicate that the wall poles were set into the bench rather than into the ground at natural grade level. This seems an especially intelligent move, because it would give additional support to the pole butts. To clear up any possible confusion, a cross section of the details accompanies the structural illustrations when individual dwelling details are discussed.

HOUSES

"In man with man against unfriendly nature and hampering circumstance we see the conquering instinct at its best." So the perceptive Amsden describes those who built the first pithouses with nothing but the materials available nearby, their bare hands, and consummate ingenuity. Such triumphs, he goes on to say, "are the real milestones of civilization,"[58] for the dwellings accommodated themselves amazingly well to the rigors of both summer and winter over a wide and varied terrain.

Everyone wonders whether the primary inspiration for the Basketmaker dwelling came from within, or from the Mogollon, the Hohokam, the fishermen of the California coast, or the earth dwellers who settled along the Missouri River. Perhaps the seeds of architecture lay in tales carried by ancestors moving down through Alaska and Canada in the dim past.

After he had wrestled with the problem of pithouse origins for some time, Amsden concluded as follows: "(1) It probably was known, in a simpler form, well back in Basketmaker II days; that is, in the earliest centuries of the Christian era—and possibly in B.C. times. (2) It probably embodies some borrowed idea, and is not a wholly local development."[59] Donald Pike says, "it is most easily assumed that the Basketmakers learned much of what they did from the Mogollon and Hohokam."[60]

Perhaps it is time to be more positive. I can only wonder how the Basketmakers could have avoided knowing about the Mogollon pithouses and even about those of the desert dwellers farther to the south. After all, it was a walk of only a hundred miles from the southern reaches of Basketmaker territory to Mogollon country. Times were peaceful. What was to prevent regular excursions? Trade and normal interest alone would guarantee contact, and simple observation would do the rest. The relative absence of diffused trade items in Basketmaker excavations may only mean that the Indians exchanged consumable goods, and that most of the goods were perishable. One interesting difference, however, that may argue against diffusion is that the Basketmaker entrance was usually placed on the south side of the dwelling, while that of the Hohokam and Mogollon was placed on the east side.

Whichever the case may be the Basketmakers did build their own houses, and with only the clumsiest of wood and stone tools and the unselfish cooperation that such ventures required.

Problems abounded. Although wood, stone, and earth were readily available, and juniper and piñon trees grew in the uplands and cottonwoods lined the valleys, the Basketmakers had no true ax, only a bludgeoning club, fire, and brute force to fell the trees. Building stones would one day be used in abundance by their Pueblo descendants, but the Basketmakers of A.D. 500 knew little about working stone and nothing at all about mortar. Earth they knew something about, however, for, as most archaeologists believe, they had already constructed cists. That would be enough for a beginning, and not surprisingly the first houses were very much like enlarged cists.

In summing up his description of the Basketmaker III pithouse, Amsden doubts that the Basketmakers invented it. Further, he even wonders whether the cist was parent to the house, or whether the house gave birth to the cist, pointing out that in Falls Creek Cave, near Durango, Colorado, Earl Morris discovered in 1940 "circular house floors with central fire-pits and traces of at least a skirting of poles, if not a whole superstructure."[61] This culture was pure late Basketmaker II.

Morris's own description of the Falls Creek find is particularly informative, in that he encountered a different structural method for the Falls Creek pithouses from the one described by Amsden for those of Phase III. It was not a discovery easily made. Morris and his co-workers repeatedly trenched and traced the cave and hillside, finding layer after layer of subsequent occupation, but none of the familiar postholes indicating former locations of posts and walls. Months went by and frustration increased. Finally they found the answer to the missing wall and roof supports. A small section of wall some 15 inches (38 cm) high and 5 or 6 feet (1.5–1.8 m) long revealed the method of construction. Timbers had been laid horizontally, log cabin style, and the interstices were filled with mud. There was no need for the customary vertical roof supports. This, then, was apparently the earliest manner of wood construction—at least in some places.[62]

To build the typical dwelling of mid–Basketmaker III, on the other hand, the family used digging sticks and pieces of stone for scoops to excavate a round or oval pit anywhere from 10 to 25 feet (3–7.5 m) in diameter. The depth depended upon soil conditions and location, but they dug down 5 feet (1.5 m) or more if they could. On hardpan, the excavation might be quite shallow. Earth is good insulation, and this was the primary reason for the deep hole. The secondary reason was to avoid using any more wood than necessary, for the Basketmakers did not have the tools to handle it. Still, the dirt itself posed problems. Even the firmest walls tended to crumble, and so most were plastered with clay or lined with stone slabs after the manner of cists; if slabs were not available, support branches would be resorted to.

The builders soon learned that better ventilation would be a blessing, and their excavations included a short horizontal tunnel at floor level extending out to a small vertical shaft. The shaft-head opening was protected by a circular stonework wall, and sometimes a movable flat stone cover was leaned against the inner end of the shaft tunnel. More frequently a stone slab was set upright in the floor a foot or two out from the ventilator tunnel entrance. This served as a deflector to shunt incoming air away from the firepit. This fresh-air intake system, working together with the entrance hole in the roof, provided a reasonably good form of ventilation.

Once the pit was finished, the house was completed with wood and mud. Techniques varied, but usually four 8-inch (20 cm) posts, forked at the top, were set up in as large a square as possible within the pit, and then connected with four horizontal beams. Clearance from floor to beam top was about 6 feet (1.8 m). Smaller poles, set at right angles to and on top of the main beams, finished the roof framing. Next smaller poles, spaced about a foot apart, were set at an angle from a foot or so back of the top edge of the pit to the main beams. This formed the basic framework for slanting walls and created an interior shelf around the perimeter of the pit. An entrance hole was left in the middle of the roof, and the hole also served as a smoke vent. Other poles framed the tunnel and any gaps that occurred in the shaft windshield.

Gaps between the framing of the walls, roof, and tunnel were covered over with anything handy: branches, brush, grass, or bark, all lashed to the poles. For a final seal, the earth from the excavation was turned to mud, mixed sometimes with grass, and plastered in a thick coating over all the walls, ceiling, and tunnel. The completed dwelling was hardly distinguishable from the landscape surrounding it, a camouflaging factor which contributed to its safety if there were marauders and which has frustrated findings by archaeologists to this day.[63] Unless the sun is just right, it is almost impossible to spot the remains of a pithouse.

There were no doors or windows. Occupants simply walked rapidly up the slanting sides and entered the house by a hardwood ladder that extended from the floor through the hole in the roof. Early ladders were more than notched poles or posts with projecting stubs. They were forerunners of the modern style, fashioned of two parallel poles, with cross-rungs lashed to them with willow or chokecherry strips. It can be assumed that such strips were also

Postulated architectural details of pithouses: plans and perspectives of pithouses with roof entrance and with tunnel entrance and antechamber. *Top,* late Basketmaker III pithouse of La Plata District, Colorado. From Morris, 1939. *Bottom,* early Basketmaker III pithouse from Chaco Canyon, New Mexico. From Roberts, 1929.

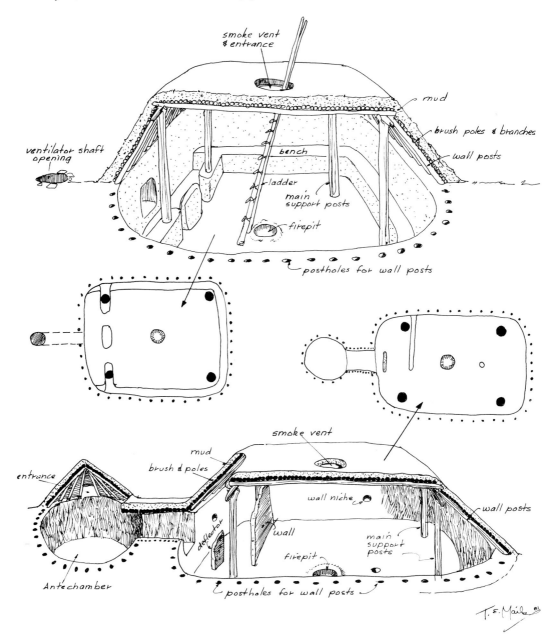

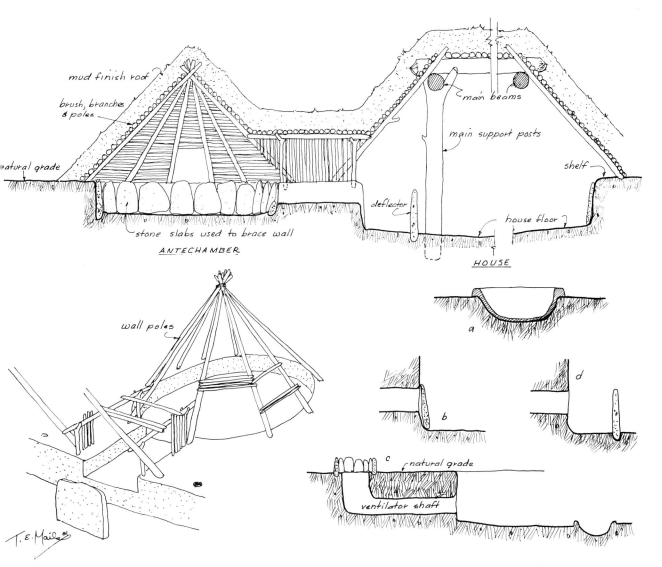

Postulated architectural details of Basketmaker pithouses. *Top and left,* possible framing method for constructing antechambers. *Bottom right: a,* firepit with clay liner. *b* stone slab used to close off interior ventilator opening. *c,* stone slab shield for exterior ventilator opening. *d,* stone deflector slab.

used to lash the entire framework of the house together, since other cultures are known to have done that.

The floor of the house was alternately scraped, watered, stamped down, and smoothed until it was packed hard. In the center a shallow round firepit was dug for cooking and heating, although much of the cooking would be done outside. The firepit was sometimes lined and rimmed with mud, which, as fires were made, would ultimately be baked until it was like brick. Aided by the ventilator tunnel, the entryway in the roof served as a smoke hole for the fire.

Somewhere along the way as villages developed, personal ritual practices and beliefs led to the inclusion of a sipapu in the floor. This small round hole was usually placed about halfway between the firepit and the north, or rear, wall.

Interior furnishings were meager. A pottery cooking vessel might be set flush into the floor, its top covered with a stone slab. Another sunken vessel provided a place to keep meal. Several niches might be dug in a firm wall to hold a few objects; the rest would be placed on the shelf at the top of the dirt wall. Cooking vessels, pots, cradles, dried meat, and baskets full of seeds and berries would be hung on stubs projecting from the slanting wall posts and from the roof beams and poles. Several manos and metates rounded out the furnishings. There were no chairs, tables, or beds. Family members simply wrapped themselves in fur robes and lay down to sleep on the floor or on a bed of leaves.

In sedentary times, corn storage required a disproportionate amount of space. The Basketmakers could not keep it all in the house, and they dared not store it too far away, since they needed to get to it in all weathers. This combination of demands led to a further development of the dwelling. The first step, it is thought, was to build a miniature house nearby. The second was to connect it to the main house by a large tunnel, after the manner of the ventilator shaft. Soon, then, after crawling back and forth for a time, some creative Basketmaker realized that the larger tunnel could also serve as an entryway to the house.[64] At Shabik'eshchee village in Chaco Canyon, New Mexico, the house so planned became the prevailing type. Some late Basketmaker III pithouses had one additional feature, a dirt bench that compassed the full perimeter of the house. This was achieved by stepping the wall as the pit excavation was made.[65]

A signal manner of wall construction and a method of retaining earth, both of which reveal engineering talent, came to light as Earl Morris worked in Mummy Cave, Canyon del Muerto, in 1923. To hold the refuse slope in place and thus increase the livable area of the cave, transverse cedar, piñon, and cottonwood poles were made to serve as braces for a wall of dry-laid stone and horizontal pine logs. Hard-packed sand was then dumped over the refuse to make a level surface. Cists built in the new floor contained caches of gourds, other vegetal matter, and, in one instance, seven hundred ears of corn.

The pit dwellings ranged from 12 feet to 25 feet (3.6–7.5 m) in diameter and had the traditional slanted walls. Some dwellings were intact enough to reveal their construction details. Four main posts with forked tops were set up, and four main beams were used to connect them. Small posts, spaced not more than 6 inches (15 cm) apart, were placed at a seventy-degree angle from grade level to the main beams around a scooped-out, slab-lined stepped pit rim. These were plastered over with mud. Next a mass of reeds was laid on top of the posts in horizontal layers. This was covered in turn with vertical sticks, and then another horizontal layer of reeds was laid. The whole of this—reeds and poles—was lashed firmly together, and the entire structure was covered with 3 inches (7.5 cm) of mud reinforced with vegetal substances and coarse sand. While no roof has survived, it is assumed that its construction was the same as that of the walls. Interestingly enough, this same stepped-rim technique was discovered at Badger House Community, Mesa Verde, during excavations in 1963.

We are in a position now at least to theorize about the evolution of the Basketmaker house. From vertical wood walls in the very late Basketmaker II stage, it progressed in Basketmaker III to the round dirt pit and angular wood walls, from there to a combination of round and rectangular pits, and finally to the stepped-rim pithouses of Mummy Cave and Mesa Verde typifying late Basketmaker III.

In Chaco Canyon, workers under the direction of Neil M. Judd in 1920 and 1922 unearthed two circular pithouses with evidence of benches, a four-post framework, and angular brush-and-mud-covered wood walls. The details are set forth in the Chaco Canyon chapter, but it can be said now that Judd's finds compare closely with those just discussed.[66] Alfred V. Kidder and Samuel J. Guernsey describe a pit dwelling in the Monuments district of northeastern Arizona in which a combination of roofing and wall poles, driven into a narrow bench at an angle, appeared to have met in tipi fashion above the middle of the dwelling.[67] Jesse Walter Fewkes discovered a similar method of construction in Mesa Verde National Park.[68] Walter Hough,[69] describing pit villages near Luna, New Mexico, and Earl Morris,[70] reporting on excavations between the San Juan River and the Continental Divide in Colorado, both noted the occurrence of large posts as roof supports, but say little about encircling benches or smaller poles set at an angle. Frank Roberts found pithouses with and without benches, and with sloped walls above grade (above ground level) at Whitewater District in eastern Arizona.[71] Judd found in southwestern Utah cave dwellings similar to, but more elaborate than, the Chaco pithouses in that the benches were faced with stone slabs and the upper walls were of jacal (mud and brush).[72]

The subject of protokivas has been considered, and it was noted that two kinds of kiva came into being in Basketmaker III. One was the clan, or at least a more personal and smaller, ritual center; the other was a huge community center where larger ceremonies involving the entire village would take place.[73] I say "entire village" in the full realization that men, as is modern Pueblo custom, would play the feature roles, but every ceremony involves women and children—even if the part played seems minor to outsiders. (Incidentally, there is no proof that clans existed in Basketmaker times, although some authorities do refer to the smaller chambers as clan kivas.)

You will recall that the Basketmaker Great Kiva found by Roberts at Shabik'eshchee, Chaco Canyon, New Mexico, was 40 feet (12.2 m) in diameter and 4 feet 2 inches (1.27 m) deep—almost twice the size of a personal kiva. At Broken Flute Cave, Earl Morris found a wall he believed had been part of a bench of a "Great Kiva," the floor level of the structure having been at natural grade level.[74]

These two finds alone are sufficient to indicate the increasing importance of religion in the life of the Basketmakers. Agricultural life was causing them

to think in new directions as the need for soil fertility, water, and growth
became dominant. The pursuit of ways to propitiate the supernatural forces
controlling the renewal of these things became essential, and, with the sedentary life as its midwife, the sophisticated ceremonial complex pursued so avidly
by the modern Pueblos was being born. Its fullest expression would not come
rapidly, but the child would grow and develop as surely and engagingly as
does the human kind, with maturity close to being reached by the advent of
historic times in A.D. 1540.

POTTERY AND NEW FOODS

Houses were only the first item that marked the change to sedentary life; pottery was the second, and it replaced the squash vessels and some baskets of
Basketmaker II. Rather than struggle once more through the fathomless question of how such new ideas came about, suffice it to say that enough evidence
exists to show the Basketmakers obtained some pieces from the Hohokam and
Mogollon, enough perhaps to provoke them into pursuing the creation of their
own. Yet, strange as it seems, they failed to acquire the technique and had to
fumble and grope their way to proficiency.[75]

Most archaeologists now believe that pottery-making was introduced into
the American Southwest from Mexico, although the earliest known fired pottery in the Western Hemisphere was made in coastal Ecuador.[76] The Mogollon
are believed to have received it from Mesoamerica by 100 B.C., and then to
have passed it on to the Anasazi around A.D. 300 or 400.[77]

From reconstruction of the findings, it appears the Anasazi endeavor went
something like this: already familiar with mud-lined baskets, they first tried
sun-drying clay pots, but found these dissolved when filled with water. Next
they fired plain clay by some means, but it cracked anyway and turned to
powder. A mixture of clay, juniper bark, and grass held together well, but the
grass burned during firing. Finally victory was achieved by mixing sand and
grit with the clay—either that, or some frustrated woman went, or sent her
husband, back to Mogollon country to find out exactly how they did it. Maybe
a Mogollon visitor was held as a friendly hostage until he or she explained the
tempering method.

Earl Morris saw the evolution of Anasazi pottery as follows: First, mud
liners were added to trays and bowls used for parching seeds. Second, fiber-
tempered (i.e., fibers mixed with mud), basket-molded mud bowls were used
as containers for dry foods. Third, the accidental burning of one of the mud
vessels proved it could hold water. Fourth, true pottery was made by intentional firing.[78]

Experts have speculated, because of the color differences between Basketmaker III pottery and that of the Mogollon and Hohokam, that different firing
methods were used. Since the ware of the two southern cultures was predominantly brown, yellow, and red, it is assumed they fired in the oxygen-rich

Pottery: *a*, Basketmaker III bowl of unfired clay, the base of which was molded in a coiled basket. *b*, Basketmaker III nonculinary squash pot from La Plata District, Colorado. *c*, Basketmaker III black-on-white bowl. *d*, Basketmaker III bowl from La Plata. *e*, Basketmaker III bowl from Pueblo Bonito, New Mexico. *f*, Basketmaker III bowl with panel design. *g*, Basketmaker III bowl from northeastern Arizona. From Earl H. Morris, 1927.

atmosphere that produces these colors. Most Basketmaker III pottery was a dull gray, indicating an oxygen-free firing atmosphere.

In seeking an answer that accounts for the difference in color, and with no eyewitness record at hand, one can only guess at how the Basketmaker women actually did their firing. Donald Pike reasons that, not having kilns, which would exclude oxygen, they baked their pottery in the middle of "a small, flaming pyre of dry wood and brush."[79] This rapidly burning fire would consume all the available oxygen and produce the gray vessels.

Amsden prefers to cite the modern Pueblo practice; I assume he chose to cite it as a carry-over from ancient times. A platform of firewood would be laid, perhaps in a shallow hole. The platform would be loosely covered with flat stones to prevent direct contact between the pots and the embers. Unfired pots would be stacked on the stones, bottom up, and a dome of firewood would be stacked evenly around and over the pile, being kept from direct contact with the pots by buffers of large potsherds, to prevent smudging. The lighted pyre would burn itself out in a few hours, and the firing would be complete. Amsden does not speculate on what percentage of pots might be lost in the process—but judging by modern standards it might amount to two out of twenty. He adds that "investigators have recorded maximum temperatures ranging from 400 to nearly 1000 degrees centigrade in the process, 500 degrees being the minimum needed to achieve the fusion of clay particles that make pottery durable."[80]

There are yet other possibilities. The potters of modern Colombia, some of whom still employ ancient techniques for ground firing, place a number of pots in a circular mound on top of any available wood and cover it with wood branches and twigs, set in a cone shape. The wood is ignited and kept blazing with additional wood for about two hours.[81] Also used for fuel is guada, a thick, hollow-tubed plant similar to bamboo that burns rapidly with a very hot flame.[82] The Basketmakers may have used a somewhat similar process, since reeds were plentiful in their homeland.

The pot-making technique itself need not be speculated about. With pot in hand, the authority can tell it was made by the coil-and-scrape method. No potter's wheel was yet known in the Americas. The potter simply took a large lump of clay and pressed it into a suitable mold, such as a gourd dish, a basket, or a previously formed clay mold. The walls were then built up with coils of clay, welded together by finger pressure. Later in the period a longer roll of clay was used and coiled upon itself to produce spiral coiling.[83] Joints would be scraped smooth with a piece of gourd shell or a sherd. Once the desired form was achieved, a final smoothing would be done with a handful of moistened grass, which left telltale striations on the surface to instruct the inquisitive archaeologists who would come along a millennium later and wonder how they did it.

The earliest vessels were neither polished nor slipped. And, as attested to by the hundreds of whole pots and millions of sherds found by archaeologists, the basic character of the ware remained constant for the entire Four Corners region. It was a dirty gray, the color of the component clay being smudged in varying degrees in the firing process. Its usual tempering matter was coarse sand, whose granules flecked and roughened the surface. Vessel walls were a quarter-inch thick, durable and quite hard. The typical form was a round body, although some vessels had elongated necks and handles, suggesting they were modeled after the gourd vessels in earlier use. A few twin-necked pots similar to modern Pueblo wedding jars were found, but so few as to suggest they were not in common use.[84] Ladles also appeared in late Basketmaker III.

A number of bird-shaped vessels have been found in Basketmaker III sites. The earliest of these were not decorated, and in form were gourd-like and quite simple, although aesthetically pleasing. Later on, more realistic shapes were fashioned and the vessels were painted with washes of red ocher, black lines, and black circles. Some of these pots had bird's heads, while others had only a rotund bird body and an opening for filling and pouring.[85] Some pots were found in graves, but it is not known whether any were used for ceremonial purposes.

Decoration came with competence and the passage of time. In its simplest form it consisted of a coating of a red ocher earth paint that was not fired on and rubs off easily, causing archaeologists to call it "fugitive red." You will recall that some earlier basket colors were also rubbed on, and rubbing would be a logical first means for the Basketmakers. Next they tried vegetable colors. These carbonized and turned black when fired, bringing to pass the black-on-gray that would typify the first designed vessels of the Anasazi, and later the black-on-white of Pueblo times.

It may be that black was precisely what the Basketmakers wanted, since it is still popular with Pueblo artists today. Two regional formulas for black are used. The Rio Grande pueblos obtain their black paint by boiling certain green plants to extract their sap. The sap carbonizes during firing, and a film of silica from the vessel's clay impregnates and hardens it. The Zuñi and Hopi add a ferruginous clay to the boiled sap, producing a brownish tinge. Both techniques are known to have existed far back in prehistoric times, but how far no one knows.[86] Interestingly enough, the distinction in color tone begins to play an important role as the story of Pueblo pottery unfolds.

One further advance in color application took place before the time of Pueblo I. Intrigued by the rich colors of Mogollon and Hohokam pots, the Basketmaker women sought to produce them themselves, but couldn't. They solved the problem by applying a slip of red vegetable dye to the pot exterior after the pots were fired. It was neither permanent nor particularly attractive, but it was at least a splash of color.

For the most part, the designs employed by the potters were those already being used for their baskets—dots, circles, straight lines, and angular geometric figures, forebears of a tradition that continues today. Some creative artists added crude human and animal figures individually and in blends of the two, but these additions soon lost popularity and were revived only in later centuries when artistry had improved considerably.

The Basketmaker's paintbrush was a leaf of shredded yucca, worked to a fine point. With this simple device, narrow lines could be drawn and then embellished. Usually the first potters began, as with their baskets, at bottom center and worked the design out from there. Later the rim replaced the center as the point of departure for the decorative scheme. It is virtually impossible to describe adequately in words the designs used, and so my illustrations will show what exactly the typical Basketmaker artist accomplished. It was not fine art at its best, but it was the beginning that led the way to magnificent things.

The advent of pottery did not end the making of baskets, although some items such as storage bags and water baskets declined in favor. At the same time, the baskets that were made became more elaborate in design, serving both utilitarian and aesthetic purposes.

With pots to cook them in, beans were added to the Basketmaker diet, soon becoming an important source of protein for the burgeoning population.[87] The Basketmakers had no doubt known about beans for some time before they put them to use. But boiling beans in baskets at altitudes above a mile was a slow and exasperating business. Pots solved the problem. Now the beans could simmer for hours over coals, with only an occasional stirring and the addition of water.

Where did the beans come from, and when did the Basketmakers begin their cultivation? That, too, lies in the realm of mystery. Presumably the sources were the same as those that brought them corn and squash, although it is certain that corn preceded the arrival of beans by several centuries. Corn is found regularly in early Basketmaker ruins, beans never. When at last a few beans were found in sites, they proved to be light brown and a bit smaller than the red-brown bean known in the Southwest as the "Mexican bean."[88]

It is vital to note that, at this point in their history, the Anasazi were blessed with the two most important food plants in native America. Amsden puts their situation well: "Whole nations have flourished on little but corn and beans. Like corn, the bean is a two in one, a succulent green vegetable first, a long-keeping dry food after maturity. It is hardy, requiring little water and enduring much abuse by sun and wind, yet the yield is liberal for such a little waif of a plant. Beans are easily harvested, easily stored, easily prepared as food. The world's gardens harbor many a plant less deserving of human gratitude than the common bean."[89]

A species of wild turkey, known as Merriam's turkey, is native to the higher forested regions of the Southwest. The early Basketmakers captured some for their feathers, but it was only in the Basketmaker III Period that they domesticated the bird. Thus it is that we in America probably owe the domestication of this popular Thanksgiving dish to the Basketmakers. Turkey pens found in late Basketmaker village sites indicate that the bird was kept and presumably bred as a domestic fowl. Earl Morris found ample evidence of turkey pens in Basketmaker caves. Under one such pen at Tseahatso, Canyon del Muerto, Arizona, he made a most stimulating discovery, a 16-inch-long hollow cylinder of wood, wrapped with a yucca cord that held a piece of cloth over a slit opening in the top. Inside the tube "lay an unbelievable assortment of colored feathers and bird skins which had successfully defied the centuries."[90]

Some secretive person had hidden it there one clandestine night and never had an opportunity to retrieve it.

Opinions vary about whether Basketmakers used the turkey for food. Donald Pike thinks not.[91] Amsden thinks they did, arguing that great numbers of turkey bones found in the ruins of the Zuñi pueblo of Hawikuh testify in its favor. Hard as meat was to come by, I find it difficult to believe they didn't eat turkey. No taboo, to my knowledge, has existed against such use in the historic pueblos.[92]

Everyone does agree that turkey feathers were used in abundance for making delightfully light wrap-arounds. The method of fabrication was virtually identical to that of rabbit-fur robes. The feathers were first split along the quill and then wrapped spirally around lengths of yucca cord. The finished strings were placed in parallel rows and cross-twined with cordage to complete the assembly. Sometimes an especially beautiful product was made by combining feather ropes and fur ropes in a single garment.

A NEW WEAPON

Sometime after A.D. 450 and before A.D. 700, the bow and arrow came by diffusion to the Basketmakers. The men still hunted to supplement their farm crops, and we can assume they especially appreciated this new arrival, more effective in many ways than the atlatl. Anyone who has tried to use the spear throwing-stick knows it would require a skilled and patient man to throw the spear with force and accuracy for any distance, and that its killing range for large game was probably no more than 75 feet.

The bow common to the Basketmaker and his contemporary cultures was the simplest type known in ancient America—the arc, or self-bow, made of a single piece of hard wood and about 3 feet long. The outer face was flat and the inner face was rounded, so as to give the cross section a D shape. Bow strings were made from rolled strips of sinew, but the early bows were not reinforced with layers of sinew strips as was commonly done on the Great Plains. The estimated pull was fifty pounds.

Arrows were made in the same fashion as spears, but were shorter, slimmer, and lighter. Most were compound, with an inserted main shaft of hard wood. Sometimes this shaft was tipped with a flaked-stone projectile point, at other times the wood itself was sharpened, sometimes a blunt wood point was fashioned. They were fletched with three split feathers, and they averaged 24 inches in length. Many Basketmaker III flaked-stone points were fashioned with barbed edges and stemmed like those of the Hohokam. The arrow manufacturing method was sound. Desert-dwelling Apache were still using compound arrows in their wars against the whites in the late nineteenth century.[93]

In earlier pages, when Basketmaker weapons were first discussed, I pointed out that the atlatl remained popular long after the bow and arrow arrived. That is understandable. The hunters knew the atlatl's capabilities and would be reluctant to trade it instantly for a weapon whose mettle was not fully known. It would be several hundred years before all the Basketmaker hunters laid down their atlatls for the last time.

In 1923, at Tseahatso, Earl Morris found a deep cist he dubbed the "Chief's Grave" because of its apparently important occupant. An aged man had been clothed in beautifully tanned buckskin garments and wrapped in a feather robe. With the skeleton were shell bracelets, an abalone shell pendant, a stone pipe, flutes, and atlatls and spears. Presumably this man of late Basketmaker III had been given several of his favorite weapons to accompany him into the netherworld.[94]

ARTS AND CRAFTS

With secure homes to dwell in, a food surplus readily at hand, and less time required to maintain that surplus, for the first time the Basketmakers had leisure hours to devote to arts and crafts. What the artisans created led to new ideas about personal adornment. A timorous style-consciousness began to creep in, and a few new garments were added to the ancient wardrobe.

Reference has been made to the advent of turkey-feather wraps, apparently worn by women and men alike. The breechclout, so common among other Indians, still was not worn by most men, but the women began to elaborate upon their aprons. The unadorned string or fiber apron of earlier days gave way to a new model, a woven strip of yucca cord about 6 inches long and 2 inches wide, decorated with painted or woven geometric figures done in red and black. From this panel, which hung horizontally from a waist cord, were left to dangle the warp ends, the long strings that completed the apron.

An even later version of the apron enlarged the panel to a square and allowed for more decoration, but the long warp ends were still included to provide adequate cover, movement, and texture.

The idea of design movement is noteworthy, in that Indian garments of many cultures exhibited from earliest times a sensitiveness to the singular qualities of motion and kinetic design: the graceful movement as one walks and breezes blow, the catching of light to create ever-changing shadow patterns, and the capturing of admiring eyes. The modern artist Alexander Calder by no means invented the mobile sculpture. It was in vogue throughout the Americas for more than a thousand years before he fashioned the first of his delightful creations. The same can be said about texture and the tactile sense, for that, too, was consciously included by Indian craftspeople from the earliest days. We find it in their clothing, in pottery, in architecture—indeed, in all the arts ranging in degree from the simpler forms in North America to the grand garments, carved façades, and stelae of Mesoamerica and South America.

Sandal styles also changed in Basketmaker III. The earlier fringed, square-toed type was replaced by a scalloped-toed irregular form whose different shapes defy description and can be made clear only by illustration. The new sandals were decorated after the manner of the new aprons and, of all places, on the upper surface of the sole, where the design would be hidden by the wearer's foot. On the bottom of the sole, an elaborate system of knots and overlaid strands formed neat patterns, and just as the upper designs were so mysteriously hidden, so too the knots and strands on the underside would soon be worn off. Amsden observes that hundreds of worn-through and discarded sandals have been found in the caves—revealing, he thinks, that they were made for regular, daily wear.[95]

Sandals: *a,* Pueblo III plaited and twilled. *b,* Basketmaker III cord sandal with raised designs on sole. *c,* Basketmaker II: *right,* 4-ways wickerwork; *left,* multiple-warp cord. *d,* Basketmaker III sandals from Canyon del Muerto, Arizona.

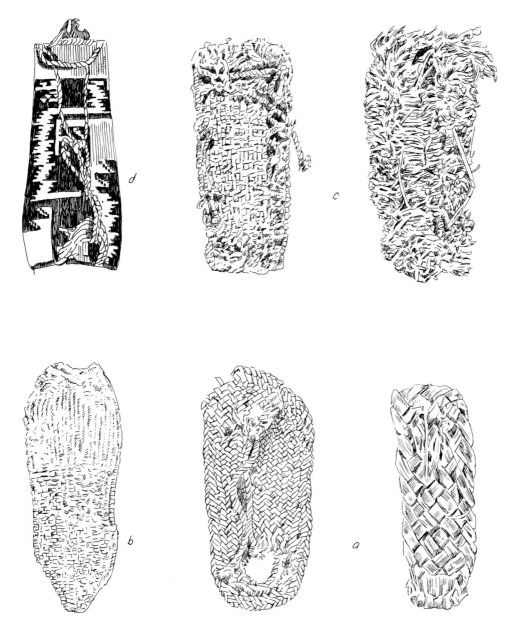

Why so much work on a sandal when the designs couldn't be seen and the sole lasted but a short while? Amsden saw it as foolishness "of an exalted kind," the "persistent, laborious creation of beautiful things," an "esthetic sense that will one day find richer expression."[96] Such fine sensuous thoughts tend to rule out argument, yet I think it entirely possible that religious and status connotations were involved. The classic footwear of the Maya was a status symbol, and in North America certain items appended to the feet during ceremonies are thought to ward off evil powers. True enough, the Pueblo women dance barefoot today to "gather power," but the men don't. Their moccasins are fraught with symbols representing life, such as colored tabs and skunk skins. The sandal was about all that the early Basketmaker people wore, hence their only opportunity for personal expression.

Donald Pike is less inspiring in his appraisal of the textured sole of the sandal. He thinks it gave better traction—quite a sensible thing for a cliff- and hill-dwelling people—and he might be right.[97]

A wholly new and more portentous item appearing at this time was the woven sash. Working with Earl Morris and others in Obelisk Cave, Arizona, in 1930, Marjorie Trumbull triumphantly came up with a bark-lined cache of six exquisitely made sashes. Two were white, two brown and white, and two brown. They were still soft and pliable, in virtually perfect condition. All were made of dog hair by a finger-weaving technique called flat or plait braiding. The narrowest was 1½ inches wide, the broadest 3 inches. They varied in length from 6 to 9 feet. All had squared-off fringe strips that were braided and strung with olivella shell beads.[98] Later two sashes of lesser quality were discovered in Broken Flute Cave, Arizona. Lister and Lister state: "Few scholars could have distinguished any of them from sashes produced by Pueblo hands [today]."[99] A number of sashes included in the display at the Mesa Verde Museum are impressive in quality, although none are so broad or dramatic as the grand rain-sash models worn by some Pueblo dancers now.

Since the Modified (Late Period) Basketmaker sashes are so similar to present-day rain sashes, they might be the first clear indication of rain and fertility cults; their purpose when worn in ritual might be an unspoken prayer to ensure adequate water for crops, the renewal of all life, and the continuance of growth. Such speculation is not, considering other evidence, without substance: clan and great kivas also made their appearance before the end of Basketmaker III, along with two other items of consequence not yet treated—effigies and flutes.

Beads were popular with the early Anasazi, who conceived during Basketmaker II and III a choice variety of necklaces of disk beads and subspherical beads of stone and various kinds of seeds. These were both single- and multiple-strand creations, often with a pendant dangling on the front or back. Some shell necklaces were fashioned of disk and saucer beads. Bead bracelets were found in a few sites, and also a bracelet of claw beads.[100] One Basketmaker infant had a shell disk attached to the left ear.[101] Strings of beads were also worn as earrings.

Tab pendants of shell, turquoise, gypsum, and hematite were used as earrings and as necklace decorations. Entire necklaces were made from whole seashells, such as olivella, conus, turritella, and cerithidea. Since the Basketmaker selection of shells was more limited than that of the Hohokam, E. Wesley Jernigan guesses that the shells were received in trade from the Hohokam, who first siphoned off the more select pieces. Rings and bracelets were never popular with the Basketmakers.[102] Some bone tube beads and decorative wooden hairpins were created.

Turquoise, absent from Basketmaker II findings, made its appearance during Basketmaker III. Ornaments of this splendid blue or blue-green stone so popular in Indian jewelry today were first unearthed in the caves of the Lukachukai Mountains on the Arizona–New Mexico border. One of the most beautiful discoveries was a large mosaic pendant, a thin piece of wood covered with bits of turquoise set in pitch.[103]

Several sources of supply for turquoise were well within reach of Basketmaker territory: in New Mexico, southern Nevada, and Arizona. All these were tapped by Indians at various times, although it is not known which of them were used by Basketmaker artisans, or when. Southern Nevada had an extensive late Basketmaker III occupancy, and turquoise jewelry was plentiful in their ruins.

The most likely source of mosaic ideas was the Hohokam, who were already flourishing by A.D. 600 and were already masters of inlay work. What few bracelets of glycymeris shell there were appeared in Basketmaker land simultaneously with the turquoise work, and these were assuredly a Hohokam ornament. Glycymeris is found only in the Gulf of California, from which the most direct trade route in ancient times lay through Hohokam country. It therefore seems probable that the two cultures exchanged raw turquoise for raw shell and that in the bargaining some finished items were also traded. No doubt turquoise went south from the Hohokam into Mesoamerica as well, reaching even the Maya hundreds of miles away on the Yucatán Peninsula; at the ancient city of Chichén Itzá a large mosaic plaque of turquoise was found. It is impossible not to wonder whether the turquoise of that plaque might have come from Basketmaker hands, as well as the stones of the bracelets worn by Tarascan kings, the turquoise mosaics of the Mixtecs and western Mexicans, the Toltec turquoise beads, and Teotihuacan turquoise masks.[104]

Just as sandals, aprons, and wraps were woven and decorated carefully, so, too, were other items, such as tumplines, or burden straps, and baskets.

As the Basketmaker III Period wore on, fewer baskets were made, but their decorative quality was improving. Some items were no longer made, and the round woven bag so popular in early times had become a coarse, plain, utilitarian item. The techniques, forms, and patterns used by weavers remained the same, but textures became finer and color was added. Red as well as black was featured in the designs, and the basket became a true art object.

An entirely new basket, called the ring basket, came into being, and it is still being made by Pueblo women. Whole leaves of yucca were plaited to produce a circular mat a foot or so in diameter. The edge was then curved up to form a shallow basin. This was accomplished by pushing the mat through a ring made by bending a flexible stick until its ends met in a circle. The edges of the mat were turned back, lashed to the ring, and then trimmed.[105] The ring baskets were easily made and serviceable, but not nearly so beautiful as the coiled mats we are more familiar with today.

Although bone awls were in common use in Basketmaker II times, only during Basketmaker III did the bone needle make its appearance. Some of the early awls had a hole drilled through them to provide for a suspension cord, but one fine day a creative inventor realized that the cord could become thread, and a size reduction and streamlining would make the bone an item far more versatile for sewing. Soon the needle-and-thread idea was spreading rapidly throughout the Basketmaker realm and becoming a boon of some magnitude to those in dire need of just such an item.

It took a full two weeks to grind down, drill, and sharpen a piece of bone to make a single awl, and a primitive sewing kit was no simple item to put together. Basketmaker women must have put in considerable time keeping their awl and needle supply adequate and in good repair.

EFFIGIES AND FLUTES

Among the Basketmaker remains at Tsegi Canyon, Arizona, Samuel Guernsey recovered six clay figurines that excited considerable interest. Shortly thereafter Earl Morris found five figurines at Canyon del Muerto, and then another twenty-three at Red Rocks, Arizona, bringing the total to thirty-four. Without prototype in the culture, these figures appeared out of nowhere, "scattered through the dry cave-dirt like crude dolls cast off by children," Amsden says.[106]

The dolls were only a few inches long. Some were made of fiber, but most were fashioned of unfired clay. All of them represented the human figure in the abstract, usually the female, with pinched-up areas forming nose and breast features. Some had a crotch cleft. One wore a grass sash, others had a punched pattern of indentations, and some had thorns and cactus spines stuck into them. Archaeologists assume that the clay effigies had something to do with a fertility cult, except those pierced by thorns. These suggested the witch-craft or hex practices of other cultures, wherein a witch seeks to injure or de-stroy someone by stabbing his image.

In Mesoamerica, human effigies made of clay were turned out by the thou-sands, and the Hohokam made them too. Possibly the idea, with its religious associations, made its way north. The practice of making effigies appears to have flourished in Basketmaker territory for only a brief time and then ceased. The rain and fertility cults by no means ended, though; they would continue without faltering as the culture passed through, and ascended from, one stage to the next up to the present.

Ceremonial items: *a*, bone flute from White Dog Cave, Arizona. *b*, pictograph of hump-backed flute player. *c*, 30-inch-long wooden flute found in Big Cave in Canyon del Muerto. *d*, ceremonial wand with bird head found in White Dog Cave. *e*, Basketmaker II deer hoof rattle from White Dog Cave. *f*, painted wooden bird and two of many wooden sunflowers found in a cache in Sunflower Cave, Arizona. *g*, *h*, unidentified pictographs.

Seldom mentioned when findings are treated in Basketmaker literature are the nipple-shaped objects that Earl Morris described as cornucopias. These tiny two- or three-inch-long, unfired-clay objects were found in Tsegi Canyon. Like the clay effigies, most of the cornucopias had patterns of indentations punched in them. They are mysterious enough to rate as ceremonial objects of unknown purpose and are similar to items used in healing by the medicine persons of other cultures; as such, they merit special interest on the part of those seeking to unravel the mysteries of Basketmaker life.[107]

Simple end flutes, common to all ancient cultures of the Americas, also appeared in the findings associated with Basketmaker III. The earlier one-stop birdcall of bone was still in service, but real flutes capable of producing real music were now being made. These consisted of the hollowed-out shell of an elder branch and had from four to six stops. One discovery was ornamented with a ruff of bright feathers neatly bound to the outer end.[108]

The flute had no vibrator or sound plug of any kind, only a plain barrel and finger holes. It may have been used for secular purposes only, but modern comparisons indicate a religious purpose as well. Many an evening in Oklahoma I've listened for hours to Doc Tate Nevaquaya, America's premier artist on the Indian flute, as he played the ancient compositions of his Comanche people. While many are secular in nature, riding songs and the like, not once did the plaintive flute fail to lift me into the spiritual realm of those proud and pensive people. The flute speaks in a special way to and of the supernatural, and there is little doubt it played a similar role for the Basketmakers.

ROCK ART

While it is exceedingly difficult to date rock art, it is generally accepted today that the Basketmakers did take up this avocation in a tentative way in Basketmaker II, and then more actively in Basketmaker III.[109] The usual form of identification has been either to associate the art with a pure Basketmaker site or to relate it to datable materials found nearby. There is also a style typical of Basketmaker artists.

At Marsh Pass, Arizona, Kidder and Guernsey found pure Basketmaker sites at which there were numerous cave paintings. Most were frontal views of square-shouldered human figures with long, triangular bodies. Heads were round and small, with an indication of a headdress or feathers in the hair. Both arms were held straight out from the shoulders and bent at the elbows, the forearms hanging straight down. Some had no hand or finger details. Legs were short; some feet had lines indicating toes, others had no foot details at all. The exposed penis of one figure was indicated by a line. Necklace lines were drawn on some figures.[110]

The other common motif at Marsh Pass was the hand print, although a number of bird figures were present also. Together with the human figures

Anasazi Child

Kiva Leader at Santo Domingo

San Juan Game Animal Deer Dancer *(original egg tempera)*

Female Buffalo Dancers of Santa Clara *(original egg tempera)*

Cochiti Man in Ancient Attire

The Eagle Keeper of Old Picuris Pueblo

Grandfather's Favorite

Harvesttime at San Ildefonso

Sun Basket Dancers of San Juan, 1930

Chaco Canyon's Pueblo Bonito Ruins

Antelope House in Canyon del Muerto

Morning of the Corn Dance at Santo Domingo

Mummy Cave in Canyon del Muerto

Corn Dancers of Cochiti Pueblo

Santa Clara Blue Corn Dancers

Young Potter of Santa Clara

Tuampomosino of San Juan

San Ildefonso Women's Chorus

Santa Clara Female Corn Dancer

just described, these are taken by authorities as typical Basketmaker designs, mostly from the Basketmaker III stage.

Some of the figures were solidly painted, others done in outline. The colors were red, yellow, and white, with some polychrome designs drawn on the human torsos. At other sites thought to be definitely Basketmaker, human torsos have zigzag lines and hand prints on them, as well as lines for necklaces. Some in Canyon de Chelly have mysterious appendages on the heads and arms. One figure on a canyon wall holds what appears to be an atlatl throwing-stick.

Experts caution those who profess the ability to read rock art, believing that at this distant point in time we lack the information needed. Nevertheless, even the experts are prone to speculation and have concluded that rock art carries a religious connotation. It is an attempt to "enrich and aid his [the artist's] religious experience."[111] Therefore the large human figures "might have represented supernatural beings or shamans personifying such beings."[112] In addition to serving as personal indentification marks, hand prints are thought to be a way of establishing the "I was here" idea—and when placed upon the drawing of another figure to be a form of deriving power from that figure. The preoccupation with birds may represent nothing more than a memorial to the Basketmakers' growing dependence upon the turkey.

Two techniques were used to produce rock art—painting, or the pictograph, and engraving, or the petroglyph. The latter was the less popular, since it was far more difficult to do and desirable surfaces for it were harder to find and get to in the Four Corners area.

Petroglyphs were made by pecking or otherwise engraving the surface of a darkly patinated rock surface so as to expose the lighter rock underneath. This created a negative-appearing image. Four techniques in combination were used to do this: pecking, done with hard-pointed stones; abrading, a scraping action wherein an abrasive rock was used to scrape a large surface and give it a tone; incising, done by a sharp tool on soft rock; and scratching, to gain a contrasting tone, done by barely breaking the patinated surface with a pointed tool made of some softer material than the rock being used for the petroglyph.

Because painting was a faster, easier, and more versatile technique, paintings at Basketmaker sites considerably outnumber the petroglyphs. Moreover, artists were attracted by the great variety of colored clays available. In his survey of Canyon de Chelly, Campbell Grant discovered more than a dozen colors used in paintings: white, yellow, black, red in several shades, green, pale green, brown, orange, gray, buff, and purple. Most commonly employed were white, pale green, and red. Black was rarely used.[113]

Most of the colors, Grant says, were of mineral origin, and the rest were vegetable colors. Charcoal was used for black. Mineral colors were the most permanent; some of the vegetable colors have faded, making it seem at first glance as though some figures were only partly painted.

The binder used with the paint may have been one of many things: water, blood, the white of an egg, even urine. All have been used in experiments by researchers and are said to work quite well.

Findings show that in the mixing of paint the raw pigments were first ground to powder in stone mortars, then mixed with the binder at the painting site. The cruder paintings appear to have been done with the fingers, and the finer paintings with brushes—probably made of yucca fibers or animal hair. The fine lines could have been made with a yucca leaf, as was done for pottery decoration.

DEATH AND BURIAL

Mummy Cave, in Canyon del Muerto, Arizona, was one of the most bountiful sites ever excavated by Earl Morris. When he began his work there in 1923, he found almost immediately in the trash slopes and cists an abundance of mummies dating from Basketmaker III through the Developmental Pueblo stage.

The first of the mummies was but an indication of things to come, and a truly startling find. It demonstrated that, although traditional Basketmaker burial customs were still being carried on during late Basketmaker III, there now were several new items of apparel. Upon removal of the layers of shredded juniper bark, a small bundle emerged, tightly trussed with cord and covered with an inverted, dirty round basket. It was an old man, his body flexed and wrapped with a rabbit-fur robe. He wore buckskin leggings, a buckskin cloak and apron, and a shell bracelet. On his feet were buckskin moccasins with soles of cedar bark. With the body was an atlatl throwing-stick, a bag of dice, a pipe, and smoking materials.[114]

Unique and new were the extensive buckskin outfit, the man's apron, suggesting the beginning of breechclouts, and the most unusual moccasins. And while the basket, rabbit-fur robe, and atlatl were related to Basketmaker II and III, the shell bracelet came very late in Basketmaker III from the Hohokam. At the least, the old man remains a mysterious figure, a subject for considerable speculation.

Mummy Cave was a veritable treasure trove of Basketmaker III artifacts. There were huge, close-coiled baskets decorated in black and red geometric designs, there were the cone-shaped carrying baskets, and there were the bowl-shaped and ring baskets. Mud trays were present. Women's aprons of yucca fiber and cedar bark were decorated and had fringes that passed between the legs and were tied in back (a new style?).

Findings included small, tightly finger-woven, seamless bags, thought by Morris to be women's handbags or men's pouches. Sandals were the decorated-upper type with the knots on the under sole, but they lacked the toe fringe common to sandals from Grand Gulch, Tsegi Canyon, and Du Pont Cave in Utah. Winter sandals were different also, having sandal soles with uppers of cord meshwork and a thick lining of cedar bark.

Some of the beads consisted of tiny pieces of shell, from both the Gulf of California and the California coast. Larger beads were made from ground bits of stone and from seeds of wild plants. There were mosaic pendants of shaped and polished turquoise, mounted with pitch on pieces of wood, and there was the wooden cylinder filled with colored feathers spoken of earlier in the text.

Implements taken from Mummy Cave in 1923 included crooked digging sticks, throwing (or fending) sticks, complete atlatls, snares, and nets. Mention has already been made of the valuable dwelling finds there and, in particular, of the layered walls showing complete details of their construction.

GEOGRAPHIC EXPANSION

Geographic expansion came about slowly. There was no need to hurry. The Anasazi thought in seasons, not in minutes and hours. The Four Corners region, home of the earliest Basketmaker Anasazi, remained the territorial center during the years of village beginnings. In fact, the early and late Basketmakers occupied about the same territory, with this significant difference: early Basketmaker remains are few and far between outside the Four Corners region, while those of late Basketmakers are plentiful in areas seldom used before.

The reason for this is clear. As the sedentary lifeway took over, the population grew rapidly. Where once there were few villages, soon there were hundreds. It was expansion of an interesting kind, though, and it merits special attention, for it seems not so much the result of an increase in the Basketmaker birthrate as the result of an influx of new people, who, seeing the advantages of farming and sedentary ways, moved in with the Basketmakers and took up the good life. Physical evidence points toward these new folk as being of several different tribes. A variation in head form between the mummies of Falls Creek Cave, Colorado, and those found in sites farther west is but one indication that they were undergoing salient changes in culture.[115] Perhaps these new people brought with them the hard wooden cradleboard that was familiar in Pueblo times and accounted for the slightly flattened skulls marking the Basketmaker Period's end.

Before the Basketmakers and their immediate Pueblo descendants ran their course, they had spread their villages over a vast territory and left behind them thousands of ruins. An extensive occupancy, with Basketmaker village sites spaced only a few miles apart, occurred in southern Nevada along the lower valleys of the Virgin and Muddy rivers. In Utah there were cave and hilltop villages as far north as the Great Salt Lake, although the main occupancy was at the southeastern end of the state. The southwestern quarter of Colorado was virtually covered with Basketmaker villages.

Southward in New Mexico there are numerous Basketmaker village sites in the valley of the San Juan and its tributaries—the Animas, La Plata, and Chaco. Shabik'eshchee Village marks the southeastern frontier of late Basketmaker land. Arizona has a number of Basketmaker cave sites in Kayenta, particularly in Canyons de Chelly and del Muerto, in the Lukachukai Mountain region, and in the Red Rocks Valley.

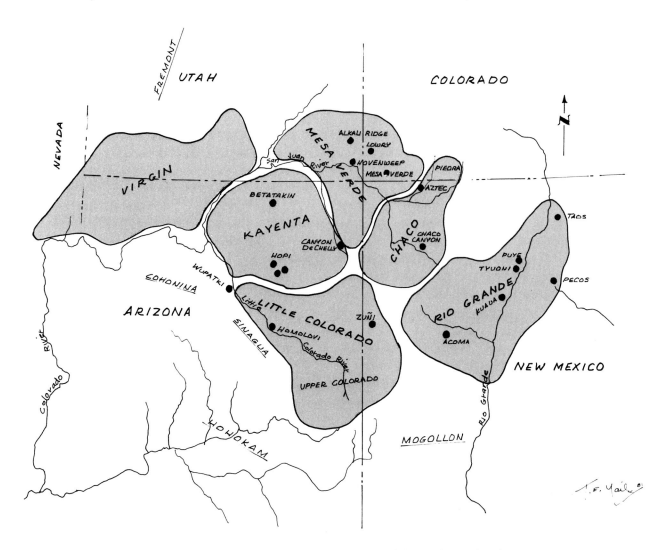

Map showing the approximate geographic areas of the six Anasazi regions.

Amsden felt there might have been a southerly extension into the mountain belt of central Arizona and western New Mexico. This was "likely territory," whose well-watered valleys were occupied by Indians in Basketmaker days. But no archaeologist as yet knows whether the occupants were Basketmaker, Mogollon, Hohokam, or some regional blend of small groups.

Timewise, Basketmaker III would embrace the greater portion of the sixth, seventh, and eighth centuries, at least in the central Four Corners area. The frontier villages would lag behind, as is natural. Communication was poor, and resistance to change was stronger in some regions than in others. At the end of the chronological period, though, the Basketmakers would flow so smoothly into Pueblo I that anyone living in those exhilarating days would not have noticed it was happening.

By the end of the Basketmaker III Period in A.D. 750, Anasazi leagues of real significance were established and progressing at varying rates in three principal regions, known today as Chaco Canyon, Kayenta, and Mesa Verde. Besides these, three lesser communities were beginning to form, one north and one south of Kayenta, and the other east of Chaco, along the Rio Grande. Pueblo settlements in the Northern Peripheral District (the Virgin Region) were gradually abandoned during the Pueblo II and III periods, and their inhabitants helped to increase the population in the San Juan area to the south.[116] While the basic lifeway of the Basketmaker III Period was still followed, each of the forming leagues began to develop, at its own pace, certain practices and characteristics that made it in time somewhat different from the others. The differences are important to those who want to know the Anasazi well, since it is here we find the true genius of the Anasazi culture in full measure. However, while it would be worthwhile to consider each of the three principal regions extensively and equally, such thorough coverage would result in an excessive duplication of specific information about such things as exact kiva particulars and details of utilitarian artifacts. Therefore, the Mesa Verde league serves in some parts as a model for the other two, and detailed information absent elsewhere is included in the Mesa Verde chapter.

Chapter 3

VIRGIN
ANASAZI

THE VIRGIN REGION

Archaeologists have, because of cultural variations, separated the developing Anasazi peoples of A.D. 700 into six cultural regions: Mesa Verde, Kayenta, Chaco Canyon, Rio Grande, Little Colorado, and, in the northwest, a region recently called Virgin, after the Virgin River. The name Virgin was also apt because the region stayed pretty much as it was from the beginning, adopting few of the innovations created and taken up by the other regions.

There are different opinions about what exact geographic areas each of these six regions should encompass. For example, some authorities extend the Mesa Verde region, because of its obvious cultural influence, at least one hundred miles north and west into Utah and include Hovenweep and Alkali Ridge in the Mesa Verde sphere. Then they assign to the Virgin region the rest of the southernmost portion of Utah plus northwestern Arizona and a small corner of Nevada. But Neil M. Judd's findings in Willard, Utah, stretch the Virgin region far to the north. Moreover, it remains a debatable question whether any significant part of the culturally laggard Utah Anasazi can fairly be listed as other than Virgin. While some aspects of Hovenweep architecture are not found on Mesa Verde, there seems no question that it does belong within the Mesa Verde range, and it is treated as such in the Mesa Verde chapter.

Least will be said herein about the Virgin Region, also called the Northern Peripheral District and Western Kayenta. But to complete the Anasazi picture a brief description is in order. The Basketmaker range is known to have included south-central and southeastern Utah, yet there the archaeological data are meager for the Pueblo periods. In the lower arid and semiarid regions of Utah from the Colorado line westward to the Great American Desert and northward to the northernmost edge of the Great Salt Lake, there are remains of numerous settlements that are assuredly Puebloan Anasazi. This is proved by the sedentary nature of the settlements and by their pottery types, dependence upon corn, and broad use of the metate.

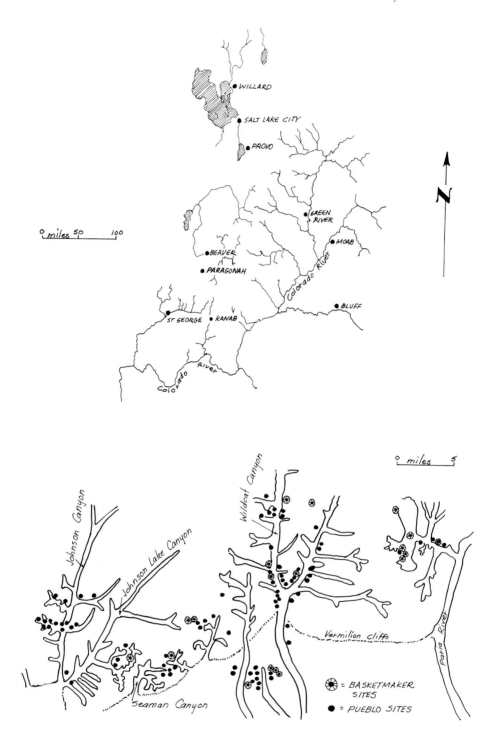

Maps showing locations of Anasazi sites in Utah located thus far and discussed in the text. *Top*, sites in western Utah in relationship to present-day cities. *Bottom*, distribution of sites of different periods in the Johnson Canyon–Paria River region east of Kanab. From Steward, 1941.

HILL CANYON TOWERS

In the wild and beautiful canyon and mesa country of the drainages of the Green and Grand rivers in eastern Utah (the Grand River is the earlier name of the upper Colorado) there are a few sites that have been briefly described by J. S. Newberry,[1] H. Montgomery,[2] and J. W. Fewkes.[3] All these sites consist of small groups of masonry rooms and towers that were built on the tops of pinnacles, the spurs of mesas, and other places easy to defend and offering good vantage points.

South of Ouray, Utah, and north of Green River lies Hill Canyon, a rugged region of eroded cliffs and deep crevasses. In 1916 Fewkes made a reconnaissance trip to the Hill Canyon area to verify reports of prehistoric Anasazi remains. He found many such sites and classified them into two types distinguished by their character: (a) true "mushroom rock ruins," which were perched on the tops of isolated rock pinnacles resembling in shape the so-called Snake Rock at Walpi, Arizona, and (b) crown spur ruins on the mesas overlooking the canyons.[4]

These ruins proved to be similar in most respects to those seen by Newberry in 1859 and by Montgomery almost fifty years later. Below the head of Labyrinth Canyon, Newberry saw a large number of masonry houses that he was certain were Pueblo because of the architecture and the red clay pottery coated with white and handsomely decorated. Some of the houses were built into the cliffsides, while other stone buildings sat like eagles on a perch, high atop detached buttes of red sandstone that rose as much as 150 feet above the canyon floor.

Montgomery found in Nine Mile Canyon similar prehistoric remains, including a tower about 50 feet (15 m) high. It was standing in an almost inaccessible spot commanding a magnificent view of several canyons and mountains.

Fewkes learned that the tower masonry was of a common Pueblo type. It was composed of natural slabs of stone, rudely fashioned by fracture, but seldom dressed in cubical blocks as had been the case with the towers in Colorado's McElmo Canyon. Exposure to the elements had led to considerable destruction, with the adobe mortar having washed out of the joints. The lower courses of masonry consisted of larger stones than in the upper courses, and they were better dressed.

On the ground plans presented by Fewkes, it is impossible not to notice the free form of the building walls compared to the more cleanly rectangular and circular units of other regions. They lead one immediately to think of Sun Temple at Mesa Verde, and to wonder whether there was some association between the structures. The essential architectural feature of the Hill Canyon towers was their roughly circular form, modified in many instances by the addition of a straight wall or a rectangular annex. In some cases the enclosing walls of two towers merged, and in a ruin designated as Eight Mile the towers were accompanied by a rectangular room a short distance away.[5]

Fewkes was intrigued by the fact that none of the towers exhibited evidence of past habitation. No fragments of pottery turned up on the surface of the tower plateaus or in their neighborhood.[6]

Except for their unusual sites, the ruins of the mushroom rock type were similar to those already described. The strange thing was that they were built on top of enormous flat-topped, free-standing pillars of rock that are often larger at the top than at the bottom and remind one in a general way of huge stone mushrooms. The pillars were once either the extensions or the spurs of

Top right, pinnacle rock in Hill Canyon, Utah. *Bottom left,* Leaning Tower Ruin in Hill Canyon. From Fewkes, 1917a.

mesas (extensions being at the end, spurs at the sides); they were cut free by erosion and in time were isolated. No one knows whether the erosion took place before or after the buildings were erected, although it seems logical to assume the latter. If erosion took place before, the question arises how the inhabitants climbed up the pillars, especially with building materials in hand. Even with ropes and ladders the task would be fearfully difficult. Fewkes found no trace of footholds, although footholds could have been worn away by wind and water.[7]

As for the purpose of the towers, the first idea that comes to mind is that they were built for defense or to serve as watchtowers. But Fewkes asks why, if that were so, the towers often exist in clusters rather than singly. He points out that towers are not limited to certain areas, as would be the case if they were defensive in nature. They are scattered randomly over a wide range of country, bounded, in the main, on the east by the Dolores River and on the south by the Mancos and San Juan rivers. Towers were also erected as far west as Montezuma Creek and as far south as Zuñi Pueblo, although they were rarely built in the sandy wastes south of the San Juan. Fewkes also observes that, while towers do possess minor differences, they are identical in essential features,[8] even to where the better-built towers of the San Juan and its tributaries are always surrounded at their bases by rooms similar in makeup to pueblo dwellings.

Fewkes was led to suppose further that the tower buildings were sacred rooms built for clan ceremonial purposes. If that was so, it would explain why several towers were united in a cluster. Each tower in a cluster would belong to a family or clan. Furthermore, the resemblance in form between the tower and the round kiva, and the relative abundance of each, suggested that one had been derived from the other, probably in the San Juan drainage basin. The idea of the towers then spread forth from San Juan southward and westward until at last, in a greatly modified state, it reached the peripheral zones of the vast Anasazi area. In plan, the earliest ceremonial tower was accompanied by dwellings separate from it. Later the dwellings were clustered closely around the tower in a compact mass. The tower by then had been reduced in height, and retained its circular form as a kiva.[9]

Thus, in Fewkes's mind the tower kiva would represent the true parent symbol of the clan, and where there were several clans there would be several towers. In further argument for clan association, Fewkes states that several circular kivas and towers he investigated had one or more incised stones bearing on their surface a coiled figure resembling a serpent. One of the best designs also had peripheral lines like the conventional symbols for feathers. Fewkes believes that, taken as a whole, the shapes and symbols give credence to an obscure legend of the Hopi which declares that the ancestral kivas of the Snake Clan, when it lived at Tokonabi, or along the San Juan, were circular in form.[10]

Not every scholar, I am certain, subscribes to these interesting opinions regarding towers. But J. W. Fewkes, the former chief of the Bureau of Ethnology, is always provocative and astute, and his ideas are seldom ignored. Simply to clarify facts that ought to be borne in mind when one is considering sources, F. W. Hodge explains that Bandelier, Cushing, the Mindeleffs, and Fewkes made most of their observations by surface inspection rather than by "spade and culture stratification." Hodge by no means wishes to decry the value of their contributions, but feels, I assume, that students should at least remember this and look to other sources for comparative and more specific data.[11]

CENTRAL AND SOUTHWESTERN UTAH

Thanks to Neil M. Judd, who began his Virgin Region research in 1915, the ruins of central and southwestern Utah are better known than the tower structures of the Green and Grand river drainages. Those ruins extend in an almost continuous line up the middle of Utah, ranging from the Utah-Arizona border on the south to the Utah-Idaho border on the north. Throughout this entire region there were once great numbers of Anasazi sites, reduced now by erosion to dirt mounds and mostly plowed over by Utah farmers.

The mounds are made up of slumped adobe from the disintegrated walls of mud houses, combined with rubbish deposits built up while the villages were still inhabited. Excavation shows that the sites were occupied for long periods and were overbuilt on a number of occasions. Judd could see no difference, however, between the architecture and artifacts of the lowest and oldest levels, on the one hand, and those of the higher and newer levels above— indicating little change in custom and culture over the years.

A principal place of archaeological investigation was Paragonah, Utah, one of several hundred villages that formerly overlooked the broad Parowan Valley.[12] These abodes were loosely grouped assemblages of rectangular one-story rooms built singly or placed end to end in contiguous sets of three or four, and all arranged around an open but unique plaza that itself contained temporary structures and kivas. The walls of the rectangular rooms were constructed of adobe, laid up in layers 15 inches (38 cm) deep to form walls about 10 inches (25 cm) thick and then smoothed to an even interior surface with bare hands. Since side-wall doorways were exceedingly rare, it is assumed that entry was made through a hatchway in the roof, closed when necessary with a stone slab. Wall heights ranged from 4 feet 6 inches to 5 feet (1.35–1.5 m). That might seem extremely low, but it does not mean that the Virgin Anasazi were unusually short. Rather, low houses were easier to build and, being windowless, afforded greater protection from the elements. Besides, the houses were intended in the main for sleeping quarters in cold weather and for the year-round storage of corn, beans, and other foodstuffs. Daily activities were performed mainly outdoors or in secondary shelters (described later).

The roof structure consisted of beams laid transversely a foot or so apart, across which shorter and smaller poles were laid at right angles. Successive layers followed of willows or brush, then grass, and finally clay. One serious defect was the lack of a sufficient overhang, and in rainy weather the water cascaded down the walls, softening the adobe until at last the weight of the heavy roof caused the whole to collapse.

The courtyard contained wholly subterranean round chambers that were dug into the rubbish and slump deposits. Each kiva had a central firepit, but there was no ventilator shaft. Judd considered the kivas to be closely allied to those of the more southerly Anasazi ruins.

The way in which the courtyard fill deposits were built up and utilized was unique. The more permanent habitations in the village were grouped to form, in a carefree way, three sides of a square. The interior of this square was then filled in over a considerable time with accumulations of camp debris, windblown earth, and parts of adobe walls that had collapsed or were collapsing because of water damage. When at last this accumulation reached almost to the rooftops, subterranean ceremonial chambers were dug into it, one for each clan in the village. Thanks to this odd arrangement, the kivas at Paragonah were entered through a roof opening at courtyard level, and even though their floor levels were the same as those of the dwellings, the isolated underground position prescribed for kivas by Anasazi mythology was preserved.

A kiva at Paragonah was an extremely simple unit. The walls and floor were surfaced with plain mud and allowed to dry. No supporting masonry or adobe wall was built, and as might be expected, the fill walls often sagged and collapsed. There was no bench, banquette, pilaster, niche, deflector, or sipapu. But there was a firepit in the kiva floor. The kiva roof was made in the same way as those of the dwellings, but now and then posts were set upright against the wall to support roof beams and coverings that were too heavy for the fill itself.

Kivas occupied only part of the central courtyard. The rest was dotted with small, flimsy huts that served as the real living and working quarters for the residents. These were temporary buildings that were torn down and rebuilt as often as the rising level of the courtyard demanded it. Usually a hut consisted of a central firepit surrounded by a square of four upright poles topped by four horizontal beams. These supported the rest of the roof structure and four sloping brush walls laid from the ground to the main beams in pithouse fashion. Within the residue of Paragonah huts Judd found small implements of bone and stone, charred corn and squash seeds, potsherds, split animal bones, and other campfire refuse.

Also found at Paragonah were the remains of rectangular courtyard shelters of jacal construction. These were larger than the huts and apparently were an attempt to gain additional space in a lodging still temporary in nature. They also employed the basic four-pole structure, but the walls were vertical instead of slanted. Small-diameter roof poles spanned the gap from the horizontal main beams to the walls, with one end resting on the beams and the other on the walls.

Included among the artifacts recovered by Judd from the Utah mounds were fragments of coiled basketry, great numbers of bone implements such as awls, antlers, gaming pieces, beads, rings, necklace pendants, and stone manos and metates for grinding corn. The metate was of a type peculiar to western Utah. At the upper, or elevated, end was a small concave depression used either as a rest for the mano or as a container for the meal.

Charred corn was obtained in considerable quantities, along with grass and squash seeds, beans, and piñon nuts. The bones of many animals show that the inhabitants of Paragonah depended in considerable measure upon hunting for subsistence. No grooved axes were discovered, but finds did include hammer stones and manos, rubbing and polishing stones, discoidal jar covers, and round stone balls presumably used for games. In addition, there were fragments from skin garments, tubular clay pipes, and red and yellow ocher clays used for paint.

Pottery embraced a crude, undecorated grayware, well-made corrugated utility vessels, and some decorated black-on-white ware. The last-named was usually a bowl, with geometric designs on the interior of the vessel only. Decorated jars and ollas were rare. The decoration styles themselves could not be positively associated with any of the specialized design systems of the San

Plot plan of the village of Paragonah, Utah, as excavated by Judd in 1916 and 1917. There are five kivas shown. The "property removed" area is that plowed under by farmers before excavation.

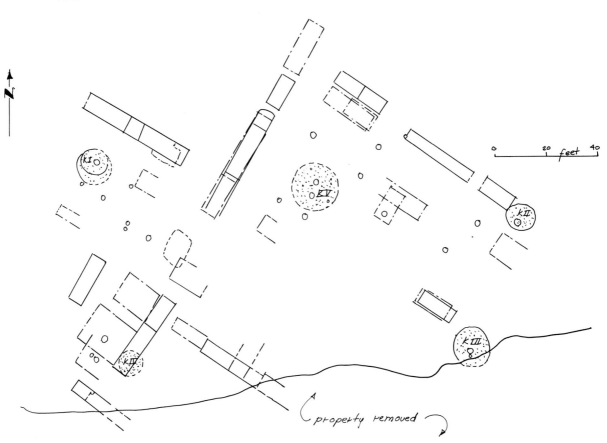

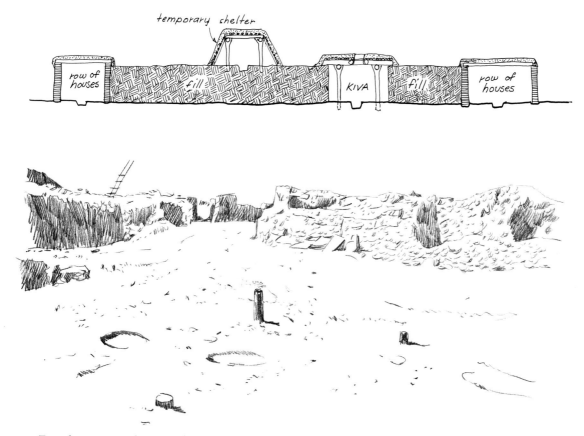

Top, the excavated ruins of Beaver City, Utah. *Middle,* section showing how fill was utilized at Paragonah to provide for subterranean kivas and elevated courtyards. *Bottom,* the excavated ruins of Paragonah.

Juan, but the geometric figures were of a type common to communities south and east of the Colorado River. Judd observed one ceramic peculiarity, the interlineal use of red paint. This was superficially applied after the bowls had been fired, the red line being drawn between black lines. Plain-ware bowls, jars, and coiled ollas were sometimes covered on the outside with a thin coat of the same red pigment.

When he finished his work at Paragonah, Judd decided that the character and ornamentation of the artifacts, along with the nature of the rectangular dwellings and the kivas, and their general relationship to one another, confirmed that a marked cultural affinity existed between the Parowan Valley people and the Anasazi inhabiting the semiarid regions east of Navajo Mountain.

Judd encountered a different kind of village site near Willard, Utah, a small town by the northeastern shore of the Great Salt Lake. The dwellings resembled the well-known winter hogan of the Navajo. Their central and most prominent feature was a shallow firepit, some 2 feet 7 inches (78 cm) in diameter. Clustered around the pit were four postholes, marking the corners of a 4-foot (1.2 m) square. The exact contour of the dwellings could no longer be traced, but it is assumed they were circular, as were most Basketmaker pithouses, and that the four main posts supported four horizontal beams. The wall poles leaned on these and provided a sloped contour. In support of his conclusions, Judd recovered fragments of charred wood and large quantities of baked clay bearing impressions of logs, willows, and grass. The structure probably did not exceed 15 or 16 feet (4.5–4.8 m) in diameter.[13]

The potsherds found at Willard were those of a coarse plain ware and a corrugated ware. Black-on-white vessels had been reported as having been found by pothunters, but Judd was unable to find any to verify the claims.

BEAVER CITY

At Beaver City, in southern Utah, Judd did find sherds of black-on-white pottery, along with fragments of plain and corrugated wares similar to those picked up at Willard. He also found the remains of circular, hogan-like dwellings, but to his surprise they had been built on top of the eroded adobe walls of a typical rectangular-roomed village. If these two types of structure had turned up at separate locations, the logical assumption would have been that the hogan-like dwellings, so Basketmaker-like in nature, dated from earlier than the rectangular structures. But this was not the case, and the find added support to the growing consensus that Utah and the Virgin Region remained a backward area, seldom affected by cultural diffusion.

One large mound at Beaver City contained fifteen rectangular rooms, plus a circular structure identified as a kiva or ceremonial chamber similar in style to those found throughout the San Juan drainage. Of the fifteen rooms, only four were contiguous, and the walls had all been constructed of adobe mud that was pressed into place while still plastic. In the northern portion of the mound, four distinct levels of occupancy were exposed, each having firepits and the usual remains of habitation. Careful examination revealed, however, that the latest residents or their forebears had occupied the lower levels and that no appreciable time had elapsed between the four building stages.[14] Exposed mounds in Johnson Canyon, about fifteen miles east of Kanab, Utah, proved to be ruins of rectangular dwellings similar to those examined near

Beaver City, with the exception that stone was freely employed in the construction of the walls.[15]

Julian H. Steward unhesitatingly describes the Johnson Canyon ruins as those of a prehistoric culture whose main features were derived from the Anasazi cultures of the San Juan drainage. Curiously, though, the cultures of the latter went through five progressive periods from Basketmaker II through Pueblo III, while Steward's findings indicated that the Northern Peripheral Utah culture consisted of only the first two Pueblo periods: neither Basketmaker II nor III was present in the sites.[16] Yet in the Johnson Canyon and Paria River region ruins, located immediately east of Kanab in southern Utah and investigated by Steward in 1932, clear evidence was found for the Basketmaker II and III and Pueblo I and II periods, all roughly comparable to the same time spans of the San Juan drainage Anasazi. Although Basketmaker II sites were few, Basketmaker III locations were common, especially in the western part of the region explored. All these sites consisted of slab cists and larger slab structures that were interpreted by Steward as dwellings. The pottery was mostly a plain ware, Paria Gray, and a Basketmaker primitive black-on-gray.

Pueblo I sites were made up of structures with crudely coursed stone walls erected on top of slab foundations. The ceramics were almost the same as those of the Basketmaker III period.

Pueblo II Period dwellings were rectangular, and coursed masonry was used for the walls. The pottery consisted of a corrugated culinary ware and a black-on-white smooth ware. The typical village had several rectangular rooms arranged in a semicircle along the northern side of a circular depression that, while not excavated, Steward was certain was a kiva. Villages were usually located on a sandy knoll, a low promontory, or a canyon rim. Habitable caves often contained traces of late-type masonry walls.[17]

Petroglyphs and pictographs with stylistic features peculiar to the region were numerous and apparently dated from all periods. Depictions included spirals, concentric circles, sun disks, wavy and zigzag lines, animals, and anthropomorphic figures. Steward thinks the latter were probably derived from Southwestern Basketmaker pictographs.[18]

The petroglyphs were mainly pecked, but some of the finer lines were incised or rubbed. Steward refers to some truly intriguing figures as round and decorated bodies. Simply to pose an alternate possibility, it may be that the round shapes are shields, since they greatly resemble the large rawhide shields known to have been carried by Pueblo warriors in historical times. It they are shields, then warfare and ceremonial uses are indicated. Steward notes that two ornamented rawhide shields were found on the Fremont River, where somewhat similar circular petroglyphs occurred.[19]

From Johnson Canyon, Steward went on to Glen Canyon, covered over now by Lake Powell. He found archaeological evidence scant there, for the river canyon and neighboring terrain were too rugged and limited in farming possibilities to attract many agricultural peoples. The ruins and petroglyphs Steward did find indicated that Glen Canyon was "a kind of no-man's land" that had been sparsely settled by outposts from both Mesa Verde and Kayenta.

Danger Cave, in northwestern Utah, was one of the seasonal homes of Desert Culture hunter-gatherers who followed a foraging lifeway stretching back 11,000 years or more. Around A.D. 1000 the Fremont culture, based primarily on agriculture, flourished briefly in northern Utah. Then warfare and drought forced it to return to the foraging pattern of the Desert Culture. Little figurines of clay and sticks such as those shown here suggest Fremont links with the Anasazi (and Hohokam) farming communities of the Southwest during its agricultural phase. From Snow, 1976.

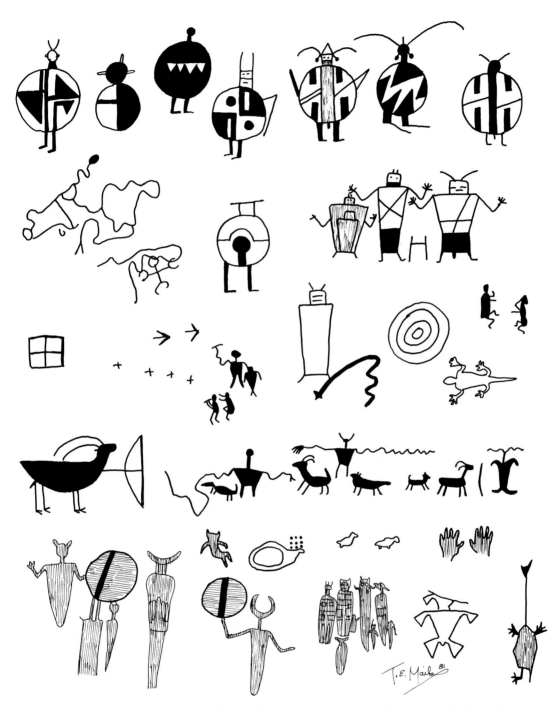

Anasazi rock art abounds in Utah. Pictured above are only a few of the petroglyphs and pictographs reported by Neil M. Judd and Julian H. Steward from White and Cottonwood canyon sites, and from near the Colorado River north of Moab.

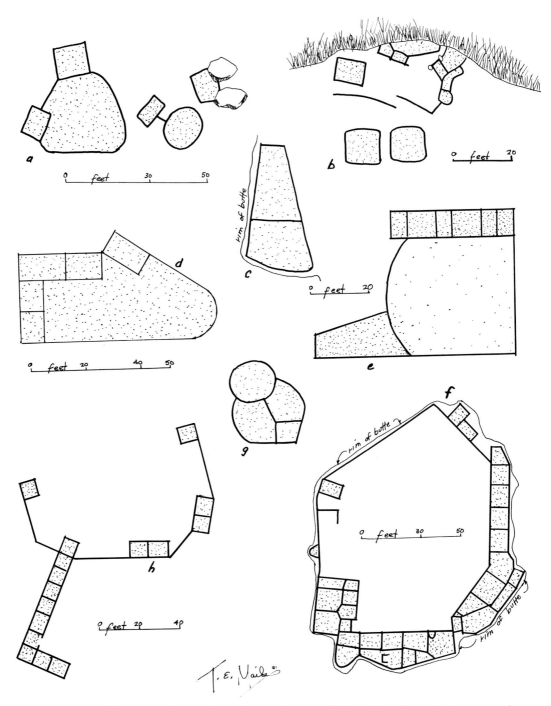

Typical plans of the unusual ruin shapes in southeastern Utah and northern Arizona. *a*, ruin near Bright Angel Creek. *b*, cliff ruin, Bright Angel Creek. *c*, ruin overlooking Nankoweap Valley. *d*, ruin high on east slope of Saddle Mountain. *e*, ruin near Cape Royal, Walhalla Plateau. *f*, ruin on White Butte, Paria Plateau. *g*, ruin north of New House Rock Corrals. *h*, ruin in lower Toroweap Valley. From Judd, 1926.

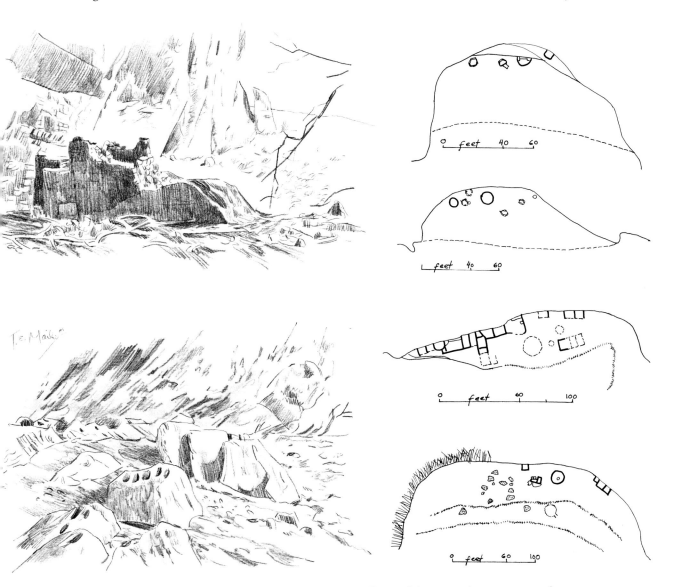

Top left, storerooms in a cave in Cottonwood Canyon. *Bottom left*, stones in same cave where tools were sharpened. *Right*, plan of four cave ruins in Cottonwood Canyon. From Judd, 1926.

These had come into contact with the Northern Peripheral Anasazi, but were little influenced by them. However, the closer the sites came to the Arizona border the more they resembled those of the Johnson Canyon–Paria River district and the Kayenta Region, to which they were geographically contiguous. Strong Tusayan (Hopi) influence was recognizable in their ceramics, use of the turkey, kivas, and elaborate textiles.[20] "Present evidence," Steward says, "also eliminates eastern Utah as the source of the Northern Peripheral culture." With few minor exceptions, eastern Utah is related to the San Juan area.[21]

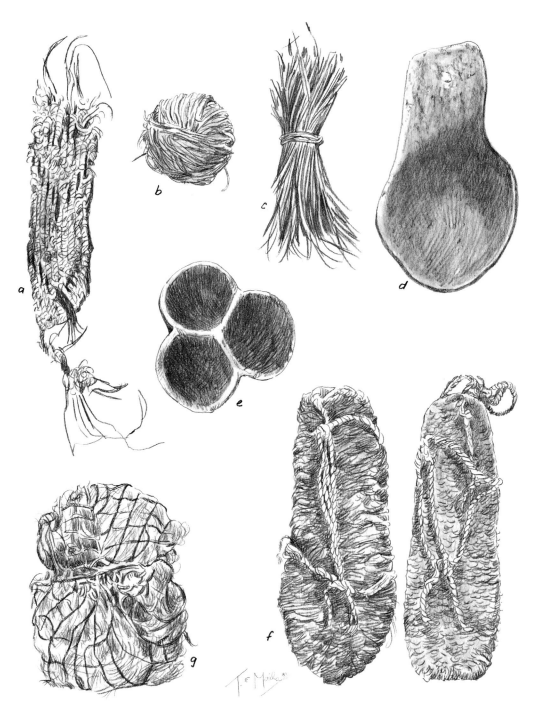

Lesser material culture objects from Utah caves: *a,* fragment of a tumpline. *b,* ball of cord. *c,* hairbrush of pine needles. *d,* dipper of mountain sheep horn. *e,* pottery paint container. *f,* woven sandals. *g,* net containing mountain goat hair. From Judd, 1926.

Lesser material culture objects from Utah: *a*, cooking pot from Heaton Cave. *b*, corrugated cooking pot. *c*, painted water jar from Kanab. *d*, small jar. *e*, decorated food bowl. *f*, pitcher. *g*, corrugated cooking pot. *h–i*, manos and metate. *j*, corn from cave in Cottonwood Canyon. *k*, stone maul. *l*, smoothing stone. From Judd, 1926.

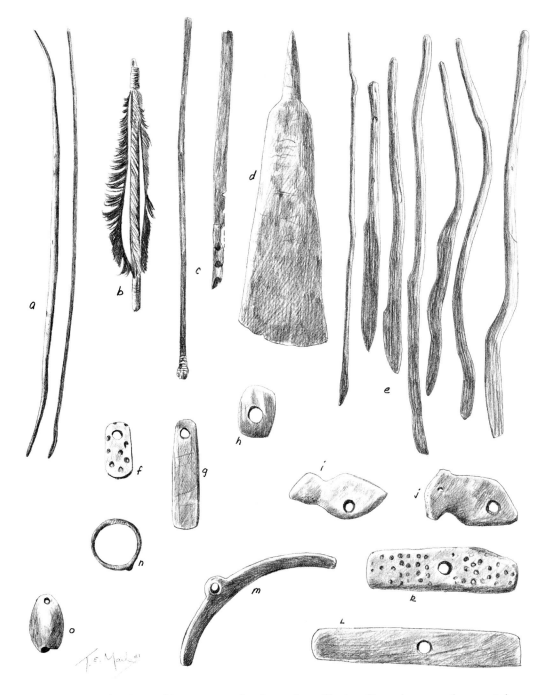

Lesser material culture objects: *a,* wooden bows from Heaton Cave. *b,* arrow fragment from Utah Cave. *c,* stone-tipped stick and wooden hearth. *d,* hoe or digging stick blade. *e,* digging sticks. *f–m,* bone, stone, and shell pendants. *n,* shell bracelet. *o,* shell necklace bead. From Judd, 1926.

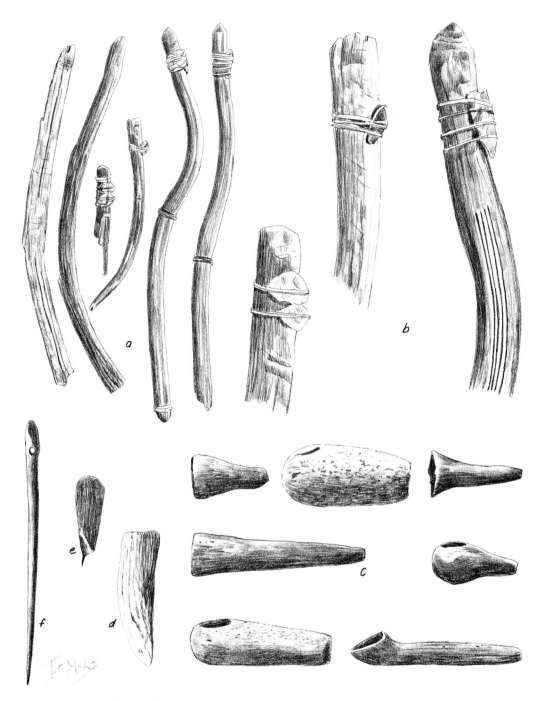

Lesser material culture objects: *a*, grooved throwing sticks from Heaton Cave. *b*, details showing stone weights attached to sticks. *c*, pipes of clay and stone. *d*, antler flaking tool. *e*, bone awl. *f*, bone needle. From Judd, 1926.

Even today, no final conclusions have been drawn about the place of the Utah ruins in the general scheme of Southwestern archaeology, although the University of Utah continues to actively investigate the state's ruins and is adding yearly to the data that will one day allow archaeologists to take an acceptable stand.

The age of the Virgin Anasazi ruins relative to those of other regions is difficult to estimate. The simple and primitive nature of the dwellings and the kivas appears at first glance to place them in the Basketmaker category. But the presence of black-on-white and corrugated ware indicates that some of the structures were built during the early Pueblo period when, as Kidder states, "the vigorous early culture of the San Juan was spreading out and exerting its influence far and wide."[22]

ABANDONMENT

No one knows how long the inhabitants of these central Utah villages managed to remain in their home country: perhaps until A.D. 1100, perhaps later. But, as with the other Anasazi, a time did come when they either decided or were forced to abandon the entire area—suddenly, it seems, because nowhere in the Virgin Region did the people have time to gather in large communities as did the Anasazi of other places when serious problems began to present themselves. That their end came early in the Pueblo Period is indicated by the fact that pottery of the early types was fashioned to the very last. No sherd associated with late-date southern wares has been found in any of the Virgin mounds.

The direction of migration is only suspected, but to assume that it was southeast is quite reasonable. All the surviving Anasazi gathered eventually in southern regions where Pueblo life continues today. It is well worth noting that, at Inscription House, which sits at the junction of the Virgin and Kayenta regions, some rooms were built with a special type of clay brick. This might be an extension of the adobe structures of central Utah, even though no examples of adobe bricks or blocks per se were found at Beaver City.

Chapter 4

CHACO CANYON

INTRODUCTION

The New Mexico plateau at Chaco Canyon where the Anasazi first flourished is not the most desolate landscape in the world, yet on a scale of 1 to 10 it would rate at least an 8. Most of the 6,500-foot-elevation desert country is barren, windswept rock and sand, and some of it is a close twin to the rugged Badlands of South Dakota. Jagged boulders jut out of the landscape at all angles. There is little color, just barren yellow, brown, and gray ground, mottled by a few small trees and an abundance of weeds, greasewood, and sagebrush. Not even the usual dry-country flora of the Southwest is present. The cliffs are not high compared to those of Canyon de Chelly or Mesa Verde, and they are not nearly so attractive. There are snakes and lizards in abundance, and only a few flowers in the spring. The riverbed is usually dry. The area is almost devoid of springs. Even flash flood water runs swiftly away. It is blistering hot in the summer and bitterly cold in winter. A new paved highway will soon pass within a few miles of Chaco, but today the last thirty miles of dirt road as you drive into the canyon from any direction has all the grace of a ravaged battlefield. It ruptures automobile tires, and it jars every inch of your body. Wind whips up the sand. It stings your face, plasters your eyes, and permeates your clothing.

Long before you reach Chaco Canyon you are asking why, by any reasonable standard, the Anasazi chose to build their dozens of villages here. Doubtless, you suppose, it must have been different in Anasazi times. There had to be enough water and vegetation to satisfy thirst and to provide fuel for homes. And there were, perhaps, even enough cottonwoods, willows, cedars, pines, and fir trees to provide thousands of sticks and logs for dwelling roofs. But an ever-increasing population depleted the supply day by day and taxed the ingenuity and determination of the people to survive. There had to be sufficient fields for corn, beans, and squash, and there were, until the insatiable demand for housing space forced the resourceful dry-farming Anasazi to capitulate. Thoughtful men and women at Chaco could never have rested easily from concern about what the future might bring. Quite plainly, though, they were at first like the talented and energetic youth who remains convinced he can overcome the world—until the hard-earned lessons of passing years teach

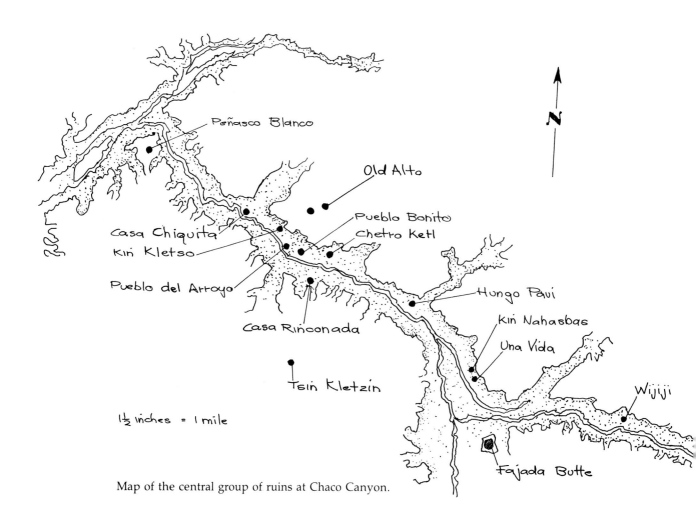

Map of the central group of ruins at Chaco Canyon.

him better. Even then the Chacoans were slow to give up. It took a full two hundred years beyond Pueblo I to bring them down, if that is an apt term to use.

Douglas and Barbara Anderson think it probable that the Chacoans developed a certain degree of specialization to survive.[1] The populace was consciously divided into groups: some to build homes, others to grow crops, some to hunt, some to produce crafts, a portion to tend to religious needs, groups to do whatever else was necessary. If the Andersons are correct, this division had to be accomplished in a remarkably short period of time for its effectiveness to be seen in what the Chacoans produced.

A second theory mentioned by the Andersons, to explain why Chaco developed in some directions not taken by other groups of Anasazi, is that "ties between Mesoamerica and Chaco were more than casual." The supposition is that Chaco Canyon was an outpost of the Toltec civilization and that such imports as macaws, other parrots, and a certain architectural style support it. If true, it would explain why Chaco declined at about the same time as the Toltecs. "It is a fact," say the Andersons, "that in the northern outpost, the new ideas presumably brought in from the South were among the first to go, and they did not survive into modern Pueblo times."[2]

A third and most intriguing theory regarding Chaco was expressed in conversation by a National Park Service employee who has served and researched at the canyon for some time. He believes that Chaco was a specialized religious center for the Anasazi of all regions, a holy place marked by ritual activity and spiritual pursuits. It was deliberately chosen for its isolation, yet connected with the Anasazi of all regions by a system of roadways that made regular communion possible. If he is correct, his view would explain the three different phases at Chaco, since each would stand as representative of a given group of distant pueblos and at the same time would provide a unity of spiritual activity for all Anasazi at Chaco itself. This idea would also give credence to the suggestion that the wider Chaco Canyon roadways were used for religious processions. In this connection, the Hopi speak of Chaco as a great crossroads for all their clans.[3]

Chaco Canyon does have a powerful aura of mystery, and it especially captivates those with some knowledge of its history. Not only are the thirteen major ruins a challenge to the imagination, but Chaco is the only Pueblo site where you can stand in one place on the edge of a cliff and see at one time such a vast panorama of huge and varied ruins. Even then you cannot see it all, for the ruins are strung out along Chaco Wash for 30 miles, while the canyon itself is 135 feet deep at the deepest point, 15 miles long, and nearly a mile wide in places. The very scope of it impresses you overwhelmingly and causes reflection about many things. Inevitably, you feel a relationship with the past that is almost eerie—a sense of a continuity of generations that reaches out and engulfs every visitor. Ancient, sprawling Chaco Canyon is such a personal and provocative place that you soon forget its barren landscape and the miserable road you endured to get there.

Chaco Canyon surrounds a southern tributary of the San Juan in northwestern New Mexico. It is generally thought that the broad watercourse was given its name by Spanish explorers who attempted to borrow a Navajo term, "tse koh," meaning "rock canyon."

The first Americans to see the canyon were nameless soldiers, merchants, and mountain men who followed a well-known trail that passed close by the spectacular ruins. In 1849 the Washington Expedition, a military reconnaissance group performing a topographical survey of Navajo country, stopped briefly at Chaco Canyon while the staff artists made a few drawings and chroniclers wrote descriptions of the ruins.

During the next fifty years the reports of Chaco's glory spread, and artists, authors, and scientists were drawn regularly to the ruins. Included among these was the well-known photographer William Henry Jackson, who, although his new experimental film failed him and his photographs were worthless, made excellent notes and drew a map of the canyon ruins.

From 1896 to 1900 Richard Wetherill, an interested amateur who had discovered many of the ruins at Mesa Verde, assisted the Hyde Exploration Expedition, called by Edgar L. Hewett a "pothunting" group, as it conducted the first serious excavations of Chaco Canyon.[4] Captivated by its uniqueness, Wetherill homesteaded in the canyon, built a permanent home and a trading post, and carried on guided trips for tourists and a trading business with the Navajo. In 1910 Wetherill was killed in the canyon, and his grave is located just west of Pueblo Bonito.

The first professional archaeologist to work at Chaco Canyon was George H. Pepper of the American Museum of Natural History in New York. Since 1905 extensive work has been done by the School of American Research, Santa Fe, New Mexico; the National Geographic Society, in conjunction with the Smithsonian Institution; and the University of New Mexico. The Chaco Canyon National Monument was established on March 11, 1907, and the National Park Service has since performed regular research in association with its Chaco Center on the University of New Mexico campus. Stabilization work to preserve the ruins from weeds, sand, rubble, and the elements goes on continually. So far, four of the thirteen major village ruins have been excavated and are being maintained: Pueblo Bonito, Chetro Ketl, Pueblo del Arroyo, and Kin Kletso. Several Hosta Butte sites have also been excavated and kept up. All the major ruins have received some stabilization, with special care being taken not to alter the appearance of the original walls.

The accomplishments of archaeologists working at Chaco Canyon have long been impressive, yet some of the truly monumental discoveries have just recently come to light. In 1978 and 1979 astonishing secrets were revealed by aerial photography. Infrared sensors have disclosed a Chaco metropolis whose scope dwarfs the canyon community previously known. They have also revealed a vast roadway system that crisscrosses the entire region.[5] Then there is Fajada.

On June 29, 1977, Anna Sofaer, one of a group of amateur archaeologists cataloging rock art in Chaco Canyon, made a serendipitous find that, to put it mildly, has excited the entire scientific community.

High up on a rattlesnake-infested butte named Fajada, she paused about midday at a mysterious, although already known, group of three mammoth stone slabs that fronted two spiral-shaped petroglyphs on the cliff face beyond them. A beam of light that passed through an opening between two of the slabs caught her eye, and she watched in utter fascination as it first struck and then made its way slowly across the surface of one of the petroglyphs. Before its course was run, she realized she was seeing in operation a unique sun calendar that had been constructed by Chaco priests a thousand years before. Specialists and photographers were hurriedly called in to check it out.

After working for two years to solve and record the exact workings of what proved to be an amazingly accurate midday sun calendar, archaeoastronomers were convinced that Fajada, as they named the device, ranks in precision, accuracy, and functional versatility with the best astronomical structures yet found in the Old and New worlds.

Fajada is unique among time clocks. In contrast to other ancient time devices that use architectural features for alignment and take their orientation from points on the horizon where the sun rises and sets, Fajada uses sunlight itself as the indicator and employs the three great stones as directional channels. These are sandstone slabs ranging in height from 6 to 9 feet (1.8–2.7 m) and in thickness from 8 to 18 inches (20–45 cm). They weigh about two tons each. Their back edges lean against the cliff, they are set roughly parallel to one another, and they are spaced a few inches apart, so that two narrow,

Top, a portion of Kimmenioli ruin situated about ten miles northeast of Chaco Canyon. About 135 ground-floor rooms are traceable. Originally the building was three or four stories high. The site is typical of the many ruins in the greater Chaco area. From Fewkes, 1920b. *Bottom,* another typical ruin of the greater Chaco area.

pointed shafts of sunlight pass through the gaps and strike the petroglyphs, marking the seasons in this manner by singling out the equinoxes and solstices. Not only does the calendar divide the year into the four quarters, posting a unique pattern to mark the beginning of each, it also gives a rough idea of the number of days elapsing between the beginning points. In addition it can predict lunar eclipses.

The larger spiral petroglyph has nine coils. The smaller spiral has three coils, with the outer line extended to make the whole look like a coiled snake. At winter solstice, December 21, the shortest day of the year, the two shafts of light frame the large spiral exactly. At midday one band rests on the left edge and the other band rests on the right edge. At summer solstice, June 21, when the sun is at its zenith, one beam strikes the exact center of the large spiral. At midday on September 21 and March 21, the autumn and spring equinoxes marking the midpoints between the summer and winter solstices, one light beam precisely bisects the nine turns on the larger spiral's right side,[6] and at the same moment the other wedge of light descends through the precise center of the smaller spiral.[7]

Chaco Canyon and Fajada Butte.

Adding to the fascination of the stone shafts is the fact that their surfaces are double-curved. Thus, at the summer solstice, when the sun is moving horizontally in the sky, the slabs' upper edges play their own special role by translating the light into a beam that progresses vertically across the spiral petroglyph.

Fajada has taken its place today as the first midday solar calendar on record, the only one known to make use of its peculiar geometry. The skill required to build it is evident, and specialists are learning that the Anasazi and other ancient peoples of North America were far more sophisticated and knowledgeable than previously thought. Without question, this new and portentous discovery, along with others being made at Chaco Canyon, will prompt archaeologists, archaeoastronomers, and other professionals to look again, and with particular keenness, for similar wonders at Anasazi ruins everywhere.

PITHOUSES

In 1920 Neil M. Judd, curator of American archaeology at the U.S. National Museum, went on a reconnaissance trip to Chaco in preparation for a National Geographic expedition at Pueblo Bonito that would begin actual work in 1921. Probing in the area, his workmen came upon the first of two pithouses they would find. These were not by any means the earliest dwellings in the Chaco area, but they were the first documented evidence of Basketmaker presence there, and as such constituted exciting finds.[8] In 1927 a Late Basketmaker village nine miles east of Pueblo Bonito was excavated by Frank H. H. Roberts.

Judd's first pithouse was encountered near Casa Rinconada. After excavation, the pit was found to be 17 feet (5.2 m) in diameter and 3 feet (90 cm) deep. The earth walls were vertical and had been roughly finished by dampening the clay and pounding it to a hard and relatively smooth surface. The floor was hard and compact, but noticeably uneven. The superstructure had long since disappeared, but enough wood fragments were found to indicate that roof and wall construction followed the conventional pattern for Basketmaker pithouses. A firepit with a slightly raised rim was found just east of the center of the room. It was 3 feet (90 cm) in diameter at the top and sloped down to 1 foot 10 inches (55 cm) in diameter at the bottom. It was 10 inches (25 cm) deep.

Placed against the east wall were three small and irregularly shaped bins formed by upright slabs of sandstone, whose assumed function was the storage of corn and other foodstuffs. A stone mano and three stone metates lay on the pithouse floor. Two niches were cut in the west wall, their bottom levels lower than that of the room floor itself and protruding into the floor area. This feature was also noted by Earl Morris in pithouses between the San Juan River and the Continental Divide, seventy miles east of the La Plata area, Colorado.

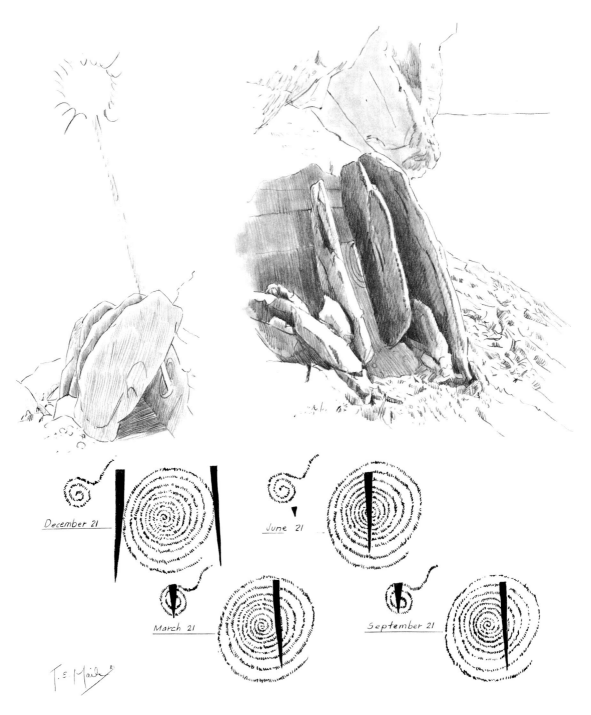

The solar calendar on Fajada Butte. *Top,* perspective views showing how the sun rays penetrate between the stone slabs to strike the spiral petroglyphs and mark the solstices and equinoxes. *Bottom,* black dagger-shaped lines show where the spirals are intersected at the critical dates. After Frazier, 1980.

The second pithouse, one that I think could well have been a protokiva, was discovered in the spring of 1922, about one mile east of Pueblo Bonito. It was dated ca. A.D. 777. Half of it had been destroyed by heavy rains, so that Judd had to make some assumptions. The room diameter was 12 feet 9 inches (3.9 m). A bench or banquette 2 feet 11 inches (88 cm) high and 2 feet 2 inches (66 cm) wide, broadening to 3 feet (90 cm) on the east side, encircled the room. The verticle rear wall of the bench measured 1 foot 4 inches (40 cm). The floor was slightly dished, and in its middle was a circular, slab-lined firepit 1 foot 10 inches (55 cm) in diameter and 9 inches (22.5 cm) deep.

More than enough evidence was found to determine the nature of the pithouse roof and walls. Four main posts, ranging from 7 to 8.5 inches (17.5–21.5 cm) in diameter, were placed in slots made in the face of the bench at the northwest, northeast, southwest, and southeast corners. Vertical sections had been gouged in the bench wall, and after the posts were set in the gouge they were wedged in tightly with stones and earth. Then the open side of the gouge was closed over with a stone slab and plastered. Several coats of smoked plaster had been applied to the face of the bench, and its level upper surface was hard and smooth, suggesting long usage.

From holes still remaining, it was learned that the basic wall structure consisted of twenty-two small posts, each about 2 inches (5 cm) in diameter, placed around the outside edge of the banquette 1 foot 8 inches (50 cm) back from the face, and at intervals of about 1 foot 2 inches (35 cm). All the postholes angled in toward the center, indicating that the post tops had once rested against four main beams and that the finished rooftop was, as with most pithouses, flat. The structural details of walls and roofs given in the Basketmaker chapters seem applicable only in a general way to this pithouse.

The decorated sherds of one bowl and the body of an unusual pipe were found amid the debris of Pithouse No. 1, along with corncobs and one squash seed. The tiny, round 2.25-inch-long pipe was shaped like a water-filled balloon, had an opening on one side, and once had a round stem. Also found were pieces of red and yellow clay of the type used for paint.

Pithouse No. 2 at Chaco Canyon yielded up many potsherds and artifacts. Pottery fragments made it possible to restore eleven large earthenware water jars and eight bowls, most of which had been given a white slip and were decorated with black designs. None of the water jars had the handles or the outflaring rim so typical of later Pre-Pueblo ollas. Also found at the site were several neckbanded pottery jars with handles or lugs, four neckbanded cooking pots, six black-on-white pottery ladles, and two pipes. The pipes appear to be the reworked hollow handles of a jar and a ladle respectively. Fragments in Pithouse No. 2 included those of a small, finely woven basket and a pair of woven sandals. Stone items consisted of two flint knives, or scrapers; several stone hammers; manos; and three broad, thin metates. There were two bone awls and a reworked fragment of a shell bracelet.

Lying among the other items on the floor of Pithouse No. 2 was the incomplete skeleton of a young female. Her shattered skull showed cranial flat-

tening, something Judd had not expected to find in a pithouse in Chaco
Canyon that dated from earlier than what some authorities prefer to call the Pre-
Pueblo Period, the time immediately preceding Pueblo II. Actually, although
Judd did not say so, the skeleton might not present a dating problem. It could
have been placed in the pithouse later by Pueblo-date people wishing only to
use the excavation as a burial site.

In Chapter 2 a description was given of Shabik'eshchee Village, excavated
in 1927 by Frank H. H. Roberts and said to be typical of the period and structures of other sections of the San Juan region. This Chaco Canyon site, nine
miles east of Pueblo Bonito, was, as Roberts classified it, the first pure "Post
Basket Maker" and "Pre-Pueblo" age village ever dug, and Roberts found eighteen pithouses there, a small low-walled plaza, forty-eight storage bins, and a
large kiva.[9] The pithouses were widely spaced, some being circular and some
oval. Common interior features included circular firepits, some of which had
low wing walls extending out from them, deflectors, and floor and wall storage

Plot plan, northern half of Shabik'eshchee Village. After Roberts, 1929.

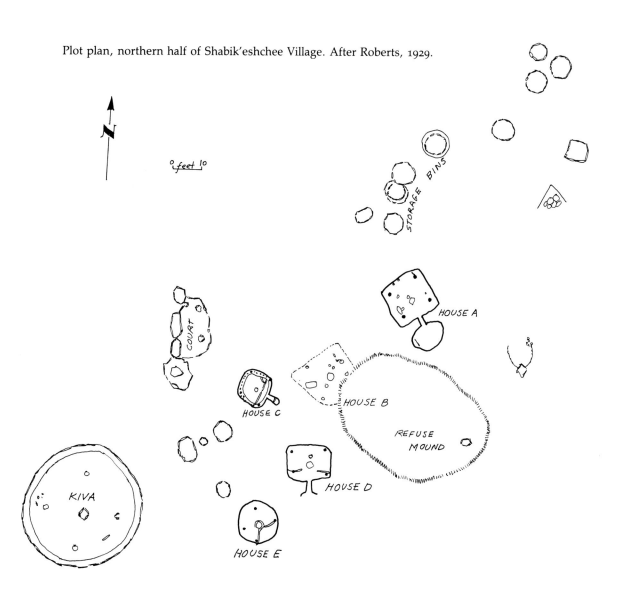

recesses. Some of the pithouses had sipapus, others did not. Entrance was gained either through a roof hatch or an entrance tunnel at whose end was an antechamber. Four main posts topped by four main beams supported the superstructure and slanting walls.

One of the Shabik'eshchee pithouses is described as a "protokiva house," since it contained so many features considered characteristic of the circular ceremonial rooms of the later pueblos to which the name "kiva" has been applied, among them circular firepit, deflector slab, ventilator, sipapu, and storage recesses and bins.

Shabik'eshchee included a large, or great, kiva that was 40 feet (12 m) in diameter and 4 feet 2 inches (1.3 m) deep. Material culture objects found at the village consisted of imperishable substances such as clay, bone, stone, and shell. No scrap of weaving was discovered. The pottery was crude when compared with that of following periods. The dead were buried in shallow graves with the body flexed and the face turned to the north. There was no cranial deformation.

Plot plan, southern half of Shabik'eshchee Village. After Roberts, 1929.

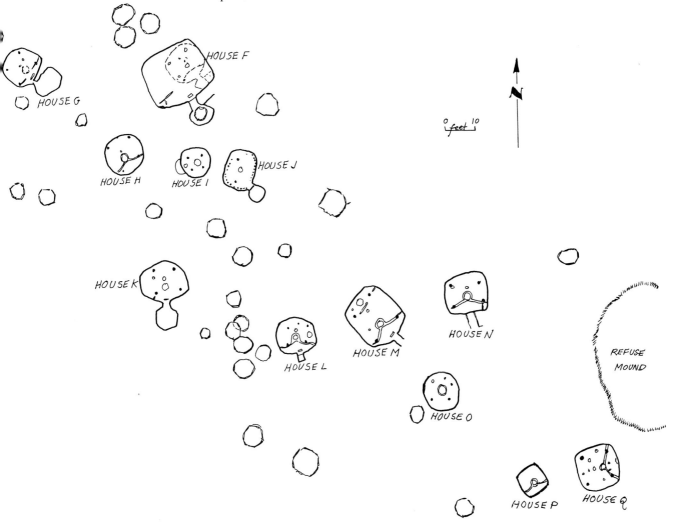

MATERIAL CULTURE

Long after Judd completed his work at Chaco Canyon for the National Geographic Society, he compiled three extensive and magnificently produced books relating to his discoveries. These were published by the Smithsonian Institution, beginning in 1954 with *The Material Culture of Pueblo Bonito* (Smithsonian Miscellaneous Collections, Vol. 124). Next came *Pueblo del Arroyo, Chaco Canyon, New Mexico* (Smithsonian Miscellaneous Collections, Vol. 138, No. 1), in 1959. The last was *The Architecture of Pueblo Bonito* (Smithsonian Miscella-

Plans and sections of four typical pithouses excavated in Shabik'eshchee Village. From Roberts, 1929.

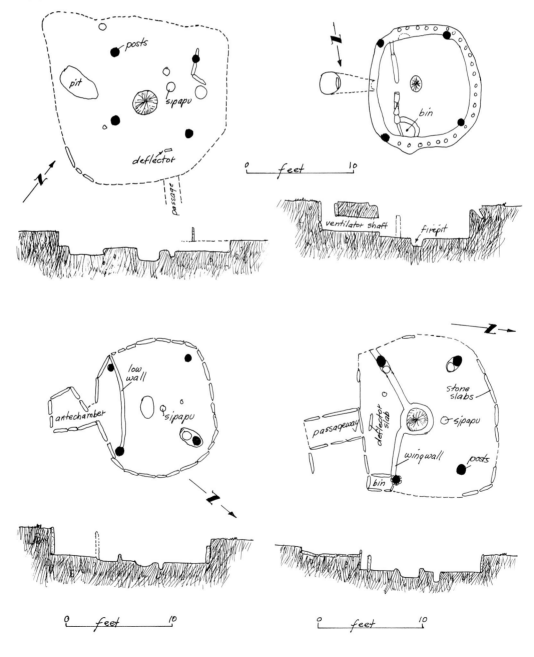

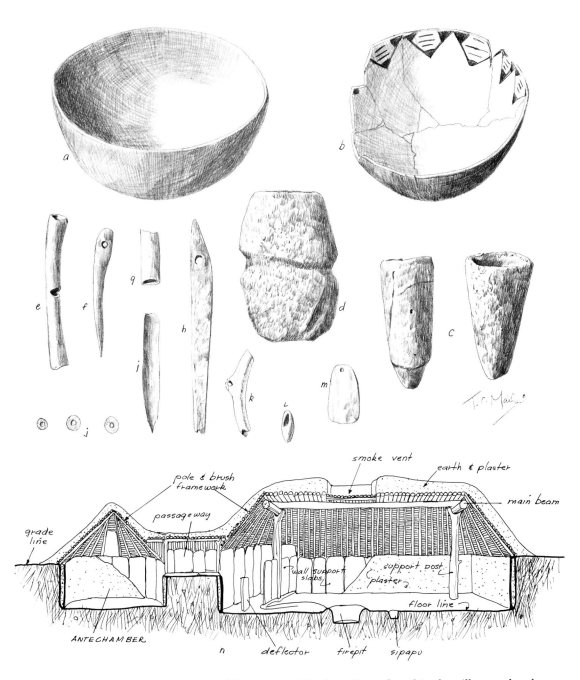

Shabik'eshchee Village. *a–m,* typical lesser material culture items found in the village: *a,* bowl with polished black interior. *b,* bowl with painted design. *c,* clay cloud-blower pipes. *d,* stone maul. *e,* bone whistle. *f,* bone needle. *g,* bone bead. *h,* bone bodkin. *i,* bone awl. *j,* shell beads. *k,* shell pendant. *l,* shell from necklace. *m,* shell earring or pendant. *n,* section through pithouse showing postulated structural details. From Roberts, 1929.

neous Collections, Vol. 147, No. 1), in 1964. These comprise an absolute treasury of information regarding the Chaco Canyon culture, and the serious student is referred to them for exhaustive details and illustrations. Space herein will permit only a summary view of Chaco's history and culture, yet even this will reveal a splendid epoch of industry and achievement.

Findings thus far indicate that, despite its formidable location, Chaco was the first Anasazi community to flower in the Pueblo I and II periods. Between

Shabik'eshchee Village. *a,* plan and section of protokiva. *b,* plan and section of kiva. *c,* front view and section of kiva wall showing how posts, beams, and stone slabs were used to hold the earth walls in place. *d,* antler flaking tool. *e,* stone cutting tools. *f,* projectile points. From Roberts, 1929.

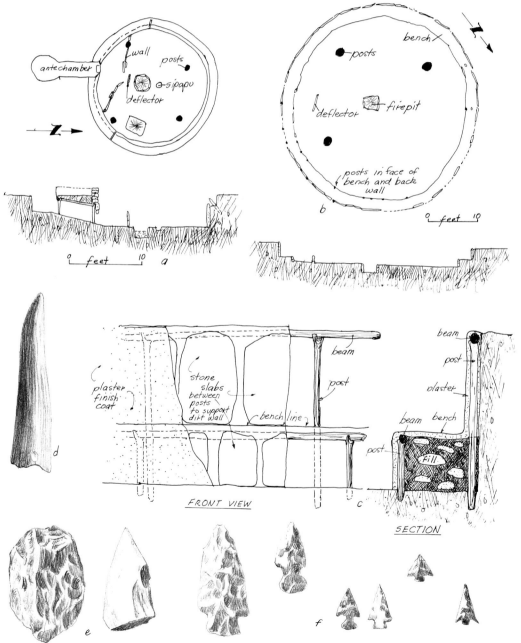

A.D. 750 and A.D. 1100 a new cultural pattern steadily emerged, marked particularly by distinct changes in architectural style. In the first step, pithouses gave way to clusters of small rectangular surface rooms whose floors were only slightly recessed below ground level. Their roofs were flat, and their earliest walls were of the type called jacal. The walls consisted of vertical poles interlaced with horizontal sticks and covered with mud. Later the jacal walls were replaced by courses of horizontal stones piled on top of vertical stone-slab

Shabik'eshchee Village: *a*, plan and section of village court. *b*, plan and section of storage bins. *c*, perspective view of storage bin with slab walls. *d*, perspective view of house with stone slab wall supports. *e*, typical metate and mano. From Roberts, 1929.

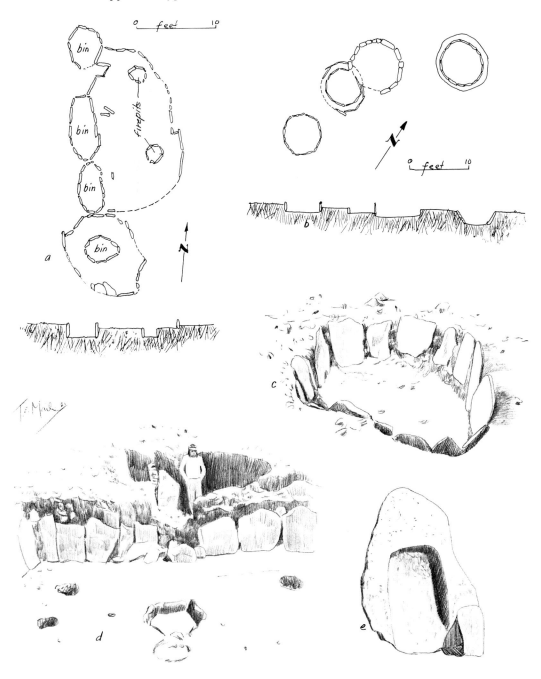

foundations. Later still the entire wall from bottom to top was constructed of rows of horizontally laid stones.

As the years passed, the clusters of rooms were regularly expanded, and each of the apartment-like buildings became in reality a monolithic village, or pueblo. In testimony to the continuing importance of religion in the lives of the people, each pueblo had one or more protokivas, whose construction style reflected that of the ancient pithouse.

The feather cloth so familiar to the Basketmakers was still being made in Pueblo I times, providing robes and blankets, as well as wrappings for burials. Large numbers of turkeys were kept to provide the feathers, although parrots, especially the red-blue and yellow macaws and other brilliantly colored birds, were now obtained through trade with neighboring cultures to the south. Fray Marcos de Niza, as he set forth from Culiacán in 1539 to search for the fabled "Seven Cities of Cíbola," met Mexican Indians returning from the north with turquoise they had purchased with the feathers of tropical birds.

Judd found only a few scraps of cotton cloth at Pueblo Bonito, and one larger cotton remnant at Pueblo del Arroyo. But it is assumed from one three-colored weaving found by George Hubbard Pepper,[10] and from archaeological inquiry elsewhere in the Little Colorado and Kayenta areas, that while cotton was not grown at Chaco Canyon, cotton fiber was imported, and fabrics woven from it increased rapidly in popularity.

Large cotton blankets are known to have been woven in those days. It was a task requiring both great skill and the use of exceptionally large looms. Colored yarns also made their appearance, and painting was done on finished fabrics. New weaving styles were employed to provide even more variation in decoration, and the wardrobes of some Chacoans included buckskin apparel. It was a time of opulent splendor for the Anasazi living in the canyon, when it is taken for granted they moved ahead of all contemporary Anasazi in this regard.

From documents written by Spanish explorers between 1540 and 1600, it is learned that Pueblo men were then wearing cotton breechclouts, painted shirts, blankets, and buckskin jackets and robes. Women wore painted cotton skirts and blankets bound at the waist with a woven sash, tanned deerskins, and footgear of buffalo hide and buckskin.[11] Yucca fibers and rabbit skins were used for blankets. Turkey-feather stockings were also made, and Pueblo men wore knee-length buckskin leggings, dyed to match their moccasins. In general, styles changed little in three hundred years of Spanish intrusion, suggesting that the styles also predated historic times.

In the field of personal ornamentation the Chacoans truly excelled. Beads of olivella shells obtained from the Pacific Ocean and the Gulf of California were extremely popular, as were abalone pendants,[12] but stone and bone beads were also manufactured, and stone and shell pendants were carved in the form of birds, animals, and rings. Splendid turquoise beads and inlaid mosaics were produced. One extraordinary necklace found at Pueblo Bonito was made up of

2,500 turquoise beads and 4 turquoise pendants. The turquoise was as well ground and finished as could be done by any skilled craftsperson with modern tools today, and it is only because few burial sites have been found that such discoveries are limited in number.[13]

Turquoise mines in Arizona and New Mexico have been diligently worked since ancient times. Possession of these deposits gave singular prestige to a community, for the mineral was a prime medium of exchange and power. Judd describes the awesome moment when the discovery of the magnificent turquoise necklace took place. Word of the find spread like magic among the Indian workers, and within minutes they had all gathered and formed a rapt and reverent audience as the archaeologist's tiny brushes deftly swept away the last particles of earth and sand.[14]

Turquoise has become for the Indians vastly more than a precious stone and a symbolic color for the mysterious powers of the ocean and sky. Visitors to the pueblos today will note that turquoise blue is the color almost exclusively used to trim windows and doors. That is because turquoise wards off witches and their evil powers and brings good luck. Whenever the stone or its color is seen, one should realize that the old beliefs are still present and alive.[15]

The sandalmaking art so familiar in Basketmaker times appears to be one of the few artistic casualties at Chaco Canyon. Decoration became less elaborate, and although a few sandals with pointed, unnotched, or notched toes were woven of fine *apocynum* (a plant related to milkweed) string, most footwear had square toes and was fashioned from plaited yucca leaves. Apparently, twined weaving had already ceased by the Bonito Phase, and at this point coiled baskets were phased out too. A few finely woven and sparsely designed baskets have been found by archaeologists, but the common basket of the day was the yucca ring variety.

The yucca ring basket was made by fastening over a wooden ring the outer edges of a bowl-shaped mat made of twilled yucca leaves. In four Pueblo Bonito rooms used for burial purposes, types of basket rarely associated with prehistoric ruins other than cliff dwellings were recovered. These included shallow, elongated trays of unusually fine weave; deep cylindrical baskets of coarser fabrics; and bifurcated (two-legged) baskets such as had been found heretofore only in cave villages of northeastern Arizona and southeastern Utah.[16] A considerable number of twilled rush or reed mats were produced for floor and roof coverings. Tumplines used at Pueblo Bonito were made of braided yucca fibers. Jar rests and head rings designed to hold water jars and other vessels were made of several materials, but primarily of cedar bark and yucca. Tubular pipes of clay or stone were designed for ceremonial smoking, indicated by the fact that many were intentionally broken, perhaps to avoid profanation by others.[17] Grooved stone axes were rarely found, although eight were obtained at Pueblo del Arroyo, and even those were poorly made.[18] Stone tools were limited to hammers, abraders, saws, rubbing and smoothing stones, hoes, arrowheads, pottery polishers, tablets, jar covers, knives, scrapers, and

milling stones.[19] Bone tools included awls, chisels, fleshers, scrapers, and flakers.[20] Wooden implements consisted of fire drills and hearths, spatulas, scrapers, spindle whorls, loom bars, bows, arrows, and children's toys.[21]

Few burials were found in the rooms of the Old Bonitian section and in
the refuse fill areas of the smaller dwellings of Chaco Canyon, the total find
representing less than 2 percent of the five thousand or more who must have
died at Pueblo Bonito alone during its 250-year history. This is unfortunate for
archaeologists, since not a single ancient cemetery has yet been discovered.
Compounding the problem, many of the revealed burials were looted by pot-

a–f, stone knives and projectile points. *g*, two tablets of fine-grained sandstone. *h*, three
manos. *i*, trough metate from Old Bonito. *j*, trough metate from Late Bonito. From Judd, 1923.

hunters before archaeologists arrived on the scene. Even more vexing is the fact that the few undisturbed burials discovered so far indicate that grave offerings at Chaco were "extremely rich."[22] This being so, and there being no evidence that cremation was in common practice at Chaco or in any other Anasazi region, archaeologists continue to search for the ancient cemeteries, hoping to learn all they can about the splendid arts and crafts of the inhabitants. Known burials have confirmed some things: cranial deformation was common at Chaco, indicating that infants were placed on hard-backed cradleboards that caused the backs of their heads to be flattened. The usual burial position was on the back, either fully extended or with the knees bent slightly. Most corpses were placed on mats with the head toward the east and were accompanied by a few of the usual mortuary offerings. The fact that seventeen of the undisturbed skeletons found by Judd's workmen had their heads to the west suggested the possibility of a Chaco taboo against doing so in life. Judd notes that the Hopi give no thought to bed orientation, but that at Zuñi, Acoma, and Laguna, among other areas, sleeping with the head to the east would be fatal, since it is the recognized position for burial.[23]

Now and then there is a stunning find that spurs the archaeologists on. At Ridge Ruin, a Great Pueblo site just east of Flagstaff, Arizona, searchers found the body of a man accompanied by more than six hundred splendid mortuary offerings. There were baskets, pottery, turquoise mosaics, stone and shell ornaments, and hundreds of finely flaked arrowheads. Many of the objects were ceremonial offerings of a type that would be placed only in the grave of an exceptional person. But the burial does give some idea of the wealth of material goods that once attended the Bonito Phase, and it promises that similar treasures await the diligent sleuth.

The main subsistence fare at Chaco Canyon was corn, beans, and squash, augmented by edible seeds taken from desert plants and by local rabbits, ground squirrels, and occasional larger game such as deer and antelope killed by hunters on distant mesas. Possibly turkey was eaten too, although the question is not settled of whether it was strictly a ritual bird kept for its feathers and not eaten even in time of famine, or whether it served both ritual and the table.[24]

Chaco Canyon pottery underwent a gradual development throughout the entire period of its manufacture, although it consisted essentially of only two main types: a corrugated ware and a black-on-white smooth ware.

Pre-Pueblo vessels included bowls with rounded bottoms and tapering rims; ladles of the half-gourd shape; globular pitchers with a squat neck and a handle that extended from rim to shoulder; small round jars with wide mouths; pear-shaped water jars with a high shoulder and a sloping neck; and cooking pots with banded necks and smooth bodies. Painted decoration included stepped and triangular elements bordered by thin, widely spaced lines often extending past corners; ticked lines; and lines and triangles with pendant dots. The decoration was applied while the slip was still damp, and it took on a blurred effect when the surface was polished.[25]

Pottery: *a*, Old Bonitian ladle. *b*, Old Bonito corrugated cooking vessel. *c*, decorated pitcher. *d*, cylindrical vase. *e*, bird-shaped bowl with T-shaped opening. *f*, beginner's bowl. *g*, olla, or water jar, from Late Bonito. *h*, rare clay pottery-maker's stamp. From Judd, 1964.

Only mineral paints were used at Chaco, and the single temper employed throughout the long history of occupation in the canyon was pulverized potsherds.

Transitional pottery at Chaco was much like that of the Pre-Pueblo Period. The bowls were a little larger and deeper, but they had the same rounded bottom and a tapering rim. Ladles were the half-gourd type, with some having a more detached, thicker, and flatter handle. The earliest water jars had a low, vertical neck; later in the period the neck was lengthened, and in some instances a secondary bulge was inserted between it and the shoulder. Duck-shaped and effigy vessels were added to earlier forms. The culinary ware was still smooth-bodied, but indented coils began to supplant the older neckbands. Painted decoration with mineral paints included the Pre-Pueblo motifs, but added whorls, checkerboard and diamond-shaped patterns, and wavy lines and hatching. In this period the pottery was polished before it was painted, and there was no blurring.

As time went on, the Transitional pottery was supplanted in part by a "Degenerate Transitional," and some Mesa Verde ware was introduced at Chaco Canyon.

Judd states unequivocally that the Classic Phase Pueblo Bonito pottery is the finest made by prehistoric peoples.[26] In this spectacular time, the corrugated ware and black-on-white smooth ware were still fashioned, but a redware appeared also in very small quantities. The method of creating corrugated ware is explained in the Mesa Verde chapter, and it will suffice to say here that Chaco corrugated ware was executed with sharp, clear indentations accomplished in a variety of ways on vessel exteriors. The prevailing corrugated form was a large jar with a very wide mouth.[27]

The identifying characteristic of Chaco Black-on-white ware is its pure white slip and the delicate lines of its black decoration. The commonest vessel forms were bowls, pitchers, and ladles. Along with these were found smaller quantities of human effigy pots and cylindrical vases.[28]

Bowls were hemispherical, with rounded bottoms and curving sides. Rims were usually rounded, but sometimes sharp. The average bowl diameter was 12 inches. Bowl exteriors were neither decorated nor slipped, although some potters ran their slip over the rim and down an inch or two below the rim. Another earmark of Chaco bowls was a black rim, sometimes interrupted by a white space or break. This was further emphasized at times by ending the black rim line in a dash or scroll shape that turned down onto the bowl exterior. Chaco ladles were either of the bowl-and-handle shape where the handle appeared to be stuck on, or of the half-gourd types, where handle and bowl seemed to be one flowing piece.

Two kinds of pitchers were made: the commoner small-bodied type averaging from 5 to 8 inches in height, and a rounder and larger pitcher with a small handle. Small pitchers had a tall neck, either cylindrical or in the form of a truncated cone. The lower one fourth of the pitcher body had a larger diameter, with a sharply angled shoulder merging into the neck. The handle was a flat strip running from a point just below the rim to a point just above the place where the neck joined the body. Rims were flat and painted black.[29]

Typical Chaco Black-on-white designs consisted of band decorations that encircled the interiors of bowls and were framed above and below by a single black line. Bands might consist of a repetition of identical units, or of an alternation of two different units. Characteristic also were lines dotted along one side, interlocking spirals, and sharp-pointed batwing figures. Besides these, there were terraced elements, and hatchings with thin lines always framed by heavier outer lines.[30]

Plain and decorated effigy vessels were made at Chaco Canyon, with depictions including birds, goats, bears, cougars, deer, tortoises, toads, and human beings. Judd states that, because of its small orifice, effigy ware would have limited utilitarian value, and so, while we have few data to justify belief in its ceremonial use, it is possible that it served in unknown rituals just as bird and animal figures do on Pueblo altars today.[31]

When they had finished their studies of Chaco Canyon pottery, Judd and his assistants concluded that Old Bonitian pottery developed out of Pueblo I practices inherited from beyond the San Juan, and that the more spectacular ceramic art of the Late Bonitians likewise drew its inspiration from the north and attained perfection in Chaco Canyon.[32]

Archaeologists have used the distinctive Chaco architecture and pottery to trace the influence of Chaco culture to many far-flung places. There are no large ruins of the Chaco type to the south, but considerable Chaco-type pottery has been found at Whitewater, Arizona, not far west of Gallup, New Mexico. Wide Ruin, which is the huge Kin Tiel Ruin on Wide Ruin Wash, a tributary of Leroux Wash, Arizona, was built around A.D. 1276 and is Chacoan in architecture though not in pottery. But not far away, just sixteen miles south of Fort Defiance, there are scores of sites containing typical Chaco pottery. North of Chaco in Montezuma Valley and McElmo Canyon, Colorado, and on the mesas of southeastern Utah, Chaco-type vessels are often found. Far to the northeast there is definite evidence of Chacoan architecture and pottery in the region of Pagosa Springs, Colorado. The famous ruin sixty-five miles north of Chaco at Aztec, New Mexico, may be either the clearest evidence of all of Chaco influence or, as Earl Morris suggested as a possibility, an actual Chaco colony.

CULTURAL DIFFUSION

Archaeologists debate the question of where the first Chacoans came from. Most of them agree that the Chaco cradle lies among the Pueblo I and II remains north of the San Juan River.[33] What is not debated is that by A.D. 1050 the Chaco people had ascended to the peak of their golden age. Living conditions were in many ways better than those of the middle classes in Europe and at least equal to the best conditions in Mesoamerica. Chacoans were prospering, and outsiders were attracted to the area. Although not all villages, or even all parts of any single village, were built or occupied simultaneously, the canyon had reached its greatest density by that time. Population estimates for the villages of the Canyon proper range from 6,000 to 15,000,[34] but the stimulating new finds of sprawling mesa-top communities will call for an entirely new estimate of the total Chaco population at its florescence. When this is accomplished, the figure should be stunning. This much is assured now: the ideas and influence of the burgeoning Chaco villages were spreading swiftly and persuasively to the Anasazi in other regions, and even to other cultures, such as the Hohokam and Mogollon.

Recent discoveries at Chaco Canyon support the contention that it was a center of incomparable importance to the Anasazi, and they reveal that the

Chaco settlements covered a far larger geographic area than heretofore suspected.

In 1979 aerial photography surveys by the National Park Service's remote-sensing division in Albuquerque, New Mexico, showed that Chaco-type communities on the periphery of the canyon were enormous in extent and size. The entire top of the mesa was covered with building sites. One site alone, fifty miles west-northwest of Chaco, near Newcomb, New Mexico, covered over 152,400 square yards, and its buildings each contained from 440 to 1,250 rooms. Another site, called Skunk Springs, spread over 594,000 square yards and had about 1,000 rooms. Both of these sites dwarf magnificent Pueblo Bonito, heretofore considered the jewel and giant of Chaco Canyon's villages. Dwight Drager of the remote-sensing center calls these discoveries "an enormous find, absolutely gigantic,"[35] and as the full extent of the Chaco culture is mapped out his comment may prove to be modest.

W. James Judge, director of the Chaco Center, is convinced that Chaco may have served as a region-wide trade redistribution center, with full-time administrative specialists in charge of storing and rerouting the region's limited resources. The overall evidence bespeaks a highly organized society, and the idea of the Andersons regarding specialization becomes highly plausible. "The whole system," Chaco Center staff archaeologist Thomas Windes says, "staggers the imagination!"[36]

Although shell ornaments and mosaic works indicate that the Anasazi had Mesoamerican and Southwestern trade contacts before the Great Pueblo Period, it was during this later time that broad evidence of expanded trade and cultural contacts appears. The Toltec civilization was at its peak in A.D. 1100 and its influence was widespread. The Aztecs, whose persuasiveness would be even greater, were just beginning their rise in power.

No one knows by what means the Mesoamerican–Chaco trade was carried out—whether direct contact through trading expeditions took place or whether some Southwestern cultures, such as the Hohokam and Mogollon, served as middlemen. Many new artifacts of Mesoamerican origin nevertheless appeared at Chaco Canyon: copper bells; parrots and their wooden likenesses similar to those still in use at modern pueblos; the feathers of many colorful tropical birds, shellwork, mosaic inlay work, new life forms in pottery and mural decoration, and certain architectural features.

The diffusion had its permanent effect. Frank Waters states that the Hopi Flute Clan still uses the heads of macaws and the feathers of other tropical birds in the Flute Ceremony, and that the Snake Clan employs seashells. Wooden parrots are placed on the altar of the Blue Flute Society. The priests carve this bird with great care, for its feathers bring the "warmth" necessary for germination.[37]

Since no newborn bird bones have been found in the Chaco ruins, it seems clear that the Anasazi did not breed or capture the birds themselves, obtaining them instead through trade. The colonnade and gallery at Chetro Ketl, along with architectural features at some other sites, are unique in the Anasazi world, and seem also to have resulted from Mesoamerican influence. At a Chaco site named Talus Unit No. 1, there are two large rooms joined by a broad three-step stairway. Archaeologists are greatly intrigued by this and wonder whether the higher of the two rooms might once have contained an earthen platform similar to the temple mounds of the Toltecs and other Meso- americans. In addition, there are several tower kivas two and three stories high that may reflect the contemporary Mesoamerican cultures.[38]

In what Judd terms "an incredible discovery," workmen in 1926 uncovered the disorderly remains of a triple-walled McElmo tower at Pueblo del Arroyo.[39] Jackson and Holmes had explored southwestern Colorado and its adjoining territory in 1874 and 1875, and were the first to describe the McElmo country and its spectacular towers, which were circular, quadrangular, oval, and D-shaped. They regarded the smaller and more numerous single-walled struc- tures as possible lookouts, and thought the D-shaped and circular towers with radiating rooms were religious in function. Holmes was especially intrigued with the multiple walls. He reported four double-walled towers on or near the Mancos River and one triple-walled tower at the headwaters of McElmo Creek. The latter was unique, for its like had not been reported elsewhere. To find one in Chaco Canyon was a happy surprise for which Judd and his party were entirely unprepared.[40]

The central room of the Pueblo del Arroyo tower was 33 feet (10 m) in diameter, and its floor had originally been paved with sandstone slabs. No trace was detected of a fireplace, deflector, or other special feature. The two encircling tiers were floored with adobe. The ten or so rooms of the outer tier were of unequal length, but averaged 6 feet (1.8 m) in width, while the inner- tier rooms averaged 6 feet 6 inches (1.95 m) in width. The only side door had later been sealed off. The outside diameter of the tower was 73 feet (22.2 m). Judd doubted the structure was ever completed, and he believed that its rooms were never roofed.[41] Archaeologists associate all double- and triple-walled tow- ers with late Pueblo III and with the Great Kivas.

CLASSIC PERIOD
ca. A.D. 1030–1130

Dendrochronology has indicated that the Classic Period, or years of greatest accomplishment at Chaco, ran from A.D. 1030 to 1130. During this century there was a mastery of engineering skills, an excellence in masonry, a height- ened proficiency in arts and crafts, an improvement in personal adornment, and a deepened sophistication in ritual. Roadways were introduced, expanded, and improved. Excellent water-control systems were installed. Trade with other cultures was broadened. Perhaps it was then that the highly complex social organization was achieved. Thirteen major villages came to fruition, as well as two hundred smaller structures.

Three groups, whose slightly different cultural remains are sufficient to cause archaeologists to speak of them as almost contemporary cultural phases, emerged ultimately at Chaco: the Bonito; the Hosta Butte; and the McElmo, who were late migrants to the canyon from the San Juan area.

BONITO PHASE
ca. A.D. 919–1100

The Bonito Phase is named for the largest and most famous of its villages, Pueblo Bonito, but it is also represented by other impressive classic towns located mainly on the north side of Chaco Canyon. These include Chetro Ketl; Pueblo del Arroyo; Wi ji ji or Wejegi; Una Vida; and Hungo Pavi. It also encompasses the outlying towns of Pueblo Pintado, Peñasco Blanco, Old Alto, Kin Ya'a, Kin Klizhin, Kin Biniola, and two isolated Great Kivas: the 72-foot (21.9 m)-diameter Casa Rinconada and Kin Nahasbas. All these village structures were either D-, E-, L-, oval-, or wedge-shaped, and they each featured a large open courtyard, or plaza, in its center. The courtyard was enclosed on three sides by multistoried rooms terraced from a single story in the front to as many as five stories in the back. The building front was usually, but not always, oriented in a southerly direction, and the outside walls were windowless.[42]

Pueblo Pintado sat on a bench some twenty-five feet or so above the valley floor. The terraced, four-story main building formed an L shape, enclosing a plaza bounded on the south side by a crescent-shaped course of one-story rooms. Two circular clan kivas, one with two pillars and the other with four, were enclosed within the square walls of the building—so as to form a double wall—and the space between the walls was filled with solid masonry. Off the southwest corner of the main building was a separate rectangular structure housing a Great Kiva more than 45 feet (13.5 m) in diameter. The masonry work, a combination of brick-sized stones and smaller stones, is so well fitted together that from a distance it looks like a plain, solid surface.

Chetro Ketl was a huge building shaped like a squared-off C, in which one dwelling room was found in a perfect state of preservation. The room measured 13 feet 11 inches by 17 feet (4.2–5.1 m), its ceiling was nearly 10 feet (3 m) high, and it had several wall niches. The roof structure of the room consisted of two main beams laid transversely, topped by small poles placed at right angles to the beams and extending from beam to wall top, a layer of cedar bast fiber, and clay. The building included a classic Great Kiva 62 feet 6 inches (19 m) in diameter.

The original walls of Peñasco Blanco formed an almost perfect ellipse, the western half containing five rows of terraced rooms, and the eastern half containing one row of contiguous single-story rooms. Between the two sections lay a great oval plaza. Just to the south, in a separate building, was the Great Kiva.

Top, a portion of the Pueblo Pintado ruin. *Bottom,* Pueblo del Arroyo ruin. From Fewkes, 1920.

Pueblo Bonito was an enormous building, set tight against a sheer cliff 135 feet high, and large enough to be called a town. It was 550 feet (165 m) long and over 350 feet (105 m) wide, covering more than 3 acres of ground and containing at least 800 rooms. Had the entire structure been occupied at once, it could have sheltered as many as 1,200 inhabitants. It was the largest building of its kind in the world until a bigger apartment building, the Spanish Flats, was erected in New York City in 1882.

Excavations of the pueblo were carried out first by B. T. B. Hyde, and then by Pepper and Judd.[43] They learned that construction had begun at Pueblo Bonito as early as A.D. 919, although it did not reach its finished state until A.D. 1067. As the ruin stands today, after excavation, it is still an exceptional structure, complete enough to allow one to envision it as it was before it was abandoned, although a hundred thousand tons of earth and stone had to be carried away to reveal it. On three sides of a vast center court the D-shaped building was terraced back from one story in front to four stories in the rear. Enclosing the southern and straight side of the D was a one-story row of rooms. In front of this was the rubbish heap, around which retaining walls were built to keep the debris from scattering. The overall plan was strictly utilitarian, for it allowed the sun to penetrate into the far reaches of the structure and ensured good ventilation for most rooms.

Plot plans: *top left*, Pueblo Pintado. *Bottom left*, Wijiji. *Right*, Pueblo Peñasco Blanco. After Jackson, 1876.

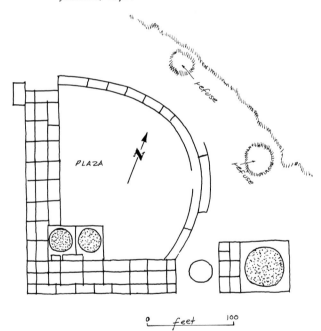

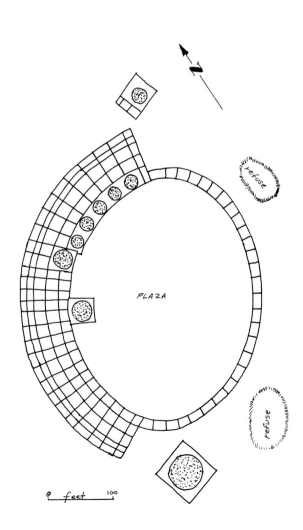

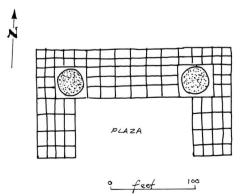

In the center court and within the Pueblo Bonito dwelling spaces themselves were numerous clan-sized kivas, whose average diameter, with three exceptions, was less than 25 feet (7.5 m). There were at least thirty-two of these clan kivas at Bonito in its late phase. The Old Bonito kivas were rectangular, had an undetermined number of pilasters, and included benches or banquettes paved with flagstones. Since the kivas were all built over, it was not possible to determine specific interior equipment.

Newer Bonito kivas were circular and alike, although not precisely so. The majority had a masonry or slab-lined circular firepit, an underfloor ventilating system, a masonry-lined subfloor vault west of the firepit, and an encircling banquette topped by six to ten log-enclosed pilasters. The banquette had a shallow recess at the south point. On top of the approximately 9-inch (22.5 cm)-high pilasters a cribwork of overlapping logs rose to form a domed ceiling perhaps 10 feet (3 m) high at midpoint. A central roof hatchway provided a smoke vent and a means of entrance. The distinctive Chaco-type ventilating system with its vent near the firepit and its underfloor duct and external air shaft made air-deflector slabs for the most part unnecessary.[44]

Late Bonito kivas built out in the courtyard were subterranean, but those placed within the terraced structure itself were at surface level and were surrounded by dwelling walls to achieve a subterranean effect. Apparently the entire community believed that its welfare depended upon the faithful performance of prescribed rituals. The influence of the ceremonial chamber took precedence over the influence of the home. Excavators at Pueblo Bonito noticed repeatedly that dwelling rooms were often sacrificed to provide space for another kiva. "Established religious rites formed the very hub about which the

Chetro Ketl, as seen from the tops of the cliffs surrounding the ruin. The Great Kiva is prominent to the left of center and out in front of the huge apartment dwelling.

Aerial view of Pueblo Bonito.

daily life and hopes of the whole village revolved."[45] It is not possible to tell how many of the clan kivas were in use at a given time, but it is certain that not all were used at once.

Besides the clan kivas, there were two Great Kivas. The kiva that Judd designated Kiva Q was the more ancient and less complicated of the two. It was subterranean and averaged 40 feet (12 m) in diameter and 12 feet (3.6 m) in depth. The interior ceiling height was about 10 feet (3 m). Four pine posts, 15 to 18 inches (38–45 cm) in diameter, supported the kiva roof structure. Each post stood on top of a foundation slab and in a neat masonry cylinder 3 feet (90 cm) in diameter and 9 inches (22.5 cm) thick, filled with shale fragments and covered by a closely fitted slab pavement 7 feet 4 inches (2.2 m) in diameter. No trace remains of the roofing timbers, but it is assumed that four heavy beams spanned the distance between the posts, and that smaller beams bridged the space from there to the walls. These would be topped by mats, sticks, or cedar bast, and clay.

On each side of the chamber was a masonry-lined sunken vault, whose top was only a few inches above the floor. The vault was packed with sand, which was topped by a thin layer of shale chips. Between the two vaults was a fireplace 4 feet 4 inches (1.3 m) square and 2 feet 5 inches (73.5 cm) high, with a recessed firepit in the center. Just north of the fireplace was a basin 18 inches (45 cm) in diameter, ringed with adobe 6 inches (15 cm) high and 3 feet 3 inches (1 m) across. Zuñi workmen identified it as the container for ashes taken from the fireplace.[46] South of the fireplace were a deflector and the butts of nine small posts that were probably the supports of a wattlework screen.

A subfloor depository of neat masonry 12 inches (30 cm) in diameter and 8 inches (20 cm) deep lay 11 feet (3.3 m) north of the fireplace. It was covered with a thin, circular sandstone slab. Because of its location, Judd was tempted to call it a sipapu, except that the sipapu was foreign to Chaco Canyon kivas.[47]

Evidence of a three-pole ladder was found between the deflector and the south point of the kiva. The Zuñi workmen said that old-time kiva ladders always had three poles.

A single bench, some 1 foot 11 inches (58 cm) wide and 2 feet 1 inch (63.5 cm) high, encircled Kiva Q. The wall masonry above the bench was 3 feet 2 inches (96 cm) thick. Behind the ladder, and 5 feet 2 inches (1.57 m) higher than the bench was a small antechamber measuring about 6 feet 5 inches (1.95 m) by 8 feet 8 inches (2.6 m). Probably there was once a stairway leading from the kiva floor to the antechamber, but collapsed walls prevented Judd from making a positive determination.[48]

Pueblo Bonito Great Kiva.

Great Kiva A, the central and most conspicuous feature of Pueblo Bonito, was excavated in the summer of 1921. The floor diameter was 45 feet 1 inch (13.5 m), and 3 feet (90 cm) above the benches the diameter was 51 feet 10 inches (15.8 m). The kiva wall was encircled by three tiers of benches that varied in width and height and merged at irregular intervals. Around the main wall and about 2 feet 8 inches (81 cm) above the highest bench were thirty-four wall niches 9 inches (22.5 cm) square by 10 inches (25 cm) deep, each capped by a sandstone slab.

Architectural details, Pueblo Bonito. Great Kiva construction. From Judd, 1964.

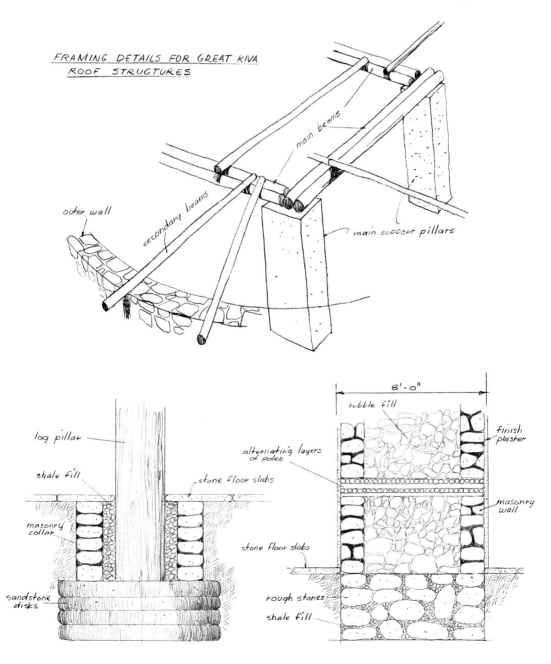

FRAMING DETAILS FOR GREAT KIVA ROOF STRUCTURES

main beams

outer wall

secondary beams

main support pillars

log pillar

shale fill

masonry collar

sandstone disks

stone floor slabs

alternating layers of poles

8'-0"

rubble fill

finish plaster

masonry wall

stone floor slabs

rough stones

shale fill

FRAMING DETAILS FOR GREAT KIVA MAIN PILLARS

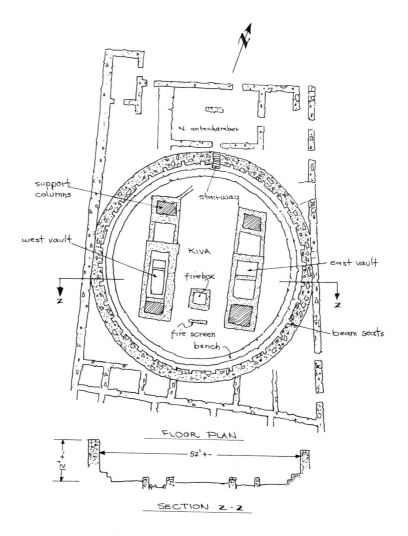

Chaco Canyon. Floor plan of Great Kiva A. From Judd, 1964.

At the north point a recessed stairway 2 feet 1 inch (63.5 cm) wide gave access to an antechamber, or altar room. The masonry altar was 4 feet 5 inches (1.3 m) long, 11½ inches (28.5 cm) wide, and 1 foot 1 inch (33 cm) high.

Four mammoth, hollow stone pillars provided the main supports for the roof. These varied in size, but were approximately 8 feet (2.4 m) long by 5 feet 6 inches (1.7 m) wide, and had walls 1 foot 6 inches (45 cm) thick. They were finished on the outside, and the space within was filled with rubblework strengthened at regular intervals by cedar poles that extended through from one exterior to the other. The poles were laid in alternating courses, about 9 inches (22.5 cm) apart: first north–south and then east–west.[49] Each pillar stood on a cylindrical foundation of coarse stonework that filled a hole 3 to 4 feet (0.9–1.2 m) deep and was packed in tight with shale chips.

Sunken masonry-lined vaults of unknown purpose abutted the north side of the two southern pillars. Originally plastered, these were approximately 9 feet 5 inches (2.9 m) long by 4 feet 2 inches (1.25 m) wide by 2 feet 6 inches (75 cm) deep.

Midway between the southeast and southwest pillars was a raised masonry fireplace 4 feet 2 inches (1.27 m) square and 1 foot 11 inches (58 cm) high. The outer corners were rounded, and the recessed basin was clay-lined and ash-filled. Also, 3 feet 6 inches (1.06 m) to the south was a wattlework draft deflector 5 feet 2 inches (1.57 m) long.

The roof structure of Great Kiva A was gone, but sufficient fragments remained to suggest what it was like. Paired peeled beams, each about 12 inches (30 cm) in diameter, spanned the distance between the pillars, and lesser timbers 3 inches (7.5 cm) or so in diameter bridged the spaces between the beams and the walls. Topping these were successive layers of peeled-willow mats, a layer of cedar splints, and a thin coat of adobe.

There are many striking similarities between Great Kiva A and the Great Kiva at Aztec, excavated and restored by Earl H. Morris in 1921. The Aztec kiva will be described shortly in the consideration of extensions or duplications, whichever the case may be, of the Chaco Canyon culture.

Several Great Kivas, no two exactly alike, were built at Chaco Canyon during the Bonito Phase. Their diameters ranged from 40 to 63 feet (12–19 m), and because of their size and features it is assumed their purpose was to serve the needs of the entire community at any given village.[50] Features common to Great Kivas included four large pillars, twin floor vaults, a raised fireplace, an encircling bench or benches, wall niches, antechambers, and peripheral rooms.

The profusion of clan kivas and Great Kivas at Chaco Canyon reveals in itself that religious life and ritual were as important to the Anasazi of the years A.D. 750–1130 as it is to the Pueblo descendants of the Anasazi today. It has always been, and is still, the hub, the leaven, and the hope of their society. It binds them together now, and it is the cord that ties them inexorably to the ancient ways. The Anasazi Pueblos live their religion; that is, the traditional Pueblos still do. It is a religion that serves both community and personal needs, although the people make no distinction between the two. Each is part of a whole, with the community needs being paramount. Anasazi religion is considered more fully in the Hopi—Pueblo V chapter, but a survey of the religious objects found at Chaco Canyon's Pueblo Bonito by Judd's National Geographic Expedition is needed to complete the present story.

Several specimens of peeled willow sticks found at Pueblo Bonito are thought to be remnants of prayer sticks. Such sticks are a central item in Pueblo religious practice today, and findings of them in every prehistoric Anasazi region confirms that this has always been so. They all require feathers in their manufacture, and turkey feathers are the most frequently used, although other kinds are employed. Judd mentions that macaw and other parrot feathers are highly prized, but I doubt their broad use for prayer sticks. In the pueblos today the colored feathers, most often, are attached in small bunches to the hair or to some part of a headdress. That macaws were important at Pueblo Bonito is evidenced by a number of skeleton finds and the discovery of a special chamber used as a cage for macaws.[51]

Since no reference to remains of macaws or other parrots from a south-western ruin earlier than Pueblo III is found in archaeological literature, it is assumed that Mexican buyers of Pueblo turquoise and buffalo hides introduced tropical feathers as a medium of exchange around the middle of the twelfth century. Yet trading itself had gone on since Basketmaker times. The shortest and most feasible routes were already well known, and the first Spanish expeditions to the Southwest were led by native guides familiar with the network of footpaths.[52]

According to Fewkes, the Hopi think of golden eagle feathers as second only to turkey feathers in importance.[53] In my personal experiences at Hopi and Zuñi, eagle feathers have seemed to rank second to nothing, being essential ceremonial paraphernalia. The Hopi are profoundly upset over current government restrictions placed upon the taking of golden eagles. They claim they must have them for success in ritual, and that eagles must be taken in the

Map showing locations of Great Kivas discovered thus far.

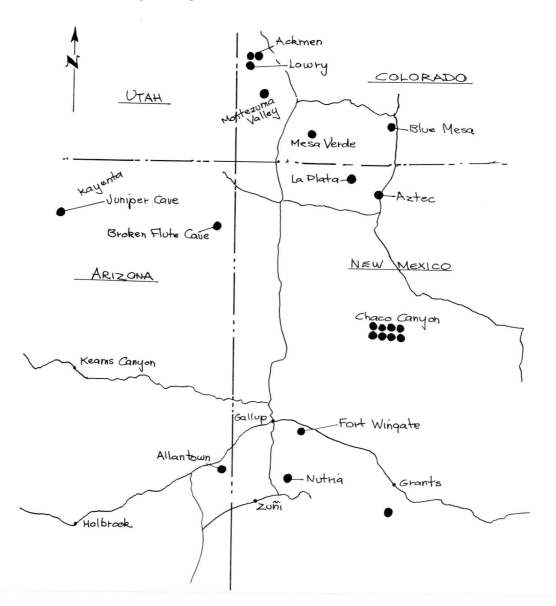

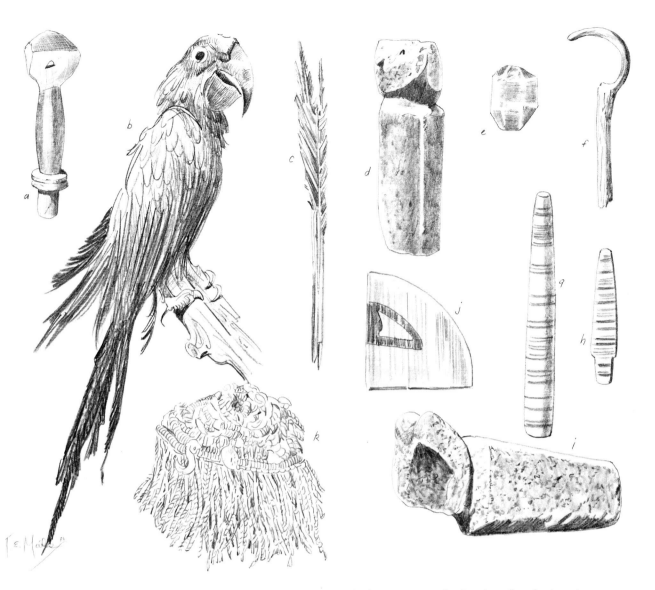

Religious objects: *a,* fragment of a ceremonial stick. *b,* macaw. *c,* feather bundle. *d,* stone fetish from Ruin No. 8. *e,* quartz crystal. *f,* fragment of ceremonial stave or paho. *g–h,* polished medicine stones. *i,* stone animal fetish from Sinklezin, a ruin near Pueblo Bonito. *j,* fragment of an altar screen. *k,* altar-stick tassel. From Judd, 1964.

ancient Hopi way, not acquired by permit from a government warehouse. Eagle nests, in their view, are clan property. When whole eagles are needed, young birds are taken directly from their nests, purified by ritual head washing, and killed by hand pressure on the sternum. Eagles are also kept in cages just for their feathers, which are plucked when necessary. The total number of birds used in a year by the Pueblos in no wise endangers the species. If it did, somewhere during the two thousand years of unceasing ritual use the golden eagle would have disappeared entirely.

Downy prayer feathers of the kind kept in bunches and attached to items, or tied individually to pieces of string, were not found at Pueblo Bonito. But since these are fragile items that would not have survived long, it is assumed they were used by the Bonitians.

Pepper found 355 prayer sticks in one room alone at Pueblo Bonito. All were carved at one end and tapered gradually at the other end. He divided the sticks into four categories: those with two knobs, the upper one sometimes perforated; those with an end shaped like a bear claw; those with a broad, spatulate end; and wedge-shaped sticks, sometimes bound with buckskin and cord.[54] Judd's National Geographic party found examples only of the bear claw, or crook, type. Such prayer sticks are still in wide use in the pueblos. For example, of thirty-one small sticks surrounding the Antelope Fraternity's Snake Dance altar, fifteen have a crook at one end and are painted black.

At Mummy Cave in Canyon del Muerto, Earl Morris found prayer sticks imbedded in the corner masonry and overlapping slightly as they extended from bottom to top of the three-story wall. Each pair of sticks consisted of one with a crook and another with a carved end, to which were attached two miniature bow-shaped sticks.[55]

In one room at Pueblo Bonito were found several specimens that could have been tasseled attachments for altar sticks. Each consisted of a main cord of yucca or cotton, coiled counterclockwise and jammed with short pendant threads made of yucca.

Shaped and painted incomplete pieces of wood were found in Late Bonitian rooms. These might have been parts of altar screens or tablitas such as those used on altars and worn by Pueblo dancers today.

When he first saw some small watermelon-shaped pieces of wood at Pueblo Bonito, Judd's "old Zuñi camp man" pronounced them to be "watermelons" such as he planted each spring to ensure a good watermelon crop.[56]

Cedar-bark bundles found at Pueblo Bonito were quickly identified by Zuñi workmen as torches like those used in the Fire Ceremony to carry fire from one room to another. Each bundle was wrapped at intervals with fine yucca-fiber string.[57]

A rattlesnake effigy made from a crooked cottonwood root with a minimum of carving and the application of black and white paint was found by Judd's workmen. Carvings or paintings of snakes often appear on Pueblo altars; Pueblo snake ceremonies are well known. The Zuñi kept rattlesnakes for arrow poisoning, and Hodge unearthed snake pens at Hawikuh.[58]

Bone, stone, and other items considered as possible ceremonial objects used at Pueblo Bonito included inlaid bone scrapers, bone dice, sandstone tablets, sandal-shaped tablets that were perhaps really celts (axlike tools), sandstone cylinders, paint cups, paints, mortars and pestles, medicine stones or fetishes, spearheads, arrowheads, stone knives, and clay plume holders. Carved stone effigies and figurines consisted of mountain lions, birds, frogs, and human figures.[59]

Among the Pueblos today, smoking is a ritual act without which a ceremony cannot be complete or efficacious. The pipe itself has special meanings. The smoke purifies, and it carries up prayers as it rises to the powers above. Bonitians made decorated stone and fired-clay pipes, some tubular and some L-shaped, including "cloud blowers" intended only for ritual purposes.[60] In

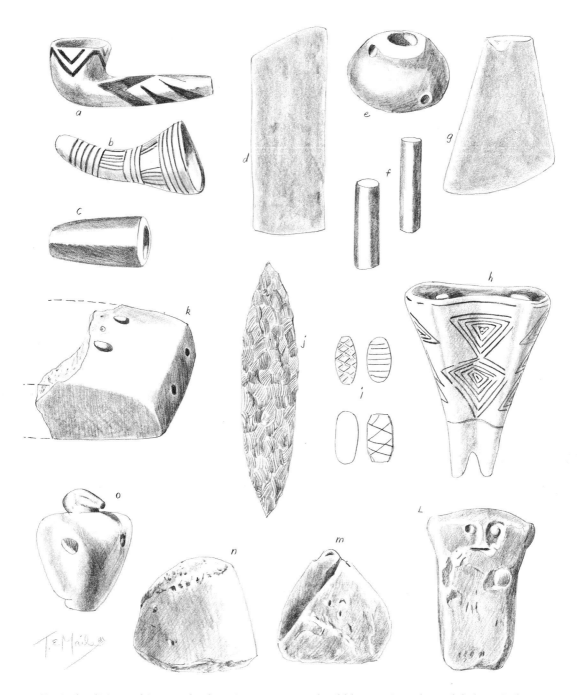

Typical religious objects: *a–b*, clay pipes. *c*, stone cloud-blower pipe. *d*, sandal-shaped, fine-grained sandstone tablets. *e*, concretionary cup. *f*, hematite cylinders. *g*, celtlike blade of hematite. *h*, clay effigy of woven bifurcated basket. *i*, bone dice or gaming counters. *j*, stone knife found in a concealed repository in a kiva. *k*, fragment of a clay prayer plume holder. *l*, clay figurine. *m–n*, sandstone heads believed to represent Mountain Lion, hunter of the north. *o*, bird effigy carved from turquoise. From Judd, 1964.

these, the smoke was not inhaled; it was blown through the pipe toward the cardinal directions to produce rain-cloud shapes, just as is done today in Pueblo ceremony.[61]

Frank H. H. Roberts, in discussing pipe specimens from the Whitewater District, says there are two main forms, one funnel-like, the other cylindrical. In his view the funnel is the older shape, common to Basketmaker III and early Pueblo I. The tubular shape was more characteristic of subsequent Pueblo stages. Reed or bone stems were often inserted in the ends of pipes. Explaining the manufacturing process, Roberts states that pipes were made from a clay paste about midway in quality between that for culinary vessels and that for painted wares. The hole in the tube was made by molding the clay around a twig or reed that was either pulled out while the clay was still moist or burned out during firing. Tubular forms were from 1⅞ to 2¼ inches in length, with maximum diameters of ¾ to ⅞ inch. Funnel-shaped forms were only slightly larger.[62]

Among the musical instruments fashioned by the Bonitians were bone whistles similar to one used today in the Oraibi Powamû Ceremony, wooden flutes, and shell trumpets.

Ceremonial basketry at Pueblo Bonito included painted cylindrical baskets, oval trays, and painted bifurcated baskets (of which there were also earthenware effigies), all used to hold objects, unidentifiable today, during ceremonies.

Taken as a whole, the artifact finds indicate that Anasazi religious beliefs and practices had matured at Pueblo Bonito and had profoundly infused themselves into the lifeway of its residents. In all probability that was equally true of the other communities of the canyon, and it is of great moment to see this same religion in full-blown practice in historical Pueblo times. For it is only by reading backwards that we come to know what ceremonial life was really like in prehistoric days.

Archaeologists agree that craftsmanship in Anasazi architecture reached its zenith at Chaco Canyon, although, aesthetically, some of the great cliff dwellings at Mesa Verde would rank as high.

A matter of continuing astonishment to those who excavate at Pueblo Bonito has been the evidence of ceaseless building activity. So much went on that it is utterly impossible to identify all the influences that prompted it. Houses were torn down and replaced; new partitions were built in; doorways were moved; walls were remodeled; new floor levels were established. First-story ceilings were further braced to receive the additional weight of later rooms erected above. At least 30 percent of the dwellings in the Late Bonito portion of the pueblo overlie the remains of unfinished or partially razed structures. Mysteries abound: in the outer northeast quarter of the village, there is a veritable maze of interlaced foundations that never received the walls for which they were prepared.

Four different types of masonry exist in the Bonito ruin. The first, oldest, and crudest is the single-coursed, accompanied by wattle-and-daub partitions and confined to the north and northwest sections. It is characteristic of a separate settlement of long standing, which was begun about A.D. 838 and formed the core unit of the later, terraced village. Those who lived here were the original, the Old Bonitians. Indications are that about A.D. 1030, when they were in a state of decline and doing little building, they invited a larger group of near-strangers to move in with them. The newcomers, known thereafter as the Late Bonitians, took over immediately, razing and replacing dwellings in such hectic continuity that they ultimately absorbed and enfolded the older settlement. They revised and enlarged the sprawling pueblo with utter disregard for the physical labor involved. What they willed to do, they did. Before the Late Bonitians were done, they had spawned Pueblo Bonito, the magnificent "City Beautiful," as we refer to it today. This is something for us all to reflect upon when we hear Indians spoken of as "inherently lazy individuals." Any such unhappy creatures are the direct product of reservation strictures, and even now they represent only a small portion of the Indians.

Curiously enough, while the new Bonitians were dominating secular and religious life of the community, the original settlers continued in the manner to which they had become accustomed, being influenced only in slight degree. They did add new ornamentation to their pottery, but retained the characteristic forms and decorative motifs. They kept their rectangular kivas, but gradually introduced into them certain special features and furnishings more typical of the circular kivas of their neighbors.[63] In essence, they remained Pueblo II people living in Pueblo III times. Another surprising matter, Judd believes, is that the Old Bonitians continued in residence longer than the Late Bonitians. Practically all the cultural material recovered by the Hyde Expeditions and by the National Geographic Society came from Old Bonitian rooms.[64]

As to where the Pueblo II Old Bonitians came from, Judd concedes they may have descended from earlier Chaco Canyon settlers, but thinks it more likely they were immigrants from southeastern Utah and southwestern Colorado, beyond the San Juan River. "They were the founders of Pueblo Bonito as we now know it, although the same site had been previously occupied by Pueblo I families."[65] Since jacal construction, the usual successor to pithouses, occurs only infrequently at Bonito, it is easier to believe that the Old Bonitians moved in from the north as a body and employed their knowledge of masonry, newly acquired, in constructing their Chaco Canyon home, beginning about A.D. 838. The traditional grouping of dwellings, storerooms, kivas, and trash piles points to southwestern Colorado as the most likely place of origin for the culture that brought Old Bonito into being. It is north of the San Juan that one finds the prototype of the Great Kiva, which is one of the distinguishing elements in what has come to be called the "Chaco Culture."[66]

The builders of Old Bonito had advanced beyond the jacal stage of Pueblo I times before their arrival in Chaco Canyon, and they built almost exclusively with distinctive masonry that is without parallel in Chaco desert country; one must go north to the La Plata area to find its mate. Old Bonitian dwellings at Chaco were rectangular and contiguous, forming a long, wide crescent with the storerooms in the rear. The kivas were deep, with flaring walls, an encircling banquette, and pilasters. Old Bonitian architecture seems to be a blend of La Plata Pueblo I and II, with certain features retained even from Basketmaker III times.[67]

Old Bonito walls were single-coursed until late in time, when some were double-coursed. They were built of wall-width slabs of sandstone, each slab spalled around the edge, and held one upon another by quantities of mud mortar pressed into place with the fingers. Ceilings were casual assemblages of whatever materials lay near at hand: cottonwood, pine, piñon, or juniper logs spaced a short distance apart and covered with brush, reeds or grass, cornstalks, and other chance gleanings. The beam ends were characteristically conical, "the beaverlike gnawing of a stone ax unmistakable."[68] Beams frequently project beyond the exterior wall for a distance of several feet, forming what are today called vigas. Twelve tree-ring dates obtained from Old Bonito beams extend from A.D. 838 to 935. Forty-four dates from Late Bonitian beams range from A.D. 1011 to 1126.[69]

Late Bonitian masonry likewise appears to be of northern inspiration, dominating both in quantity and quality that of the Old Bonitians. There was an almost measured regularity, with neatly squared corners and carefully selected ceiling timbers that were freshly cut and peeled. Identical features exist in the ruins of southeastern Utah and southwestern Colorado. At Lowry Ruin in southern Colorado, where he obtained tree-ring dates between A.D. 1086 and 1106, Paul S. Martin recognized both Chaco masonry and Chaco pottery. One La Plata ruin described by Earl Morris was a compact, Chaco-like structure that had been erected above the remains of a Pueblo II house.[70] The Great Kiva is another tie to the north, and the Late Bonito Great Kiva was of late-date construction.

Thus Pueblo Bonito, and perhaps all Chaco culture from beginning to end, may be a product of Anasazi culture that evolved along the lower Utah-Colorado border and was carried south and east by migrant groups as they searched for peace and more fertile fields. And if this point of view is pursued, it soon becomes apparent that migrations from the north began long before the northern area was totally abandoned in the late thirteenth century.[71] After the Chaco culture had itself matured, its influence spread back to the north and had its effect upon the Anasazi still living there.

The plastered dwelling rooms in Chaco Canyon structures were large and high-ceilinged for the time, some being as high as 12 feet (3.6 m), although the average was 8 feet 6 inches (2.55 m). Storage of corn and other foodstuffs took place in the inner rooms that lacked light and had the poorest ventilation, although vent holes and shafts did carry air in and down to them. Building roofs and the huge central plaza provided additional working space, and many of the activities of the Pueblo were carried on in the open.

Most Pueblo Bonito rooms did not have fireplaces, which indicates that cooking was done outside on the roofs or in the courts. In their earliest phases, many Bonito village buildings had windows in the outermost wall, but as time passed, all such walls were sealed off tight, as was the single main gateway in the building front. Entry thereafter was only by means of ladders that could be pulled up, and a constant fear of enemy attack is plainly shown.[72]

Pueblo del Arroyo, nearest neighbor of Pueblo Bonito, was excavated by the Judd-led National Geographic Expedition between 1923 and 1926. Mention has already been made of its triple-walled McElmo tower. In ground plan, the pueblo itself consists on its west side of a rectangular block of massed rooms with extensions at each end on the east side, so as to give the whole a kind of squared-off C form. In front of this unit is a large courtyard. On the east side a crescent-shaped row of contiguous one-story rooms encloses the other side of the courtyard. The outer west wall of the pueblo is 268 feet long, and the total area occupied by the building and its court is slightly more than 1 ⅛ acres.

In its original state, Pueblo del Arroyo was terraced from one story in front to four stories in the rear. The dark and poorly ventilated ground-floor rooms were used primarily for storage, and the upper rooms served as dwellings. Unlike the case of Pueblo Bonito, most rooms had fireplaces. Judd counted a total of 284 rooms housing a maximum population of 475. Like the others, this village once had an outside door, but it was blocked off early and egress thereafter was by ladders—certainly not a convenient means.

There were at least seventeen clan kivas and one Great Kiva within the walls of Pueblo del Arroyo. All the clan kivas were circular in floor plan and masonry-lined. All were enclosed within the straight walls of surface dwellings, to produce a subterranean effect. Of eight excavated by Judd's group, each had an encircling banquette, but only four had low pilasters of the type needed to bear cribbed roofs, and these were log-enclosed. Typical features included overhead hatchways, firepits, and ventilator tunnels, but no sipapus or deep south recesses of the type common to Mesa Verde kivas. Diameters at floor level ranged from 11 feet 8 inches (3.55 m) to 25 feet 10 inches (7.8 m).[73]

In general, the masonry of Pueblo del Arroyo was like that of Pueblo Bonito, although there were marked divergences. Some walls appear to have been built of secondhand materials; some exhibit more or less banding with dressed blocks of friable sandstone, while others include sections composed of selected laminate sandstone. As a whole, the building appears to be the product of individuals, each of whom built according to his personal preferences.[74] Floors in adjoining dwellings were often set at different levels, and it is clear that the builders completed each storied room, both walls and ceiling, as their work advanced. Nevertheless, Pueblo del Arroyo was a planned community. Someone coordinated the layout and work, even though individuals carried out the orders as they saw fit.

As was the case with Pueblo Bonito, evidence suggests that the original part of Pueblo del Arroyo was built by Anasazi who came early in time from the north. Later they were supplanted and dominated by new immigrants from the San Juan country. Northern influences are particularly evident at Pueblo del Arroyo. The pottery recovered there is in large measure characteristic of southeastern Utah and southwestern Colorado. Datable timbers reveal a time span for this village from A.D. 1025 to 1117, the very period when the Mancos-McElmo culture was flourishing north of the San Juan.[75]

While it was not the only method used by Anasazi builders, cored masonry is thought to have made its original appearance at Pueblo Bonito. It was a way of building high walls with reduced bulk, and some think it was a technique learned from Mexican masons. Coring was accomplished by facing on both sides an inner core of rubble. The facing was done with a veneer of horizontally laid thin tabular stones that provided a fine texture and a smooth, finished exterior and interior. The walls were extremely thick at the bottom and tapered evenly toward the top, providing a stable base and at the same time reducing the load that a uniformly thick wall would have produced. Careful detailing extended also to doorways, roofs, and sharp squaring of corners. Little mortar was needed. Except for the use of smaller stones, the stonework of the Late Bonito Phase was an echo of the astounding creations of Peru, where the stones were often so perfectly fitted together that it is difficult to insert a knife blade between them. However neat and precise the Late Bonito masonry, though, it was invariably covered with brown adobe mud.[76]

The exceedingly thick walls, some measuring 4 feet (1.2 m) or more in width at the base, required strong door lintels. For this purpose, eight or ten pine logs 5 inches (12.5 cm) or so in diameter laid side by side were bound together in raft fashion with split-willow or yucca-leaf thongs, and then used to bridge the door opening. Lintel ends extended as much as a foot into the jamb walls. The wall masonry continued above the lintel to the ceiling. Doorways between rooms were fairly small and were often placed near corners. But exterior doorways were centered, and they measured as much as 5 feet 6 inches (1.68 m) high and 3 feet (90 cm) wide. The usual doorsill was a thin sandstone slab raised 12 to 20 inches (30–50 cm) above floor level.[77] Most doorways in Late Bonito were rectangular, but T-shaped openings were also made, and a few doors were placed in the very corner.

Four distinct types of cored masonry, each type illustrating the dominant construction method in vogue at a given period during occupancy of the Pueblo Bonito village, were identified by Judd. Walls of the first type, which appeared to be the earliest and was related to Old Bonito, were crude and irregular, and the rooms they enclosed were small, with low ceilings. The next three types were all Late Bonito. The second type exhibited infinite attention to detail. It consisted of rather large uniform blocks of friable sandstone, dressed on the face only, laid in adobe mud, and chinked with innumerable small, thin chips. The third type utilized uniformly thin tablets of laminate sandstone, a minimum of adobe, and little or no chinking. Larger blocks were frequently laid in bands both for decorative effect and for bonding the masonry veneer to the rubble core of the wall. The fourth type consisted of a rubble core veneered with laminate sandstone of fairly uniform thickness laid with a minimum of mud mortar between the stones.[78] Tree-ring dates for sixty-five ceiling beams sampled at Pueblo Bonito range from A.D. 828 to 1130, and the four types date from within this period.

The fairly characteristic ceiling of the fourth type of Late Bonitian room rested on a single pine or fir beam, 10 inches (25 cm) in diameter and set transversely at a height of 8 feet 5 inches (2.54 m) at about the midpoint of the room. On top of this beam and set at right angles were forty selected and smoothed willow poles averaging 2½ inches (6.3 cm) in diameter. These were placed close together with the butt and whip ends alternating. Above them at right angles was a layer of red cedar splints, from 3 to 4 feet (0.9–1.2 m) long and 2 inches (5 cm) wide. Cross poles, spaced apart, were laid at right angles on top of the splints, and the whole was lashed together with yucca-leaf thongs to made a firm mat. A layer of cedar bark covered the mat, and the whole was finished off with a coating of mud 3 inches (7.5 cm) thick.[79] Hatchways were present in both Old Bonitian and Late Bonitian ceilings, usually in the southeast corner. Old Bonitian timbers frequently extended several feet beyond an outside wall, but few Late Bonitian timbers did so.[80] Judd observes with considerable admiration that with primitive tools Late Bonitian carpenters could cut the end so cleanly off a beam that one would swear it was done with a modern saw.[81]

The use of massive logs for the Great Kiva beams has excited considerable speculation about where they came from. The logs carry no scars to indicate they were transported over long distances, and if they were, no one has figured out how or the point of origin. Some think that conditions at Chaco then were different from those now and that the trees were local products. Willow was also in common use at Chaco, and that, too, is no longer around. Trees of any kind or consequence there are few and far between today.

The ancient Zuñi were known to have moved large logs by means of a litter. Four or more pairs of men held poles as crosspieces between them, and the log was laid upon these. I have seen Sioux men carry the Sun Dance Tree in the same manner. One clue to how transportation was facilitated at Chaco rests within another Anasazi accomplishment. With digging sticks and hoes they constructed a vast and sophisticated network of roads not duplicated by anyone else in North America. Archaeologists knew about the roads for a long time, but only with the advent of aerial photography were they able to trace their extent, which is considerable.

How considerable is only now being documented through the assistance of such space-age techniques as remote sensing and analysis. Avid research in 1979 nearly doubled the known lengths and numbers of the roads that connect as many as forty population centers throughout the San Juan Basin. They also lead to local resource areas where trees were plentiful (it is now assumed that tens of thousands of ponderosa pines were hauled over the roadways from mountain forests as much as thirty miles away); to good farming locations; to chert deposits; and to deposits of trachyte, used for pottery temper. The evidence is mounting that Chaco was an essential part of a highly interactive society of people in the San Juan Drainage Basin who traveled, communicated, and transported food and materials between widely separated points.[82]

The main roads were bordered with curbs of either masonry or earth, and some were as wide as 30 feet (9 m). Spur roads 10 feet (3 m) wide branched off from the main roads in all directions. Topsoil was removed, and road bases consisted of either packed earth or bedrock. When natural barriers were encountered, ravines were filled with rocks to make them passable in wet weather, and cuts were made through hills. Retaining walls were erected to make roads level, masonry stairways and ramps assisted movement over elevated places, and wide stairways were cut into cliff faces to make ascent easier.

Architectural details, Pueblo Bonito. House construction. From Judd, 1964.

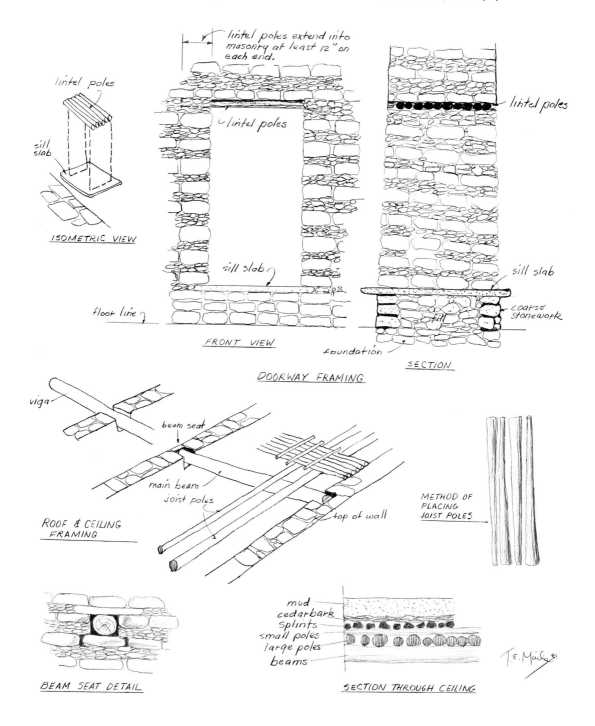

The ruins of numerous small buildings still stand like sentries at measured intervals along the roadways, suggesting they may have served as way stations.

Unquestionably, construction of the road system required an enormous labor force, and it had to be built for a good reason. Yet no one knows what that reason is. Chacoans had neither wheeled vehicles nor beasts of burden requiring roadways. Nor is there any evidence that they organized defense

Architectural details, Pueblo Bonito. Types of wall built by the Old Bonitians and the Late Bonitians. From Judd, 1964.

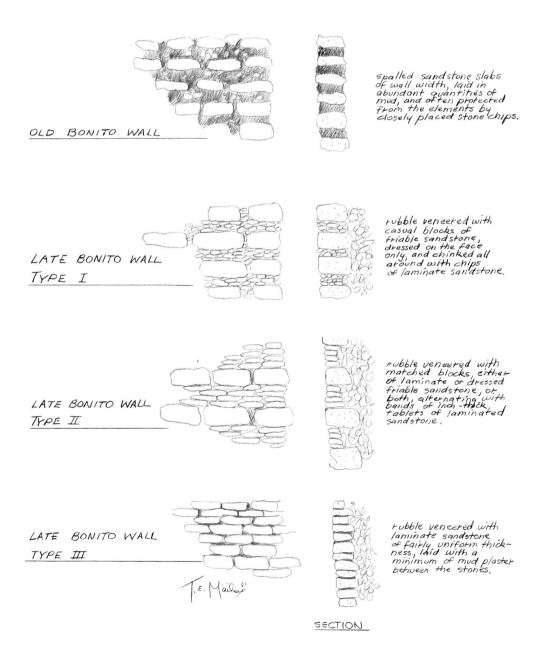

OLD BONITO WALL

spalled sandstone slabs of wall width, laid in abundant quantities of mud, and often protected from the elements by closely placed stone chips.

LATE BONITO WALL
TYPE I

rubble veneered with casual blocks of friable sandstone, dressed on the face only, and chinked all around with chips of laminate sandstone.

LATE BONITO WALL
TYPE II

rubble veneered with matched blocks, either of laminate or dressed friable sandstone, or both, alternating with bands of inch-thick tablets of laminated sandstone.

LATE BONITO WALL
TYPE III

rubble veneered with laminate sandstone of fairly uniform thickness, laid with a minimum of mud plaster between the stones.

T.E. Mails

SECTION

forces needing roadways to move swiftly from one village to another. The rapid transportation of trade goods is a possibility. Ease of communication between towns is another likelihood. Douglas and Barbara Anderson pose the interesting possibility that the roads within the canyon proper were used for ceremonial processions. I assume they mean the sort of ritual parades held by some Mesoamerican cultures on broad roadways built just for that purpose. This much is known now: hundreds of miles of roads extended north and toward the Salmon and Aztec ruins near the San Juan River, and also toward Mesa Verde. Other routes went south and west to connect Chaco Canyon with outlying villages associated with the Chaco culture. Roads toward the east probably reached Pueblo Pintado, the easternmost village of the Chacoans, which was situated on the divide between the San Juan and Rio Grande drainages.[83]

During their florescence, the Chacoans completed another engineering project that illustrates their high degree of capability and community cooperation: a water control system. The idea no doubt came to them sometime during the Old Bonito period, and the project was probably started then. But it was the Chacoans of later years who developed the system into its truly effective form.

Chaco farmers did flood farming and dry farming. They had no year-round streams for the kind of canal irrigation that was practiced by the Hohokam. The problem at Chaco was always that of capturing seasonal precipitation, storing it, and then making use of it as needed. Their solution was a good one. On both the north and south sides of the canyon they erected dams and diversion walls designed to catch the runoff from every gulch and gorge. Then they built dikes to divert the runoff into ditches that ended in gates, through which the water was distributed to the fields and on to small reservoirs near town sites. The water system did not service every part of the canyon, but it didn't need to. The areas where alluviation was good and natural moisture collected were already acceptable for dry farming like that still practiced by Hopi farmers in similar country today.

Alfred Vincent Kidder wisely points out that those who insist the climate of Chaco Canyon at its time of occupation must have been more favorable than it is today overlook an important fact: they "have failed to realize the ability of the Pueblo Indian to support himself quite comfortably in the face of conditions of dryness which would stagger the white farmer."[84] He goes on to say that such investigators have not taken into consideration how little water the Pueblo Indian actually uses, how carefully he conserves his supply, or how little he thinks of climbing up and down steep, precipitous paths to get it. Furthermore, the modern Pueblo farmer often lives miles from his cornfields, and in a like manner scores of ancient villages were located considerable distances from the nearest land that could ever have been cultivated, even under the most favorable climatic conditions. In addition, it is often forgotten that while the modern white farmer produces food for an enormous population, the Pueblo farmer produces only for himself and his family, hence no real comparison can be fairly drawn about the amounts of land needed for support.[85]

Judd mentions a serious complication caused by continual irrigation: sterility in the cultivated fields. Irrigation water of a certain type in the Southwest tends to eliminate or wash out helpful chemicals from the soil, leaving behind too high a percentage of sodium bicarbonate. The latter has a hardening effect upon the earth amd makes it impermeable to water. While excavating at Chaco, he repeatedly noticed that shallow puddles of rainwater sometimes stood for days. Testing showed alkali contamination to depths of ten feet, and if this factor became widespread in Chacoan times it would have destroyed the productivity of the soil and made farming as hopeless as it would be in the canyon today.[86]

HOSTA BUTTE PHASE
ca. A.D. 919–1100

The Chacoans of the Hosta Butte Phase were contemporaneous with the Chacoans of the Bonito Phase and lived in close proximity to them. Most aspects of their material culture were alike, except that the Hosta Butte group seemed in many ways like poor relations, and their villages were clearly inferior. Buildings were seldom more than one story high and were crudely constructed. The people built clan kivas but no Great Kivas, although it is possible they shared in the erection and use of the isolated Great Kiva at Casa Rinconada.

The difference between the Anasazi of the Hosta Butte and Bonito phases adds one more mystery for archaeologists to solve. Some have suggested that, because fewer luxury items have been found in the Hosta Butte area, artisans and craftsmen who lived at Hosta Butte may have produced items for those who lived in the more opulent Bonito villages. But the probable reason for the difference is that Anasazi settlers came from different areas and had variant ideas about life-styles. Differences in dialect could also be a factor. Such distinctions caused several other Indian nations to live in separate areas, even though they shared a common heritage and sometimes cooperated in mutually beneficial ventures. We can nevertheless assume with some confidence that the groups at Chaco shared in the construction and use of the roadways and water control systems, as well as in the ceremonials of the Great Kivas.

McELMO PHASE
A.D. 1030–1050

The McElmo Phase at Chaco is the product of yet another new people who migrated from the San Juan area in the north, joined the Bonito and Hosta Butte people living there, were welcomed, and built sizable villages of their own. These were well-planned, multistoried apartment buildings in self-contained rectangles that lacked plazas. The settlers built clan-sized kivas, all of which were enclosed within the rectangular building and were surrounded by dwelling rooms. They constructed no Great Kivas.

McElmo masonry was cored, but the walls were thinner than those of Bonito. Wall stones were also larger, less angular, and more uniform in size. They were taken from the debris of nearby sandstone talus slopes and required considerable shaping, so that the finish lacked the quality common to Bonito buildings.

The McElmo Phase at Chaco Canyon is represented by the villages of Kin Kletso and Casa Chiquita; by a part of Tsin Kletzin on the south mesa; by New Alto, known also as Pueblo Alto, on the north mesa; and possibly by a triple-walled building at Pueblo del Arroyo.

ABANDONMENT

By A.D. 1110 at the latest the Anasazi at Chaco Canyon surely knew that their time of prosperity and tenure was rapidly coming to an end. Problems had mounted and multiplied to where the people could no longer cope. It was not their nature to give up easily, and who could doubt they had come to love their canyon homes? One can easily imagine their last heroic efforts to continue on together. Judd even thinks that some groups moved a short distance upcanyon and built again to escape the ferocious arroyo cutting. From datable timbers gathered at their villages, the Old Bonitians and Kin Kletso were apparently the last survivors, with final cutting dates of A.D. 1126 and 1178 respectively. Whatever the actual truth may be, one by one small groups faced the facts and began to migrate. Sometime before the twelfth century came to its end, Chaco Canyon was empty. The last of the Chacoans were on their way to a new home and life.

The most popular theories advanced for abandonment are prolonged drought, pestilence, and constant pressure from nomadic invaders. None of these is easy to support. The Chaco residents were not strangers to droughts: they survived several. Besides, the great drought that gave the Anasazi in the north awesome problems from A.D. 1276 to 1299 came long after Chaco was a ghost canyon. Mischa Titiev surveys the evidence regarding all Anasazi and reports there is not a single instance on record of their having abandoned a pueblo on account of epidemic diseases.[87] And while raiding peoples were moving into the Chaco area, there is scant evidence in the ruins either of deaths due to warfare or of plundered villages. Pueblo Bonito and McElmo structures were closed off to outsiders in a manner indicating that those Anasazi thought they had someone to fear. But the contemporary Hosta Butte villages took no defensive measures whatsoever. Moreover, it would seem that the invading nomads could hardly have been more powerful than the entrenched villagers, and in support of this suggestion, the abandonment was not hurried. No one left Chaco Canyon in a panic.

Judd suggests that the anxieties of defensive warfare may well have hastened the actual abandonment of Chaco Canyon.[88] Sedentary and peaceful folk such as the Bonitians were always fair game for nomadic hunters, who killed the men, stole women and children, plundered the fields, and even pillaged the burial chambers. In one example, of seventy-one bodies found buried in four rooms at Pueblo Bonito, most had been wantonly disturbed at a time shortly before, or shortly after, the village was deserted by its builders. Skulls had been tossed aside; arms and legs had been torn from bodies; bones had been scattered in hopeless confusion; mortuary offerings had been overturned and trampled—all in the search for turquoise and other rich ornaments the Bonitians buried with the dead.[89] One defender had been shot with an arrow.[90] Even the fact that these Bonitians had to be interred within the rooms rather than in the accustomed burial ground is evidence that the people were living under adverse conditions.

The better reason for the exodus (excepting perhaps an important one discussed again in the next chapter) is that the Chacoans simply lost their endless battle with a hostile environment, aided and abetted by their own acts. The time inevitably came when the last mature tree was cut down for building and fuel. Then even the young timber had to be used, and its demise completed the gradual recession of the southwestern pine forest that had been taking place for centuries. It is said that more than five thousand trees were used for buildings in Chetro Ketl alone; without replenishment, nature couldn't keep up. Such heavy depletions also ensured that soil erosion became far worse than it otherwise would have been. In this wise at least, the Chacoans of A.D. 838–1178 were no better respecters of nature than we are today, and they paid a heavy price.

Some archaeologists believe that when the Anasazi first arrived at Chaco Canyon, it was blessed with rich soil. Abundant vegetation, they say, caused the precipitation from spring rains and summer showers to spread out evenly over the flat valley floor, depositing, year by year, layers of enriching silt and penetrating the earth from top to bottom.[91] Now, however, the steady consumption of trees and brush led to the formation of deep water-cut arroyos. The destructive action of such channels was continuous and enormous. Not only did the churning waters rapidly cut away the rest of the adobe earth of the valley bottoms; the ever-deepening channels carried off the flood waters before they could be captured in the water control system, and the plane of underground seepage was lowered to such an extent that the remaining land on either side of the bottoms became permanently parched.[92]

From this time on, every drop of rain found its way into a funnel-like arroyo, and every runoff quickly became a raging torrent, undermining, cutting down, and carrying away more and more of the cultivable soil of the valley. By A.D. 1100 the Chacoans were expending every ounce of energy in a vain effort to keep up. To give but one example of the geophysical changes that took place in Chaco Canyon over the centuries, when Judd excavated the two pithouses mentioned earlier, he discovered that the floor level of the 1922 pithouse was 12 feet 2 inches (3.7 m) below the valley surface, and that 6 feet (1.8 m) of silt had been deposited above the original roof level following its abandonment.[93] Compounding the alluvial problem, Anasazi dislodged from other areas began to migrate to the canyon. This expanded the labor force but at the same time increased the needs and further depleted the resources. Judd's expedition in the 1920s had to go twenty miles to obtain firewood.[94]

It seems there was no single clear-cut and final blow that demanded a sudden departure. More likely, it was the sum total of the problems that did the Chacoans in. They gathered up what was most precious to them and left.

It is believed that some of the migrating groups of northern Anasazi moved into Chaco and reoccupied some of the buildings on a sporadic basis after A.D. 1200. But they, too, found the problems insurmountable and in a short while moved on.

Where the Chacoans migrated to remains a prime question. Some archaeologists think that for about two hundred years most of the Chaco Anasazi moved aimlessly about, stopping now and then to build homes and raise crops, and searching constantly for new and permanent places to stay. They lived, possibly as individual clans, in small groups, and they experimented with various ways of dealing with the challenging environment. Perhaps they returned to the simpler life-style of their Basketmaker ancestors. Others suspect, on more plausible archaeological evidence, that some Chacoans went directly to the Rio Grande area to join Anasazi relatives already settled there, while others joined Anasazi at Acoma or Zuñi, both of which had been occupied by A.D. 1100.

Since he knows of no Classic Chaco site dating later than A.D. 1130, Harold S. Gladwin believes the Chaco culture died out at Chaco Canyon; that the once opulent lifeway was not transferable. But Judd feels the evidence suggests a dissociation and dispersal. While the Old Bonitians tarried for a time, the Late Bonitians moved on, presumably seeking farmlands where erosion was not a problem. The Chaco-like qualities in the ruins to the north suggest to Judd a common heritage rather than Chaco influence. Toward the south and east, however, the opposite is true. A Chaco influence that predominated from Pueblo I to Pueblo III times is "undeniable" at Whitewater, Arizona, and late contacts from Chaco are evident also at the Village of the Great Kivas on the present Zuñi Reservation. The pre-Zuñi kivas excavated near Hawikuh by Frederick W. Hodge are "unquestionably" of late Chaco origin. The older portion of Zuñi has always seemed to Judd to be a reflection of Pueblo Bonito. "If," he says, "I were to seek the lost trail of the Late Bonitians I should turn first of all to the Zuñi Mountains and their surroundings."[95]

This much is certain, the ancestors of the Chacoans are present among the Pueblos today, and something of the culture of Chaco Canyon continues on.

For two long centuries after the final Chacoan clan left the canyon, the abandoned villages had only the birds, the animals, the rodents, and the forces of nature for company. It is known that the earliest Athapaskans were moving into the Southwest at the time, and they might have made occasional use of the ruins. One segment of the Athapaskans, the Navajo, built a few homes in the Chaco area in the 1600s, and by A.D. 1700 they were firmly established in and around the canyon. When the Pueblo Indians had no recourse but to flee after their revolt against the Spanish was crushed in A.D. 1692, some of them returned to the Chaco vicinity and shared it for a time with the Navajo. By the late 1700s the two groups had either separated or merged, no one knows which. Only Navajo, or Navajo and cross-descendants, live in Chaco Canyon today.

AZTEC

The clearest and most interesting example of the Chaco type of culture outside the limits of Chaco Canyon is the great Aztec Ruin. Built between A.D. 1100 and 1121, its site is approximately sixty-five miles north of Chaco on the lower waters of the Animas River, a northern tributary of the San Juan, in New Mexico.

Aztec Ruin, New Mexico. View from within the court looking north at the center of the north wing where, after excavation, the walls were the highest. The Great Kiva, since restored, is shown in the foreground. From Earl H. Morris photograph.

Excavation of the site was carried out by Earl Halstead Morris during the years 1916–23. When he was done, it was clear that the general ground plan of Aztec, its manner of fortification, the room sizes, large doorways, high ceilings, and masonry work typified exactly those of the Chaco Canyon culture. The low profile on the southern side permitted the midwinter sun to penetrate the plaza and reach the higher terraced rooms in the rear. Even the structural weaknesses duplicated those of Chaco. Joints were overlapped, and corners were not bonded.[96] Morris, greatly intrigued, began to wonder whether he was onto an important discovery in the area of cultural relationships.

Aztec was an enormous rectangular apartment village, with its own kivas. There were at least five hundred large rooms, capable, if the entire facility was ever in use at once, of housing eight hundred or more people. Each terraced row of dwellings received fresh air and sunshine, and interior ventilator shafts carried air to the lower rooms, used for storage. There were no exterior openings in the outermost wall. Bearing walls were of coursed masonry, cored and tapered, although a few interior partitions were of jacal. Doorways in ground-floor rooms were either rectangular or T-shaped and opened onto the roofs or the plaza. Hatchways, sometimes with runged ladders, led to the upper stories. Ceilings were unusually high for Anasazi buildings, ranging from 9 to 11 feet (2.7–3.3 m). Two or more pine or juniper beams spanned the short dimension of a room. These were topped with peeled cottonwood branches placed at right angles to the beams and either evenly spaced or grouped in clusters. Mats made of willow sticks lashed together with yucca strips covered the branches. Then came a dense layer of cedar shakes, and over that a layer of clay, the whole forming either a finished roof or the floor of a room above.

Aztec sandstone was tough and cross-bedded, and consequently masonry quality did not equal that of Chaco Canyon. Interior walls were often plastered, and murals or geometric figures were painted on some of them with a pale red paint made from ground red sandstone. One decorated room at Aztec had a flagstone floor and white handprints on the ceiling beams, indicating possible use as a shrine or ceremonial chamber.[97]

Clan kivas were first exposed early in 1920. In the southwest corner of the plaza two clan-sized kivas, one built on top of the other, were encountered 8 feet (2.4 m) below the plaza level. In the lower kiva, sealed over by the floor of the one above it, Morris found a large quantity of sherds and restorable vessels of unmixed Chaco types, plus two special effigy finds: a seated hunch-backed figure similar to one recovered by George Pepper at Pueblo Bonito, and a sad-eyed spotted deer.[98] A mystery began to present itself, for it appeared to Morris that Aztec had had different tenants at different times. It was a puzzle that demanded pursuit.

Moving his workmen to the northeast portion of the plaza, Morris unearthed beneath 4 feet (1.2 m) of fill yet another kiva. It was plastered, had no banquette or pilasters, but contained the richest Chaco ceramic treasure he had yet come across, including an effigy of a man with genitals and a line indicating a sandal tie on one of his feet.[99]

Dwellings offered further evidence of occupation by two different groups of peoples. Beneath the floors of some of the ground-level rooms it was discovered that Chaco refuse, 5 feet (1.5 m) deep in places, had been floored over and sealed off. Above the floors the refuse was strictly Mesa Verde in nature. At this point the identity of the mysterious occupants became known: the first and original residents were related to Chaco Canyon; the second and later residents were related to Mesa Verde. Both were Anasazi. But the question of why and when the two were at Aztec in successive occupations was yet to be answered. Burials were excellent sources of information, and fortunately Aztec contained more than most sites.

Most of the burials were of either aged or young people, proving that if people could once get past the first hazards of life, they could look forward to achieving a fair age. One hundred and eighty-six burials were found, by no means representing all who had died in the Aztec area during its centuries of occupancy.[100] But, as was the case at so many other Anasazi locations, the main burial grounds escaped Morris and have not been found to this day. To my mind, this hidden burial practice of the Anasazi, as it is commonly held to be, is of great moment, since it indicates a unity of thought and action that pervaded the Anasazi culture and perhaps extended to *most* things, even though the Indian groups lived miles apart.

Most of the bodies found in the Aztec village building itself were flexed and laid out in simple fashion on the floors of abandoned rooms that thereafter served as trash bins or turkey pens. In time, accumulated waste covered the bodies, and pits were scooped in the floors or trash to hold additional corpses. Disturbance by rodents was a common occurrence.

Of particular interest was the skeleton of a man dubbed "the warrior." He was about six feet two inches tall, an extraordinary height for the time, and obviously a man of great importance. There was an ornament on his chest and a bead bracelet on one arm. He was wrapped in a turkey-feather cloth and a rush matting. On top of these was a huge basketry shield, three feet in diameter. It had a selenite-speckled rim outlined by a dark red band, and the center was blue-green. Only two others like it had been found, one at Canyon de Chelly and the other at Mesa Verde. On top of the shield were seven curved sticks, of the throwing or fending type. Other artifacts included a coiled basket, several bowls, a Mesa Verde kiva jar broken over the man's skull, bone awls, an antler, a sandstone rasping instrument, a chipped knife blade, several flakes, and two axlike weapons with heads and handles.[101]

The remains of a seventeen-year-old girl, whose pelvic girdle and left forearm had been badly damaged in an accident, revealed that splinting was being practiced in her time. A healer had attempted to set the bones and had applied six shaped splints to the arm. But the girl died from internal injuries before knitting began.[102]

The possibility that witchcraft was practiced was raised when the skeleton of a woman was found with a wooden stake driven through her pelvis and into the ground. Two other unusual finds included the skeleton of a prisoner

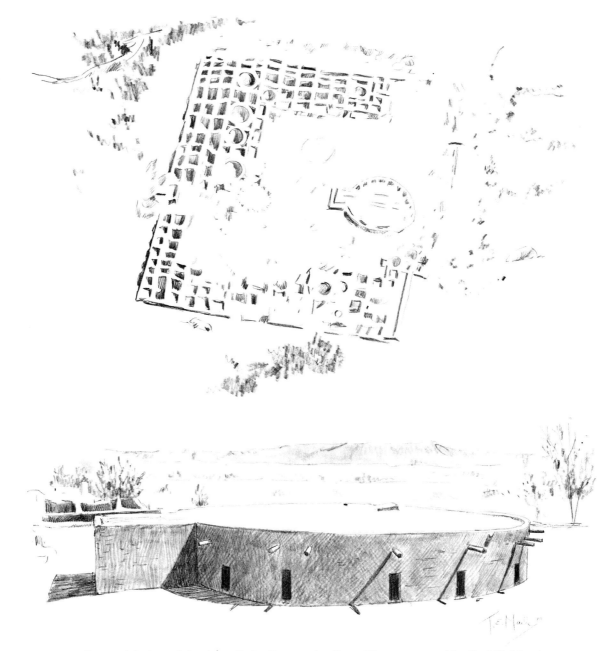

Top, aerial view of the Aztec Ruin. *Bottom*, the Great Kiva as restored by Earl H. Morris.

who had been sealed up in a room, and the residue of what appeared to be two intentional cremations—a rare occurrence in the San Juan region.

Twenty-eight clan-sized kivas were found at Aztec. Of these, twelve had shallow basal recesses, from eight to ten pilasters, and subfloor ventilators. Two had deeply recessed south banquettes that associated them with Mesa Verde influence.[103]

Late in 1920, Morris began a long-cherished project, the excavation of what he knew to be the Great Kiva of Aztec. Anxious as he was to know what its details were really like, he had also an ulterior motive. Neil M. Judd was about to dig out the Great Kiva at Pueblo Bonito, and Morris wanted to beat him to it. So he excused his covetousness by claiming the Aztec kiva would provide a type example. Morris succeeded. By the end of March 1921 the digging at Aztec was done, and Judd did not finish his Chaco task until June of the same year. When comparisons of the two Great Kivas were made, a few variations in details were noted, but in all essentials they were identical. It was another and conclusive testimony to the ties between Chaco Canyon and Aztec.

Once he could see the entire structure at a glance, Morris likened his Aztec kiva to a wheel. The kiva chamber proper formed the large hub, and the arc-shaped surface rooms encircling it were located between dividing walls that radiated out from the center like spokes. The kiva diameter at floor level was 41 feet (12.5 m), and its floor line was 7 feet 6 inches (2.3 m) below grade level. Two masonry benches encircled the ceremonial chamber. On the north and south sides were narrow stairways, the southern one leading to a passageway to the outside, and the northern one to a square alcove at surface level with such unique features that Morris attributed special ceremonial significance to the space. It had a built-in altar, a reredos of which only the stubs of three charred posts remained, and a sipapu.

Within the kiva chamber proper were the remains of four great pillars, each composed of alternating layers of masonry and mud-embedded, peeled cedar poles. The highest pillar found was only 3 feet 6 inches (1.07 m) high, but from the amount of fallen materials Morris estimated the original height of the pillars at 16 feet (4.9 m). There were two stone floor vaults, each roughly 8 feet (2.4 m) long, 3 feet (90 cm) wide, and 3 feet (90 cm) deep. With a cover, these could have served as large drums upon which participants danced, or they might have been boxes from which actors emerged as if by magic at specified points in a ceremony. (The latter was a ritual technique employed by the ceremonial actors of the Northwest Coast tribes.) A square masonry box containing a recess was placed midway between the two southern pillars to serve as a firepit. Shallow holes for pots and other paraphernalia were scattered at random over the entire floor surface of the kiva.

The slightly tapered kiva interior walls were cored with river cobbles and veneered on both sides with thin sandstone blocks, after the manner of the Bonito Phase walls of Chaco Canyon. Walls of the twelve surrounding chambers consisted of thin coursed sandstone set on a foundation of cobblestones. All the wall surfaces had been plastered over several times, the last coat having a base border of red 3 feet (90 cm) high and the natural white extending from there to the ceiling. Morris found evidence of at least nine renewals of the smooth adobe floor.

Because there were no pilasters spaced around the kiva walls, Morris assumed that the roof had not been cribbed or otherwise vaulted, but flat, with a central structural core of four main posts and beams like that of the ancient pithouse. From this core smaller but still large beams had spread out radially, spanning the gap from the main beams to the surrounding walls. These secondary beams were bridged over with still smaller poles, assembled in sets of three, spaced apart, and set at right angles to the radial beams. On top of this triple beam assemblage was laid a tight layer of split sticks and branches; a thick coat of earth topped off the whole. The ceiling of the kiva proper and that of the band of surrounding rooms was at the same level, so that the entire 1,900-square-foot roof was flat, and the finished building sat like a hatbox in the south courtyard.[104] A hatchway was made in the center of the roof for ventilation.

Taken as a whole, the Great Kiva at Aztec was another clear tie to the Anasazi at Chaco Canyon, except that Morris found some evidence that it had been remodeled by the Mesa Verde people who came late to the site in or around A.D. 1225.

In 1934, to his utter delight, Morris was asked by the director of the Office of National Parks to restore as a tourist attraction the Great Kiva at Aztec. He first made a hurried trip to Chaco Canyon to check construction details of the Great Kiva at Chetro Ketl. It had been fully excavated and examined by Edgar Hewett, and it would serve as an excellent model. Among other things he discovered there were great sandstone disks, bedded on coal shale and serving as foundations for Chetro Ketl's main pillars. This led Morris to sink pits below the Aztec pillars to see whether such slabs existed there.[105] They did, and to his astonishment, duplicating Hewett's experience at Chaco, he found that the Great Kiva of Aztec had been built on top of an earlier kiva.[106]

Obtaining extra stones from a ruin in the La Plata area, Colorado, and beams from the Aztec area, Morris and his crew went to work swiftly. At last the Great Kiva was restored, and tourists found its massive grandeur an unforgettable experience. Archaeologists, however, were somewhat critical of the flat roof and the building's newness. Some felt it was wrong to rebuild any ruin. Nevertheless, Morris believed he had done as faithful a job of reconstruction as was possible, and he was extremely proud of it. Time and the thousands of grateful people who visit the Aztec Ruin yearly seem to bear him out.

By 1923 there was not the slightest doubt in Morris's mind that people bearing the Chaco tradition had settled centuries before on the fertile banks of the Animas River and constructed a village building as fine as any in Chaco Canyon. They worshipped in the same type of clan and Great Kivas, and Aztec shared the same craft traditions and channels of trade, "even like Pueblo Bonito acquiring goods from central Mexico."[107]

Presumably, Morris thought, Aztec and the Chaco towns of the Bonito Phase were roughly contemporaneous. Aztec might even represent a colony of the Golden Age Bonitians rather than a generalized sharing of culture traits. In either event, the inhabitants remained happily at Aztec for a long time. Later, dendrochronology proved that Morris was right about a Chaco-Aztec time relationship. The dates established by Dr. Andrew E. Douglass for Pueblo Bonito were A.D. 919–1130, and for Aztec's masonry village building, A.D. 1110–21.[108]

Judd's opinion was that Aztec was not a Chaco colony but, on the contrary, built by a division of the same northern San Juan people that became the Late Bonitians. Thus the tie between Chaco and Aztec was one of heritage rather than that one was the offshoot of the other.

Of course, early Anasazi lived in the Aztec area for centuries before the main part of the Aztec village building was erected in Pueblo III times. That great venture was but the culmination of a long period of growth and development. Moreover, the compound was allowed to decay at least once, perhaps twice, with subsequent repair and reoccupation. The first Chacoan builders established the primary form, except for the one-story south-wing rooms, and then lived in it for generations. This was demonstrated by the three-to-eight-foot-deep trash piles, and also by the three-foot-deep layer of silt that had raised the land level along the north exterior wall. Then the building was abandoned. Left to the elements, the upper parts of it collapsed, filling many of the lower rooms with rubble. Around A.D. 1225, repair work was done by migrants from Mesa Verde, and the building's walls were extended into the courtyard. It was reoccupied, and the population continued to increase for a while. Finally, ongoing pressure from nomadic invaders caused the late migrants also to give up Aztec Pueblo and move away. Someone, either the last of them or the enemy, set fire to the great building and ended its usefulness forever.[109]

WHITEWATER/ALLANTOWN DISTRICT

Space will not permit a thorough examination of all the sites that came within the sphere of distinct Chaco influence, but summary information about some of the other and more important locations is needed to give an adequate picture of the greater Chaco range, which extended more than one hundred miles to the south, and one hundred miles north and northeast. Aztec has already been mentioned. To the south were Whitewater/Allantown, Kiatuthlanna, and the Village of the Great Kivas. To the northeast was the Piedra District.[110]

Chaco cultural influence spread southwest as well as north. Frank H. H. Roberts did considerable archaeological work at the Whitewater District site, located three and a half miles south of Allantown, Arizona, fourteen miles northwest of Zuñi, and ninety-eight miles southwest of Chaco. What he found convinced him that the numerous villages of the Whitewater residents were culturally and physically typical of the Anasazi province, and represented one variant of the pattern stemming from the Chaco Canyon area.[111] On the basis of data collected, it seemed "quite clear" that the Whitewater ruins represented a peripheral lag in the Chaco pattern and that the flow of influence was from Chaco toward Whitewater and not the reverse. The flow was slow at first, but by the time the Great Pueblo stage was reached the lag was barely discernible.[112] The ruins, Roberts declared, are on the very periphery of the westward expansion of the Chaco culture and at the eastern edge of influence from Little Colorado Region centers farther west.

Structures erected at Whitewater spanned the years from A.D. 814 to 1014, and during that time the residents progressed through three architectural stages: from Basketmaker III to pithouse and unit types to large masonry structures. However, the traces of Basketmaker III sites were so disturbed and mixed by the activities of subsequent occupants that little could be learned about them.[113] Most of the digging was done in Pueblo I and II remains, and a

Whitewater. *a*, three bone gaming pieces. *b*, projectile points. *c*, plan of surface building with pit oven. *d*, section through pit oven. *e*, mano and metate. *f*, bone needle. *g*, plan of a group of Whitewater pithouse and surface remains. From Roberts, 1939 and 1940.

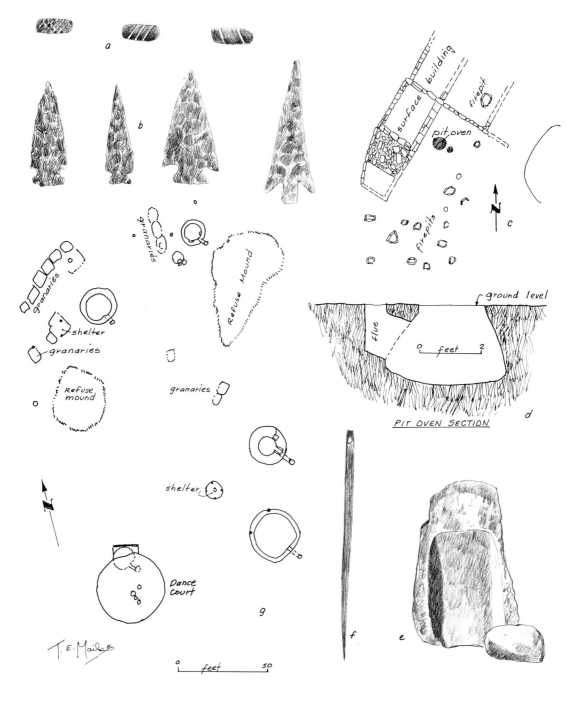

fairly complete picture of the nature and trends of these periods was gained from twenty pit structures, with their accompanying granaries and surface shelters, and from three unit-type ruins with associated ceremonial chambers.

Beginning about A.D. 814, single-roomed pit dwellings comparable in shape and style to those of other Anasazi locations were built. A few local structural differences of a minor nature revealed the personal whims of the

Whitewater. *Top left*, plan and section of pithouse. *Top right*, pithouse view showing stone collar used for aperture of ventilator shaft. *Center right*, stone axhead. *Bottom*, postulated reconstruction of framing method for pithouse shown top left. From Roberts, 1939.

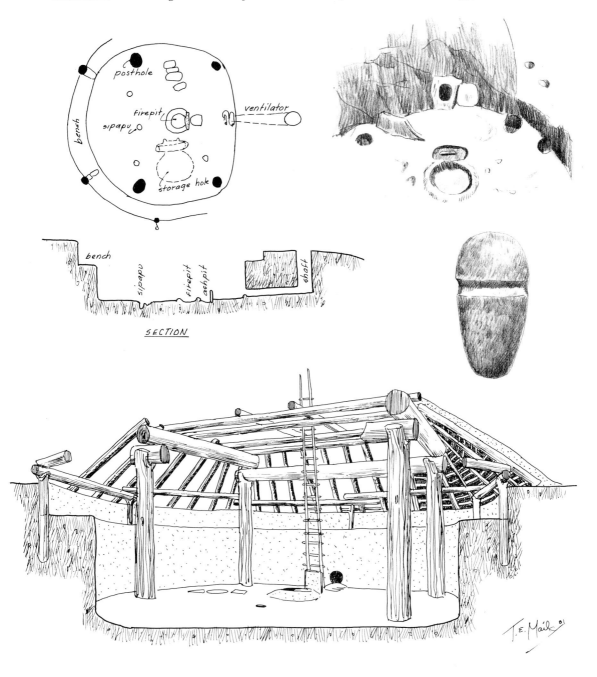

owners. But other features foreshadowed significant developments to come. Three of the dwellings were encircled by a bench and probably represented the final stage of the pithouse. Most authorities believe the bench did not occur until shortly before the transition step, or protokiva, that itself culminated in the subterranean kiva. Even after the bench was introduced, pithouses with and without benches were constructed side by side. The bench was at first nothing more than an item of preference.[114]

Two of the pit structures at Whitewater contained a prototype of the pilaster and illustrated how that architectural feature might have developed in the Southwest. In one of these a pillar of mud and stone had been placed between the main support post and the wall, presumably as a brace for the post. In the second dwelling, two posts were braced. Using this idea as a catalyst, Roberts sets up a possible evolution: the earliest main posts were placed some distance from the walls. Next, the posts were placed almost against the wall. The weight of the roof caused these to shift, and led to reinforcement with blocks of stone and mud plaster. Shortly thereafter it was learned that the stone and mud pillar could itself support the roof and upper walls, and the wood posts were eliminated.[115]

In the series of Whitewater dwellings as a whole there was a change in function of the floor basin adjacent to the firepit, and it was possible for Roberts to trace this change in the one set of ruins. In what he believed were the earliest pithouses, there was a shallow floor depression where the butts of the ladder poles rested. To improve this feature and better avoid slippage of the ladder, the sides of the basin were plastered. Then stone slabs were used to line the basin, and it became a kind of box. Now the space between the ladder poles could be used as a repository for excess ashes until they could conveniently be removed from the pithouse. So valuable did this idea prove to be that the ladder ends were thereafter embedded in the ground to ensure firmness, and a separate slab-lined box was fashioned whose sole purpose was to hold ashes.

Another unique feature, and in Roberts's view the first example of such in the Southwest, was that of combining several pithouses into one larger structure.[116] Nevertheless, each unit was complete in itself, even to the point of having its own sipapu. Presumably the people were not yet ready to give up the personal dwelling features to which they had become accustomed. Roberts makes reference in this connection to an old archaeological theory that the rectangular-roomed communal buildings of the Pueblo people were an outgrowth of combining several circular houses into a single structure. But he concluded the combining of pithouses was simply the logical first step in house development peculiar to Whitewater, and that it had no direct bearing on the growth of the communal type of building in general.[117]

The step-by-step evolution of the unit-type dwelling that became the basic component of the great communal buildings of the Anasazi is amply illustrated at Whitewater by several dwelling groups. First in the series was a semisubterranean oval pit structure with sloped walls above grade, entered by a ladder placed in a small shaft connected to the main chamber by a pole-, brush-, and earth-covered trench or passageway. Oval wattle-and-daub granary pits, located west of the main chamber, appear to have been used as shelters or makeshift habitations.

The second step in the series found the passageway serving as a ventilator, with entrance to the pit dwelling made via a ladder and a hatchway in the roof. The granaries were now rectangular in form, had stone walls, and were contiguous, and some were being lived in. Outdoor firepits, pit ovens, and

Whitewater. *a,* postulated reconstruction of cribbed roofing erected over pit of structure designated by Roberts as No. 3, one side omitted to show method of laying timbers. *b,* plan and section of structure No. 3. *c,* plan and section of No. 16 house and granary assemblage. From Roberts, 1939.

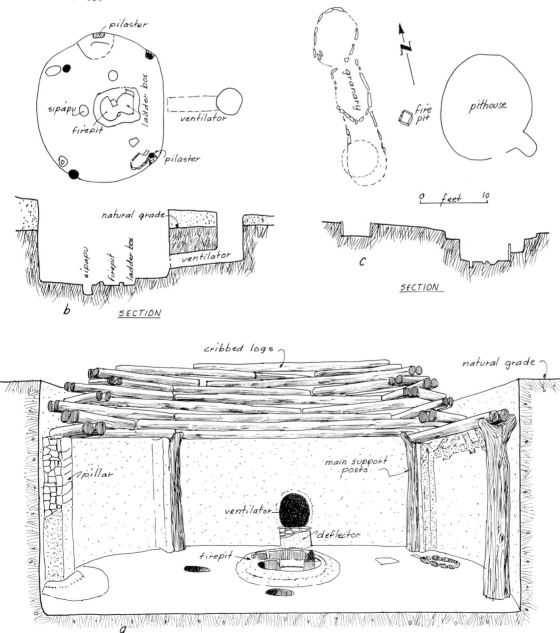

arbor-type brush shelters were associated with the granaries, and a rude kind of porch was erected in front of one of them. With each change the floor level of the granaries became shallower, until finally they were true surface structures.

Pit ovens merit special notice. The pit was underground, with its opening at grade level. It was jug-shaped and had a narrow orifice. A distinctive feature was a flue extending out from one side and turning up to ground level. A disk-shaped walkway surrounded the oven. It consisted of a layer of sand topped with a layer of adobe clay. It is possible that the ovens functioned in the same way as the *pi-gumme* (cornmeal mush) ovens of the Hopi. Victor Mindeleff explained that in the Hopi version the flue was used to poke and arrange the fire. He also suggested that such pits were probably the model upon which the domelike Spanish ovens found today in all the pueblos were based. The main difference is that one is above the ground, while the earlier one is below it. The Hopi custom was to light large fires in the pits and heat the walls to the desired temperature. The coals and ashes were then removed, the material to be cooked was placed inside, and the opening was sealed.[118]

The third group in the unit-type series was the first unit in the Pueblo I village. The pit structure was still traditional in its details and used the four-main-pole and beam system. But the granaries had become a contiguous row of rooms, and Roberts found that some of them contained marked evidence of habitation. A portico was provided at one end of the row, and there was a small court with a firepit at the other end. Some pit structures became proto-kivas, and were increasingly used for (clan?) ceremonial purposes.

The fourth in the series was the second unit in the Pueblo I or II village. The subterranean pit structure was now a full-blown kiva with a cribbed roof resting on a bench, and the rectangular granaries had all become dwelling spaces.

The fifth and last in the development series was the third unit, a fully mature Pueblo II form with its surface dwelling, court, and subterranean ceremonial chamber.[119] After the adoption of the large communal houses, the kiva sometimes became a circular surface unit enclosed by a second set of walls, square or rectangular in form, to give it a subterranean essence.

Another unique feature of the main site at Whitewater was a large, shallow, adobe-paved, and slab-bordered circle that, for want of a better name, was called a "dance court." The court was 37 feet (11.3 m) in diameter. Near the center were three depressions placed in a row. What its real purpose was is not known. Roberts found no evidence of a roof, and he speculated that the court had served as a temporary place for community rites while the Great Kiva, 38 feet 6 inches (11.7 m) in diameter, at the north end of the nearby Great Pueblo ruins was being built. No closely comparable court had been found in the Anasazi province at the time of Roberts's investigations, and he tended to reject the suggestions of others that the dance court represented a variation of the ball courts of the Hohokam.[120]

The Pueblo III ruins, which Roberts describes as the Great Pueblo Period at Whitewater, were not excavated. But from what he could see of the remains, the community consisted of two large buildings and a Great Kiva 62 feet 10 inches (19.15 m) in diameter placed in such a way as to form a partially enclosed court, in which two rectangular towers were located. Cored and well-dressed masonry, potsherds, and other visible evidences reinforced his view that Whitewater had certain affinities with Chaco Canyon and was "roughly contemporaneous" with a Great Pueblo village on the Zuñi Reservation. The double-tiered and two-storied smaller building appears to have been erected first. The terraced larger building might have been built by groups of Anasazi withdrawing from scattered units in the district. In Roberts's opinion, all indications are that the Great Pueblo ruins fall within the twelfth century, and that while their main features point to a northern and eastern influence, there are traces of other influences, such as the sipapu, reaching them from the Little Colorado region to the west and from the south and southeast.[121]

Whitewater. *Top left,* kiva interior. *Top right,* stone ornament, clay pipe, bone whistle. *Bottom,* plans of two Whitewater subterranean kivas. From Roberts, 1939 and 1940.

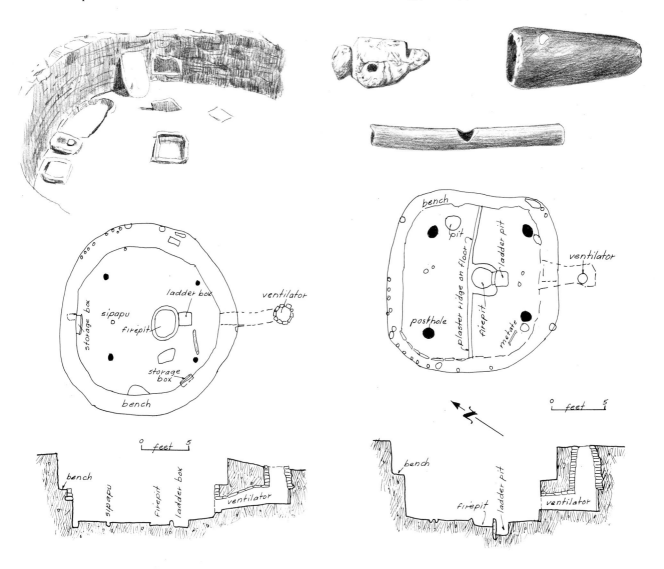

Most of the Whitewater burials were made in the refuse mounds, although some were in rooms or other occupied areas. No traces of cremation appeared in any of the diggings. Usually bodies were flexed; often they were accompanied by funerary offerings such as dogs and turkeys. Some of the skulls in the Whitewater series were undeformed, but the majority showed artificial lambdoid flattening. Of particular significance is Dr. T. D. Stewart's comment: "This type of deformation cannot be explained solely by the weight of the head upon a hard cradle board." He discounts the popular idea that cranial deformation among the Pueblos was entirely accidental in that it was due solely to the weight of the head upon the cradleboard. Burials at Whitewater and other places in New Mexico and Colorado demonstrate that Pueblo deformation was more than accidental.[122] The reason I stress this is that, as one looks at deformed skulls, it is apparent that the flattened area is at much too sharp an angle to have resulted from pressure on an infant's head from the flat cradleboard. Despite the fact that only flat boards have been found, it must be inferred that something was added to the board or otherwise applied against the head.

The bodies of fowl and animals also received regular burials, even to the point of accompaniment by offerings common to their kind. For example, placed with turkeys and dogs were such things as miniature vessels, corn, animal bones, and potsherds fashioned to form shallow dishes.[123] Esoteric religious views are certainly indicated by such practices. Roberts wonders whether the Whitewater Anasazi had somewhat similar conceptions to those of the Aztecs, who believed it was necessary to have the soul of a dog guide the soul of a person on the journey into the world beyond the grave.[124] Perhaps the turkey, so valuable to the Anasazi for clothing and for prayer feathers, served a like purpose.

Subsistence at Whitewater consisted of corn, beans, wild grass seeds, piñon nuts, rabbit, deer, and antelope. Indications were that turkeys were kept for their feathers and not for food. In general, the Whitewater residents followed the same economic pattern as the rest of the Anasazi. They were mainly agriculturists who supplemented their diet by as much hunting as the country afforded.[125] Population for the community was probably 250 at the point of maximum growth.

It has been mentioned that, while possible causes of abandonment in other Anasazi areas include enemy attacks, most areas lacked specific evidence of this. Whitewater was an exception. The remains of several individuals revealed that they met violent ends. Some had their skulls crushed, others had body bones fractured as if by clubs, and projectile points were found in association with skeletons in positions indicating they had been in the bodies when these were interred.[126]

Artifacts recovered at Whitewater consisted of pottery, additional objects of fired clay, bone and stone implements, minor articles fashioned from those materials, and shells carved for personal adornment. Perishable materials were virtually absent from the site, and so the information obtained is incomplete and one-sided. There was no evidence of the kinds of clothing, textiles, or wooden implements that unquestionably played a prominent part in daily life.[127] A few potsherds bore basketry impressions, and several pieces of charred cord were found. One cord was made from cotton, the other from *apocynum* fiber. Because of their fragmented and charred condition, the use of the cords could not be determined.

Stratigraphic tests at Whitewater revealed a definite progression in pottery forms, and a certain sequence in the appearance of types. The earliest main type was Basketmaker III of the eastern variety, also called La Plata Black-on-white. It is a type common to an area extending from western New Mexico to the northeastern San Juan Basin. The second main type is known as Chaco I or Kiatuthlanna Black-on-white. It was typical of the Chaco cultural pattern beginning about A.D. 840. Subsequently, the Little Colorado style made its appearance. This type seemingly originated in the area between the Puerco and Little Colorado rivers, although it evidences a strong Chaco influence. The third main type was Kana-a Black-on-white. It found its center in the Kayenta Region and spread slowly toward the southeast.

Most of the pottery developments during the middle and late phases at Whitewater were an outgrowth of the three main types, with additional introductions from certain Little Colorado centers, from central-western New Mexico, and from the Chaco Canyon area.

In culinary vessels, smoothed exterior surfaces gave way to banded necks with smooth bodies, smooth-bodied vessels with manipulated neck coils, and allover corrugated ware of a coarse quality that was ultimately replaced by vessels with narrower coils and fine indentations. Black-interior pottery progressed along two lines: the earliest forms, contemporary with Chaco I wares, had a black interior and gray exterior. One group branched off from here and developed successively lighter exteriors, until at last they had vessels with black interiors and white exteriors. Another group progressed from gray, to gray-brown, to brown-red, and finally to pure red with a black interior. This type had widespread distribution along the southern borders of the Anasazi area, and Roberts thinks it originated in the south.[128] Redwares with black painted decoration played a minor part in the Whitewater District,[129] and those that were found may not have been of local manufacture.

In Roberts's opinion, the really significant feature about Whitewater pottery is that "it demonstrates an early southwest extension of influence from the Chaco Canyon area with a subsequent spread toward the northwest from Little Colorado centers and toward the southeast from the Kayenta or Tusayan Region. The movement was contrary to that postulated by many southwestern workers. . . ."[130] He adds that throughout the entire period represented by the material from the Whitewater District the Chaco cultural pattern predominated, and that while a cultural lag was present in the beginning, by A.D. 950 the gap was exceedingly small. Also, there may have been considerable travel

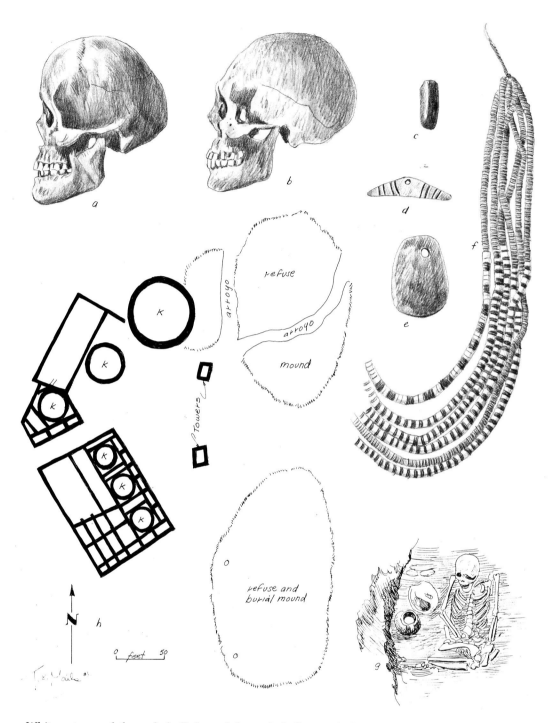

Whitewater. *a*, deformed skull. *b*, undeformed skull. *c–e*, shell and stone ornaments. *f*, stone necklace. *g*, flexed burial. *h*, plan of large ruins of Great Pueblo period. From Roberts, 1939 and 1940.

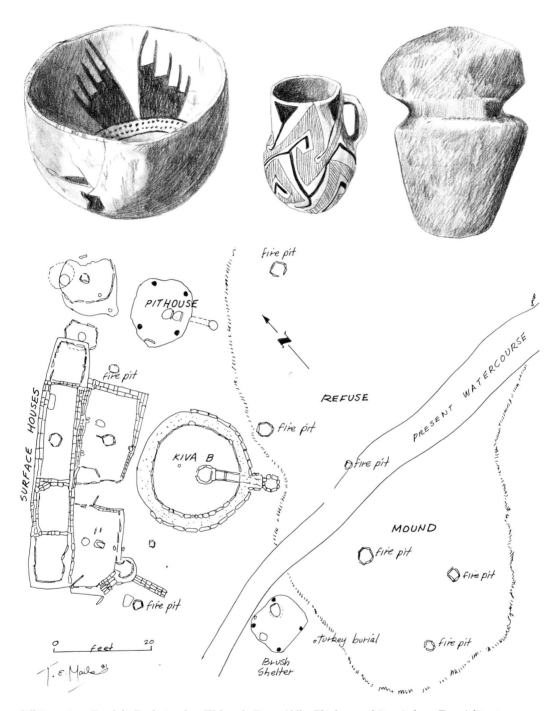

Whitewater. *Top left*, Basketmaker III bowl. *Top middle*, Black-on-white pitcher. *Top right*, stone hoe. *Bottom*, partial plan of Whitewater Developmental village. Refuse mound was also used for burials. From Roberts, 1939 and 1940.

back and forth along the Puerco from the outlying precincts to the main centers of the Chaco group.[131] With the help of dendrochronological dating, Roberts gives the following periods for Whitewater pottery:

Early ninth century	Chaco I, banded culinary wares
Mid-ninth century	Little Colorado, Kana-a
Late ninth, early tenth century	Chaco Transitional, manipulated coils
Very early tenth century	Escavada Black-on-white, coarse corrugated
Late tenth century	hachured wares, developed Little Colorado, fine corrugated
Early eleventh century	Tularosa[132]

KIATUTHLANNA

From May to September of 1929, Frank H. H. Roberts and his Zuñi assistants conducted archaeological investigations at Kiatuthlanna, at the Twin Salt Lakes in Apache County, eastern Arizona. The site is approximately thirty miles southwest of Zuñi and twenty-five miles south of Chambers. The name is Zuñi, and it means "Place of the Big Water."[133] The Zuñi believe it is one of the sites where their ancestors stopped briefly during the migration from their place of origin to the present location of Zuñi Pueblo. A half-mile from Kiatuthlanna are two small lakes to which the Zuñi still attribute special ceremonial significance. One is red and very salty. The other is green and only slightly salty. The Zuñi have legends to explain the differences between the lakes. Roberts noted that at stated intervals while the work was going on, two of his older Zuñi workmen deposited turquoise offerings in the reeds encircling the green lake and sprinkled sacred cornmeal on its waters. They scattered pollen on the red lake. Shortly after June 21, the summer solstice, while a special ceremony was taking place at Zuñi, prayer feathers were placed in the tall grass on the southern bank of the red lake.

Every four years, during the summer solstice ceremonies at Zuñi, a party of priests makes a pilgrimage to the Place of the Big Water. They stop along the way, build fires, and chant to the spirits to petition for life-giving rain. On their arrival at Red Lake they dance around it, sing, and sprinkle cornmeal on the water. If their ceremonies are properly performed and there is no evil in the hearts of those who bless the water, a great turtle who lives in the lake will surface, hear their prayers, and transmit them to the proper spiritual powers. Similar and additional ceremonies of thanksgiving are then performed at the Green Lake.[134]

According to the migration story told to Roberts, the Zuñi ancients lived at Kiatuthlanna for four years. Then they moved on in search of the middle of the world, where they had been told to settle permanently. Eight miles north of the Twin Lakes they found watercress growing, and built there the village

Pitkiaiakivi. Setting out again, they stopped and built Hantlipinka, a most sacred place of the Zuñi, where their first war god figures were created and the
people were divided into clans. Matilda Coxe Stevenson, who wrote extensively about the Zuñi, visited this place and describes it and the clan symbols
that were pecked into the canyon walls.[135]

While searching for the middle of the world, the Zuñi separated into three
groups, to accomplish their mission more quickly. One group went southeast,
one east, and one north and east. Roberts's informant insisted that the last-

Kiatuthlanna. *a*, plan of Pithouse Group 1. *b*, structural section showing how two pithouses
were combined. *c*, Black-on-white ladle. *d*, Black-on-white dipper. From Roberts, 1931.

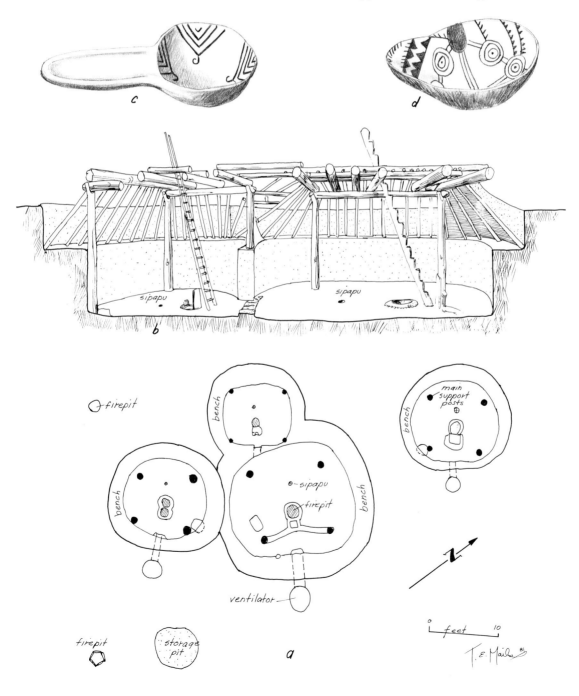

named group, the Winter People, built the villages of Chaco Canyon and then continued northward to a point above the San Juan, to places where they built other villages, including one near a hot spring. After this they turned east to the Rio Grande area. In time they moved again, following the Rio Grande to the south, finally turning west, and building the old Zuñi village called Nutria. From here they moved on down the valley to join the other Zuñi groups and built the present-day village known as Zuñi.[136]

Roberts thought it especially interesting that the area described in the story coincides with the known range of the Chaco culture, touching upon Kiatuthlanna, Chaco Canyon, Aztec, the ruins at the famous Pagosa hot springs in Colorado, Bandelier monument, and Pecos in New Mexico. However, beyond the coincidence of the locations, the archaeological evidence indicates that the sites mentioned were more or less contemporary; hence it does not seem that they resulted from a migratory group passing in chronological order through the regions. In fact, some of the more northern sites are dated earlier than the southern locations. All that Roberts could conclude to justify the Zuñi story was that after an original expansion of the Anasazi a contraction took place, during which some of them wandered down the San Juan drainage in the beginnings of the great movement that culminated in the abandonment of the northern frontiers at the close of the Pueblo III Period.[137] In consequence, Roberts suggests that students should not place too much reliance upon primitive myths and legends, "especially when they deal with events viewed through the haze of great antiquity." He goes on to say that workers in the Southwest have found that traditions concerning archaeological sites are for the most part unreliable, and that if they are referred to at all, "they should be interpreted with great discernment."[138] I think it only fair to point out, however, that Roberts's view, even though accurate, leaves unanswered the question of how the Zuñi knew about all these sites *before* such helpful information as archaeological evidence came into being. Without this modern aid, how did they draw so discerning a picture of the Chaco cultural range? Is it no more than coincidence?

Eighteen pithouses, three jacal structures, and a pueblo ruin with forty-nine rooms and four kivas were excavated at Kiatuthlanna, all apparently built in the order named.

The pits of the pithouses were found to be of two kinds. The subterranean portion of the first and earliest kind consisted of an oval with its dirt walls rising more or less vertically from the floor to grade level; the second kind had larger pits that were either oval or round, with an encircling bench. The roof structure of both kinds was supported by four main posts and beams, with sloping side walls and a flat roof. In the earlier models the side-wall poles extended from grade level to the horizontal beams. Later structures had the pole butts resting at the intersection of the back of the bench and the dwelling wall. An opening in the roofs of both types served as the entrance and smoke hole. The wall and roof framework was covered with leaves, brush, bark, branches, reeds, and a final thick layer of mud.[139]

Architectural features of the pithouses included a wall-opening type of ventilator shaft at the southeast side of the room, fire and ladder pits near the room center, a deflector located between the ventilator opening and the firepit, a sipapu hole, and holes and recesses for the storage of objects. The ventilator-firepit-sipapu complex was continued in the later ceremonial chambers of the communal dwellings, indicating that what were once family rites practiced in the privacy of one's own home had given way to communal ceremonies whose aim was to meet the needs of the clan or community as a whole.[140]

Pithouses at Kiatuthlanna were built in clusters of from four to six that together constituted a small village made up of a single family group or clan. In three of the villages the central structure was larger than the pithouses surrounding it, suggesting that from earliest times a definite ceremonial significance was attached to the larger unit. This would make it in fact a protokiva.[141]

The smaller pithouses were typical of Anasazi structures of the late Basketmaker III Period, and the later and larger pithouses were similar to those of the Pueblo I Period found at Chaco Canyon and in southwestern Colorado.[142]

Little was left of the jacal dwellings. But the walls consisted of vertical poles covered with mud, and it is supposed that the roofs were flat. The dwellings ranged in size from one to several rooms and were similar in nature to the jacal houses of southwestern Colorado during the Pueblo I Period. Indications are that the jacal structures were contemporary with the later-date pithouses, and it is also possible that the jacal units served as summer dwellings and the pithouses were occupied during the winter.

Actually, a variety of dwelling types existed within a given community. Continuity accompanied change. This was a characteristic of early Anasazi times, and there was always fluctuation in structural detail at any stage of development. For example, while the sedentary culture was evolving, a shift was made from subterranean to surface houses. But the shift was accompanied by an inevitable state of instability. Some people continued to live in pithouses while others were experimenting with the newer styles. It took considerable time for people to accept the new ideas and to take the final step of making the conversion. Moreover, some never did make the change.[143]

The pueblo ruin at Kiatuthlanna had stone, adobe, and stone-veneered exterior walls. The adobe was not shaped into bricks, but seemed to have been laid up in the form of nodules of about the size that could be conveniently held in a person's two hands. As each nodule was placed, it was further molded and patted down. When the wall was dry, the cracks were filled in with clay. When the clay had set, a final wash or plaster was spread over the entire surface.[144] Walls of this kind are still being built by the Rio Grande Pueblos.

From an original six rooms and one kiva, the pueblo evolved through five successive stages, until at last it contained forty-nine rooms and four kivas. The final stage is of particular interest to archaeologists in that, while interior and exterior walls were mainly of adobe, the exterior walls were faced with stones. It seemed to Roberts that throughout all its stages the building was more like those of the San Juan than of the Little Colorado area.[145]

The D-shaped, early type of partially subterranean kiva was rare for this district, and it would remain for future excavators to decide whether, as it seemed to Roberts, it represented a northern intrusion.[146] Later kivas were typically circular. The earliest kiva at Kiatuthlanna had no sipapu. Also, there were no interior posts, pilasters, or piers to support the roof. Hence the roof timbers must have rested directly on the walls.[147] The second kiva, which was also D-shaped, did have three pilasters and a sipapu.

Kiatuthlanna. *a*, plan of Pithouse Group No. 2. Typical pithouse pottery: *b–e*, culinary vessels. *f*, bowl with quartered decoration. *g*, pitcher. *h*, seed jar or canteen. From Roberts, 1931.

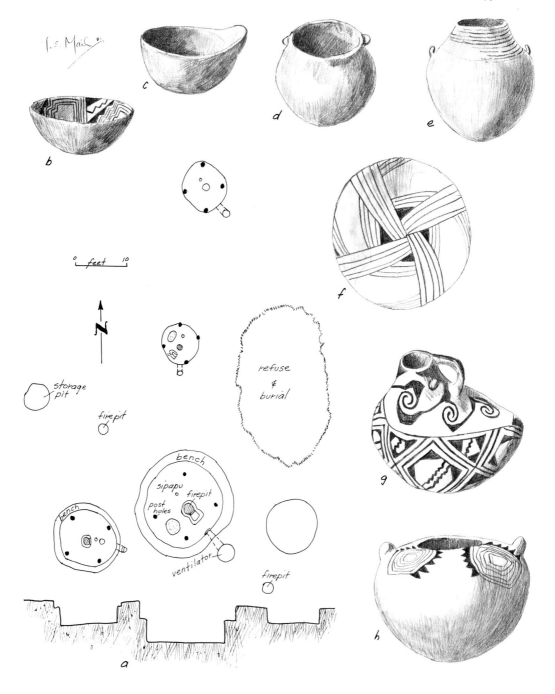

In addressing himself to the presence or lack of a sipapu in the kivas, particularly in kivas of the Chaco cultural group, Roberts sees a plausible suggestion in modern sources. He notes that Victor Mindeleff found among the Hopi two classes of kiva, whose only distinction was that some had sipapus and others did not. The more important rites were held in those with sipapus. Hence it was concluded that the sipapu distinguished the kivas that were strictly consecrated for religious observances from those that in the early period

Kiatuthlanna. *a*, plan of Pithouse Group No. 3. Pithouse artifacts: *b–e*, shell pendants. *f–h*, stone pendants. *i*, stone drill. *j*, stone knife. *k*, *n*, stone projectile points. *l*, bone tool. *m*, bone awl. From Roberts, 1931.

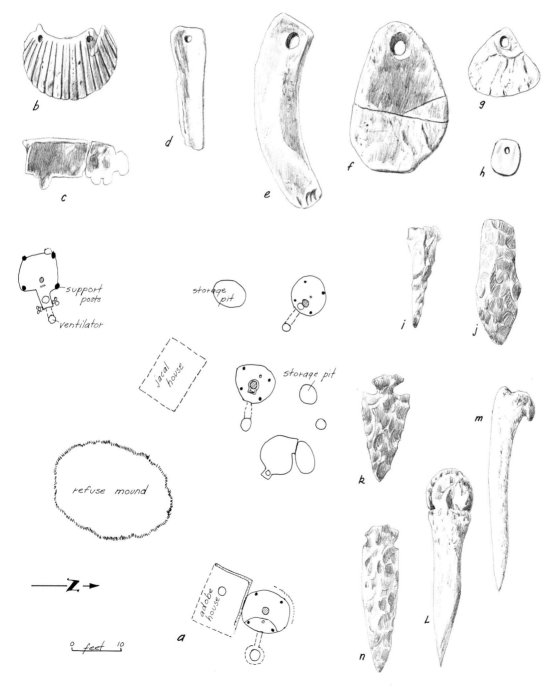

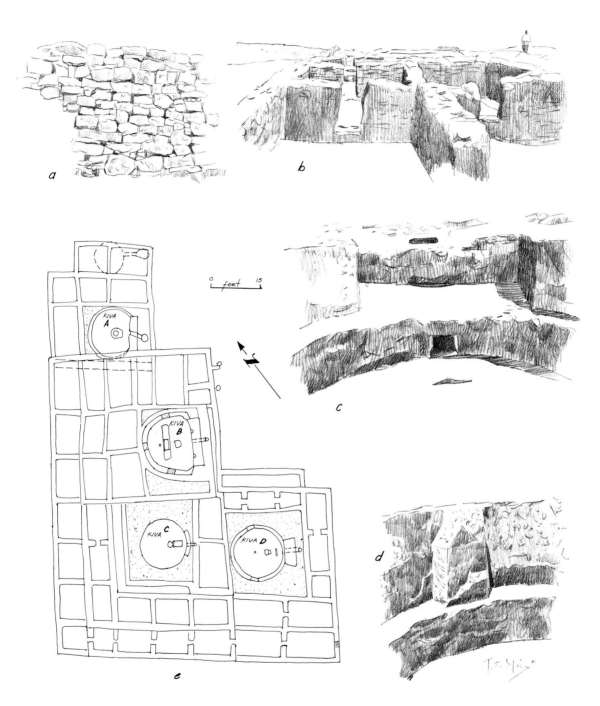

Kiatuthlanna. *a*, typical wall in pueblo ruin. *b*, row of rooms with connecting doorways. *c*, ventilator and recess in Kiva D. *d*, bench and pilasters in Kiva D. *e*, plan of completed pueblo ruin. From Roberts, 1931.

Kiatuthlanna. Typical artifacts found in the pueblo. *a*, stone bowl. *b–d*, projectile points. *e*, bone awl. *f*, stone pipe. *g–i*, shell beads. *j*, *k*, shell bracelets. *l*, corrugated culinary jar. *m*, Black-on-red pitcher. *n*, Black-on-red bowl. From Roberts, 1931.

were designed to serve mainly as clubrooms for men. Later, the clubroom as a distinct entity gave way to the true kiva, which served both purposes.[148]

The sipapu of the third kiva built at Kiatuthlanna was, like many found at Mesa Verde, filled with clean sand, and encased in the sand was a smooth, slim stone cylinder. When the stone was found, the Zuñi laborers immediately stopped work and gathered to examine it. All insisted it was a kiva stone, but no further information could be obtained from them, and nothing about the stone indicated what its function might have been.[149]

Roberts found evidence that the Kiatuthlanna site was abandoned after the pithouse and jacal stages, and later reoccupied by the group who built the large pueblo. There were pithouse and jacal remains from the early and middle Pueblo I Period and no remains from the Pueblo II Period; the large pueblo was typically Pueblo III.[150]

As was the case at Whitewater, material culture objects other than the buildings consisted only of those made of imperishable materials. There were pottery, stone and bone implements, and stone and shell ornaments. Some of these showed marked differences between the pithouse and pueblo stages, while others were much the same for both. The broadest variations took place in pottery, axheads and mauls, arrowheads, awls fashioned from specially pre-pared bones, and beads. Pottery displayed a distinct northern influence of the Chaco cultural type in its early period, but a fusion of influence from Chaco Canyon and the Upper Gila area, New Mexico, in its late period. Bone implements were northern in style, while stone objects exhibited both south-ern and western traits. All objects found in the pithouses were definitely Pueblo I Period, while those associated with the surface structure were clearly Pueblo III.[151]

Pithouse Anasazi at Kiatuthlanna buried their dead with the body flexed and placed on its back. Pueblo dwellers laid the body on its side. Pithouse bodies had the heads pointing in various directions, while pueblo bodies were invariably placed with the heads toward the east. Pithouse mortuary offerings consisted uniformly of three distinct kinds of pottery, which were randomly placed in the grave. Pueblo offerings included a random selection of objects, but they were always placed next to the head of the deceased.

There were striking contrasts in the skeletal remains of the different peri-ods. The skulls of the pithouse residents were either long or broad, either undeformed or only slightly deformed. To Roberts, this was proof of a mixture of stock and customs, the long heads representing Basketmakers and the broad heads representing Pueblo migrants. Pronounced deformation of the occipital region of some skulls testified to a new form of hard cradleboard that produced the head flattening. The deformation in this case was so severe that it was impossible to tell whether the deceased had come originally from a long-headed or a broad-headed stock, or from a mixture of the two.[152]

In concluding his Bureau of American Ethnology report on Kiatuthlanna, Roberts states that the material culture of the residents indicates they adopted features from each of the several centers near them. That most features were reminiscent of the Chaco culture he attributes to Chaco's long leadership in the development of the Pueblo pattern, while the Little Colorado and Rio Grande cultures had yet to attain their prominence of the Pueblo IV Period.[153]

VILLAGE OF THE GREAT KIVAS

During the summer of 1930, Roberts directed the excavation of a group of ruins at the mouths of Red Paint Canyon and Lonesome Canyon on the north side of Nutria Valley, sixteen and a half miles northeast of the town of Zuñi, on the Zuñi Reservation in western New Mexico. The site was composed of three communal dwellings and two Great Kivas. Accordingly it has been given the name Village of the Great Kivas.[154]

The high plateau upon which the village was located illustrates the judicious selection of dwelling places made by some of the Anasazi. Except for

Plot plan of ruins of Village of the Great Kivas. From Roberts, 1932.

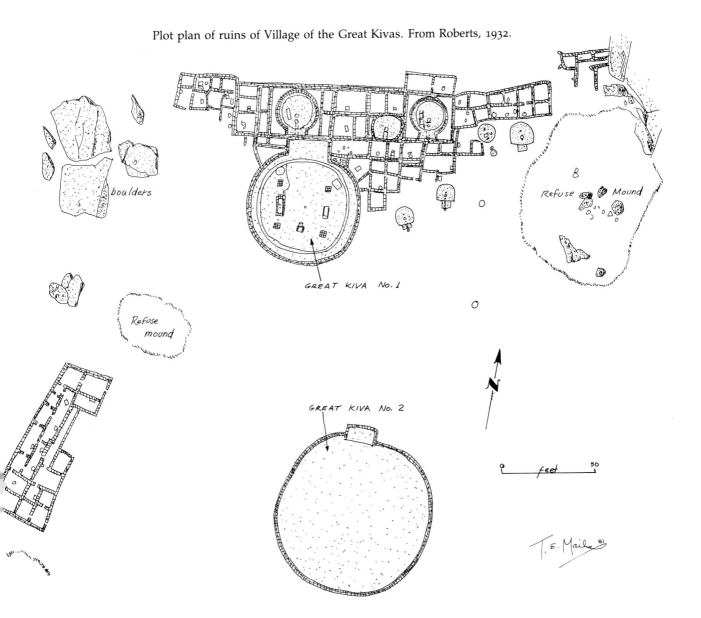

cliffs on the north and east sides that protected it from winter winds, the village was situated considerably higher than most of the surrounding territory. Therefore all surface water from rain and melting snow drained away rapidly from the dwelling area. Ample farming land was immediately available, since the mouths of the two canyons had broad, flat bottoms, perfect for planting. In addition, an even larger expanse extended from there across the Nutria Valley. Drainage water spread out from both canyons over the valley and pro-

Village of the Great Kivas. *a,* bird's-eye view of the village looking south. *b,* black-on-white bowl design with Kokopelli, the humpbacked flute player, in the bottom. *c,* section through *pi-gumme* oven. *d,* some of the petroglyphs on the cliffs near the village. From Roberts, 1932.

vided all the moisture needed to grow corn, beans, and squash. Roberts calls our attention to the fact that most prehistoric and modern Zuñi villages were so placed, and the Village of the Great Kivas was typical in this regard.[155]

The largest dwelling included three clan-sized kivas, one Great Kiva, and sixty-four other rooms. Sixty of the rooms were on the ground level, and four comprised a second story. Besides these, there were four detached subterranean rooms in front of the east end of the dwelling unit. As was the case at other sites, the building grew to its ultimate size through several stages or periods of constructional activity. The first stage consisted of a rectangular block of thirteen rooms and two clan-sized ceremonial chambers. Next, five more rooms and a Great Kiva were added, and at the same time some of the first-unit rooms were remodeled. After some time a landslide forced the abandonment of a ceremonial chamber and several rooms, and a new addition was built to replace them. This consisted of fifteen rooms located east of the Great Kiva and south of the first unit. Two of the original rooms were remodeled to make a new ceremonial chamber.

Up to this point the dwelling structures were Chacoan in style. Walls consisted of horizontal courses of large stones separated by layers of smaller ones. Rooms were large and ceilings high. The new east- and west-wing additions were characterized by irregular outlines and inferior masonry. Rooms were smaller and numbered thirty-one rooms and four subterranean kivas. Since the growth was far too rapid to be accounted for on the basis of natural increase, it is thought that the original settlers, who probably came from the north, were joined by a new group of migrants. Because of the character of certain of their material culture objects, such as red and polychrome pottery, it appears that the late group came from the south, "possibly as a backwash up the Zuñi River of a migration down the Little Colorado from the Upper Gila region."[156]

The early clan-sized kivas were of two types. One, a stone form of the surface variety, was incorporated within the building proper. The other was subterranean and placed in front of the building. Two of the incorporated kivas had benches, ventilator recesses, subfloor ventilators, firepits, deflectors, Katcina niches, and subfloor vaults at the west side. Only one kiva had a sipapu. Pilasters were absent, as was characteristic of the district. The third kiva, formed by the remodeling of the two rooms, lacked many of the standard features: there was no sipapu, bench, Katcina niche, or subfloor vault.[157]

The four subterranean kivas located outside and in front of the largest dwelling unit in its final stage were more D-shaped than circular or oval. The earth walls were plastered, but they had no stone lining. The kivas featured intrawall ventilators rather than the subfloor variety, sipapus, firepits, deflectors, and Katcina niches. Three of them had recesses above the ventilator. The one that did not had geometric paintings on the walls. Roberts saw in some of the kivas a suggestion of the rectangular room that replaced the circular form in some districts in late prehistoric times.

Two of the rectangular rooms in the original dwelling unit contained features generally found in kivas and were possibly a prototype of the fraternity room or clubroom as opposed to the true kiva. At modern Zuñi the various fraternities have headquarters in ordinary living rooms, where they perform rites pertaining solely to the fraternities. Community rituals are enacted in the kivas.

At its point of peak development, the second dwelling unit contained twenty rooms. The walls were constructed of cubical blocks of stone, and they were more carefully worked than those of the first dwelling. This unit had no kivas, and Roberts speculates that the occupants joined the earlier residents in the use of their kivas.

He also believes that the presence of two Great Kivas at one location in the Zuñi district is very important, since they demonstrated that what he calls the "superceremonial chamber" had a wider distribution than had been sus-

Village of the Great Kivas. *a,* plan and section of kiva designated by Roberts as No. 2. *b,* stone ring used to face off ventilator shaft. *c,* plan and section of Great Kiva No. 1. *d,* interior of vault at the west side of the kiva. *e,* west subfloor vault, dais, and pillar base. From Roberts, 1932.

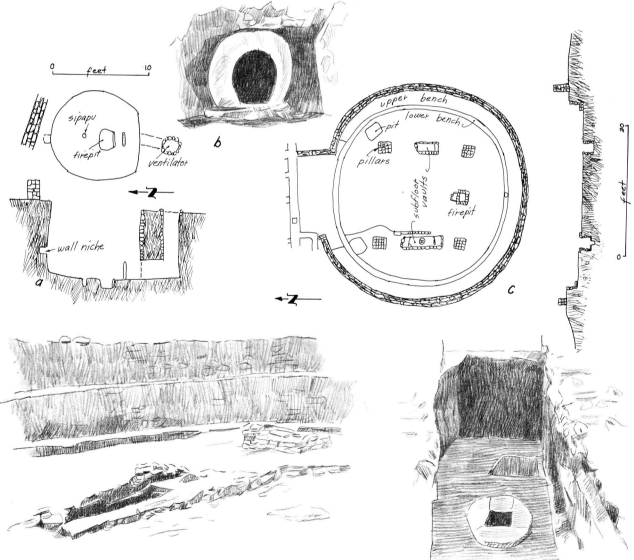

pected before 1930. In addition, they added materially to the evidence of a strong northern element in the village.[158] Only one of the Great Kivas was excavated. It measured 51 feet (15.5 m) in diameter above its double bench, making it somewhat larger than the Great Kiva at Aztec, and it contained four masonry pillars or pilasters, a north alcove or altar room, a firepit, a possible sipapu, and two subfloor vaults. The pillars were similar to those of the Great Kiva at Aztec. They consisted largely of blocks of stone carefully laid in adobe mortar, with an occasional course of cedar poles placed horizontally side by side and imbedded in mud plaster. There were several courses of stone, a course of poles running north and south, several more courses of stone, then a course of poles running east and west. This sandwich pattern was repeated for the full height of the pillar. At Aztec, every other course consisted of wood

Village of the Great Kivas. *a*, plan and section of kiva designated by Roberts as A. *b*, view of south side of kiva. *c*, view of north side showing Katcina niche with corn goddess stones in place in front of it. From Roberts, 1932.

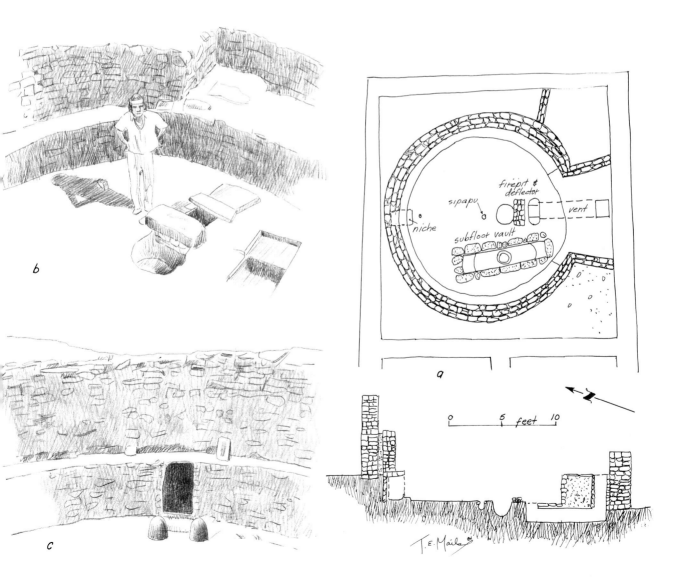

poles. There were no true peripheral rooms as at Aztec, but there were a few bordering rooms. The other Great Kiva was much larger, having a diameter of 78 feet (23.8 m). At the time of Roberts's work there, it surpassed in size all other known structures of the type.[159]

In Roberts's opinion, the presence of two Great Kivas in a community of this size is unusual "and might be considered an indication that the religious side of its life was overemphasized."[160] He does not clarify his meaning, and I am puzzled as to how an Indian culture could ever overemphasize religion, since it has always been the very core of traditional Indian life. It is more often the non-Indian who stresses the need for balance and who worries about those who become overly zealous in religious matters.

Since the excavated Great Kiva had been destroyed by fire, it is entirely possible that the second Great Kiva was built to replace it. Without excavation, this could not be posited for certain, so Roberts hazards two explanations for a possible dual presence. One is that the village was the ceremonial center for the entire district and everyone gathered here to perform the major ceremonial rites. The other is that the village was divided into two large groups, each having its own Great Kiva. The enclosed present-day dance courts may represent the survival of the idea.[161]

As at Kiatuthlanna, with few exceptions only the objects fashioned from imperishable materials survived at the Village of the Great Kivas. Artifacts recovered included pottery, stone and bone implements and ornaments, fetish heads carved from stone, and stone objects employed as tools in their natural form. The perishable finds consisted of scraps of unidentified cloth and bits of charred basketry.[162]

A few pottery specimens could be associated with the Pueblo II Period, but most were forms typical of Pueblo III. They consisted of the usual two types: culinary and nonculinary. The culinary jars were of the corrugated variety, most having indentations that covered the entire vessel. A few pieces had indentations only on the neck portion. Wide-mouth and globular bodies were common shapes, and pitchers with handles were also found.[163]

The nonculinary vessels were characterized by smooth surfaces and painted decoration. Included were black-on-white wares, red vessels with black designs, red vessels with designs in black and white, buff or cream-colored bowls and jars with red decorations bordered with black, yellow or buff bowls with red interiors bearing black designs and with red designs on the exterior, and red bowls with burnished black exteriors. Nonculinary shapes included short-necked, globular-bodied water and storage jars; globular canteens; seed jars; jars with stirrup handles; pitchers; ladles or dippers; bowls; and mugs.[164]

Black-on-white vessel designs exhibited patterns common to all regions except the Kayenta and Virgin. Red vessels with black decoration were also typical of several regions. Red vessels with black interiors and white decorated exteriors were similar to Little Colorado bowls. Polychrome bowls were most closely related to the Little Colorado area.[165]

From the few charred basketry remains it was determined that both coiling and twilling were employed. Twilling is rarely found in prehistoric ruins, but it is a method still employed by modern weavers. The bone implements were typical of those found in the more northern Anasazi ruins: awls, punches, scrapers, bone tubes, turkey whistles, beads, and ornaments. The only bird bones found were turkey. Bone fleshers were of a type common to Chaco,

Stone artifacts found at the Village of the Great Kivas. *a–b*, paint mortars. *c*, small pestle for grinding paint. *d*, jar stopper. *e*, arrow smoother. *f–h*, fetish heads. *i–j*, corn goddess effigies. From Roberts, 1932.

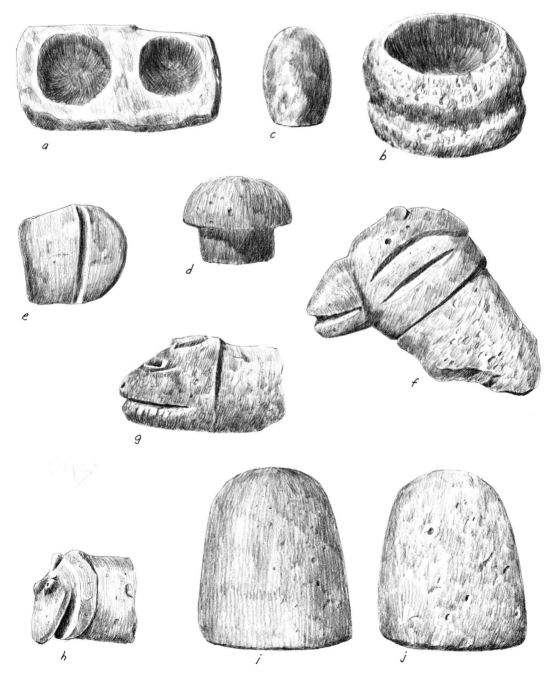

Aztec, and Mesa Verde and represent a type known as the San Juan flesher.[166]

Stone objects included manos, metates, mortars, mauls, jar stoppers, arrow-shaft smoothers, axheads, small mortars and pestles for grinding paint, arrowheads, spearpoints, ornaments, effigy heads, and unworked pebbles and stones.

Two types of metate were found: the northern trough form, and a southern flat type that was introduced about the time alterations to the original portion of the village were completed. Likewise, finds included two types of mauls. The first, related to the north, was short and cylindrical with flat striking surfaces and an encircling hafting groove. The second, related to the south and west, was a flat tabular-shaped stone with either rounded or blunt-pointed ends and having either a completely encircling hafting groove or a groove on only three sides. Most axheads had short cutting edges and a fully encircling hafting groove.[167]

Roberts states that the paint mortars, sandstone jar stoppers, and arrow shaft polishers were more like those commonly found in the Upper Gila and Little Colorado regions than those recovered in the northern areas.[168] But similar artifacts at Mesa Verde are reported by Gustaf Nordenskiöld, J. W. Fewkes, and Arthur H. Rohn.[169] The rounded conical objects found at the village and designated as corn goddesses, but quite similar to the so-called god of germination stone found by Fewkes at Pipe Shrine House, Mesa Verde, seemed in Roberts's view to have been introduced from the north, although they, too, have been found in Little Colorado ruins.

Weapons finds were not numerous at the Village of the Great Kivas, nor at other sites in the general area. The reason is not known. Arrowheads were all of the same type. They had a broad, square tang; notches for hafting were cut at right angles to the long line of the blade.

Stone beads were all of the disk variety still made by the Pueblos, and were carved from southwestern alabaster. Larger pendant disks were either round or oval and had a single perforation. Some pendants were fashioned from alabaster and others from ferruginous shale.[170] Only a few small, unworked fragments of turquoise were found, indicating either that it was difficult to obtain or that the modern Zuñi fascination for it had not yet come into vogue at the village. Yet sites of a slightly later date in the Zuñi region yielded considerable amounts of turquoise, and its popularity at Chaco Canyon has already been emphasized.[171] The present-day turquoise pendants worn by some Shalako Ceremony impersonators are the largest and purest stones to be seen among the Pueblos.

Fascinating sandstone effigy heads were carved by the artisans of the village. It was not possible for Roberts to tell in all cases what the effigies were meant to represent, perhaps because effigies depict mythological as well as actual creatures. Nor was he able to learn their exact function. Someone suggested they served as fetishes in ceremonies, or that they were clan symbols. Details indicated that the heads were formerly attached to bodies made from perishable materials.[172] In every instance the head features were well defined, but the neck or stem was no more than an unfinished cylinder. A shallow groove on the stem just behind the head provided a means for attaching it to the body with a thong. One head was very suggestive of the plumed serpent used in some of the more important ceremonies at modern Zuñi.[173] Another carved head seemed to resemble a frog.

The frog plays an important role in Zuñi mythology because of its association with water. Members of the rain priesthood at Zuñi keep fetishes made from four hollow reeds filled with water. In the largest of these a small toad (called a frog by the Zuñi) is kept. Bowls used for certain ceremonies have either painted or carved frogs on them. In rain ceremonies, members of the Frog Clan sing special songs. Considering all this, Roberts decided the stone frog head he found at the village might have been used for rain rituals, or was the fetish of a water clan, or both.[174] Roberts thought it noteworthy that cloud-blower pipes were not found at the site.[175]

Rock art was plentiful on the cliff faces behind the village. There were symbols and figures, the latter occurring in groups and as single petroglyphs, including both geometric and life forms. Some of the art was of late date and probably represented the work of Zuñi and Navajo of historic times. The plainly ancient art included depictions of two of the humpbacked flute players found in all Anasazi regions. As to the art taken as a group, there was nothing about it that could definitely be attributed to people migrating to the village from any particular region.[176]

In an instructive description of the rock art, Roberts reveals that, as of 1930, there was considerable comment and argument over the meaning of petroglyphs and the extent to which they could be regarded as symbolic of definite things associated "with the life of the Indian."[177] Many writers had attempted to make a written language of them and had read more into them than they should—this is still the case today. Others had gone too far in the opposite direction, calling them recreational drawings and, as such, meaningless. The truth probably lies somewhere in the middle, with some symbols no doubt possessing definite meaning and others simply the artistic expressions of creative people.

The Zuñi did offer explanations and interpretations of some of the symbols, a fact of some consequence since it represents their understanding from within the same culture that created the rock art. Roberts found some of these to be logical and others to be farfetched, and he did not know whether they represented the views of the original artists.[178] It might be said, though, that Anglo logic is not the best measure of the Zuñi explanations that follow.

Among the insect drawings, the Zuñi identified the centipede, the scorpion, and the ant. All these are endowed with poisonous stings, and they were depicted as part of a ceremony during which the spirit powers were called upon to wreak vengeance upon their enemies. Whenever a war party left the village, the war priest sang at night a song in which these insects and certain animals were asked to bite and sting the enemy. The depictions at the ancient village might well represent just such occasions.[179]

The three main figures of another group consisted of a horned toad, an unidentified insect, and the humpbacked flute player. The Zuñi said the flute player represents a rain priest, pictured on the rocks to attract clouds and moisture to the area. The toad and insect assist him. The flute player is called Chu'lu'lanch, which is the name of the flute he uses.[180]

Spiral figures were explained by the Zuñi as referring to the period when the ancients were migrating in search of the center of the world so that they might settle down and build their permanent home. A deer figure was said to be the record of an unusually successful hunt. It was drawn on the rock to propitiate the spirits of the dead animals and to attract others to the region. The turtle figure was important because of its association with water, and because it occurs often in the creation myths. A drawing in which a zigzag line connects an owl with the moon and a star represents a historic folktale commonly told to Zuñi children. The line traces the flight of the bird. In the story, an owl comes to the war chief and leads him to where the hogans of Navajo enemies are located. Donning a headdress of piñon jay and quail feathers that makes him invisible, he then enters the hogans and assesses the Navajo strength. Returning to Zuñi, he gathers sufficient warriors and goes back to attack the enemy, either capturing them or stealing their belongings. The owl is capricious, however, for sometimes he flies on ahead and warns the Navajo to flee before the Zuñi arrive, hence the zigzag line.[181]

Sixty burials were uncovered at the Village of the Great Kivas. Most were found in the refuse mounds, a few in the earth elsewhere. Several infants had been placed close to outdoor firepits, and one body was buried in an abandoned pit oven. More than a third of the corpses were those of infants and young children. Bodies were flexed, and forty-six of the bodies had heads pointed toward the southeast. Pottery mortuary offerings were usually placed near the head or the upper part of the body. Skeletal material revealed that cranial deformation was in common practice and that the people suffered considerably from decayed teeth. On the basis of occupied rooms and the number of burials found, it is estimated that the maximum population of the Village of the Great Kivas was one hundred. Through the use of charred beams, Dr. Andrew Douglass established a mean date of A.D. 1015 for the site, and Roberts assumes that it was built and occupied during the years A.D. 1000–30. This was also a time of intense building activity at Chaco Canyon, and evidence in general suggests there was some correlation between the two areas. "There is no doubt," Roberts says, "but that the Village of the Great Kivas was inhabited in the days when the Pueblo cultures were forging toward the peak of their classic era and that it was built by groups migrating from two different regions."[182] Since Great Kivas are generally associated with the Chaco culture, the presence of two at the Village of the Great Kivas is a persuasive indication that it was founded by a Chaco group or one directly influenced by that center.[183]

PIEDRA DISTRICT, COLORADO

The San Juan area remained one of the most important in the Southwest up to the end of the Pueblo III Period in A.D. 1300. It was a center from which many of the characteristic features of the sedentary cultures were diffused, and for an extended time it was the leader in their development. Reference has already been made to two of the Anasazi regions, the Virgin and Chaco Canyon. Kayenta and Mesa Verde will be considered next, and after that the somewhat less important areas, the Little Colorado and Rio Grande regions.

There was also a number of minor districts or localities of varying importance. These were peripheral to and flourished under the influence of one of the major centers. Aztec was one of the minor districts. Others that have just been treated were within the greater Chaco culture sphere. Another area

Piedra. *Left,* map of the A village on Stollsteimer Mesa. *Top right,* plan and section of Unit C-3 showing relationship of dwellings to depression. *Bottom right,* map showing location of the Piedra District in relation to Mesa Verde and Aztec. From Roberts, 1930.

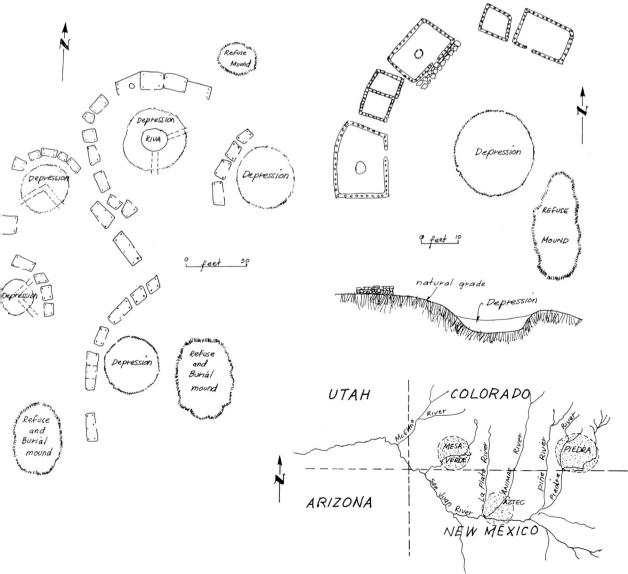

showing distinct affiliations with the Chaco culture was the Piedra District, consisting of an impressively large group of ruins that ranged along the Piedra River in southern Colorado. Its center lies about seventy miles due east of Mesa Verde, and it includes the upper reaches of the San Juan River as far east as present-day Pagosa Springs.

The district was practically unknown archaeologically before the summer of 1921. At that time a joint investigation was undertaken there by the State Historical and Natural History Society of Colorado and the University of Denver. The greater part of two field seasons was spent in excavating a portion of a large pueblo ruin on top of the Piedra Parada or, as it is otherwise called, Chimney Rock. This investigation, plus a few minor ones in the surrounding territory, convinced archaeologists that it was an important section for study.

Piedra. *Left*, plan and sections of House Group 2 in the A village. *Top right*, postulated method of kiva construction. *Center right*, rows of stones used to support base logs in type A dwelling. *Bottom right*, postulated method of constructing type A houses. From Roberts, 1930.

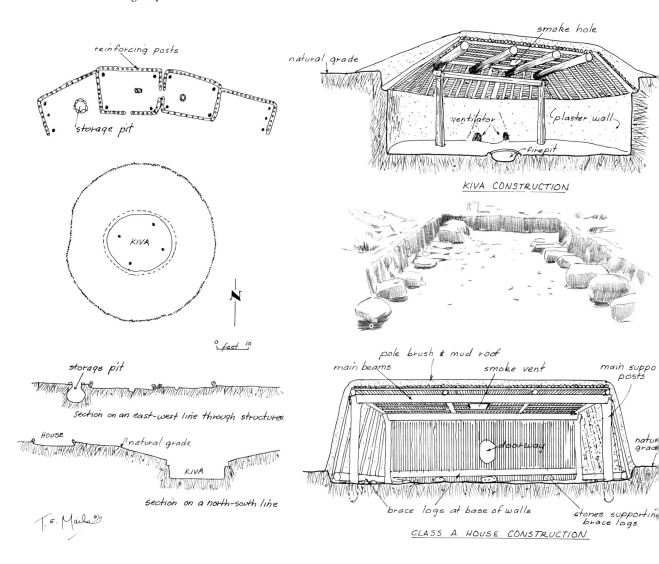

In 1923 Frank H. H. Roberts, who would become in time so familiar with the general range of Chaco culture, was sent to conduct a reconnaissance of the district and to locate and map the village sites and ruins. When he was done, the importance of the sites was at last appreciated. From the junction of the Piedra and San Juan rivers, just below the town of Arboles on the Colorado–New Mexico border, there was an almost unbroken line of former Anasazi sites extending northward on both sides of the river for over fifteen miles.

A majority of the sites were remains of jacal villages of the Pueblo I and II periods. But many other heaps of debris from the Pueblo III Period unquestionably covered the ruins of large stone dwellings of the Pueblo II Period. Chimney Rock Mesa and its lower spurs were literally covered with the ruins of stone buildings. The large pueblo previously mentioned was there, and on the lower level of the same formation were 110 mounds, each marking the location of a former unit-type or one-clan village. The cultural center of the district was on and around Chimney Rock Mesa.[184]

Also represented in three localities at Piedra were dwellings from the Pueblo IV and V periods. Two of the sites, one on the mesa top just above the town of Arboles and the other on the west side of the river six miles upstream, were occupied by Jemez people during and after the Rio Grande Pueblo revolt of A.D. 1680–92. Following their decisive defeat by the Spanish in the battle of San Diego Canyon on June 29, 1696, the Jemez people fled to Navajo country and remained there for several years.[185] That small groups of them should drift northward into the Piedra District is not surprising, since the region was known to them either through tradition or from knowledge gained from hunting parties.

The Piedra mountain region is one of the richest and most beautiful in Colorado. Pagosa Springs and its environment form a splendidly fertile recreational center, with motels, mountain lodges, ranches, golf courses, and streams filled with trout. Game and timber are as abundant today as they must have been in the days of the Anasazi dwellers. Abandonment of the area was not because of desiccation. The only plausible causes would be nomadic raiders, internal dissension, or religious considerations. Roberts found that the oldest villages were scattered and unprotected, whereas those of late Pueblo II were placed on higher and more defensible locations and were concentrated within smaller areas. Both factors indicate pressure from hostile or covetous invaders.[186]

The investigations of Roberts were almost wholly restricted to sites on the upper level of Stollsteimer Mesa. The only exception was a small village on the first bench above the river at the foot of the southern end of the mesa. In all, his excavations included the ruins of eighty dwellings, two kivas, six circular depressions, and seven burial mounds.[187]

Three kinds of houses were uncovered, all belonging to the general type called jacal. They had lateral doorways and flat roofs with central smoke holes and were grouped around the pit from which the dirt had been taken for their construction. Each house group seemed to represent a unit and the home of a single clan, a prototype of the unit-type dwellings of the Pueblo II Period.

The earliest of the three kinds of house revealed a late Basketmaker inheritance. It had sloping walls, a flat roof, and interior support posts and beams. But its general features moved it into the early Pueblo I Period. The next two types of dwelling to be built were surface types of rectangular shape, having vertical walls that were definite forms of the Pueblo I Period. These made possible the joining of single-roomed dwellings into compact communal units that consisted of contiguous rooms.[188]

Piedra. *Left,* plot plan of the B village. *Top middle,* detail of method of passageway construction for kiva entrance. *Top right,* house and kiva combination in B village. *Bottom right,* postulated construction of B-type houses. From Roberts, 1930.

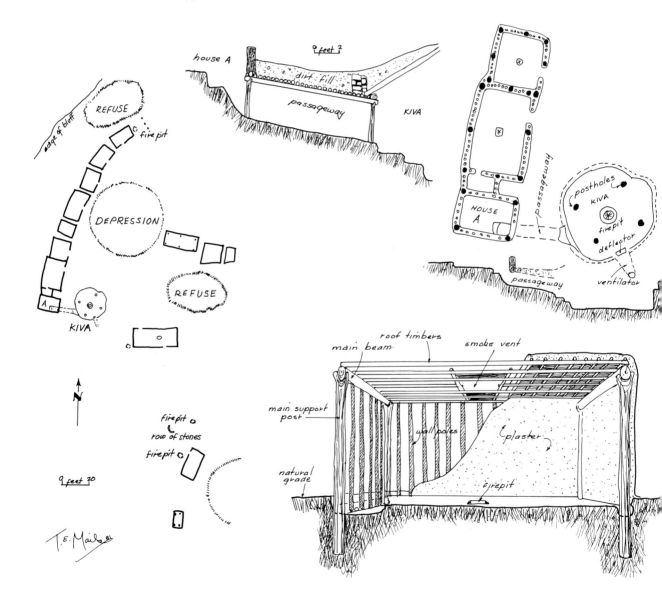

Piedra pottery: *a,* pitcher. *b,* bowl. *c,* water jar. *d,* culinary vessel with banded neck. *e,* cooking bowl. *f,* black-on-red seed jar. *g,* duck vessel. *h,* seed jar. From Roberts, 1930.

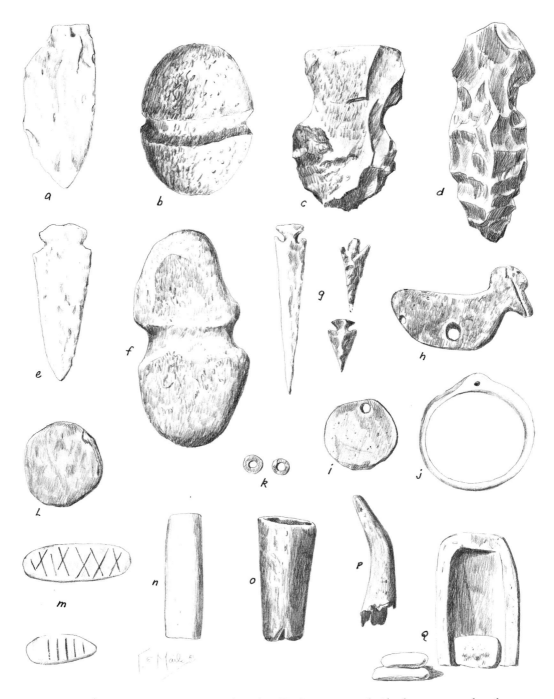

Typical lesser material culture objects found at Piedra: *a,* stone knife. *b,* stone maul or hammerstone. *c,* stone hoe. *d,* stone pick. *e,* stone projectile point. *f,* stone ax. *g,* chalcedony and obsidian arrowpoints. *h–i,* stone pendants. *j,* shell bracelet. *k,* stone beads. *l,* stone pot lid. *m,* bone gaming pieces. *n,* bone bead. *o,* stone pipe. *p,* antler flaker. *q,* manos and metate. From Roberts, 1930.

The pits mentioned earlier served secondary purposes. They were also used as reservoirs, as the subterranean portions of kivas, and possibly as dance plazas. Roberts could find the ruins of only two clan-sized kivas, and he thought it an unusually small number for so many dwellings. But it was a feature comparable to that of communities of the same period in the La Plata district farther west, and it possibly suggests that the circular kiva was still in a developmental stage.[189]

As was so often the case in the south, the lesser material culture objects found at Piedra were limited to those made from imperishable materials: pottery, bone and stone implements, stone and shell items for personal adornment, and small fossils and stones that because of their unique forms were saved and possibly used for ritual purpose.[190]

The ceramic craft was clearly in a transitional stage. Features of the late Basketmaker III Period continued as new features characteristic of Pueblo I ware were being added. These included banding on the necks of culinary vessels; a shift from banded to coiled pottery; variations in vessel shapes; the discovery of the slip wash; the elaboration of painted decoration; the turning to new sources for design elements; and the extending of painted decoration to the surfaces of large jars, pitchers, seed jars, and other vessel forms in addition to bowls and ladles. Pottery designs were characterized by boldness and by a marked lack of skill in execution. The potters were in no way bound by convention. They worked freely, and they demonstrated amply that the clay and paint media were still not mastered.[191]

A few bone and stone implements were turned up, such as awls, knife handles, punches, beads, whistles, gaming pieces, manos and metates, cutting stones, hammers, projectile points, and ornaments. The arrow points in particular showed that considerable skill had been developed in the art of stone flaking.[192] Four glycymeris shell bracelets could have come only from the south, and so represented trade relations between the Piedra Anasazi and other peoples.

Burial customs were identical to those practiced throughout the San Juan area, except that most bodies were oriented with heads to the north, and the rest in any direction. Two forms of crania were found in the skeletal material, including those with occipital deformation.[193] The refuse mounds were used as cemeteries and were randomly located.[194]

Roberts believes that the data he gathered from the Piedra excavations give "a clear and distinct picture" of life in the Pueblo I Period in the Piedra portion of the San Juan archaeological area. Plain evidence of the wholesale destruction of villages by fire revealed to him that the stage was one of disturbance and instability. Skeletal remains showed a mixing of peoples, and the material culture as a whole evidenced that it resulted from the adaptation of already established practices, to which new features were added. As time went on, some customs were changed and others were completely discarded.

Chapter 5

KAYENTA

INTRODUCTION

Kayenta is an incredible land of twisted, shadowed, seamed, and crossbedded sandstone mountains surrounding deep green canyons. It looks in some areas like gigantic piles of pulled taffy. Upon experiencing it, the archaeologist Jesse Walter Fewkes felt that the environment must have had a marked influence upon the character of its architecture and upon its arts and crafts. "We can hardly imagine a people living any length of time in this region without being mentally influenced by the precipitous cliffs that rise on all sides. The summits of these heights are eroded into fantastic shapes resembling animals or grotesque human forms. The constant presence of these marvelous forms, of awe-inspiring size and weird appearance, exerted a profound influence on the supernatural ideas of the inhabitants. Here were born many conceptions of earth gods and the like, survivals of which still remain among the Hopi."[1]

Although it has not been emphasized here, the early Kayenta Anasazi culture is already well known to us, for it was in the Kayenta area and nearby La Plata that much of our archaeological information regarding the Basketmakers was obtained. From A.D. 500 on, the Kayenta farmed the bottomlands of Tsegi Canyon and occupied most of the region north of the Little Colorado River in the high desert country of northern Arizona. In Pueblo III times they built several significant cliff dwellings and a host of surface pueblos somewhat similar to those existing at Hopi today. But no round towers have been found in the Kayenta area.[2]

Excepting certain of the structures erected in Canyon de Chelly and Canyon del Muerto, the best-known Kayenta cliff dwellings are Betatakin and Kiet Siel of the Marsh Pass area. Two smaller cliff ruins are also worthy of attention: Inscription House and Three Turkey Ruin. Archaeologists judge that the farmlands of Kayenta were more constricted and less productive than those of Mesa Verde and Chaco Canyon. The population remained relatively small, and the artisans were either slovenly or did not have the time to build as well as their Anasazi relatives did elsewhere. Kayenta masonry work was decidedly inferior. For the most part, irregularly shaped stones, neither dressed nor smooth, were laid in random patterns and interspersed with great quantities of adobe mortar that cracked badly with the passage of time. Walls of flimsy wattle and daub (jacal) were erected alongside walls of stonework, and the pithouses common to the Basketmaker III Period were at times still being built side by side with the masony pueblos of Pueblo III.[3]

The kivas of Kayenta differed considerably from those of Mesa Verde and Chaco. Circular kivas were built, but they lacked pilasters and were sometimes semisubterranean, sometimes entirely aboveground; contemporary with them were the rectangular surface ceremonial rooms that archaeologists call *kihus*. These had many of the traditional kiva features, but were entered by a doorway rather than through a hatchway in the roof.

In describing the kivas of the Marsh Pass area in 1909, Fewkes notes they are of two types: one circular and subterranean type allied to those of Mesa Verde; the other rectangular, aboveground, and entered from the side.

He also states that the key to the life-style of the people from which the cliff dweller culture was derived is probably the kiva, which furnishes also an excellent basis for the classification of the Anasazi into subordinate groups. Architecturally, he says, the kiva reached its highest development in the Mesa Verde region (Chaco enthusiasts may properly dispute this, but the major Chaco excavations came a full dozen years after Fewkes wrote, and he was without benefit of this information), where it is a circular subterranean room with pilasters and banquettes, ventilators and deflectors, fireplaces, and ceremonial openings. As the San Juan River is followed down to its junction with the Colorado, there is a gradual simplification of the circular type of kiva by the elimination of pilasters, ventilators, and other features, until at last, in some places, the round kivas consist of rooms in which almost the only architectural feature remaining is a large banquette.

The question naturally arises whether the circular kiva in the eastern part of the Mesa Verde region was an adaptation of a simpler form that began in the western part, or whether the latter was a degenerate form of the eastern. In other words, in which direction did the spread of kiva ideas go? Some authorities believe there was no spread as such, that in the beginning circular kivas lacking pilasters extended simultaneously along the entire course of the San Juan, and that as the kivas of the Mesa Verde became highly specialized in function, pilasters were added there while the kivas of regions lower down the river still lacked them. Fewkes disagrees, contending that from the evidence "it would seem that the circular form of kiva originated in the eastern section and gradually extended westward,"[4] where in time the pilasters were developed.

He supports his belief by noting also that the modern Hopi rectangular form of ceremonial room situated underground seems in some instances to have derived certain features from the circular subterranean kiva. Yet the chief kiva at Walpi, that used by the Snake Fraternity, is rectangular and subterranean, while that used by the Flute priests is practically a ceremonial room and is entered by a side doorway. In fact, though, ceremonial rooms of both forms, circular and rectangular, exist side by side in many ancient cliff dwellings, and the puzzle of some aspects of the course of kiva-*kihu* development remains.

POTTERY

Archaeologists believe that the knowledge of true pottery-making reached the Kayenta Anasazi by A.D. 400, although there is evidence of a local development of the ceramic craft about the same time. Some baskets were being lined with clay, and while the result was not yet true pottery, the idea was at least germinating. The discovery of a few free-standing unfired clay vessels indicates that a second step was taken also: from that point on, the coiling technique was practiced, and it appears that thereafter the craft developed rapidly.

A well-made fired grayware called Lino Gray was in production by A.D. 500. Its shapes included globular jars, flat-topped hemispherical ollas, ladles, and gourd forms, all quite similar to forms being manufactured at the time by the Hohokam and Mogollon. Less common forms were jugs and seed jars, and Kayenta ollas had no handles. In an apparent attempt to copy the red-slipped vessels of their Southwestern neighbors, the Kayentans even coated a few vessels with a powdery red pigment called fugitive red. But the pigment was not fired, and some of the red rubbed off whenever the vessel was used. Not until A.D. 800 did the Kayentans master the art of manufacturing a true red-colored pottery of their own.

Some of the early Lino Gray pots were painted with black decorations, most likely inspired by basket designs of the period. This style was called Lino Black-on-gray and featured triangles, squares, circles, bands of triangles, zigzag lines, and some human and animal figures. A common depiction was a line of people holding hands in such a way as to form a large circle.

Many of the motifs seen on Hohokam and Mogollon pottery of the A.D. 100–500 period were prominent in Kayenta pottery of the years A.D. 600–1000. These included hatched lines, crosses, scrolls, and chevrons and triangles painted along bowl rims. Whether these were local creations developed by the Anasazi, whether it took a long time for the ideas to spread north, or whether the Anasazi were simply slow to accept the designs of others is not known.

In spite of the similarities between Kayenta ceramics and those of their southern neighbors, a distinct pottery-making tradition emerged early in Kayenta history. White-firing kaolin clays occur in Kayenta country, but not in southern Arizona, and so by A.D. 700 a black-on-white pottery unique to the Kayentans was begun. Although decorations included life forms and life designs similar to those of the southern peoples, Kayenta potters established at the same time their own rigid geometric styles, and elaboration upon these became the standard for almost all elements used by the Kayentans throughout their cultural history.

Kayenta bowls were hemispherical and ranged from 4 to 13 inches in diameter. Rims were either straight or curved out slightly to form a lip. A common feature, never seen elsewhere among the Anasazi, was a single, horizontally placed loop handle. All decoration was done on the bowl interior. Ladles were of the bowl-and-handle type and averaged 9 inches in length. Handles were both hollow and solid and sometimes were elongated loops. Only the Kayentans manufactured a colander. This was a small seed-jar-shaped vessel with a fairly large orifice. It ranged from 3 to 6 inches in diameter and had a number of small holes in the bottom that enabled it to serve as a sifter or strainer.

Kayenta—Black Mesa. *Top,* pitchers: *left,* Dogoszhi Black-on-white; *right,* two Tusayan White-ware. *Center,* Tusayan Polychrome ladle. *Bottom left,* Sosi Black-on-white. *Bottom right,* Tusayan Whiteware. From Gumerman, 1970.

During the Pueblo I Period, the Kayentan artisans advanced from the earlier basketlike designs to thin lines with dots and triangles. The style is called Kana-a Black-on-white and was made from about A.D. 725 to 950. During the Pueblo II Period the shift was to circular scrolls, large triangles, and broad dotted lines, classified today as Black Mesa Black-on-white. This form of decoration began about A.D. 900 and continued until A.D. 1100. Toward the end of the period the dotted lines were replaced by interlocking-triangle scrolls, in a style called Sosi Black-on-white.

During the Pueblo III Period, from A.D. 1100 to 1300, the Kayenta design elements became far more complex as smaller individual designs were combined to provide an intricate pattern of decoration. Almost none of the white background was allowed to appear, and the line work was extraordinarily accurate.[5] Some of the most beautiful decoration of the prehistoric Southwest was done by Kayenta artists between the years A.D. 1250 and 1300. Curiously enough, in these late pottery types, called Tusayan and Kayenta black-on-whites, the potters returned to design elements abandoned by their ancestors hundreds of years before. Some new vessel shapes, such as mugs, also made their first appearance at this time, perhaps because of influences from the talented potters of Mesa Verde.

The Kayenta region was unique in the Southwest in that three different kinds of clay were available to its potters. This stroke of good fortune enabled them alone to produce wares that fired white, orange, and gray. Other potters had to coat their brown- or gray-firing pottery with a red slip to produce redware, while the Kayentans were able to manufacture a true orange pottery called Tsegi Orangeware. At first they did their decoration directly on the orange surface, but by A.D. 900 they were coating the entire orange vessel, save perhaps the bowl bottom, with a red slip, and then painting their black designs over the red. From here they moved to polychrome ware by incorporating the natural orange into the decoration scheme.

Polychrome finds were abundant at Kiet Siel, Betatakin, and the surface pueblos of Marsh Pass. These included bowls and handled jars, but no ollas, ladles, or seed jars. The base color was yellow or orange, and the decorations were done in black, red, and white. The bowls averaged 10 inches in diameter, but some were as large as 14 inches. They had outcurving rims and a single handle. Exterior decoration was confined to one or two heavy and carelessly drawn lines that encircled the bowls just below the rim. Interior designs covered, more or less completely, the inner surface.[6]

The designs for orangeware were similar to those for black-on-white ware of the same period, although they were combined in different ways. Hatched lines were drawn on Tusayan Black-on-red, and broad black lines were applied to Medicine Black-on-red. Common to the polychromes were broad red bands outlined either in black or in combinations of broad black lines outlined in white and hatched black lines. These are known today as Kiet Siel and Tusayan polychromes.

The whiteware and orangeware vessels of Kayenta are thought to have served a variety of functions, but grayware pots were used mainly for cooking, and they followed a simpler course of development. After A.D. 700 the plain Lino Gray vessels were replaced with jars whose necks were decorated with either a corrugated band or incised lines that tended to emphasize the clay coils that formed the neck. By A.D. 900 the pinched corrugations were extended to cover the entire vessel. Grayware bowls remained quite rare. Typical for the Pueblo II Period were pear-shaped or globular jars with large apertures, called Tusayan Corrugated. By A.D. 1075 the clay coils were no longer pinched, but just overlapped in a siding-like effect entitled Moenkopi Corrugated. Most Kayenta corrugated wares were inferior in execution to those of Mesa Verde and Chaco Canyon.[7]

As the Kayenta culture neared its end, corrugated pottery gave way to a new style of grayware with a bumpy texture called Kiet Siel Gray; it is quite similar to Hopi utility pottery. In fact, many aspects of the Kayenta culture are common to what archaeologists recognize now as early Hopi, including the whiteware and orangeware pottery traditions.

After A.D. 1300, whether as a result of trade contacts or as a result of a southern migration of the Kayenta Anasazi, it is apparent that some Kayenta designs were adopted by the Mogollon. Kinishba polychromes were quite similar to the Jeddito Black-on-yellow and Sikyatki polychromes being fashioned at Hopi at the same time. Kayenta influence is also seen as far south as the Tucson area, causing experts to believe the Kayentans split up as they moved, some joining the Hopi and others settling in Mogollon and Hohokam country. Where the latter group went after that remains anyone's guess.

CANYON DE CHELLY AND CANYON DEL MUERTO

Ancient Kayenta can be subdivided for study purposes into three major areas: Canyon de Chelly, Marsh Pass, and Black Mesa. Today the Hopi pueblos occupy what was once Kayenta's southernmost edge.

Canyon de Chelly is pronounced "Canyon d'Shay." It sits in the middle of the Navajo Reservation and cuts through the Defiance Plateau, an eroded, gently sloping plain that separates Black Mesa Basin on the west from San Juan Basin on the east. From the Tunicha Mountains come the streams that continue to carve out thirty-mile-long Canyon de Chelly. Joined to de Chelly like one arm of a giant wishbone is Canyon del Muerto, Canyon of the Dead, eighteen miles in length. Not so well known as the Grand Canyon, the colorful Canyons de Chelly and del Muerto are nevertheless photographed by professionals as often, and in my view the multihued cliffs and stone monoliths of these canyons are far more inspiring and worthwhile. On any given day the Grand Canyon looks about the same from each of its plateau view stations. It alters its appearance only as the weather changes. The Canyons de Chelly and del Muerto, both of which have countless side canyons and caves, present new and breathtaking sights every half mile as they twist, turn, and soar.

Beginning as a shallow, cottonwood-lined cut just beyond the Navajo town of Chinle, the great sandstone cliffs of de Chelly continue to rise steadily until at Spider Rock the rim of the plateau is almost one thousand feet above the canyon floor.[8] To stand at any one of the score of lookout points on the sheer edge of the precipice and look down into the broad canyon with its streams, cottonwoods, peach orchards, ruins, rock art, and Navajo hogans is an experience like no other, and it draws you back again and again. The best known of the Anasazi ruins are White House in Canyon de Chelly and Mummy Cave and Antelope House in Canyon del Muerto.

Sometime after 1880, the first written reports of the astonishingly beautiful Canyon de Chelly began to appear, and before long scores of people were making their way to the canyon to observe its wonders and to collect what they could of the relics there. For years thereafter, vast quantities of artifacts

Map of the Canyon de Chelly National Monument.

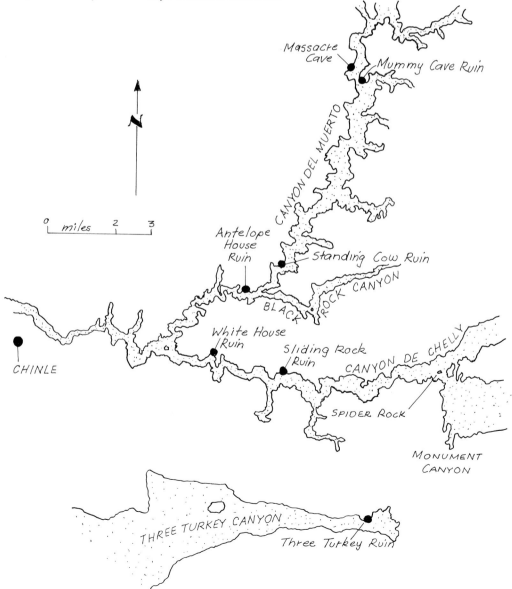

Canyon del Muerto: cliff dwellings abound on nearly every ledge.

were removed for personal collections and to be sold to wealthy collectors, museums, and traders.

In 1879 Colonel James S. Stevenson had led an exploration of the Southwest for the newly created Bureau of American Ethnology (BAE). It included a visit to Canyon de Chelly, and he returned to Washington, D.C., with twenty-one pieces of pottery from the area. In 1882 Stevenson and his party made a second and more extensive examination of the canyon, making sketches and taking photographs. (It was his discoveries of Anasazi mummies that caused him to give Canyon del Muerto its name.)

Cosmos and Victor Mindeleff, employees of the BAE, made many maps, diagrams, and photographs of Canyon de Chelly between the years 1882 and 1897. Victor's monumental work on pueblo architecture was published in the BAE Eighth Annual Report (1886–87), and Cosmos's extensive investigation of the canyon was published in the BAE Sixteenth Annual Report (1894–95). Authorities credit Cosmos's work with being the "best broad study" of Canyon de Chelly's cliff dwellings.

Next to come were sightseers and writers, including Dr. Theophil Mitchell Prudden, a pathologist-bacteriologist whose observations concerning Canyon de Chelly were published in 1903. The writer and photographer Frederick Monsen made many trips to the canyon in the middle 1880s and explored many ruins. Caught up by the excitement of the Southwest, he lived among the Indians for eighteen years and made a superb photographic record of the people and the environment. Regrettably, to put it mildly, Monsen's entire collection, including 10,000 photographic plates, was lost in the San Francisco earthquake and fire of April 18, 1906. All that survives is some enlargements in the Huntington Library in San Marino, California, and in the Museum of the University of Oslo, Norway.[9]

Chinle trader Samuel E. Day and his sons Samuel, Jr., and Charles did considerable relic hunting in Canyons de Chelly and del Muerto between the years 1902 and 1905, selling parts of their collections to the Smithsonian Museum, Washington, D.C., and to the Brooklyn Museum, New York.

The best known of any archaeologist for his association with Canyons de Chelly and del Muerto is Earl Halstead Morris, who did prodigious work at the canyon ruins between 1923 and 1932. In particular, his exceedingly fruitful excavations at Mummy Cave and nearby Big Cave are known to every student of Southwestern literature. Here he found such an abundance of material that it allowed him to see at a glance everything from pure Basketmaker to late Pueblo, a time span covering a thousand years. Among his many contributions, Morris restored portions of the three-story tower at Mummy Cave. Thanks to him, tourists see the tower today much as it was when first erected in A.D. 1284. Morris's wife, Ann, made the original studies of Canyon de Chelly rock art and thereby supplied her own valuable contribution to Anasazi lore.

Harold Sterling Gladwin's main offering to Canyon de Chelly archaeology was his tree-ring studies, which accurately dated some of the ruins. These enabled him to show that, in his view, drought was not so much the cause of the ultimate abandonment of San Juan drainage basin as was the more likely intolerable harassment by the Apache and Navajo.

David L. DeHarport devoted six seasons of fieldwork to Canyon de Chelly between 1946 and 1951. His findings were described in a 1,600-page report for his Ph.D. at Harvard University, as yet unpublished and deposited in the Peabody Museum files. In all, he recorded 369 sites, of which 153 included rock art in various amounts.

In 1949 and 1950, Charles R. Steen, an archaeologist employed by the National Park Service, excavated Tse'-ta'a, a badly damaged Canyon de Chelly surface ruin that proved to be inhabited from late Basketmaker times through the Pueblo III Period, and occupied sporadically thereafter by Hopi between A.D. 1300 and 1700. From what at first seemed to be a stream-cut and hopelessly eroded ruin, Steen unearthed pithouse remains, sherds, parts of charred beams, masonry walls, grooved axes, hammerstones, projectile points, and blades of petrified wood. Two kivas were found, both about 12 feet (3.6 m) in diameter. One was entirely subterranean, with a banquette 3 feet (90 cm) high. The other was about 7 feet (2.1 m) high, being half below ground level and having niches and a firepit. A larger kiva, about 20 feet (6 m) in diameter, had been built on top of a previous kiva, and a group of thirteen contiguous masonry rooms adjoined it that showed Mesa Verde and Chaco Canyon influences. Rock paintings high above the ground surface at Tse'-ta'a indicated to Steen that multistoried structures had once existed, enabling residents standing on third- or fourth-story roofs to do the artwork. Late in its history, Navajo residents were also at Tse'-ta'a, but that is another story. Our concern is with the Anasazi.[10]

On April 1, 1931, Canyon de Chelly National Monument was established by President Herbert Hoover. It covers 131 square miles and is administered today by the National Park Service of the U.S. Department of the Interior, "working closely," Campbell Grant points out, "with the Navajo Tribal Council at Window Rock, Arizona."[11]

Because of their surpassing beauty and ecological advantages, the Canyons de Chelly and del Muerto were natural attractions for prehistoric Indians. Not surprisingly, then, the two dramatic canyons became parents to hundreds of prehistoric Indian sites, including especially those of the Anasazi. Some of the sites can be recognized today only through pottery sherds lying on the surface. Others are visible cliff dwelling ruins that perch in high, shallow caves along the cliff faces, or are crumbled ruins lying at surface levels hard by the present stream beds.

Like so many of their relatives who seem to have drawn inspiration and invigoration from spellbinding landscapes, the Basketmaker Anasazi came early to Canyons de Chelly and del Muerto. Canyon farmers had ideal growing conditions for corn and squash, and there were abundant nuts, seeds, berries, roots, bulbs, and plant greens. Turkeys may have been the chief meat resource, followed by jackrabbit and deer, although many other animals were included in the dwellers' diet.[12] The population of the two canyons in the Basketmaker II Period is thought to have reached approximately two hundred, the settlements being concentrated in the lower sections and a few middle and upper reaches.

During the Basketmaker III Period, from A.D. 500 to 700, the typical canyon dwelling became the pithouse, placed in rock shelters, in caves, and in the open. Pithouses were often built in clusters, each cluster with its own group of storage cists. The earliest pithouses of Mummy Cave were circular and recessed. Diameters ranged from 12 to 25 feet (3.6–7.5 m), and pit depths ranged from 3 to 5 feet (0.9–1.5 m). Later houses were more oval. Ordinarily, but not always, four posts topped by four main beams provided the main structure, and the walls were slanted and completed in the classic pithouse manner. Kivas were not built during this period, but it is assumed from such finds as clay fertility figures that rituals were being conducted in homes or in the open. The great number of rock paintings near the habitation sites indicates that open areas were the most likely places.[13] Toward the end of the Basketmaker III Period a few surface houses with contiguous rooms were built in peripheral areas, and some archaeologists suspect this might be because of cultural diffusion, since the canyons offered a logical route for new ideas to travel.[14]

As A.D. 700 and the beginning of the Pueblo I Period arrived, the inhabitants of the Southwest embarked on perhaps the most vital century in their history. For many, it was a time of shifting about, of the blending of cultures and cultural patterns. The northern Anasazi of the Durango area ventured south and west into the La Plata Valley, onto Mesa Verde, and west to southeastern Utah. Simultaneously, the Anasazi already south of the San Juan began to create new communities in the Marsh Pass region, in the Red Rocks Valley, and in Canyon de Chelly. Campbell Grant points out that these new areas of habitation acted thereafter as corridors for the passage of peoples and ideas from north to south and vice versa, although cultural changes resulting from the exchange of ideas often took a long time to develop. Moreover, in some peripheral areas such as central Utah and the Fremont culture region of southeastern and eastern Utah, the new ideas seem never to have arrived at all.[15] Life there in Virgin territory went on pretty much as it had done.

One of the first consequences of the population shifts and the influx of new ideas was a change in building styles, although, as one might expect, the Anasazi who were already fond of a certain style would at first resist change. Later, as they observed certain advantages in the new ideas, they would begin

Ruin on bottomland, Canyon del Muerto. After Cosmos Mindeleff, BAE 16th Annual Report, Pl. 45, 1897.

with tentative modifications rather than effecting an immediate and total change. Even then the final product would be an adaptation rather than a duplication. For example, pithouses were built for centuries after other building styles were introduced, although certain of their features would vary from region to region. Early in the Pueblo I Period some of the Anasazi began to build surface rooms. Jacal and then jacal and masonry construction were employed in open sites, and toward the end of the Pueblo II Period the typical dwelling in the Four Corners region was made up of masonry walls and contiguous rooms. When dwellings were located in a cave or alcove, the masonry rooms were placed tightly against the back wall, with the kivas out in front. All the unit-type buildings in Canyon de Chelly were set well back under the overhang to protect them from frequent and disastrous rock falls. While the caves served as excellent shelters, they were dangerous in many ways. The recesses were created by a combination of water wear and exfoliation, the latter continuing to occur while the Anasazi lived there. Over the ages, weather changes had caused the face of the cave arch to fracture, and sometimes large shingles of stone would break off and crash onto the cave front and down into the canyon, thereby forming the valuable talus slopes that would facilitate access to the cliff dwellings and provide building material for the dwellings.

The protokiva came into being in Pueblo II, and by the end of the period it had been replaced by the kiva. But considerable reference to the development of ceremonial chambers has already been made in the Chaco Canyon chapter, and a detailed consideration of kiva construction is set forth in the Mesa Verde chapter that follows, so nothing further need be said about kivas at this point.

Grant believes that a "rather rigid social system" had come into being by A.D. 1100, the end of the Pubelo II Period, and that this in turn had its effect on the development of contiguous unit-type dwellings. The people were dividing into clans, each clan being known by a name, usually that of some animal, plant, or object. Descent was matrilineal, the house belonging to the woman and the kiva to the man.[16]

In 1950 DeHarport estimated that the population of Canyon de Chelly had reached a peak of five hundred by late Pueblo II. Three hundred and one sites were found, the largest having eight dwelling rooms and six storage rooms. He found true circular kivas at all the larger sites. His population estimate did not include Canyon del Muerto, and so the total population of the two canyons may have been eight hundred or more.

In late Pueblo II, pottery-making became increasingly important to the Canyon de Chelly Anasazi, who followed the general trends familiar to other Anasazi regions. They made a plain ware, small decorated ladles, a bird-shaped vessel with the neck serving as the spout, corrugated ware, and a coiled black-on-white decorated ware. Pottery found at the Tse'-ta'a excavation included Kana-a, Mancos, and Mesa Verde black-on-whites. Excavations at Canyon de Chelly reveal that the pottery of late Pueblo II was mainly a type common to the region northeast of the canyon. Being peripheral to the powerful centers of Mesa Verde and Chaco Canyon, the residents of Canyon de Chelly seem to have adopted pottery styles rather than developing styles of their own.

There are only three books that contain extensive material on Canyon de Chelly's Anasazi culture. One is *Earl Morris & Southwestern Archaeology* by Florence C. and Robert H. Lister. Another is Cosmos Mindeleff's report in the Bureau of Ethnology Sixteenth Annual Report (1894–95). But the best by far is Campbell Grant's 1978 *Canyon de Chelly: Its People and Rock Art*, which has,

White House Ruin. *Top,* plot plan of upper part of ruin. *Center,* plot plan of lower part of ruin. *Bottom,* view of the ruin. After Cosmos Mindeleff, 1897.

along with other data, a splendidly illustrated section on the rock art of the canyon people. Covering more than eighty pages, the pictographic data provide a panoramic view of the life and environment of those who lived in the canyons, revealing in particular the extent of their cultural development over a thousand years.

Wishing to detract in no wise from Mr. Grant's stellar contribution, I redrew in the Basketmaker III section only enough of his illustrations to give a sample of rock art and its meaning in those times, and I redraw enough in this chapter to accomplish the same end in completing the study of Anasazi life in Canyons de Chelly and del Muerto. The manner of creating rock art was explained when the subject was first treated in earlier chapters.

As Paul Martin points out, less is known of the prehistory of cotton than of any other major cultigen. Cotton was present in Arizona by A.D. 100 to 300 and may have been there earlier, since it has been found in Mogollon, Hohokam, Anasazi, and Hakataya sites.[17] But cotton was not in broad use by the Anasazi until the Pueblo II Period. In discussing its use at Canyon de Chelly, Grant states flatly: "The knowledge of cotton and loom weaving certainly came from Mexico and probably was first passed on to the Hohokam and thence to the Anasazi by the same people who had brought them red polished ware and cranial deformation."[18] Kilts, blankets, and breechclouts were now woven of cotton, while yucca and *apocynum* were used to make sandals with round toes.

Turkeys were domesticated and might have become a primary meat source. The atlatl was at last supplanted by the bow and arrow for hunting, although corn ground on trough metates remained the core of the Anasazi diet. Rock paintings and petroglyphs were executed in greater numbers in Pueblo II than in any other period. Burials during this time were usually in the trash deposits, although some were made under dwelling floors and in abandoned storage units. The main mortuary offerings were pottery. One fact made clear by the skeletal remains was that cranial deformation, so common to all other Anasazi at the time, was also practiced at Canyon de Chelly.

During the last half of the eleventh century, problems similar to those that led to the final abandonment of other Anasazi regions began also to affect the residents of Canyons de Chelly and del Muerto. Whatever actually happened there, the peace that marked a thousand productive years was beginning to erode. Perhaps it was due to constant pressure from the nomadic and non-agricultural peoples moving in from the north and east. Athapaskans and the Shoshoneans, particularly the warlike Utes who ultimately dominated the entire Great Basin and Colorado Plateau, are usually cited as the culprits.

Nevertheless, protected as they were by the natural barriers of the Grand Canyon and the Chuskas, the Kayenta Anasazi were able to overcome for another thirty years whatever pressures had caused, by A.D. 1250, the entire northern frontier to begin to collapse. While life went on at Kayenta, the Anasazi of the Mesa Verde culture were filtering out of the cliff dwellings and on their way to join relatives living in other places. It is believed that some stopped for a while at the Canyon de Chelly and Marsh Pass areas. Others drifted south to join the already growing settlements at Antelope Mesa that ultimately became the Hopi villages. Some went west to Wupatki. Aztec was reoccupied by Mesa Verde Anasazi in A.D. 1225, but they quickly left there and moved on to the Rio Grande. By the end of the thirteenth century, no one was left at Mesa Verde, and as we know, Chaco Canyon had been standing empty for a hundred years.

In contrast, the last part of the thirteenth century was a time of growth at Kayenta. Several large cliff dwellings were built or enlarged, including Betatakin and Kiet Siel. About A.D. 1284 a three-story tower was erected at Mummy Cave in Canyon del Muerto by migrants from Mesa Verde. Its masonry is Mesa Verde in style, and an abundance of Mesa Verde pottery has been found at the site. Grant believes that, since the rooms were built in a previously unoccupied portion of the village, the occupants considered themselves distinct from the other residents of the cave. He also claims that a number of bodies showing evidence of violent deaths found in the tower indicate a severe clash between an enemy force and the canyon Anasazi, "who were about to abandon the

The petroglyph maker at work.

region."[19] There is, however, scant evidence to indicate such clashes between Anasazi in prehistoric times.

DeHarport identified sixty-seven masonry sites related to the Pueblo III Period at Canyon de Chelly, and estimated the population to be more than eight hundred. Noting the defensive locations chosen by the canyon builders, he mentions also what he thinks were defensive walls with loopholes guarding the way to several sites.[20] Most of the multistoried buildings had collapsed, but enough walls and rubble remained to indicate that many structures had been three or four stories in height. As with the rest of the Kayentans, Pueblo III

Top, plot plan of Mummy Cave in Canyon del Muerto. After Cosmos Mindeleff, 1897. *Center,* close-up of Mummy Cave Tower, as restored by Morris. *Bottom,* general view of the twin caves that together make up Mummy Cave.

masonry work at Canyon de Chelly was by and large inferior to that of Chaco and Mesa Verde.

Most of the beams in the tower at Mummy Cave were cut in A.D. 1284, the latest known building date in the canyon. The final dates from Marsh Pass also fall in the A.D. 1280s, making it obvious that the exodus time for the Kayenta Anasazi was at hand. Migrations from the entire region began soon thereafter, and by A.D. 1300 the last of the three great Anasazi leagues was gone from its beloved home region. Along with the others it was in the process of becoming a revitalized people in new places. Pottery types found in various ruins suggest that eventually some, if not most, of the Kayenta Anasazi wandered south onto Antelope Mesa, where they became the catalyst for a major era of pueblo-building. Several large and important villages of that district date from this time, including Kokopnyama, of the late A.D. 1200s to 1300s; Kawaikuh, or Kawaika-a, of the middle A.D. 1300s to 1400s, and Awatovi of the A.D. 1300 to 1700 period.[21]

It is generally believed that the present populations of the Pueblo villages in Arizona and New Mexico consist mainly of various clans whose ancestors once lived in the ancient villages of the Four Corners region. Problems solved only in part are, first, that of locating accurately the ancestral villages where the clans lived in prehistoric times and, second, that of plotting the migration routes followed from location to location on their way to where they currently live. In this effort, comparative archaeological studies are of prime importance, and the Pueblo migration legends, while accepted for what they are, are of considerable value as guides. Roberts finds that the myths often seem to be at variance with archaeological data.

Jesse Walter Fewkes states that the early legends of the Hopi Snake Clans tell how bags containing their ancestors were dropped from a rainbow in the neighborhood of Navajo Mountain (in southern Utah). Here the people built a pentagonal home. One of their young men married a Snake girl who gave birth to reptiles that bit the children and compelled the people to migrate. They left their canyon homes and went southward, building houses at the stopping places all the way from Navajo Mountain to Walpi. Legends declare that some of these houses, probably their kivas and *kihus,* were round, and others were square. The original Snake kivas were circular, but these gave way to rectangular shapes before the Hopi arrived in the valley below Walpi.[22]

Concerning the ancient site of Laguna Canyon, Victor Mindeleff summarizes the Hopi traditions still preserved by the Horn and Flute clans of Walpi. They declare that the Horn people, to which the Lenbaki (Flute) belonged, came from a mountain range in the east. Its peaks were always green. From the hillside the people saw the plains over which roamed the deer, the antelope, and the bison, feeding on never-failing grasses (possibly the Horn people were so called from an ancient home where horned animals abounded). Meandering through these plains were streams of bright water, beautiful to look upon. It was a place to which none but Hopi ever gained access.

The description suggests a region like that of the headwaters of the Rio Grande, and, as with the Snake people, the traditions tell of a halting kind of migration, not of continuous travel. For they remained many seasons in a given place, where they would plant crops and build permanent houses. One stopping place is described as a canyon with high, steep walls, in which was a flowing stream. This, it is said, was the Tségi (Mindeleff inserts here "the Navajo name for Canyon de Chelly," but Fewkes corrects him, stating that Laguna Canyon, likewise bordered by high cliffs, was meant). Here they built a large house in a cavernous recess high up in the canyon wall and devoted two years to ladder-making and to cutting and pecking shallow holes up the steep, rocky cliff by which to mount to the cavern. Three years more were employed in building the house.

The legend also relates that after they had lived at Tségi for a long time a stranger happened to stray into their vicinity. He proved to be a Hopituh (Hopi), who said that he lived in the south. He remained for a time and left, accompanied by a party of the "Horn" (clan), who wanted to visit the land occupied by their kindred Hopituh and return with an account of them. But they never came back. After waiting a long time, another band was sent out. These people did return, and they said the first Horn group had found wives and built houses on the brink of a beautiful canyon, not far from the Hopituh dwellings. After this, many of the Horns grew dissatisfied with their cavern home, dissensions arose, everyone left, and in this way all the Horn people reached Hopi country, first known to archaeologists as Tusayan.[23] Thus ends the summary by Mindeleff.

Mischa Titiev picks up and emphasizes the intriguing idea of internal dissension as a primary reason for the constant moving of the Hopi and, by inference, of the Anasazi as a whole. He does not deny that drought, war, and disease were contributing factors in the decay of the Anasazi, insisting in fact that Anasazi mobility and Anasazi decline were interrelated. Both were caused by the same set of factors. At one time, he says, the Pueblo peoples were living in small, probably autonomous, villages within which the social system seems to have been dominated by units no larger than a clan. When enemy or economic pressures caused the small units to gather into larger towns, the people did not give up their social and ceremonial integrity. Their reluctance to do so prevented the development of strong villages, and in time caused divisions. Thus a point always came when groups separated and went off to found settlements more in accord with their personal views and lifeway. In this manner, Titiev accounts for the abandonment of the great pueblos, the large number of Anasazi ruins, and the puzzling phenomenon of Anasazi mobility. "It is highly probable," he declares, "that the Great Period of the Pueblos in the San Juan district was quickly terminated not so much by the operation of external forces as by internal disintegration arising from a weakly-knit social structure."[24]

Deric Nusbaum, son of a former superintendent of Mesa Verde National Park, relates a somewhat different story told to him at Mesa Verde by a Hopi medicine man. The Hopi said his people had lived on the mesa "way back," and he told Nusbaum he wanted to see the ruin shaped like a D (Sun Temple). Asked why, he explained there was a legend stating that after his people had lived on the mesa many years they became so powerful and brave they thought they were as powerful as the gods, and didn't need them anymore. To get rid of them, the Hopituh decided to put up a special building with two kivas and a passageway between them (Sun Temple). They would then invite the gods to a contest to see which could make the best medicine—their own medicine men or the gods. Each group would go into a kiva and make medicine. When the gods lost the contest, as the Hopituh were sure they would, the Hopituh could catch them in the passageway and kill them.

The gods were extremely angry when they learned of the plan, and decided to teach the Hopituh a lesson. They came down as requested, and each group went into its kiva. Almost immediately consternation raged in the Hopituh kiva, because the gods had changed the language of each village and the medicine men could accomplish nothing together. The displeased gods then drove the people out of their beautiful homes and down the canyons to the desert country south of the mesa. When the children and the old people couldn't keep up with the others, the gods took pity on them and changed the children into bluebirds and the old ones into turkeys.[25]

Whatever the truth may be, the Anasazi did, over a period of time, leave their ancestral homes and migrate southward; they included the Anasazi who once inhabited the spectacular Canyons de Chelly and del Muerto.

Most of the Navajo hogans seen on the canyon bottoms today are occupied only during the planting and harvesting seasons. The extreme temperatures in summer and winter make living on the canyon rims or at the town of Chinle far more desirable. Summer temperatures in the canyons reach a high of 104° Fahrenheit, and temperatures in winter can drop to −30° F. Winter winds increase the chill factor, and canyon ice can make travel extremely hazardous. But in spring and fall Canyon de Chelly is the perfect place to live in or visit, and thus to experience the wonders wrought by nature and the Anasazi. Yet, despite such adverse weather conditions, it appears that the Anasazi lived year-round down in the canyons and up on the canyon sides. If so, they had to be a hardy race, not easily given over to discouragement.

After A.D. 1300, and for the next four hundred years, small parties of Indian foragers and hunters traveled back and forth through Canyon de Chelly, for it remained an oasis-like thoroughfare connecting the Black Mesa area and the Chuskas, with watered camping places and ample shelter in the abandoned Anasazi villages. Evidence also points to sporadic use of the canyon by small groups of Hopi. The ideal growing conditions continued to make the canyon attractive to farming peoples, and sherds found in the canyons indicate the Hopi visited there often between A.D. 1300 and 1700. They were well received by the Navajo residents, even to the point where intermarriages took place, and such descendants are known today as "High-House People."

Those who planted the first peach orchards in the canyons were in fact migrants from the Rio Grande area, and were known as the Asa. Eventually the Asa and the Navajo quarreled, and the Asa people moved to the Hopi area known as Walpi. In support of their presence at the canyons, fragments of Katcina masks and other ceremonial items of the Asa were found by the Day brothers in Bee Hive Ruin in Canyon de Chelly in 1904. In addition, at three of the canyon rock art sites there are paintings that appear to be Hopi in origin. In time all the Hopi sojourns came to an end, and sometime after A.D. 1746 Canyon de Chelly was permanently taken over by the Navajo.[26]

THREE TURKEY RUIN

Three Turkey Ruin is typical of Kayentan cliff dwellings. It rests in a wind- and water-worn cave in 500-foot-deep Three-Turkey Canyon, a wild and wooded hideout once used by the Navajo to escape the scourge of Kit Carson's Utes and Mexicans in the Navajo war of 1864. It can be reached today by following a very rough road south for fifteen miles or so along the mesa top from the rim of Canyon de Chelly. It is the best-preserved small ruin of those built by the Anasazi, and thus is the counterpart to the larger well-preserved Kiet Siel. Its association of dwelling cubes nestled into the small cave that shelters it is so beautifully blended into the rough, striated sandstone rocks that it would bring accolades to any modern architect. Architecturally, the structure is Kayentan, but Mesa Verde Black-on-white pottery sherds and the kiva suggest it was built by migrants from Mesa Verde in A.D. 1250.

The ruin takes its name from what appear to be three red, brown, and white turkeys painted on the exterior wall of the uppermost room. No one knows who the first white person was to see Three Turkey Ruin, but in 1938 Harold S. Colton found there the remains of several wall inscriptions dated 1898 and 1900. Sam and Charlie, sons of the Chinle trader Samuel E. Day, who was at Canyon de Chelly from 1902 to 1905, are the first documented visitors to investigate Three Turkey Ruin, and it is certain they removed whatever worthwhile artifacts they found. In 1906 the Days sold a large collection of Pueblo artifacts to the Brooklyn Museum.[27] Richard F. Van Valkenburgh, an ethnologist with the U.S. Indian Service who did fieldwork at Canyon de Chelly, was taken by Navajo acquaintances to Three Turkey Ruin in 1937, finding it in such perfect condition he could scarcely believe the Anasazi weren't still living in it. Trying without success first to scale the cliff by climbing up some ancient hand- and toeholds once used by the Anasazi, and then to swing nearly a hundred feet down into the cave from the cliff ledge above, Valkenburgh gave up and in 1938 guided a party from the Museum of Northern Arizona at Flagstaff to the ruin. Ladders were set up, and the party made its way excitedly into the ruin, expecting to find a plethora of artifacts. Astonishingly enough, and despite its difficulty of access, the ruin had been virtually cleaned out by pothunters. The archaeologists had to content themselves with corrugated and smooth gray utility potsherds, tree-ring borings, the making of a map, and a careful inspection of the premises.[28]

They learned that the main part of the ruin rests on a ledge more than sixty feet above the canyon floor, although the stream bed was undoubtedly much higher at the time of occupancy. Access is presumed to have been by ladder, and there is a stone parapet with a loophole, built apparently to guard

Three Turkey Ruin. *Top right,* the pictograph that gives the ruin its name.

against an enemy attempting to scale the ladder before it could be pulled up. The remains of steps made of stone masonry, logs, and fill lead from the parapet up the steeply sloping ledge to and between the buildings.[29]

At one time there were at least eighteen rooms in Three Turkey Ruin, plus a large surface kiva that may be the only perfectly preserved kiva in existence. It is roughly circular in shape and enclosed by thick masonry walls. There are no pilasters. The main support for the kiva roof structure was provided by two large Douglas fir beams. Entry was through a hatchway. There were a ventilator opening, a large wall niche, a central hearth, and a deflector. The interior wall was mud-plastered and decorated with two parallel, dot-bordered white bands having triangles extending up at intervals in sets of three.

All the exterior walls at Three Turkey Ruin were either roughly coursed or angled and uncoursed sandstone slabs set in generous amounts of mud mortar. While some rooms were entered by rooftop hatchways, exterior doorways were placed in the side walls where they would not be vulnerable to frontal attackers. They are jogged so as to be slightly T-shaped, and some openings have pole lintels similar to those used at Mesa Verde. A few rooms have small windows. The main roof beams were set into the walls a few courses below the wall tops, and they projected in most cases four or five feet beyond the walls. Pine and fir poles were laid side by side at right angles to and over the main beams. These were in turn covered by a dense layer of juniper bark, and a thick layer of mud was smoothed over the bark to complete the roof. Some

Map of the Navajo National Monument/Marsh Pass area. Redrawn from official reports by U.S. General Land Office, 1910.

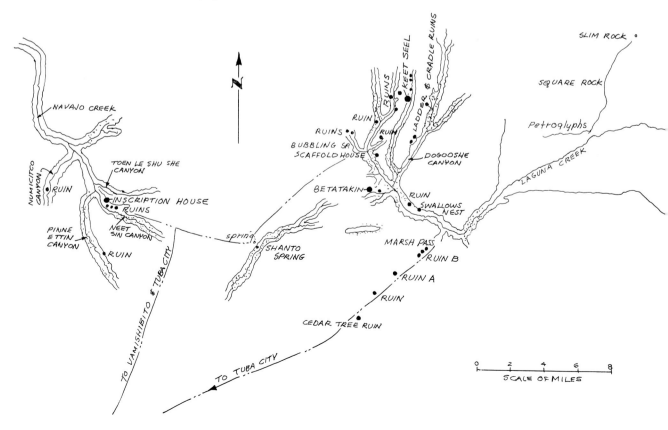

of the finished roof levels were even with the top of the walls. Other dwellings had a slab or mud coping that extended, as at Zuñi, slightly higher than the roof. Several vertical posts rise above the outer walls of two rooms. These may have been used for drying meat or produce. Noteworthy, too, are the jacal (wattle-and-daub) interior partitions used to subdivide some living areas. These were fashioned from vertical split or whole juniper poles lashed to a few horizontal poles and covered with mud.[30]

Above and just east of the main section of Three Turkey Ruin is a second ledge bearing a small ruin that consists of one large masonry room with rounded corners and two flanking masonry storage rooms. The remains of a two-story, two-room house are situated in a cave some eight hundred yards or so from Three Turkey Ruin. Built about A.D. 1200, this structure was burned and abandoned around A.D. 1250, about the same time the Three Turkey complex was built. Archaeologists wonder whether the fire was accidental, or whether it was perpetrated by enemies and forced the move to the higher and more defensible Three Turkey Ruin cave.

MARSH PASS

Thus far only Canyon de Chelly and its immediate environment have been described. But the vast Kayenta region contains many village sites inhabited by the ancient Anasazi. These include cave, surface, and cliff structures, all of which are of special interest to those who seek to trace origins, migrations, and cultural developments. Marsh Pass, in northwestern Arizona, is one of the most important areas, for it lies on a logical route between Mesa Verde and the modern Hopi pueblos. More important still are the resemblances shown by its masonry construction features to those of other regions. The builders of the Marsh Pass structures brought their craft with them, they did not develop it. All indications are that the ancient inhabitants came from higher up the San Juan River, and evidence gathered thus far supports Hopi legends that the last inhabitants were Hopi belonging to the Flute, Horn, and Snake clans.[31] Probable dating for these would be in the late Pueblo III and the early Pueblo IV periods, excepting, of course, the earlier Basketmaker sites also common to the area.

RUIN A AND CLIFF-HOUSE B

Although it is near the flourishing town of Kayenta and is crossed by a major highway running from Tuba City, Arizona, to Cortez, Colorado, Marsh Pass has received relatively slight attention from archaeologists. Yet it is one of the most important archaeological regions in the Southwest, for much of it is covered with ruins. Fewkes made a long-deferred visit to several of the Marsh

Pass sites in 1909 and began his report with two in particular. He designated these Ruin A and Cliff-House B. Ruin A was a surface pueblo of considerable size, although so little of it remained that its true extent could not be known. Still-standing walls rose to a height of 10 feet (3 m), indicating a two-story building. The walls were composed of roughly laid masonry and had been plastered on the interior. An unusual fact was that a number of the stones had been decorated on the exterior surface with deeply incised geometric figures.

The architecture and site choice were similar to those of the ruins at Wupatki and also to the structures at the Hopi village of Old Walpi. Navajo guides told Fewkes they knew of other ruins in the neighborhood that were comparable in structure and situation.[32]

Cliff-House B was a picturesque ruin that occupied the entire floor of a low, narrow cave situated in an almost vertical cliff forming one side of a canyon that extended deep into the mountain. It was exceedingly difficult to enter, and the last twenty feet of the cliffside trail consisted of nothing more than a series of footholes pecked in the rock. The rooms included a three-story square tower, both masonry and jacal walls, and one possible kiva.[33] In general, the condition of the ruin was very poor, as was the case with Swallows Nest, a poorly preserved small cliff dwelling that Fewkes found in a niche high up in an open cave.[34] Then he visited Betatakin and Kiet Siel, the high points of his arduous but rewarding survey of the Marsh Pass area.

BETATAKIN

Betatakin, considered along with Kiet Siel to be in the Marsh Pass area, but actually situated about six miles north of Marsh Pass, is one of the most majestic cliff dwelling sites ever occupied by the Anasazi. A visitor must make the awkward descent a mile and half down into a canyon and then of course master the even more difficult climb back up. A switchback trail drops into the recess at a point where its walls are almost sheer and rise nearly six hundred feet above the floor. The sides of the canyon are a salmon-red sandstone, weathered by wind-blown sand and water into beautifully rounded projections, arches, and caves. The wooded floor is covered with growth that becomes quite dense near the head of the canyon. There are Douglas firs, oaks, box elders, wild rose bushes, and many other plants, all watered by a small clear stream.

The cliff dwelling itself sits in one of nature's largest arches, a simply awe-inspiring cave 236 feet high in a 500-foot cliff wall. It is big enough to contain the Capitol Building of Washington, D.C. Frank Waters's Hopi informants told him it was built by the Fire Clan.[35] It once was a village of more than 100 ground-floor rooms, and 135 rooms in all, masonry walls, mud-plastered roofs, storage rooms, open-roofed courts, six rectangular *kihus* (ceremonial chambers), no kivas, and a good spring at the mouth of the cave.[36] Excellent farmland once existed down on the canyon floors and above on the mesas. Both fuel and building material were plentiful in the canyon.

Betatakin village was first seen by Dr. Byron Cummings in 1909. Subsequent examination by dendrochronology and restoration by Neil M. Judd revealed that Kayentan Anasazi had built and remodeled it over a period of forty years, from A.D. 1242 to 1286,[37] after carrying most of the construction materials laboriously up a steeply slanting rock-and-talus slope. Betatakin was aptly named by the Navajo ''Hillside House,'' because there were only a few square yards of level floor. The sharp sandstone slope required the construction of several large retaining walls, behind which dirt and rubble were piled to make level surfaces.

Fewkes explains how the irregular floors and shallow, high-vaulted caves of Kayenta came into being. As opposed to Mesa Verde, where deep caves

Marsh Pass. *Top,* Ruin A. *Left,* exterior view. *Right,* interior wall. *Bottom,* Ruin B. From Fewkes, 1911a.

Betatakin.

were formed by horizontal rock cleavage, the tall Kayenta rock pinnacles had simply broken away and toppled over, leaving broken bases that later became foundations for rooms and exposing flat cliff faces that, because of the limited space, had to form one or more walls of most dwellings. The contiguous houses, built upon bases of fallen rocks at different heights, often seem to stand one above the other, presenting a preview of the well-known terrace form that marks some modern Hopi pueblos.[38] Since most house walls were built tight against the back wall of the cave, the refuse courts in back of the buildings that were so characteristic of the Mesa Verde cliff dwellings are missing. This method of construction is also common in the cliff dwellings of the Red Rocks country, at the headwaters of the Verde and its tributaries, and in a few cliff dwellings of the Gila area. It is a typical form that is referred to as a dependent village, as distinguished from villages like Cliff Palace, where most of the dwelling walls are independent of the cave wall.

Betatakin can be entered from one end only, over a difficult pathway where one is in constant danger of falling. Just at the edge of the ruin, two pictographs are encountered. One is a large shield-like white circle with a human figure on it with outstretched arms and legs. On each side of the body is a yellow circle and rainbow-like crescent of red, yellow, and green. The other pictograph is of a horned animal, possibly a mountain sheep.

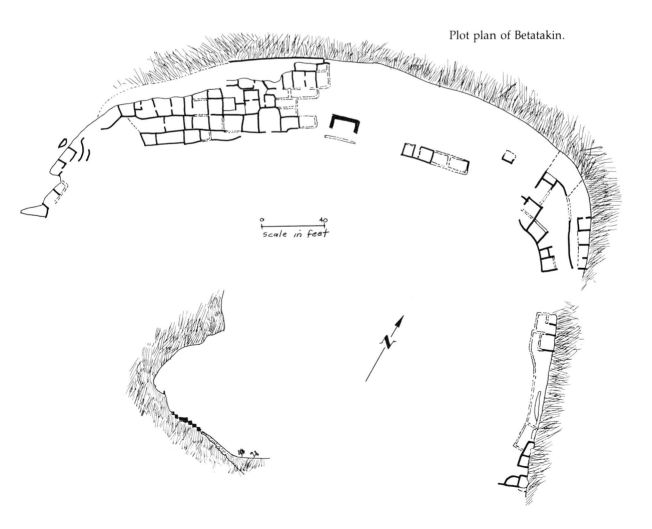

Plot plan of Betatakin.

scale in feet

Betatakin's rooms are rectangular, and only a few are more than two stories high. The masonry is crude, and a marked feature is its wattle-and-daub walls. Interior walls were probably plastered, and some exterior walls were covered with mud. There are no towers or round rooms. All doors and windows are rectangular. In 1917 the ruin was restored and prepared for visitors by a work party under Judd's direction.

KIET SIEL

Eleven miles from Betatakin and ten miles north of Marsh Pass is Kiet Siel (also spelled Keet Seel). Boasting more than 150 rooms and five kivas, it is the largest cliff ruin in Arizona and possibly the best-preserved large ruin of all those built by the Anasazi. It, too, sits in an enormous egg-shaped cave, six miles up Kiet Siel Canyon from Dogozhobiko. The trail to it is enchanting, winding through sun-warmed piñon trees and past waterfalls, and crossing a meandering stream bed many times, while the ravens glide slowly up above, like hang gliders, across a pure blue sky. The Navajo have refused to build hogans in

Kiet Siel ruins.

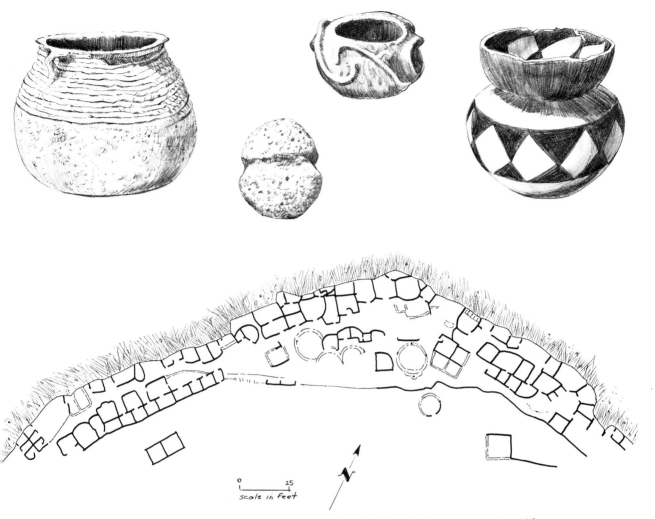

Marsh Pass. *Top,* corrugated ware, stone maul, bowl with relief ornaments, jar with constricted neck. *Bottom,* ground plan of Kiet Siel. From Fewkes, 1911a.

Kiet Siel Canyon, saying the spirits of the ancient Anasazi are still too alive there. Kiet Siel means "Broken Pottery" in Navajo. Waters reports it as having been built by the Spider Clan.[39]

Kiet Siel Ruin is reached today by climbing a forty-foot ladder. Exactly how the Anasazi themselves got up to it is not known for certain, although a pecked way in from both cliff ends is possible. The cliff ceiling is lower than the great arch sheltering Betatakin, hovering closely over the rooms like the wing of a mother hen over her chicks, and then turning like a billowing sail sharply up to meet the sheer cliff face above. The ruin is not high enough up for perfect defense, but the slanting rock wall leading up to it is much too smooth for good footing with a weapon in hand.

Kiet Siel's dwellings are a more loosely knit assemblage than those of Betatakin and are more spread out than most of the cliff dwellings of Mesa Verde. The length of the ruin is about 300 feet (90 m). Rooms include circular kivas and rectangular *kihus.* Towers are absent, and in general there is a strong resemblance to modern Hopi villages. The wall stones are smaller and rougher than those at Betatakin, and considerable rubble mortar was employed in their construction. Jacal walls were also built, and several are well enough preserved to show how such were made at Kayenta. Medium-sized poles were set vertically into the ground at random intervals. Other horizontal poles, or branches, were then laid across these at intervals of 24 inches (61 cm) or so, and the basic framework was lashed together. Long branches, stripped of their leaves, were then woven vertically into the framework to fill out the walls, and a final thick coating of mud was applied on both sides to seal the wall off.

Top, jacal masonry as employed in wall construction at Pueblo Bonito in Pueblo I and early II times. *Bottom,* while not all pure jacal walls were built in precisely this way, this is a perspective view and section showing how a typical jacal wall was constructed. "Jacal" is alternately described as "wattle-and-daub" or "sticks-and-mud."

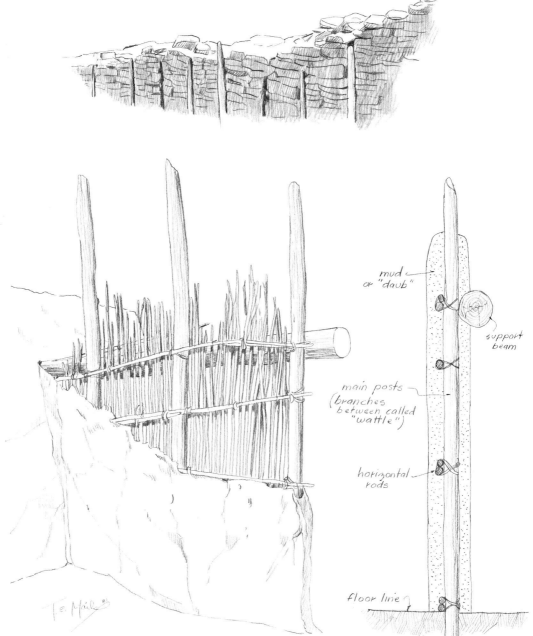

Fewkes reduces the walled enclosures of Kiet Siel to six types:

(1) Kivas, or circular subterranean rooms with a large banquette on one side, the walls being generally broken down and without pilasters or roof-supports.

(2) *Kihus*, or rectangular rooms with doors on one side, each having a low bank, or "deflector," rising from the floor between the doorway and the fire-hole. Instead of this bank being free from the wall, as they are at Betatakin, it is generally joined to it on one side, the floor at the point of junction being raised slightly above the remaining level [to form a low bench]. Smoke-holes are sometimes, but not always, present in the roof. These [*kihu*] rooms, like the circular rooms, are ceremonial in character. The only opening in their floors that can be compared with the *sipapu* is a shallow depression a few inches deep. The diameters of these opening are greater than in the case of the *sipapus* in Cliff Palace kivas.

(3) Rectangular rooms, some of which have benches and show evidence of having been living rooms.

(4) Large rooms each with a fireplace in the middle of the floor.

(5) Rooms with metates set in bins made of stone slabs (milling rooms).

(6) Courts and streets. The longest street extends from the middle of the ruin to the western end and is lined on both sides by rooms many of the roofs of which are still intact.[40]

SCAFFOLD HOUSE

Scaffold House, another large ruin measuring about 300 feet (90 m) in length, sits in a cavern four miles north of Betatakin. It received its names from an unusual wooden scaffold constructed in a vertical, diamond-shaped cleft in the cliff about fifty feet above the west end of the main ruin. To make this scaffold, the builders pecked holes into the sides of the crevice and laid several large logs horizontally, their ends fitted into the holes, forming a bridge. On top of these, smaller poles were laid at right angles; then came coverings of sticks, bark, and clay, the whole being constructed after the manner in which pueblo roofs were made. A hatchway was left in the middle. Fewkes calls it "probably as daring a piece of aerial building as can be found anywhere among cliff dwellings," and he assumes it was an outlook or a place of defense.[41] Later, another scaffold structure like it was found in Sand Canyon, Colorado.[42]

Scaffold House was fairly well preserved, and it contained at least two circular kivas. The larger one was about 15 feet (4.5 m) in diameter and subterranean, with a deep banquette on one side. There were no pilasters, and the inner walls were plastered. Details included a firepit, deflector, wall pegs, and wall niche. Most of the roof was still in place, and its construction was the first of its kind Fewkes had seen. Three main beams, a large center one and two smaller side beams, were laid from wall to wall. Smaller transverse beams were placed on top of these and covered with sticks, bark, and a final layer of adobe. No hatchway was to be seen but, as the covering over the banquette was missing at one point, it is assumed the entrance was there.

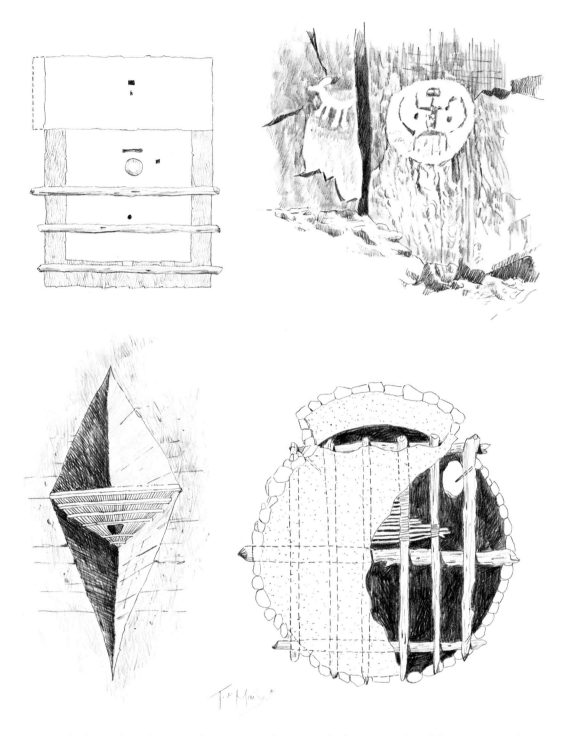

Top left, floor plan of rectangular ceremonial room and placement of roof beams. *Top right*, pictographs at Betatakin. *Bottom left*, the cave scaffold at Scaffold House. *Bottom right*, Scaffold House kiva showing roofing details. From Fewkes, 1911a.

The roof of the second kiva was supported in part by four freestanding posts. It was a feature that reminded Fewkes of one of the kivas of the Rio Grande region described by Castañeda, the historian of the Coronado expedition of 1540–42.[43] Also included in the ruin were a rectangular room that appeared from its kiva-like features to be ceremonial in nature, and a *kihu* much like those of Betatakin. There were many pictographs at Scaffold House, the most conspicuous of which represented human hands, snakes (including one 15 feet [4.5 m] long), mountain sheep or other horned mammals, and figures representing human beings with tails.

Other Marsh Pass cliff dwellings given brief coverage by Fewkes are Cradle House, which had fifty rooms and at least three circular kivas without pilasters; Ladder House; Forest-Glen House; Pine-Tree House, which had two very large kivas from 20 to 30 feet (6–9 m) in diameter; and Trickling-Spring House. The unique feature of this last and tiny ruin was a small plaza surrounded by rooms that open onto it.[44] This is a common characteristic of the modern pueblos, and its occurrence might be an evidence of the plaza feature in its embryonic stage.

Together with a few pottery jars, vases, and food bowls, Fewkes collected in the Marsh Pass area several perforated clay disks and a similar disk of mountain sheep horn that he thought were spindle whorls, although they could have been gaming implements. Another clay disk, which had a row of holes near the rim, is similar to a type of modern Hopi votive offering. A rare find by W. B. Douglass, which gave Cradle House its name, was a Pueblo III bifurcated basket, one of the finest examples of prehistoric basketry of the Southwest. Fewkes thought it was an unusual kind of cradle, but it probably was not. A similar basket with practically identical decoration was found in San Juan County, Utah, and it is possible the two baskets were made by the same woman.

Miscellaneous objects collected in the Marsh Pass cliff dwellings included stone axes, hatchets, and pounding implements. Kiet Siel yielded up a curved stick identical to those placed by the Walpi Snake priests around the sand painting of their altar. Near the curved stick were a planting stick and a horn spindle. A flute identical with those used at modern Walpi by Flute priests was found at Betatakin, which tends to support their legend that the Flute Clan once lived at the cliff dwelling.

In drawing together his views regarding the Marsh Pass area, Fewkes points out that the nature of the cliffs favored the construction of cliff dwellings rather than surface pueblos. The cliffs are replete with sandstone caverns, large and small, as is the case at Mesa Verde and Canyon de Chelly. There were fragmented rocks, springs and creeks, abundant clay, and wooded areas. In short, everything needed for cliff house life was at hand, although flat areas for farming were at a premium. The neighboring Sethlagini Mesa is of a different geological formation, having no caverns. Its mesa top is broad, and it called for surface pueblos built on promontories or on low hills.[45]

Fewkes believes that the caves were selected for habitation not because they could be better defended than surface pueblos but because of their constant creek-water supply and the associated land patches that could be cultivated. Small numbers of marauding Indians could have raided the Anasazi cornfields, but the cliff dwellers kept enough food in store to last more than a year, and even a prolonged siege could not have run them out or caused their surrender. Nor could the high cliff villages have been successfully assaulted. The defenders were too securely in place.[46]

SURFACE PUEBLOS

Alfred V. Kidder and Samuel J. Guernsey excavated several of the surface pueblos of Marsh Pass and reported their findings in Bureau of American Ethnology Bulletin 65, in 1919. These pueblos were above-grade, loose aggregations of structures, each of which consisted of an apartment building ranging from 50 to 100 feet (15–30 m) in length and made up of a single or double row of two-story rooms. The masonry work was as a rule better than that of the Kayenta cliff dwellings, and it was done with evenly coursed large stones. The kivas of the Marsh Pass area were round and subterranean, lacking pilasters for roof beam supports but having firepits, deflectors, and ventilator shafts. The kivas were located near the dwellings but, unlike the clan-sized kivas of Mesa Verde and Chaco Canyon, were not contained within the apartment buildings proper.[47]

The findings of Kidder and Guernsey at Marsh Pass included a few burials also. The bodies were placed in shallow oval pits dug in the refuse fill piles situated near the houses. They were closely flexed and were usually accompanied by ceramic offerings.[48]

BLACK MESA

As part of an ongoing training project carried out in 1968, 1969, and 1970, an archaeological investigation team from Prescott College, Arizona, excavated and surveyed parts of Black Mesa in the western Kayenta Area. The team findings to date have been summarized in two excellent volumes published by the Prescott College Press, and these contribute greatly to our knowledge concerning this hitherto minor but unknown segment of the Anasazi culture.*

Black Mesa lies between the Kayenta–Marsh Pass region and the historic Hopi pueblos. It is one of the few large areas of the Southwest that have not been extensively explored by archaeologists, probably because there are only a handful of the dry caves that could hold substantial amounts of perishable material. It also lacks the scenic grandeur of other Anasazi locations, and it is at best a marginal area of Anasazi development.

*It is a survey done none too soon, since the Peabody Coal Company of St. Louis is strip-mining coal from Black Mesa. The college acknowledges its gratitude to the Peabody Company, which initiated the archaeological project and is paying for it, and the kindness of the Navajo and Hopi tribes in allowing the archaeological work to be done.

The Prescott team has confirmed what was already suspected, that the archaeology of Black Mesa is at its best unspectacular. "The masonry architecture is poor even by Kayenta standards and the majority of rooms are jacal (wattle and daub) rather than masonry. Artifacts are scarce, and luxury goods are virtually non-existent. The settlements are small and usually have very little depth."[49]

Nevertheless, the research team sees two valuable side factors in the very "backwardness" of the Black Mesa Anasazi: the opportunity to study the culture in a germinating form, without its having been overbuilt and buried, and the opportunity to establish a series of time phases for the area.

After excavating 9 sites and surveying 193 more, researchers have determined that the prehistoric cultural tradition on the mesa is indeed Kayenta Anasazi, dating from A.D. 500 or before to ca. A.D. 1200, when the area was entirely abandoned.

Left, map showing location of Black Mesa. *Top right,* Tusayan Corrugated. *Bottom right,* Dogoszhi Black-on-white. From Gumerman, 1970.

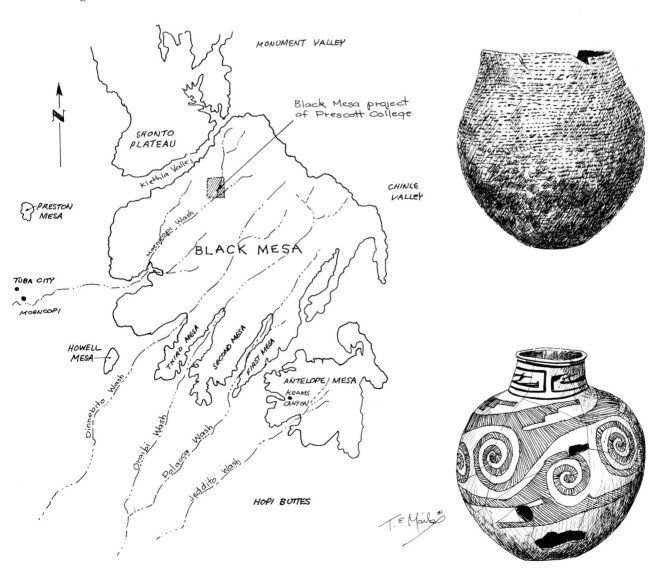

The earliest phase has been entitled the Dot Klish Phase, and it is associated with Basketmaker III. The sampling made there was much too small to permit anything more than generalizations. Indications are that Black Mesa settlements were placed on low knolls and terraces along the major drainage, Moenkopi Wash. But at the same time, other Dot Klish Phase Anasazi villages were built beyond the confines of Black Mesa. Some of these to the north, in the Klethla Valley, have been excavated by a team from the Museum of Northern Arizona at Flagstaff. They say that Dot Klish Phase village sites were scattered and small, a condition that would remain constant during the occupation of Black Mesa. "The primary social unit was most likely the extended family or several extended families which occupied a single site."[50] No pattern of village orientation or architectural style was followed, and they did not duplicate the linear villages of other Basketmaker III sites. Dwellings were usually shallow oval pithouses or small jacal structures. Storage rooms were either slab- or masonry-lined, and semisubterranean.

Manos held in one hand were the usual grinding tools. Pottery included Lino Black-on-gray, Lino Fugitive Red, and Lino Gray. There is evidence that coal was used for some firing and for home fuel. Charred corn and the bones of animals were found, and it appears that two types of agriculture were practiced: floodwater farming and dry farming. No Dot Klish burials were found, but human fecal material was studied—indicating, among other interesting things, the presence of a highly infectious spiny-headed worm that can cause severe internal bleeding.[51]

Another phase, the Tallahogan, is equivalent to the Basketmaker III–Pueblo I transition period. It ended around A.D. 852. Building sites were located on slightly higher terraces than in the Dot Klish Phase, possibly to allow use of the former building areas for farm plots. Only one pithouse was excavated, and it proved to be better constructed than both earlier and later buildings. Storage cists were in use, along with the same tools as were common to the Dot Klish Phase. Pottery types added to those of the earlier phase were Lino Tradition, Kana-a Black-on-white, and Kana-a Black-on-gray.[52]

Dinnebilo Phase settlements, covering the approximate years A.D. 875–975, evidenced yet another shift in location. Kayentans still lived along the main drainages, but the movement now was to the uplands. Specialized activity sites were in use by now, as different parts of the mesa were employed at different times for hunting, collecting, and farming. Some sites were so small and poorly arranged they can hardly be called villages, while others evidence a classic Pueblo I unit village kind of orientation. This was a crescent-shaped row of contiguous slab-lined storage cists on the northwest, pithouses to the southeast, and trash deposits farther southeast. Somewhat similar arrangements were followed at Badger House on Mesa Verde, and are treated in detail further on. Artifacts found at the sites were similar to those of earlier phases, although there were more chipped-stone artifacts. Pottery was typical Pueblo I Period Kana-a Black-on-white, Kana-a Gray, and Lino Gray. No burials were encountered.[53]

Black Mesa. Pithouse and two outside storage pits. Note the postholes that surround the pit-house. From Gumerman, 1970.

The Wepo Phase, dating from ca. A.D. 1000 to 1050, saw a fourth shift in areas of occupation and the first kivas. After nearly half a millennium of occupation, the Kayentans of Black Mesa moved away from the confines of the Moenkopi and its major tributaries and up to the upland region. Now there was an increased reliance on dry farming. Village plans began to stabilize, marking a transition from subsurface to surface structures that varied to a marked degree in either their arrangement or their lack of it. One village might have surface dwellings on the north side of the site facing south, a kiva in front of these, and a trash deposit out in front of the kiva. Another village might have kivas, storage rooms, and dwellings—consisting both of pithouses and of jacal structures—scattered all over the site. Considerable experimentation in architecture is apparent. Jacal and masonry were combined, and pithouses were Mogollon-like in style, consisting of shallow pits, rectangular rooms with rounded corners, and ramped entryways. Large, sometimes circular, multi-room jacal structures were common. Kivas were circular and occasionally masonry-lined. They varied in banquette or recess style, and some-

Black Mesa. Plan, section, and perspective view of kiva. From Gumerman, 1970.

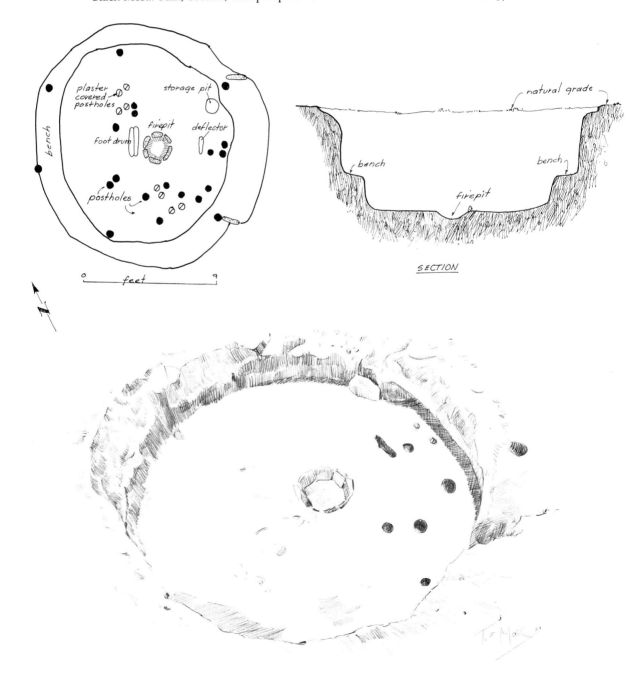

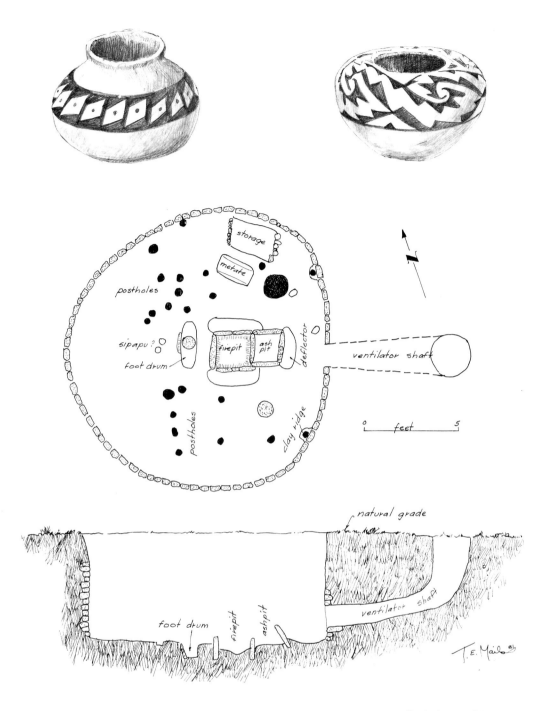

Black Mesa. *Top left,* Black Mesa Black-on-white pot. *Top right,* Flagstaff Black-on-white pot. *Bottom,* plan and section of subsurface ceremonial room. Redrawn and revised from Gumerman, 1970.

times had what might have been a foot drum located behind the firepit. There was a high ratio of kivas to dwellings.

Wepo Phase artifact finds included many worked sherds, bone awls, and chipped-stone tools. Pottery consisted of Kana-a Black-on-white, Kana-a Gray, Wepo Black-on-white, and Black Mesa Black-on-white. Tusayan Gray Ware was banded both on the neck and on part of the vessel body, sometimes being indented or incised. One complete burial was discovered. The body was placed
indented or incised. One complete burial was discovered. The body was placed

in a sitting position, with legs crossed and arms folded across the chest.[54] There was definite cranial deformation, revealing that this common Anasazi practice was being carried out at Black Mesa by A.D. 1040.[55] Three other burial skulls exhibited the same lambdoidal flattening trait. Also manifest in the skeletal remains was evidence of severe dental wear, and of osteoporotic pitting, possibly due to congenital anemia.[56]

The Lamoki Phase, covering the years from A.D. 1050 to 1100, was a time of population increase. Occupation of the uplands continued, along with dry

Black Mesa. *Left,* plan and section of stone and jacal structure. *Right,* plan and section of room block and jacal structures. From Gumerman, 1970.

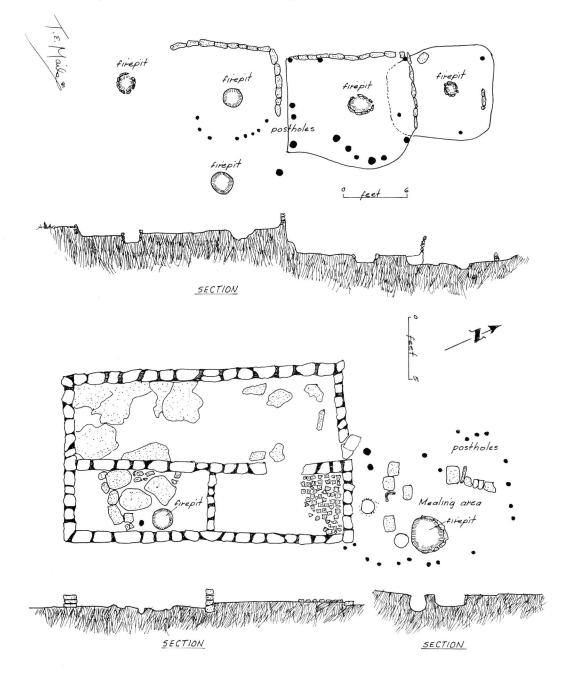

Top, partially excavated Toreva Phase site showing pithouse, two-room masonry structure for storage that was converted to a mealing room, and a second mealing room in the background. *Bottom*, Black Mesa from the northeast at the mesa's highest elevation, about 1,000 feet above the desert.

farming. In addition, the northeast corner of the mesa was now inhabited, and a relatively large cliff dwelling, Standing Fall House, was begun. The village plan that would also characterize the following Toreva Phase was adopted. It consisted of a masonry room block fronted by a kiva, and beyond that the trash heap. Site orientation was generally along an east–west axis. More masonry was employed than previously, although it is assumed that jacal structures were attached to the masonry. Pottery styles for the period were mainly Black Mesa Black-on-white and Tusayan Corrugated.[57]

The Toreva Phase, lasting from A.D. 1100 to ca. 1200, ended the prehistoric occupation of northeastern Black Mesa. It was attended by an increased shift of villages to the uplands. There was also a decided clustering of sites in certain locations, particularly around the edges of low sage-covered flats suitable for dry farming. The change in settlement pattern was due, apparently, to the environmental situation. Sites were now of two kinds: primary villages with dwellings, storage rooms, and kivas; and secondary sites with "habitation rooms and limited activity areas."[58]

The secondary sites are thought to represent a branching out to make full use of the surrounding resources, while retaining social and religious relationships with the primary sites. In other words, the secondary sites were like

Black Mesa. *Top left,* male skull with lambdoid flattening. *Top right,* stone finger ring and pendants. *Bottom,* Moencopi Wash. From Gumerman, 1970.

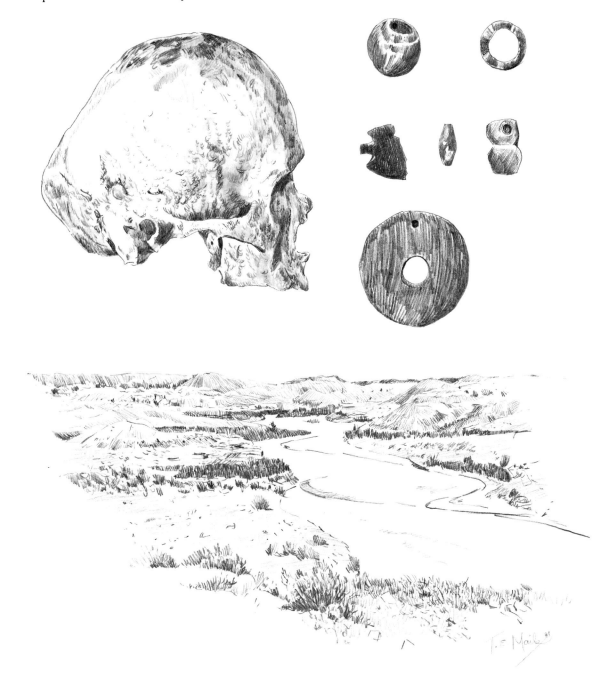

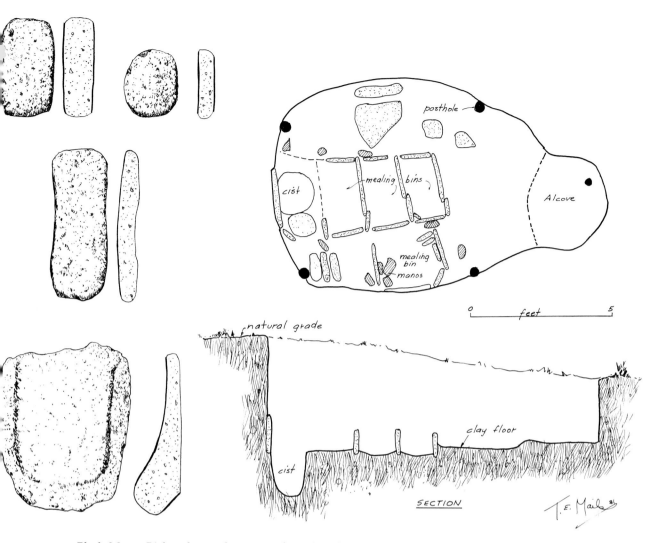

Black Mesa. *Right*, plan and section of a subsurface mealing room. *Top left*, face and section of one-hand almost rectangular mano. *Top right*, face and section of one-hand oval mano. *Center left*, two-hand mano with convex use surface. *Bottom left*, trough metate, open on one end. From Gumerman, 1970.

satellite stations for a central unit. Village plans duplicated those of the Lamoki Phase, but usually included a rectangular subsurface mealing room containing mealing bins (in which the meal was ground). Village plan variations include the absence of masonry surface structures and mealing rooms or both.

Jacal rooms served ordinarily as dwellings, and masonry rooms were in use for storage. Hearths were sometimes found in the mealing rooms, and some of the smaller jacal rooms could have served storage purposes. Warehouse rooms usually occupied the central area of a village, with the dwellings placed on either side.

Artifacts continued to resemble those of earlier phases, although most manos were now two-handed, "hinting at the possibility of an increase in dependence upon cultivated and noncultivated plant foods."[59] Primary pottery types for the Toreva Phase were Sosi, Dogoszhi, and Flagstaff black-on-whites, and Tusayan Corrugated. Several burials were discovered. Most of the bodies were semiflexed with no particular directional orientation of the head. One burial pit was covered with a slab, and another contained a fetus placed on top of a large sherd and buried in the trash fill. Most of the burials were in a poor state of preservation and had been badly disturbed by rodents.

For reasons yet to be agreed upon by anthropologists and archaeologists, the Anasazi began to move out of Black Mesa, and it was entirely abandoned by the end of the Toreva Phase in A.D. 1200. Everything of value was taken along by the migrating people, and the discovery of a whole artifact is rare. Even the heavy stone metates were removed, suggesting that the Kayentans of Black Mesa did not plan to move far. Surely it is no coincidence that the pueblos of the modern Hopi are only thirty miles south of Black Mesa.

As a final note, the Prescott College team has concluded that the Black Mesa Anasazi were in "continual interaction" with other Kayenta peoples, a fact testified to by the remarkable similarity of pottery design style and design attributes. Isolation or a lack of relationship would have led to greater differences in pottery techniques, shape, and design.

Inscription House.

INSCRIPTION HOUSE

Inscription House lies almost thirty miles west of Betatakin, on the western-most edge of the Kayenta region. It is a medium-sized ruin, housed in a spectacular cliff hollow that sweeps upward from it like a vast corrugated wash-board. The floor of the canyon is hot in summer, and the climb back to the rim is steep and long. But Nit Sin, or Nitsi, Canyon is a truly lush and enchanting place to visit. According to the Navajo, Nit Sin means "Antelope Drive," because the form of the canyon resembles such a drive layout.[60]

The fifty-room ruin received its name from an inscription that was scratched into the plastered wall of one of the dwellings in A.D. 1661. It is generally believed to be of Spanish origin, but far too little remains for anyone to be certain. Archaeologists have been particularly interested in the combined wattle-and-daub and mud-brick construction of Inscription House, in its exaggerated T-shaped doorways and tiny T-shaped windows, and in its rock art pecked and painted on the cliff walls. Frank Waters reports that it was built by the Hopi Snake Clan,[61] and Fewkes agrees. He states that the geographical position of this and nearby ruins in relation to Navajo Mountain led him to believe they were built by the Snake clans in their migration south and west from Tokonabi, which an old Snake chief described as "the ancient home of my ancestors,"[62] to Wukoki, which was at Black Falls (Wupatki).

Extremely interesting to Fewkes was the fact that the walls of some Inscription House rooms were built of elongate cylinders of clay "shaped like a Vienna loaf of bread." These bricks consisted of a bundle of twigs packed in thin red clay and flattened on two faces. The walls were laid up after the fashion of brick walls, and were held together so tenaciously by clay mortar that a portion of one room had fallen as a single mass. The use of straw-strengthened bricks was new to Fewkes, who had found plain cubical clay blocks in use at Mesa Verde and knew of true adobe structures at Canyon de Chelly and Awatovi.[63]

We move now to the magnificent Mesa Verde Region, where the concentration will be upon the Anasazi sites within the national park proper. There is little to be gained by seeking to describe every known Anasazi site within the Mesa Verde Region. If I even tried, the reader would soon be dizzy with data and close to exhaustion. My purpose is to give a substantial but only representative picture of the Anasazi as they passed through their various periods in each region. Students desiring more than this should go to the detailed ethnographic data, of which, as the bibliograpy shows, there is an amazing amount. Even so, I have by no means cited them all.

There are, though, several noteworthy subcenters in the region, including Alkali Ridge and Hovenweep in the present state of Utah, and the Montezuma-McElmo districts in southwest Colorado. The La Plata, Colorado, area was touched upon frequently in the Basketmaker chapters, and will be looked at now for Pueblo material, as will be nearby Johnson Canyon. Both are immediately adjacent to Mesa Verde on its southeastern side.

Chapter 6

THE MESA VERDE REGION

The majestic Anasazi ruins within Mesa Verde National Park are internationally known. But the Mesa Verde culture encompassed a much larger geographic area than the park. What is now the park complex served apparently as the regional center for a vast number of sites to the east and west, most of which are never seen by visitors. Ruins west of the park fit within a broad arc that reaches first to what is now the Colorado–New Mexico border on the south, then westward some distance into present-day southeastern Utah, and finally north to Cahone and Dolores, Colorado. It is an area filled with Anasazi ruins of varying sizes. On the opposite, eastern side of the park a lesser but similar situation exists in the Mancos and La Plata drainages.

WESTERNMOST SECTOR

Attention was first called to the westernmost sector by William H. Jackson, W. H. Holmes, and L. H. Morgan between 1875 and 1877.[1] Gustaf Nordenskiöld offers some information about it in his 1893 report.[2] T. Mitchell Prudden wrote a summary record of the region in 1903.[3] And Jesse Walter Fewkes contributed his perceptive views of the western area in his Bureau of American Ethnology Report of 1919.[4] Other data, such as those of Morley and Kidder, have tended to deal with individual western sites.[5]

Prudden divided the ruins he surveyed into twelve geographic areas that are most helpful to students. In addition, he constructed a detailed map of the country. It is, however, quite complicated to read, and I have attempted to simplify it and make it more instructive.

The first of Prudden's divisions was Montezuma Valley in Colorado. It lies between Ute Mountain and the sharp western crest of the Mesa Verde. Low upon the eastern slope of the main peak of Ute Mountain is Aztec Spring Ruin. Its main part, large enough to compare favorably with the great ruins of Chaco Canyon, measures more than 400 feet (120 m) square, according to Prudden. Besides Aztec, he noted a few small scattered sites in the valley between Mesa Verde and the southern spur of Ute Mountain, a few ruins far down on the southern and western slopes of Ute Mountain, and a few ruins high up among the piñons on its northeastern shoulder.[6]

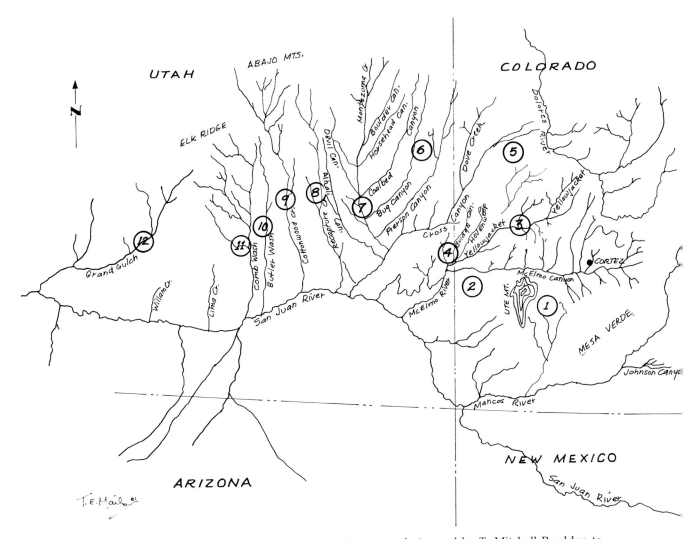

Map showing locations of the twelve geographic areas designated by T. Mitchell Prudden to describe the Anasazi ruins in the Westernmost Sector of the Mesa Verde Region.

Fewkes describes the Aztec Spring Ruin as a huge village consisting of a cluster of unit pueblos of the "pure type" in various stages of consolidation. By "pure type" he means a site where several unit types, each consisting of a dwelling block and a kiva, are clustered and consolidated.[7] He quotes the lengthy descriptions given of Aztec by Jackson and Holmes and adds some comments of his own. Most valuable of these are that the village lacked towers and that it consisted of two sections: a west and an east. The west, or Upper House, was a compact, rectangular, multistoried building with circular kivas and with dwelling rooms of different shapes. Several rubble mounds in the vicinity are the remains of former pueblos and kivas. The Lower House was a rectangular structure located east of the spring, having a large court on the south side whose long dimension measured 218 feet (66.5 m). Fewkes saw no ruined prehistoric village in the Montezuma Valley that so stirred him to properly excavate and repair as that at Aztec Spring.[8]

The second Prudden division was the McElmo Group, which straddles Utah and Colorado. Lying immediately west of the Mancos drainage area, the

McElmo Canyon has Ute Mountain on its south and east and a high mesa on its north. The country falls away as the river runs westward, and after receiving the Yellowjacket River, the McElmo turns southwesterly through broken hill country to join the great San Juan at a point about twenty-five miles below the mouth of the Mancos. The broad McElmo Valley, before it passes into the canyon at the northern foot of Ute Mountain, contains a considerable number of scattered ruins. The largest of these forms a group located in the upper part of the valley where it slopes against the Dolores divide. The main building is about 135 feet (41 m) long and was once two or three stories high at the back.

Top, plot plan of McLean Basin ruin with towers. *Bottom,* round and D-shaped towers in McLean Basin. From Fewkes, 1919a.

It faces southward, and in front are a court and a trash mound. The masonry is of superior grade. The large Burkhardt's Ruin is located at the head of McElmo Canyon. Fewkes situates it at Mud Spring, mentions that it contained a triple-walled stone tower, and adds that its cluster of mounds forms a village with many kivas that covers a considerable area. He quotes Holmes and Morgan at length concerning the details of "the great tower."[9] Besides these large remains, Prudden found many small ruins, mostly of the unit type, scattered along the western base of Mesa Verde and near the present town of Cortez, Colorado.

A series of unit-type ruins are dispersed along the bank of the McElmo Creek (or McElmo River) from the head of the canyon to the entrance of the Yellowjacket. A few small cliff dwellings are also scattered along the valley. In the valley bottom, near Battle Rock, is an isolated rock around which cluster the ruins of many small dwellings.

When Prudden speaks of "unit type" houses, he means those constructed in a simple block consisting of from six to eight rooms, usually in a double row, with a nearby kiva that ordinarily was in front, and a trash dump beyond the kiva. When unit types are referred to by Mesa Verde archaeologists, the dwelling block is usually on the north side, with the kiva in front and the trash mound to the south of the kiva.

Branching off from the high mesa at the north end of the McElmo is a series of short, rugged canyons. Several of these, notably Sand Canyon and Rock Canyon, contain many small, well-built cliff dwellings. The area also exhibits rock art, and there are two fairly well preserved towers on a rocky bench to the east of the mouth of Sand Canyon.

At the heads of two of the side canyons there are large ruins. These are villages that were built on the edge of the cliffs and partially down the slopes. They stand virtually on top of the great mesa bordering the McElmo to the north. One is known as Goodman Point Ruin or Goodman Lake Ruin; the other in Prudden's time had no name. The Goodman Point Ruin consists of three compact and impressive clusters of rooms, two of which form buildings that face each other across a narrow wash. Prudden states that the smaller cluster of these two is more than 100 feet (30 m) long, and the larger over 300 feet (90 m). The dimensions given by Fewkes are somewhat less.[10] Each building consists of from four to six rows of rooms, each room measuring from 12 to 15 feet (3.6–4.5 m) square. Prudden could not determine the original number of stories. Back of the main group of ruins and lying upon the slope on one side is yet another and almost equally large building, apparently of another period of construction. A trash mound stands between the two facing structures. Several small, isolated buildings surround the larger main building, and nearby is an enclosure 60 feet (18 m) in diameter that Prudden could not identify. It appears from his description to be the remains of a Great Kiva. It has low walls of inferior masonry, with "four small stone heaps" that are probably pillar remains, since they are "set within and near the wall in such positions as to form a square."[11]

Fewkes refers to a circular depression, 56 feet (17 m) in diameter, in the midst of the largest mounds at Goodman Point; it has four piles of stones arranged regularly on the floor. In his view it was once roofed and was a Great Kiva serving the community at large.[12]

About half a mile up the wash from the ruin is an ancient man-made reservoir that still holds water and is called Goodman Lake.

Prudden's unnamed ruin, on the southern edge of the great mesa a few miles west of Goodman Point, is of considerable size. It, too, consists of two large blocks of rooms separated by a wash. Each block is several rooms deep and originally rose two or three stories in height. Behind one of the blocks is a wall that might have been built for defensive purposes. Beneath the overhanging ledge upon which one of the large blocks stands are two small cliff houses.[13]

Fewkes speaks of a Johnson Ruin, which is four miles west of the Goodman Point Ruin at the head of Sand Canyon. It may be Prudden's unnamed site. Fewkes says the remains of former houses skirt the rim of the canyon head for fully half a mile and once included towers, great houses, other types of buildings, and numerous depressions indicating subterranean kivas. He also mentions a small cliff house that sits directly under the mesa rim.[14]

Prudden visited several smaller and isolated ruins located between the larger Goodman Point and the unnamed ruins, and he believed there might be more, since he had not yet explored all the exceedingly rough, piñon-clad country.

He did find a large ruin on a rocky slope at the junction of the McElmo and the Yellowjacket. It contained many rooms and several kivas. He received no reports of ruins on the McElmo below the mouth of the Yellowjacket, but stories were told to him of a few small ruins along the district drained by the East McElmo.[15]

Fewkes calls attention to some mysterious megalith and slab-house ruins on the bluff situated at the junction of the McElmo and Yellowjacket canyons. These are of two kinds: small rectangular enclosures made of slabs of stone set on edge, and semicircular structures also constructed of upright stone slabs, or megaliths.[16] Similar structures exist at Sandstone Canyon (which joins the Yellowjacket from the north), at other places to the north, in Montezuma Canyon to the west, and on the Mesa Verde. At the time, no one knew what purpose the rectangular structures served. Suggestions were storage bins, burial places, and cremation places, none of which seemed to fit as they were examined further.

The third in Prudden's division is the Yellowjacket Group of Ruins in Colorado. The Yellowjacket is the main tributary to the McElmo from the north. The more important ruins in the lower portion of Yellowjacket Canyon are few in number and small, and several small ruins are scattered along the valley bottom from the mouth of the Sandstone to three or four miles above the mouth of the Dawson, which joins the Yellowjacket farther upstream, from the east. Near the mouth of the Dawson, and high on the northern bluff of the

Top left, plan and perspective of megalithic stone enclosure, McElmo Bluff. *Top right*, Great House at the head of Holly Canyon. *Bottom*, cliff dwelling, Sand Canyon. From Fewkes, 1919a.

Top, petroglyphs on wall of Yellowjacket Canyon. *Center,* kiva in unit-type house. *Bottom,* Stronghold House, Square Tower Canyon. From Fewkes, 1919a.

Yellowjacket, stands a considerable group of ruins built partly on the edge of the bluff and partly down the upper portion of the higher slopes, plus a series of towerlike structures reaching down into the valley. There are two long buildings, each two to three rows of rooms deep, separated by a shallow wash descending from the mesa top behind. One of these buildings is more than 300 feet (90 m) long, the other nearly 200 feet (60 m). Both contain several kivas, and behind both ruins is a fairly well preserved zigzagging stone wall. In a slight depression on the mesa top is a man-made reservoir. It is formed by a low dam of earth and measures about 90 feet (27 m) across.[17]

Fourteen miles west of Dolores, Colorado, at the head of Yellowjacket Canyon where its walls are only a few feet high, are the Yellowjacket Spring Ruins. Since these are situated on the line of the old Spanish Trail, they were seen often by early explorers, who called them by the Indian name Surouaro, meaning "Desolation." The main ruin consists of a series of five clusters of irregularly placed houses of the unit type. Though they are close together, each set of houses has its own kiva in front and a trash mound to the south; Prudden calls this a "burial mound." Burials were commonly made in trash heaps, but it is doubtful that burial was the primary purpose for their formation. The lateral wings of many of the houses are quite long, and sometimes they enclose a court that contains several kivas. In some of the houses a low wall connects the lateral wings, and several house groups include a small tower. Prudden estimates that the village contains no fewer than three hundred rooms, and adds that several structures of irregular shape, one of considerable size, sit at the edge of the canyon above the main group of buildings. In referring to burials, he states that a thin stone slab was laid over many of the bodies, and that others were enclosed in a loosely laid stone cist.[18]

In his description of Surouaro, Fewkes states that the village contained both large and small houses of the pure pueblo type, and covered an area only slightly less than the impressive Mummy Lake group on the Mesa Verde. He adds that the individual houses were not so grouped as to enclose a rectangular court, and that the intervals between them were of considerable extent. All the houses were built of stone and were hammer-dressed (pecked) on the exposed faces. Pottery sherds of great age were plentiful, and metates were abundant. Also there were ruins of several large reservoirs and traces of acequias (water ditches) that led to them.[19]

Fourth in Prudden's division are the Colorado Ruins on the tributaries of the Yellowjacket. In these short canyons in the high country, which end abruptly in cliffs of varying height, and on the sharp mesas between them are various kinds of ruins. Some are the unit type, others are small cliff dwellings. Some are towers, and there are irregular clusters of ruins on the edges of the cliffs. Of the latter, the best known are the Cannonball Canyon Ruins, which are randomly placed clusters of rooms and towers built around the heads of shallow gulches.

In describing the Yellowjacket area in general, Fewkes thought it contained the most valuable collections of rock art in that part of the country.

Petroglyphs and pictographs were most often located near ruins, but sometimes occurred far from building sites. They consisted of geometric shapes, with rectangles and spirals predominating: representations of human beings, birds, animals, bird tracks, human hand prints, bear claws, snakes, rain clouds, and other forms. Those on the cliff surfaces had been pecked with rude stone chisels, but some found in sheltered cave sites were painted. These last may not have been done by Anasazi.[20]

Prudden believed that the first three of the northern tributaries, Ruin, Bridge, and Hovenweep canyons, contained the most noteworthy ruins. Those of the two terminal branches of Ruin Canyon consist of towers and large and small buildings, some skillfully built on top of isolated rocks. They are similar to the mushroom rock types encountered by Fewkes in Hill Canyon, Utah. Where Bridge Canyon boxes, there are clusters of well-preserved tower and room complexes and clusters of rooms located near the edge of the cliff. This region is known locally as the Hawkberry or Hackberry. On the top of the great mesa that extends northward between the headwaters of Bridge Canyon and the Hovenweep is a long line of unit-type ruins spaced at varying distances apart.[21]

Above the point where the Hovenweep opens out into a level valley, along the cliffs and up on the high mesas, are several small ruins, a few large clusters, and several towers. Less than a mile away, where a small side gulch enters the Hovenweep from the west, are two groups of ruins situated on a projecting point at the forks of the valley. Each group contains at least fifty rooms, and the original buildings were two or three stories high at the back. On the mesa top, to the west of the ruins just mentioned, are two more ruins, one small, but the other measuring 175 feet (53 m) in length.

Far up the Hovenweep are a pair of large ruins facing each other across the valley. High up on the west side is a rambling mass of rooms partly erected on a projecting rock and partly extending down the slope. The ruin on the east side is built mostly upon a low, narrow rock tongue. Its grouping is irregular, the main section consisting of some twenty rooms, each averaging 10 feet (3 m) square. A low wall runs across the base of the rock tongue and bars access to the ruin from the back. Above the east ruin is a man-made ditch designed to conduct water to it from another area. The hillside across which this conduit runs is marked with a series of reversing zigzags designed to turn the water abruptly back and forth at short intervals, so as to lead it by gradual stages down the slope to the point of delivery.[22]

So interesting and instructive is this area that, at the urging of archaeologists, President Harding issued in March 1923 a proclamation creating the Hovenweep National Monument.[23] Fewkes considers the monument especially valuable in that, while the relationship of Hovenweep buildings to those on the Mesa Verde is practically identical, there are forms of buildings unique to each of the localities. Therefore the areas complement one another and make an interesting comparison of pithouses, jacal structures, masonry dwellings, kivas, shrines, and towers.[24]

Fifth in the Prudden division are Ruins in Piñon Clearings, on the uplands of the Yellowjacket and Montezuma Creek region. While Prudden is fascinated by questions involving the clearings and does not identify all the types of ruin he found, some were of the unit type with four to eight rooms and one or two kivas surrounded by a clearing ranging from 50 to 150 feet (15–45 m) across.[25]

In 1937 a group led by Paul S. Martin excavated what proved to be an important site in the Ackmen-Lowry region, Colorado, just east of the head of Cross Canyon. It consisted of early Pueblo I sites, dated A.D. 747–68, having

Top, map of ruins located in Hovenweep National Monument. *Bottom,* Hovenweep Castle ruin.

one or two surface dwellings of jacal or masonry associated with a pithouse that was probably a protokiva or kiva, and of later sites dated A.D. 855–72, whole multiroomed dwellings were built of coursed masonry and whose pithouses were definitely kivas. A large pueblo found in the area and known as Lowry Ruin seems to have been occupied throughout Pueblo II.[26]

The sixth Prudden division is the Ruins of the Montezuma Creek Group in Utah. This creek drains the barren Utah upland lying between the Dolores River and the Abajo Mountains. It is an arid and forbidding country, and there are only a few ruins, consisting mainly of scattered small valley sites and small cliff dwellings. Exceptions to this are the Pierson Lake and Bug Lake ruins. Pierson Lake is situated on top of the lofty piñon- and sage-covered mesa that rises between Cross and Pierson canyons a little northwest of the point at which Dove Creek enters Cross Canyon. Pierson Lake is man-made, by the Anasazi, and it was still being used by cattle herders in 1903. Close by the reservoir are two ruins of the unit type, each with several rooms located on the north side of the village, short wings, and a kiva in front.

The Pierson Lake Ruin is a short distance away from the lake. It contains between 250 and 300 rooms forming a compact group about 300 feet (90 m) square. About 300 yards west of the main ruin is a second ruin measuring about 100 feet (30 m) long at the back. A few hundred yards northwest are several unit-type ruins.

The Bug Lake Ruins resemble those of the Pierson Lake group. They are located east of Pierson and stand upon a high mesa between Pierson and Bug canyons. Bug Lake is another Anasazi-made reservoir that is still in use today. The main ruin sits quite near the lake, and it is composed of two groups of buildings facing each other across a small watercourse. Both are well preserved, with parts of walls still standing and roof timbers present among them. The larger group is made up of many units that together form a fairly compact mass. The mass faces southeast. It is about 450 feet (137 m) long, and includes a number of circular kivas surrounded by irregular masses of rooms. Some kivas are located side by side; some are separated by narrow passageways that lead from the building rear to a court 60 feet (18 m) wide on the southeast side of the pueblo.

Across the wash from the largest group are several smaller and isolated structures. Two of them are about forty feet apart and stand on ground that slopes toward the wash. An earthen dam has been built between the buildings, forming a reservoir of considerable capacity. There is also a large dam across the wash itself.

West of the main ruin are two extensive gravel benches, each a few feet in height, that rise like steps one behind the other. The piñons have been cleared from these over an area five hundred yards long and three hundred yards wide. On the first bench there are five isolated ruins of the unit type. Each has one row of southward-facing rooms with short wings, and also has from two to four circular and subterranean kivas in front of the rooms. Prudden notes there are fewer building stones here than is usual in ruins of this size. On the second bench is another assemblage of widely scattered unit-type sites, each with two or three of its own circular kivas.

Prudden found the Bug Lake group of ruins to be of "peculiar interest," because it confirmed his impression of different periods of occupancy in a single locality, and it excited his curiosity about the relationship of time and culture within the associated ruin groups.[27]

At Alkali Ridge, Utah, thirteen sites have been excavated that have yielded valuable information about architectural development. Ten of the sites reveal that in this locality, even as early as the eighth century, pueblos with as many as three hundred surface dwelling and storage rooms were being built contemporaneously with large and small pithouses. Pueblo buildings of the time consisted of long curving rows of contiguous rooms, with the dwellings and open plazas in front and the storage rooms in back. A variety of wall types were built, often in combination, including upright stone slabs, jacal, some coursed masonry, and some simple adobe.[28] By tree-ring dating, it was learned that Alkali Ridge sites and Piedra sites both date back to the 770s, yet the former were associated with Basketmaker III and Pueblo I, while the latter were related solely to Pueblo I.

Next, and seventh in the Prudden division, come the Ruins in Montezuma Creek Valley, Utah. They are mostly of the unit type, standing on the alluvial bottom or on the low cliffs at the sides. Scattered about the valley are a few buildings of considerable size, several fortified rocks, and a few small isolated dwelling ruins. Pictographs are also present in several places.

At the entrance to Coalbed Canyon there is an isolated butte about fifty feet high that has a flat top two or three acres in area. It is known locally as "the Island," and its top and sides are covered with irregular and complex buildings. Just outside one of them is a row of erect slabs set 5 to 6 feet (1.5– 1.8 m) apart, measuring from 4 to 6 feet (1.2–1.8 m) high, 6 to 7 inches (15– 17.5 cm) thick, and 14 to 18 inches (35.5–45 cm) wide. A lower loose-stone wall fills the gap between the slabs, and the whole forms a continuous wall barring access to the ruins on this side of the butte. A similar wall is placed at the opposite end of the butte. At intervals along the stone trail leading to the butte top, Prudden found heaps of stones he believed were placed there for defensive purposes. He also found that at several other places in the valley similar stone slabs were used in construction.

One of the largest of the valley ruins lies east of the stream bed between the mouths of Bug and Pierson canyons in Utah. It measures about 375 by 190 feet (114–58 m) and probably contained at its peak development more than two hundred and fifty rooms and ten or more circular kivas.

At the upper part of Montezuma Creek Valley, unit-type ruins are numerous, including at the uppermost end a compact group of ruins about 300 feet (90 m) long, with from six to eight kivas. At the mouths of several of the creeks running into the Montezuma from the high mesa on the west are a few small cliff dwellings and a few insignificant ruins on the mesa tops. At the head of the short canyon north of the Alkali, which Prudden calls Jackson Canyon, is another large ruin consisting of two buildings facing each other across a shallow wash. Each building consists of an irregular mass of rooms about 200 feet (60 m) long, having low towers among them. Together the two buildings enfold more than 150 rooms.[29]

While I have not yet come across it in the literature, I assume that some authority has noted the many instances in the westernmost sector wherein single large buildings, or clusters of unit types, are separated by washes or gullies so as to form two main parts, and then has gone on to speculate that as of this early prehistoric period the dual division found in many present-day pueblos had already begun.

The matter of dual division is considered in some detail further on, but the pueblos of Zia and Taos, in the Rio Grande area, can serve as modern examples. Zia has two kivas. All those who live north of an imaginary east–west line, drawn through the village between the north and south plazas, belong to the Wren kiva; those who live south of this line belong to Turquoise.[30] Taos has six kivas, but they are divided equally into a north and south division, although until recently each of the two pueblos also shared a communal ceremonial structure.

The eighth of Prudden's divisions is the Ruins on Recapture Creek, Utah. This creek is the principal drainage stream for the southern slope of Abajo Peak. Its valley sites and cliff dwellings, while fairly numerous, are mostly small. A few ruins, though, are of considerable size. One of these contains from thirty to forty rooms. Another consists of three groups. The largest is about 180 feet (55 m) long, another about 60 feet (18 m), and what appears to be the oldest of the three is made up of scattered buildings.

The ninth of the divisions is the Ruins on Cottonwood Creek, Utah. This extensive creek enters the San Juan at the town of Bluff, and it drains the western slopes of the Abajo Mountains. The lower reaches of the creek are low-walled and contain only a few small ruins, including both valley and cliff dwellings. Some twenty miles or so above the creek mouth, the valley sites become more numerous, and they are scattered along the bottom for several miles. One ruin that sits on a high gravel bench below the mouth of Dry Wash contains from fifty to sixty rooms. In some branches of the Cottonwood near its source, particularly the Allen, Hammond, and Cottonwood canyons, there are many cavelike recesses in the cliffs bordering the valley. In these caves some of the earliest burials of the Basketmakers were found. There are a few small ruins on the high mesa between the Recapture and the Cottonwood at the foot of Abajo Peak, and Prudden received reports of other scattered sites southward along the mesa.[31]

The tenth in the geographic division is Ruins on Butler Wash, Utah, which is a narrow, dry, shallow valley having on its western side the sloping uplift of a great fault. Along the eastern side and situated mostly at the mouths of short canyons are a series of small valley sites, and in many of the canyons are various-sized caves containing cliff dwellings. One cave far up the valley contains a large ruin with many burials. In the upper reaches of the Butler, Prudden found no noteworthy ruins, but he did find painted rock art in the caves,[32] and others have discovered Basketmaker remains in the area.

The eleventh division consists of Ruins on Comb Wash, Utah. This dry, shallow valley ranges from one to six miles in width. It is bordered on the east by a great fault that runs between the Abajo Mountains and Elk Ridge, and on the west by swells that run up to the high mesa at the foot of Elk Ridge. The valley possesses only a few small ruins at the mouth of the wash, several scattered sites near the head of the valley, and a few small cliff dwellings in the side canyons of Elk Ridge.[33]

The twelfth and last in Prudden's geographic division of the westernmost Mesa Verde Region ruins are those situated in Grand Gulch, Utah. This is the westernmost of the large northern tributaries to the San Juan. It heads in the long mesa slopes south of Elk Ridge and is a narrow, tortuous canyon with walls several hundred feet high. Most of its ruins are clustered in large caves at and below the main forks of the canyon. A host of Basketmaker relics similar to those of Cottonwood Creek and Butler Wash have been found here. The walls and caves of the gulch are a mecca for pictograph hunters. In one instance a certain spiral figure common to the region was carved into still-soft adobe that had been spread on the face of the rock. Extensive excavations have been carried on in the Grand Gulch caves, and a large amount of Basketmaker material has been removed from there to the American Museum of Natural History in New York and to the Field Columbian Museum (now the Field Museum of Natural History) in Chicago.[34]

The single note of regret appended to Prudden's survey report is his lament concerning the great injury that had already been wrought upon the interests of archaeology by the widespread, unlicensed, random digging of relic hunters. By 1903 it was epidemic, and even the Navajo, who at first had balked because of a superstitious dread of the ancient Anasazi ruins, had begun to enter the ruins and wreak havoc at the urging of unscrupulous merchants of relics. Seldom did Prudden come upon a ruin in the Mesa Verde Region that had not been seriously looted, with reconstruction of the culture made most difficult thereby. Of course, archaeologists do not indict all the early relic hunters. Archaeology itself was but a fledgling science then, and many of the amateurs were deeply interested in what they found. Some passed their relics on to museums, where they have been preserved. But data regarding the finds were not recorded, and the connections of finds with sites were forever lost.

To illustrate how rampant relic hunting was at the time, Fewkes was able to reconstruct the minor antiquities of the westernmost part of the Mesa Verde Region by turning to local collections, "one of which, owned by Mr. Williamson, of the First National Bank of Dolores, is comprehensive."[35] In the main, the objects he examined presented no essential difference from those referred to in detail later in this chapter.

In his sweeping survey, Prudden concentrated on the locations and general characteristics of Anasazi sites, omitting for the most part the structural details of buildings. Fortunately, Fewkes compensates for this by providing some structural information in his 1919 BAE report. He discovered that cliff dwellings in the westernmost district were smaller as a rule than the "magnificent" examples of the Mesa Verde park area. Yet they were built along the same architectural lines. Kivas were circular and subterranean, "similarly constructed to those of Spruce-tree House," with pilasters to support cribbed roofs and containing ventilators and deflectors. As a rule, the cliff dwelling masonry was excellent and identical with that of Mesa Verde. The absence of very large cliff houses in the McElmo area he ascribed to a lack of immense caves. He thought it noteworthy that McElmo cliff dwellings were generally accompanied by large open-air (unroofed) pueblos, towers, or great houses on the cliffs above, while on the Mesa Verde proper open-air buildings were usually situated some distance from the cliff dwellings. Sun Temple was a seeming exception.[36]

Extensive reference is made to great houses and towers. Fewkes states that, while towers differed in arrangement from pueblos of the pure type, they were often combined with dwelling rooms to form composite houses arranged in clusters, called villages. A tower might be an isolated structure, or it might be surrounded by one or more rows of concentric curved walls divided by partitions into rooms.[37] In Fewkes's opinion, the best towers were localized in three canyons: Square Tower, Holly, and Hackberry. There were many other towers in the Yellowjacket-McElmo areas, but there was no other locality where so many different forms appeared in equal numbers in a small area.

The Horseshoe and Emerson ruins in Colorado were the most dramatic examples Fewkes found of D-shaped buildings. The latter ruin was named after the forest ranger who first visited it and called it Sun Dial Palace. It was an intriguing assemblage of spaces, with an elliptical center chamber surrounded on all but the south side by four rows of rooms. Some of the outside walls were deliberately staggered so that the light cast by the sun caused shadows to strike different walls at different hours during the day.[38]

The masonry of the westernmost area varied in style and in excellence, not only between buildings, but in different parts of the same building. Some walls exhibited what Fewkes believed was the best-constructed masonry north of Mexico, while others were crudely made. In the central structure of the Holly group the lowest courses of wall stone were larger than those above. At Hovenweep the order was reversed. In the Round Tower in McLean Basin, stones of various sizes were introduced purely for ornamentation.

Fewkes recognized masonry of two basic types. The first type was not coursed, and stones of different sizes were employed in random fashion. Intervals were filled with masses of adobe. Stones, if dressed at all, were dressed on the exterior only. The second and more common type consisted of courses of well-dressed stones of uniform size that were carefully pecked, and the thickness of the stones might vary from course to course. As a rule, the inner walls of kivas were better constructed than the walls of other rooms, and their masonry courses were uniformly horizontal. As at Mesa Verde proper, the sides, lintels, and thresholds of doorways received the most careful attention of the builders. With rare exceptions, evidence of plastering had disappeared, but Fewkes believed that the interiors of all the great houses and towers were formerly plastered.[39]

a, schematic group plan of Emerson Ruin. *b,* ground plan of unit-type house. *c,* plot plan of Holly Canyon Ruins. *Bottom,* southern part of Cannonball Canyon Ruin, McElmo Canyon.

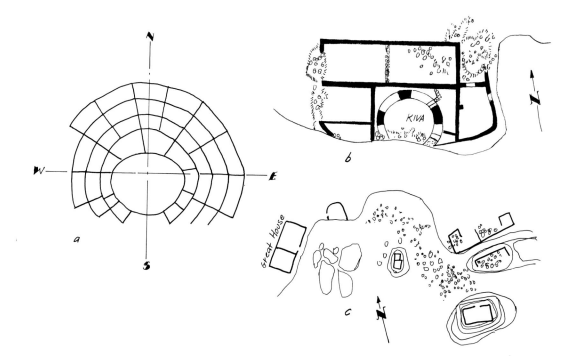

THE MANCOS AND LA PLATA SECTOR

East of the Mesa Verde and also within the sphere of its cultural influence lies the Mancos and La Plata Sector. It consists of a triangular plateau bounded on the west by the Mancos Canyon, on the east by the La Plata River, and on the south by the Colorado–New Mexico boundary line. Its elevation varies from 6,000 to 7,000 feet above sea level. Running from the northeast to the southwest is a low divide composed of a series of broken hills. The canyons that drain to the Mancos are exceedingly deep and rough, while the arroyos running to the La Plata are much less precipitous. Most of the country on the eastern side of the divide is a rolling tableland. The entire area is replete with piñon, cedar, cottonwood, aspen, pine, and spruce, with gooseberries and chokecherries everywhere present. Earl Morris found the land to be abundant and fertile, and believed that at the time of his first work there in 1913 corn could have been grown successfully on the mesas without irrigation. "The region offered all the conditions indispensable to primitive culture."[40] One thing missing was an adequate source of fresh drinking water. Morris found only one good spring, at a place called Mancos Spring.[41]

The La Plata River begins in Colorado, just northwest of Durango, and extends southward to meet the San Juan in New Mexico at a point slightly west of Farmington. The Mancos River is a long but relatively small stream that originates a few miles north of the town of Mancos, Colorado. It follows a southwest course along the east side of the Mesa Verde, and then as it approaches the northern border of New Mexico it curves westward to intersect with the San Juan River at a point just east of the Four Corners marker. The large side canyons on the west of the Mancos are those that run upward into the Mesa Verde proper. Fewkes examined the towers in the southwestern part of the canyon and valley and found that in all essential features they resembled those of the Mesa Verde, McElmo, and Yellowjacket canyons. He concluded they were built by the same people at the same time.

Thanks again to the untiring work of Earl Morris, the ruins on the east and southeast sides of the Mesa Verde, in the region between the Mancos and La Plata rivers, are fairly well known. He explored and excavated there in 1913 and 1914, subdividing his BAE report into "Cliff Ruins" and "Ruins on the Mesas."

In summarizing what he discovered, he claims there once existed in the cliff ruins of Johnson Canyon, which is a southeast tributary of the Mancos River, a typical example of the culture of the Mesa Verde Region. The materials for building, weaving, and ceramics were obtained in the immediate vicinity, and the fruits of wild trees and plants, as well as the cultivated crops, came, with few exceptions, from the nearby canyons and mesas. The general characteristics of the masonry and details of kivas and dwellings, the methods of burial, the pottery and other lesser material culture items all indicated that the cliff dwellings in Johnson Canyon were "culturally and approximately chrono-

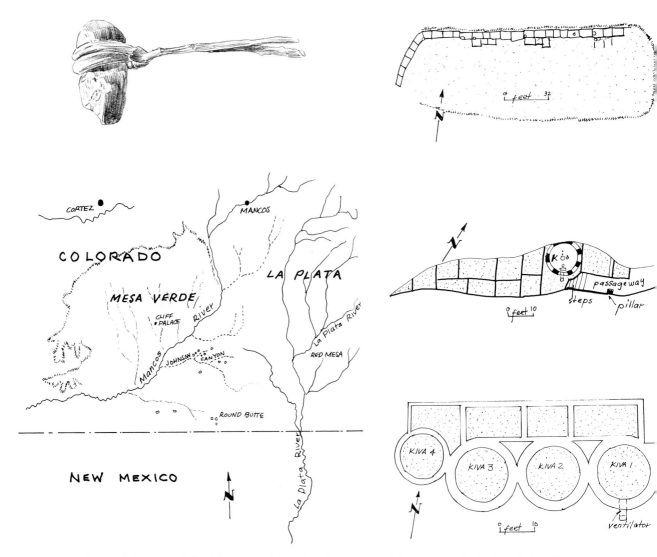

Bottom left, map of the Mancos and La Plata Sector. *Top left*, stone ax hafted with handle of skunkbush found in area. *Top right*, plot plan of Ruin No. 17 in Johnson Canyon. *Center right*, plot plan of Eagle Nest House. *Bottom right*, plot plan of Ruin No. 20. From Earl H. Morris, 1919.

logically contemporaneous with the large ruins of Mesa Verde National Park."[42]

The inhabitants of the mesas were an agricultural people whose homes were single-storied aggregations of cell-like chambers, usually grouped to form a rectangle. As a rule, the building floors were recessed in the earth, with jacal walls above grade that "were covered with plaster." Morris found no kiva in connection with a jacal dwelling, but thought future excavations might prove that certain of the circular pits contained features linking them unmistakably to the kivas of "of later time." Pottery from the mesas exhibited a wide range of form and surface treatment, but it was structurally inferior. Less than half of it was decorated with painted designs, and true coil ware was not found. The symbolism was unlike that of the Mesa Verde, and it displayed less conventionalization. Stone implements were few, but specimens were of the same general type and workmanship as those of the cliff dwellers. "Of the work in bone, wood, and other perishable materials almost nothing could be learned."[43]

Within Johnson Canyon, at the mouth of Spring Canyon, Morris found several cliff ruins, designating the best as Nos. 1, 2, and 3. The first two ruins were small and poorly constructed. Some walls were of mud, and either spalled with small stones or chinked with pottery sherds. Near these were many small ledge enclosures that probably served as storage sites for corn and other produce. The third ruin was larger, with four kivas and a tower. A number of artifacts were recovered at this site, and all were similar to those described further on in this chapter.

In Lion Canyon, Morris came upon a site he named Eagle Nest House, for it was a picturesque and majestic ruin sitting high up on the cliff in a large

The Mancos and La Plata Sector. Cliff dwelling designated by Morris as Ruin No. 6 in Johnson Canyon. From Earl H. Morris, 1919.

The Mancos and La Plata Sector. Eagle Nest House, Johnson Canyon. From Earl H. Morris, 1919.

cave. If one ever wonders what archaeologists often went through in their quests for knowledge, Morris's description of how he climbed into this almost inaccessible ruin answers the question:

> A hard but not dangerous climb of 400 feet brings one to the base of the cliff below the ruin. Here the observer is impressed with the force of Nordenskiöld's statement, for the ruin seems indeed inaccessible. . . . The cliff overhangs above and below the shelf which supports it, and as the distance is too great to permit the casting of a rope over one of the protruding beams, direct access is impossible. However, from the east end of the ledge a crevice continues along the cliff for some distance. Near its end the wall below drops back to the perpendicular. Here two large poles had been leaned against the cliff and fastened to the stump of a cedar which had grown conveniently at the bottom. I climbed to the end of these, pushing a pole ahead of me until only 3 feet of it overlapped the top of the first pair; after lashing this to them and binding another pole beside it I clambered up these and repeated the process. The top of the fourth pair of poles reached to the ledge. Even after they had been securely fastened at the top it was not until the next day that my workmen could be prevailed upon to attempt the ascent.[44]

Eagle Nest House contained twelve rooms and a kiva, all in an excellent state of preservation and quite like the cliff dwellings of the Mesa Verde in construction. The kiva had a banquette, pilasters, deflector, ventilator, and firepit. Unique, though, were what Morris believed were two sipapus and, in the east wall, a niche. The kiva walls were plastered with brown clay and had a white line surmounted with triangles and other figures, much like those found in the square tower of Mesa Verde's Cliff Palace.[45]

Four other ruins in Lion Canyon were thought worthy of mention. One was the largest cliff dwelling in Johnson Canyon or any of its tributaries, being

The Mancos and La Plata Sector. *Top,* largest masonry structure of the La Plata area. Excavated by Morris in 1930. Pueblo III Period on surface with early strata below. *Bottom,* typical pithouse of the La Plata District. From Earl H. Morris, 1919.

The Mancos and La Plata Sector. *Top,* pit room with wall support slabs in Ruin No. 17. *Bottom,* subsurface rooms in Ruin No. 17. From Earl H. Morris, 1919.

more than 200 feet (60 m) long, with six kivas and thirty-one rectangular dwelling rooms still standing. Before its demise it probably contained as many as eighty rooms. The ruin had been thoroughly ransacked by relic hunters long before Morris got to it, and practically every nook and cranny had been pried into.[46]

The pottery found in Johnson Canyon was of three varieties: coil ware, plain smooth ware, and decorated smooth ware; all were constructed by the coiling process.[47] Morris also found grinding stones, axes, pot lids, griddles (upon which meal cakes were fried), bone implements, articles of wood (including digging sticks, prayer sticks, and compound arrows), fire sticks, a reed quiver, a hairbrush, pot rests, rush matting, feather cloth, cotton cloth, baskets, plaited yucca sandals, and miscellaneous other articles of unknown purpose.

Morris was the first to do excavations among the inconspicuous ruins that are numerous in the upper La Plata Valley and on top of the mesas westward to the Mancos Canyon. Here he found the remains of Basketmaker pithouses (already described in the Basketmaker village and house material), and also the remains of what were essentially jacal houses. A few stone walls were built, and upright stone slabs were sometimes used either to brace jacal walls or to provide an actual wall base.

Morris's description of jacal construction at Site No. 11 is most informative. Shallow trenches had been dug where it was desired to place the walls. In these trenches, poles averaging about 4 inches (10 cm) in diameter were set up side by side, held upright by stones wedged into the trenches on both sides of the pole butts. The exposed surfaces of the poles were coated with mud till they were almost, if not quite, hidden, and a strong wall superficially resembling one of adobe was formed. It is probable that the roof consisted of beams, twigs, and bark covered with clay.[48]

A ruin on Red Mesa, listed as Site No. 20, proved to be quite unusual. In its clean plan it was a reminder of Fire Temple at Mesa Verde. It was a stone ruin, 77 feet (23.5 m) long and 32 feet (9.7 m) wide, its long axis extending east and west. In plan it consisted of four connected kivas in a row, flanked on the north by a row of four contiguous rooms, none of which had side openings, although the entire structure was above grade. The masonry was excellent, with walls of dressed sandstone blocks chinked with tiny spalls. Most unusual were the shallow pilasters, being but 5 inches (12.5 cm) deep. Morris had no opportunity for extended investigation, but he thought the relationship of this masonry building with the surrounding jacal was worthy of further study.[49] It did appear to be a special ceremonial center or shrine, and it was not surprising that many slab-enclosed stone boxes similar to those found on the Mesa Verde and thought to be shrines were found near the ruin.

Lesser material culture items turned up on the mesas included pottery that was inferior to that of the cliff dwellings; there were four classes: smooth ware, smooth ware with banded necks, smooth polished ware without decoration, and smooth polished ware with decoration.[50] There were also bone tools, stone axes and hammers, stone pottery smoothers, pounding stones, and chipped implements such as arrowpoints, knives, drills, and scrapers.

In the spring of 1916 Morris returned to continue his explorations along the La Plata drainage, and he came back to the area several times after that. In 1916 he made what were at the time startling finds at a site that provided him with important stratigraphic information. The Basketmaker-Pueblo relationship was suspected by now but not yet positive. Here, though, eight feet below masonry dwelling foundations he discovered a honeycomb of pithouses either piled on top of one another or standing side by side. In all, he obtained at the site evidence of three distinct but continuous periods of occupancy by those who would shortly be classified as Basketmakers and Pueblos: pithouses, dwellings built of cobblestones and adobe, and dwellings built of coursed masonry.[51]

The Mancos and La Plata Sector. *Top,* La Plata kiva ruin with masonry bench and pilasters. *Bottom,* Great Kiva at La Plata site. In center are the remains of one of the huge logs that served as main roof supports. Pueblo I Period. From Earl H. Morris, 1919.

THE MESA VERDE PROPER
PUEBLO I, II, AND III, A.D. 700–1300
(DEVELOPMENTAL AND GREAT PUEBLO PERIODS)

HISTORY

At the Pecos Conference in 1927, five successive periods were established for the Pueblo time sequence, and each of the periods was given a summary definition. As we move to the magnificent era at Mesa Verde proper, it may be helpful to quote the definitions for Pueblo I, II, and III.

Pueblo I, A.D. 700–900, was defined as "the first stage during which cranial deformation was practiced, vessel neck corrugation was introduced, and villages composed of rectangular living-rooms of true masonry were developed."

Pueblo II, A.D. 900–1100, was "the stage marked by widespread geographical extension of life in small villages; corrugation, often of elaborate technique, extended over the whole surface of cooking vessels."

Pueblo III, A.D. 1100–1300, was characterized as "the stage of large communities, great development of the arts, and growth of intensive local specialization." This period is also known as *Classic Pueblo* and, more recently, as *Great Pueblo*, since it marks the peak of florescence for the ancient Anasazi.

Nowhere are these three periods seen more clearly than at the Mesa Verde proper, midway between the westernmost and easternmost sectors of the Mesa Verde Region. Basketmakers lived in what is now the spectacular Mesa Verde National Park area before the Pueblo I Period, although documented habitation by the Basketmakers dates no earlier than A.D. 600. They probably lived in the park area before that, but all except their final dwelling sites either eroded away, were covered over, or have not yet been found. Contributing to the absence of early sites was the common Anasazi practice of repeatedly looting, burning, and leveling abandoned buildings and then reusing what they could of the earlier materials as sites were overbuilt. This practice poses problems for archaeologists and for the dendrochronologist who seeks true dates for a site. For example, a given building, the majority of whose timbers date from A.D. 914 and 915, might also include two beams dated A.D. 879 and 884. The question then arises whether the building was begun in A.D. 879 and finished much later or was actually built in A.D. 914 with the help of borrowed timbers.

The Mesa Verde is situated on the Colorado Plateau and is an erosional remnant created by the uplifting of the San Juan and La Plata mountains. Its elevation ranges from 6,000 to 8,575 feet. It is bounded on the west and south by the Ute Mountain Indian Reservation; on the west, north, and east by the vast and magnificent Montezuma and Mancos valleys, and on the southeast by the Southern Ute Reservation. There are simply no words adequate to describe the view from the mesa top, which extends for a hundred miles or more out over the immense green valleys.

After living on the mesa top for an unbroken span of at least seven hundred years, from A.D. 600 to 1300, the Anasazi left the mesa and all they had accomplished there and went away, taking few material goods with them. For nearly six hundred years after that the ruins decayed, the small cornfields lay fallow, and the trees and shrubs once again took possession of their natural home.

The history of the discovery of the great mesa has been told in so many books and articles that it would be superfluous to retell it in detail here. After the Anasazi departed, marauding Ute and Navajo Indians occupied the entire

Top, Mesa Verde as seen from Yucca House National Monument in Colorado. *Bottom,* one of the canyons of Mesa Verde National Park.

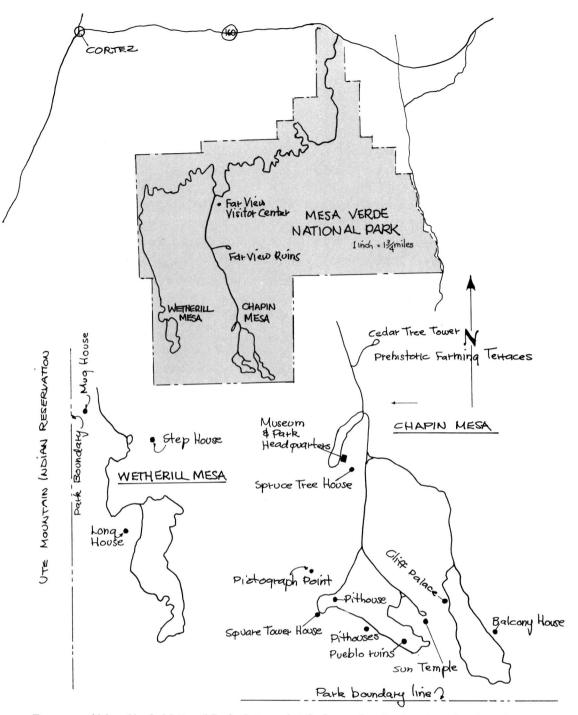

Top, map of Mesa Verde National Park. *Bottom,* detail of map showing location of major ruins.

region and the great mesa itself, but did no farming there. Spanish explorers were in all parts of the Southwest during the late 1500s and the 1600s, and in 1765 Don María de Riveria led a pair of expeditions into the La Plata Mountains east of the mesa. One of the groups named it Mesa Verde, Green Table, because it resembled a vast, flat green tableland.

On August 10, 1776, a party led by two Spanish priests, Francisco Atanasio Domínguez and Silvestre Vélez de Escalante, camped on the Mancos River at a point near Mesa Verde. They were searching for a short route to Monterey, California, and their journal includes an entry describing an ancient ruin on the rim of the Dolores River, together with a record of the abundant trees, pastures, and flowers.

In 1829 Antonio Aramijo made his way down the Mancos Canyon on his expedition from Santa Fe, New Mexico, to Los Angeles, California. In 1848 ownership of the Mesa Verde Region passed from Mexican to American hands, and the new owners began to explore it to find out what they had.

In 1859 Professor J. S. Newberry, a geologist with the J. N. Macomb Expedition, climbed to the top of the north rim of the mesa, was absolutely thrilled with what he saw, and although he mentioned no ruins, gave a glowing report of the geological wonders of the mesa.

In 1868 the United States made a treaty with the Ute Indians, ceding to them large areas of southwestern Colorado, including what is now the Mesa Verde National Park area. But in 1873, when extensive mineral deposits were discovered in the region, the Utes were persuaded to relinquish the San Juan district.

In 1874 the renowned photographer William Henry Jackson, leading a government survey party guided by John Moss, followed Aramijo's route down the Mancos Canyon, where he excitedly investigated and photographed a structure he named Two Story Cliff House. It was the earliest known discovery of a Mesa Verde cliff dwelling by white men. If only Jackson had gone four miles farther up the nearest side canyon, he would have found the far greater Cliff Palace. But a band of Utes frightened him away, and he did not see it.

In 1875 the geologist W. H. Holmes visited, named, and briefly described some of the ruins in the Mancos Canyon.

In 1886 a woman named Virginia McClurg visited Balcony House, and in the winter of 1888 the electrifying discovery that soon caused Mesa Verde to become a household name was made by Mancos Valley ranchers Richard Wetherill and Charles Mason, who found and explored Cliff Palace, Spruce Tree House, and Square Tower House. Even in a fallen state the ruins constituted the most spectacular finds imaginable. Shortly thereafter the Wetherill family and their friends began to excavate systematically and to collect artifacts in the grand cliff dwellings. Then, as word spread and local residents saw what the Wetherills were finding, others began to emulate them, not resting until the finest of the artifacts were cleaned out. My own father, Fredrick Mails, who lived until 1921 on a ranch outside Cortez, Colorado, told me he made several horseback trips to the mesa ruins, and that while he did not collect anything, he once knew several families who had rooms filled with Mesa Verde artifacts. Some they kept for personal pleasure, but selling them was also a big business.

It was not long before scientists also began to make pilgrimages to Mesa Verde, and survey and restoration work there has been carried on continuously ever since. The first to come was Baron Gustaf Nordenskiöld in 1891, and extensive reference will be made to his work shortly. Then came Jesse Walter Fewkes of the Smithsonian Institution, followed by the National Geographic Society, the National Park Service, Gila Pueblo (Arizona), and the universities of Colorado and Arizona.

From 1953 to 1956 the University of Colorado, under the direction of Robert H. Lister, conducted research on Chapin Mesa, in the Far View locality. Three surface pueblos were excavated and reported upon.

From 1958 to 1963 the important Wetherill Mesa Project was carried out. Six major mesa-top and cliff-dwelling sites were excavated and reported upon, including Long House, Step House, Big Juniper House, Two Raven House, Badger House, and Mug House. The last two are given extensive consideration later in this chapter.

In 1965 the University of Colorado Mesa Verde Archaeological Research Center was established, and continuous projects in the Mesa Verde Region are being undertaken by the center. The work projection is endless. In 1951 Don Watson, then the park archaeologist, surveyed Chapin Mesa and recorded more than one thousand sites. The Wetherill Mesa group of 1958 recorded more than eight hundred. This total of eighteen hundred sites represents an area amounting to only 20 percent of the entire park.

As was the case at Chaco Canyon, life at Mesa Verde could never have been child's play, either for those who first lived on the mesa tops or for those who later built the cliff dwellings. The area is cut and divided by gullies and canyons one can easily get lost in. It is also evident that the vegetation on the mesa was more dense by far in early Pueblo times than it is today, since the Anasazi cleared away much of it for agricultural and building plots, burned great quantities for fuel, and used still more to build their thousands of buildings. What had taken centuries to grow would not replace itself quickly, yet even at the turn of the twentieth century, pothunters making their way from Cortez to the cliff dwellings would report that narrow pathways led either along the edge of a precipice or through low-growing piñons with clutching limbs. Palmer Henderson, who made the trip in 1893 in the company of the Wetherill brothers, said, "Most people think piñons are trees; they are cunningly disguised demons delighting to flick out a bit of cheek, turn back a foot, or even pull a man off his horse if he's not wary. I could grow eloquent over the meanness of piñons."[52] He goes on, though, to praise piñons for their beauty, for their small nuts to roast and to grind for flour, and for wood "that burns more brilliantly than driftwood and smells sweeter than incense."[53]

The point is, however, that if it was that hard to ride along the trails and through the piñons in 1893, what must it have been like for the Anasazi to make their way with all manner of loads on their backs and heads when the piñons and brush were far thicker?

There are different opinions regarding the amount of drinking water available on the mesa for the six-hundred-year period from Pueblo I through Pueblo III. There are no permanent streams or ponds, but some say that, except in time of drought, there was ample water because of an abundance of springs and seeps. Others believe there were relatively few ground water sources. Weather conditions would, of course, have altered the situation from year to year or decade to decade. Yet the diligent efforts of the Anasazi to husband precipitation and to catch the water from melting snow by building reservoirs would seem to indicate that water was always in short supply. If it was a precious commodity, we can be certain that religious views and ceremonial life were oriented toward obtaining and preserving it. Some cliff village caves had either open springs or seepage points. Other villages could not have survived without springs close by. But nowhere in the archaeological records do we find evidence of abundant springs within the cliff dwellings themselves. Most water had to be carried for some distance, although there were times each year when the people had more than they needed.

Palmer Henderson described the Mesa Verde in 1893 as "almost waterless country," but it is obvious that he was not on the mesa in late summer, when the weather can vary dramatically and occasional torrential rains form raging streams of water that flow swiftly along the gullies and then jet like waterfalls out over the rims of cave roofs. Fewkes, stated, after experiencing these, that the visitor in the dry season can hardly imagine the amount of rain that occasionally falls during the summer months. Therefore it is difficult to appreciate the destructive force it exerts when it flows over the cliffs.[54] The torrents gain force from the distance of the fall, sweeping everything before them and bringing down earth, stones, small trees, and bushes. The bottoms of the canyons are soon filled with roaring torrents fed by waterfalls that can be seen at intervals far down the gorges. Observers caught in cliff dwellings during such downpours behold a vast curtain of water falling over the projecting cliff in front of them. The cataracts never last long, but so long as the rain falls their power is irresistible. The cliff-dwelling Anasazi had constantly to cope with this, and repair work was always going on. Once the Anasazi left and the dwellings were abandoned, nature took its inexorable yearly toll.

Two major mesas exist within the national park, Chapin and Wetherill, and excavations have mainly been confined to these areas. Arthur H. Rohn, as expert concerning Mesa Verde as anyone is today, reports that as of 1976 at Chapin Mesa eleven pithouses of the Basketmaker III Period had been excavated, eighteen others had been partially excavated, and twenty-six mesa-top sites that were surveyed were thought to include thirty-six or more unexcavated pithouses. In addition, Basketmaker III remains had been found in several sites, all the known house sites being located along the low ridges of the mesa top.[55]

No complete village or cluster of Basketmaker III pithouses had been excavated, but indications were that typical village sites consisted of from six to eight separate structures situated in close proximity. Dwelling floor shapes ranged from roughly squarish to circular in plan, and floor levels were from 2 to 4 feet (0.6–1.2 m) below grade. Common features included an antechamber that was connected to the main room by a raised passageway, a crude bench or banquette, a central clay-lined circular firepit, storage pits, irregular wing walls, and the typical Basketmaker four-post-and-beam roof support. Stone slab deflectors and clay-lined sipapus were typical, but not always present. A four-post arrangement also held up the antechamber roof. Upright sandstone slabs were often used to line and support the dirt walls, to serve as deflectors, and to make storage bins. The later pithouses were the squarish variety, and they had smaller antechambers and more extensive wing walls. All pithouses were oriented toward the south, and trash was randomly scattered about the dwellings. Construction dates determined through dendrochronology range from A.D. 587 to 700, and a terminal date for the period of A.D. 750 is postulated.[56]

Lesser material culture objects found in the ruins are similar to those of Wetherill Mesa's Badger House Community and Mug House, both of which are considered in detail later. Of five burials associated with the sites just mentioned, four bodies were flexed and one was extended. The preserved skulls were undeformed. Mortuary offerings accompanied the four bodies that faced upward. The meager economic evidence indicated an agricultural base consisting of corn and beans. Piñon nuts were also found, along with the unworked bones of mule deer and turkey, although Rohn notes that evidence to indicate domestication of the turkey is lacking. Pottery associated with the period consisted of Chapin Gray and Chapin Black-on-white.[57]

PUEBLO I AND II AT CHAPIN MESA

The Pueblo I Period for Chapin Mesa extended from A.D. 750 to 900. Dwellings continued to be located along the low ridges of the mesa top. No complete village or cluster of houses had been dug as of 1976, but excavations that were made and surface indications suggested plans similar to those of Alkali Ridge (in the westernmost part of the region) and of the La Plata on the eastern side. The plans consisted of several roughly parallel rows of contiguous surface rooms and deep pithouses scattered to the south of the rooms. Surface dwellings were essentially rectangular, with combinations of jacal and adobe walls. Thin sandstone slabs were sometimes set upright to support the wall bases. Beams usually rested directly on the walls, but in some structures additional support was provided by posts set in the floor at the four corners. Floors were recessed as much as 12 inches (30 cm) into the ground and often contained circular, dirt-lined firepits. There were also outdoor fireplaces. Storerooms, whose dimensions were smaller than those of the dwellings, sometimes formed a second row of rooms behind the dwellings.

The pithouses of the period were squarish, with rounded corners. Their excavations ranged from 5 to 7 feet (1.5–2.1 m) deep and averaged 12 feet (3.6 m) square. Typical details included ventilator tunnels, jacal deflectors, wing walls, circular clay-lined firepits, and numerous floor pits for pot rests and storage. Sipapus were not found, and a bench attended only one site. Walls were of earth, and the roof was supported by the four-main-post-and-beam system.[58]

With the exception of several pottery changes, the lesser material culture remained much the same as that of the previous Basketmaker III Period and similar to that of Badger House Community. Pottery consisted now of Chapin Gray, Moccasin Variety of Chapin Gray, Chapin Black-on-white, Piedra Black-on-white, Abajo Red-on-orange, and Bluff Black-on-red. Far more artifacts were found than in the Basketmaker excavations. The economy base continued to be agricultural, but animal bones were turned up in much greater quantities and varieties.[59]

Rohn divides Pueblo II at Chapin Mesa into early and late phases, the first with an uncertain dating of about A.D. 900 to 1000, and the second also questionable and extending from about A.D. 1000 to 1100. Sites excavated in part were in the same locations as those of their predecessors. As with the Basketmakers, villages still consisted of clusters of from six to eight small but separate dwelling blocks, each probably having its own clan-sized kiva. Surface structures were of jacal, with small stones sometimes embedded in the adobe to make it more durable. Floors of excavated dwellings were in such poor condition their original features could not be determined. Kivas were subterranean and circular, and walls were unlined, except where the dirt was loose. Standard features included ventilators, firepits, sipapus, banquettes, and, again, the four-post support system for the roof.[60]

The lesser material culture and economy varied little from those of previous periods. Pottery included Cortez Black-on-white, Mancos Black-on-white, Mancos Gray Corrugated, Mesa Verde Corrugated, Chapin Gray, and Bluff Black-on-red—La Plata Variety.

Late Pueblo II found most house sites still situated along the low ridges on the mesa top. But others were being placed on talus slopes; some of these were located where broad benches occurred, and others beneath the cliffs in the deeper canyons toward the southern end of the mesa. Village clusterings of separate dwelling blocks and kivas duplicated those of the early Pueblo II phase, but walls were made now with sandstone masonry one stone thick, with an occasional post for additional support. Most stones were dressed by bifacial chipping on both the interior and exterior sides. Large upright stone slabs formed the base of some walls. A few rooms contained firepits.

Kivas were circular and subterranean, and their walls were partially lined with masonry. Typical features included ventilators, sipapus, firepits, slab deflectors, and wall niches. A banquette and six masonry pilasters supported the roof, which was probably cribbed. At least two specialized ceremonial buildings were constructed, each with kiva and tower combinations. One large kiva had eight pilasters and those often mentioned vaults commonly described as "foot drums."[61]

Of particular interest in this period was the use of many shrines. Rohn defines these as technically any structure, natural formation, or place held in some degree of sacred esteem. "This means that some unusual rock formation where a legendary event took place can be as important a shrine as a purposely-built structure."[62]

One type of shrine consisted of varying assemblages of sandstone slabs and blocks, designed to form either boxes or niches of various dimensions. These in turn contained special stones or fetishes having special ceremonial significance. A second type of shrine consisted of mesa-top structures, actually buildings, of possible ceremonial use. Examples of these are the famous Sun Temple (mentioned in greater detail elsewhere), Cedar Tree Tower, and Far View Tower or House.

Fewkes directed the excavation of Cedar Tree Tower in 1920. About a mile north of Spruce Tree House he found a tower and a kiva connected by a tunnel that had a small rectangular subterranean alcove on its southwest side. The circular kiva possessed all the typical features, except the sipapu, which was drilled in the tower floor. The tower was expertly built of double-coursed masonry, in which virtually every stone was dressed by pecking to fit the curvature of the walls. A low retaining wall supported a level plaza-like space over the kiva roof. The absence of refuse indicated that the tower had not served as a habitation, and it is assumed today that it was a place where sacred paraphernalia were kept and specified rituals were performed. Not the least of its attributes was the spectacular view southeastward into Soda Canyon.[63]

Far View Tower or House was excavated by a Fewkes-led party in 1922. This proved to be a circular tower that had been built on top of the ruins of a Pueblo II house. It was related to one kiva and possibly two. One of the kivas appears to have been built at the same time as the tower, the other to have resulted from a remodeled structure. Unfortunately, vandals or pothunters had destroyed a large portion of the Tower/House complex before Fewkes excavated it, and so only guesses could be made as to its purpose. Suggestions are that it might have housed the deceased from the earlier pueblo or from adjacent pueblos, or it might have been a specialized burial place associated with the tower-kiva complex.[64]

One hundred feet south of Far View House is Pipe Shrine House, a mysterious and remarkable structure also excavated in 1922.[65] A saucerlike depression on the surface proved to be a central kiva, without firepit, ventilator, or deflector. The fireplace was but a segment of the floor area separated from the rest by a low, curved ridge of clay. It was also a shrine, for it contained many artifacts mixed with the ashes. Included were twelve decorated clay pipes, several fetishes, a small black-and-white decorated bowl, chipped flint stone knives, and other objects.

The pipe discovery was a significant one, for it indicated that the Anasazi priests of the mesa, like the Hopi, smoked ceremonially and after smoking threw their pipes into the firepit. The kiva was 24 feet (7.3 m) in diameter and equally deep. It had eight pilasters and probably a cribbed roof, although the entire kiva had been ravaged by a great fire and no traces of beams survived. There was no banquette on the south side.

A circular tower once rose above the Pipe Shrine House rooms. Fewkes thought it was an observatory. South of Pipe Shrine House were several rectangular shrines, one built in a retaining wall that contained a number of carved stone fetishes or idols quite similar to those found in the Chaco Canyon Region. Such stone images are rarely found on the Mesa Verde.[66]

Pottery underwent a great deal of individual experimentation and variation during late Pueblo II at Chapin Mesa. Principal types were Mancos Black-

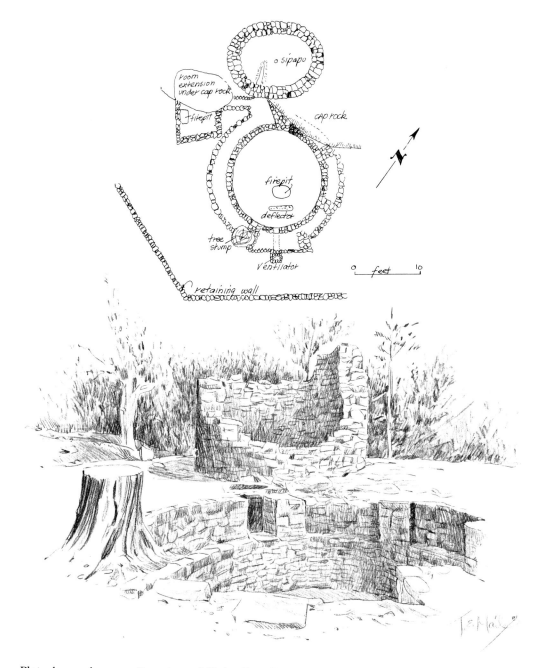

Plot plan and perspective view of Cedar Tree Tower and kiva. From photo by G. L. Beam, 1920. Plan by Fewkes, 1920b.

on-white, Mesa Verde Corrugated—Mancos Variety, Cortez Black-on-white, and Chapin Gray—Mummy Lake Variety. Other lesser material culture objects were consistent with preceding and following phases. Corn still dominated the economy, and many terraced fields were in use.

As he does with Pueblo II, Rohn divides the Pueblo III Period into two parts: the early period dating from A.D. 1100 to 1200, and the late period from A.D. 1200 to 1300.

Most house sites of the early period were located toward the ends of the low distributary ridges on the mesa top and so were closer to the rims of the canyons than to the center of Chapin Mesa. More and more Anasazi shifted their dwellings to the talus slopes at the cliff bases and on the broad benches. Some cave sites were now occupied. Village site makeups began to vary: some continued the pattern of Pueblo II, others pulled the dwellings and kiva together into a single structure, and still others grouped several multiple-kiva sites together. In the majority of sites, kivas were wholly or partly enclosed by

a, plan of Far View House. *b,* rare Mayan-type arch in flue of Kiva at Far View House. *c–d,* serpent symbols incised on rocks in masonry walls. *e,* stone corn goddess fetish found in ruin. *f,* second stone fetish. *Bottom,* south side of Far View House Ruin. From Fewkes, 1916.

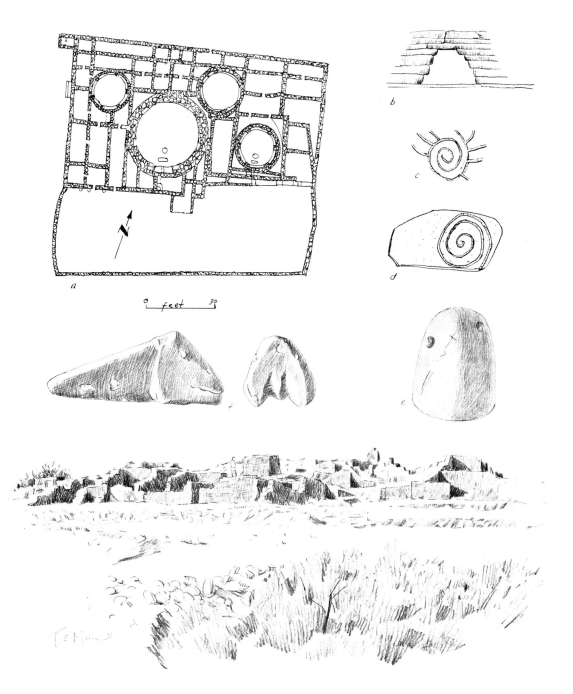

Pipe Shrine House. *Top left*, Mountain Lion Shrine or Shrine of the South. Square enclosure is shrine as found. (Cochiti Pueblo on the Rio Grande has a stone lion shrine.) The building in the background is Pipe Shrine House. *Top right and center*, stone mountain sheep and bird effigies. From Fewkes, 1922c. Similar effigies were found at the Village of the Great Kivas at Zuñi. *Bottom*, Far View Tower, looking north, showing the tops of two kivas. From Fewkes, 1922c.

rooms and walls. Dwelling walls were often several stones thick, roughly spalled, and occasionally pecked.[67]

Buildings were built two and three stories high and in oblong, L-shaped, and horseshoe arrangements like many of those already described for the westernmost Mesa Verde Region. Specialized ceremonial buildings, such as Far View Tower, came into being.

Kivas of this period were circular and masonry-lined and possessed ventilators, sipapus, firepits, stone-slab or masonry deflectors, wall niches, banquettes, six masonry pilasters, a southern keyhole recess at banquette level, and probably cribbed roofs. Several kivas originally had a Chaco Canyon type of subfloor ventilator, but this had been replaced by the more typical wall-opening type. Floor vaults were found in the larger kivas.

Also employed in this period were retaining walls to support and circumscribe plazas, steps, and trash mounds. Continued use was made of shrines, reservoirs, and stone check dams. Field houses were also built. Corn, beans, and squash were grown, hunting for game continued, and there is evidence that turkeys were domesticated.

Late Pueblo III, covering the years A.D. 1200 to 1300, was the cliff-dwelling period at Mesa Verde. Almost all the Anasazi dwelling sites were located in the various-sized caves and rock shelters along the vertical sandstone cliffs. Some ceremonial sites were in use on the mesa top, and it is possible that a few mesa-top village buildings were still occupied, but these would be exceptions to the rule. For such an archaeologically important time as this, a summary view is not sufficient, and Mug House, on Wetherill Mesa, serves as an excellent example both of the architectural marvels wrought by the cliff-dwelling Anasazi and of the lesser material culture objects. In addition, a detailed look will be taken at the many sites and findings of Gustaf Nordenskiöld, together with those of Fewkes not already mentioned.

Fire Temple, in Fewkes Canyon on Chapin Mesa, merits particular consideration. It was first known as Painted House, but excavations done in 1919 and 1920 revealed its true purpose, to Fewkes's satisfaction at least, and the name was changed. Fewkes thought it proved to be one of the most exceptional cliff ruins yet recognized in the Southwest, for he regarded it as a temple of the eternal fire. "Attention," he says, "should be called to the importance of the discovery that the cliff dwellers had a New Fire Cult and possibly that rites of new fire and conservation of the same existed among prehistoric people of the Mesa Verde."[68]

In July and November the Hopi perform the rites of kindling the new fire, known as the Lesser and Greater Fire ceremonials. The act is performed by rotating a fire stick or drill in a notched board, and just such fire equipment has been found in Spruce Tree House, Square Tower House, and elsewhere.

Fewkes thinks the Lesser Fire Ceremony at the East Mesa of the Hopi is the closest survival of the cliff dweller's fire rite, since in it is the personification of a phallic being, Kokopelli. His picture was well preserved up to a few years before the excavation on the wall of the secret Fire Temple Chamber

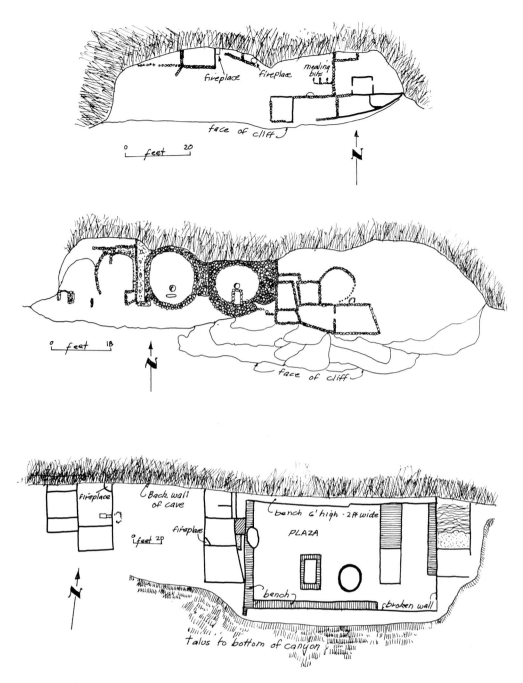

Top, ground plan of Upper Cave of Fire Temple House. *Center,* ground plan of Lower Cave of Fire Temple House. *Bottom,* ground plan of Fire Temple House central court. From Fewkes, 1920b.

where fire was created. This Lesser New Fire, called *Sumykoli,* is celebrated by a fraternity of fire priests, now extinct, known as the Yaya priesthood. The Yaya priest at Hopi carries in his hand during this ceremony a rattle of exceptional construction. Two such rattles, now in the Brooklyn Museum, were found in a cliff dwelling in Canyon de Chelly.

The masonry of Fire Temple indicates it was contemporary with the first settlement of Cliff Palace, and the architectural plan is as clean as that of our most modern buildings. The general form and arrangement of rooms at the east and west ends of the central court of Fire Temple differ from any other cliff ruin or pueblo in the Southwest. No cooking places, grinding bins, or household implements were found at the site. Moreover, there are no kivas, and nowhere else is found a large circular firepit filled with ashes and standing in the center of a rectangular court. Calcined human bones were absent, and the pit was not used as a crematory. Further, since ashes were found elsewhere in the court, it appears that great fires once raged over all parts of the court.

Top, bins for grinding corn in upper cave of Fire Temple House. From photo by J. A. Jeancon. *Bottom*, western end of Fire Temple Court. From photograph by G. L. Beam.

On the east and west ends of the court are banquettes or benches, with those of the east end serving as seats for spectators. Niches in the rear wall provided places where sacred objects may have been placed. A wall of the cliff bears triangle and zigzag paintings that Fewkes interprets as symbols of sex life. But, most important, on the wall of one room at the west end of the court there are paintings done in red. One of these, now erased, represented a phallic being still associated with New Fire ceremonies among the Hopi, while others represent fire itself. One of the four fraternities that celebrate this ceremony is the order of Horn priests, who wear on their heads imitations of the horns of mountain sheep. Paintings of mountain sheep cover the walls of the west room of Fire Temple.

The massive-walled buildings at the east and west ends of the court originally reached to the roof of the cave, and although they were two stories high no wooden beams for flooring occur. Wherever a lower story existed it was filled in with rubble and paved over with adobe to make a second-story floor. On the white wall plaster there are many figures painted in red. Most of these are triangles and symbols for lightning, which Fewkes describes as female and male symbols similar to those in Hopi sacred rooms.

Immediately west of Fire Temple is a group of rooms from which household utensils were excavated, and east of the temple are two low caves that may have served as residences for the fire priests and their families, since they contained dwelling spaces, granaries, mealing bins with metates still in place, and several kivas.[69]

BADGER HOUSE COMMUNITY

From 1958 through 1965 the National Park Service, with generous support from the National Geographic Society, conducted a comprehensive field study of the archaeology and ecology of Wetherill Mesa. At Badger House Community, a mesa-top site whose maximum population never exceeded one hundred individuals, findings were made that represent the cultural and physical remains of a community of sedentary farmers during a span of more than six hundred years, from roughly the mid-seventh through the mid-thirteenth centuries A.D.[70] When the work was done, the researchers concluded that the beginning of the Basketmaker III Period at Mesa Verde dated, for that site at least, no earlier than A.D. 600.[71] This earliest period of Mesa Verde occupation for which there is solid evidence is designated as the La Plata Phase, A.D. 600–750.

Pithouses typical of this phase had an almost circular main room and a small antechamber. Roofs were supported by the traditional four main posts and four beams. Narrow benches held the butts of slanting sidewall poles, and low wing-wall partitions were set up on the south side to subdivide the main room. Small surface storage rooms, probably of jacal construction, were scattered about in a random pattern behind the pithouses.

Basketmaker life at Mesa Verde was consistent with that already described for Basketmakers in general, but the Anasazi were on the threshold of significant advances. A.D. 750 was to be the eve of experimentation and assertion that would cause archaeologists to give the Anasazi a new descriptive name, Pueblo.

Pueblo I is distinguished by portentous new habits, products, and practices. During the Piedra Phase, beginning in A.D. 750 and lasting until A.D. 900, lambdoidal cranial deformation was adopted for the first time. Whereas Basketmaker cradleboards were previously padded and soft, Pueblo-period infants were placed on hard boards that flattened the upper back portion of the

Badger House Community: *a*, pithouse dated A.D. 650. *b*, pithouse dated A.D. 620–31. *c*, shallow pits of adobe-walled surface house dated A.D. 650–832. *d*, protokiva with antechamber. From Hayes and Lancaster, 1975.

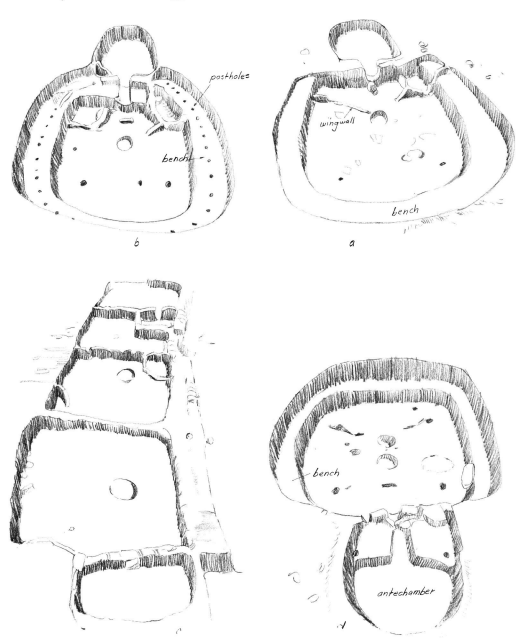

head and broadened the face. No one knows why this was done. Perhaps it was suggested by outsiders who joined the Anasazi already dwelling at Mesa Verde. Perhaps it became a means of common identity for a people just beginning to recognize themselves as a nation. In any event, the practice quickly became popular, possibly even religiously significant, and fashionable. Everyone did it, and cranial deformation continued for centuries.

Most La Plata pottery was a slightly polished plain ware, Chapin Gray, done in a variety of shapes. But in the Piedra Phase, potters added some interesting changes. Neck-banded culinary pots made their appearance as the clay coils around the necks of jars were left unsmoothed. Bowls that were to be decorated were given a coat of white slip to cover the interior surface. This provided a contrasting base for the black designs, and the product is called Chapin Black-on-white. The Black-on-white decoration of closed vessels, virtually unknown previously, became more and more popular.[72] Red ceramics with black designs have also been traced to the early Pueblo I Period, but some authorities think the natural gray clays and techniques of Mesa Verde would not have accounted for these. Thus they are believed to have come to the mesa as alien trade items from other areas.[73] Those who excavated Badger House Community state that Bluff Black-on-red pottery was introduced early in the Piedra Phase and increased in popularity to a degree slightly greater than black-on-white pottery.[74] Tubular gray pottery pipes were also found in the Badger House ruins.[75]

Cotton made its first appearance in Pueblo I, coming to the Mesa Verde by means of trade with southern neighbors. As the Anasazi began to grow cotton for themselves, they also constructed looms and fashioned cotton textiles. In the modern pueblos, men are the weavers, and it is assumed this was the case in Pueblo I times.

New strains of corn were introduced. These, too, came from the south, probably originating in Mesoamerica.[76] Such strains were of no small importance, since the Anasazi population was steadily expanding and the new corns could withstand arid conditions and had shorter growing seasons. This, more than anything else, enabled the Anasazi to exist and flourish even in marginal agricultural areas.

Other changes notwithstanding, the advent of the Pueblo I Period and Piedra Phase at Mesa Verde is best identified by significant architectural innovations. On the one hand, pithouse construction methods were employed to fashion small aboveground or "surface" villages whose contiguous, single-storied rooms were joined together to form slightly L- or U-shaped apartment structures whose actual shape was little more than an arc. On the other hand, the pithouse itself was dug deeper to form an underground ceremonial chamber, or protokiva.

The plot plan employed for the earliest surface villages became standard for all such villages to be built over the next 350 years: surface dwellings and storage buildings occupied the northwest portion of a site and faced southeast. Kivas occupied the southeast portion. Archaeologists call this plan "front orientation." Trash was dumped to the southeast of the kivas.

Reconstructed views of Basketmaker III pithouse located near the Step House Ruin at Mesa Verde. *Top,* interior view showing roof construction. *Bottom,* exterior view showing wall construction and house interior.

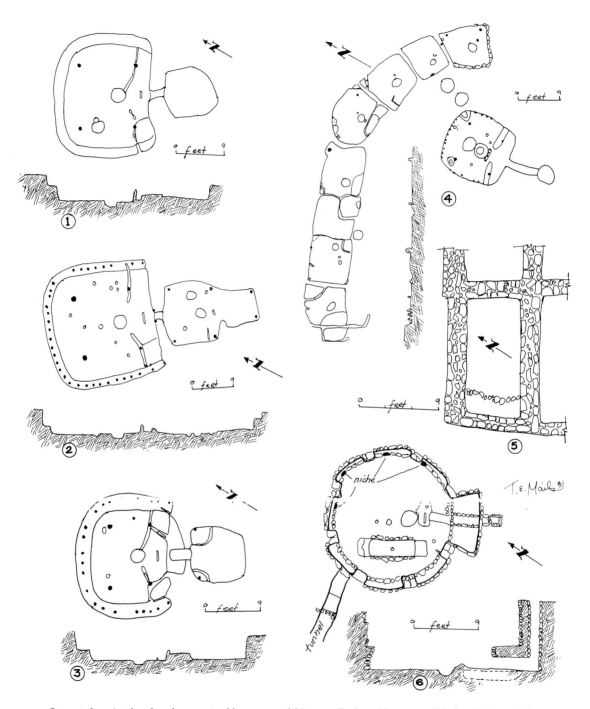

Steps taken in the development of houses and kivas at Badger House on Wetherill Mesa. Nos.
1, 2, and 3 are plans and sections of pithouses with antechambers dating to the La Plata Phase,
Basketmaker III, ca. A.D. 620 and after. House and Protokiva 4 are from the Piedra Phase, ca.
A.D. 860. Block stone house 5 dates to the Ackmen Phase, early Pueblo II, ca. A.D. 920. The
fully developed kiva No. 6 is of the Mesa Verde Phase, Pueblo III, ca. A.D. 1258. From Hayes
and Lancaster, 1975.

The construction method employed for Pueblo I surface buildings is sometimes referred to as "wattle and daub," and other times as "jacal" or "adobe and jacal." Whereas some walls were simple adobe, usually vertical posts were set into the ground at intervals of 2 feet (61 cm) or so. These posts were forked at the top to receive roof beams 4 to 8 inches (10–20 cm) in diameter. Clear beam spans were short, ranging from 6 to 14 feet (1.8–4.2 m), because the beams were relatively light, and the posts and beams were lashed together with strips of bark.

Walls were completed by interweaving the vertical posts with sticks and brush and then coating both sides with layers of mud. Roofs were finished by placing a tight layer of branches and brush at a right angle across the beams, and then covering this raftlike mat with a thick layer of earth. The final roof was flat. Window openings were small and the number held to a minimum. There was no door. The typical access opening was in the center of the roof, as in the original pithouse. A dweller climbed up one ladder to his roof and then down another ladder into his house.

Some builders braced their walls with flat stones set on edge and wedged against the posts. Room divisions were made by placing flat stones upright in a line.

Douglas fir, juniper, and piñon were the preferred woods used for construction. Fir was the early Pueblo I favorite because it was straight and easily cut and trimmed. But it grew only at the foot of the cliffs on the northern slopes and had to be carried up to the mesa tops. When centuries of building eliminated the more accessible firs and made their transportation even more difficult, the use of fir virtually ceased. By the end of the Ackmen Phase (ca. A.D. 1100)[77] only juniper and piñon were still in service. This fact as much as any may have led to masonry construction.

Sometime after A.D. 750, the first "protomasonry" made its appearance. This consisted of courses of flat but unshaped stones alternating with layers of adobe, a method that became increasingly common by the late ninth century.[78]

At certain locations on the great Colorado Plateau, archaeologists have found structural remains from the early Basketmaker II Period, including a few that appear to be religious in nature. But none of these discoveries have been made at Mesa Verde, where the earliest protokivas and kivas found so far are associated with the late Basketmaker III and Pueblo I periods.[79] In recognizing this, however, it should be noted again that comparatively few investigations of Mesa Verde sites of the Basketmaker periods have been carried out, and the possibility is left open that future research will yet reveal earlier Basketmaker protokivas and kivas. The exciting promise is always there, for ongoing work at the mesa continues day by day to bring new and informative discoveries to light.

When at last the Mesa Verdeans began to convert some of their pithouses to protokivas for clan religious purposes, over a period of time the antechamber was replaced by a ventilator shaft, the pit was dug deeper, and the bench was eliminated.

Thus it is seen that the earliest protokivas were originally pithouses that had served as family dwellings. Once surface apartments were constructed, the pithouse could become a clan kiva for five families.[80] Studies of Badger House Community show this 5:1 ratio to be relatively consistent for the Piedra Phase, as well as for the remainder of Anasazi occupation of Mesa Verde.[81]

The protokiva designated as C was dated A.D. 752 or before. The main room was nearly rectangular and had rounded corners. The depth of the main room excavation was 3 feet 4 inches (1 m), and a banquette, 2 feet (61 cm) high and 1 foot 6 inches (45 cm) wide, lined all the walls. There were no traces of wall postholes on the banquette, and the sidewalls were vertical. A posthole for a main roof-support post was set in from each of the four corners.

Protokiva C had two shallow firepits placed in line with the main axis. There had once been a deflector stone and wing wall, although it was missing at the time of excavation. Eight small pits in the floor probably served as pot rests, and three larger pits may have been used for warming food.

The 9-by-7-foot (2.7 × 2.1 m) antechamber lay to the southeast of the main room. It had no bench, but there were two triangular shelves. As with the main room, there were holes for roof-support posts at the four corners. The Badger House Community account makes no mention of a Protokiva C sipapu, but it does state that although the typical kiva form had not yet developed, the structure functioned as a kiva.[82] Evidence showed that the antechamber had burned, as well as the passageway and south corner of the main room, after which the protokiva was abandoned.

Protokiva E, dated ca. A.D. 860, revealed something of the evolution of the protokiva over a 150-year period. The pit was nearly rectangular, 16 feet 6 inches (5 m) long by 13 feet (3.9 m) wide and 4 feet (1.2 m) deep. A narrow ventilator shaft extended out from the south wall of the pit. Pit walls were perpendicular and retained traces of plaster. Four main postholes in the floor indicated the locations of the main roof supports. Each hole was about 3 feet (90 cm) in from the corner and from 9 to 15 inches (22.5–38 cm) deep. Sandstone spalls were used to wedge the posts.

A D-shaped firepit was located just south of the center of the room. It was rimmed with a collar of adobe 4 inches (10 cm) high, giving an effective depth to the pit of 9 inches (22.5 cm) and a width of 2 feet 6 inches (75 cm). An adobe deflector joined together two wing walls that separated the main part of the room from a narrow area along the south wall.

A sipapu, 4 inches (10 cm) wide and 9 inches (22.5 cm) deep, was located on the main axis of the room between the firepit and the north wall. It was filled with yellow sand. Four other small pits were also filled with yellow sand and probably served as pot rests.

Protokiva E was only one of five subterranean kiva structures located in front of what ultimately became an apartment building consisting of twenty-eight rooms, or seventeen sets of family living quarters. Built in stages, the final surface building was 180 feet (55 m) across the front and 257 feet (78 m) across the back.

Archaeologists note that the protokiva signifies an important change in the social life and outlook of the Anasazi. Whereas they once performed their routine religious functions in their own subterranean homes, several families now shared the protokiva. Whether these five families were an extended family—a grandfather and his grown sons or daughters—or the beginnings of a clan organization is not known.[83]

This much is certain: with the inauguration of the Pueblo I Period a whole new spirit of cooperation was evident. This is best seen in terms of cooperative food production and religious activities. United efforts reached even beyond the limits of any single family or village. Intercommunity ceremonial structures, Great Kivas, began to appear on the Mesa Verde. Two have been found by archaeologists—one at Wetherill Mesa and another in Morfield Canyon—and others may yet be found.[84] Since these spectacular semisubterranean chambers often had floor diameters larger than 50 feet (15 m) their construction and usage indicate more than local interest, and it is assumed that the Great Kivas were built as cooperative efforts and used for harvest festivals and other ceremonies involving several area villages.

With evidence like this at hand, it is tempting to speculate about the total Mesa Verde population during the Pueblo I Period, and thus to imagine better what life was like on the great mesa. Unfortunately, the practice of overlaying one site with another was so broad as to make such estimates difficult, if not impossible. We know only that the population, although very small by today's standards, was expanding and that important progress was being made. A village might number from fifty to one hundred inhabitants—seldom more. If we knew how many villages there were at a given time, we might compute an approximate population.

Rohn states that the population of Chapin Mesa—and I assume the situation was similar on Wetherill Mesa—appears to have reached two distinct peaks, one during Pueblo I and one during late Pueblo III, with a relative low occurring between them sometime during Pueblo II.[85] His guess is that the maximum population for the mesa at its peak period of growth in Pueblo III was 1,600.

Throughout the Piedra Phase, and indeed into the thirteenth century, Anasazi farmers supplemented corn and other staples with wild game for subsistence. Lesser material culture items such as projectile points, baskets, corn-grinding tools, and bone tools were made and used in the same way as in earlier periods, but notched axes and hammers, pitted rubbing stones, and stone fetishes were added to the tool and worship kits. Clothing styles changed very little, and the practice of burying the dead in a flexed position continued. Most of the burials were made in the trash mounds of the village.

The Pueblo II Period, spanning the years A.D. 900–1100, was a transition step to the Great Pueblo (Pueblo III) Period, when the magnificent cliff dwellings were erected at Mesa Verde. Archaeologists have divided Pueblo II into two phases: the Ackmen Phase, A.D. 900–ca. 1000, and the Mancos Phase, ca. A.D. 1000–ca. 1075.

The Ackmen Phase saw a rapid evolution in architecture and pottery. The protokiva having set the stage, the true kiva now came into being. Incorporated into the confines of the village, kivas acquired great religious and social significance. Basing their conclusions upon modern Pueblo kivas, anthropologists believe that in the Ackmen Phase each kiva was used only by members of the same social unit, the clan. Clan rituals were performed on special occasions related to the planting, growing, and harvest seasons, and the kiva served as a kind of clubroom and workroom for the men the rest of the time.

In Pueblo society today, members consider themselves descendants of common ancestors and share common names. Pueblo society is matrilineal. Members are associated with the distaff side of the family, and property rights and line of descent are related to the mother's side. Accordingly, it is believed that Mesa Verde women owned the home and most of the items therein. Property passed from mother to daughter, and when a couple married, the groom was expected to live with his wife's relatives. This may answer the question why the clan kiva became a sanctuary for men, and why women were allowed to enter it only on special occasions.

Three kivas were excavated at Badger House Community. The kiva designated C is dated, by inference and by comparison with others similar in construction, sometime near A.D. 1000.[86] Kiva B is Mancos Phase, and Kiva A is Mesa Verde Phase (ca. A.D. 1200–1300)—dating from A.D. 1258.

Kiva C was an oval pit 16 feet 2 inches (4.9 m) wide at the floor level. It was dug with digging sticks in sloping ground, so that the wall height was 7 feet (2.1 m) on the west and 6 feet (1.8 m) on the east. There was a banquette 18 inches (45 cm) wide and 3 feet (90 cm) high around the entire circumference. Only three of an original seven rock and mortar pilasters remained. These were roughly shaped, about 1 foot (30 cm) wide and 1 foot 10 inches (55 cm) high, allowing for a kiva ceiling 5 feet (1.5 m) high at the outer edge. There is clear evidence that the roof was cribbed by laying poles from pilaster to pilaster around the circumference of the kiva.[87]

For ventilation, a pear-shaped hole was dug in the south bank, extending at its widest point 5 feet 6 inches (1.65 m) beyond the kiva wall. A subfloor tunnel was dug to connect the shallow, D-shaped firepit with the back of the hole. The tunnel was 1 foot 6 inches (45 cm) wide and 1 foot 2 inches (35 cm) deep. Its sides were lined with vertical stone slabs, and its top, which was several inches below the kiva floor, was bridged over with small poles and finished with an overlayer of adobe. Stone walls erected over the tunnel roof connected with and completed the banquette, and a vertical opening in the stone walls provided a chimney extending from the ventilator tunnel to the ground surface.

There were two firepits, the D-shaped one already mentioned and a roughly circular one 2 feet 2 inches (66 cm) across and 6 inches (15 cm) deep. The circular one was in the exact center of the kiva. It had been filled with clay and floored over before the D-shaped pit was built. A vertical sandstone slab projecting a few inches above the floor level formed the south end of the D-shaped pit.

The kiva floor was left unplastered, but it was reasonably level and covered with a fine coat of golden sand. A sipapu, 4 inches (10 cm) wide and 9 inches (22.5 cm) deep, was placed midway between the fireplace and the north wall. Several other small holes, each filled with clean yellow sand, were probably used as pot rests.

Badger House Community: *a*, plan and section of circular tower. *b*, Great Kiva associated with adobe-walled surface house and dated after A.D. 650. *c*, stone fetishes found on floor of kiva. *d*, block-wall surface houses of the late Pueblo II Period. *e*, plan and perspective view of fully developed kiva. From Hayes and Lancaster, 1975.

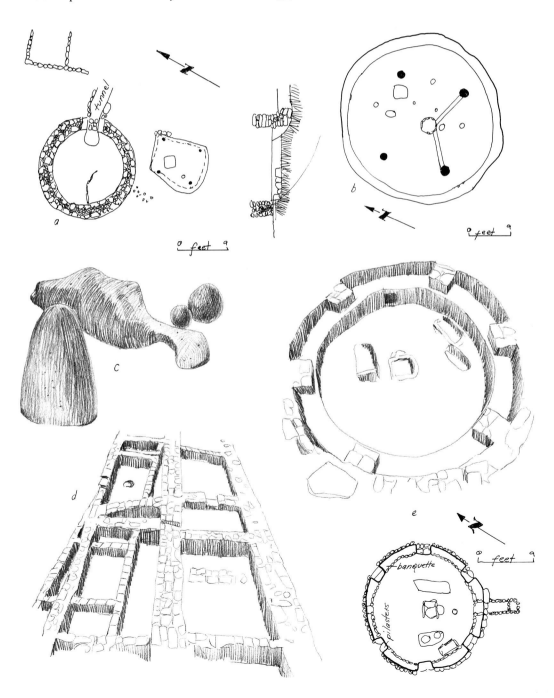

After an unknown period of occupation, Kiva C was abandoned. Much of its structural material was removed, and the open pit served thereafter as a trash dump.

Kiva B was built sometime after A.D. 1000. The excavators of Badger House believe that Kiva C may have served as a pattern for it, and that the missing material from Kiva C may have been used in Kiva B.

Kiva B was circular and 14 feet 7 inches (4.5 m) in diameter at floor level. Its wall height was 4 feet 7 inches (1.4 m), and the roof was cribbed with poles. The banquette was 3 feet (91 cm) high and averaged 1 foot 6 inches (45 cm) in width. Six stone pilasters above this supported the roof timbers.

A masonry liner extending from the floor to the banquette was made of well-laid, fairly uniform blocky stones, some of which had been pecked with a hammerstone. A minimum amount of mortar was used, and where it had to be thick, small chinking spalls were first inserted. A single coat of reddish brown finish plaster was spread over the wall stones.

The pilaster stones were also pecked. The wall lining separating them consisted of large stone slabs standing on edge and topped by 1 foot (30 cm) or more of chipped-edge stone masonry. This part of the wall above the banquette was also plastered.

A ventilator tunnel 6 feet 6 inches (1.95 m) long extended out from the south side of the kiva. It was 1 foot 5 inches (43 cm) wide and 1 foot 10 inches (55 cm) high. The floor was earth, and the first 2 feet (61 cm) was bridged over with sandstone slabs. The rest is thought to have been bridged with poles. A stone-lined shaft led up from the tunnel floor to the surface.

Subfloor ventilator tunnels are common in McElmo (ca. A.D. 1075–1200) and Mesa Verde phase kivas in the Mesa Verde area and are often attributed to Chaco influence. But subfloor ventilators in the Chaco country are not clearly earlier in time, even though they are more numerous there. Most of the kivas of the Bonito Phase of Pueblo del Arroyo had subfloor tunnels, and dates from this ruin range from A.D. 1052 to 1117.[88]

A rectangular firepit was built a little to the south of the Kiva B center. It was lined with stone slabs on three sides and had an adobe rim on the fourth (west) side. There was no deflector.

A small slab bin was built against the southwest wall of the kiva. Its purpose is unknown, but it may have held the metate found in the kiva. There was no sipapu, but a small niche in the masonry of the lower liner and located on the main axis of the kiva may have substituted for one.[89]

Also found were two rectangular subfloor pits that flanked the fireplace, one to the west and one to the east. About 4 feet 6 inches (1.35 m) long, 1 foot 6 inches (45 cm) wide, and 1 foot 3 inches (38 cm) deep, these pits are thought to have contained large ollas whose neck rims were set flush with the finished floor. Clay was packed around the installed ollas and topped off with a coat of adobe.[90]

Once abandoned, Kiva B became a trash dump and was even used for a burial. The remains of a child were found at the junction of the tunnel and shaft.

It is natural to ask why clan kivas were abandoned and then subjected to such seemingly irreverent uses as trash dumps. This might have happened when the villagers decided it was safer to build them inside the village walls. Or it might have been because of deterioration of one kind or another or fire damage that made it easier to build a new kiva than to repair the old one. Perhaps it was because circumstances indicated a relocation was needed to a fresh, new place of worship free of bad omens. Possibly it was because the Anasazi had come to realize by intuition what believers know to be so today— that the church is not ever a building, it is people. An empty church building may contain good associations and remembrances, but it is consecrated only by the religious activity and devotion of its members. Once those members choose to move on, the building loses its force, and aside from nostalgia, what happens to it thereafter is of no consequence.

As the kiva developed and its relationship and ratio to clan units became constant, it became an integral part of the village. Eventually it was incorporated into the confines of the village itself. Placed in front of the dwelling block, it provided a solidification of front orientation that has given rise to the terms "unit houses" and "clan houses," as being descriptive of the evolving social interaction of the Anasazi.

The houses of the Ackmen Phase (A.D. 900–ca. 1000) were similar in size and construction to those of the Piedra Phase (A.D. 750–900). Most walls were jacal, with spall-filled adobe, and were reinforced at the base with stone slabs, although true masonry walls of rough stones began to appear in sufficient number to suggest a growing popularity. During the Mancos Phase, ca. A.D. 1000–ca. 1075, fully lined kivas were built, in addition to apartment buildings with straight rows of rooms, whose walls were made of scabbled (roughly worked) stone, often with chipped edges.[91] These were the real forerunners of the cliff dwellings, and it is probable that the construction techniques learned during the Ackmen and Mancos phases made the cliff dwellings possible.

The earlier masonry structures had, in their lower 1 foot (30 cm) of wall, extremely rough masonry or unshaped rock in various sizes, with additions of many spalls and considerable mortar. This foundation was topped with one or two courses of scabbled stone of fairly uniform size, which made up an entire wall thickness of 6 inches (15 cm) or so. The stones had the bifacial spalling of the edges that became typical during the late Pueblo II Mancos Phase. Average room dimensions were 10 feet 8 inches by 6 feet (3.25 × 1.8 m).[92]

In the Mesa Verde Phase masonry structures, walls were compound and of classic finished masonry. The stones were large, exposed surfaces were flat, and most stones were dressed by pecking. The area between the two finished faces was filled in with rough rock, earth, and pieces of scabbled stone taken from earlier structures. The interior and exterior wall surfaces were dressed, and some corners were butted while others were tied together by broken joints. Floors were clay, some rooms and benches (perhaps to sleep on), and a few rooms had firepits in the center.[93]

Just off the southwest corner of the Mesa Verde Phase house at Badger House Community, a tower was built. Only the base remained for archaeologists to use in determining its original nature and size, and so conclusions regarding it are limited. It averaged 12 feet 5 inches (3.75 m) in diameter. Its wall, like those of the houses of the same phase, was compound, with a core of rough rock and adobe, and double-faced. Facing stones were pecked and fairly uniform in size. Some outside wall stones were shaped to conform with the tower's curvature. The wall was undergirded by a footing of large, flat, chipped-edge stones laid in a shallow trench and made wider than the wall itself. A small doorway was fashioned on the east side, and it stood over the entrance to a tunnel that connected the tower and the surface dwelling unit.[94]

Circular, D-shaped, and sometimes rectangular towers were characteristic of Mesa Verde architecture of the McElmo and Mesa Verde phases. The ruins of more than sixty towers have been found, and there were no doubt many more. By far the most are adjacent to or very near kivas.[95]

Early in the Ackmen Phase, Mesa Verde pottery went through a rapid transition in design style, and it evolved in short order into Cortez Black-on-white. By now most bowl interiors were slipped and well polished. The designs of Bluff Black-on-red evolved into a short-lived Deadman's style, often with a red slip. Likewise, the first culinary pottery changed from the familiar banded-neck to a narrower, more finely applied fillet pattern, and in time this, too, was supplanted by indented corrugated pottery.

Pottery of the Mancos Phase is known as Mancos Corrugated and Mancos Black-on-white. Culinary pots were pinched with the fingers to create a systematic corrugated surface. Anasazi pots were always hand-molded, never wheel-turned, and crafted from concentric coils of clay. Culinary vessels were not painted, but serving dishes were. These were smoothed, coated with a white slip, and then decorated.

Some of the pottery found at Mesa Verde reveals that contact with adjacent areas was being made at this time. Fragments of intrusive vessels fashioned to the south and west of Mesa Verde have been excavated. Their designs, shapes, paints, and clays were not native to Mesa Verde.

There was no change in the manufacture or style of stone artifacts during the Ackmen Phase. But the blunt awl with a narrow tip was replaced by a gradually tapered awl that often bore wear grooves across the shank near the tip.[96]

By A.D. 1000, though, trough metates with their grooves open at both ends were being used in slab bins. The fully grooved ax and hammer began to replace notched tools, and projectile points with wide bases were notched on the sides rather than at the corners.[97]

In considering the ecological evidence at Badger House Community, archaeologists found that the Mesa Verde climate of the seventh through thirteenth centuries was essentially the same as it is today. The same juniper, piñon, Douglas fir, ponderosa pine, oak, fendlerbush, and sagebrush still abound, and the same birds and mammals, with few exceptions, are still present. Jackrabbits are gone, and bison—probably present in the form of small migrant herds in southwestern Colorado until a century or so ago—no longer exist there. Since most of the bison bones discovered were ribs, it is assumed that after descending to the plains to kill bison, the Anasazi cut away sides of ribs and carried only these back to the mesa tops. Eagle bones were found in the ruins, and during Pueblo II bighorn sheep specimens outnumbered those of mule deer.[98]

Great Kivas have already been mentioned as evidences of intercommunity cooperation at Mesa Verde. Water management systems are other such evidence. Two systems have been found, and it is expected that others will come to light as research continues.

Mummy Lake, near Far View House on Chapin Mesa, was an extensive project designed to collect precipitation and control its distribution. It was begun in the Ackmen Phase, grew to 90 feet (27 m) in diameter, and continued in use until ca. A.D. 1200. The interior of the basin was lined with a masonry wall everywhere but at the inlet, which was on the west side. A second stone retaining wall braced an earth bank on the east side, and there were stone steps in the center of the south interior wall. The sensibly built inlet channel completely reversed the intake flow, causing silt to be deposited where it could be easily cleaned out rather than in the reservoir itself. Collecting ditches were dug to bring rainwater down from the higher northern elevations of the mesa. These fed a control gate consisting of a stone wall and basin that shunted the water either into the basin or into a ditch that led to Mummy Lake. Water stored in the basin could be let out by means of a distributary ditch either for domestic use or for use in the fields. The lake itself had no outlet, and so water was taken from there in vessels for domestic use. The ditch system was designed so that Mummy Lake could be bypassed and the water sent on to the Far View House community. Not surprisingly, with a ready supply of water the Mummy Lake community became one of the largest and strongest of its time.

Morfield Reservoir, at the northern end of the park area, was an elaborate water management system that was begun during the Piedra Phase and remained active for two centuries until sediment buildup caused its abandonment. Ditches collected rainwater from slope runoff and shunted it into an earthen tank in a canyon bottom. There was no outlet from the tank, and so the Anasazi living in the vicinity must have used vessels to extract the water for domestic purposes, as they did from Mummy Lake.

Both water management systems just mentioned are truly impressive, but archaeologists have learned that nearly every drainage on the higher elevations of the Mesa Verde had a series of check dams. These were lines of man-laid rock walls that checked the flow of water and held the sediment, thus providing for and feeding small agricultural terrace plots. The walls were started low and then added to as the sediment accumulated behind them. Maintenance would have been a particular problem, and the majority of dams recorded are partially washed out.[99] Nearly a thousand of these dams have been found on Wetherill Mesa, and nine hundred on Chapin Mesa, allowing the Anasazi to develop many desirable mesa-top areas and smaller marginal plots. The significance of the water resources is best seen when one recognizes that the natives were able to survive severe drought conditions more than once during the Pueblo I and Pueblo II periods.

PUEBLO III

As previously noted, sometime before A.D. 1200 the Anasazi began to move from the mesa rims into coves and caves of every size that nature had carved in the cliff faces below. Archaeologists, among others, have puzzled at length over why they did this. The move was in no wise an easy one to make, and once they were down there, life in the cliff dwellings was hazardous and inconvenient. Residents had to climb up and down to tend their fields, to obtain fuel, to forage, and to hunt. Maintaining a sufficient water supply was always a problem. In winter the caves were cold and dank. Archaeologists believe that fires may have burned twenty-four hours a day during the coldest months. Fuel had to be stored in large amounts. Infants at play had to be watched constantly. The aged or infirm were virtually trapped. And so archaeologists think it was fear of (not necessarily direct confrontations with) invading warlike tribes that forced the relocation, and when the way in which the move came to pass is traced, the idea becomes at least plausible.

As Rohn has indicated, the fact that at the beginning of the Great Pueblo Period the people lived in relatively small and scattered villages suggests that it was a peaceful time. The kivas were still located outside the village walls, and had there been raids, men could easily have been caught helpless inside them. But early in the period something caused the Anasazi to relocate their kivas inside the village walls. At the same time, the first towers were built, either alongside the outer walls of the village unit or adjacent to an exposed kiva and connected to it by a tunnel. Thus the tower became both a ceremonial structure and a communication-watchtower.

The village pueblos began now to increase in size as most Anasazi abandoned their small compounds and gathered together in more concentrated and defensible units. This was one of the outstanding characteristics of the time, and pueblos of great size resulted.[100]

In Mesa Verde proper and among the Anasazi living in other sectors of the region the trend was the same. Toward the end of the twelfth century, sizable village buildings were found in many places on the mesa tops and in the shallow drainages at the heads of canyons. Sometimes several clusters of small pueblos were built in close proximity to one another. At other times several smaller pueblos were gathered, litter fashion, around a much larger one. Most of the assemblages enclosed or centered around a spring, so that, whatever happened, a water supply was assured.[101]

Two possibilities come to mind to explain the contraction: either the Anasazi had discovered material and religious advantages in closer communal living, or their security was threatened. Some authorities have speculated that

Pueblo Period winter clothing: buckskin cap, buckskin shirt, rabbit-fur or feather robe, stockings of woven hair, moccasins of hide.

divisions were arising among the Anasazi themselves, and a few native mythological stories do give credence to that idea. But there is scant evidence of a people scattering as one would expect them to in such circumstances: at least, not right away. And so for the moment defense remains the best reason, both for the communal villages and for the move into caves.

If you have not seen the amazing ruins of a Mesa Verde cliff dwelling, you might picture in imagination an almost sheer sandstone cliff rising anywhere from several hundred to a thousand feet from the canyon below to the mesa top above. A quarter to halfway or more up the cliff surface, the churning waters of ages past have cut enormous chunks from the cliff wall, and exfoliation has done the rest. To get to the cave, one must climb up or down, using narrow pathways in a few instances, but more often by far employing a combination of rude ladders and crude handholds or steep steps cut into the rock. The Anasazi had to have clear heads. In some places it is perilous to make the climb at all. One simply clings like a fly to the rock face and dares not look up or down. Yet the Anasazi managed the climb daily, and usually with a burden of some kind carried on their heads, sides, or backs with the aid of a head ring, a sling, or a tumpline.

The cliff dwellings consist in the main of stones, tree timbers, and adobe. All these materials are heavy and awkward to transport by human means alone. Yet such quantities were moved about and into the caves of Mesa Verde, Kayenta, and Canyon de Chelly as to boggle the mind, and in a relatively short period of time. Everything from single dwellings and storage places tucked into small crevasses, to huge and spectacular stone villages in immense caves, came rapidly into being as the resolute and ingenious Anasazi burst forth into their age of florescence.

Inevitably, one asks how they did it. And even when some of the answers have been learned, amazement remains. Nowhere in North America is there a feat of ancient architecture to rival that of the cliff dwellings, built without the aid of nails, bolts, trusses, or any tool of consequence.

In the summer of 1891 an energetic, inquisitive twenty-two-year-old budding Swedish scientist named Gustaf Erik Adolf Nordenskiöld and a small staff of workers, assisted and guided by the famous Wetherill brothers, explored Mesa Verde, carefully measuring, photographing, and diagraming ruins and describing the artifacts they found there. Included in his brief investigation were such well-known sites as Square Tower House, Spring House, Cliff Palace, Long House, Mug House, Kodak House, Step House, Spruce Tree House, and Balcony House. In 1893 Nordenskiöld published in Stockholm a report of his findings entitled *The Cliff Dwellers of the Mesa Verde*. Although Nordenskiöld was not a trained archaeologist, that was the first major report of an archaeological work in the United States, and his methods became the standard for all archaeological endeavors at Mesa Verde from that time until now. He was also responsible in part for the Act of Congress that created Mesa Verde National Park on June 29, 1906. More recent investigations notwithstanding, *The Cliff Dwellers of the Mesa Verde* continues to supply some of the finest descriptions of the dwellings and lifeway of the Pueblo III Period.

Nordenskiöld's first significant excavations were undertaken at Long House, whose long row of ruins lay in a vast high-vaulted cave in a steep cliff of Wetherill Mesa. Rohn calls Long House a "Fire Temple-like structure."[102] To get to it, Nordenskiöld followed the access route used by the onetime residents

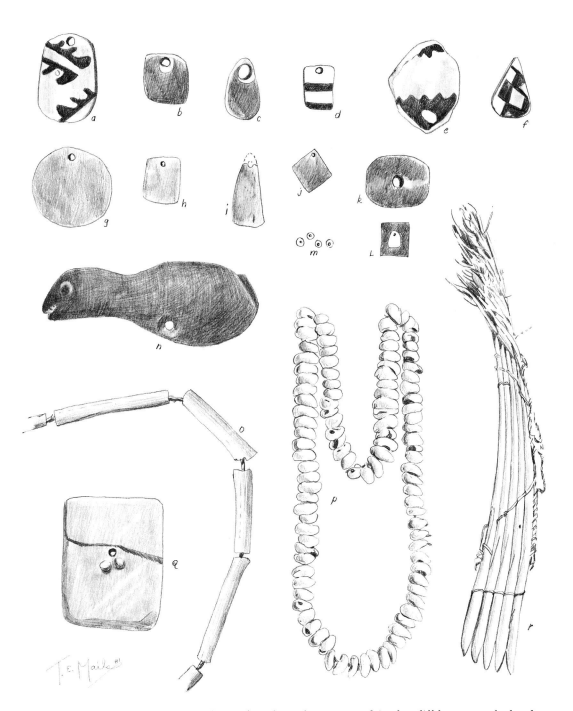

Typical lesser material culture objects found on the mesa and in the cliff houses: *a–f*, sherd pendants. *g–l*, stone pendants. *m*, stone beads. *n*, effigy pendant of black lignite or jet. *o*, bird bone beads. *p*, shell beads. *q*, stone pendant. *r*, Nordenskiöld identified this as a feather headdress, the Mesa Verde Museum describes such items as feather brushes used by medicine men to drive away illness. From Nordenskiöld, 1893, and the Mesa Verde Museum.

themselves. He followed notches hewn in the sandstone to descend 198 feet (60 m) down the cliff face to a talus slope, and then walked laterally for 300 feet (91.4 m) to reach the westernmost part of the cave. Here he found a skillfully built four-story-high triangular stone tower, one wall of which was formed by the cliff.

The tower stones were brick-sized, rough-hewn, mortared, and spalled with rocks and potsherds. The east part of the second story was a niche, and the floor of the niche was pierced by a narrow passage leading to a nearby kiva. The third story was quite small, and the top room so tiny it could have been used only as a storeroom.

Beyond the tower was a continuous row of six kivas set close to the cliff on an upper ledge; the first kiva was the one connected to the tower. All the kiva interiors at Long House were similar in dimension and arrangement: there was a central circular hearth, a deflector, an L-shaped ventilator tunnel and shaft, a banquette, and six stone pilasters. Each kiva was further enclosed by a quadrangular stone wall, with the space between this wall and the exterior of the kiva wall being filled in with dirt and stone rubble.

Below the row of kivas was a series of rooms. At the time of Nordenskiöld's visit, these were nearly buried under heaps of rubble and stones. Farther east on the same ledge as the kivas was a block of rooms that extended up to the cave roof. The innermost room was more than 19 feet 8 inches (6 m) long, but otherwise constricted and dark, having only a narrow entryway on the west side. In front of this room were two more that once were two stories in height. The first-floor ceiling beams projected a foot or two on the outerside—perhaps to provide for a balcony, but Nordenskiöld thought they might have served as handholds for people passing along the narrow ledge in front of the rooms.

Next, and appended to those just mentioned, was a group of three more rooms. Then came a long open space or passageway, whose back wall was the cave itself. It reached clear to the east end of Long House. In front of this space were the remains of a long row of contiguous rooms that originally were a single story in height. None of these had doorways on the front side, a fact that led Nordenskiöld to wonder whether they were for defensive purposes. Possibly, however, the ledge in front of the rooms was much too narrow to use for a walkway, and the absence of doorways prevented children from falling out of an opening and down the steep talus slope. Beyond the contiguous rooms were the ruins of six more kivas, interspersed with various walls and rooms. These completed Long House. The stone walls of the dwellings there were built like those of the triangular tower, and their thickness was the same, averaging 10 inches (25 cm). Room dimensions averaged 7 feet 2 inches by 8 feet 3 inches (2.2 × 2.5 m), with a height of about 6 feet 7 inches (2 m). Doorways measured 1 foot 7 inches by 2 feet 4 inches (48 × 70 cm) and were similar in construction to those of other cliff dwellings.

Nordenskiöld notes that the kivas never had an upper story and that kiva floors, when the nature of the ground permitted, were sunk "lower than that of the adjoining rooms of the ordinary type." Other rooms were also haphazard in arrangement, and it seemed as though the size of Long House had increased as population growth demanded it.

A spring was situated at the innermost part of the cave. Although it was only a small pool, the Nordenskiöld party believed that when diligently worked it could have been made to produce a considerable supply of water. "Similar aquiferous strata," Nordenskiöld said, "are of frequent occurrence in the depths of the caves in which the cliff-dwellers built their houses."

At several locations in the sandstone rock faces of Long House there were shallow, broad, and oblong grooves about 8 inches (20 cm) in length. These were present at most of the cliff dwellings, and were the places where stone axes were ground. There were also grooves that were long, straight, and narrow but crossed each other in all directions; other tools, such as bone awls and scrapers, were sharpened there.

About 50 feet (15 m) above the main ruins of Long House, in an overhanging vault, were two low walls pierced with fifteen loopholes, each only a few inches wide, and skillfully oriented in all directions. Nordenskiöld decided they were loopholes for arrows, allowing archers to command all the approaches to Long House. There was no apparent way to ascend to the ledge, although a high wall might once have reached up to it; ladders of yucca rope could also have been used. In connection with the idea of the low walls being breastworks, nowhere did Nordenskiöld find literal evidence that Long House residents had engaged in warfare. Therefore the possibility must be held open that the wall apertures had to do with solar observation, or observation for other purposes. The ledge holding the walls was also quite narrow and the crevice top so low that an archer would be required to crawl on hands and knees, leaving one to wonder how several archers could handle bows and arrows successfully and effectively in such a restricted space.

Four hundred and fifty feet south of Long House were the ruins of two rooms. These contained the fragments of several human skeletons and a quantity of yucca cord.

From Long House, Nordenskiöld moved three-quarters of a mile south to Kodak House. Although smaller in size, it resembled Long House in many respects. It consisted of thirty to forty rooms and five or six kivas. Several hundred feet from Kodak House and at the bottom of the canyon was a fairly good spring, which undoubtedly afforded an adequate supply of water for the village inhabitants.

After Kodak House came the cursory examination of several ruins on Wetherill Mesa. Some were so precarious to get to that Nordenskiöld was left marveling at how the residents conducted their regular lives there. He was also amazed at how the Anasazi could build so skillfully in such difficult places. At this point Nordenskiöld decided that, generally speaking, all the ruins on Wetherill Mesa were so like one another in size and structure that a description of any one of them applied to most of the rest.

When he had concluded his investigations on the west cliffs of Wetherill

Mesa, Nordenskiöld moved to the east cliffs. Here he found a ruin "of exceedingly great interest." It was named Step House, after a stairway built of great blocks of stone that led to the ruin. The cave was about 240 feet (73 m) long and 50 feet (15 m) deep, with the ruins occupying only 100 feet (30 m) of the north end. The open space was covered with refuse, turkey droppings, leaves, and corncobs, mixed with rubbish and dust.

Finds in the Step House ruins proper were few, but several graves were discovered, and a hiding place where it seemed "evident that on some occasion of imminent danger jars and other objects of value had been buried."

As a rule, the graves unearthed by Nordenskiöld had been prepared with great care. Close to the Step House ruin he came upon the half-mummified body of a child with the traditionally flattened head. The corpse was in a crouching position and wrapped in a feather robe.

Near the child and in a second grave was the body of an adult whose face was turned toward the cliff. It was in a flexed position, with the knees drawn up to the chin, and was wrapped in a mat made of long, narrow withes that had been split in two and pierced with fine holes at intervals of about 4 inches (10 cm). Long cords of yucca were passed through the holes to tie the withes together. Four earthen vessels had been placed in the grave: a bowl had been turned upside down over the head, a larger bowl was placed on top of the first one, and a small mug and small bowl sat on the ground in front of the face.

North of the previous grave was the interred body of a completely mummified adult who seemed to have been a person of importance, judging by the care with which the body had been buried. The head was covered with a hide cap and the feet were sheathed in hide moccasins. The body was wrapped in a net of cords spirally wound with strips of hide on which the hair was still partly preserved. The cords were further held together by strips of yucca leaf, under which thick bunches of cedar bast had been inserted. Under the body was a mat similar to the one found in the grave previously described, and a second mat was spread over it. The head rested on a short, rounded block of wood. The body was flexed, with the head turned toward the cliff and facing the southeast. In front of the face stood a basket half full of cornmeal and covered with a beautiful bowl turned upside down. Alongside the basket was a small ladle or spoon, and between the two a corncob. Generally the clothing was quite like that of the Basketmaker III corpse that Earl Morris found at Mummy Cave in 1923. Custom had changed very little in the intervening period.

Several other graves were found by Nordenskiöld. Special finds in these included digging sticks and more feather-robe-wrapped bodies. Some of the graves were shallow oval holes dug in reasonably hard ground and roofed over with short poles. The poles were in turn covered with a mat of withes, a sandstone slab, and then a foot of dirt. The apparent purpose of this arrangement was to prevent loose soil from falling onto the body. All the corpses were flexed and lay on their sides, with mortuary offerings similar to those already described placed in front of the faces.

Kidder states that, as of 1924, the main cemeteries of the large Mesa Verde dwellings had never been discovered, and that the few graves found thus far were not enough to account for a hundredth part of the bodies that had been disposed of.[103] Reference was made earlier to this identical circumstance at Chaco Canyon and Aztec, and to the puzzle it presents.

Fewkes addresses the question also, pointing out, for whatever it is worth, a possible solution for the missing bodies. He begins by noting that cremation was practiced by Indians dwelling along the lower Colorado River, and also by the Hohokam. Then he adds that Castañeda, chronicler of the Coronado expedition to Cíbola that is identified with Zuñi, says that the inhabitants burned their dead. But so far as is known to modern archaeologists, the ancient Anasazi did not as a rule practice cremation, and no record of the practice has attended historical times.

The broadest exception to this is found in a few places at Mesa Verde. Nordenskiöld discovered calcined bones in a stone cist at Step House,[104] and the Wetherills claimed they found evidence of cremations elsewhere among the Mesa Verde cliff dwellings. Fewkes exposed a special room in the depths of the Cliff Palace cave that he said was set aside for cremation purposes. In it he found bushels of what proved to be human ashes, and the cave roof was densely smoke-blackened. He also discovered, on the mesa top, round stone enclosures several feet deep, in which occurred great quantities of bone ashes. All this he offers as possible evidence for the absence of graves. As a rule, he says, the poor people were cremated, and the more important persons were buried in the places where bodies are found.[105]

As Nordenskiöld continued his research at Mesa Verde, he discovered grave sites in three types of location: in the general neighborhood of a ruin, in the ruins within the caves, and on the mesa top.

The open space or inner court of the more extensive cliff dwellings was often employed as a burial ground, where graves were found in the soil deposits that consist of turkey droppings and miscellaneous refuse. Other graves were encountered in small hollows worn by water in the sandstone cliffs. The corpses were often wrapped and covered in the same way as those mentioned earlier, and they were accompanied by similar funerary offerings.

The dead were also buried within dwellings. Some of these inner tombs had been walled up, but at Spruce Tree House Nordenskiöld found, in a little room, "the doorway of which did not seem to have been walled up," the bodies of three children. In a ruin in a subdivision of Johnson Canyon, John Wetherill came across a remarkable room sepulcher. Finding a door that had been sealed up, he chipped out a rock and saw it was indeed an entrance. Removing the rest of the rocks, he found some burial wrappings and then a piece of a woven sash that was red, white, and black. He broke through the wall on another side, dug down to the floor level, and discovered more matting and an arrow with an agate point, the first ever found in a cliff dwelling in Johnson Canyon. Further digging revealed first a basket and then seventeen arrows lying across the heads of five bodies. Interspersed among the skulls were four bowls. One body lay on top of a mat with a bow on one side and a mug and a basket on the other. The body was not covered, but moccasins were on the feet and a feather cloth was under the head. Nearby was a hollow stick 2 feet (61 cm) long with both ends wrapped with sinew and having a bone point 6 inches (15 cm) long at one end.

The skeletons of three infants had pieces of buckskin with them, and one had a mug by its head. Removing the infants, Wetherill discovered that a large mat covered the entire floor. When he lifted the mat up, he found that the infants had rested on top of an adult of some importance. This man was covered with a willow mat, under which were two more mats made of grass, then a mat of feather cloth, then a buckskin jacket with fringes. Also found were a stick with a loop at one end, which Wetherill thought was a medicine stick, two prairie-dog-skin pouches, two awls, a walnut, and several buckskin bags.

Nordenskiöld also saw many burial sites on the mesa tops, but he was undecided whether or not these were the graves of people who had inhabited the cliff dwellings. Such burial sites were usually indicated by a slight elevation and by quantities of pottery fragments and flint chips strewn on the ground. In two such mounds on Wetherill Mesa, excavations were instituted. The graves were shallow, and in them were a few objects, including bone awls and stone axes similar to those used by cliff dwellers. There was also a plain little pottery bowl with a handle. Not far from Long House was a skeleton that was not flexed, but its legs were bent back at the knee. Nordenskiöld says that, as a rule, no pottery was buried with the mesa-top dead, adding that it might have been the custom to smash vessels on top of the grave, thus accounting for the fragments mentioned earlier and relating to a custom prevailing later among the Hopi.[106]

The pottery sherds found on top of the mesa-top burial sites were of the same sort as those occurring in the cliff dwellings. Similar, too, were the skulls, causing Nordenskiöld to assert finally that the burial places belonged either to the cliff dwellers or to a people "nearly akin" to them who lived in villages on the mesa top.

Richard Wetherill, however, pointed out a difference in the method of flattening the head. Mesa-dweller skulls were flattened by pressure applied obliquely from above, so that it principally affected the parieto-occipital region, whereas cliff-dweller skulls were flattened from straight behind, the occipital region being the most affected.

Nordenskiöld visited the ruins on Chapin Mesa several times during the summer of 1891, but did excavations at only two. Here he found the largest structures on Mesa Verde; in size and excellent state of preservation they were "certainly the most important in the whole of the United States."

Spruce Tree House is the first of these ruins that he mentions, and he worked there only a few days. It sat in a cave 240 feet (72 m) long and 92 feet (28 m) deep. Its height was small in comparison with its depth, and the interior of the cave was quite dark. A great part of the ruin was in an excellent state of preservation, and Spruce Tree House remains so today. It has about 114 rooms and housed about one hundred people. It is usually the first ruin seen and visited by tourists at Mesa Verde, especially since the main facilities and museum are just across the canyon from it. The third-largest cliff dwelling on the mesa, it was constructed between A.D. 1200 and 1276.

The architecture of Spruce Tree House was much the same as that found on Wetherill Mesa, although in some parts the stonework was better. It was clear that not all parts of the village were built at the same time. Many new walls had been added to older ones, and the arrangement of rooms was determined by the shape of the cave.

The cave was oriented in its long direction on a north–south axis, and it contained two groups of rooms divided by an east–west passageway running from the front to the back of the cave. Each group of rooms had an open space behind it, and the ground there was covered with turkey droppings. Each group also had its own kivas, five of these in the northernmost group and two in the southernmost. Nordenskiöld thought that more kivas might be buried under fallen buildings. He was right; later one more was found, making a total of eight.

Spruce Tree House.

Kiva construction details were the same as those already described. The kivas were from 13 to 16 feet (3.9–4.8 m) in diameter, stood in front of the other rooms, and were subterranean. Some of the kivas have since been restored and can now be entered by visitors, but at the time of Nordenskiöld's visit all the kiva roofs had fallen in. As with the kivas on Wetherill Mesa, kiva roofs provided the courtyards for community activities.

Dwellings and storerooms were entered by small doorways, most of which were rectangular but others T-shaped. The arch was unknown and not used by Anasazi builders. The doorsill consisted of a long stone slab, and the lintel of a few sticks laid across the top of the opening to support the wall stones above. Long stones also served as lintels. Along both sides of the doorway and across the top, some builders added an inset frame. This consisted of a few sticks covered with plaster and formed to receive a thin sandstone slab that was used to close the doorway. The frame angled in as it moved toward the top, so that the weight of the slab rested against it and the slab stayed in place. Wooden loops were set into the masonry wall, one on each side of the doorway on the exterior, so that a stick could be passed through them to bar and secure the slab.

No one really knows why T-shaped doorways were built, since they would be difficult to close. A Hopi suggested they were shaped to accommodate a person wishing to enter the room bearing a wide burden on his back. Most archaeologists, however, think the T-shaped design offered hand supports that were used as "boosts" to help one move more easily through the small entryways.

The walls and roofs of some rooms were covered with thick soot. Light came only from the doorway, although a few rooms had tiny quadrangular loopholes that admitted a little light and air. It would seem that comfort in the dwellings was at a premium. Access from a lower to an upper story was generally gained by a small square hole in the ceiling, located at the corner of the lower room. When not in use, the hole was probably closed off with a stone slab. Stones projecting from the walls provided a ladder to the upper stories. Roofs serving both as ceilings and as the floors for upper rooms usually consisted of log beams covered with small poles laid close together and at right angles across the beams. Thick layers of twigs and adobe finished the job. In some cases, though, pairs of larger poles spaced a few feet apart were laid across the main beams. The poles were covered with a layer of twigs and cedar bast, and the whole was coated with adobe. In several buildings the beams were extended through the walls and were used to form balconies. One assumes these provided places for rest and recreation, but they also made communication between the upper-story rooms easier.

Kiva walls at Spruce Tree House, as well as the walls of some dwellings that Nordenskiöld thought might have belonged to persons of rank, were covered with a thin coat of yellow plaster. In one instance they were further adorned with two painted birds. One room of unknown purpose was elliptical, and another was pentagonal. This last had a closet made of stone slabs, a rare item in cliff dwellings. Spruce Tree House was opened for visitation by tourists following the removal of debris and stabilization by a work party led by Fewkes in 1909.

Not far from Spruce Tree House, hard by a trail that tourists follow to get to the ruin today, was a fairly good spring. This was a valuable asset to the community and no doubt played a large part in the longevity of the village. Also near the ruin were several small, isolated rooms, situated on ledges exceedingly difficult to get to. Nordenskiöld felt they were much too small to be

Top, bird's-eye view of Sun Temple. *Bottom,* ruin of Megalithic House.

lived in and might have been meant for defensive purposes. But he adds that Fewkes thought they more likely were shrines where offerings to gods were deposited, even though no offerings at the time of his writing had been found to confirm his opinion.

Nordenskiöld believed that the cliff dwellings were erected at an earlier period than the stone buildings on the mesa tops, an opinion that would be hotly contested by modern archaeologists. But the Swedish explorer was correct in assuming that the villages on the mesa and the cliff dwellings were the work of the same people. Pottery fragments corresponded, as did construction methods. He did few mesa-top excavations and offers only a few descriptions of what he found. Included were notes concerning D-shaped towers and two special towers: a round one placed on top of a conical, isolated rock "and probably a lookout," and a rectangular one hidden in the piñon forest that he felt should be regarded as a religious edifice. The excavators of Badger House add that many of the towers at Mesa Verde are located so as to afford a view of another tower. Therefore signals from tower to tower could have rapidly linked most of the larger settlements across the entire mesa.[107]

While he does not specifically mention it by name, Nordenskiöld might have seen Sun Temple, to be excavated by Fewkes in 1915. It is one of the best known and most visited of the mesa-top ruins. It sits on top of a lofty point overlooking Cliff Palace Canyon and is in an excellent state of preservation. The carefully dressed walls, 4 feet (1.2 m) thick, still stand an average of 6 feet (1.8 m) high. There was no roof, and the building was open to the sun. Its first known discovery was in 1915, but its purpose and symbolism remain a mystery to this day, except that Frank Waters believes he knows what it was: its D shape shows that it was a ceremonial building erected for the conduct of ceremonies belonging to the Bow Clan. He goes on to describe most persuasively how each part of the building, including its four circular kivas (Rohn says three) was used by the One Horn, Two Horn, Flute, and Wuwutcim societies. Of particular value is his explanation of the small stone or shrine that sits at the southwest corner. It has four dots with grooved lines extending out from them. According to Waters, this served as a sundial, by which a specific part of the Wuwutcim Ceremony, still performed by the Hopi today, was timed to begin.[108] All the kivas at Sun Temple are equipped with subfloor ventilators like those of Chaco Canyon, a trait that strongly suggests a tie between Mesa Verde and Chaco Canyon.

Also mentioned by Nordenskiöld are Anasazi-built reservoirs where water was collected for irrigation and as a hedge against drought, as well as small natural tanks worn in the rocks from which cliff dwellers drew their supplies. He thought the water conservation projects were especially noteworthy, since they seemed to be conclusive evidence that the Anasazi of A.D. 1100–1300 were able to contend with the same dry climate and scarcity of water that prevailed at the time of his visit in 1891. In this connection, he found the assertion of Holmes that a dense agricultural population could not have inhabited the region under the same arid climatic conditions "to be absurd."[109] Proof that ag-

Balcony House, showing kivas and door openings.

riculture was widely practiced was shown also by the quantity of corn found in the ruins and by several level terraces, divided by stone walls, that Nordenskiöld discovered near Step House. They were, in fact, terraces quite similar to those he had seen in the wine-producing districts of southern Europe.

Don Watson describes the logical and clever way in which these garden-plot terraces were built. Rather than exhaust themselves by hauling in hundreds of loads of fill dirt, the farmers let nature do the heavy work. The men, he says, liked to farm in the rich soils of the low draws above the heads of the canyons, for these made excellent farming areas. But the Anasazi enlarged their plots by building terraces where the draws were too narrow and steep for normal farming. Low dams of stone were erected across the drainage cut; these were seldom more than 3 or 4 feet (0.9–1.2 m) high and 20 or 30 feet (6–9 m) long. The heavy rains of summer washed the rich soil down from the mesas and deposited it behind the dams. Soon each dam supported a flat plot of soil large enough to grow corn, beans, or squash. Sometimes there were a hundred or more terraces in a single small draw, and even in mostly dry years the farmers could produce an adequate crop.[110]

Nordenskiöld decided that Balcony House was the best preserved of all the ruins he had investigated on Mesa Verde and that cliff-dwelling architecture reached its culminating stage here. He did not draw a plan of the ruin, but he observed that more care had been bestowed on the walls than even in Cliff Palace. Stones were hewn and fitted together with utmost care. Wall surfaces were perfectly smooth, and corners were turned at perfect right angles. He might have added that the ruin included more and larger windows than most other ruins.

He also thought that Balcony House was better situated and designed for defense than any other large ruin, since a handful of men posted in it could easily repel a large enemy force. Of all the cliff dwellings, this one seemed to offer the strongest argument in favor of the idea that toward the end of their Golden Age the Anasazi were indeed being pressured and threatened by marauding bands of intrusive Indian tribes.

In summing up his remarks concerning Balcony House, Nordenskiöld mentions a place where the inhabitants went up and down a wall by means of wooden pegs either set or driven into the mortar. Having found in all his research the pieces of only one ladder—that one at Balcony House and suspect because a cut had been made in it by a metal implement—he concluded that ladders were seldom employed by the cliff dwellers. In his view, the perilous climbs that attended daily life "had inured them to difficult pathways." Nevertheless, it seems certain that entrance to the kivas was made by a ladder that extended up through the roof hatch. Kidder even refers to the kiva opening as "a combined ladder hole and roof vent."[111] Other evidence indicates that ladders of several varieties were in general use.

In a long and somewhat shallow branch of a thickly wooded cliff canyon, a "wild and gloomy" gorge named Cliff Palace Canyon, Nordenskiöld came upon Cliff Palace, the largest and most spectacular of the Mesa Verde park ruins. "Strange and indescribable," he says, "is the impression on the traveller, when, after a long and tiring ride through the boundless, monotonous piñon forest, he suddenly halts on the brink of the precipice, and in the opposite cliff beholds the ruins of Cliff Palace, framed in the massive vault of rock above and in a bed of sunlit cedar and piñon trees below. This ruin well deserves its name, for with its round towers and high walls rising out of the heaps of stone deep in the mysterious twilight of the cavern, and defying in their sheltered site the ravages of time, it resembles at a distance an enchanted castle." Nordenskiöld's plan of the ground floor of the ruin shows more than 100 rooms, but once it was thoroughly examined by the National Park Service and Fewkes, Cliff Palace was found to contain 220 rooms and 23 kivas. Fewkes decided that Cliff Palace was composed of many clans, and that its population grew from without and within. "New clans joined those existing, and new births continually added to the number of inhabitants."[112] Fewkes established a classification of secular rooms at Cliff Palace that was based on their function: living rooms, milling rooms,[113] storage rooms, rooms of unknown function, towers, and round rooms. Kivas he separated into two types: generally circular or cylindrical subterranean rooms, with pilasters to support the cribbed roof, and with fireplace, deflector, and ventilator; and circular or rectangular surface rooms with rounded corners, without pilasters, fireplace, or deflector.[114] However, the latter kivas might better have been designated as *kihus*, the special ceremonial surface chambers.

In a valuable footnote Fewkes explains that the word "kiva," now universally employed in place of the Spanish "estufa" to designate a ceremonial room of the Pueblos, is derived from the Hopi language. "The designation is archaic, the element *ki* being both Pima and Hopi for 'house.'" Attempts have been made to connect this word with a part of the human body; esoterically, the kiva represents the Underworld, or womb of the earth from which the races of man were born. Fewkes thought it highly appropriate that ancient ceremonies should take place in a kiva, the symbolic representation of the Underworld, "for many of the ceremonies are said to have been practiced while man still lived within the Earth Mother."[115] Indeed, the Hopi believe that the ritual calendar is still followed there. Some of the Cliff Palace kivas had no sipapu. The Hano kivas of the East Mesa of the Hopi lack sipapus also, and the Tewa of the Rio Grande are said to have no such openings in their kiva floors.

Fewkes thought there was every reason to conclude that the kivas preserved the oldest types of building of the cliff-dweller culture, "and it is believed that the form of these archaic structures is a survival of antecedent conditions."[116] He assumes that, in A.D. 1250 as at present-day Hopi, secular houses were owned by the oldest women of the clan, that kivas were the property of the men of their respective clans, and that courts, plazas, and passageways were common property.[117]

Cliff Palace kiva deflectors were made in four ways: some were a low stone wall, free at both ends; others were a curved wall that connected with the kiva walls on either side, with orifices to allow the passage of air; a few were a stone slab set upright in the kiva floor; some were jacal, free at either end and consisting of slender upright poles, between which were horizontally woven twigs, the whole being plastered over with clay.[118]

Modern kiva fires have special ceremonial import, but for practical purposes they are kindled for light rather than heat. They are kept small, since a large fire would produce so much smoke and heat it would drive the society members out. The kiva fuel, as is the case at Walpi now, has always been small twigs and brush. No evidence of a lamp has ever been found in a cliff dwelling, although torches were used to transfer fires and perhaps for walking or working in dark places.

As a rule, the kivas of Mesa Verde proved to be much smaller than those of the modern Hopi pueblos. They ranged in size from 9 to 19 feet (2.7–5.8 m) in diameter, whereas the chief kiva at Walpi measures 15 feet (4.5 m) wide and

Cliff Palace.

25 feet (7.5 m) long. It is evident, then, that the Mesa Verde kivas could accommodate only a few clan members at a time, probably the clan leaders and not the fraternity as such. The religious fraternity as it occurs in modern pueblos had in all probability not yet developed. "Nevertheless," Fewkes points out, "the smallest kiva in Cliff Palace is as large as the room in Walpi in which the Sun Priests, mainly of one clan, celebrate their rites."[119]

Of special interest to Nordenskiöld were two rooms at Cliff Palace that he thought were kivas, yet they deviated in floor plan from the common type. To

a height of 3 feet 4 inches (1 m) from the room floor they were square, approx-imately 9 feet 10 inches square (3 × 3 m), with rounded corners. Above this the room widened. Walls were set back so that a banquette was formed whose shelf varied in width. The upper walls were rectangular, with square corners, and were the exterior walls of dwellings that surrounded the kiva. There were five niches in the lower wall and a narrow passage, open at the top, that was probably a tunnel. The floor was covered with so much rubble that it could not be determined whether there was a central fireplace, a deflector, or a sipapu.

Nevertheless, Nordenskiöld was made to wonder whether these kivas were the transitional step between the round kivas of the cliff dwellers and the later, rectangular kivas of the Hopi.

In 1909 Fewkes was able to determine that the rooms lacked firepits, deflectors, sipapus, and even roofs. He thought the rooms were a new type rather than a transitional form and were not a modification of the circular or the rectangular kivas.[120]

Fewkes refers to the walls of Cliff Palace as having the finest masonry known to any cliff dwelling and as possessing the best stonework in prehistoric ruins north of Mexico.[121] In full agreement, Nordenskiöld says that the Anasazi at Cliff Palace were found to be further advanced in architecture than their western relatives on the Mesa Verde. Building stones were carefully dressed, and often laid in regular courses with chinking. Dwelling walls were perpen-

Plot plan of Cliff Palace. Open shaded areas are multistoried structures. Solid shaded areas are kivas, twenty-three in all. After Fewkes, 1919c.

Cliff Palace, showing kivas, round tower, and storage areas in rear.

dicular, sometimes were laid without mortar, and as part of the conscious design sometimes leaned slightly inward at the same angle all around the room. Some interior and exterior walls were plastered. Corners formed almost perfect right angles, including those of the doorways. Nordenskiöld posited two slightly different methods of wall construction. Some lower foundation walls that were rough-hewn and laid horizontally without order were often topped by walls of carefully dressed stones in regular courses. In other instances, the foundation stones were set on edge. Fewkes mentions the custom of laying stone foundations on top of wooden beams, especially in cases where it was necessary to bridge the intervals between projecting rocks.[122] Thanks to frequent small apertures that were left in the walls, Cliff Palace rooms had better lighting and ventilation than most cliff dwellings. Doorways were either rectangular or T-shaped, the latter being larger than usual. Most doorways were slightly narrower at the top and had high sills. One kiva, 12 feet 9½ inches (3.9 m) in diameter, was entered by a doorway in the wall, one of the few instances anywhere in which Nordenskiöld observed this arrangement.

Evidence of sun-dried adobe bricks in prehistoric buildings in the Southwest is rare. But Fewkes discovered such bricks in the wall of one room at Cliff Palace. These were cubical, but there was no indication that they had been molded in forms or frames, nor was there a core of sticks and straw as in the bricks used in the construction of Inscription House.[123]

As in other large ruins, Cliff Palace had open spaces behind the dwellings and at the rear of the cave where turkeys were kept. The rooms of the village were set on several different levels, and a number of well-built retaining walls and terraces provided level ground to build on. Remarkably, all but a few of the roof timbers in Cliff Palace were missing. Only holes were left in the walls to show where they had been. Since there were no traces of fire, Nordenskiöld decided finally that the timbers had been deliberately removed and used for some other purpose. Fewkes says they were either used for other buildings or were burned as firewood by pothunters, who often stayed for weeks looking for artifacts.

Cliff Palace has several towers. Of particular interest is a cylindrical one at the southern end whose circular lower-floor wall is perpendicular, but whose upper walls slope in, so that the top has a smaller diameter than the floors below. It is a three-story structure. Taller still is a four-story rectangular tower, with a rectangular doorway at the first floor and T-shaped doorways on the top floor. It also has several windows. Part of the original white plaster still adheres to the wall exterior, and some painting was done on the interior walls. Dwelling walls flank it, and just in front is a kiva. Since 1909, when the original excavation and repair of Cliff Palace was undertaken by fifteen workmen directed by Fewkes, the village has undergone considerable reconstruction and stabilization by the Park Service, and it is an astonishing place to visit.

A plaintive statement made by Fewkes in his report to the Smithsonian Institution (Bureau of American Ethnology Bulletin No. 51) in 1911 is well worth quoting:

> The reader is asked to bear in mind that when the repair of Cliff Palace was undertaken the vandalism wrought by those who had dug into it had destroyed much data and greatly reduced the possibility of generalization on the character of its culture. The ruin had been almost completely rifled of its contents, the specimens removed, and its walls left in a very dilapidated condition. Much of the excavation carried on under the writer's supervision yielded meager scientific results so far as the discovery of specimens was concerned; throughout the summer earth was being dug over that had already been examined and cult objects removed. Had it been possible to have begun work on Cliff Palace just after the ruin was deserted by the aboriginal inhabitants, or, as that was impossible, at least anticipated only by the destruction wrought by the elements, these explorations might have illumined many difficult problems which must forever remain unsolved.[124]

Square Tower House received its name from a four-story-high tower whose erection required great skill. There are many dwelling rooms in the ruin, all of which follow the construction methods of other cliff dwellings. The ruin measures 140 feet (42.5 m) in length, averages three stories in height, and has seven circular subterranean kivas. The most striking feature of Square Tower House is the tower. Its rear wall is formed by the perpendicular cliff. The inner plastering of the lowest story is painted white, with a red dado.[125] Two kivas were of particular interest to Nordenskiöld, since to his knowledge they were the only cliff dwelling kivas still retaining even part of their roofs, although the remnants threatened momentarily to give way. One kiva he entered had a cribbed roof, the partially fallen flat part of which covered about half of the roof surface, and had once had an entrance hole in its center, since there was no other access to the kiva. The cribbing consisted of five courses of poles resting on six pilasters. The flat part of the roof was made by laying poles 6 inches (15 cm) in diameter parallel and close together, with the ends resting on the cribbing. These poles were assembled in two groups, spaced 1 foot 10 inches (55 cm) apart, in what appears to make two sides of an entrance hole. The gap between them was covered by two groups of smaller sticks laid crosswise on top of the first poles, the groups again spaced apart so as to form the other two sides of the entryway. Another kiva at Square Tower House had a flat roof made by laying poles across the room after the common manner of dwelling construction.

Lesser material culture objects discovered at Square Tower House were for the most part like those found elsewhere on the mesa. Some, though, merit special mention. One was a cloud-blower type of unburned clay pipe. Another was an undecorated stone shaped like a bullet point that may represent Muyingwa, the God of Germination. On their Soyal altar at the great winter solstice ceremony at Walpi, a major object of which is the continuance of life by calling back the sun, the Hopi employ a similar design shape, half oval, its surface painted with symbols of corn.[126] Found with the Germination God stone was an unusual cubical stone bearing an incised design, and a carved stick.

MUG HOUSE

While profoundly impressive, Nordenskiöld's observations of the Mesa Verde cliff-dweller ruins by no means provide all the detailed information one might wish. For that, it is necessary to turn to more recent data.

In 1960 and 1961 the National Park Service excavated and cleared of rubble a Wetherill Mesa cliff dwelling given the name Mug House because of an abundance of pottery mugs discovered there. Arthur H. Rohn, leader of the archaeological party, wrote an account of the findings in a U.S. Department of the Interior book entitled *Mug House,* one of the most recent and thorough descriptions of a cliff dwelling ruin.

Mug House cave is 200 feet (60 m) long and 40 feet (12 m) deep. It consists of a main floor 600 feet (180 m) above the canyon bottom and a shelf 15 feet (4.5 m) higher that protrudes from the back wall of the cave. The mesa rim is 90 feet (27 m) above the roof of the cave. About the middle of the eleventh century, the first inhabitants of Mug House used chipped-edge stones, mortar, and timbers to build a small apartment dwelling on the shelf and a kiva below it on the main floor. The two structures were probably connected by a wooden ladder. Later, parts or all of these first structures were dismantled, and the

Mug House. Perspective view.

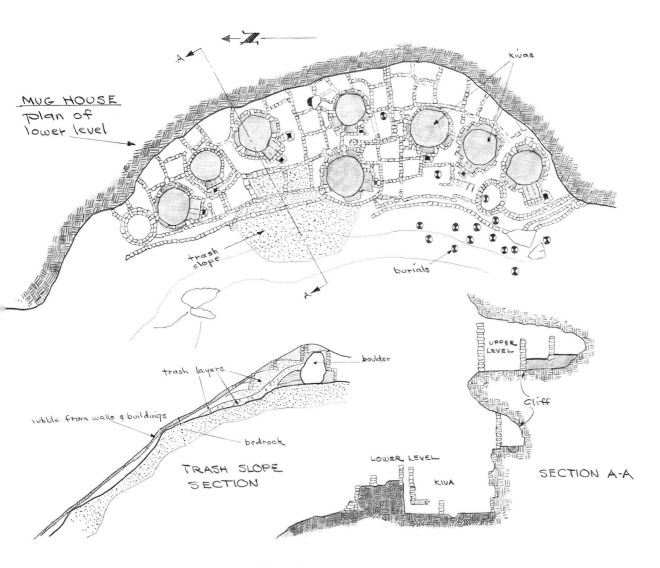

MUG HOUSE
plan of
lower level

kivas

trash slope

burials

trash layers

boulder

rubble from walls & buildings

bedrock

TRASH SLOPE
SECTION

UPPER
LEVEL

cliff

LOWER LEVEL

KIVA

SECTION A-A

Mug House. *Top,* plot plan of cliff dwellings. *Bottom left,* section through trash slope. *Bottom right,* section through, showing walls in relationship to cave.

materials were combined with new timbers and stones to form new rooms. This was a standard technique, for any abandoned stone house would quickly become a major source of supply for a new dwelling, and the practice of razing and combining would continue over the decades until A.D. 1277, a total period of about two hundred years.

Rohn and his associates concluded that while building, remodeling, and repairing went on continually at Mug House, there were actually three major waves of construction. This was true in a general way of all cliff dwellings. They evolved rather than being built in their entirety at one time, as buildings are today. For the usual addition, only a wall or two would be added to an existing dwelling or to the back wall of the cave.

It was not until the thirteenth century that the Mug House Community rooms and kivas covered the entire cave floor and ledge. At its peak there were about one hundred rooms housing perhaps the same number of residents, two towers, one room believed to be used for special ceremonial purposes, and eight kivas. Many of the rooms were exceedingly small and used only for storage.

In his interpretation of social groupings at Mug House, Rohn recognizes four levels of complexity that are most informative, for they present solid evidence of the excellent social progress being made by the Anasazi:

> 1. Clusters or *suites* of three to nine contiguous rooms with some adjacent outdoor space in an area or courtyard quite probably represent household living quarters.
> 2. Several households, or one unusually large household cluster, may share a single courtyard space and are called *courtyard units.*
> 3. The total plan of the ruin further suggests a *dual division,* both in the layout of the routes of access between the two parts and in the nature of construction seen in the kivas.
> 4. Finally, Mug House forms the nucleus of a larger *community,* which at one time at least included occupants of the two small caves lying immediately north of the ruin.[127]

Using these four groupings, Rohn found he could correlate "in varying degrees" some aspects of social organization at Mug House with modern Pueblo society, especially with the Keres Pueblos in central New Mexico. He believes the parallels are striking and that they suggest little change. "The household," he says, "occupies the most prominent role in both, and some degree of dual organization is indicated. The modern Pueblo community has apparently grown in size, and has isolated itself in response to inroads by alien people, including the bearers of Western European culture. . . . The courtyard unit, however, seems to represent a social unit that no longer exists in modern settlements, and the kiva is now entirely separate from associated houses."[128]

The fact that modern Pueblo communities of the Rio Grande have isolated themselves, particularly in regard to ceremonial activities, makes one all the more grateful that we can examine the ancient ruins of the Anasazi and find there, by careful analysis, much of the information not otherwise obtainable.

The floor space of the largest room in Mug House measures 105 square feet (9.6 m²). Excepting kivas, all the rooms, including those placed against the cave wall, are rectangular, the second largest covering 88 square feet (8.1 m²), being 8 feet 6 inches by 10 feet 6 inches (2.5–3.2 m), and the average running between 40 and 50 square feet (3.6–4.6 m²). Except for storage spaces, no horizontal wall dimension is less than 5 feet 6 inches (1.7 m), which suggests they were always designed to permit a person to lie down and stretch out; Mug House adults ranged from 5 feet to 5 feet 8 inches (1.5–1.7 m) in height. Ceiling heights averaged 5 feet 6 inches (1.7 m), the highest being just over 7 feet (2.1 m). Depending upon location, storeroom ceilings might be lower, yet there was enough room for a person to climb in and crawl around.

Cliff dwellers found it convenient and useful to throw most of their trash down the slopes that fell away at various degrees from the front of the cave floor. As a result, after years of occupation the fill raised and extended that portion of the cave floor. Trash was also deposited in some of the abandoned

Architectural details, Mug House. *Top*, roof details. *Center left*, T-shaped doorway. *Middle right*, corner hearth. *Lower left*, typical room plan, showing doorways and hearths, at Mug House. *Lower right*, rectangular doorway and compound wall. From Rohn, 1971.

rooms, and this formed a union with the rubble and dirt that washed over the edge of the cliff above Mug House to fill them completely. Accordingly, while the first Mug House kivas were dug in the existing sand and dirt on the cave floor, later kiva pits were dug in the more easily excavated trash-filled areas. Stone retaining walls were then needed to prevent the kiva walls from collapsing. Kiva roofs consisted of cribbed beams topped with brush and a final coat of adobe. When they were completed, the roof added a new courtyard space to the cliff dwelling complex.

As time passed, more and more stone retaining walls were erected along the front of the cave to hold the existing trash and to make even deeper deposits of refuse and dirt possible. Then, when a new kiva was excavated, the fill from its pit was also dumped behind a retaining wall to provide more room for buildings and walks.

Cliff dwellings blended so perfectly with the cliffs and caves housing them that visitors often stare at a site for some minutes before realizing the ruins are actually there. Since the buildings were made entirely of the natural materials that surround them, they seem organic, just as though they grew like live plants out of the caves and cliffs—which indeed they did. Only masonry and no wattle-and-daub (jacal) or plain adobe walls were found in Mug House cave.

The first building supplies were readily at hand. Over the millennia prior to occupation and even as the centuries of occupation themselves passed, the forces of nature caused great sections of the cave roof to break away and fall, shattering as they struck the cave floor below and then cascading in part over the front edge of the cave to form a talus slope. Some of this shattered rock was still too large for the Anasazi to move or to use for wall construction, and they had as yet no tools to work it. But other pieces of sandstone were small enough to be tapped and trimmed to useful sizes.

One advantage was that sandstone commonly fractured with one side flat. So the builders searched first for flat-sided stones, whose usual size was anything from that of a present-day brick to a large loaf of bread. These were used in the average instance to build the walls of their dwellings, although, for the lower courses of some walls, stones so heavy that two men would be needed to lift them were pressed into service.

A few walls of later date were undergirded with footings of large stones, but the earlier and majority of walls of Mug House were set directly on the cave or trash floor. Exterior walls were not plastered. The stones were laid with the flat side facing out, forming as smooth and uniform an exterior surface as was possible and producing square corners. This meant, however, that the interior surfaces of single-course walls were irregular. To compensate for this, builders filled the depressions and gaps with small sandstones in a technique called "spalling." The small stones were mortared into place and then plastered over until the interior wall surfaces were reasonably smooth. Such walls are referred to in literature as either "single-coursed" or "simple." Approximately two thirds of all Mug House walls were single-coursed.

Some builders solved the problem of irregular interior walls by erecting compound, or "double-coursed," walls. To make these, an outside wall of the regular stones was completely backed by a wall of carefully chosen smaller stones whose flat sides produced a smoother surface. At intervals, the compound wall was bonded by a large stone as wide as the total wall, but the outside course of stones still bore the weight, and the inside course could be removed at any time without impairing the structural quality of the building.

Whenever spalling or double coursing failed to satisfy the aesthetic sense of the builders, stone surfaces might be pecked by hammering them with a stone hammer. This removed protrusions and left texture marks on the stone surfaces. Other stones were ground to fit, especially around doorways. The grinding was accomplished by rubbing a harder stone against the softer sandstone. It was a time-consuming process, but not a difficult one.

Wall stones at Mug House were laid in mud mortar. In the earliest and crudest buildings, the stones were set with a red loess adobe taken from the mesa top. Unless sand or a sandy-soil grout was added, this adobe shrank away from the rocks when it dried. So the masons turned to a yellow-buff mesa-top adobe containing fine loam and sand, which dried without shrinking.

Somewhere along the way the builders of Mug House discovered a nearby cave known today as Adobe Cave. When explorers found this cave in the twentieth century, the puddling pits and digging sticks for digging and stirring were still in place. The largest adobe pit was flanked by depressions in the cave floor the size of bushel baskets that still retained a veneer of fine dried mud.

Researchers assume that the adobe was processed in the following manner: raw adobe was broken loose with digging sticks and then scooped out into the cave floor with the bare hands. Water was added, and with their feet the workers kneaded and tramped the chunks of adobe into a pliable mass. Foreign matter was then removed, and the adobe was carried to Mug House either in baskets or in slip form in pottery vessels. Park Service researchers note that this must have been a difficult and hazardous task, since the trail from Adobe Cave to Mug House is, at its very best places, terrifying.

Later still, the residents of Mug House began to use crushed shale as mortar. It assumed a handsome pinkish gray tone when it dried, and when softened with water, ground, and mixed with grout, it became a satisfactory clay for pottery.

Room floors were leveled and smoothed. Depressions were filled with dirt and protrusions were pecked. Then in most rooms a layer an inch or so thick of the same mortar as that used for the walls was spread over the entire floor surface. Even smooth rock floors were covered with mortar as an insulation against cold. Where the floor joined the wall the mortar was coved and rounded off, to join the two surfaces neatly together. A few Mug House floors were covered with loosely set sandstone slabs.

Evidence of conscious wall decoration still exists in some rooms at Mug House. Chinking and spalling was either laid in rows or done with pieces of deep red sandstone that contrasted with the larger buff sandstones. Corncobs and corncob impressions were also pressed into the mortar, and ornamental borders of chinking were set in the walls just below the ceiling beams. Even potsherds were used for chinking.

The interior walls of many homes were completely plastered, and the plastering was redone whenever the walls became dirty or smoke-blackened. Since there are no hand prints or fingermarks in the wall plaster, it is assumed that the mortar was puddled into a thick slip and then brushed onto the stone with a type of brush common to many Indian tribes. This consisted of blades of dry grass lashed together to form a small round bundle. The finished walls were pink or tan, and some were painted over with red, white, and black designs. One room in Mug House was adorned with a purplish red lower zone topped with an overall pattern of dot-outlined triangles. Another had the lower half of its walls done in a "railing" design with red paint.

The innermost rooms of the cliff dwellings could at times employ the sloping back walls of the cave as a roof, as could the uppermost rooms of multi-storied dwellings. But other rooms required conventional roofs. For these, the cave ceiling in itself did not provide sufficient shelter against the cold, nor did it offer privacy. We have also seen that, in many instances, roofs furnished additional work and recreation spaces or became the floors for upper rooms. About half of the first-story rooms at Mug House were roofed with timbers and adobe, and these provided a sturdy enough surface for a number of terraces and second-story rooms.

As new stone walls were erected for rooms, roof beams were set into their tops and the wall was built around them. Where walls were being added to an existing room or rooms to make a new dwelling space, rocks were removed from the existing walls to provide the seats for the beam ends.

Ceiling beams were laid on the walls at Mug House in two different ways. The first was to place a single beam down the center of the longitudinal dimension of the room. The second was to place several smaller and equally spaced beams so as to span the narrower, or transverse, dimension of the room. On top of these, anywhere from four to six poles 3 or 4 inches (7.5–10 cm) in diameter were laid at right angles, spanning the long dimension. Whenever a single large beam was used, pairs of beams of smaller diameter were placed at right angles over it on approximately 2-foot (61 cm) centers. These smaller beams usually spanned the space from the main center beam to the side walls, rather than from wall to wall. One pair of secondary beams was laid against each end wall, and the other pairs were equally spaced between them. Sometimes beams extended through a wall in such a way as to provide the framework for a balcony. No evidence was found to indicate that beams were lashed together at points of intersection. All ceilings and roofs rested directly on the wall tops and did not require additional support from posts set in the floor.

The largest of the beams still existing at Mug House is 12 feet 7 inches (3.8 m) in length and 6 inches (15 cm) in diameter. The smaller beams average 3 inches (7.5 cm) in diameter. Juniper was employed for beams more often than any other wood. Next in popularity were Douglas fir and piñon. As mentioned earlier, this might have been because Douglas fir had become hard to obtain.

Whichever structural system was employed, the roof was finished in the same way. Shingles or short lengths of split logs were laid in closely packed order at right angles to and above the uppermost beams. Over these the builders placed a matting of juniper bark and finished the roof with a coating of adobe 3 or 4 inches (7.5–10 cm) thick. When smoothed and dried, the combination provided a flat, solid, durable roof, capable of serving as a strong terrace or second floor. As an exception to the foregoing, a few rooms at Mug House had only twigs and brush bridging the beams, and then a final coating of adobe. Small rooms did not require large beams. These were roofed with small poles spaced from 1 foot 6 inches to 2 feet (45–61 cm) apart, a layer of shingles, and the traditional adobe finish.

Two types of doorway were built at Mug House. The rectangular opening was the more popular. There was a sill averaging 2 feet 6 inches (75 cm) above floor level, and the opening averaged 1 foot 6 inches (45 cm) in width and 2 feet (61 cm) in height. The lintel then was 4 feet 6 inches (1.35 m) or so above the floor. Rectangular doors for storerooms were even smaller. Five doorways at Mug House were T-shaped and were of a type common to many of the dwellings of Mesa Verde, Chaco Canyon, and elsewhere. T-shaped doors averaged 1 foot 6 inches (45 cm) in width and 3 feet 6 inches (1.05 m) in height. The offset is 1 foot (30 cm) above the sill, which itself is 1 foot (30 cm) higher than the floor level. Archaeologists say that with practice the small doorways are easily entered.

Doorsills consisted either of carefully fitted wall stones or of separate slabs fashioned for the purpose. Door lintels in the earliest houses consisted of several sticks placed close together in parallel. In later houses, a long block of sandstone bridged the space from wall to wall.

It is apparent that builders took great care in constructing their doorways. The stones were pecked and ground until smooth, and then they were squarely edged. Some builders used two upright slabs as door frames and rested another long slab across these as a lintel.

All the doorways could be closed from the outside with a sandstone slab that was ground to fit the opening. Some slabs were as thin as a half inch. To hold the slab in place, builders either fashioned a stone collar for the doorway or placed a bar of wood across the top of the opening for the slab to lean against. Sometimes two bars were spaced to form a groove at the top of the door into which the slab could be inserted. Since closure was from the outside, it would appear that door slabs were put in place when the owner was away and that, when present, the owner draped a hide or mat over the wooden bar to close the opening.

One doorway at Mug House has two oak loops set into the stone frame in such a way they are thought to have once held a crossbar. Some other doorways have oak loops on the outside of the doorframe that probably supported a stick used to hold the closing slab or hide firmly in place.

Wooden loops were regularly placed wherever a hanger or a handhold was needed. To make a loop, a slim rod of green wood was bent till the ends crossed, and these were lashed together with yucca strips. While the walls were being laid, the crossed ends of the loop were pressed into the mortar. When the mortar was dry, the loop was fixed permanently in place. One valuable use for loops was to provide a series of handholds along narrow and dangerous ledges within the cliff dwelling. Loops served also as clothes hangers. Long suspension poles and short pegs were also inserted in the wall mortar to serve as hangers. In most instances they were placed near the ceiling.

Mug House dwellings had no windows, although small holes were made in the walls at floor or ceiling level to improve ventilation for rooms with fireplaces. None of these holes are thought to have served as peepholes. Some rooms had wall niches of various sizes, and built-in stone shelves made by slightly offsetting the interior face of a masonry wall.

Every group of rooms serving a Mug House family included at least one with either a central or corner fireplace that consisted of nothing more than a ridge of adobe or a line of stones to wall it off and form an ashpit. Inside this fireplace three large stones would be set on end in a triangle to serve as a pot rest. Fireplaces were also built against courtyard walls and along rock shelves that were used at times as spare living spaces, perhaps as guest rooms. As mentioned earlier, fires were always needed for warmth in the cold Mesa Verde caves, and it is probable that Mug House fires were kept burning constantly in the winter months. The cave faces due west and so receives virtually no sunlight until afternoon; some portions of it are shaded more than nine tenths of the time. The warmth of the sun's rays would penetrate the dwellings only when air temperatures were already at their peak. The cave formed a natural funnel for the strong mesa winds, and this contributed further to the discomfort of Mug House residents.

Eighteen grinding bins were also found in the ruins at Mug House, none in good condition. Rohn assumes that at one time all these were lined with large shaped, dressed sandstone slabs similar to the slabs used to close doorways. The metate itself was propped up in a sloping position by stones and adobe, and it was surrounded by a mud collar about 4 inches (10 cm) wide. At the lower end, the basin in which ground meal was collected had a rectangular shape with rounded corners, and it was usually floored with small shaped sandstone slabs, often including a well-worn mano. One room contained six grinding bins, indicating its use as a community mealing house.

Wide-mouthed corrugated jars were frequently buried beneath courtyard and room floors, with the orifice at or near floor level. Presumably these were storage vessels that took the place of storage cists found in other Mesa Verde sites but not at Mug House. Sandstone slab covers, some shaped, others unshaped, were used to close each jar mouth. One room at Mug House still had, at the time of excavation, two buried storage jars, a stone table, and several pottery items resting on the floor.

Mug House kivas were circular and subterranean with the exception of one that was at first rectangular but was later changed to a round form. The pits ranged from 11 to 13 feet (3.3–3.9 m) in diameter, and some were 9 feet (2.7 m) deep. Each kiva had a banquette whose flat shelf-like top was about 3 feet 5 inches (1.04 m) above the floor level and 1 foot (30 cm) or more deep, except for a recessed section above the ventilator shaft that was considerably deeper. Since these were much too high for seating, they were used as storage places for ceremonial items and other objects such as tools. Three Mug House

Bird's-eye view of kiva at Mug House. Rectangular and T-shaped doorways in wall and background.

kivas could not have had cribbed roofs because they had no pilasters. Therefore large roof timbers must have rested directly on the tops of the kiva walls. However, in most Mug House kivas there are six stone pilasters, and they are remarkably uniform in size, averaging 1 foot 8 inches (50 cm) in width and 2 feet (61 cm) or more in height. The addition of the pilasters to the benches allowed a man of average height to stand erect at the outside wall of the kiva.

The pilasters supported cribbed roofs of juniper, Douglas fir, or piñon poles. A first course of these was laid from one pilaster to another to form a hexagon. Then progressively smaller hexagons were created by laying more courses, each consisting of six more poles placed on top of the next lower layer, with their points meeting on the straight sides of the layer below. In this way, from three to eight layers were built up to close the ceiling in like a dome. At its highest level of cribbing the central area was closed in, except for an entrance opening, with parallel poles laid flat and side by side. A thick layer of branches and brush was piled on top of the cribbing to bring the roof almost to ground level, then dirt fill and a coat of adobe completed the job. The finished roof provided a courtyard for religious and social functions. Entrance to the kiva was made by ladder, and the roof hatch served also as a smoke hole for ventilation. Some of the Mug House kivas had little tunnels, 1 foot 6 inches (45 cm) wide by 2 feet (61 cm) high, that led up to ground level, but they must have been exceedingly difficult to get through.

Kiva walls were lined with smaller stones than those used in dwellings, and they were set in mortar and plastered over. Researchers say that after the

Top left, section showing details of entrance hatch framing of kiva at Spruce Tree House. *Top right*, top view showing typical method of framing a cribbed-roof kiva (beams were sometimes paired). *Bottom*, section showing postulated construction details of the "pure type" crib-roof kiva. After Prudden, with alterations.

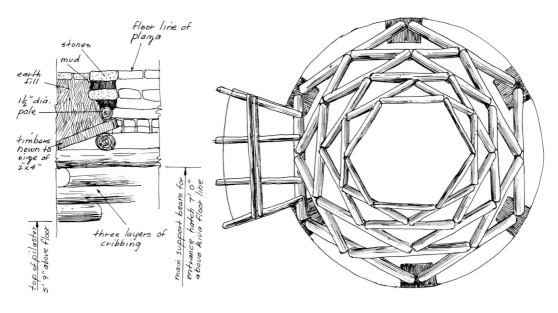

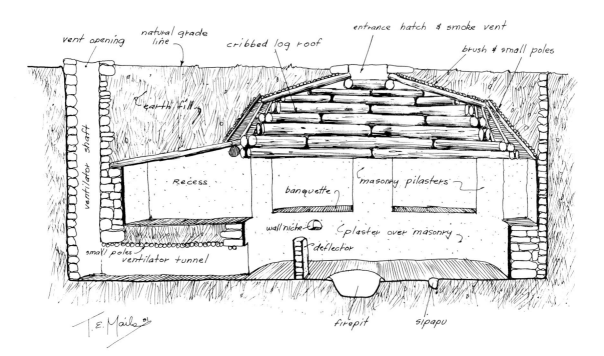

kiva walls were erected, dirt and other fill was packed in so tightly against the exterior face that it absorbed much of the weight imposed on the walls by the roof. In some instances, designs or single-color tones were painted on the front, or wall, surface of the banquettes. The plastering was redone many times, as kivas were refurbished each year, and it is assumed that on each occasion newly painted religious designs or colors were added. Nine successive coats of plaster were found in one kiva in Mug House.

Almost all individual plaster coats consisted of a thin natural brown or tan adobe body, probably obtained from Adobe Cave. This was brushed on and smoothed with bunches of dried grass. It was customary to apply white plaster to the upper portion of the banquette wall, and either to leave the lower portion its natural color or to apply an additional coating of red or red-orange paint. Figures and designs were found by early explorers in some Mug House kivas. One had a pair of red birds facing each other on a white background, plus a blue-green bird and a bird track. Sometime after 1935, a great sandstone rock slid into the kiva and destroyed these. In another kiva, a band of deep red encircled the lower 2 feet (61 cm) of the wall, and this was topped by a band of white 3 inches (7.5 cm) wide. On an earlier plaster coat a white band had been topped with white triangles.

Kiva floors were leveled, packed, and then finished with a thin coat of adobe. Some kivas had sipapu holes in the floor, others didn't, indicating that beliefs regarding the need for a sipapu varied at Mug House. In the center of each kiva floor was a roughly circular firepit, averaging 9 inches (22.5 cm) in depth and 2 feet (61 cm) in diameter. Usually the hearth walls were lined with flat stones and clay, and pot-support stones were commonly used. In Mug House it was customary to use the broken-off neck of an olla as a lining for the opening of the sipapu. Some of these openings had been filled with clay plugs and smoothed over at floor level. The plug of one was loose, as if to indicate that it was removed when the sipapu was to play a role in a ceremony. This is a practice currently followed by the Hopi.

In each kiva an L-shaped ventilator tunnel passed under one wall of the banquette and then turned up vertically as a shaft or flue to courtyard level. The tunnel and shaft walls were lined with stones to prevent the dirt from collapsing, and split juniper shakes laid side by side, occasionally capped with smooth sandstone slabs, roofed the tunnel beneath the adobe floor. Ordinarily, the ventilator shaft was placed on the side of the kiva nearest the opening of the cave. But if the kiva itself was close enough to the cave opening, the ventilator was placed on the traditional south side.

Between the firepit and ventilator shaft was a low stone wall that served as an air deflector. The stone averaged 1 foot 8 inches (50 cm) in height and 3 feet (90 cm) in length. Heated air from the fireplace moved upward toward the smoke hole, at the same time drawing in fresh air through the ventilator shaft. Since the deflector shunted this air away from the fireplace, fires were easier to control and air was circulated throughout the kiva. Smoke-blackening on kiva-ruin walls reveals, however, that the roof method of smoke expulsion was not always efficient.

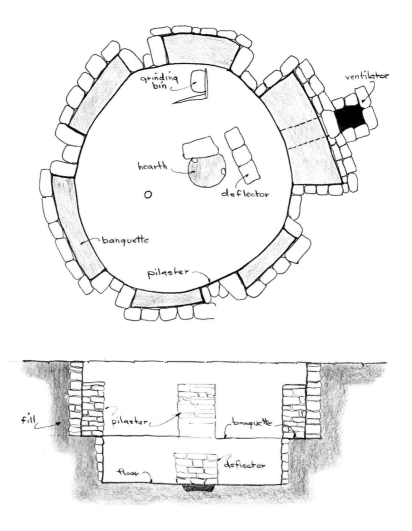

Mug House. *Top,* plot plan of kiva. From Rohn, 1971. *Bottom,* section through kiva showing wall surfacing with stones, and banquettes (or benches) and pilasters.

A feature common to all kivas at Mug House was the wall niche. Anywhere from one to eight of these were built into each kiva wall. Most were constructed in the lower part of the banquette, where they could easily be reached by persons sitting on the floor, although others were found in all locations save the pilasters. In seven of the eight kivas a special niche was found in the lower lining wall directly opposite the ventilator opening. Such consistency always implies significant ritual purpose, and one, in a kiva called D, contained a hematite paint stone.

Niches were made in several sizes and shapes, although many were nearly square. Sizes ranged from a few inches wide and high to 1 foot (30 cm) square. All were storage places used by the kiva society members. Objects found in the niches of Mug House included the already mentioned paint stone, potsherds, bone awls and needles, stone scrapers, knives, hammerstones, stone flakes, and acorns. All these point to kivas as places of considerable activity where members prepared for and carried out complex rituals.

Squirrel, rabbit, and turkey bones were found in the shafts of several kivas, causing archaeologists to wonder whether these animals and birds were sometimes kept in the shafts for ritual purposes. Researchers also suspect that kiva-roof courtyards determined in large part the social life-style of the cliff dwellers. The kivas are often surrounded by surface rooms that open out onto the courtyard. These assemblages, Rohn says, can easily be divided into family groups and then into extended groups or communities. Although, at peak development, Mug House had eight kivas, they seemingly were not all in use at the same time.

As to the orientation of kivas, in most of them a straight line can be drawn through the center of the ventilator, recess, deflector, hearth, center of the kiva proper, sipapu, and, where one exists, the niche in the wall opposite the ventilator. This line establishes the orientation or axis of the kiva. Wherever Pueblo builders were not restricted by topography, they consistently oriented their kivas toward the south or southeast. In the Mesa Verde cliff dwellings, however, the orientation was usually toward the open side of the cave, whatever axis direction resulted, although an almost southerly axis might be maintained when a kiva could be located outside the cliff overhang. If the builders had so desired, Mug House kivas could all have been built with a southern orientation. Yet they were not, and so it seems to be indicated that a traditional southern orientation is important, but not a sacred matter.

One Mug House room, which Rohn prefers to call a *kihu,* or special ceremonial chamber, stands out from all the others in construction and features. It has better facing on the interior walls and lacks chinking. There is a centrally located hearth, wall plaster, a bench, a niche, and loom loops. Nowhere else do all of these occur in a single room. In particular, the only other centrally located hearths are in the kivas, in one of the towers, and in one other room.

There has been considerable discussion about the role of towers in Mesa Verde sites. Mug House has two. They could be defensive structures, but evidence indicates a ceremonial purpose in association with the kivas, and since tunnels often connected towers and kivas, a popular theory today is that towers also served as escape routes for the members of kivas who might otherwise have been trapped in the subterranean structures when an enemy attack took place. The south tower is the first structure encountered by a person entering Mug House via toeholds pecked into a large sandstone boulder. The north tower presents a solid masonry wall to anyone coming from the north, forcing one to traverse a path three feet wide between the tower wall and a retaining wall that drops sharply away to the trash slope below. Yet there are no openings in the tower walls that could be used for defensive purposes.

Both towers are placed in locations that clearly associate them with one or two kivas, although no evidence of tunnels connecting the towers with kivas was found. Construction details of the towers duplicated those of the kivas, except that the towers were aboveground.

Tower walls were set on top of a footing consisting of rough stones wedged into a shallow trench and slightly thicker than the wall itself. Tower walls were double-coursed. The stone faces on both interior and exterior were dressed by pecking. No chinking was needed. A red-brown loess was used for mortar in the north tower and a blue-gray shale for mortar in the south tower.

The north tower was almost a perfect circle, 8 feet 6 inches (2.6 m) in diameter. The south tower was oval and measured 7 by 9 feet (2.1 × 2.7 m). Little remains of the south tower, but there is enough of the north tower to determine that it was at least two stories high. Both towers contained hearths with pot supports, and wall niches. The north tower had a rectangular doorway that opened into a kiva courtyard.

Stone towers made their first appearance late in the Pueblo II Period and became common in the early part of the Pueblo III Period. Many, as at Mug House, were built inside the villages, next to the kivas, and sometimes were connected to them by a tunnel. But a number of round towers in Mesa Verde were not part of villages, and to this day their use remains a mystery. Whether they were ceremonial structures, lookouts, or even way stations used by traders on their journeys to and from the mesa is open to speculation.

About two hundred yards south of Mug House, at the base of a nearly vertical sandstone cliff, is a man-made reservoir. Runoff water from approximately six acres of mesa top spills over the cliff above it. The Anasazi dug away the top part of a talus slope where it joined the cliff, and then formed a basin by erecting a rock-and-rubble dam 10 feet (3 m) high and 4 feet (1.2 m) thick across the front. The inside wall was lined with coursed masonry, in which smooth-faced stones were set close together in reddish brown mortar without chinking. A layer of the same kind of mud covered the reservoir bottom. The basin measured 22 feet (6.7 m) long by 10 feet (3 m) wide, and about 4 feet (1.2 m) deep. It held between 6,000 and 7,000 gallons of water.

A trail leading south from Mug House passed along the base of a cliff and by the reservoir. It then ascended a talus fan to the mesa top. Near the point where the trail reached the mesa, archaeologists found a large pile of rough sandstone blocks they believed to be a stockpile of future building materials, still awaiting transportation to the ancient dwelling place.

LESSER MATERIAL CULTURE ARTIFACTS

Pottery

Gustaf Nordenskiöld came upon and collected countless fragments of pottery on the mesa tops and in the cliff dwellings of Mesa Verde. Yet he rarely found whole vessels, and managed to collect only 60 perfect or nearly perfect specimens, most of which were found in graves associated with the cliff dwellings of the Pueblo III Period. Most of the pots had already been taken away by those of whom Earl Morris spoke as "inexperienced pothunters" who did "aimless gophering,"[129] and the balance would remain until professional expeditions were able to do excavations sufficient to expose them. Mug House, for example, would yield up 439 whole and restorable vessels in 1960 and 1961.[130]

Nordenskiöld classified his finds into two main groups: coiled and indented ware, later to be called corrugated ware by archaeologists; and coiled ware or ware of ordinary manufacture with the surface made quite smooth. He subdivided this second group into four smaller divisions: plain ware undecorated; plain ware with indented or incised ornament; ware painted in black or black and white; and ware painted in black, white, and red.[131] Archaeologists now refer to the painted ware as either McElmo or Mesa Verde Black-on-white, with the McElmo designation representing that found in earlier sites.[132]

Kidder classifies Mesa Verde vessels quite simply, as "corrugated, black-on-white, and a very small percentage red."[133] In reviewing his own discoveries and comparing them to those of Nordenskiöld, Fewkes, and Morris, Kidder states that corrugated vessels are of two sorts: large jars with wide mouths and egg-shaped bodies, and small pitcher-like jugs with single handles. Mesa Verde Black-on-white ware is distinguished by its clear, pearly, grayish white slip, which seems to have a certain softness and depth not found in other Anasazi pottery. Also, vessel surfaces were polished to a high gloss. Kidder postulates four basic shapes: ollas, bowls, mugs, and ladles. Besides these he lists, as less common, kiva jars, pitchers, seed jars, and canteens.[134]

Corrugated vessels have been treated to some extent in the section on Badger House Community, Mancos Phase, but Nordenskiöld, with his customary enthusiasm for scientific answers, examined corrugated ware closely and reports his findings at length.

He says that vessels were made of the fine clay that occurs along the beds of the canyons, mixed with sand consisting of the grit left by the erosion of volcanic rock. A single spiral coil formed the concave bottom of each pot, and more coils were added to build up the walls to the desired shape. As the work advanced, the inside walls were smoothed either with the fingers or with some implement. The outer surface of the bottom was also smoothed, otherwise the corrugations were carefully retained for exterior ornamentation; small, regular dents were made in some of the corrugation by pinching with the fingertips. Variety was obtained by different arrangements of impressions and by alternation of plain and pinched coils. Nordenskiöld felt that the work required great experience, since even the walls of large jars were seldom more than a fraction of an inch thick, and could easily be pushed out of shape or broken by an amateur.[135]

Corrugated ware was probably used for water storage, and its secondary employment when it was cracked was as a receptacle for corn. Nordenskiöld found some jars sunk in room walls at the bottoms of niches, and some that were set on the hearths for culinary purposes, the outside being coated with soot.[136]

Rohn's National Park Service workmen at Mug House found 129 corrugated jars that were classified as Mesa Verde Corrugated. Rohn agrees with Nordenskiöld's analysis of the method of manufacture, but adds that coil bonding was done only on the inside of the jar, and that tempering was accomplished with relatively coarse particles of crushed dark-colored igneous rocks, along with plentiful amounts of quartz and sandstone.[137] His published work on the Mug House excavation done in 1960 and 1961 contains sixty-eight pages devoted solely to pottery. The details are most enlightening, but far more exhaustive than is necessary here. A summary of the more useful information that should be added to Nordenskiöld's will suffice for our purposes.

Corrugated vessel shapes range from that of a crude spheroid to that of an egg. The greatest diameter is below the midpoint of the vessel, and the mouth diameter ranges from one-half to two-thirds the maximum diameter. There are many variations on this basic shape. Rims were formed by adding another band of clay around the mouth, so that the mouth turned sharply outward. Crimping, Rohn says, was sometimes done with tools. Appliqué was common on Mug House corrugated jars. This consisted of clay coil designs such as scrolls being pressed onto the exterior surface of the vessel. Painting was limited to crude lines or splotches drawn just inside the rim, and usually pendant from the lip. Jar capacities range from 2 to 35 quarts. Most of the Mug House jars had served originally as cooking pots, others for storage. Eight jars were found in kivas, and Rohn thinks that small corrugated jars may have served as receptacles for valuable personal articles or for ceremonial items.[138]

Smooth-ware vessels were so even that Nordenskiöld could not determine exactly how they were made. He assumed, however, that the coiling technique was used. Ladles, spoons, and small bowls were presumably molded by hand from a lump of clay. The grain was much finer than that of corrugated ware, and the material consisted "probably of clay mixed with fine quartz sand and crushed bits of pottery."[139]

No guess was made as to the method of firing. Nordenskiöld observes only that vessels were baked with varying success and had a surface so hard it couldn't be scratched with steel, yet seldom could a metallic ring be produced. Craftsmanship was virtually flawless, and the symmetry of bowls almost perfect.[140]

As a rule, only small vessels were left undecorated. Indented or incised ornamentation on large vessels, probably very early in date, was accomplished by pressing the clay into a basket, whose plaited basketwork impression would then show on the exterior surface of the clay bowl. These were rare finds, though, and most decorated ware discovered by Nordenskiöld in the cliff dwellings was painted in black or black-and-white. For these, the molding had been done in the same manner, but the baked vessel was harder and more durable. The surface often had a glazed appearance obtained by intensified baking, and probably by the application of a fusible substance before the black ornament was applied. In two of the ruins he found lumps of a white kaolin-like substance, easily crushed to a fine white powder, which he thought might be the coating material. By chemical analysis he determined that the black paint used was red oxide of iron mixed with a resin that converted it into black magnetic oxide.[141]

Since it differed greatly from black-on-white ware, Nordenskiöld felt that ware painted in red, black, and white might well be work obtained by barter from the more southern Anasazi. The material was clay with a slight admixture of crushed potsherds. Ornamentation was somewhat more intricate, and the shape deviated from the norm, with the top rim of the bowl curved in slightly.

He thought it probable that the bowls, being so rare, were intended solely for religious purposes.[142]

After considering the painted designs on Mesa Verde ware, Nordenskiöld decided that the pottery represented a more ancient type than that of the southernmost Anasazi. Mesa Verde designs were relatively simple, while the others combined their ornamentation into complicated patterns, so that Mesa Verde was probably the "first link in a long chain of development." If this opinion was correct, all the ornamentation on cliff-dweller pottery could be traced backward through intermediate forms to patterns originally derived from textile fabrics, and the great majority of these from basic patterns.[143]

Kidder identifies what he believes are the distinguishing marks of Mesa Verde Black-on-white ware. With the exception of certain zoomorphic figures on bowl exteriors, the decoration is mainly geometric, bold, and free. Earmarks are the use of balanced sets of framing lines above and below band decorations; the prevalence of patterns—either continuous or of repeated units—on bowl exteriors, and the common occurrence of large designs in solid black and hatching that cover the entire interiors of bowls. Mesa Verde hatching, he points out, can be distinguished from that of Chaco Canyon by the coarser quality of the component lines and by the fact that edge lines have virtually the same weight as the hatching lines. Border lines at Chaco were much heavier than the hatching.

Once again, Mug House data provide us with comprehensive details regarding painted ware. Rohn assigns one hyphenated-type name to the group found at Mug House, recognizing in it two pottery varieties known as McElmo and Mesa Verde, and McElmo–Mesa Verde Black-on-white. The clay for this was obtained from ground and sorted shale. Four major tempering materials were used: crushed potsherds, crushed rock, crushed sandstone, and sand. A majority of vessels contained two or more kinds of temper. The color of the fired clay body was predominantly a neutral gray, ranging from an almost white to dark gray, and pointing to direct exposure "in an open fire to which the supply of oxygen was intentionally restricted during the early stages." Since a brown tone would have resulted from high temperatures maintained over an extended period, Rohn assumes that the firing period was short, and done with enough oxidation in the late stages to burn out all or part of the carbonaceous core. The presence of firing clouds on many vessels indicated that fuel was piled completely about the vessels, and that burning embers frequently fell against them as the fuel was consumed.

Rohn agrees with Nordenskiöld's comments regarding vessel hardness, pointing out that seven hundred years in the ground, plus considerable handling during excavation and in the laboratory, barely affected the broken edges. He also agrees that smooth-ware vessels were constructed by the coiling method, the coil joints being pressed together with the fingers. In his view, the final shaping and thinning of vessel walls was done by scraping with pottery fragments or squash rinds, and polishing was accomplished with a hard tool such as a waterworn pebble. Rohn adds that the high polish increased the

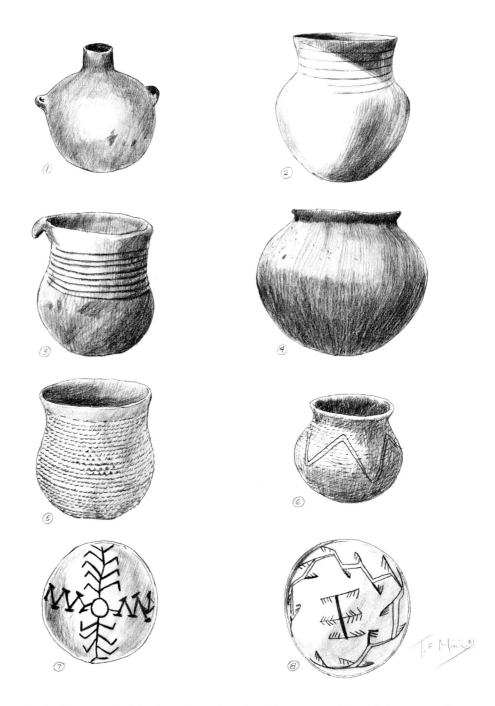

Mesa Verde. Lesser material culture items found on the mesa and in cliff houses: pottery: *1*, Chapin Gray, Basketmaker III–Pueblo I. *2*, Moccasin Gray, Pueblo I. *3*, Mancos Gray, early Pueblo II. *4*, Mummy Lake Gray, Pueblo II–early Pueblo III. *5*, Mancos Corrugated, Pueblo II. *6*, Mesa Verde Corrugated, Pueblo III. *7*, Chapin Black-on-white, Basketmaker III–Pueblo I. *8*, Piedra Black-on-white, Pueblo I. From Rohn, 1971 and 1977.

Lesser material culture items found on the mesa and in cliff houses: pottery: *9*, Cortez Black-on-white, early Pueblo II. *10*, Mancos Black-on-white, Pueblo II. *11*, McElmo Black-on-white, Pueblo III. *12*, Mesa Verde Black-on-white, Pueblo III. *13*, Abajo Red-on-orange, late Basket-maker III–Pueblo I. *14*, Abajo Polychrome, Pueblo I. *15*, Bluff Black-on-red, Pueblo I. *16*, Deadman's Black-on-red, Pueblo I. From Rohn, 1971 and 1977.

ability of the pot to hold liquids, and that surfaces to be painted generally received a coat of light gray or white slip, probably made from the same clay as the body. Mineral paint appeared on only one double mug. The balance of 294 vessels were decorated with carbon paint. The bright red or reddish brown tone on a few vessels was "probably due to the reaction of alkalies in the vegetable juices of the organic paint with iron in the clay body."[144]

Mesa Verde bowls varied in size from 3 to 15 inches in diameter. The smaller bowls usually had flat bottoms and steeply rising sides. The large bowls curved evenly from rim to rim and were uniformly a full quarter of an inch thick. This resulted in a flat rim that is a characteristic feature of Mesa Verde ware.[145]

Bowl shapes were remarkably alike. They resembled the contour of an inverted mushroom without its stem. Some bowl bottoms were flattened slightly while others were rounded. Sorting by sizes at Mug House revealed two distinct diameter-size classes, one at 11 inches and the other at 6½ inches. Capacities ranged from ½ quart to 6 quarts. The most common form of rim was a squared-off one, although a few were rounded or beveled or had a lip. Bowls did not have handles. Virtually every bowl surface was decorated on one or more fields—interiors, rims, and exteriors—with each having its own particular types of design common to the Mesa Verde Anasazi.

Rohn asserts that the Mesa Verde style is "characterized by a tendency to subdivide spaces within the decorative field until the resultant pattern is achieved. Symmetry and balance—expressed by decorated versus undecorated spaces, solids versus fine lines—are a part of every decoration." Band layouts predominate on late Mesa Verde vessels, but there are also centered designs and sectored fields. McElmo pottery has more halved, quartered, and offset-quartered arrangements. Nearly all bowls include a small space in the center of the bowl bottom that is either undecorated or carries a small independent figure that is less complex than those used on bowl exteriors in other regions. Most of these interior figures appear to be symbols for the four cardinal directions. Exterior figures, on the other hand, are biomorphic: figures often done in facing pairs—birds, bird tracks, lizards, and some human representations. Of particular interest are figures that seem to be the male and female aspects of Kokopelli, the humpbacked flute player so important in Hopi Katcina lore.[146]

At Mug House, bowls and bowl fragments were discovered in the fill in dwellings, kivas, trash deposits, and graves. Some of the bowl sherds had soot on them, indicating they were used primarily for preparing meals and for storage.[147]

Mesa Verde mugs were shaped much like mugs today. They ranged from 3 to 7 inches in height, had flat bottoms, and had either straight or slightly convex sides that grew smaller toward the mouth. They had a single flat handle that ran from the base to a point just below the rim edge, which was usually flat.[148]

Twenty-seven mugs were recovered at Mug House, and two were found in burial sites in nearby Adobe Cave. Only four of the total can be classifed as

McElmo Black-on-white. Rohn separates the mugs into three main shapes, all with flat bottoms: a cylinder with either straight or convex sides, a truncated cone with a mouth smaller than the base, and a double mug consisting of two truncated cones joined by two hollow tubes, one near the base and one near the rim. As a rule, rims are flattened or rounded and not tapered. Handles are a single strap extending from a point just below the rim to a point just above the base. Decoration was done on the exterior walls, lips, and outsides of handles.[149] All layouts are bands, with the patterns running horizontally on the walls and vertically on the handles. Only eight basic motifs were employed, all of which were common to bowl interiors. Rims were done with groups or continuous runs of dots or dashes. Mug heights ranged from 2¼ to 4⅝ inches, diameters from 2⅞ to 4¾ inches. Capacity varied from a cupful to ½ quart. Mugs were obviously drinking vessels. They were found in dwellings and in burial sites, but not in kivas.[150]

The Mesa Verde olla, or water jar, was generally 12 to 14 inches high, and had a full, rounded, or globular body with a short cylindrical neck set on top. At or slightly below the point of greatest diameter were two loop handles, or lugs, that usually bent slightly downward.[151]

Of the twenty-one ollas found at Mug House, seven were McElmo Black-on-white and fourteen were Mesa Verde Black-on-white. Wall curvature was always rounded and sometimes sloped inward toward the top. Height equaled but never exceeded the maximum diameter. Maximum diameter was always at a point below half the total height. All vessels had small necks and mouths. Vessel bottoms were indented, enabling them to stand level. The ends of the lugs, or strap handles, were set into holes cut or left in the body, after which the joints were smoothed over. Decoration was applied to the rim, neck, upper part of the body exterior, and lugs.[152] Virtually all decorations are the familiar cultural patterns with one or more horizontal bands encompassing angular geometric designs. Rohn found more hatching on water jars than on other utensils, but could decipher no reason for it. It appears that the long hatching lines, angling down on the jar sides, could have represented rain in the minds of the potters, and thus would be a prayer for rain. Jar diameters at Mug House ranged from 9¼ to 14 inches, and an average jar held 12 quarts of water—about 35 to 40 pounds.[153] That, plus the weight of the pot, would make a heavy load when transported on one's back, side, or head from spring to dwelling. Jars were also used for storing meal and seeds or whatever could be poured from one container to another.[154]

Mesa Verde ladles, or dippers, were all of the bowl-and-handle type. Each had a small bowl measuring from 3 to 4½ inches in diameter, and a handle from 6 to 8 inches long, which was round and usually hollow. Sometimes the handle contained pebbles or balls of clay, so that it rattled.[155]

Dippers collected at Mug House had the same shapes as small bowls, their height being consistently less than half the diameter of the bowl. Handles were usually attached between the bowl rim and the bottom, although for some the underside of the handle formed a straight line with the bowl base. Many dipper bowl bases were flattened. Most dipper rims were flattened or rounded but not tapered. The typical handle was round and hollow. Only two of thirty-four handles contained clay pellets for rattles. Dipper sizes were relatively uniform, maximum bowl diameters ranging from 4½ to 5⅞ inches and heights from 1⅞ to 2¼ inches. Average capacity was a third of a quart. Dippers were decorated in the same manner and style as bowls, with the handle decorations consisting of simple line patterns applied to the upper surface. Dippers were used to extract substances from larger containers and to fill water jars at shallow springs. Those with rattles may have been made for specific purposes, perhaps ceremonial, yet we can easily imagine housewives enjoying their gentle rain-sound music or mothers using them to entertain children. Only a few of the dippers found at Mug House had holes in the handle ends large enough to accommodate cords by which they could be hung on a peg.

Kiva jars, so called because a few were found in kivas, seem to have been fashioned only at Mesa Verde sites or at locations clearly related to the Mesa Verde culture.[156] They were from 6 to 18 inches in diameter, but were uniform in shape. The body was a flattened spherical form with an orifice 3 to 3½ inches in diameter at the top. The rim edge was stepped, providing a recessed ridge to hold a lid—much like that of a modern teapot. The lid had either a small knob or a loop for a handle. Jar capacities averaged 3 quarts.

Mesa Verde seed jars were what the name implies: vessels designed to hold seeds. They averaged 7 inches in height and 11 inches in diameter.[157] They had a rounded bottom and became gradually larger toward the top. The top, or rim, was not quite flat, and the opening was small. Bodies were spherical, walls were sometimes depressed toward the mouth and other times slightly raised, but there was never a true neck or lip. Some seed jars had from four to eight holes around the opening that held thongs used to hang them up, thus protecting the contents from rodents. Parts of only two such jars were found at Mug House. The simple design work on the upper part of the slipped jar exterior is reminiscent of Mancos Black-on-white, although Rohn feels that a case can still be made for classifying them as Mesa Verde Black-on-white—which he does.[158]

Twenty-nine kiva jars were obtained at Mug House, three being identified as McElmo Black-on-white, and all but one of the rest as Mesa Verde Black-on-white. The one jar resisted classification. Shapes were identical to those of seed jars, but with the addition of an inset rim to hold a lid. Diameter always exceeded height. Some jars had a series of small holes around the neck for suspension. These were formed by pushing small sticks through the clay before firing: the wood burned out and left the holes. Like the water jars, kiva jars were decorated on the rim and the upper part of the body exterior. In addition, the inside of the lip was decorated. With only a few exceptions, the motifs were the same as those most commonly found inside the bowls. While Rohn does not mention it, it appears that the design work on kiva jars is as a rule older than that on other jars. The patterns are quite powerful. Only a few of the jars include unique designs that indicate a special use for the vessel.

Not many of the kiva jars found at Mug House were in kivas, even though the name implies a direct association with them. Rohn believes there can still be a connection, since in modern pueblos ceremonial objects are usually kept in secular dwellings and are taken into the kiva only when needed.[159] Perhaps the best argument in favor of the kiva connection, if such an argument should be made at all, has to do with the fact that, because of their small mouths, these jars were impractical for culinary use and much too small to hold worthwhile quantities of food. The lids were another factor. These were decorated and could be held firmly in place by cords passed through the holes around the jar rims. It might have fitted ceremonial custom to seal off certain sacred items between ceremonies.

The Mesa Verde Black-on-white canteen was a small spherical vessel 7 or 8 inches high. It had a short neck and a small orifice. Just below each side of the neck and set at an angle was a small loop handle to which a cord loop, such as one made from yucca, could be attached for carrying.[160] Capacities ranged from 1¼ pints to 3 quarts of water. Three canteens with globular bodies and constricted necks were discovered at Mug House.[161] Designs are similar to those of many Mesa Verde Black-on-white jars, with bands above and below an inner core of geometric, mostly triangular, constructions. Canteen rims were sometimes painted with lines or dots, and handles were decorated with straight or zigzag lines.

Only two restorable pitchers were found in fill deposits at Mug House, both Mesa Verde Black-on-white. These were slipped, polished, and decorated with organic paint.[162] One had a globular body, a short cylindrical neck, and a flat rim. Decoration ran from top to bottom, with two horizontal design belts separating three groups of horizontal lines. The other was decorated in normal fashion on the upper part of the body, which was without its neck. Both pitchers had a strap handle about half as long as the pitcher was high, and set about two thirds of the way up the vessel side. The strap was also decorated, and one had opposed stepped triangles. Both pitchers had flat bottoms.[163]

Mug House yielded up four black-on-white jars that could not be categorized. They resembled other jars, but either lacked their characteristics or had certain characteristics not common to the others.[164] Several undecorated utensils were also found, including jars, bowls, mugs, canteens, and ladles.[165] They may represent pieces that the potter did not have time to fire, or they may have been left undecorated on purpose. Five Mancos Black-on-white vessels were unearthed in the older deposits in and around Mug House, as well as part of a Cortez Black-on-white dipper. The rubble fill of the Kiva F ventilator shaft contained an undamaged Chapin Gray bowl. Rohn feels it could have been an heirloom or one found by a Mug House resident in the ruins of an earlier dwelling. He notes, and thus excites one's curiosity, that "historic Pueblo Indians employ in both secular and ceremonial activities various items found among the ruins of previously occupied buildings. Old stone arrowpoints impart 'power' to fetishes because of their age."[166]

Rohn observes that, "whether for sentimental reasons or economy," the residents of Mug House frequently mended broken pots. One method was to drill small holes in pairs on both sides of the break and then draw the pieces together with twine or yucca strips. Piñon pitch was used at Mug House to seal the seams and to line the entire pot bottoms of corrugated jars that held liquids. The pitch ranged in color from a clear orange through a dark red-brown to a brown-black. Its glassy-textured core suggests that the pitch was heated and applied to the pots while it was fluid. Mend holes are common in black-on-white sherds, indicating that the Anasazi were diligent in getting the utmost service from what they made. More than 50,000 sherds were collected at Mug House, and in several respects supported and added to the information garnered from the complete or nearly complete vessels.[167]

Headrings and Pot Rests

Rohn describes two headrings found at Mug House. The first ring was made from the interwoven whole leaves of narrow-leafed yucca. It was 6½ inches in diameter and 2⅜ inches thick. The three surfaces—top, bottom, and sides—were concave, the sides being designed to absorb shifting weight as the bearer walked, the top to receive the round bottom of the bowl, and the bottom to fit the bearer's head. It is an especially clever item. The second ring, which is in the Wilmarth Collection at the Colorado State Museum, was made in the same way. It was 4¾ inches in diameter and 1½ inches thick, having been considerably compressed by use.[168]

Three doughnut-shaped bundles of split yucca leaves were also found. These had served at pot rests and still retained impressions of the vessels that had rested on them. To make the pot rests, a bundle of yucca strips or fibers some 1⅜ to 2 inches in diameter was formed and then bent into the shape of a ring, after which varying numbers of split yucca strips were wrapped around it and tied in square knots to keep the fibers together and to fix the shape permanently.[169]

One small cornhusk ring was collected at Mug House. A small bundle of cornhusks was spirally wrapped with other husks and secured around the perimeter by pulling one end of each husk through another. It was 4¾ inches in diameter and ⅜ inches thick, suggesting its use as a headring.[170]

Rohn mentions that large lumps of piñon pitch found on the exterior bases of pots could have helped to seat the pots in a permanent storage position beneath a floor.[171]

Basketry

One complete coiled basket and the fragments of four similar to it were found at Mug House. Either few baskets were being made during Pueblo III or pot-hunters had already removed the rest. The complete basket was hemispherical, being 5 inches in diameter and 2 inches in height. The standard coiling technique was used to make it. One or more foundation elements were formed into a spiral, and each successive row was attached to the preceding one by simple loop stitching. Most of the foundation rods used in the baskets were willow, and the rest were rabbit bush. Strips of willow were used for the stitching elements. These passed over each new coil and through the topmost rod of the preceding coil. In most cases, each new stitch passed between two previous stitches of the row below. Sometimes one split an earlier stitch. At the rim, the willow strips were pinched or pulled out as they passed over the topmost coil, so as to form a lip, and no alteration was made in the ordinary stitching.[172]

Two small twilled ring baskets were also found. In both cases, split yucca strips were woven in an over-three, under-three diamond twill, with the ends of half the strips passing over a ring made of an oak twig. The ends of the yucca strips were held in place by twining groups of three and four of them together, additional yucca strips being added just below the oak ring. A narrow plaited band of yucca strips, just below the oak ring, covered the raw ends of the main elements and added a decorative touch. This plaited band was made by looping yucca strips through some of the basketry and twining elements, interweaving the two ends of each strip with similar ends from other strips, and finally tucking the ends under. One basket was left in its natural colors, and the other had a simple pattern made by using black-dyed elements in one direction and natural-colored elements in the other.[173]

Nordenskiöld discovered a few baskets made of willow. To make these, a thick round rod was laid in a spiral and smaller rods were then braided at right angles to it. The braiding was so tight that it required only a coat of pitch or some other substance on the outer surface to make the basket watertight. Some baskets were fashioned by braiding strips of yucca leaf, often arranged in handsome patterns. The pattern was sometimes further elaborated by placing darker strips in one direction and lighter strips at right angles to them.[174]

Manos and Metates and Grinding Stones

One hundred and five whole and fragmentary sandstone metates were found at Mug House. The stones were shaped by spalling, or chipping off flakes, and by pecking. Most were either rectangular with rounded corners or ovate: rectangular but entirely rounded on both ends. The grinding surface took up one face and was usually concave in long section and convex or flat in cross section. Troughed metates were almost completely absent. Traces of eighteen grinding bins were found in the ruin, but none of them contained metates. The metates were discovered in the fill of rooms and kivas. This suggested either that the last residents used metates outside grinding bins, or that the metates and their bins had collapsed together into the rubble.[175]

Four hundred and ninety-two manos were found scattered throughout the fill in Mug House, and they consisted of thirteen styles or substyles according to material, size, and shaping.[176]

Grinding stones were also discovered. These were of either sandstone or

Mesa Verde. Typical lesser material culture items found on the mesa and in cliff dwellings: *a*, woven yucca headring for carrying pots. *b–c*, woven yucca pot rests. *d*, pot rest or headring of wrapped cornhusks. *e*, yucca torch. *f*, yucca hairbrush. *g*, yucca torch. *h*, willow basket lid or tray. *i–k*, plaited willow baskets. From Nordenskiöld, 1893, and Rohn, 1971.

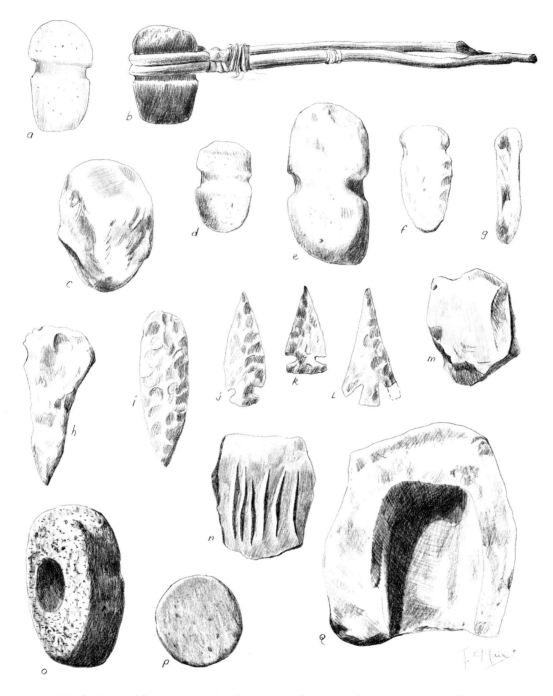

Mesa Verde. Typical lesser material culture items found on the mesa and in cliff dwellings. Stone: *a*, ax. *b*, hafted ax. *c*, hammerstone. *d*, hammer. *e*, maul. *f–g*, hafted implements. *h*, drill. *i*, knife. *j–l*, projectile points. *m*, scraper. *n*, grooved abrader. *o*, pounding stone. *p*, jar lid. *q*, metate. From Fewkes, 1916, and Hayes and Lancaster, 1975.

volcanic rock and appear to have been nether stones on which other tools were rubbed for sharpening or shaping. Shapes were irregular, but they were spalled, pecked, and/or ground.[177] Grinding stones included small rounded handstones. These were pecked, ground, and highly polished. Some were found in trash deposits and some on kiva floors.[178]

Abraders

When all the metates and grinding stones had been sorted out, there still remained at Mug House a small number of shaped sandstone pieces that did not fit the regular classifications. Rohn calls these abrading stones, because at least one surface had been modified by use grinding. The abrader could be held in one hand while it was rubbed back and forth against the object to be ground. Soft abraders were made from gritty sandstone. Hard abraders were somewhat larger and made from tougher sandstone. Since they were found on floors and banquettes of kivas, Rohn assumes they were used by men for ceremonial and work purposes.[179] The relatively small number of abrading stones is accounted for by the fact that natural cave surfaces were also used for grinding and sharpening tools. Details regarding this technique have already been given.

Polishing and Rubbing Tools

Excavations at Mug House turned up a number of small waterworn pebbles, not over 2¾ inches in diameter, which were probably used for polishing pottery. They are principally of quartz, quartzite, chert, basalt, and hard sandstone and are similar to stones being used for polishing in the Pueblos today. One stone in this category was thought to be part of a possible medicine kit because it was found with other medicine items in a burial.[180]

Pounding Tools

Rohn separates the pounding tools from Mug House into mauls, notched and grooved hammerheads, pitted pounding stones, and hammerstones. Mauls were large hammerstones used for heavy-duty pounding. A pecked groove encircles the stone, suggesting it was originally hafted. Hammerheads were notched or grooved to receive a haft or handle. Six different styles were made by pecking, grinding, and chipping cobbles of granite, quartzite, basalt, porphyry, and diorite. Only one hammerhead still had its handle, which was made from a peeled branch of green oak wrapped twice around the groove, with the two ends extending about 12 inches to make the handle. Lashing was done with yucca-fiber cord tied in a square knot. Wear marks show that wrapping was also done near the butt of the handle. Pitted pounding stones were smooth rectangular or oval stream cobbles of the same materials as hammerheads, and their well-battered ends suggest repeated use in pounding, pulverizing, and rubbing. Since they were commonly found in kivas, they were used primarily by men. A great number of hammerstones were found in Mug House. These were made from cores or waterworn pebbles, could be held in the hand, and were used for pounding and pecking.[181]

Mortars and Paint Pestles

Two mortars, one complete and one fragmentary, were made from waterworn cobbles of diorite by creating a small oval depression in the center of a flat surface. Rohn states that similar items from Pecos Ruin in New Mexico were called "paint-grinding stones" by Kidder.[182]

Paint pestles at Mug House were manufactured from pebbles of milky quartz. Red stains on the polished flat surface indicate the stones were used to grind pigments.

Chopping Tools

Stone chopping tools taken from Mug House are classified as axheads, adz heads, celts, fragments of bitted tools, choppers, utilized flakes, and utilized cores. All axheads were made from stream cobbles taken from the gravel beds of the Mancos River. Fine- or coarse-grained igneous rocks, quartzites, hard sandstones, and clay stones were roughly chipped and then finished by pecking and grinding. Several styles were made. Notches or grooves were worked into the stone to facilitate hafting. The sharpened bit had a convex head and the poll was rounded. Many polls are battered, indicating their use as hammers.

One stone found at Mug House had an asymmetrical bit formed by two ground faces of unequal size, causing Rohn to call it an adz. Beveled wear facets are visible on both faces adjacent to the bit. A true adz is used in shaping wood and is a cutting tool that has a curved blade set at right angles to the handle. One celt, probably a kind of ax, was found in a kiva. It had a symmetrical bit and a rough, round head, but no groove or notches to hold a handle. Bitted tools made from shale or chert had narrow bits and are classed by Rohn as miscellaneous, problematical objects.[183]

Fewkes reports that the few timbers remaining in Cliff Palace at the time of his excavation in 1909 showed they were probably cut with stone hatchets aided by the use of fire. He goes on to say that the labor of hauling these timbers and of stripping them of their branches must have been great, considering the rude tools at hand. Indications were that wedges were used for splitting logs, since the surfaces of split timbers and sticks were always more or less fibrous, and never smooth.[184] Moreover, all transportation was manual and done with the assistance of only the rudest mechanical contrivances. Even our best mechanical minds have not yet figured out how the logs were moved from cliff tops or canyon bottoms to the caves in the cliff surfaces. It remains a feat to be marveled at.

Choppers

Numerous stone artifacts had the coarse and sinuous chipped edge of items often used by prehistoric peoples for chopping, and so Rohn calls them choppers. Most are little more than utilized cores and flakes, with a minimum of flaking applied to produce the chopping edge. The larger ones would be held in the hand, the smaller ones with the fingers. They were rough, crude, poorly made general-purpose tools of chert, clay stone, quartzite, basalt, granite, and diorite. While only one utilized flake from Mug House seemed to have been used for chopping, all the utilized cores were choppers.[185]

Cutting Tools

Cutting tools from Mug House are classified as knives, utilized flakes, chipped saws, and ground saws. Rohn defines knives as any tool with one intentionally prepared sharp edge. Twenty-four chipped-stone knives were found at Mug House; some of them could have been held in the hand without hafting, whereas others were thought to have originally been hafted. Most are shaped like large arrow or lance points and have no distinguishable serrated edge. Flakes were the most commonly employed implements for cutting and were simply pieces of stone with naturally sharp edges. The flakes were of chert, clay stone, chalcedony, quartzite, and basalt. Chipped saws were stone tools characterized by the presence of at least one saw-toothed edge. Ground saws were small pieces of flat sandstone with thin edges beveled on one or two faces by grinding. Tools of this sort were ideal for cutting small bones and pieces of wood.[186]

Scraping Tools

Many scraping tools were found in the rubble and refuse deposits of Mug House, on room floors, on banquettes, and in the niches of kivas. There were eight different kinds in all: stone scrapers, utilized flakes, utilized cores, humerus scrapers, a tibia scraper, bone side scrapers, sherd scrapers, and squash rind scrapers.

Stone scrapers were made from ordinary stone flakes of chert, clay stone, and quartzite by retouching one or more edges. These were, in fact, little more than utilized flakes, which were natural pieces of chert with sharp edges used as found for scraping. Utilized cores were usually chert pieces saved and shaped to be used for scrapers.[187]

The humerus scrapers of Mug House, ordinarily referred to in the literature as "fleshers," seem to have been too delicate to use for that purpose, and their thin edges would have gouged into a hide. Perhaps they were a general-purpose tool used in preparing various vegetal materials for food and household needs. Most were fashioned from the distal (knee) ends of bighorn sheep and mule deer humeri. Sheep scrapers ranged from 4¾ to 7 inches in length. Deer scrapers were longer and heavier. One tibia scraper, 10 inches long, was made from the nearly complete left tibia of a mule deer. It could have been used for fleshing animal hides, because it had a thick, strong edge and sufficient length. Bone side scrapers consisted of splinters of long bones that had sharp edges along their sides. Some were deer and some were turkey.

Sherd scrapers were pottery fragments used for scraping. Their convex edges were well suited for scraping pot interiors, but sherds were also used on plant fibers and animal hides. Squash rind pieces were sometimes employed for smoothing and thinning pottery.[188]

Perforating Tools

Classified by Rohn as perforating tools, since they were used to make holes in items, were chipped-stone drills, utilized-flake drills, bone awls, bone reamers, bone needles, yucca-leaf needles and thread, wooden awls, and wooden punches. Chipped-stone drills were pieces of chert and quartzite that were chipped bifacially to a typical drill shape. They measured from 1⅜ to 2¼ inches in length. Utilized-flake drills, ordinary stone flakes with a very sharp point, were employed for most drilling. Bone awls were used mainly for making baskets and for stitching materials together. These were pieces of bone with sharp, evenly tapered points, some being ground to achieve their shape and others simply splintered. Many were turkey bones, others the bones of bighorn sheep, rabbit, bobcat, and coyote. Bone reamers differed from awls by having an elongated, slender point to one side rather than in the middle of the bone. The tool was designed to be twisted during use so as to enlarge a hole. Bone needles were bone splinters ground to a point at one end and having a hole drilled in the other end. The sides were also ground smooth.[189]

Another type of needle was the sharp natural tip of a yucca leaf; the attached fibers of the rest of the leaf served as cordage. Beyond the first 1⅜ inches of the leaf the rest was split and stripped of pulp. Then the fibers were separated into two groups that were first twisted together and then plied together. It was a clever and readily available device that saw widespread use in the Southwest in prehistoric times.[190]

Wooden awls, ranging in length from 4⅜ to 9⅜ inches, were fashioned from fendlerbush, mountain mahogany, and chokecherry. The bark was removed from a branch, the wood was smoothed, and then it was ground to a tapered point at one end. The wooden punch was a fendlerbush stick, 2⅜ inches long, with a blunt, flattened tip and the other end rounded.[191]

Weaving Tools

Tools found at Mug House that were used for weaving included bone awls with transverse grooves, bone matting tools, bone weaving tools, wooden battens, and wooden spindle whorls. Rohn believes that bone weaving awls differed from ordinary awls only in that they had highly polished shallow transverse grooves on the shaft toward the pointed end. Some authorities think the grooved awls were used for making coiled baskets rather than for weaving. Bone matting tools were crafted from the splinter of a long bone and possibly were used to lift strips during the manufacture of plaited yucca baskets or matting. The bone weaving tool was made of the proximal (knee) end of the right ulna of a mule deer. It had no sharpened point, and a deep groove worn in one side near the tip gave it a hook shape.[192]

Wooden battens were made from juniper and mountain mahogany and have the characteristic shape and wear of implements still used by weavers to beat down the wefts. They were about 9 inches long, 1⅝ inches wide, and ½ inch thick. Ends were beveled, and some smoothing of the surfaces was done. One part of a circular wooden spindle whorl made from ponderosa pine was recovered at Mug House. Its faces were ground smooth and a hole was drilled in the center. It was 3¼ inches in diameter.[193]

Miscellaneous Tools

Miscellaneous tools resting in the debris at Mug House included composite utilized flakes that were employed for both cutting and scraping; composite rubbing and pounding stones; lapstones or anvils that were large unmodified cobbles of coarse-grained igneous rock and hard sandstone that provided firm surfaces to work against; what Rohn calls "shaft straighteners," which had a long shallow groove in the stone face, but which seem to me more likely to have such grooves for smoothing arrow shafts, since bone or stone wrenches with a single round hole were ordinarily employed by Indians for straightening objects; bone spatulas made from the tibias and scapulas of bighorn sheep, mule deer, and turkey (the specific function of which is not known); and, finally, antler flakers that were used to chip out stone tools by pressing the antler point against the stone.[194]

Mats and Matting

The commonest form of matting in Mug House consisted of groups of long, straight willow sticks laid side by side and sewed together with yucca cordage. The bark was left on the sticks, whose ends were rounded off. They were pierced at intervals ranging from 2⅞ to 5½ inches and then strung on series of yucca cords that at the very ends were knotted to keep the sticks from sliding off. Finished mat sizes included widths of 14 and 45 inches and lengths of 20 and 40 inches. Evidence indicated that willow mats were common floor coverings in all rooms and kivas, where they were laid side by side to cover large areas at places where people were likely to sit or lie on the floor. Also, fragments were present in all burials where any sign of perishable material remained. Rohn feels they may have been the standard casing in which corpses were laid to rest. Willow-rod mats may also have served as door curtains, since the loops above one Mug House doorway indicated that the opening was closed by some other means than a slab.[195]

Twilled mats of rushes were made by three over-two, under-two twilling. Finds indicate that this kind of mat was also used as a floor covering, although fragments recovered at Mug House were not sufficient to indicate finished mat sizes. Rush strips were either interwoven at right angles to one another or plaited, so that two styles were produced.

Reed mats were made by twining. The reeds were laid side by side and held together by double rows of interwoven wefts of two-ply two-twisted yucca cords, evenly spaced apart. The weft pairs in the double rows paralleled each other, catching two warps in each twist. Weft ends were cut or broken off just beyond a joint to prevent splitting.

Cradleboards

Rohn believes that one small pine board found at Mug House was the side-board of a wooden cradle. It measured 1 foot 1⅞ inches long, 4⅜ inches wide, and ½ inch thick. All surfaces had been ground smooth. Two holes were drilled in it, one near a corner and the other on the opposite side about three fourths of the way down. The side hole still contained a fragment of yucca cordage, and a notch indicated that some wrapping had been regularly passed over it.[196]

Pillows

A well-finished wooden pillow, 13 inches long, 4 inches wide, and 1¾ inches thick, was found in a burial at Adobe Cave. While the corpse seems to have been turned over as it was placed in the grave, and thus had the pillow block resting on top of his head, Guernsey found in another instance a body with a mummy's head resting in proper position on top of the pillow.[197]

Fire-making Equipment

The standard fire-making equipment used at Mug House was a simple round-stick fire drill of the type that was rotated between the hands while its point rested in a cupped notch cut into a narrow, rectangular piece of wood. Woods used for this purpose were sagebrush and serviceberry. No evidence on the drill shaft indicated that a bowstring or other device was used to turn it. Rohn thinks that some kind of "slow match" was used to transfer fire from one fireplace to another, and that charred cornhusks and grass crowns found at Mug House may have served this purpose.[198]

Paddles and Pokers

Slightly curved split-oak sticks, some 1 foot 3¾ inches in length, were peeled and ground smooth to serve as stirring tools for mixing mortar and plaster, and other peeled sticks, slightly longer, were used (as their blunt, charred ends

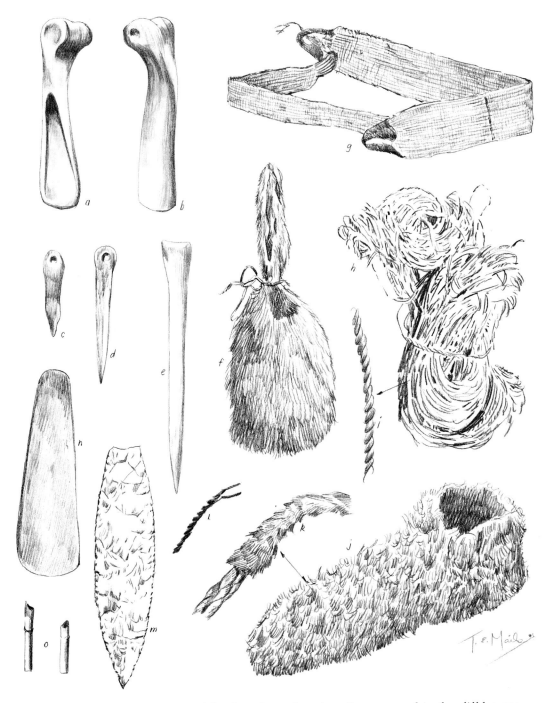

Mesa Verde. Typical lesser material culture items found on the mesa and in the cliff houses: *a–b,* bone fleshers. *c,* bone awl. *d,* bone needle. *e,* bone bodkin. *f,* hide pouch filled with salt. *g,* woven yucca and cotton tumpline. *h,* large hank of yucca cord, more than 1,100 feet long. *i,* enlarged detail of yucca cord. *j,* feather-cord sock. *k,* enlarged detail of feather-wrapped yucca twine. *l,* detail of human-hair cord. *m,* large stone knife. *n,* stone knife. *o,* reed cigarettes. From Nordenskiöld, 1893, and Rohn, 1971.

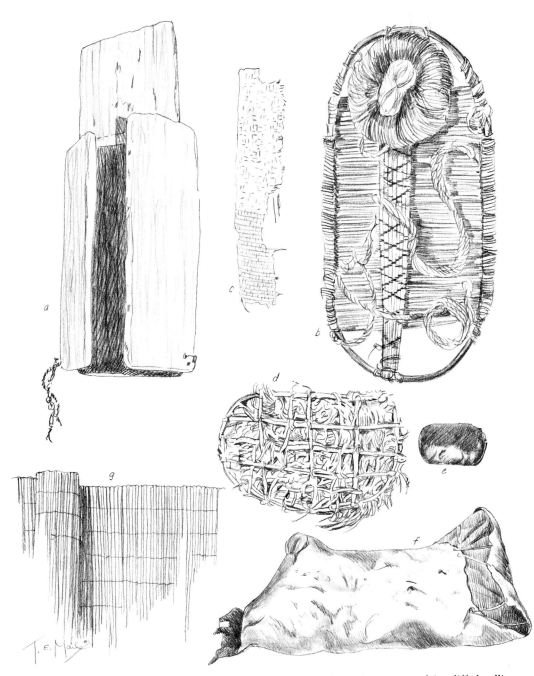

Mesa Verde. Typical lesser material culture items found on the mesa and in cliff dwellings: *a*, wood cradleboard of the Pueblo Period type that flattened the back of the child's skull. *b*, padded cradleboard from Basketmaker III Period. *c*, portion of mat made of plaited reeds. *d*, snowshoe of twigs joined together with yucca leaves and having a filler of cedar bast. *e–f*, stuffed hide-covered pillows. *g*. mat made of split willow rods held together with yucca cords. From Nordenskiöld, 1893, and Mesa Verde Museum.

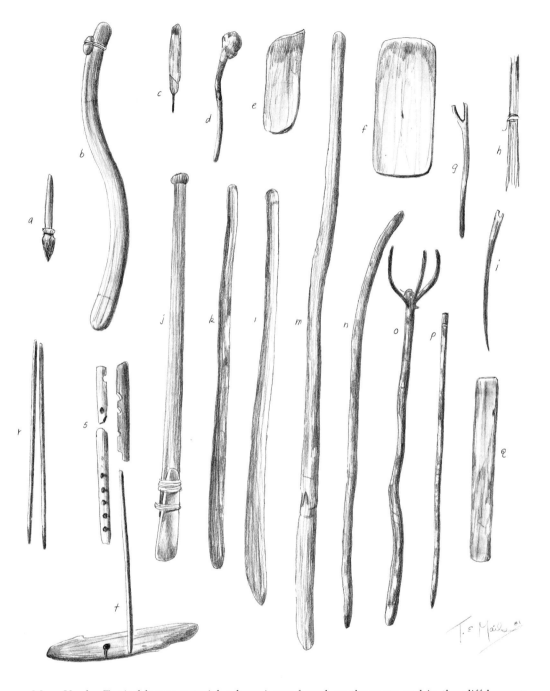

Mesa Verde. Typical lesser material culture items found on the mesa and in the cliff houses:
a, foreshaft of atlatl dart. *b,* rabbit throwing-stick with stone weight. *c,* wooden awl.
d, wooden pounding stick. *e–f,* wooden scoops. *g,* wooden fork for rack or placing items.
h, bundle of hardwood sticks with one pointed end, possibly a weaving tool. *i,* end of a bow.
j, wooden digging stick with stone blade attached. *k–n,* wooden digging sticks for farming.
o, wooden fork. *p,* long stick with a carved cross on top. *q,* possible wooden weaving tool.
r–t, wooden fire drills and hearths. From Nordenskiöld and Mesa Verde Museum.

indicated) to poke fires and keep them burning.[199] Mountain-mahogany sticks with a fork at one end may have served to lift and carry hot rocks, as was the custom for Plains Indians.[200]

Worked Sandstone Slabs

Thin slabs of sandstone served in many ways: to line niches, hearths, doorways, and other wall openings; to build bin liners and closets; to make paint palettes, pot covers, jar lids and plugs; and as door slabs. The thin beds of hard sandstone at Mesa Verde produced these slabs—many of which could be used without alteration, while others had to be ground and otherwise altered.[201]

Tumplines

From Basketmaker through Pueblo times, the Anasazi carried burdens on their backs by means of tumpline straps hooked over the forehead. Six tumpline fragments, no two alike, were found at Mug House. All were fashioned from yucca fibers and in some cases were covered with hide that was sewn in place. The commonest technique was twining, although one found by Nordenskiöld was made in the same manner as willow-rod matting. A complete twined headband taken from Mug House sometime before 1960 had a total length of 1 foot 5 inches and a width of 3 inches. The Nordenskiöld tumpline was 1 foot 11¾ inches long and 1 inch wide. All the tumplines had loops at the end to receive a yucca cord that was fastened by means of clove hitches. A few tumplines consisted of a basically narrow strap that broadened only at the point that made contact with the forehead.[202]

Yucca Strips and Cords

The quantity of yucca used by the Anasazi at Mesa Verde was astonishing, and the uses to which it was put were nothing short of ingenious. It was used for plaiting sandals, baskets, ropes, cords, threads, nets, fabrics, and other weaving. Commonly found both on the mesa tops and in the canyon beds, the plant has long, narrow leaves with extremely sharp points made brown and harder by aging, and composed of extremely tough fibers. Nordenskiöld thought it was the most important material employed in the resourceful cliff dwellers' textile industry. The leaves were cut, harvested, and dried, then stored in large bundles. He found in the ruins bundles of leaves, prepared fibers, cords already twisted, and fabrics already knotted. Even the fruit was used for some purpose; in one cliff dwelling he came upon a quantity of yucca threaded on a stalk to dry.[203]

Rohn points out that while yucca strips were strong, drying made them brittle, and they could not be used again once they had lost their flexibility. Leaves reached a maximum of 2 feet 3½ inches in length, and so to increase this the Anasazi knotted strips together. Being everywhere available, yucca was always handy to patch and to repair breaks. Bundles had yucca-strip wrappings. Ears of corn were strung together with yucca strips for storage. Harness nets made of the wider strips were used to carry jars. Twilled head-rings and sandals were made of yucca, and pot rests were lashed together with the plant.[204]

Probable Ceremonial Paraphernalia

For a long time there has been a tendency to assign any article whose functional use is not known to a ceremonial category. And if the article seemed at all strange in its construction, it was assuredly a ritual piece! It is gratifying, then, that as Rohn and his associates classified the items at Mug House, he listed, under the general heading of "Miscellaneous Objects," what he calls "Probable Ceremonial Paraphernalia," and he established some sensible standards for the choices. Researchers as a whole would do well to adopt the standards for all archaeological work.

Rohn states: "The identification of ceremonial paraphernalia requires more than observation of form and appearance. The absence of a recognizable physical function is virtually a first requirement." Possible ceremonial objects at Mug House were selected as such (a) because of where they were found, (b) because similar objects are identified as having ceremonial significance among historical Pueblo Indians, and (c) because no practical economic function can be proposed for them. Items whose use is simply indecipherable are set off in a category by themselves.

A few flat slabs of shale and sandstone were distinguished from ordinary worked sandstone slabs because of extensive grinding on their faces and edges. Rohn calls these "stone tablets," but warns against confusing them with wooden tablets set in altars or worn on the head during modern Pueblo ceremonies. While some other authorities assign such stones to utilitarian purposes, Rohn believes that those he found were used for some ceremonial function, in part, perhaps, for their bell-like sounds when struck. Supporting this belief is the use of long, thin, basically unmodified bell stones among both protohistorical and historical Pueblo Indians along the Rio Grande in New Mexico.[205]

Among the stone objects considered by historic Pueblo Indians to be sacred and to possess supernatural power are pieces of fossilized wood. Nine such small pieces, partly ground on their faces, sides, and ends, were found at Mug House.

Four small, well-worked stones found at Mug House are listed as effigies because they seem to represent some animal or object. Besides these, there were two small cones that are virtually identical to a fetish from Zuñi said by Frank H. Cushing to represent the relic of the weapon or the tooth of a god. Both are polished except for the flat base, which was ground. Because they show evidence of having been worked into special shapes, such as small bowls, a few concretions found in Mug House were listed as possibly ceremonial, although others clearly served utilitarian needs, such as pot supports. Some waterworn pebbles, because they had not been worked, were also classified as possibly ceremonial.[206]

Modern Pueblo Indians use reed cigarettes in their ceremonies. Eleven such reed cigarettes were found in the rooms and kivas of Mug House. These consisted of a section of reed that was pierced to allow air to pass through. As the tobacco in the reed burned, the reed burned also. Wild tobacco of several species grows in the Mesa Verde area today, but it is not known whether these same plants were smoked by the Anasazi. The absence of pipes in Mug House suggests that all ceremonial smoking was done there with reeds.[207]

Ears of corn are most important items in modern Pueblo ritual. They are often built into prayer offerings and fetishes, and they are carried in dances and placed in offering trays. One corncob found at Mug House had a large wing-feather quill inserted in one mud-packed end. Another had a similar hole where a quill might have been.[208]

A bundle of ten small, bare twigs of sagebrush, wrapped with a split yucca strip, was found at Mug House. Since sagebrush is used as a remedy by some modern Pueblo Indians, the Mug House bundle could also have served in curing rituals.[209]

Toys and Gaming Objects

Classified as "Probable Toys and Gaming Objects" at Mug House were miniature clay bowls, clay figurines, small sherd disks, and sherds reworked into unusual shapes. The clay bowls were far too small to have any practical use, and they were not fired. Some accompanied the burial of an infant, others the burial of a child. Several small figurines of unfired clay bore markings that suggest they were human representations. These are similar to Basketmaker III figurines from the San Juan drainage. But figurines of post–Basketmaker III manufacture are virtually nonexistent from the Four Corners country, except for some described as babes-in-cradles. Nevertheless, Rohn will consider his finds to be toys until evidence is found to the contrary.[210]

Objects of Unknown Purpose

Listed among "Objects of Unknown Purpose" found at Mug House were several items that might be explained. One is a cornhusk bundle.[211] At Step House, Nordenskiöld found lumps of a white kaolin-like substance for which cornhusks served as a container. It is possible that husks made suitable containers for a number of like items.[212] A second item consisted of small sticks wrapped with yucca strips or twine.[213] One of these had two lengths of feather-wrapped yucca twine attached to its side and bent in a U shape to give it the curved form of a shepherd's crook, and the other stick once had something attached to it, but it is now gone. Rohn finds it tempting to think of these as

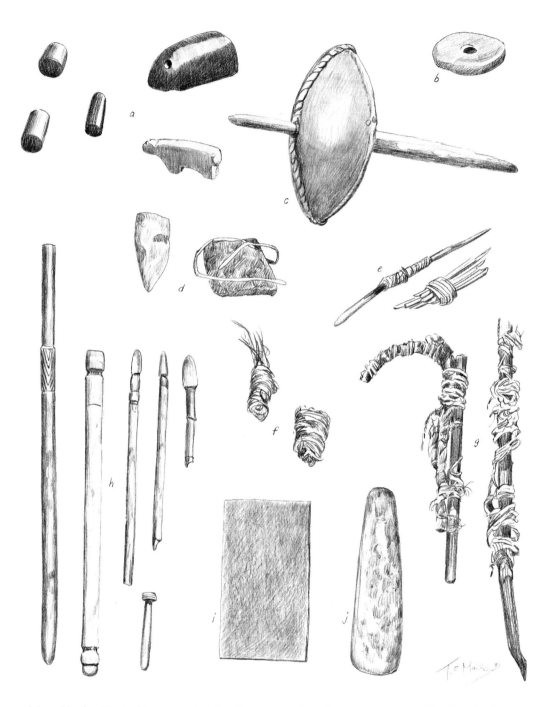

Mesa Verde. Typical lesser material culture items found on the mesa and in cliff dwellings: *a*, stone fetishes. *b*, soapstone ring—a type sacred to present-day Zuñi. *c*, rawhide rattle. *d*, stone lightning knives—Pueblos believe that one such stone is at the head of each lightning bolt. *e*, feather prayer plumes. *f*, medicine bundles consisting of dried plants, found on a kiva bench. *g*, pahos consisting of sticks wrapped with yucca. *h*, wooden pahos. *i*, stone tablet. *j*, tchamahias, ancient stone hoe used as altar fetish. From Mesa Verde Museum and Rohn, 1971.

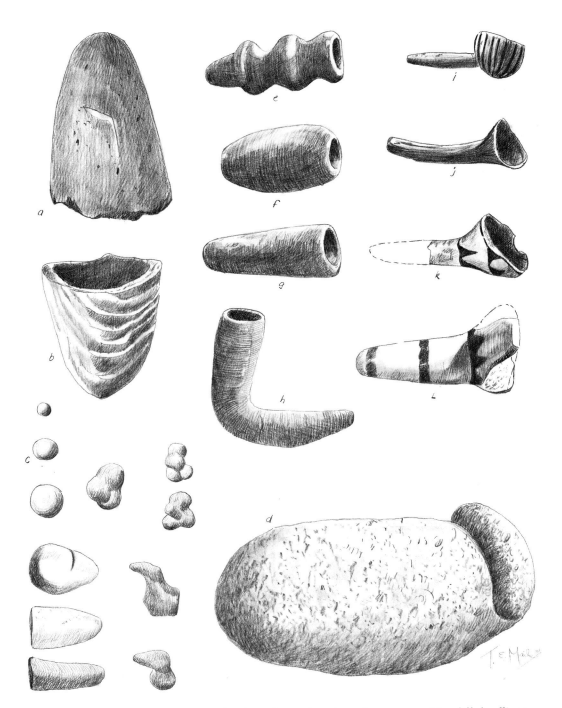

Mesa Verde. Typical lesser material culture items found on the mesa and in cliff dwellings: *a*, conical corn goddess fetish stone found in kiva. *b*, stone concretion fetish. *c*, fetish stones. *d*, carved sandstone phallus fetish. *e–l*, stone and clay pipes. From Fewkes, 1920b, and Hayes and Lancaster, 1975.

prayer sticks.[214] The association is certainly a credible one, since the Hopi use small canes on their altars and as pahos, or prayer sticks. Members of the Singers Society carry a short crook, and canes are often employed by other Katcina societies.[215] A third item that may be explained is a small bundle of five sticks, four of which were tied together with yucca strips to form a square, with the fifth set at a right angle in the center of the other four. Rohn thinks the bundle had a ceremonial purpose.[216] Perhaps, though, it was nothing more than a version of a bird-hunting arrowpoint common to many prehistoric and historic tribes.[217]

ABANDONMENT

The demise of the Mesa Verde Region has been mentioned many times. There is no need to treat it in detail now. Whatever combination of happenings brought it to pass, by the mid-1200s individual groups or clans in all parts of the region were beginning to abandon their beloved homes on the mesa tops and in the cliffs, and were mking their way south or southeast in the search for new homes. It appears that the exodus continued at a steady pace over the last half of the century, and the awesome drought of A.D. 1276–93 was the final straw. By A.D. 1300 only the ghosts remained to haunt the sandstone castles.

No one yet knows precisely why the Anasazi left or for certain where they went. Evidences of Mesa Verde architecture occurring at Aztec, Canyon de Chelly, Marsh Pass, and Chaco Canyon mark in vague fashion some of the trails they followed. Which of the Mesa Verde Anasazi left each one of these markers behind may never be proved, but present-day Pueblo customs make it clear that Mesa Verde residents were among their ancestors as the various Pueblo IV and V villages of Arizona and New Mexico either came into being or increased in size. The ancients are not gone. They live on today, and they can be dramatically seen in the faces and lives of their descendants.

Chapter 7

THE LITTLE COLORADO REGION

It is remarkable that, of the six Anasazi regions of prehistoric times, two of the three lesser ones, the Little Colorado and the Rio Grande, would alone survive the problems attending the late Pueblo III Period and emerge as the only regions where Anasazi life continues today.

THE UPPER LITTLE COLORADO SECTION

Neither the Little Colorado nor the Rio Grande region began to assume an importance commensurate with their present status until after A.D. 1300, during the Pueblo IV Period. But ancient ancestors of the Anasazi inhabited the two areas long before that.

The Little Colorado Region is divided by archaeologists into two geographic parts or sections, the Upper Little Colorado and what is alternatively called the Middle, Central, or Lower Little Colorado. That seems simple enough to follow, but the boundaries of each section have not been cleanly defined. It is understandable, for several factors can complicate the attempt. Boundaries shifted through time, and Mogollon influence was strong in the lower part. J. Richard Ambler's map shows a greater Little Colorado Region of prehistoric time that extends from Wupatki, Arizona, on the west to beyond Zuñi, New Mexico, on the east, and from Cross Canyon trading post, Arizona, on the north to Springerville, Arizona, on the south.[1] The northernmost line swings south of the present-day Hopi pueblos. If the map is accurate, it raises some interesting questions, for it passes some distance north of the Kinishba Ruin on the Fort Apache Indian Reservation and leaves the ruin hanging, and in encompassing Zuñi it argues with Frank H. H. Roberts's assignment of Whitewater, Kiatuthlanna, and the Village of the Great Kivas to the Chaco Canyon culture sphere. Moreover, Paul S. Martin places Springerville and nearby Snowflake in the Upper Little Colorado Region.[2]

George J. Gumerman and S. Alan Skinner, in their commendable 1968 "Synthesis of the Prehistory of the Central Little Colorado Valley," pull in the borders of that section appreciably. But they, too, are vexingly vague about boundary lines. They delineate the section as "the poorly known distribution of 'pure' Little Colorado White ware sites," and verbally sketch a southern line that extends from Grand Falls, Arizona, on the west, to Holbrook on the east. Their eastern boundary is established by a line that runs almost straight north from Holbrook to Indian Wells, a distance of about thirty miles. They give no western border line and say that the "indistinct northern limits are placed south of the foot of Black Mesa."[3] Whether this refers to the part of Black Mesa whose three southern fingers or mesas terminate at the present-day Hopi villages, or instead to the south edge of the higher and more northern part of the mesa (usually known as Kayenta country) is not explained. I assume the former.

What, then, do the archaeologists do with the Anasazi who are known to have lived to the south of the region just delineated? According to the authors mentioned and to Paul S. Martin, these southern neighbors are properly known as the Upper Little Colorado, even though they sit geographically south and below the Central Little Colorado Valley. The "Upper" in the title, I assume, comes from its association with the 8,000-foot-high Mogollon Rim that divides the more southern Tonto and Coconino national forests, and from the White Mountains almost due south of Holbrook. Martin describes three Upper Little Colorado sites that were excavated near the towns of Snowflake, St. Johns, and Springerville.[4] Gumerman and Skinner mention pottery types from an Upper Little Colorado–White Mountain area source.[5]

If we draw a western border line from Two Guns, Arizona, to a point south of the Kinishba Ruin near Cedar Creek, then add to this a curving southern border line that passes around Springerville and then loops north to St. Johns, and continue on northwest from there, enclosing the Petrified Forest National Park and turning slightly westward to connect with Indian Wells, we have circumscribed the Upper Little Colorado area. If we then put together this section and a Central Little Colorado section that includes the Hopi mesas, we will have established, within reason, the total Little Colorado Region, some 160 miles long and 67 miles wide. It would not include the Zuñi district or the Kin Tiel Ruin (Wide Ruin), but the latter is believed to antedate the greater Chaco Canyon cultural region and would properly be added to the Little Colorado Region in late Pueblo III or thereafter. My map should clarify the picture somewhat.

Compared to the prehistory of the major regions already considered, that of the Little Colorado Region, and particularly that of its lower section, is poorly known, although efforts are currently being made to remedy the situation. Particularly active in this regard is the Museum of Northern Arizona, at Flagstaff. Three factors have conspired to produce the lack of information. The first is that the region was peripheral to the major centers of cultural development and was once thought of as a cultural vacuum.[6] The second is related to the first, in that survey and excavation have been neglected because of its mi-

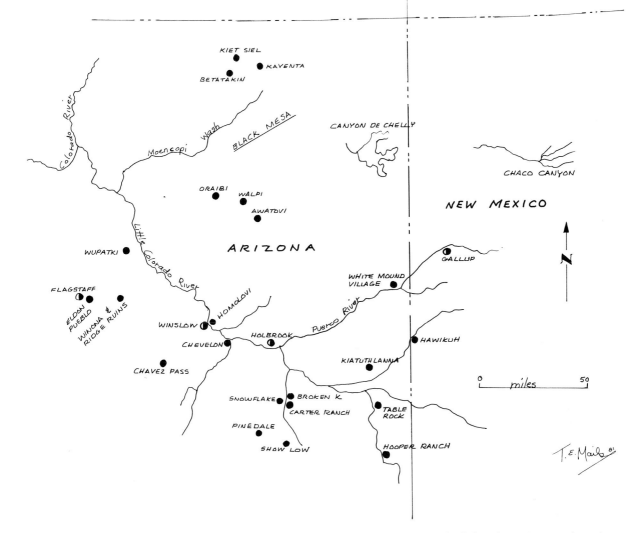

Map showing location of major ruins in the Little Colorado/Upper Little Colorado regions, and their geographical relationship to the Kayenta and Chaco regions.

nor nature. The third is that cultural complexity has had to be dealt with. From B.C. times until Pueblo II there was an intermingling of prehistoric subcultures whose effect is just now being explored and appreciated. For instance, it is certain that a mixture of Anasazi and Mogollon traditions was to some degree taking place as early as Pueblo III in both the Little Colorado and the Rio Grande regions. So profound was this amalgam that it resulted in a fascinating alloy that, together with environmental adaptations, eventually led to the cultural distinctiveness that marked both regions.

HAY HOLLOW

At the Hay Hollow Valley site east of Snowflake, the Field Columbian Museum of Chicago (now the Field Museum of Natural History) excavated five houses dated about 300 B.C.–A.D. 300. Excavators speculate that the original village plan consisted of two clusters of such dwellings together with their storage and cooking pits. Floor recesses were shallow, being only 4 to 10 inches (10–25 cm) below grade. A centrally located, basin-shaped recess in the floor appears to have served as a firepit, and the dwellings had a short tunnel entrance that was located on either the east or the south side.

White Mound Village. *Top,* lesser material culture objects: *a–f,* projectile points. *g,* bone and shell pendants and ornaments. *h–i,* black-on-white pottery. *Bottom,* plot plan and section of one of the house clusters of White Mound Village—pithouses fronting surface rooms. From Martin and Plog, 1973.

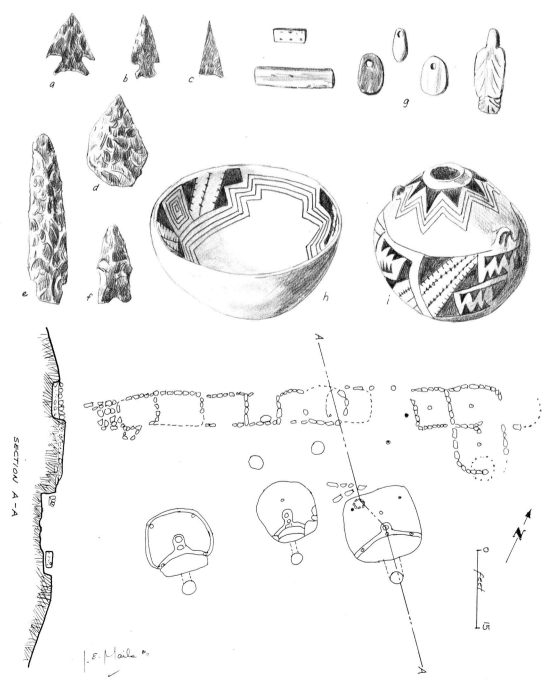

Later the museum excavated three comparable dwellings that were part of a large village situated on the alluvial flat bordering Hay Hollow Wash. At one time this village might have included as many as twenty dwellings. When an area survey had been completed, it appeared that the alluvial flat could actually have contained several such villages, which were occupied simultaneously. The three dwellings that were examined dated from about A.D. 500 to 700, and as such were placed in the Basketmaker III Period.

Lesser material culture objects recovered at the Hay Hollow site of 300 B.C.–A.D.300 included many troughed metates, basin metates, and one-hand manos. A report by Vorsila L. Bohrer on the paleoecology of the area states that the valley received higher effective soil moisture at A.D. 1, that a piñon-juniper woodland belt enclosed the valley, and that wild plants were used by the residents.[7] More than 250 storage and roasting pits were found at Hay Hollow. This indicated to Martin that the storage of surplus food and the roasting of corn, cholla, other food plants, and meat were an important part of the subsistence pattern, and that the site constituted a fairly permanent village.[8]

Other items recovered were pottery, choppers, bifacial blades, stone pounders, and hammerstones. A puzzling fact is that no bone tools were found.

The Basketmaker III village at Hay Hollow of A.D. 500–700 yielded bits of corncobs, Mormon tea, beeweed, mustard, beans, and amaranth, and the bones of deer, rabbits, gophers, and prairie dogs, all of which supplemented the vegetal diet.[9]

Using the Basketmaker villages from the Chaco Canyon Region as a comparative example, Martin reasons that the Upper Little Colorado Anasazi villages of the Basketmaker III and Pueblo I periods, A.D. 500–900, consisted also of clusters of round, oval, or rectangular pithouses accompanied by storage pits. As previously stated in the Chaco Canyon chapters, the dwellings of Shabik'eshchee Village at Chaco Canyon were grouped in a semicircle, and the pithouses of Kiatuthlanna were arranged in clusters of from three to six dwellings with accompanying storage structures. Martin and his associates add to these a third arrangement, a double row of contiguous rooms forming a crescent or arc that usually faced south or southeast and embraced pithouses or kivas. The rear row of storage rooms was built with crudely done masonry walls, and the front row of dwelling rooms had jacal walls. Upper Little Colorado villages included anywhere from three to fifty pithouses, and from four to a hundred or more surface rooms.[10]

WHITE MOUND VILLAGE

White Mound Village was excavated by Harold S. Gladwin in 1936.[11] This site overlooks the Puerco River at a point one-half mile west of White Mound, Arizona. It was occupied between A.D. 750 and 850, in the Pueblo I Period.

A total of six pithouses, three blocks of surface storage rooms, numerous storage and cooking pits, and various other features were excavated and examined. Pits ranged in depth from 2 feet 6 inches to 6 feet 7 inches (0.75–2 m) in depth and in size from 12 to 18 square yards (10–15 m²). Standard dwelling features were ventilators, firepits, deflectors, and low partitions that separated the entrance area from the rest of the room. Three of the pit dwellings had floor storage cists, and most roofs were supported by the traditional four-main-post-and-beam system. Storage rooms ranged in size from 2.4 to 7.3 square yards (2–6 m²) and had crude masonry walls. In some structures almost the entire floor was excavated to provide more storage space.

Villages of this period consisted of from one to twenty dwellings, four being the average number. Most sites were located on ridges and mesas, but some were situated in caves.

White Mound potsherds were mainly Lino Gray, with only two other types, White Mound Black-on-white and a polished red ware, being present in any noteworthy quantity. Other lesser material culture objects found were manos, metates, axes, mauls, hammerstones, projectile points, shell and turquoise ornaments, sandals, and baskets; bone items consisted of awls, scrapers, needles, and tubes. Bodies were buried in a flexed position, and mortuary offerings varied from nothing to small amounts of pottery and ornaments. Judging from these lesser finds and the architecture, life at White Mound Village was very much like that already described in the Basketmaker sections.

Metates of this period were not enclosed in bins. The upper end of the metate was propped up on a stone, so that the ground meal slid down into a container. Utility pottery was fashioned for cooking, and decorated ware was used for serving and storage. Mauls were employed for battering and pounding. Hammerstones were used to peck troughs into metates and to fracture large stones into smaller pieces that then were flaked, such as arrowpoints, knives, and scrapers. Stone axes were used to cut and shape wood. Stone bowls served various purposes, such as mortars and paint grinders. Knives and choppers were used for butchering. Drills were made to pierce wood, bone, shell, jet, and turquoise. It is assumed that the tubular stone pipes found on pithouse floors were used in ceremonies. Bone tools included awls, needles, and fleshers for work on baskets, sandals, mats, robes, and hides.

Vast storage and roasting pits such as those already described at Kiatuthlanna and Whitewater were in common use. Depths ranged from 1 foot 6 inches to 6 feet (0.45–1.8 m), and diameters from 3 to 6 feet (0.9–1.8 m). Either a conical roof of poles, brush, and mud, or a large stone slab was used as a cover for the pit to keep its contents dry. Some pits had stone slab-lined walls and floors.

In sum, between A.D. 500 and 900, Anasazi life in the Little Colorado Region consisted of hunting; planting; harvesting; grinding; cooking; manufacturing tools, baskets, pottery, jewelry, clothing, and ritual items; building homes and storage places. The inhabitants performed personal and community rituals, played games, carried out the special activities of family life, and coped with nature and with one another. Life centered in constant learning and adaptation, in particular toward a harmonious accommodation with the whole of creation. The longevity of the Anasazi suggests they managed to do this quite well.

The Anasazi villages of the Pueblo II Period, A.D. 900–1100, became increasingly larger than the villages of Pueblo I. Buildings were often multistoried and ranged in scope from twenty to two hundred rooms. The pithouses in some of the villages were separated from the pueblo building block itself, and in others were enclosed within the pueblo block.[12]

Manos and metates were abundant in Pueblo II, indicating an increasing reliance upon agriculture. Mealing bins came into existence, with as many as four being placed side by side in a single room or in a courtyard. In such instances, the texture of the stones ranged from coarse to fine. Investigations have also revealed that individual metates with special surfaces, such as sandstone or volcanic rock, were used for grinding different kinds of foods—one for corn, another for cactus, and a third for piñon nuts.[13] The arrangement of mealing bins in pairs, in rows, or facing one another makes it probable that several women made the work less difficult by turning it into a social occasion. This became especially obvious when excavators discovered that late in the period grinding rooms were built in centrally located places.

Concerning cloth manufacture, Keith M. Anderson speaks of Kayenta weaving tools that suggest the true loom was present in Pueblo II, together with loom holes in kiva floors for tying down the bottom of the loom. His finds included raw cotton, spindle whorls, cotton plants from which cotton was carded by wooden combs, and loom parts such as bent-stick floor anchors, warp rods, roller bars, battens, shuttles, and shed and heddle rods. It is assumed that similar looms and attachments were in use in all parts of the Little Colorado Region.

During the years A.D. 700–1000 the Anasazi were dependent to some degree upon corn, beans, and squash, but Indian rice grass, piñon nuts, prickly pear cactus, and beeweed were also consumed, along with deer, rabbit, mountain sheep, and antelope. Storage facilities reveal that variations between wet and dry years caused the residents to plan ahead, and led to attempts to forecast weather cycles. Yet experience with the land was perhaps their best ally. It taught them where rain- and groundwater were more likely to be found, and how best to make use of the land as a whole. It has been seen that water control devices were in broad use at Chaco Canyon and Mesa Verde, and we can assume that some such methods were in use at Little Colorado.

KINISHBA

Kinishba pueblo, dated A.D. 1160 to anywhere from 1350 to 1400, was excavated as a joint project by the Arizona State Museum and the University of Arizona, both of Tucson, between 1931 and 1939. Once the pueblo itself and the pithouse and small house ruins near it were surveyed, along with those that partially underlie the pueblo, it was determined that the village site had been occupied from A.D. 900 to 1400.[14]

As might be expected, then, Kinishba was one of the largest pueblo sites, if not the largest, in the Upper Salt River area. Throughout its existence, the pueblo undoubtedly continued to increase in size, reaching its peak about A.D. 1350.

The group of ruins comprising Kinishba is situated in a broad valley a few miles southeast of Cedar Creek on the Fort Apache Indian Reservation, and just north of Highway 73. Its name is Apache and means "Brown House," being derived from the color of the stone walls. The forested Mogollon Rim lies only twenty miles to the north of Kinishba, and the pueblo actually occupies a peripheral position between the Mogollon and Upper Little Colorado

Kinishba. *a–b*, stone axes. *c–f*, arrow shaft smoothers. *g*, typical masonry work in wall construction. *h*, Tonto Polychrome bowl. *i*, Fourmile Polychrome bowl. From Baldwin, 1939.

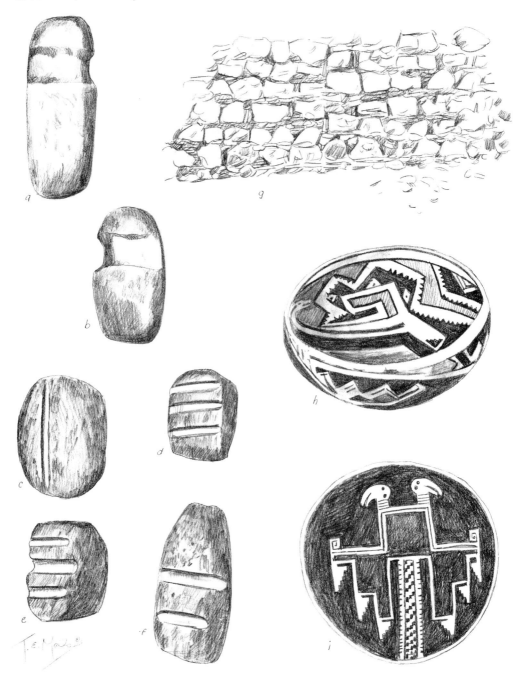

regions. One would expect under these circumstances to find a blending of cultures.

This proved to be the case. Gordon C. Baldwin, who directed some of the excavation work, concludes that Kinishba is a long-occupied site about midway between the Anasazi, Hohokam, and Mogollon areas. "Yet it is basically, fundamentally, and essentially a typical Anasazi pueblo." There undoubtedly was Mogollon influence in the earlier periods, and Hohokam influence at that time also, but certainly the later development, at least that from about A.D. 1000 to 1400, was "dominantly Anasazi." All the characteristic pueblo traits were in evidence: stone masonry, ceremonial rooms, and corrugated and black-on-white pottery.[15] The pueblo seems to conform quite closely to the pattern of those located to the north of the Mogollon Rim, such as Show Low, Pinedale, and Fourmile.

Kinishba consisted of eight structures, the two largest of which were situated on opposite sides of a wide, deep wash. Since the wash broadened after abandonment to the point where some of the rooms bordering it were carried away, it is impossible to determine whether the two largest groups ever formed a single pueblo.

The large group on the eastern side of the wash was compact and rectangular. Its length was 336 feet (102 m), and the maximum width of the portion remaining was 113 feet (34 m). The plan consisted of a rectangular block of rooms with plazas toward the northern and southern ends, and there were entrances in the western and southern walls.

The large group on the western side of the wash followed a more random plan. Its length was 443 feet (134 m), and its maximum width was 159 feet (48 m). Indications were that it once boasted more than two hundred ground-floor rooms.

The six smaller groups clustered closely about the two larger groups: three on one side of the wash and three on the other. No excavation of these groups was done, but from surface indications Baldwin assumes that all eight groups were occupied contemporaneously. A short distance away, however, were several small house groups that were occupied just before the time the main pueblo groups were built.

While no second-story rooms remained in place at the time of excavation, there was evidence that practically the entire pueblo had been at least two stories in height. Most of the rooms uncovered by excavators were large, averaging 10 by 14 feet (3 × 4.2 m), and they featured rectangular slab or clay-fired firepits, mealing bins, and other household artifacts. Excavators decided they were dwelling rooms. Surprisingly enough, only a few small rooms seem to have been used for storage.[16]

Three types of masonry were present: rubble, with rocks of various sizes laid in abundant mortar; ashlar, or coursed masonry, with large rock courses alternating with thin layers of shale and sandstone; and cyclopean, with rocks of different sizes laid in uneven courses. All three types occurred in all sections of the pueblo groups, and sometimes even in the walls of the same room. The only regularity in construction was in outside walls exposed to the weather, where large regular blocks of stone in even courses formed the only type of masonry.[17] No roofs were found in place, but there was evidence that they consisted of main beams topped by smaller poles laid at right angles, a layer of brush or split logs, and a 3-to-4-inch (7.5–10 cm) layer of clay on top. Room floors were normally finished off with hard-packed clay. Entrance to rooms was by means of a roof hatchway and a ladder. As at Chaco Canyon, there were no exterior doorways other than those leading to the plazas.

True kivas, such as the circular subterranean structures common to the San Juan area, were not found at Kinishba. But a number of rectangular rooms seemed to contain some of the features of kivas.

One of these rooms was located in the north plaza. It was subterranean, its floor being 5 feet 6 inches (1.7 m) below grade. It measured 10 by 11 feet (3 × 3.3 m), with a small chamber along the south end 2 feet 9 inches (83.5 cm) wide. The chamber floor was 2 feet 4 inches (71 cm) higher than the main floor. It was set off by a wall, with a doorway in the center that was reached by a single step. The room walls were both dirt and masonry, and they were plastered. Support posts carried the roof beams. A small rectangular firepit was near the center of the room, and a shallow depression that may have held the butts of ladder poles was just north of the pit. A round, flat stone was imbedded in the floor next to the south wall. The few artifacts found in the room were largely ceremonial. From its general conformation, Baldwin thinks the room may well have represented a prototype of the Old Hopi kiva.[18]

A second ceremonial room was of a different type. It fronted the main plaza on the western side and measured 12 feet 11 inches (3.9 m) by 14 feet 10 inches (4.5 m). In the center was a square firepit, and east of the pit was a stone slab deflector. In the east wall was a ventilator shaft. Along the south wall was a banquette or bench of rocks and clay, and plastered. It was 1 foot 10 inches (55 cm) high and 12 inches (30 cm) thick.

Lesser material culture objects found consisted in the main of items made from imperishable material only, and the report is accordingly incomplete.

Subsistence consisted of a small flint (hard-surface) type of corn, at least two types of beans, and walnuts, chokecherries, and other wild products. Many remains of animal and bird bones in the rooms and trash heaps show the inhabitants relied heavily upon hunting for their food.

Kinishba's ceramic industry was highly developed, with excellent forms typical of the Great Pueblo Period. Almost all the ware was manufactured by the coiled process. There were two classes: plain and decorated. The plain consisted of corrugated vessels, either red or grayish black, and of plain red or reddish brown types, some having a burnished black interior. The decorated class included black-on-white; black-on-red; Pinto, Gila, and Tonto polychromes; St. Johns, Pinedale, and Fourmile polychromes; Jeddito Black-on-yellow; and several other types represented mainly by sherds.[19]

Besides the Kinishba-made types, a number of trade wares were found, showing that Kinishba had trade connections with several other areas. These included Jeddito Black-on-yellow, the Old Hopi ware from the north, many examples of the Hawikuh or Old Zuñi series, green glaze on white, black-and-green glaze on white, black outlined either with purple-on-white or black-and-red-on-white, and a few red-on-buff sherds from the Hohokam area. Baldwin thinks Kinishba was the center for a number of ceramic developments in the Upper Salt and Little Colorado area.

Clay objects found included scrapers, round flat disks, and prayer-stick bases. Stone implements consisted of manos, metates, mortars, bowls, rubbing and polishing stones, axes, hammers, arrow-shaft smoothers, hoes, jar covers, paint palettes, arrow and dart (or spear) points, knives, scrapers, and drills. Bone and horn implements included awls, needles, daggers, fleshing tools, punches, chisels, arrow straighteners, and whistles.

Ornaments were numerous. Stone was the chief material, but shell was also extensively employed. Beads, pendants, and rings were abundant, but bracelets were not common. One peculiarly shaped object, much like the lip plugs of Mesoamerica, was found. It was fashioned from green soapstone and had a small hole drilled through the plug part.[20]

Only a few textile specimens were discovered, but these included baskets, matting, and cloth. The basket and matting fragments were yucca, and the cloth was cotton done in several different weaves.[21]

Ceremonial objects included painted stones, painted deer bones, quartz crystals, perforated bear claws, worked stone items, and a single tubular greenstone pipe four inches in length.

Most burials of the Kinishba people were made, in accordance with regular Anasazi custom, in the trash mounds surrounding the pueblo. Inhumation was almost the only form practiced, but three cremations were unearthed. Of seventy-six burials, only thirteen were flexed; the body ordinarily lay on its back. The head was commonly pointed to the east, with the face turned up. Mortuary offerings of pottery were found in slightly more than half of the graves, although ornaments frequently accompanied the remains of children. The vast majority of offerings were placed near the head or close to the body on either side. The crania were brachycephalic (short or broad), with marked occipital deformation.

Two of the cremations were of the pit type characteristic of the Hohokam who lived in the Gila Basin until the end of the Sedentary Period, about A.D. 1100. The third cremation resembled more closely those of the Classic Hohokam, from A.D. 1100 on, where the calcined bones were placed in a small jar. A number of burned bones had been scattered over the surface of the ground, probably by pothunters, and these were thought to represent other cremations.

Just why Kinishba pueblo was abandoned can only be conjectured. Baldwin's view is that it may have been due to pressure from incoming nomadic tribes, such as the Apache. This could have driven the Kinishba and other regional inhabitants north into the Hopi and Zuñi areas. The more logical explanation, however, is that the gradual drying up of the main spring that furnished their water ultimately forced the migration.

SHOW LOW

The Show Low Ruin (A.D. 900–1375+) holds a special place in the hearts of archaeologists, since it provided the charred timbers that allowed Dr. Andrew E. Douglass to link his first prehistoric and historic chronologies into a single time span that reached from A.D. 700 to 1380.

In 1929 Emil W. Haury, under the auspices of the U.S. National Museum, was placed in charge of expeditions to the Show Low and Pinedale ruins, and his findings are reported in the Smithsonian Miscellaneous Collections, Volume 82, Number 11 (1931), entitled *Recently Dated Pueblo Ruins in Arizona.*

Show Low Ruin is located about fifty-five miles south of Holbrook, in Show Low, Arizona. It is situated on a low elevation on the edge of a narrow valley formed by Show Low Creek. The beautiful countryside is thickly wooded with western yellow pine and several species of juniper and oak. Adolph F. Bandelier examined it in April 1883, and Walter Hough in July 1901. Edson Whipple, who purchased the land on which most of the pueblo stood, removed much of the masonry and used it for his own building purposes. He also removed a number of artifacts that fortunately were acquired by Gila Pueblo, Globe, Arizona. What still remained indicated that Show Low pueblo had an overall "roughly-rectangular" shape, its longest axis running north–south. Several rows of single-story rooms occupied the western side, from which three short projections extended eastward to form an E within the rectangle. The intervening spaces were used as plazas, of which the southernmost still had in 1929 a large depression in its middle. Part of the northeast section of the pueblo was abandoned and covered with debris while dwellings on the western side were still occupied. Sometime subsequent to the abandonment, the remaining part of the pueblo was destroyed by fire. Observers think such wholesale burning was probably the work of marauders, since domestic utensils and stores of corn found in nearly every room indicate that the pueblo was hastily evacuated.

The masonry was of various types, and excavated rooms indicate at least two, and perhaps three, successive levels of occupation: a tree-ring date of A.D. 1204 has been assigned to the first, and A.D. 1375 to the later. The earliest masonry walls consisted of large, carefully selected stones that were chinked, and they were well constructed. The later walls were poorly built of random-sized stones. An even older occupation may be indicated by walls in the northeast part of the pueblo. These were formed by a basal row of upright slabs topped by small stones placed in rude, horizontal courses—a type already seen at Badger House Community at Mesa Verde and in buildings of the westernmost Mesa Verde section. In all types of masonry, the walls averaged 12 inches (30 cm) in thickness and were laid up with an abundance of clay mortar.

Dwelling rooms averaged 11 by 12 feet (3.3 × 3.6 m), the largest room being 11 by 17 feet (3.3 × 5.2 m). Floors were finished with hard-packed clay and broken only by a square, slab-lined firepit. Roofs consisted of supporting beams topped by reeds or split logs and a final layer of clay. Entry was through the roof. No kivas were discovered at Show Low, but archaeologists who were there in 1929 and did partial excavation felt that kivas might one day be found in other parts of the pueblo.

There was an abundance of shelled corn stored in ollas and ear corn piled row upon row, as is the custom with modern Pueblos, indicating that maize played an important role in the subsistence pattern of the Upper Little Colorado Anasazi. Beans, berries, and walnuts showed that foodstuffs in general paralleled those of Kinishba. Bones of deer, rabbit, turkey, and dog were also found in the rooms and trash mounds.

Lesser material culture objects found at Show Low were similar to those marking the Pueblo IV Period in the overall Little Colorado Region. Items of special interest included a sandstone loom block like those used in present-day Hopi villages, and a potter's kneading slab not unlike those used by present-day Zuñi.

Ceramic styles representative of Hopi, Zuñi, and Gila culture areas were found at Show Low, proving that considerable mixing of local and foreign types had taken place. Ceramics associated with the lower level of occupancy included black-on-white, black-on-red, an orange-red ware decorated in both black and white paint, corrugated, and a small amount of intrusive material. The black-on-white sherds fall roughly into two groups, the first and earliest showing a definite Chaco Canyon affinity with a mean date of A.D. 1200, and the second replacing the Chaco type with pottery having an Upper Gila influence.[22] By A.D. 1375 Show Low Black-on-white ware was no longer in vogue, and Fourmile Polychrome predominated. Its glaze-paint sometimes lacked luster and was vitreous and gritty.[23]

PINEDALE

Pinedale Ruin is situated in Navajo County, Arizona, about one-half mile southeast of Pinedale and sixteen miles west of the Show Low Ruin. It is dated at A.D. 1132–1330.

The pueblo consisted of two building units. One was a large rectangular court surrounded by single rows of one-story rooms. The other was a more compact structure, its rooms encircling a central rectangular plaza. The east, west, and south rooms of the second unit were two stories in height, and they terraced away from the plaza, while the north end of the plaza was either open or only partly closed by single-storied rooms. Extending eastward for approximately one hundred feet from the northeast corner of the main pueblo was a wing of contiguous rooms several rows in width. Trash heaps were found on the east and west sides of the main portion and along the north side of the east wing. As in the case of Show Low, many of the wall stones had been removed by settlers, and the ever-present pothunters had worked the ruin to good effect.

Pinedale's masonry was, on the average, far better than that of Show Low.

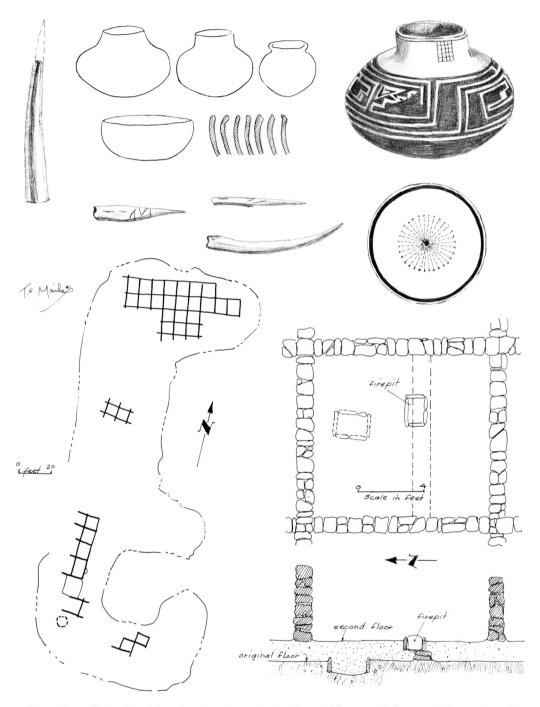

Show Low Ruin. *Top left and center,* bone tools. *Top middle,* vessel forms of Fourmile poly-chrome. *Top right,* Fourmile Polychrome olla dating from ca. A.D. 1375. *Center right,* Design on Fourmile Polychrome bowl interior. *Bottom left,* plot plan of ruin. *Bottom right,* floor plan and section of house. From Haury and Hargrave, 1931.

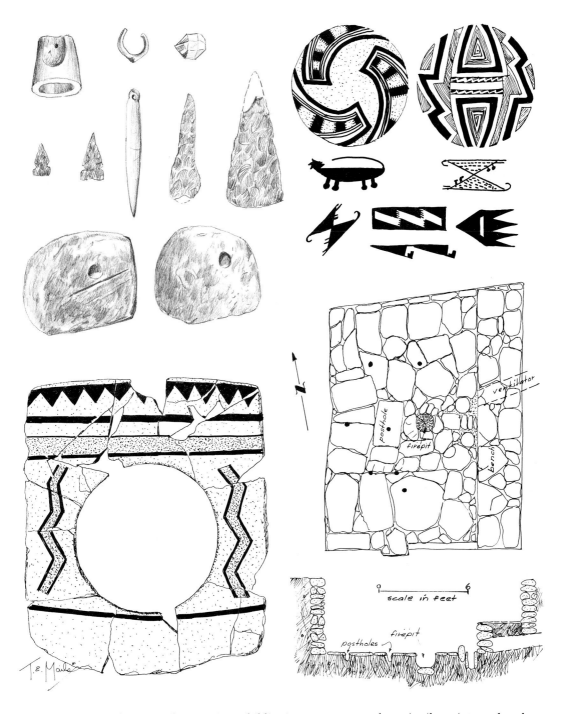

Pinedale. *Top left*, stone objects: pipe, child's ring, quartz crystal, projectile points and awl with eyehole, drill point. *Top right*, Pinedale Polychrome bowl decoration and Black-on-white interior and exterior bowl decorations. *Center left*, two loom blocks found in a kiva. *Bottom left*, painted stone altar slab. *Bottom right*, floor plan and section of kiva.

In spite of the fact that much of the structure was two stories in height, the walls were seldom more than a foot thick. Stones were carefully dressed, they were chinked with thin spalls, and the rooms were quite large.

The most interesting structure uncovered at Pinedale was an almost rectangular surface kiva on the southwest corner of the plaza. Its north and south walls measured 13 feet 3 inches (4 m) in length, the west wall was 15 feet 5 inches (4.7 m), and the east wall was 17 feet 3 inches (5.3 m). The kiva masonry was inferior to that of the dwelling rooms. There was no coursing, and ample mortar was employed. A stone-faced platform about 3 feet (90 cm) wide and 2 feet (60 cm) high ran the full course of the east wall. It is similar to the Hopi platform in style, but the Hopi version typically runs across the shorter dimension of the south or southeast end of the kiva. The bench could originally have contained sand to be used in the groundwork for sand paintings, as was suggested by the finding of two sand-filled ollas under a kiva floor at Kokopnyama.[24] The kiva bench and walls were plastered with at least eleven coats of adobe.

The kiva floor was recessed about 4 inches (10 cm) below grade and was completely paved with flagstones of varying sizes. Cracks between the stones were filled with clay. Other kiva features included a small shelf on the south wall, a central circular firepit, a ventilator with a wall opening in the front of the platform, a small subfloor depository, and six small holes pecked in the floor stones that may have served as loom anchors. No true sipapu was found. The chamber roof seemingly was flat, and built like those of the dwelling rooms. Tree-ring dating assigned a construction time to the kiva of between A.D. 1293 and 1330, and so its use occurred in the Pueblo IV Period.[25]

Stone implements largely duplicated those found at Show Low. Of special interest was a painted stone slab whose shattered parts were found in an abandoned room. Restored, it measured 16 by 19 inches (40 × 48 cm) and was ¾ inch (2 cm) thick. Its colors were white, yellow, and black, and there was a circular hole 10 inches (25 cm) in diameter in the middle. Haury and Hargrave thought it safe to say the slab formed part of an altar decoration or was otherwise used in religious rites. Painted slabs are still used by the Hopi in the construction of the Antelope altar in the Snake Ceremony. Relatively few painted slabs of this nature have been recovered, and nearly all were found in ruins in the Silver Creek drainage or its environs. Fewkes unearthed an excellent specimen of rectangular form in a grave at the Chevelon Ruin. Whipple discovered four well-made slabs at Show Low. Fewkes also cites the presence of one in a grave at Sikyatki Ruin in the Jeddito Valley.[26]

The period of ceramic productivity at Pinedale was sandwiched between the two levels found at Show Low. Dating procedures signified that an interval of seventy-five years had occurred between the earliest Show Low level and the major Pinedale occupation, and then a difference of more than seventy-five years between Pinedale's peak and the final Show Low occupation. Applied to the pottery sequence, the dates would be A.D. 1204 for Show Low, A.D. 1290 for Pinedale, and A.D. 1375 for late Show Low. Pinedale pottery as a whole is assigned to the late thirteenth and early fourteenth centuries, and it is classified into black-on-white, black-on-red, black-and-white-on-red, plain, corrugated, and intrusive.[27] Black-on-white was abundant, with a thin black glaze-paint commonly being used. Pinedale Polychrome was even more plentiful, the black paint in this instance consisting of a lead glaze that seldom merged into the other colors.[28]

THODE, CARTER, BROKEN K, AND HOOPER

In the 1950s and 1960s Paul S. Martin, in association with other specialists, excavated a number of pueblos in the Upper Little Colorado section, all of which were in the vicinity of Springerville, Snowflake, Show Low, and St. Johns.[29]

Perhaps the earliest of these, with a mean date of A.D. 1100, was the Pueblo II and III Thode Site, on Mineral Creek near Highway 60, about twenty miles west of Springerville. Martin thought it could represent a transition phase between pithouses and surface pueblos. It consisted of eleven small irregularly shaped rooms with slightly recessed floors built close enough to one another to be virtually contiguous. All were one-story, and the masonry was crudely done. Thode's population is estimated at from twenty to twenty-five persons.

The earliest positive date is assigned to the Carter Ranch Site. This was a forty-room, two-story pueblo, with two clan-sized kivas and a Great Kiva, that flourished in Pueblo II and III from about A.D. 900 to 1200. It lies nine miles east of Snowflake, and overlooks Hay Hollow Wash, a tributary of the Little Colorado River. The rooms enclosed a plaza that contained a medium-sized kiva, a small rectangular kiva with a platform on its east side, various cooking pits, and a large storage pit 6 feet (1.8 m) deep and 6 feet (1.8 m) in diameter at floor level. The storage pit had once been covered by a stone slab. The circular Great Kiva was located about 40 feet northwest of the pueblo. It was 55 feet (16.7 m) in diameter and had five masonry pillars, a firepit, and a ramp entryway on the east side. Thirty burials were discovered in a plot east of the eastern boundary wall, attended by pottery mortuary offerings. Of particular interest was the fact that males of status were buried in the central part of the plot. The estimated population for the pueblo is two hundred.

Broken K Pueblo, in Hay Hollow Valley on the James Carter Ranch, is nine miles east of Snowflake and about five miles north of the Carter Ranch Site. Pueblo III in vintage, it contained about ninety one-story rooms enclosing a square plaza. Within the house block were two clan-sized kivas whose floors were paved with slabs. The plaza contained two larger kivas and several cooking pits. By analysis, James Hill concluded that the pueblo was once inhabited by five matrilineal subgroups that fell into two larger units or clans. Carbon 14 and tree-ring dating revealed that Broken K Pueblo functioned from about A.D. 1150 to 1280. The population estimate is from 150 to 200. A mealing room at

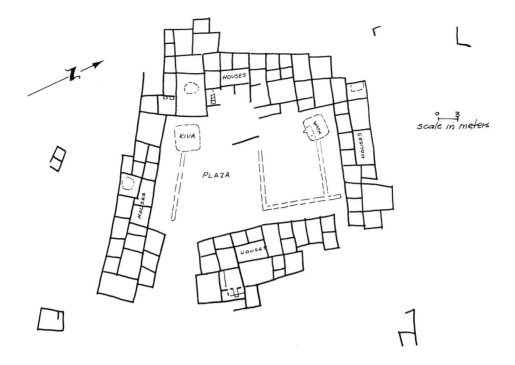

Plot plan of Broken K Pueblo—doorways omitted. Redrawn from Martin and Plog, 1973.

the pueblo contained at one of its ends four slab compartments, each with its own metate. At the lower end of each bin was a hollowed stone that served as a receptacle to collect the ground meal. In the middle of the room was a rectangular firepit, and next to it a slab-lined ashpit.

Hooper Ranch Pueblo was given a mean date of A.D. 1230. It is east of Rim Valley Pueblo and on the east bank of the Little Colorado River. Part of this two-story pueblo may have been washed away by floodwaters, but its original size is estimated at sixty rooms, and its population at about 250. It had three kivas: one small and one medium-sized kiva and a Great Kiva, all of which were rectangular. The small kiva had a flagstone floor, a bench on the west side, and a ventilator. Adjoining it on the south side was the medium-sized kiva, which had a dirt floor, central firepit, floor vault, ventilator, and a bench on its south side. Adjacent to the second kiva was the Great Kiva, measuring 47 by 50 feet (14.3 × 15 m). On its east side was a ramp entryway 7 feet (2.1 m) wide and 7 feet (2.1 m) long. Between the ramp and the firepit was an enormous deflector slab, 3 feet (90 cm) high and 7 feet (2.1 m) long. Benches lined all four walls. Vaults were located on the north and south, in both halves of the room. In the south half was a floor crypt 15 inches (38 cm) long by 14 inches (35.5 cm) wide and 11 inches (27.5 cm) deep. It was roofed with a ring slab that was capped with a solid slab. Within the crypt were a female effigy, 8¾ inches (22 cm) high, painted with yellow, blue, red, and black stripes, and a miniature pottery jar that held black and white stone beads. The effigy is of a type rarely found and is considered to be a cult deity rather than a proto-Katcina.[30] Some aspects of the Hooper Ranch Pueblo indicated a relationship with the Zuñi pueblos about sixty miles northeast.

During the Pueblo III Period, and specifically after A.D. 1200, the walls of the Little Colorado surface pueblos were built better and straighter. Whenever rooms were added, the new walls were aligned with the older ones, and the room corners were squared. Rooms were arranged in a straight line, an L shape, or a semicircle. Wing walls were sometimes added to enclose a court or plaza, or a row of rooms accomplished this purpose.[31]

Martin provides some revealing insights concerning the uses made by the Anasazi of their villages. He says that in one of several "firsts," Freeman and Brown ran for him a statistical analysis of the pottery on a Univac computer and demonstrated, first, that four groups of pottery may have been used for functionally diverse purposes; and second, that there were four room types, each of which was devoted to a different cultural activity.[32] The Anasazi of A.D. 950–1200 were already following an organized life pattern. Additional computations revealed that, prior to A.D. 1050, the number of activity areas in dwellings declined, while those in kivas increased threefold.[33] Quite plainly, the importance of the village religious center was on the upswing.

TABLE ROCK

Table Rock Pueblo (Pueblo IV—A.D. 1350) was excavated by Martin and company in 1958. The site is two miles east of St. Johns and on the east bank of the Little Colorado River. It consisted of between sixty and one hundred one-story rooms and at least two rectangular kivas. The buildings were separated into two sections, each of which was three rooms wide; the sections were parallel. Most of the southernmost-section rooms had firepits and may have been the living quarters. The average room size was 7 feet 6 inches by 9 feet (2.25 × 2.7 m). One kiva measured 12 by 13 feet (3.6 × 3.9 m). It was incorporated into a house row and was floored with fitted slabs. It had an altar on the south side, a rectangular firepit and an ashpit, and loom postholes in the floor east of the firepit. The other kiva was situated below the mesa, and it was poorly constructed. The architecture and pottery of Table Rock Pueblo bore a pronounced relationship to that of the Hopi and the Zuñi. Its mean date was A.D. 1350, and its population was between 100 and 125.[34]

CHAVEZ PASS

The last site to be mentioned in association with the Upper Little Colorado section is Chavez Pass, about thirty miles southwest of Winslow and about twenty miles southeast of Mormon Lake. It consisted of a large mesa-top pueblo built of lava rock; two dwelling groups were arranged around two courts and together enclosed as many as two hundred rooms. Martin gives it a mean date of A.D. 1375.[35]

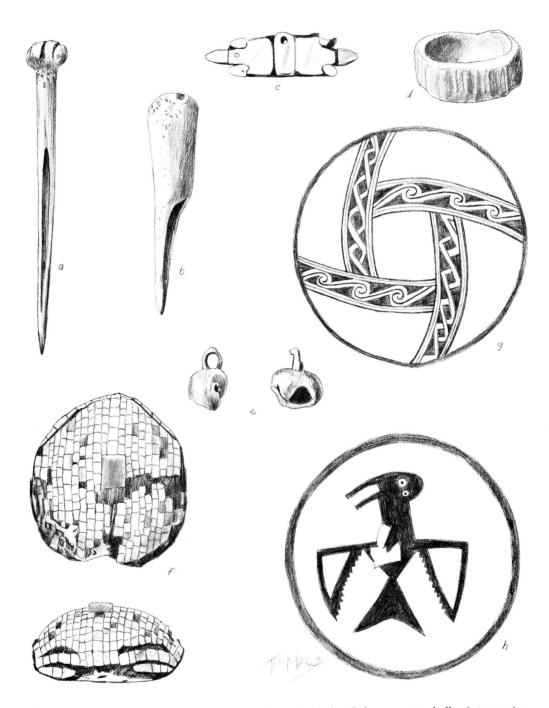

Chavez Pass. *a–b*, bone awls. *c*, mosaic pendant. *d*, kaolin disk. *e*, copper bells. *f*, turquoise mosaic frog. *g*, geometrical decorated bowl interior. *h*, mythic bird on bowl interior. From Fewkes, 1896a.

THE CENTRAL LITTLE COLORADO SECTION

The essentially barren terrain in the Central Little Colorado section is quite similar to that of Chaco Canyon. Flat areas abound. Elevations above sea level range from 4,500 feet on the Little Colorado River to 6,500 feet on some of the higher buttes. Precipitation averages eight inches a year, and much of it is quickly lost as runoff. It contrasts sharply with the Upper Little Colorado section, which is mountainous, tree-covered, and far wetter. Show Low, Pinetop, and the Fort Apache Indian Reservation have become the centers of one of the finest recreation areas in Arizona, and people from all over the world are familiar with its beauty through the colorful pages of *Arizona Highways* magazine.

The earliest archaeological work in the central section was done by Fewkes, who was there several times between 1896 and 1904. Walter Hough was in the central section in 1901 as part of the Museum-Gates Expedition, but he concentrated mainly upon exhuming burials associated with large Pueblo IV sites.[36] Harold S. Colton made some sporadic site surveys in 1939 and added what he learned to the reports of Fewkes and Hough to make his own report on the area.[37]

Nothing further happened until a few limited excavations were carried out in the late 1940s and early 1950s. In the early 1960s, William Wasley performed salvage archaeology along the proposed route of Highway 66 in eastern Arizona, and at that time he confirmed that an Anasazi-Mogollon blending had taken place in the Puerco and Little Colorado valleys.

In 1949 Fred Wendorf, under the auspices of the Museum of Northern Arizona, had excavated a pithouse village on the Flat Top site, which is located on a high mesa at the southern end of the Petrified Forest National Park. Thought to be Mogollon, the dwellings were slab-lined, with an entrance oriented toward the northeast. The pottery proved to be a Mogollon brown ware, Adamana Brown, and, taken together with other evidence, it suggests that until the middle of Pueblo II the Lower Little Colorado section was mainly Mogollon territory.

Then in 1966 the Museum of Northern Arizona performed two series of excavations, one in the southwestern Hopi Buttes locality and the other several miles east of Holbrook. Eleven sites were dug in all, and in the Hopi Buttes locality a survey recorded 211 sites in a twenty-five-square-mile area. Also in 1966, two pre-ceramic, pre–A.D. 500 pithouses were excavated near Dilkon. These established the first positive Basketmaker II presence in Central Little Colorado.

The Hopi Buttes survey recorded three Basketmaker III sites, only one of which was excavated. Most of the pottery was Lino Black-on-gray, revealing a Kayenta influence, and it dated the sites somewhere between A.D. 600 and 800. The three Basketmaker dwellings were circular surface rooms that appear to have had the familiar four-main-post-and-beam support system, covered with brush and earth. Floors were finished with a coating of clay and had central clay-lined firepits. In addition to the dwellings, two roasting pits and a slab-lined storage pit were unearthed.

PUEBLO I

A single Pueblo I site consisting of three pithouses was excavated at Hopi Buttes, along with two Pueblo I dwellings at other locations. Kana-a Black-on-white pottery places the Buttes site within the Kayenta range of cultural influence and dates it in the A.D. 800–950 period.

The three pithouses differed enough from one another to suggest to Gumerman and Skinner a Mogollon and Anasazi relationship. The first pithouse was circular, with an eastward-oriented ramp entryway of Mogollon vintage. The second pithouse was also circular, but had the typical Anasazi bench, ventilator, and partitioned floor. The third pithouse was more rectangular, with a northward-oriented alcove entry, and it lacked the typical roof-support pattern.

Two other pithouses of the Pueblo I Period were excavated in the Hopi Buttes area. These were circular and had northeast-oriented ventilator shafts, partitioned floors, and the four-post roof-support system. One had a dual ventilator shaft similar to those of the early Kayenta pithouses. David A. Breternitz excavated in 1956 and 1957 a Pueblo I site near Winslow. Its brownware, black-on-white pottery, and a Kana-a Black-on-white containing the ashes of a cremation emphasize once again the amalgam of Mogollon and Anasazi during the Pueblo I Period.

Archaeologists feel that the Pueblo I Period in the Central Little Colorado section was strongly influenced by the Kayenta Region. Its architecture and pottery were Kayenta in style. Gumerman and Skinner think the two regions formed "a uniform subculture" during Basketmaker III, Pueblo I, and early Pueblo II. Little Colorado variations from the Kayenta culture are explained "by the necessary adaptation to the more arid environment and to the high degree of interaction with the Mogollon people to the south."[38]

PUEBLO II

The Pueblo II Period in the Central Little Colorado section spans the years A.D. 900–1100, but it is best understood when it is divided into two phases. During the first phase, from A.D. 900 to 1075, it continued to be strongly marked by Kayenta influence. The second phase opened in A.D. 1075 with the introduction of Holbrook Black-on-white pottery. This was the beginning of the Winslow branch, which marked a time of movement away from Kayenta influence.

Five unexcavated sites at Hopi Buttes represent the early part of Pueblo II. All the painted pottery is Black Mesa Black-on-white. A single site excavated near Holbrook represents the Winslow branch. This was an L-shaped five-room pueblo with adobe walls. A short distance to the east was a D-shaped pithouse, with a firepit, ventilator, and a four-post roof-support system. Pottery included Little Colorado and Tusayan White and Gray ware, Holbrook Black-on-white, and Sosi Black-on-white. The Little Colorado ceramic tradition had been established, but the pottery characteristics were still Kayenta Anasazi. Ultimately, Little Colorado wares unique to the area would develop out of Kayenta styles.

The reason for the change is not certain, but a dramatic increase in sites at Holbrook in early Pueblo II indicates that considerable population growth was taking place. Whether this growth was due to an influx of new people or to a shift of Little Colorado residents is not known. While it is possible that the Central Little Colorado inhabitants had become in time a distinct sociocultural group, they continued to maintain a high level of interaction with Anasazi to the north and Mogollon to the south.[39] As has been seen in earlier chapters, the latter part of the Pueblo II Period was for the Anasazi a time of unrest and a beginning of movement. Departures were already taking place from Aztec and the Virgin regions to the north, and from Chaco Canyon to the west. Presumably the Little Colorado and Rio Grande regions began to receive some of these migrants, along with their cultural influences.

Holbrook Phase sites were relatively small. They consisted of two or three pithouses and a surface storage room that was rectangular and crudely built. It had a foundation of basalt or sandstone slabs that probably carried mud or jacal upper walls. The pithouse entrances were ramped, the pits were rectangular, and a four-post roof-support system was employed. Interior details included circular firepits and various other pits used for pot rests and storage. No kivas were found, but that may be because of the limited number of Pueblo II excavations carried out.

PUEBLO III

Pueblo III at Central Little Colorado dates from A.D. 1100 to 1250 and is known as the McDonald Phase. Representative of the pottery is Holbrook Black-on-white, Walnut Black-on-white, Flagstaff Black-on-white, and Padre Black-on-white. A Leupp Black-on-white was manufactured between A.D. 1200 and 1300. Walnut and Padre black-on-whites are thought to be the result of Upper Little Colorado influence, particularly that of the White Mountain area south of present-day Show Low.

In the Hopi Buttes survey mentioned earlier, sixty sites were assigned to the early part of the McDonald Phase and eighty-one to the late part. This indicates another increase in area population after A.D. 1175. Pueblo III sites in the Central Little Colorado section remained small, although somewhat larger than those of Pueblo II. A typical village consisted of four or five pithouses and several surface dwellings. Some of the sites included kivas, and some did not. No large cluster was found. Instead, small settlements were scattered over all parts of the area to take advantage of the numerous arroyos and dunes that made the best farming places, and of the limited water sources needed for everyday purposes.

Some Pueblo III pithouses still had the shallow rectangular pits and ramped side entrances that reflected Mogollon influence and were common to Pueblo II. But deeper pits with square shapes and roof entrances became in time the more dominant form. Instead of the familiar four-post support system, two main posts were recessed into the walls like the posts in the pithouse found by Neil Judd at Chaco Canyon. Other interesting deviants from the norm included ventilator shaft openings placed at or in the room corners, and perforated sandstone slabs used for roof smoke holes and for ventilator shaft openings.

Gumerman and Skinner report that, in the 1960s, pithouses identical to the later and unusual forms just described were excavated at Neskahi Village on Paiute Mesa near Navajo Mountain in southern Utah. These were dated A.D. 1000–1100, and as such were somewhat earlier than those of Central Little Colorado.[40]

The surface structures of Pueblo III at Central Little Colorado also varied in form and construction. Most of the surface rooms were rectangular, but other room shapes were devised to conform to topographical demands. A typical building consisted of five contiguous rooms and clay walls that were spalled with small sandstones to slow down deterioration. At the Sundown site near Holbrook, a clay-walled kiva was built within a masonry room. Masonry walls of the McDonald Phase varied. Depending on the site, they were either dressed sandstone or crudely laid unshaped basalt rocks.

Kivas of this phase were D-shaped, keyhole-shaped, and rectangular, with platforms at one end like those of present-day Hopi. At the Hopi Buttes Plaza site a rectangular Great Kiva was discovered that was 35 feet (10.5 m) wide. The Sundown site included a shallow, circular, and benched Great Kiva measuring 40 feet (12 m) in diameter. Both sites were well constructed, had several clan-sized kivas enclosed within the room blocks, and had walled plazas. It is assumed they served as greater community centers.

Burials associated with the McDonald Phase were both flexed and extended. Most bodies were accompanied by mortuary offerings consisting of Little Colorado Whiteware bowls and of corrugated utility jars.

Toward the end of the Pueblo III Period, somewhere between A.D. 1250 and 1300, the Anasazi population distribution of the Central Little Colorado section experienced a pronounced contraction. Most of the area was abandoned as the section's inhabitants began to accumulate in ever-expanding pueblos along the Colorado River and on the Hopi mesas. Reasons given for this include changes in climate, an increasing refugee population, and pressures by invading peoples. The seemingly defensive nature of some locations support the last-mentioned idea, but probably a combination of the problems caused the contraction.

Experts also puzzle over why the Anasazi migrating from other areas would come to the arid Central Little Colorado Valley. A settled existence there had always been precarious, especially at a distance from the Colorado River valley. Perhaps they came because Anasazi relatives were already living there and surviving. Perhaps it was the only alternative to the Rio Grande Region. Some of the first migrants did make their way past Hopi country and south into the Upper Little Colorado section, where accommodation with the Mogollon, as has already been seen, would not have been a problem. But that changed drastically when the Apache and Navajo decided they wanted the territory, for it was not long after that that all the Anasazi in the Little Colorado Region decided the Hopi mesas were the only secure place to settle down. Thanks to a combination of factors, not the least of which were the intrusions and circumscriptions by Spanish, Mexicans, and Anglos, they have remained there ever since.

Pertinent to this, John T. Hack emphasizes a factor of some consequence. He states that the Hopi region seems, when first one experiences it, to be nothing but a barren, windswept desert. But, paradoxically, it is this very barrenness that gives it superiority. Its exposed position and broad valley flats enable windstorms to pile up great mounds of sand that inhibit arroyo cutting, allow floodwater to spread, and provide a permanent groundwater supply in or beneath the large dune areas.[41]

PUEBLO IV

Pueblo IV in both the Little Colorado and Rio Grande regions is known to the anthropological subsciences as the period of redistribution and the establishment of new communities. Properly regarded, it has two phases. The first covers the time of instability, migrations, and the inauguration of new cultural centers. It extends from A.D. 1250 to the time just preceding the arrival of the Spaniards in A.D. 1540. The second phase is of shorter duration and spans the interval from the appearance of the first explorers to the final subjugation of the Pueblo peoples in 1692, when their temporarily successful revolt against the Spaniards that began in 1680 was ended. Early Pueblo IV was formerly referred to in the literature as a period of regression or cultural decline. But subsequent study has shown that the designation is no longer appropriate.

Because of a lack of archaeological information, it is difficult to name Little Colorado ruins that are solely representative of the earlier Pueblo IV Phase. Distinct sites on the border between the Central and Upper parts include Puerco, Chevelon, Homolovi, and Chavez Pass. There are, however, many other examples that had their beginnings early in Pueblo IV and continued on to practically the end of the phase. And in the Hopi country of Arizona there are many Jeddito Valley sites that date to this period.

Later stages of the early phase are represented by Sikyatki in the Hopi area, or district, and perhaps by whatever associations can reasonably be made with the more southern Casa Grande villages.

The second phase of Pueblo IV is regarded as the early historic. It is best represented by Awatovi in the Hopi district and by Hawikuh, near the present-day village of Zuñi, New Mexico. These were thriving villages long before the Spaniards arrived in A.D. 1540, and they continued to function for some time thereafter. Hawikuh was not abandoned until A.D. 1670, and Awatovi was destroyed in the autumn of A.D. 1700.

Hopi Buttes

A single Pueblo IV site, located on top of a precipitous cone-shaped volcanic plug named Chimney Butte, was excavated during the Hopi Buttes survey mentioned earlier. It consisted of one rectangular room whose walls were of double-coursed unshaped basalt boulders. There was no finished floor and no definite firepit. Sherds of Holbrook Black-on-white, Tusayan Black-on-red, and corrugated utility ware indicated occupation of the butte as early as Pueblo II, giving it a possible date range of A.D. 900–1350. The inaccessibility of this 6,553-foot-elevation ruin that rises 1,000 feet above the surrounding plain prompted Gumerman and Skinner to suggest it was a shrine. Supporting this idea are the frequent mention of Chimney Butte in Hopi legend and the fact that it is regularly associated with present-day Second Mesa ceremonies.

Kin Tiel

A number of large and interesting ruins that show Hopi affinities are located within the Central Little Colorado section of the Pueblo IV Period. One of these is Wide Ruin, or Kin Tiel, as the Navajo call it. The ruin is on an upper and eastern tributary of Leroux Wash called Wide Ruin Wash, eighteen miles north of Chambers, Arizona. On early maps Kin Tiel is designated as Pueblo Grande, and it first became known through the work of Victor Mindeleff and Fewkes. It is dated about A.D. 1264–85.

In 1929 Lyndon L. Hargrave, in search of datable beams for Dr. Andrew E. Douglass, excavated at Kin Tiel, and also at Kokopnyama, which is on Antelope Mesa about a mile east of the Jeddito trading post. In looking at the Kin Tiel ruin itself, and at a reconstructed floor plan, one can easily see why it was called Pueblo Grande and Wide Ruin. It was an immense pueblo, sometimes referred to as the "Butterfly Ruin," because it formed a compact assemblage of rooms that in plan were shaped like a butterfly.

Hargrave reports that, unlike other ruins in the immediate area, Kin Tiel had an outer wall unbroken except for narrow passageways. As in the case of Pueblo Bonito at Chaco Canyon, terraced dwelling rooms looked down upon open courts. The courts were separated by a stream channel that appeared to have been crossed by extensions of the outer wall of the village. As with the Show Low and Pinedale ruins, local settlers had removed virtually all the Kin Tiel wall stones for their own building purposes. In consequence, no primitive masonry stands above ground today. The ruin has been leveled, and all that remains is a low, widespread mound of sandstone blocks and adobe mortar.[42]

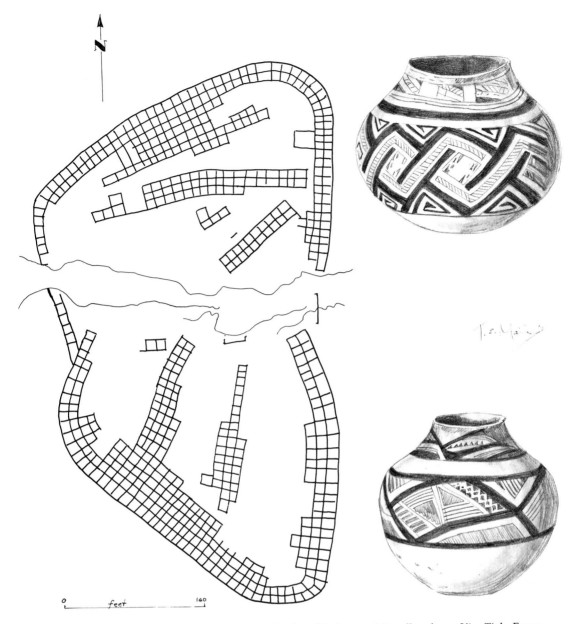

Left, general plan of Kin Tiel Pueblo. *Right,* late black-on-white ollas from Kin Tiel. From Smithsonian photographs, and from Haury and Hargrave, 1931.

Hargrave excavated two kivas that proved to be quite similar to Jeddito Valley kivas (to be discussed in detail shortly). The significant thing is that the Kin Tiel kivas represent what are believed to be the earliest and most easterly examples of kivas of Hopi character.[43] Both were built in A.D. 1275 or 1276. Watson Smith, who describes the Jeddito kivas in detail, found these dates to be "somewhat surprising," in that it places the Kin Tiel kivas in a period prior to the assumed time of construction of the earliest excavated kivas at Awatovi, which were not built before A.D. 1300. He believes that earlier kivas might yet be discovered at Awatovi, but he thinks it remarkable that Hopi-style kivas should occur so far from what has been regarded as the Hopi homeland. Of course, the even more distant rectangular Pinedale kiva already described is Hopi in style and was dated between A.D. 1293 and 1330.

The Hopi type of kiva chamber is divided by a rise in floor elevation into what is called the kiva room proper and the platform, or alcove. The kiva room is the larger portion. It contains the altar appropriate to each ceremony, and the ritual is enacted there by the society members. The platform space, along with side benches, is reserved for spectators who are permitted to witness certain parts of ceremonies, and for novices during the tribal Initiation Ceremony. Both kivas at Kin Tiel seem to have followed this pattern. Pueblo custom also decrees that the kiva be partly, if not wholly, underground. Even

Plan and perspective views of Kin Tiel kivas. The kiva on the right is the oldest of the Hopi type of rectangular kiva yet reported. It was constructed and destroyed in the same year, A.D. 1276, after the roof collapsed on and killed five men. From Haury and Hargrave, 1931.

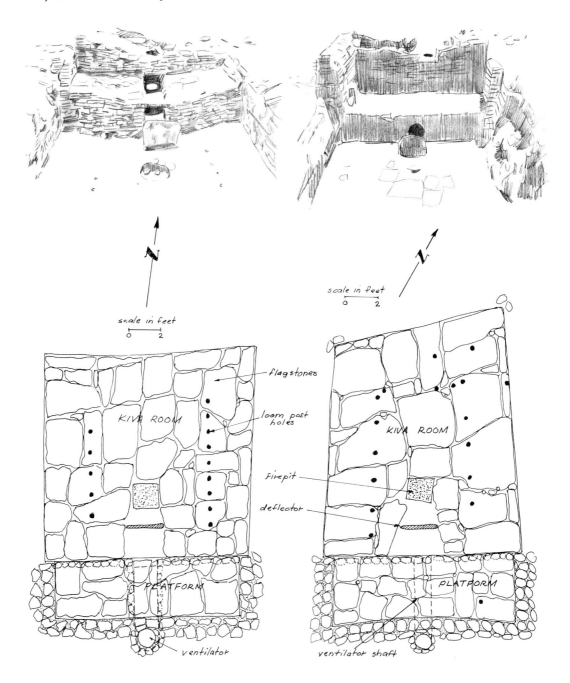

where villages stand on solid rock, kivas are built on lower ledges or set into crevices so that the side of the kiva that is against the cliff permits in essence the fulfillment of the subterranean aspect.

The kivas at Kin Tiel were subterranean. One kiva had masonry-lined walls in traditional fashion, but the other had walls that were simply dirt plastered over, reminding one of the kiva walls found by Judd at Paragonah, Utah. The price ultimately paid for the dirt walls at Kin Tiel proved to be quite high. One day the walls and roof collapsed and buried five men, whose bodies were uncovered by the excavating party in 1929. The platform walls were of well-built masonry, however, and the kiva floor and platform were covered with flagstones.

The Kin Tiel kivas featured firepits, deflectors, and a ventilator shaft that passed under the platform. The orientation was such that the altar would be placed at the north end of the kiva room. Banquettes, benches, and pilasters were absent, and the presence of a sipapu was questionable.[44] From available evidence, it appeared that the roof consisted of main beams overlaid at right angles with smaller poles, which were topped by a layer of brush, grass, and several inches of adobe mud. Entrance was by means of a ladder that extended through a hatchway and whose butts rested on the platform floor.

Of particular interest to Hargrave were two parallel rows of small holes drilled in the flagstone floor of both kivas. In his opinion, the holes were used to anchor the lower end of looms, since "it is well known that Hopi men have long woven blankets in their kivas."[45]

Pottery recovered from the fill in both kivas is described as black-on-white, black-on-orange, and corrugated, indicating the period to be one of transition from Pueblo III to Pueblo IV.

Puerco

Puerco was once a large pueblo. It included about 125 rooms arranged in a rectangle, with three kivas situated in a plaza in front of the rooms. The kivas were rectangular, and each had a bench at its south end. The pottery was mainly a development of Homolovi, but the Hopi influence was greater than that of Zuñi. The pueblo appears to have been built as a unit rather than in stages, and it is dated A.D. 1250–1350.[46]

HOMOLOVI

The Homolovi ruin was partially excavated by Fewkes in 1896 and by Gordon G. Pond in 1965. This was an especially large masonry pueblo, having two plazas surrounded by dwelling rooms, into which were incorporated several ceremonial structures. The original building was two stories in height, and many of the lower-floor rooms were paved with sandstone slabs. A rectangular kiva inspected by Pond featured a slab-lined bench and wall murals. Pond also reports that a large number of Hopi pottery types were found, including Jeddito Black-on-yellow and Sikyatki Polychrome. In general, Homolovi sherds are indistinguishable from those of Awatovi.[47] Burials were made outside the pueblo walls, and bodies were usually covered with a flat sandstone slab. Most bodies were extended rather than flexed, and mortuary offerings consisted of many and varied goods.

Possible dates for the Homolovi site are A.D. 1200–1300. Hopi informants recognize Homolovi as a Hopi site, and they support their assertion with legends referring to the village, which say that the founders of the Hopi village named Shipaulovi once lived there.

CHEVELON

The Chevelon ruin was excavated by Fewkes in 1896. It is fifteen miles east of Winslow and south of the Little Colorado River. Large amounts of shell were unearthed at Chevelon, suggesting it had trade and ties with the Hohokam. Pottery was similar to that of Homolovi, Jeddito Black-on-yellow being a common type. Burial methods were identical to those of Homolovi.

HOPI—TUSAYAN

An assessment and description of the Hopi culture, once improperly identified as "Moki," could not commence until the advent of the historic period in A.D. 1540. But the Hopi story may have begun as early as A.D. 1120, at the end of the Pueblo II Period, when some specialists believe the pueblo known as Old Oraibi was founded. Since excavations are not permitted by the Hopi, no one knows for sure.

The Hopi language is Uto-Aztecan (Shoshonean), and thus connected with those of the Ute and Comanche. The town of Hano is the single exception, as it maintains its Tewan dialect. Hopi, or *Hopituh Shi-nu-mu*, means "the Peaceful People," or some variation of that. Yet the name may be no more than a reference to peaceful early Anasazi years, or else the expression of a creed or a wish. Edward P. Dozier states that war was "despicable" to the Hopi,[48] and their name might be understood in this context. They also practice, with amazing success, passive resistance. But the Hopi, as will clearly be seen, could and would stand up to a challenge, and could become contentious and violent if in their view the situation justified or demanded it. Further, Mischa Titiev makes it clear that, while the Hopi had "a horror of wanton killing" and were rarely the aggressors in warfare, it seems it was their custom to go on the warpath each fall after the harvest was gathered. Upon returning, they would celebrate by dancing with the scalps they had taken, and even when their war parties ceased they continued to perform either the Kaleti, or Warrior Dance, or the Howina' aiya, or Market Dance.[49]

Archaeologists are not certain when the next Hopi villages after Old Oraibi were begun. Certainly a few of them, such as Shongopovi, were in embryo form shortly thereafter, and when the contraction of the Little Colorado Region of the early 1200s got under way, many villages that still exist today began to grow at an appreciable rate. Adding to the difficulty of pinning down their

Homolovi. Lesser material culture objects: *a*, shell ornament. *b*, stone pendant. *c*, bone tube. *d*, stone knife. *e*, carved bone awl. *f*, decorated jar with bird design. *g*, mythic bird figure from food bowl. *h*, bowl with mythic spider emblem on interior. *i*, bowl with bird design on interior. From Fewkes, 1896a.

original locations is the fact that a considerable shifting about of sites took place. The Hopi were and are sedentary people, but in typical Anasazi fashion, for sedentary did not mean stationary. They continually reconstructed and added to sites and sometimes moved entire villages to one or more new locations. That was especially true after the Pueblo revolt erupted in 1680 and they feared the consequences.

Chevelon. *Top left,* rush matting, often used for wrapping bodies for burial. *Center left,* plaited basket fragment and *(center)* detail of plaiting technique. *Top right,* gaming reeds. *Bottom,* stone slab painted with rainclouds and bird symbols. From Fewkes, 1896a.

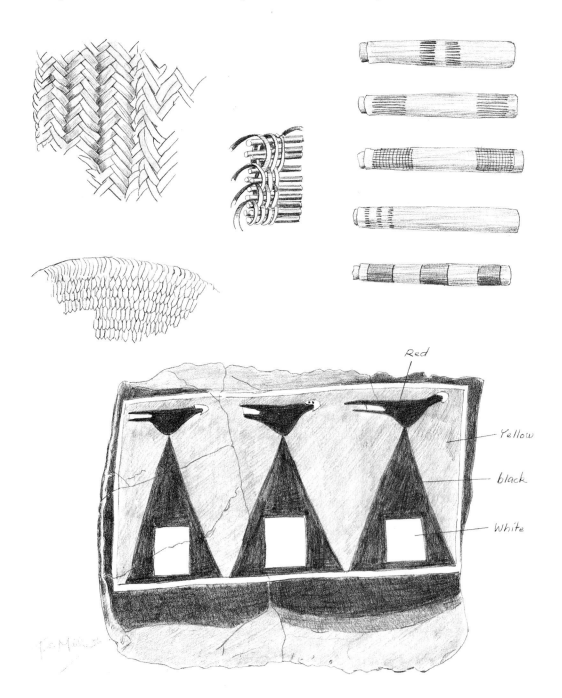

Ultimately, the Hopi towns, forming an overall community first known to outsiders as Tusayan, came to occupy three high and virtually barren mesas that are the southwesternmost extensions or spurs of Black Mesa, known today as the Central Little Colorado section. Since Old Oraibi, on the westernmost mesa, was the earliest settlement, the Hopi considered these mesas, beginning there, as the first, second, and third mesas. But after the Englishman Thomas

Chevelon. Lesser material culture objects: *a–b*, shell armlets. *c*, incised shell ornament. *d*, shell frog. *e*, shell pendant. *f*, enlarged detail of shell used as rattle or bandolier. *g*, disk of turtle-shell. *h*, bone ear pendants. *i*, dipper with divided handle. *j*, decorated bird pot. *k*, stick used by Stick-swallower. From Fewkes, 1896a.

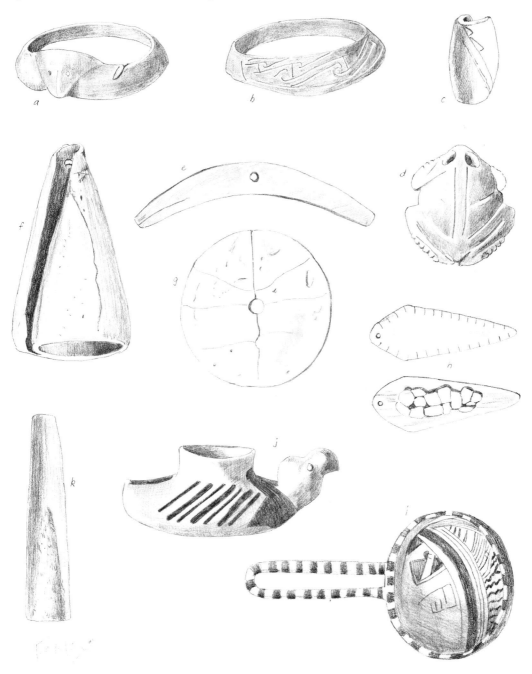

V. Keam established a trading post east of the mesas in 1878, and the U.S. Government built its agency at Keams Canyon in 1887, the mesas were numbered from east to west, and they are so known today.

Since the names of the Hopi villages and other Hopi words occur fairly often in the following chapters, it might be helpful to explain that Hopi is always written precisely as it is spoken. Most of the letters in the English and Hopi alphabets stand for the same sounds, and Hopi letters are always pronounced the same, although there are differences in dialect between mesas.[50] For example, the present-day Hopi villages and their pronunciations are as follows:

First Mesa	Walpi *(Wahl-pee)*
	Sichomovi *(Seet-chew-moh-vee)*
	Hano *(Hah-noh)*
	Polacca *(Poh-lah-ka)*
Second Mesa	Shipaulovi *(She-paul-oh-vee)*
	Mishongnovi *(Mee-shong-noh-vee)*
	Shongopovi *(Shung-oh-po-vee)*
Third Mesa	Old Oraibi *(Oh-rye-bee)*
	New Oraibi *(New Oh-rye-bee)*
	Hotevilla *(Hoh-tah-vill-ah)*
	Bacobi *(Bah-ko-bee)*
Other village	Moencopi *(Moh-en-koh-pee)*

There are three villages on First Mesa: Walpi, Sichomovi, and Hano. Polacca sits at the foot of the mesa on the eastern side.

Walpi, the most interesting of the villages to any visitor because of its dramatic setting on the tip of a stark, six-hundred-foot-high mesa, was built about A.D. 1700. Its name means "Place of the Gap." Walpi has five kivas. One is enclosed within a house block, and the other four are detached.

Sichomovi, alternatively spelled Sichimovi, "Place of the Mound Where Wild Currants Grow," lies between Walpi and Hano, and it is separated from Walpi only by a narrow bridge of rock. The present village was begun about A.D. 1750 by a group from Walpi, said to be the Patki, Lizard, Wild Mustard, and Badger clans. After being devastated by a smallpox epidemic, the Sichomovi people moved to Tsegi Canyon and to Zuñi. Later, though, they returned and resettled in Sichomovi.[51] The present village has two kivas, placed back to back in a plaza.

Hano is a Tewa village that was founded sometime after A.D. 1696 by people who fled the Rio Grande country after the reconquest of the pueblos by the Spanish. The people of Hano still consider themselves Tewa, even though they have adopted many Hopi customs and intermarried. Hano and Sichomovi are contiguous in appearance, but the Tewa and Hopi are keenly aware of an unmarked boundary line that separates the two villages. Hano has two kivas. Albert Yava, a lifetime resident of the village, has furnished us with an excellent inside account of Hano, and further reference to this is made shortly. Edward P. Dozier gives us the anthropologist's view of Hano's development in an account published in 1966.[52] Taken together, the two books offer an excellent treatment of the differences and similarities between the Hopi and Rio Grande worlds, and sharp insights into the cultural adjustments made by the Hano Tewa as they melded into the Hopi lifeway while at the same time seeking to retain their Tewa identity.

Polacca is named after Tom Polaccaca, a Hano-Tewa who built the first store below the mesa. The village grew up around the First Mesa day school in the 1890s. It has had no political or ceremonial status, but so many people have now moved down to it from Walpi that this venerable mesa-top village is virtually abandoned as a dwelling place. Ceremonies are still held up in Walpi, and the kivas remain, but one wonders whether eventually some important political changes will be made. By ancient custom, ceremonies will always be held at Walpi, because it is the ceremonial center for First Mesa by virtue of its length of residence.

Second Mesa is twelve miles west of First Mesa, and it is split at its extreme end into two spurs. Shipaulovi (sometimes spelled Shipolovi) and Mishongnovi are on one spur, and Shongopovi is on the other.

Shipaulovi is the word for a small fly or gnat, whose petroglyph was on a stone brought to the village by a Katcina and preserved in a shrine. Harold S. Colton and others subscribe to a legend that says the founders of Shipaulovi once lived at Homolovi and were driven out by swarms of mosquitoes; hence, to Colton, the petroglyph is a mosquito and the name means just that.[53] Harry C. James believes that beams taken from the old Franciscan mission at Shongopovi argue that people from there settled Shipaulovi after a schism. Shipaulovi has three detached kivas.

The name Mishongnovi is defined by Colton as "Place of the Black Man."[54] The reference is to a chief named Mishong, who was a member of the Crow Clan. Mishong led his followers from the San Francisco Peaks region, near Flagstaff, to Shongopovi. They were not allowed to settle there, but were permitted to begin a village below the shrine at Corn Rock, a prominent sandstone pillar at the end of Second Mesa, on condition that the Mishongnovi would forever protect the shrine from desecration.[55] Archaeologists believe that Mishongnovi was occupied from A.D. 1250 to 1800, and that it moved to its present site on the end of the mesa (from the lower position near Corn Rock shrine) during the 1700s.[56] The present village has four detached kivas.

A Franciscan chapel was established at Mishongnovi in 1629, and it was cared for by a priest from Shongopovi until 1680.

Shongopovi, or Shungopovi, means "Place by the Spring Where the Tall Reeds Grow." According to tradition, it is the oldest of the Hopi villages, but the original site was not where the present one is today. Shongopovi was established by the Bear Clan. According to Bertha P. Dutton, Shongopovi people built a new pueblo on top of Second Mesa in 1680.[57] An excellent spring, named Gray Spring, is said to have been the result of the ceremonial prayers of the Cloud Clan. It is walled in with masonry and has been used by the villagers for several centuries. The original site of Shongopovi was just north of Gray Spring. Pottery sherds found there by Colton led him to conclude that it was established before A.D. 1250, and then occupied until the early part of the 1400s.[58] James states that the Franciscan mission of San Bartolomé was built on a ridge about five hundred yards above the spring, and that from 1629 to 1680 a substantial portion of Shongopovi was situated near the mission. Fol-

Hopi. *Top,* Mishongnovi in the foreground, and Shipaulovi crowning the mesa in the background. *Bottom,* street scene in Old Oraibi in 1921. Both scenes from Earle R. Forrest photographs.

lowing the Pueblo revolt of 1680–92, the present village was built, and some of the mission beams were incorporated within it.[59] It has five detached kivas.

Third Mesa is ten miles west of Second Mesa. Old Oraibi sits on the tip of the spur, with New Oraibi at its base. Eight miles or so beyond Old Oraibi and on top of the mesa is Hotevilla, and a half mile northeast of Hotevilla is Bacobi, or Bakabi.

The original, or Old, Oraibi was founded by the Bear Clan around A.D. 1100. Its name is connected with a rock called "orai," and the original village would become, along with the pueblo of Acoma, the oldest continuously occupied town in the United States. Although it undoubtedly began as a small cluster of dwellings, by historic times it had evolved into a sprawling community. The center of Old Oraibi consisted of two main masonry, multistoried buildings located on the east and west sides of a long, narrow plaza, with slightly smaller room clusters situated at the north and south ends of the plaza in such a way as to complete the plaza enclosure. An additional thirty or more small-house clusters were grouped about the main buildings, each cluster being so laid out as to provide for a village with seven streets oriented north and south. At one time the village had thirteen rectangular kivas that were detached from the dwelling units.

Most of Old Oraibi is in ruins. Yet when Victor Mindeleff examined it in 1882 and 1883, he discovered that it was the largest of all the Hopi villages and contained half of the entire Hopi population. In 1899 George A. Dorsey spoke of Old Oraibi as the largest and most ancient of all Hopi pueblos, and in many respects the best preserved and most interesting community in the world.[60] It was a proud village without a church, spurning the advances of the U.S. Government, and separated from its nearest neighbor by a broad, deep valley. There was only one white man within twenty miles, and the nearest trading post was thirty-five miles away. In 1929 Lyndon L. Hargrave found ample evidence that Old Oraibi was very old. Beneath the town were the remains of dwellings, room on top of room. Some years before, the edge of a road had been cut through a trash mound at the bottom of which were found the buried remains of older and better houses.[61]

Old Oraibi remained the largest of the Hopi towns until 1906, when dissension over leadership, government pressures, and Christianity split the community and brought about the founding of Hotevilla. The withdrawal of other residents from Hotevilla led to the founding of Bacobi in 1907, and to the establishment of New Oraibi at the foot of Third Mesa in 1910.

New Oraibi was to become the most progressive of the Hopi villages. It has accepted more white man's innovations than any other village, and it has abandoned many Hopi customs. Many of the houses are more modern, having electricity and modern furnishings. Well water is even available, and there are outdoor toilets. The residents have adopted white people's dress. Children play baseball, basketball, and the like. But the economic life parallels that of other villages, and while there are no Katcina initiations, some vestiges of the Katcina cult are still present.

By 1932 the population of Old Oraibi had been reduced to 87,[62] and the ceremonial organization had suffered a serious decline. Since then the population has increased some, reaching 167 in 1968, but Old Oraibi has become a bitter place. Today a sign at the village entrance tells whites flatly to "Keep Out." It was not always so. In his report on Kokopnyama in 1929, Hargrave says there was hardly a room, either above or below ground, in Oraibi or the villages of Second Mesa, that at some time he had not been permitted to enter.[63]

Hotevilla means "skin the back." The original reference was to a low cave housing its main spring. The entrance was so tight that persons using it usually skinned their backs on the rough cave roof.[64] It was founded in 1906 by Youkeoma and his followers after the schism at Old Oraibi. The chief stubbornly refused many of the demands of Bureau of Indian Affairs officials, and the village has remained one of the most conservative of the Hopi. It is said that part of the ruined condition of Old Oraibi is explained by the fact that when the dissenters moved away they literally took their houses with them.[65]

Bacobi, "Place of the Jointed Reed," was established in 1907 after a schism at Hotevilla.

Moencopi (also spelled Moenkopi) means "Place of the Flowing Stream." It is about forty miles north of Old Oraibi and is a colony of the ancient town. It is built in the midst of sites said to have been occupied by the migrating Hopi clans of early days. Moencopi was founded about 1870 by an Old Oraibi chief named Tuba, or Toovi, and the traditional Hopi people who live there still recognize the authority of the village chief of Old Oraibi. Moencopi is actually two communities; Upper Moencopi is the more modern one, and it surrounds a day school in the old village. Lower Moencopi is a traditional community. Not far from Moencopi, the U.S. Government established an agency that was run by Mormon missionaries. This has become a fairly large and active center, named Tuba City, but Mormon efforts to convert the Hopi have met with limited success.

Almost nothing is known of Hopi life in the more than six-hundred-year period between the establishment of Old Oraibi and the early 1800s. We do know that by the fourteenth century they were contending with the herculean problems of survival in a challenging environment, of nomadic wanderers such as the Navajo who were making their first probes into the region, and of absorbing other Anasazi and Southwesterners who were abandoning their home regions. In A.D. 1540 a detachment from the Coronado expedition under Don Pedro de Tovar visited the Jeddito Valley and other parts of Hopi country. This first encounter was a friendly one, and it was here that the Spaniards first learned of the great stream that played a major role in Hopi mythology, the Colorado River. Almost immediately Don García López de Cárdenas was dispatched to search for it.

It was 1583 before the Spaniards came again. This time the expedition, led by Antonio de Espejo, was seeking gold. There was none to be found at Hopi, and so the second meeting was cordial also. The Spanish went on with their search.

Juan de Oñate visited the Hopi villages in 1598 and again in 1604. Apparently he came seeking something other than gold, for the padres followed in 1629 and began the attempt to convert the entire Hopi nation to Christianity. It was shortly thereafter that the missions already mentioned were established, and they remained in operation until the Pueblo revolt took place in 1680.

Since the revolt was begun in New Mexico, and since the Spanish were to exert a far greater influence over the Rio Grande Anasazi than over the Hopi, a more complete story of the revolt is told in the Rio Grande Region chapter. For now, it will suffice to say that the missionary efforts concerning the Hopi did not go at all well. Some converts were made, but these became a nagging thorn in the sides of the traditionalists. Dutton describes the overall period from 1629 to 1870 as one of great unrest among all of the Pueblo peoples.[66] They resented the overt interference with their religion and the demand for acceptance of a foreign faith, they detested the enforced labor required of them for purely Spanish purposes, they smoldered as their women were raped and abused, and their distrust and hatred mounted at a steady pace.

Rebellion saturated the Hopi mind long before the Rio Grande Pueblos themselves had enough of Spanish rule, and the Hopi joined in the battle with willing hearts. They immediately killed four Roman Catholic priests and demolished the missions and chapels. For twelve years thereafter not a Spaniard was to be seen in Hopi. Then in 1692 an arrogant Don Diego de Vargas returned to Hopi, and visited Awatovi, Walpi, and Second Mesa. He met with only passive resistance, consecrated the people to the Roman Catholic faith as loyal subjects of the King of Spain, declined to visit militant Old Oraibi, and went home in short order, satisfied that the problems were over.

They weren't. Not much happened for a few years, for the isolation and aridity of Hopi country did not attract Spanish colonists. Moreover, the reconquest meant little to the Hopi except for the handful that had been truly converted. But in 1700 all that changed. Franciscan Fathers Fray Juan de Garicochea and Fray Antonio Miranda set out with resolute intent for Hopi country. They arrived at Awatovi in the Jeddito Valley, where they somehow subdued or persuaded the Anasazi, and baptized many of them. It was an act that would bring to pass the direst of consequences, and it would mark indelibly a day of infamy in Hopi history as relative turned against relative and Awatovi, the Sistine Chapel of the Anasazi, was destroyed.

AWATOVI

The Jeddito Valley, a few miles east of the Hopi mesas and not far south of Keams Canyon, became like the Hopi villages proper an important culture center in prehistoric times. Natural water reservoirs and broad valleys filled with alluvial deposits, together with herbs, grasses, shrubs, timber, sandstone, and clay and coal deposits, combined to make the area one of the most desirable for dwelling places in the Central Little Colorado section. The remains of an-

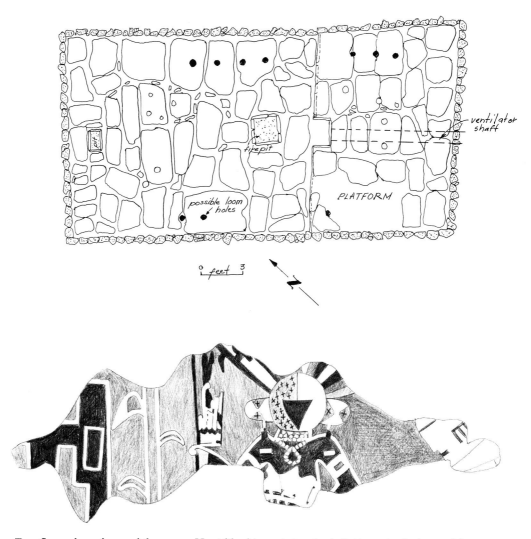

Top, floor plan of one of the many Hopi-like kivas at Awatovi. Bottom, typical mural fragment. Represented is almost certainly Ahöla Katcina, who appears at the Hopi Powamû Ceremony and symbolizes the coming of the sun. After Watson Smith, 1972.

cient habitations are found tucked in considerable number under the mesa rims.

Paul S. Martin reports pithouse sites in the valley dating from A.D. 670 to after 800,[67] but the excitement of archaeologists has centered in the large pueblo ruins of Awatovi, Kawaika-a, Chakpahu, Pink Arrow, Nesuftonga, Kokopnyama, and Kululongturqui. Victor Mindeleff mapped the five largest Jeddito ruins in 1882 and 1883.

Awatovi, alternatively spelled Awatobi, was situated on the old trail that connected the villages of Cíbola (the Zuñi area) and the villages of Hopi. Consequently, it was the first to be discovered, in 1540, by the previously mentioned Tovar and Cárdenas. Espejo visited the Jeddito Valley in 1583, Oñate in 1598, and de Vargas in 1692. In the first half of the seventeenth century a Roman Catholic Franciscan mission was established at Awatovi, and it remained in operation until its destruction during the Pueblo Revolt of 1680. In

1700 an attempt was made to reestablish the mission. But it collapsed when the Awatovi pueblo was abruptly terminated by traditional Hopi under circumstances that were almost inevitable, and reprehensibly sad. Missionaries cannot always be proud of what they set into motion.

The sum of injustices heaped upon the Indians by invading Europeans was crushing. But worse by far is what happens when the frustrated and disrupted Indians, boxed up and unable to cope any longer with their conquerors, begin to turn upon one another. The most wretched part of the removal of the Cherokees from their native home in the south to Oklahoma Indian Territory was not the long march in which almost a third of the Cherokees died. It was when in Oklahoma the agonized and hopeless Cherokees disputed with and assassinated one another. Now at Hopi and at Jeddito we see another such tragedy whose memory can never be erased.

The story is told that during the winter of 1700–1, after the people of Awatovi had permitted the Franciscan priests to return and to reestablish their mission, a swarm of angered Hopis from other mesas, with the chief of Awatovi as an accomplice, attacked Awatovi. They trapped and burned most of the men, who had been asked by their chief to meet in their kivas before sunrise, captured the remaining men, abducted the women and children, and then tortured and dismembered the Awatovi male captives and some of the women and children at a place near Second Mesa. The documentation for this is given in nearly a dozen publications,[68] but for a vivid and heartrending account I recommend that of Harry C. James, *Pages from Hopi History,* pages 61–64.

In 1892 Fewkes excavated part of a kiva he thought was one of those where killings took place, but his findings were inconclusive. In 1895 he tried again, but still did not find enough evidence to be certain, although he suspected he was in or near the sites in question. However, in 1964 Rex Gentry discovered a mass burial about fifteen miles southwest of Awatovi and ten miles south of Second Mesa that upon examination by experts tended to corroborate the wholesale massacre of Awatovi men, women, and children.[69]

Fewkes was followed to Awatovi by Russell, Hough, Kidder, the Cosgroves, Gladwin, Morris, and Hargrave. Each of these men learned something more about Awatovi and its environment. But it remained for the next expedition to strike gold.

From 1935 to 1939 an expedition from the Peabody Museum did extensive work in the Jeddito Valley area. Twenty-one sites were excavated entirely or in part; they dated from the sixth century A.D. to the early part of the eighteenth. At these sites approximately fifteen hundred rooms were uncovered, thirteen hundred of them at Awatovi, and the rest at other sites on Antelope Mesa and in the Jeddito Valley. The expedition was led by John Otis Brew, but a number of prominent archaeologists, such as Paul S. Martin and Watson Smith, participated in the project.

Two of the earliest sites were of particular note: Site 4a and Site 264. The first was a Basketmaker III–Pueblo III site near the Jeddito trading post. It consisted of subterranean and surface ruins whose history could be traced for at least six hundred years. During the 1938 and 1939 seasons, the excavation of this and Site 4a were under the direction of Charles Avery Amsden of the Southwest Museum at Los Angeles. Site 264 was a village about a quarter of a mile long, situated on a point that projected out into the Jeddito Valley below Kawaika-a. Its main occupancy was Basketmaker III–Pueblo I, with pithouses, slab-lined storage rooms, outdoor firepits, and one Pueblo II house built inside an earlier pithouse. Especially instructive was the fact that the site exhibited traits comparable to Basketmaker III–Pueblo I sites of the San Juan area, and to contemporary sites of the Upper Little Colorado section along the Mogollon Rim.

As for Awatovi itself, the only walls still standing in 1935 were those of the southeast corner of the old mission. Elsewhere nothing but great mounds of building debris lined the former plazas.

But by the time the Peabody Museum archaeological investigations ended in 1939, Awatovi had proved to be the ruin of a large pueblo that once had covered twenty-three acres on the rim of Antelope Mesa overlooking the Jeddito Valley. Its occupancy period ranged from Pueblo III to the early part of Pueblo V, and more expressly to the A.D. 1701 date of the massacre. Besides the pueblo, there was the ruin of the seventeenth-century mission, San Bernardo de Aguatubi, although according to Brew, Anasazi occupation of the site had reached its peak in the fourteenth and fifteenth centuries and was already in decline when the mission was founded.[70]

As at Old Oraibi, trenching revealed room built upon room, one house being built on the ruins of another after the earlier ruins had been filled in and smoothed over with trash. The buried rooms, happily enough, had actually been preserved by the topping process, and their walls were in excellent condition. They consisted of well-shaped stones and their plaster was intact, promising that, although the kivas excavated so far had unpainted walls, the kivas yet to be uncovered might well contain long-desired and elusive wall murals. Open and sealed doorways alike were encountered, and one room had a bench at its south end. Flagstone floors were common. Brew states that, on the whole, construction was "quite impressive," except for the poor quality of the Mesa Verde sandstone, which disintegrated quickly when exposed to the elements.[71]

In addition to the dwelling and storage rooms, five rectangular kivas were excavated in 1935. Four were in open plazas, and one was incorporated in a large building. The first kiva was the most elaborate encountered in the history of Anasazi archaeology, save the Great Kivas. Its floor consisted of a smooth layer of hard-packed adobe mud, topped by a layer of clear sand, over which large, thin flagstones were laid. A bench encircled three walls and expanded to become a platform at the south end. It, too, was slab-lined, and its back wall was hung with matting. There were two firepits. One contained coal ash and the other wood ash. There was a sipapu consisting of a large, plain utility pot. A big circular stone with a hole in the center rested on the floor near the sipapu, and it was probably placed over the opening during certain ceremonies. Two well-made loom weights with recessed hand grips were found on the kiva floor. Tiny hemispherical pits were worked in the floor and wall slabs as ornamentation, and each of the largest slabs had a single hole piercing it. The remains of two domestic sheep found on the floor made it clear that the chamber belonged to the later, or Spanish mission, period; and of the kivas uncovered, it most closely resembled the modern Hopi kiva. The other kivas were all slab-lined, but had benches on only one wall. One kiva was in a Sikyatki-period house block. Timbers from Sikyatki levels were dated by Emil Haury from about A.D. 1504 to 1550.

Many artifacts were discovered in 1935, including bone and stone implements and beads made of clay, bone, stone, and shell. Unusual were pottery imitations of shell that were painted and pierced for use as beads, pendants, and earrings. Brew also discovered a "surprisingly frequent" occurrence of life forms in the pottery decoration. Especially gratifying was the discovery of Katcina mask portrayals and what seemed to be representations of ceremonial dances. In their sum, these finds alone promised that some of the modern Hopi ceremonials might now be traced "into the archaeological past."[72]

The year 1936 was to be propitious. The "Western Mound" of Awatovi was excavated, and testing was done elsewhere on the site. Almost immediately, differences in construction and pottery indicated the excavators were into an earlier period.[73] None of the brilliant Sikyatki and Mission polychrome wares were present. Instead the pottery was black-on-orange or black-on-white, all characteristic of the latter part of the Pueblo III Period. Moreover, walls were double-coursed and well laid. Many rooms contained two firepits, and it was clear that coal was being burned in these prehistoric times. Early in the second month of the season, pieces of painted wall plaster were found in a kiva fill. Intensified examination revealed many painted layers on the kiva walls. Anticipation heightened appreciably, and it was by no means misplaced, for this was to become one of the most remarkable and valuable discovery times in the history of Southwestern archaeology, as spades sank deep into kiva after subterranean kiva in Awatovi and Kawaika-a. Until this moment came to pass, most information regarding ancient ceremonial life could only be guessed at. Archaeologists had speculated about what uses were made of mute artifacts, they read backward from modern times after observing present Pueblo customs, and they studied petroglyphs. But there was no written language to assist the guesses they made, and hints of wall paintings, wherever they were found, tantalized them and encouraged them to continue searching for more informative murals.

A few examples are the following: at Alkali Ridge, in the westernmost section of the Mesa Verde Region, fragments of murals were found in a Pueblo II site. At Mesa Verde proper a few geometric designs and simple representative bird figures still remained in fragmentary form on some kiva walls. Paul S. Martin discovered geometric kiva paintings at Lowry Ruin in Colorado.[74]

Then, after the Museum-Gates Expedition was concluded in 1901, Walter Hough published in the annual report of the National Museum for that year a description of an illustrated mural at Kawaika-a, in the Jeddito Valley.

But now twenty-three paintings were found on those famous first-kiva walls at Awatovi. The searchers moved on to an adjoining kiva, and then on to another. Soon the mural total was forty-one. The archaeologists and their Hopi crew were ecstastic. Yet the findings were only a sample of what was yet to come. All told, murals were to be discovered in eighteen kivas in Awatovi and Kawaika-a.

Even at this juncture, though, Brew noted that surprising variations were to be found in subject and technique. Depictions included pure geometric designs, realistic human figures, and formalized bird and animal representations much like those on Sikyatki pottery.

Brew was convinced that a study of these, along with pottery paintings, would add much to our knowledge of the history of Pueblo art. Beyond this, it seemed probable that some of the figures could be identified with modern ceremonies and legends. And since the paintings occurred on kiva walls, it might also be possible to obtain information from them regarding the societies or clans by whom the kivas were used.[75]

Every mural element was carefully photographed and a scale drawing made. The color was then recorded as closely as possible by comparing it with a color dictionary that was being compiled as they went along. Black, white, reds, and yellow were the most common colors, but orange, green, blue, and pinks also augmented the brown of the adobe plaster background.

As far as could be determined, the mural paintings were done with an unknown kind of brush and the fingers on reasonably smooth masonry-and-mortar walls that were plastered over.[76] Since entry was through the roof, unbroken walls were available for the murals. At Awatovi, some of the mortar had been reinforced with a matting of reeds or grass, as at Hopi and Zuñi. Several finish coats of a fine-textured reddish brown plaster completed the job and provided the working surface for the murals.[77] The paint was mixed with a mordant and uniformly done on dry plaster in the manner called fresco secco, as opposed to fresco, which is done on wet plaster that bonds and holds the paint.

It is provocative to see how discoveries of magnitude seem to parallel and augment one another. The simultaneous discoveries of the relationship of Basketmaker and Pueblo types, and the excavations of Great Kivas, have already provided us with typical examples of this. Now, while archaeologists probed for long-sought murals in the kivas of Awatovi and Kawaika-a, the same thing was happening over in New Mexico. Details regarding this lie in the chapters ahead, but it should be mentioned here that in 1935, during the excavation of Kuaua, near the town of Bernalillo, other important murals were found in a single kiva. They are treated in the book *Sun Father's Way* by Bertha Dutton, as well as in numerous other reports.[78] According to Smith, as of the time of his 1952 report on Awatovi, the Kuaua murals were better preserved than those of

Jeddito, and because of their broad content they constituted by far the most valuable and extensive collection of prehistoric mural art outside Awatovi and Kawaika-a.[79] In 1975 Frank C. Hibben's book *Kiva Art of the Anasazi at Pottery Mound* was published on the splendid murals painted on the walls of kivas found in a ruin known as Pottery Mound, in central New Mexico. This village was occupied between A.D. 1300 and 1475, placing it in the same period during which Awatovi reached its florescence.

In his summary remarks on the general history and distribution of kiva mural paintings, Smith sees wall painting as a persistent trait in Pueblo cultural development. It began, simply at least, as early as Pueblo II, perhaps in the middle San Juan area, and grew gradually in complexity as it spread throughout the entire Anasazi realm. It flowered in Pueblo IV, at the same time that ceramics and architecture reached their climax of vigor.[80] After that a decline in all three media of expression began, and only ceramics and wall art, now translated to easel art, have experienced within this century any kind of renaissance.

As I take reluctant leave of fabulous Awatovi, it should be said that Watson Smith's extensive book *Kiva Mural Decorations at Awatovi and Kawaika-a, with a Survey of Other Wall Paintings in the Pueblo Southwest* (1952) must be ranked with the finest publications available on the Anasazi. It reads easily, but it is utterly perceptive and thorough about Pueblo life in general during the Pueblo III, IV, and V periods.

Casting about for the significance of the Jeddito wall paintings as a whole, Smith gingerly suggests a relationship with kiva altars. Altar backs, like the altar reredos in a Christian church, are often painted with symbols and may be hung with many objects that are meaningful to the ritual. In some instances an upright slat altar is replaced by a painted screen that is unrolled and hung on the wall to provide a backdrop. Smith wonders whether the wall mural might have served the same purpose, as either a screen or an altar back.[81] The geometric and Sikyatki-style designs may have been purely decorative, while the pictorial designs seem, almost inescapably, intended as representations of actual ceremonial performances, including the altar, the regalia, and the human and superhuman participants.[82]

In 1972 the Peabody Museum published Smith's report on the kivas of Awatovi and Kawaika-a, kivas at other sites in the Jeddito area, and Hopi-like kivas in adjacent areas. It treats the architecture of the kivas, focusing upon those at Awatovi and Kawaika-a.[83]

At Awatovi twenty-three kivas were either excavated or tested. At Kawaika-a twelve more were excavated. The report contains diagrams for most of these, together with sections and photographs that spell out in careful detail the final transitional step from the earlier circular kiva to the modern kiva.

Smith concludes that all the kivas were constructed and occupied during the Pueblo IV Period, and more expressly between A.D. 1300 and 1630. All but one of the kivas were characterized by a predominance of Pueblo IV black-on-yellow pottery found on the floor and in the fill. This does not mean there were no earlier kivas at Awatovi or Kawaika-a. It means only that further excavation would be required to uncover the earlier kivas "almost certainly there."[84]

The kivas were apparently subterranean or partly so, but it was not possible to determine whether the roofs were level with the grade or, as at modern Hopi, had their entryways projecting a foot or so above grade. Some kivas appear to have been located in plazas; in many instances they were built in clusters. At least three clusters at Awatovi were located on the cliff edge, just as at modern Hopi, so that the rear walls were almost entirely above ground and exposed to the elements.

All the kivas were essentially rectangular, with lengths ranging between 13 and 23 feet (3.9–7 m), and widths averaging 12 feet 4 inches (3.75 m). Some kivas had corner pilasters, but bays or alcoves were rare.[85] Most kivas were laid out in an approximately northerly orientation. Walls indicated at least three major building stages during Pueblo IV, with the best masonry being done in the earliest stages and a subsequent deterioration in quality in the later stages. The walls of all stages were coated with plaster composed of the same mud as that used for the mortar. The base-coat plaster was not sifted, and it contained many bits of rubbish. In some instances, reeds and mats were used to reinforce the plaster. Thin coats of clean finish plaster were applied over the base coat, and the murals were painted directly on the final finish coat. Some front walls featured small niches. Only two kivas had side doorways, and both had been sealed during occupation.[86]

Indications were that all the kivas had a bench that extended fully across the rear wall. Benches averaged 4 feet 7½ inches (1.4 m) in width, and 1 foot 4 inches (40 cm) in height. Their surfaces were paved with large, smooth sandstone slabs. Some kivas at Awatovi had front or side benches, but none at Kawaika-a included these, suggesting a possible difference in ritual between the two villages. Cists were inset in several rear benches. Most of them contained a globular utility jar, its wide mouth canted toward the front, and often the jar contained food or objects of ceremonial significance.[87]

Every kiva had a ventilator shaft consisting of a rectangular tunnel running beneath the rear bench, with a rectangular vertical shaft rising to the surface just outside the rear wall. The shaft floors were earth, roofs of sticks supported the overlying bench slabs, and the side walls were stone slabs. Virtually every kiva floor was paved with sandstone slabs. All the kivas had firepits near the center of the room, and stone-slab deflectors. Sipapus were present in only half of the kivas and were about halfway between the firepit and front wall. At Awatovi and Kawaika-a, sipapus were elongated pits sunk into the floor, with a recessed ledge around the mouth of the pit into which a plank or slab fitted so that its upper surface was flush with that of the floor. This resonator or foot drum is common to some of the Hopi kivas, and during ceremonies the participants at prescribed times stamp on the plank to send messages to the spirits in the underworld.[88]

Small circular holes were found in the floors of nearly every kiva. These were sometimes arranged in parallel rows, with from three to five holes in each row, and other times randomly placed. It is thought that most served as loom anchor holes, since in modern Hopi kivas vertical weaving looms are often set up near the side walls.[89] Two of the kivas had incised designs on the floor or rear bench, and three had small pits in the floor that held the ladder butts in place. Two kiva roofs were still intact at Awatovi. The roof structure consisted of two main beams laid across the narrower dimension of the room, topped at right angles with five or six smaller beams spaced to leave a rectangular opening in the center. This hatchway opening was bordered by a low parapet of stone blocks and adobe. A layer of small poles was placed on top of the small beams, and over the poles was laid brush, grass, or matting and a final coat of adobe. Ceiling heights measured from the floor to the bottom of the main beams varied from 6 feet 3 inches (1.9 m) to 7 feet 6 inches (2.3 m). It is assumed that a ladder provided access, but no ladders were found.

Generally speaking, the kivas at Awatovi and Kawaika-a conformed to prescribed pattern in architecture and function. Their style remained constant for three centuries, and the modern Hopi kivas resemble them closely. Smith decided, on the basis of his kiva studies, that "the basic pattern of Hopi ceremonial life was well established during early Pueblo IV times and has changed little since."[90] The pattern represented the attainment of a relatively well-stabilized ceremonial and cultural scheme, following several earlier centuries of fluidity and change.[91]

KAWAIKA-A

Kawaika-a, or Kawaikuh, so often referred to in the Awatovi material, is dated A.D. 1350–1469 and is the largest pueblo ruin in the Jeddito area. It is on the southwestern edge of Antelope Mesa, about three miles east of Awatovi. The pueblo was of irregular arrangement, having a number of kivas and plazas or courts enclosed by room clusters of various sizes.

Walter Hough visited the ruin in 1901, in conjunction with the Museum-Gates Expedition, and recorded a wall elaborately decorated in color: the painted wall showed part of a human figure and a bird, both done in yellow, green, and white.[92] However, the far more significant work at Kawaika-a was done by Watson Smith and the Peabody Museum expedition of 1935 to 1939.

SIKYATKI

Sikyatki has also been mentioned several times. It holds a prominent place in legends still told at Walpi. Its ruins are about two miles north of Polacca, and its primary renown comes from the extraordinary pottery created there.

According to legend, the village was founded by the Kokop, or Fuel, people at a time when Walpi was possibly the only other town on First Mesa.

Rivalry and disputes between the two pueblos escalated to where a Walpi man cut short the hair of a Sikyatki youth. Later, the humiliated and headstrong youth, while masked and participating in a ceremony at Walpi, took a knife and went looking for his enemy. When he couldn't find him, he cut off the head of the man's sister instead. He escaped, tore off his mask, and ran along the cliff top boasting of his deed. In reply, the infuriated men of Walpi waited until the men of Sikyatki were out in their fields, then attacked the village and destroyed it.

In the summer of 1895 Fewkes and his crew of Hopi workmen excavated some parts of the infamous Sikyatki ruin. Only the slightest traces of the village remained above ground. The roofs had collapsed, sand had drifted into and filled the open spaces, and sagebrush and other desert plants had taken root in the debris. Modern melon and squash fields covered part of the ruin area. There was little to suggest that just below the surface were ceramics that would rank with the finest ever created. Even Hopi who came to visit while work was in progress were transfixed by the beautifully decorated vessels that came to light. In fact, the finest potter of the mesa, a woman from Hano named Nampeyo, proclaimed that her best work was inferior to the worst by the women of Sikyatki, and she begged permission to copy some of the designs for her own use.[93] Lesou, her husband, helped decorate the pottery that resulted and assisted her further by gathering sherds to be used for inspiration. In this way a whole new era in Hopi ceramics was begun.

As the ruin itself was exposed, it proved to be rectangular in plan, with its northern and western buildings being much higher than the southern and eastern units. Walls were masonry, carefully plastered over. The largest rooms were about 8 feet (2.4 m) square, and doorways connected series of adjacent rooms that apparently were occupied by a single household. Rooms contained wall niches and storage jars, and some had firepits.[94]

Most of the lesser material culture objects obtained by Fewkes were taken from burial plots. The greater part of the burials had been made in sandy places that occurred a few hundred feet beyond the outer walls of the dwelling units. But people of special standing were buried under dwelling floors. Mortuary offerings included pottery, food, stone implements, fetishes, prayer sticks and other ritual paraphernalia such as tubular pipes, personal ornaments, and in one instance a textile fabric resembling a feather cloth.[95]

The prayer sticks, properly called pahos, were numerous and of different kinds, varying in form from wooden slats to pencil-like rods bearing carved ferules. Most were painted in green and black and resemble those used today by the Flute Fraternity at Walpi. Fewkes believes this resemblance supports the claim of the fraternity that their ancestors were among the first to settle in Hopi country and were among those who once populated Sikyatki pueblo.[96]

Coal was not used only as fuel; in the form of lignite it was polished and shaped for jewelry. Turquoise beads gave evidence of trade with Rio Grande Anasazi, and shell indicated trade contacts with Gulf peoples. The most common form of necklace was made of short pieces of bird bones strung together and stained green. Slabs of mica and selenite were drilled and shaped to make pendants and earrings.[97]

Many of the mortuary pottery bowls contained smooth stones similar to those still employed to polish pottery. Also found were concretionary quartz crystals like those used by medicine men, stalactite fragments, one fossil ceph- alopod, white kaolin disks, and a cylindrical clay corn fetish.[98]

By all odds, though, the most artistic of the objects found at Sikyatki was the pottery, and its forms were so symmetrical that Fewkes could hardly be- lieve they were done without a potter's wheel. He thought it "not too much to say" that the Sikyatki collection included ceramics more finely made and elab- orately decorated than any ceramic work of any aboriginal tribe of North America, and that it compared favorably with the best work of Mesoamerica.[99] It was vastly superior to pottery being made in the adjacent pueblos in 1895, in form, in fineness of parts, and in beauty of decoration. It was ornamented with an elaborate and symbolic polychrome decoration that differed in charac- ter from that of any pueblo near or far. Beyond its surpassing beauty as an art form, there was knowledge to be gained from its symbolic decorations, for never before had such a variety of ancient picture writing been discovered in any one ruin in the Southwest. Fewkes was certain that if anyone could inter- pret this Pueblo pictography correctly, our understanding of the ancient Pueblo mind and acts would be vastly enriched and enlarged.[100]

The pottery types at Sikyatki included utility ware and decorated smooth ware. The latter consisted of food basins, bowls, jars, vases, dippers, and other household items. Both the black-and-white and red ware were thought to be intrusive, but the predominant yellow ware was clearly a Sikyatki product. Colors used for decoration were red, brown, yellow, and black. Spattering with pigment was popular, and the details of some of the more elaborate figures were sharpened by finely incised lines. Food basins were most elaborately dec- orated on their interiors, while vases were decorated on their exteriors. For purposes of study, Fewkes grouped the pottery under three headings: (1) fig- ures of anthropomorphic gods and human beings; (2) figures of animals and plants; (3) geometric designs, terraces, bars, frets, and spirals.[101] His articula- tion of these in his articles and books is most interesting and instructive, and his writings are recommended reading for those who wish to pursue the mat- ter of Anasazi symbolism more deeply.

KOKOPNYAMA

Kokopnyama, dated A.D. 1269–1430, is situated one mile northeast of the Jed- dito trading post and a few miles south of Keams Canyon, on the north side of the Jeddito Valley. Lyndon L. Hargrave did some work there in 1929, the same year he investigated Kin Tiel. He reported that a surface survey indicated a ruin about ten acres in area, with architectural features "not unlike those of modern Hopi pueblos, if recent influence in the latter is disregarded."[102] The

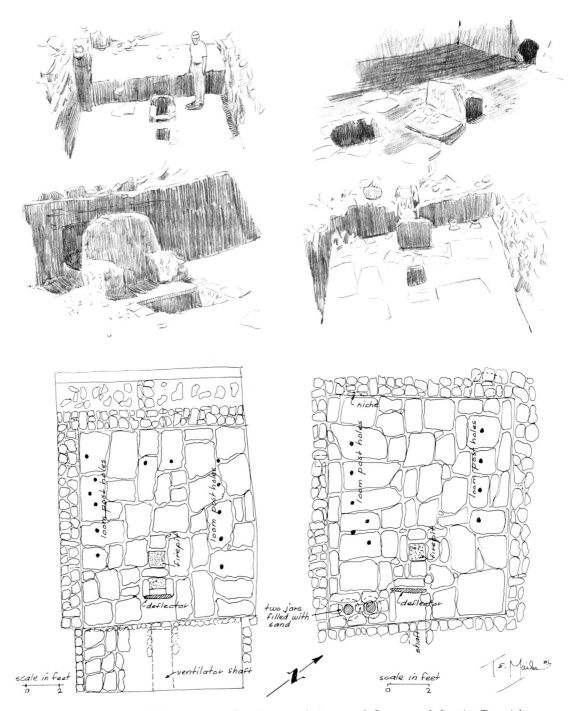

Kokopnyama. *Top left,* kiva views showing armchair-type deflector and firepit. *Top right,* house interior and, below it, kiva interior with two storage jars. *Lower left,* plan and perspective view of kiva. The armchair-type deflector and firepit combination shown is still found in some Rio Grande kivas today. From Haury and Hargrave, 1931. *Lower right,* kiva plan and perspective. Two buried jars containing sand for ceremonial use can be seen in the southwest corner.

general plan was essentially the same, with house groups that were two or more stories in height enclosing open courts. In addition to having a main quadrangular plaza surrounded by room blocks, the pueblo stretched north for nearly six hundred feet along the mesa's edge. The Pueblo III dwellings and the Pueblo IV kivas were on the slope below the mesa edge.

Hargrave thought the distinctive characteristic of Kokopnyama masonry was the poor quality of its friable sandstone. This accounted for the crumbled condition of its exterior walls, even though Kokopnyama was of more recent vintage than many other ruins whose stone walls were better preserved. The interior walls were in somewhat better shape, since their granular surfaces had been protected by coats of natural yellow-clay plaster, a practice common today among the Hopi.[103]

Room sizes averaged 7 by 8 feet 6 inches (2.1 × 2.55 m). Floors were of clay, with a finish thickness of from one to several inches. Firepits were placed either in a corner or against a wall at a location very near a corner. Boxlike caches with plastered interiors used for both domestic and ceremonial storage were found. Only seven doorways were uncovered, some square, some rectangular, with height greater than width, and some T-shaped. Lintels were either of split juniper sticks set in adobe mortar or of sandstone slabs. Entrance was most often made through the roof, and until the early 1900s practically all first-floor rooms of historic Hopi pueblos were entered in this way. Mealing bins were also found in Kokopnyama rooms. One perfectly preserved ceiling was discovered. It consisted of two large main beams that supported three smaller crossbeams. Split juniper was laid between the smaller beams to fill in the gaps. Above this was laid brush or grass and a final coat of adobe. Only the main beams were imbedded in adobe pockets in the walls.

Hargrave reports the finding of four kivas, and he excavated three of these.[104] Two were virtually identical to those of Awatovi and Kawaika-a in size and features. Exceptions were that neither contained a foot drum or a sipapu, and one had a fireplace unique for this area in addition to its square subfloor firepit. In essence this fireplace resembled an upholstered armchair without legs. The deflector constituted its back, and a sandstone extension at each side its arms. Between the arms was a fireplace that had two levels. Fireplaces like this are also found in the kivas of the Rio Grande pueblos.

The third kiva excavated was unusual only in that it was almost square and had no rear bench. Its ventilator shaft entered the rear wall at floor level and then intersected a vertical circular shaft within the core of the masonry wall itself.

SUMMARY

Summing up what archaeologists have learned thus far, it appears that the Hopi region at the southern end of Black Mesa was not occupied during Basketmaker II times, though there were scores of cave sites in the adjacent Kayenta Region. The earliest occupancy of the Hopi country is represented by a few pithouse sites in the Basketmaker III Period of A.D. 500–700 and by many sites in the Basketmaker III–Pueblo I transition period of A.D. 700–800. During the latter period the pithouses were enlarged, and isolated slab-lined storage chambers were arranged as contiguous surface units. The villages grew larger and more complex, and there is clear evidence their inhabitants were influenced by the Mogollon in architecture, in ceramics, and perhaps in religion.

The form of Pueblo I Period culture from A.D. 700 to 900 is not clearly identified in the Hopi region as yet, at least as compared to the development sequence in the San Juan. According to Colton: "Until about 900 A.D., north of the Little Colorado River, the Anasazi in Northern Arizona seemed to have had a more or less uniform culture, Kayenta Branch."[105] During this period there was considerable change: the bow and arrow replaced the atlatl and there were improvements in metates and manos. Cotton was added to the other sources of textile fibers, and beans augmented the corn and squash crops.

With the advent of Pueblo II, ranging from A.D. 900 to 1100, the Hopi culture assumed an individuality that has resulted in its being given a separate archaeological classification, the Tusayan Branch. During this period there was an increase in the number of sites and an appreciable increase in population. The Hopi pithouses of this time strongly resembled the Pueblo II pithouses of the San Francisco Mountain district, and there was an infusion of Tusayan wares from the Kayenta area. The masonry-lined pithouses varied in form from circular to rectangular to D-shaped, and a D-shaped kiva developed from the house types. The sites were still small, consisting of from two to nine rooms, and they were located both on the rim of hills and on the river benches.

The individual early Pueblo III Period sites were also small, and they remained similar in nature to those of the Kayenta Region, except for the D-shaped kiva. But an increase in the number of sites indicates an expanding population. Later in Pueblo III, small masonry pueblos such as Oraibi developed. One of these, called Pink Arrow, had thirty-two rooms and a kiva. At this time a number of pottery types indigenous to the Little Colorado area appeared, particularly St. Johns Polychrome, as did the first square kivas. The Pueblo III Period covered A.D. 1100–1300, and it is divided by Colton into the Kioko, Polacca, and Hukovi phases. As he sees it, during most of this period the Tusayan Branch developed in relative isolation.

Pueblo IV, dated by archaeologists from A.D. 1300 to 1600, was the first culture phase sufficiently known and comparable to the modern to be labeled Hopi. As the fourteenth century began, there was an impressive increase in the size of some sites and at the same time a contraction in their number while the overall population continued to grow. The San Juan Region was abandoned, and southern migrations took place coincidentally with the great drought of A.D. 1276–99. Later, all or part of the Kayenta population moved south to join their cultural relatives on the spur tips of Black Mesa. Later still, another population influx came from the Winslow area. New pottery types were developed from intrusive models. Large masonry pueblos came into being, with rectangular kivas of the historic type. As evidenced by the magnificent kiva wall paintings of Awatovi and Kawaika-a, a religious life similar to present-day practices characterized the period, although sometime after A.D. 1500 the Jeddito area was gradually abandoned, with Awatovi surviving until A.D. 1700.

During Pueblo V, from A.D. 1600 to the present, some documentary data became available on the historic Hopi pueblos. They reveal that the early Spanish explorations had relatively little effect on Hopi culture, though some believe that the psychological effect was profound, and that the introduction of missions after A.D. 1629 began to modify Hopi life in some respects. The Pueblo revolt of 1680 brought a temporary end to Spanish rule and a considerable influx of Pueblo people from the Rio Grande to Tusayan. A group of Tiwa-speaking people settled on Second Mesa at Payupki. They remained until 1742, when they were removed and later resettled at Sandia in New Mexico. A Tewa-speaking group came to First Mesa, where they exist today as the village of Hano. Other refugees were probably incorporated into the Hopi villages, and it is believed that groups returned to the Rio Grande at various times.

After 1680 the Hopi villages, excepting Old Oraibi, moved up to the mesa tops where we now find them, and during this process a number of what Fred Eggan calls "satellite villages" developed, such as Sichomovi and Shipaulovi.[106] The Hopi were least affected by the reconquest and managed to resist successfully Spanish efforts to reconvert and control them, except for that brief and infamous period at Awatovi. During the historic period, epidemic diseases periodically reduced the Hopi population. Navajo and Ute pressures restricted geographical expansion, and occasional famine periods led to temporary migrations of segments of the population to Zuñi and to the Rio Grande pueblos.

Spanish rule over the Hopi ended in 1821, when Mexico gained its independence. Internal problems plagued the Mexicans, however, and they paid little attention to the Pueblo Indians. No missionaries were sent, and no aid was offered. The Navajo continued to harass the Hopi, and Anglo-American mountain men began to move into the area, causing at least one incident in 1834 when they raided some Hopi gardens and were turned away only after a loss of about twenty Hopi lives.[107]

The United States terminated Mexican sovereignty over the Hopi in 1848, and after constant complaints by the Hopi about Navajo depredations, American forces, under the command of Colonel Kit Carson, finally subdued the Navajo. Drought and smallpox besieged the Hopi in 1853, 1854, and 1864. During this period the population decreased by an estimated 60 percent. Mormon missionaries came in 1858, but failed to win a single convert before 1870, the same year the first Protestant mission was built at Keams Canyon. The first U.S. Indian agent came to Hopi country in 1869, and in 1882 a 3,863-square-mile reservation was established.

An approximate dating for the Jeddito and Hopi area villages is as follows for the Pueblo III, IV, and V periods:

JEDDITO		HOPI	
Awatovi A.D. 1200–1700		Old Oraibi A.D.	1100–present
	original	Shipaulovi	1200–1680
	late	Shipaulovi	1680–present
	original	Mishongnovi	1250–1800
	late	Mishongnovi	1800–present
	original	Shongopovi	1250–1680
Kokopnyama 1269–1430	late	Shongopovi	1680–present
Kawaika-a 1350–1469	original	Walpi	1300–1700
Sikyatki 1300–1500	late	Walpi	1700–present
		Hano	1696–present
		Sichomovi	1750–present
		Moencopi	1870–present
		Tuba City	1870s–present
		Polacca	1880–present
		Hotevilla	1906–present
		Bacobi	1907–present
		New Oraibi	1910–present

POPULATION FIGURES*

	1891	1932	1948	1968
Old Oraibi	903	87	199	167
Shipaulovi	126	123	152	142
Mishongnovi	244	266	298	530
Shongopovi	225	307	423	475
Walpi	232	163 ⎫		80
Hano	161	309 ⎬	1285	241
Sichomovi	103	315 ⎭		364
Moencopi			640	710
Tuba City				
Polacca				
Hotevilla			644	
Bacobi			176	
New Oraibi			590	401

*The 1891 and 1968 figures are taken from Harry C. James, *Pages from Hopi History* (p. 16), and the 1932 and 1948 figures are from Stanley A. Stubbs, *Bird's-Eye View of the Pueblos*, pp. xv and 95–117.

NOTES

INTRODUCTION

1. Arthur H. Rohn, *Cultural Change and Continuity on Chapin Mesa*, p. 247 ff.
2. Charles Avery Amsden, *Prehistoric Southwesterners from Basketmaker to Pueblo*, pp. 116–17.
3. Campbell Grant, *Canyon de Chelly: Its People and Rock Art*.
4. Florence Curtis Graybill and Victor Boesen, *Edward Sheriff Curtis: Visions of a Vanishing Race*, p. 91.
5. Ibid.
6. Ibid.

CHAPTER 1 SOUTHWEST BEGINNINGS

1. James A. Maxwell, ed., *America's Fascinating Indian Heritage*, p. 53.
2. Alfred Vincent Kidder, *An Introduction to the Study of Southwestern Archaeology*, p. 40.
3. Ibid., p. 41.
4. Florence H. Ellis and Laurens Hammack, "The Inner Sanctum of Feather Cave, a Mogollon Sun and Earth Shrine Linking Mexico and the Southwest," p. 42
5. Paul S. Martin and Fred Plog, *The Archaeology of Arizona*, p. 79.
6. Ibid., pp. 337–41.
7. Nigel Davies, *Voyagers to the New World*, p. 179.
8. Ibid., p. 135.
9. Ferdinand Anton, *Pre-Columbian Art: And, Later Indian Tribal Arts*, by Frederick J. Dockstader, p. 118.
10. Ibid., p. 119.
11. Ibid., p. 181.
12. *World Book Year Book*, 1967, p. 190.
13. Anton and Dockstader, op. cit., p. 119.
14. *World Book Year Book*, 1968, p. 174.
15. Anton and Dockstader, op. cit., pp. 114–15.
16. Davies, op. cit., p. 137.
17. Ezra B. W. Zubrow, Margaret C. Fritz, and John M. Fritz, comps., *New World Archaeology*, p. 173.
18. Campbell Grant, *Canyon de Chelly: Its People and Rock Art*.
19. *Arizona Highways*, Vol. 52, No. 1 (Jan. 1976).
20. *Arizona Highways*, Vol. 27, No. 5 (May 1951).
21. *Arizona Highways*, Vol. 54, No. 3 (Mar. 1978).
22. J. Richard Ambler, *The Anasazi*, p. 5.
23. David Muench and Donald G. Pike, *Anasazi: Ancient People of the Rock*, p. 69.
24. Hugo G. Rodeck, "Mimbres Painted Pottery," pp. 44–53.
25. Ibid., p. 48.
26. Ibid.
27. R. L. Carlson, book review, *American Indian Art* (Autumn 1976), p. 71.
28. Ibid.
29. Ibid., p. 72.
30. Rodeck, op. cit., p. 48.
31. Ibid., p. 51.

CHAPTER 2 THE ANASAZI

1. Campbell Grant, *Canyon de Chelly: Its People and Rock Art*, p. 24.
2. David Muench and Donald G. Pike, *Anasazi: Ancient People of the Rock*, p. 45.
3. Experts are still debating which of the two, Mogollon or Hohokam, received and developed maize.
4. Florence C. and Robert H. Lister, *Earl Morris & Southwestern Archaeology*, pp. 170–71.
5. Charles Avery Amsden, *Prehistoric Southwesterners from Basketmaker to Pueblo*, p. 52.
6. H. M. Wormington, *Prehistoric Indians of the Southwest*, p. 31.
7. Ibid., p. 35.
8. Margaret M. Wheat, *Survival Arts of the Primitive Paiutes*, pp. 74–76.
9. Amsden, op. cit., p. 58.
10. Lister and Lister, op. cit., p. 149.
11. Muriel Porter Weaver, *The Aztecs, Maya and Their Predecessors*, p. 258.
12. J. Richard Ambler, *The Anasazi*, p. 45, and Thomas E. Mails, *The Mystic Warriors of the Plains*, pp. 135–38.
13. Amsden, op. cit., pp. 71–72.
14. Ambler, op. cit., pp. 5, 45, 80.
15. Weaver, op. cit., p. 278.
16. Matilda Coxe Stevenson, "The Sia," p. 88.
17. Weaver, op. cit., p. 279.
18. Lister and Lister, op. cit., p. 171.
19. G. H. S. Bushnell, *The First Americans*, p. 93.
20. Stewart Peckham, *Prehistoric Weapons in the Southwest*.
21. Ibid.
22. Ibid.
23. Ibid.
24. Ibid.
25. Wheat, op. cit., p. 14.
26. Amsden, op. cit., p. 73.
27. Lister and Lister, op. cit., p. 137.
28. Ambler, op. cit., p. 45.
29. Mails, op. cit., p. 532.
30. Wormington, op. cit., p. 41.
31. Amsden, op, cit., p. 88.
32. Wormington, op. cit., p. 44.
33. Amsden, op. cit., p. 91.
34. Weaver, op. cit., pp. 55–59.
35. Ibid., pp. 78–81.
36. Lister and Lister, op. cit., p. 132.
37. Amsden, op. cit., p. 80.
38. Ibid.
39. Ibid., p. 92.
40. Ibid.
41. Ibid., p. 74.
42. Ibid., p. 47.
43. Thomas E. Mails, *The People Called Apache*, p. 418.
44. Ambler, op. cit., p. 95.
45. Wormington, op. cit., p. 30.
46. Amsden, op. cit., p. 96.

47. Ibid., p. 106.

48. Ibid., p. 107.

49. Muench and Pike, op. cit., p. 98.

50. Lister and Lister, op. cit., p. 71. Earl Morris letter of November 3, 1921, to Clark Wissler.

51. Ibid., p. 78.

52. Grant, op. cit., pp. 25–27.

53. Amsden, op. cit., p. 113.

54. Lister and Lister, op. cit., p. 78.

55. Frank H. H. Roberts, Jr., "Archeological Remains in the Whitewater District, Eastern Arizona" (1939), p. 23.

56. Lister and Lister, op. cit., p. 79.

57. Ibid., p. 76.

58. Amsden, op. cit., p. 111.

59. Ibid., p. 112.

60. Muench and Pike, op. cit., p. 98.

61. Amsden, op. cit., p. 112.

62. Lister and Lister, op. cit., p. 166.

63. Amsden, op. cit., pp. 108–10.

64. Ibid., p. 52. See also Muench and Pike, op. cit., p. 99.

65. Amsden, op. cit., p. 49.

66. Neil M. Judd, "Two Chaco Canyon Pit Houses," pp. 399–413.

67. Alfred Vincent Kidder and Samuel J. Guernsey, *Archeological Explorations in Northeastern Arizona*, p. 44.

68. Jesse Walter Fewkes, "Field-Work on the Mesa Verde National Park," p. 58.

69. Walter Hough, "Explorations of a Pit House Village at Luna, New Mexico," p. 415.

70. Earl H. Morris, "Preliminary Account of the Antiquities of the Region Between the Mancos and La Plata Rivers in Southwestern Colorado," p. 186.

71. Frank H. H. Roberts, Jr., op. cit., pp. 1–265.

72. Neil M. Judd, "Archeological Investigations at Pueblo Bonito, New Mexico" (1922), p. 66.

73. E. Wesley Jernigan, *Jewelry of the Prehistoric Southwest*, p. 151.

74. Lister and Lister, op. cit., p. 149.

75. H. M. Wormington and Arminta Neal, *The Story of Pueblo Pottery*, p. 13.

76. Grant, op. cit., p. 42.

77. Robert H. and Florence C. Lister, *Anasazi Pottery*, p. 9.

78. Ibid.

79. Muench and Pike, op. cit., p. 100.

80. Amsden, op. cit., p. 121.

81. Gertrude Litto, *South American Folk Pottery*, p. 141.

82. Ibid., p. 145.

83. Wormington and Neal, *The Story of Pueblo Pottery*, p. 11.

84. Lister and Lister, *Anasazi Pottery*, p. 14.

85. Ibid., pp. 11–12, 18.

86. Amsden, op. cit., pp. 121–22.

87. Lister and Lister, *Earl Morris & Southwestern Archaeology*, p. 152.

88. Amsden, op. cit., p. 132.

89. Ibid.

90. Lister and Lister, *Earl Morris & Southwestern Archaeology*, p. 120.

91. Muench and Pike, op. cit., p. 101.

92. Amsden, op. cit., pp. 131–32. See also Grant, op. cit., p. 53.

93. Mails, *The People Called Apache*, pp. 263–69.

94. Lister and Lister, *Earl Morris & Southwestern Archaeology*, p. 125.

95. Amsden, op. cit., p. 128.

96. Ibid.

97. Muench and Pike, op. cit., p. 47.

98. Lister and Lister, *Earl Morris & Southwestern Archaeology*, p. 152.

99. Ibid.

100. Jernigan, op. cit., pp. 162–64.

101. Kidder and Guernsey, op. cit., p. 164.

102. Jernigan, op. cit., pp. 178–79.

103. Lister and Lister, op. cit., pp. 152–53.

104. Weaver, op. cit., pp. 131, 137, 199, 217, 266, 272.

105. Amsden, op. cit., pp. 128–29.

106. Ibid., p. 134.

107. Wormington and Neal, *The Story of Pueblo Pottery*, p. 15.

108. Amsden, op. cit., p. 134.

109. Grant, op. cit., p. 164.

110. Ibid., pp. 162–63.

111. Ibid., p. 167.

112. Ibid.

113. Ibid., p. 157.

114. Lister and Lister, *Earl Morris & Southwestern Archaeology*, p. 116.

115. Amsden, op. cit., p. 114.

116. Alfred Vincent Kidder, *An Introduction to the Study of Southwestern Archaeology*, p. 40.

CHAPTER 3 VIRGIN ANASAZI

1. J. S. Newberry, *Report of the Exploring Expedition from Santa Fe, New Mexico, to the Junction of the Grand and Green Rivers of the Great Colorado of the West, in 1859.*

2. H. Montgomery, "Prehistoric Man in Utah."

3. Jesse Walter Fewkes, "Prehistoric Remains in New Mexico, Colorado, and Utah" and *Archeological Investigations in New Mexico, Colorado, and Utah.*

4. Fewkes, *Archeological Investigations in New Mexico, Colorado, and Utah*, p. 23.

5. Ibid., p. 29.

6. Ibid.

7. Ibid., pp. 29–30.

8. Ibid., p. 34.

9. Ibid., p. 35.

10. Ibid., p. 36.

11. F. W. Hodge, Foreword to Emil W. Haury, *The Excavation of Los Muertos and Neighboring Ruins in the Salt River Valley, Southern Arizona*, p. vii.

12. Neil M. Judd, "Archeological Investigations at Paragonah, Utah," pp. 1–22.

13. J. W. Fewkes, "Prehistoric Remains in Arizona, New Mexico, and Colorado," pp. 64–65.

14. Ibid., pp. 65–67.
15. Ibid., p. 70.
16. Julian H. Steward, "Archeological Reconnaissance of Southern Utah," p. 281.
17. Ibid., pp. 287–88.
18. Ibid., p. 332.
19. Ibid., p. 333.
20. Ibid., p. 300.
21. Ibid., pp. 353–55.
22. Alfred Vincent Kidder, *An Introduction to the Study of Southwestern Archaeology*, p. 251.

CHAPTER 4 *CHACO CANYON*
1. Douglas and Barbara Anderson, *Chaco Canyon*, p. 32.
2. Ibid.
3. Frank Waters, *Book of the Hopi*, p. 42.
4. Florence C. and Robert H. Lister, *Earl Morris & Southwestern Archeology*, p. 11.
5. Kendrick Frazier, "The Anasazi Sun Dagger," pp. 56–67.
6. Ibid., p. 59.
7. Ibid.
8. Neil M. Judd, "Two Chaco Canyon Pit Houses," pp. 399–413.
9. Frank H. H. Roberts, Jr., *Shabik'eshchee Village, a Late Basket Maker Site in the Chaco Canyon, New Mexico*, pp. 10–150.
10. George Hubbard Pepper, *Pueblo Bonito*, p. 108.
11. Neil M. Judd, *The Material Culture of Pueblo Bonito*, pp. 69–70.
12. Ibid., pp. 87–96.
13. H. M. Wormington, *Prehistoric Indians of the Southwest*; and Alfred V. Kidder, *An Introduction to the Study of Southwestern Archaeology*.
14. Neil M. Judd, "Everyday Life in Pueblo Bonito," p. 246; and Judd, *The Material Culture of Pueblo Bonito*, pp. 80–87.
15. Marc Simmons, *Witchcraft in the Southwest*, p. 2.
16. Neil M. Judd, "Archeological Investigations at Pueblo Bonito, New Mexico" (1926), p. 87.
17. Wormington, op. cit., p. 89.
18. Kidder, op. cit., p. 173.
19. Judd, *The Material Culture of Pueblo Bonito*, pp. 117–39.
20. Ibid., pp. 139–52.
21. Ibid., pp. 152–59.
22. Wormington, op. cit., p. 90; and Kidder, op. cit., p. 172.
23. Elsie Clews Parsons, *Pueblo Indian Religion*, Vol. 1, Part 1, pp. 98–99.
24. Neil M. Judd, *Pueblo del Arroyo, Chaco Canyon, New Mexico*, p. 126.
25. Judd, *The Material Culture of Pueblo Bonito*, p. 177.
26. Judd, "Everyday Life in Pueblo Bonito," p. 239.
27. Kidder, op. cit., p. 176.
28. Ibid.
29. Ibid., p. 177.
30. Ibid., p. 178.
31. Judd, *The Material Culture of Pueblo Bonito*, p. 227.
32. Ibid., p. 234.
33. Judd, *Pueblo del Arroyo, Chaco Canyon, New Mexico*, pp. 169–70.
34. Kidder, op. cit., p. 184.
35. Frazier, op. cit., p. 64.
36. Ibid.
37. Waters, op. cit., pp. 43–44.
38. Anderson, op. cit., p. 28.
39. Judd, *Pueblo del Arroyo, Chaco Canyon, New Mexico*, pp. 109 ff.
40. Ibid., p. 109.
41. Ibid., p. 107.
42. Kidder, op. cit., p. 170.
43. Lister and Lister, op. cit., pp. 46–48. See also Judd, "Everyday Life in Pueblo Bonito," pp. 227–62.
44. Neil M. Judd, *The Architecture of Pueblo Bonito*, pp. 177–80.
45. Judd, "Everyday Life in Pueblo Bonito," p. 249.
46. Judd, *The Architecture of Pueblo Bonito*, p. 208.
47. Ibid., p. 209.
48. Ibid.
49. Ibid., p. 201.
50. Wormington, op. cit., p. 86.
51. Judd, *The Material Culture of Pueblo Bonito*, p. 264.
52. Ibid., p. 265.
53. Jesse Walter Fewkes, "Sky-God Personations in Hopi Worship," pp. 26–27.
54. Pepper, op. cit., p. 143.
55. Lister and Lister, op. cit., p. 144.
56. Judd, *The Material Culture of Pueblo Bonito*, p. 276.
57. Ibid., p. 278.
58. Ibid.
59. Ibid., pp. 279–99.
60. Frank H. H. Roberts, Jr., *Archeological Remains in the Whitewater District, Eastern Arizona* (1940), pp. 110–11.
61. Judd, *The Material Culture of Pueblo Bonito*, pp. 299–304.
62. Roberts, *Archeological Remains in the Whitewater District, Eastern Arizona*, p. 111.
63. Judd, "Everyday Life in Pueblo Bonito," pp. 259–60.
64. Judd, *The Material Culture of Pueblo Bonito*, p. 20.
65. Ibid., p. 29.
66. Ibid., p. 30.
67. Ibid., p. 32.
68. Judd, *The Architecture of Pueblo Bonito*, p. 26.
69. Ibid., pp. 50–51.
70. Lister and Lister, op. cit., pp. 59–66.
71. Judd, *The Material Culture of Pueblo Bonito*, pp. 34–35.
72. Wormington, op. cit., p. 88.
73. Judd, *Pueblo del Arroyo, Chaco Canyon, New Mexico*, pp. 57–95.

74. Ibid., p. 6.
75. Ibid., pp. 5–6.
76. Judd, *The Architecture of Pueblo Bonito*, p. 162.
77. Ibid., p. 163.
78. Ibid., p. 25; and Neil M. Judd, "Archeological Investigations at Pueblo Bonito, New Mexico" (1922), pp. 109–10.
79. Judd, *The Architecture of Pueblo Bonito*, p. 163.
80. Ibid., p. 27.
81. Ibid.
82. Frazier, op. cit., p. 64.
83. Anderson, op. cit., p. 49; and Kidder, op. cit., p. 185.
84. Kidder, op. cit., p. 182.
85. Ibid.
86. Judd, "Everyday Life in Pueblo Bonito," p. 201.
87. Mischa Titiev, *Old Oraibi: A Study of the Hopi Indians of the Third Mesa*, p. 99.
88. Judd, "Everyday Life at Pueblo Bonito," p. 261; and Judd, "Archeological Investigations at Pueblo Bonito, New Mexico" (1926), p. 87.
89. Judd, "Everyday Life in Pueblo Bonito," p. 245.
90. Ibid., p. 261.
91. Kidder, op. cit., p. 184.
92. Judd, *The Material Culture of Pueblo Bonito*, p. 3.
93. Judd, "Two Chaco Canyon Pit Houses," p. 404.
94. Judd, "Everyday Life in Pueblo Bonito," p. 230.
95. Judd, *The Material Culture of Pueblo Bonito*, p. 35.
96. Lister and Lister, op. cit., p. 35.
97. Ibid., p. 34.
98. Ibid., p. 43.
99. Ibid.
100. Ibid., p. 31.
101. Ibid., p. 32.
102. Ibid., p. 33.
103. Judd, *The Architecture of Pueblo Bonito*, p. 42.
104. Lister and Lister, op. cit., pp. 50–51.
105. Waters, op. cit., p. 127.
106. Lister and Lister, op. cit., p. 53.
107. Ibid., p. 44.
108. Ann Axtell Morris, *Digging in the Southwest*, p. 262.
109. Lister and Lister, op. cit., p. 38.
110. Frank H. H. Roberts, Jr., *Early Pueblo Ruins in the Piedra District, Southwestern Colorado*, p. 12.
111. Roberts, *Archeological Remains in the Whitewater District, Eastern Arizona* (1940), p. 139.
112. Frank H. H. Roberts, Jr., *Archeological Remains in the Whitewater District, Eastern Arizona* (1939), p. 263.
113. Ibid., p. 253.
114. Ibid., p. 254.
115. Ibid., pp. 35–36.
116. Ibid., p. 96.
117. Ibid., pp. 254–55.
118. Victor Mindeleff, "A Study of Pueblo Architecture: Tusayan and Cibola," pp. 163–64.
119. Roberts, *Archeological Remains in the Whitewater District, Eastern Arizona* (1939), pp. 256–57.
120. Ibid., p. 258.
121. Ibid., pp. 258–59.
122. T. D. Stewart, appendix, "Skeletal Remains from the Whitewater District, Eastern Arizona," in Roberts, *Archeological Remains from the Whitewater District, Eastern Arizona* (1940), pp. 153–63.
123. Roberts, *Archeological Remains in the Whitewater District, Eastern Arizona* (1939), p. 264; and Roberts, *Archeological Remains in the Whitewater District, Eastern Arizona* (1940), pp. 134–35.
124. Roberts, *Archeological Remains in the Whitewater District, Eastern Arizona* (1940), p. 135.
125. Roberts, *Archeological Remains in the Whitewater District, Eastern Arizona* (1939), p. 264.
126. Roberts, *Archeological Remains in the Whitewater District, Eastern Arizona* (1940), p. 136.
127. Ibid., pp. 1–2.
128. Ibid., pp. 137–38.
129. Ibid., p. 138.
130. Ibid.
131. Ibid., pp. 138–39.
132. Ibid., p. 139.
133. Frank H. H. Roberts, Jr., *The Ruins at Kiatuthlanna, Eastern Arizona*, p. 1.
134. Matilda Coxe Stevenson, *The Zuñi Indians*, pp. 153–58.
135. Ibid., pp. 34–43.
136. Roberts, *The Ruins at Kiatuthlanna, Eastern Arizona*, pp. 7–8.
137. Ibid., pp. 8–9.
138. Ibid., pp. 9–10.
139. Ibid., pp. 16–59.
140. Ibid., pp. 31, 43–86.
141. Ibid., pp. 52–111.
142. Ibid., pp. 16–86.
143. Ibid., pp. 173, 86–90.
144. Ibid., pp. 92–93.
145. Ibid., pp. 90–113.
146. Ibid., pp. 97, 108.
147. Ibid., p. 93.
148. Ibid., pp. 94–95.
149. Ibid., p. 52.
150. Ibid., p. 174.
151. Ibid., pp. 163–70.
152. Ibid., pp. 168–71, 174–75.
153. Ibid., p. 175.
154. Frank H. H. Roberts, Jr., *The Village of the Great Kivas on the Zuñi Reservation, New Mexico*, p. 158.
155. Ibid., pp. 103, 164.
156. Ibid., pp. 158–59.
157. Ibid., p. 159.
158. Ibid., pp. 86–98.
159. Ibid., pp. 96–97, 160–61.
160. Ibid., pp. 98, 161.
161. Ibid., p. 162.
162. Ibid., p. 134.

163. Ibid., pp. 104–6.

164. Ibid., pp. 107–33, 164–65.

165. Ibid., p. 165.

166. Ibid., pp. 135–39, 166.

167. Ibid., pp. 139–49.

168. Ibid., p. 167.

169. Arthur H. Rohn, *Cultural Change and Continuity on Chapin Mesa*.

170. Roberts, *The Village of the Great Kivas on the Zuñi Reservation, New Mexico*, pp. 146–47.

171. Ibid., p. 147.

172. Ibid., pp. 147–49, 167–68.

173. Stevenson, op. cit., pp. 94–95, 101.

174. Roberts, *The Village of the Great Kivas on the Zuñi Reservation, New Mexico*, pp. 148–49.

175. Ibid., pp. 133–34.

176. Ibid., pp. 149–52, 168.

177. Ibid., p. 149.

178. Ibid., p. 150.

179. Ibid.

180. Ibid.

181. Ibid., pp. 151–52.

182. Ibid., p. 169.

183. Ibid., p. 86.

184. Roberts, *Early Pueblo Ruins in the Piedra District, Southwestern Colorado*, pp. 12–16.

185. Ralph Emerson Twitchell, *Leading Facts of New-Mexican History*, p. 410.

186. Roberts, *Early Pueblo Ruins in the Piedra District, Southwestern Colorado*, pp. 17–18.

187. Ibid., pp. 164–65.

188. Ibid., pp. 21–71, 166.

189. Ibid., pp. 166–67.

190. Ibid., p. 167.

191. Ibid., pp. 74–141, 167.

192. Ibid., pp. 144–55, 167–68.

193. Ibid., pp. 70–71, 168–69.

194. Ibid., pp. 155–64, 168.

CHAPTER 5   KAYENTA

1. Jesse Walter Fewkes, *Preliminary Report on a Visit to the Navaho National Monument: Arizona*, p. 31.

2. Alfred Vincent Kidder, *An Introduction to the Study of Southwestern Archaeology*, p. 215.

3. Fewkes, op. cit., p. 32.

4. Ibid., pp. 23–24.

5. Kidder, op. cit., p. 224.

6. Ibid.

7. Ibid., p. 220.

8. Campbell Grant, *Canyon de Chelly: Its People and Rock Art*, p. 5.

9. Ibid., p. 136.

10. Ibid., pp. 148–50.

11. Ibid., p. 9.

12. Ibid., p. 32.

13. Ibid., p. 39.

14. Ibid.

15. Ibid., p. 46.

16. Ibid., pp. 47–48.

17. Paul S. Martin and Fred Plog, *The Archaeology of Arizona*, p. 280.

18. Grant, op. cit., p. 53.

19. Ibid., p. 61.

20. Ibid.

21. Ibid., pp. 65–66.

22. Fewkes, op. cit., p. 3.

23. Jesse Walter Fewkes, "Tusayan Snake Ceremonies," pp. 299–311.

24. Mischa Titiev, *Old Oraibi: A Study of the Hopi Indians of the Third Mesa*, pp. 96–99.

25. Deric Nusbaum, *Deric in Mesa Verde*, pp. 119–22.

26. Ibid., pp. 71–73.

27. Grant, op. cit., p. 137.

28. Stephen C. Jett and Dave Bohn, *House of Three Turkeys: Anasazi Redoubt*, pp. 22–26.

29. Ibid., p. 52.

30. Ibid., pp. 52–55.

31. Fewkes, *Preliminary Report on a Visit to the Navaho National Monument: Arizona*, p. 34.

32. Ibid., p. 10.

33. Ibid., pp. 10–12.

34. Ibid., p. 12.

35. Frank Waters, *Book of the Hopi*, p. 44.

36. Kidder, op. cit., p. 219.

37. Grant, op. cit., p. 37.

38. Fewkes, *Preliminary Report on a Visit to the Navaho National Monument: Arizona*, p. 13.

39. Waters, op. cit., p. 45.

40. Fewkes, *Preliminary Report on a Visit to the Navaho National Monument: Arizona*, p. 17.

41. Ibid., p. 18.

42. Jesse Walter Fewkes, "Archeological Field-Work in Southwestern Colorado and Utah," pp. 71–73.

43. Jesse Walter Fewkes, *Preliminary Report on a Visit to the Navaho National Monument: Arizona*, p. 19.

44. Ibid., pp. 20–22.

45. Ibid., pp. 30–31.

46. Ibid., p. 34.

47. Kidder, op. cit., p. 219.

48. Ibid.

49. George J. Gumerman, Deborah Westfall, and Carol S. Weed, *Black Mesa: Archaeological Investigations on Black Mesa: The 1969–1970 Seasons*, p. 1.

50. Ibid., p. 190.

51. Ibid., pp. 189–91.

52. Ibid., pp. 191–92.

53. Ibid., pp. 192–93.

54. Ibid., pp. 193–94.

55. Ibid., pp. 239–41.

56. Ibid., p. 244.

57. Ibid., p. 196.

58. Ibid., p. 197.

59. Ibid., pp. 196–98.

60. Fewkes, *Preliminary Report on a Visit to the Navaho National Monument: Arizona*, p. 4.

61. Waters, op. cit., p. 45.

62. Fewkes, *Preliminary Report on a Visit to the Navaho National Monument: Arizona*, p. 2.

63. Ibid., pp. 4–5.

CHAPTER 6 MESA VERDE

1. William H. Jackson, *Ancient Ruins in South-western Colorado;* W. H. Holmes, *Ancient Ruins of Southwestern Colorado;* L. H. Morgan, "Houses and House-life of the American Aborigines."
2. Gustaf Nordenskiöld, *The Cliff Dwellers of the Mesa Verde, Southwestern Colorado: Their Pottery and Implements.*
3. T. Mitchell Prudden, "The Prehistoric Ruins of the San Juan Watershed of Utah, Arizona, Colorado, and New Mexico."
4. Jesse Walter Fewkes, *Prehistoric Villages, Castles, and Towers of Southwestern Colorado.*
5. Sylvanus G. Morley and Alfred V. Kidder, "The Archaeology of McElmo Canyon, Colorado."
6. Prudden, op. cit., p. 257.
7. Fewkes, op. cit., p. 16.
8. Ibid., pp. 23–28.
9. Ibid., pp. 20–21.
10. Ibid., p. 17.
11. Prudden, op. cit., pp. 259–60.
12. Fewkes, op. cit., p. 18.
13. Prudden, op. cit., p. 260.
14. Fewkes, op. cit., p. 18.
15. Prudden, op. cit., p. 261.
16. Fewkes, op. cit., pp. 60–64.
17. Prudden, op. cit., p. 262.
18. Ibid., pp. 262–63.
19. Fewkes, op. cit., pp. 16–17.
20. Ibid., pp. 65–66.
21. Prudden, op. cit., p. 264.
22. Ibid., pp. 264–65.
23. Jesse Walter Fewkes, "The Hovenweep National Monument," p. 467.
24. Ibid., pp. 469–80.
25. Prudden, op. cit., pp. 266–67.
26. Paul S. Martin, Carl Lloyd, and Alexander Spoehr, *Archaeological Work in the Ackmen-Lowry Area, Southwestern Colorado,* 1937, p. 624.
27. Prudden, op. cit., pp. 267–71.
28. Florence C. and Robert H. Lister, *Earl Morris & Southwestern Archaeology,* p. 100.
29. Prudden, op. cit., pp. 271–73.
30. Leslie A. White, *Zia: the Sun Symbol Pueblo,* p. 183.
31. Prudden, op. cit., pp. 274–75.
32. Ibid., p. 275.
33. Ibid.
34. Ibid., pp. 275–76.
35. Fewkes, *Prehistoric Villages, Castles, and Towers of Southwestern Colorado,* pp. 66–67.
36. Ibid., pp. 37–38.
37. Ibid., pp. 40–44.
38. Ibid., pp. 34–35.
39. Ibid., pp. 40–41.
40. Earl H. Morris, "Preliminary Account of the Antiquities of the Region Between the Mancos and La Plata Rivers in Southwestern Colorado," p. 163.
41. Ibid., p. 164.
42. Ibid., pp. 180–81.
43. Ibid., pp. 202–3.
44. Ibid., p. 167.
45. Ibid., pp. 167–71.
46. Ibid., pp. 171–73.
47. Ibid., pp. 174–76.
48. Ibid., p. 187.
49. Ibid., pp. 192–93.
50. Ibid., pp. 192–203.
51. Lister, op. cit., p. 66.
52. Palmer Henderson, "The Cliff Dwellers," pp. 80–81.
53. Ibid.
54. Jesse Walter Fewkes, *Antiquities of the Mesa Verde National Park: Cliff Palace,* p. 24.
55. Arthur H. Rohn, *Cultural Change and Continuity on Chapin Mesa,* p. 233.
56. Ibid., pp. 233–35.
57. Ibid., pp. 233–34.
58. Ibid., pp. 235–36.
59. Ibid., p. 236.
60. Ibid., p. 237.
61. Ibid., pp. 238–39.
62. Ibid., p. 109.
63. Ibid., pp. 116–17; and Jesse Walter Fewkes, "Field-Work on Mesa Verde National Park" (1921b), pp. 91–94.
64. Rohn, op. cit., pp. 116–17.
65. Jesse Walter Fewkes, "Archeological Field-Work on the Mesa Verde National Park, Colorado" (1923), pp. 93–98.
66. Ibid., pp. 99–101.
67. Rohn, op. cit., p. 241.
68. Fewkes, "Field-Work on Mesa Verde National Park," pp. 80–81.
69. Ibid., pp. 75–90.
70. Alden C. Hayes, and James A. Lancaster, *Badger House Community,* p. v.
71. Ibid., p. 186.
72. Ibid., p. 183.
73. Michael D. Yandell, editor, *Rocky Mountain and Mesa Verde National Parks,* p. 61.
74. Hayes and Lancaster, op. cit., p. 183.
75. Ibid., p. 182.
76. Yandell, op. cit., p. 62.
77. Hayes and Lancaster, op. cit., p. 185.
78. Ibid., p. 183.
79. Ibid., p. 186.
80. Ibid., p. 23.
81. Ibid., p. 183.
82. Ibid., p. 23.
83. Ibid., p. 183.
84. Yandell, op. cit., p. 62.
85. Rohn, op. cit., p. 290.
86. Hayes and Lancaster, op. cit., p. 78.
87. Ibid., pp. 75–76.
88. Neil M. Judd, *The Material Culture of Pueblo Bonito,* pp. 59, 172.
89. Hayes and Lancaster, op. cit., p. 83.
90. Ibid.
91. Ibid., p. 184.
92. Ibid., p. 81.
93. Ibid., p.84.
94. Ibid., p. 93.
95. Ibid., pp. 95–96.
96. Ibid., p. 184.
97. Ibid.

98. Ibid., p. 185.
99. Rohn, op. cit., p. 91.
100. Don Watson, *Indians of the Mesa Verde*, p. 183.
101. Ibid., pp. 183–84.
102. Rohn, op. cit., p. 293.
103. Alfred Vincent Kidder, *An Introduction to the Study of Southwestern Archaeology*, p. 197.
104. Nordenskiöld, op. cit., p. 49.
105. Fewkes, *Antiquities of the Mesa Verde National Park: Cliff Palace*, pp. 38–40.
106. Nordenskiöld, op. cit., p. 76.
107. Hayes and Lancaster, op. cit., p. 96.
108. Frank Waters, *Book of the Hopi*, pp. 94–96; and Watson, *Indians of the Mesa Verde*, p. 113.
109. Nordenskiöld, op. cit., p. 73.
110. Watson, op. cit., p. 65.
111. Kidder, op. cit., p. 196.
112. Fewkes, *Antiquities of the Mesa Verde National Park: Cliff Palace*, p. 12.
113. Ibid., pp. 33–34.
114. Ibid., p. 48.
115. Ibid.
116. Ibid.
117. Ibid., p. 34.
118. Ibid., p. 50.
119. Ibid., p. 51.
120. Ibid., p. 63.
121. Ibid., p. 29.
122. Ibid.
123. Ibid., p. 30.
124. Ibid., pp. 11–12.
125. Jesse Walter Fewkes, *Field-Work on the Mesa Verde National Park* (1920b), pp. 49–57.
126. Ibid., pp. 62–63.
127. Arthur H. Rohn, *Mug House*, p. 31.
128. Ibid., p. 41.
129. Lister and Lister, op. cit., p. 78.
130. Rohn, *Mug House*, p. 171.
131. Nordenskiöld, op. cit., p. 78.
132. Rohn, *Mug House*, p. 145.
133. Kidder, op. cit., p. 198.
134. Ibid., pp. 198–99.
135. Nordenskiöld, op. cit., pp. 78–79.
136. Ibid., p. 80.
137. Rohn, *Mug House*, p. 131.
138. Ibid., pp. 131–45.
139. Nordenskiöld, op. cit., pp. 80–81.
140. Ibid., p. 81.
141. Ibid., pp. 82–84.
142. Ibid., pp. 84–85.
143. Ibid., p. 91.
144. Rohn, *Mug House*, pp. 145–47.
145. Kidder, op. cit., p. 199.
146. Rohn, *Mug House*, p. 171.
147. Ibid., p. 172.
148. Kidder, op. cit., p. 199.
149. Rohn, *Mug House*, pp. 175–76.
150. Ibid., pp. 177–78.
151. Kidder, op. cit., p. 199.
152. Rohn, *Mug House*, pp. 182–84.
153. Ibid.
154. Ibid., p. 184.
155. Kidder, op. cit., p. 199.
156. Ibid., p. 202.
157. Ibid.
158. Rohn, *Mug House*, pp. 178–79.
159. Ibid., p. 181.
160. Kidder, op. cit., pp. 202–3.
161. Rohn, *Mug House*, p. 178.
162. Ibid.
163. Ibid.
164. Ibid., pp. 184–85.
165. Ibid., pp. 185–86.
166. Ibid., p. 188.
167. Ibid., pp. 189–91.
168. Ibid., p. 194.
169. Ibid., pp. 195–96.
170. Ibid., p. 196.
171. Ibid., p. 257.
172. Ibid., p. 192.
173. Ibid., p. 194.
174. Nordenskiöld, op. cit., p. 102.
175. Rohn, *Mug House*, p. 203.
176. Ibid., pp. 203–6.
177. Ibid., pp. 206–7.
178. Ibid., p. 207.
179. Ibid., p. 208.
180. Ibid., p. 209.
181. Ibid., pp. 209–12.
182. Ibid., p. 207.
183. Ibid., pp. 212–16.
184. Fewkes, *Antiquities of the Mesa Verde National Park: Cliff Palace*, p. 34.
185. Rohn, *Mug House*, p. 216.
186. Ibid., pp. 216–19.
187. Ibid., p. 219.
188. Ibid., pp. 219–22.
189. Ibid., pp. 222–26.
190. Ibid., p. 226.
191. Ibid.
192. Ibid., pp. 226–28.
193. Ibid., p. 228.
194. Ibid., pp. 229–30.
195. Ibid., pp. 231–32.
196. Ibid., p. 233.
197. Ibid., p. 234.
198. Ibid.
199. Ibid.
200. Thomas E. Mails, *Sundancing at Rosebud and Pine Ridge*, p. 91.
201. Rohn, *Mug House*, p. 235.
202. Ibid., pp. 235–37.
203. Nordenskiöld, op. cit., p. 94.
204. Rohn, *Mug House*, p. 239.
205. Ibid., pp. 241–42.
206. Ibid., pp. 242–44.
207. Ibid., p. 244.
208. Ibid., pp. 244–45.
209. Ibid., p. 245.
210. Ibid., pp. 245–46.
211. Ibid., p. 252.
212. Nordenskiöld, op. cit., p. 83.
213. Rohn, *Mug House*, p. 252.
214. Ibid.

215. Barton Wright, *Hopi Material Culture*, pp. 92–93.
216. Rohn, *Mug House*, p. 251.
217. Thomas E. Mails, *The Mystic Warriors of the Plains*, p. 428.

CHAPTER 7 LITTLE COLORADO

1. J. Richard Ambler, *The Anasazi*, p. 6.
2. Paul S. Martin and Fred Plog, *The Archaeology of Arizona*, p. 136.
3. George J. Gumerman and S. Alan Skinner, "Synthesis of the Prehistory of the Central Little Colorado Valley, p. 185.
4. Martin and Plog, op. cit., pp. 136–40.
5. Gumerman and Skinner, op. cit., p. 191.
6. Harold S. Gladwin, *A History of the Ancient Southwest*, p. 154.
7. Vorsila L. Bohrer, as quoted by Martin and Plog, op. cit., p. 198.
8. Martin and Plog, op. cit., pp. 198–99.
9. Ibid., p. 199.
10. Ibid., pp. 197–98.
11. Harold S. Gladwin, *The Chaco Branch Excavations at White Mound and in the Red Mesa Valley.*
12. A. J. Lindsay, Jr., as quoted by Martin and Plog, op. cit., p. 198.
13. Martin and Plog, op. cit., p. 202.
14. Gordon C. Baldwin, "Material Culture of Kinishba," p. 324.
15. Ibid., p. 326.
16. Gordon C. Baldwin, "Excavations at Kinishba Pueblo, Arizona," p. 13.
17. Ibid., pp. 14–15.
18. Ibid., p. 14.
19. Baldwin, "Material Culture of Kinishba," pp. 314–16.
20. Ibid., pp. 320–21.
21. Ibid., p. 321.
22. Emil W. Haury and Lyndon L. Hargrave, *Recently Dated Pueblo Ruins in Arizona*, pp. 27–28.
23. Ibid., p. 78.
24. Ibid., pp. 48–52.
25. Ibid., p. 53.
26. Jesse Walter Fewkes, "Two Summers' Work in Pueblo Ruins," p. 162.
27. Haury and Hargrave, op. cit., pp. 61–71.
28. Ibid., p. 78.
29. Martin and Plog, op. cit., pp. 136–40.
30. Martin et al., *Chapters in the Prehistory of Eastern Arizona, I*, pp. 168–207.
31. A. J. Lindsay, Jr., as quoted by Martin and Plog, op. cit., p. 198.
32. Martin and Plog, op. cit., p. 138.
33. Ibid., pp. 197–98.
34. Ibid., pp. 136–37.
35. Ibid., p. 375.
36. Walter Hough, "Archaeological Field Work in Northeastern Arizona," pp. 279–358.
37. Harold S. Colton, *Prehistoric Culture Units and Their Relationships in Northern Arizona*, pp. 66–69.
38. Gumerman and Skinner, op. cit., p. 189.
39. Ibid., p. 190.
40. Ibid., p. 192.
41. John T. Hack, *The Changing Physical Environment of the Hopi Indians of Arizona*, p. 80.
42. Haury and Hargrave, op. cit., pp. 80–81.
43. Watson Smith, *Prehistoric Kivas of Antelope Mesa*, p. 157.
44. Haury and Hargrave, op. cit., pp. 81–85.
45. Ibid., p. 87.
46. Albert H. Schroeder, "Puerco Ruin Excavations, Petrified National Monument, Arizona," p. 93.
47. Gumerman and Skinner, op. cit., p. 196.
48. Edward P. Dozier, *Hano, a Tewa Indian Community in Arizona*, p. 30.
49. Mischa Titiev, *Old Oraibi: A Study of the Hopi Indians of the Third Mesa*, p. 162.
50. M. A. and J. O. Ekstrom, *How to Read and Write Hopi*, pp. 4–6.
51. Harry C. James, *Pages from Hopi History*, p. 10.
52. Dozier, op. cit.
53. Harold S. Colton, as cited by Harry C. James in *Pages from Hopi History*, p. 12.
54. Ibid., p. 12.
55. Harry C. James, op. cit., pp. 12–13.
56. Bertha Dutton, *Indians of the American Southwest*, p. 40; Harry C. James, op. cit., p. 13.
57. Dutton, op. cit., p. 40.
58. Colton, as cited by Harry C. James, op. cit., p. 12.
59. Harry C. James, op. cit., p. 12.
60. George A. Dorsey, "The Hopi Indians of Arizona," p. 734.
61. Lyndon L. Hargrave, "Excavation at Kin Tiel and Kokopnyama," p. 100.
62. Stanley A. Stubbs, *Bird's-Eye View of the Pueblos*, p. 17.
63. Hargrave, op. cit., p. 100.
64. Harry C. James, op. cit., p. 14.
65. Stubbs, op. cit., p. 117.
66. Dutton, op. cit., p. 39.
67. Martin and Plog, op. cit., pp. 376–77.
68. Watson Smith, op. cit., p. 73.
69. Ibid., p. 74.
70. John O. Brew, Foreword to Watson Smith, *Kiva Mural Decorations at Awatovi and Kawaika-a.*
71. John O. Brew, "The First Two Seasons at Awatovi," p. 125.
72. Ibid., p. 126.
73. Ibid., pp. 128–37.
74. Paul S. Martin, *Lowry Ruin in Southwestern Colorado*, pp. 42, 201.
75. Brew, op. cit., p. 135.
76. Watson Smith, *Kiva Mural Decorations at Awatovi and Kawaika-a*, p. 31.
77. Ibid., pp. 13–21.
78. Ibid., p. 76.
79. Ibid., p. 77.
80. Ibid., pp. 104–5.
81. Ibid., pp. 319–20.

82. Ibid., p. 321.
83. Watson Smith, *Prehistoric Kivas of Antelope Mesa*, pp. 1–124.
84. Ibid., p. 104.
85. Ibid., p. 107.
86. Ibid., pp. 108–14.
87. Ibid., pp. 114–16.
88. Ibid., p. 120.
89. Ibid., pp. 121–22.
90. Ibid., p. 123.
91. Ibid.
92. Hough, op. cit., pp. 279–358.
93. Jesse W. Fewkes, "Preliminary Account of an Expedition to the Cliff Villages of the Red Rock Country, and the Tusayan Ruins of Sikyatki and Awatobi, Arizona, in 1895," p. 577.
94. Ibid., p. 578.

95. Ibid., p. 579.
96. Ibid.
97. Ibid., p. 580.
98. Ibid.
99. Ibid., p. 582.
100. Ibid.
101. Ibid., pp. 582–83.
102. Hargrave, op. cit., p. 96.
103. Ibid., p. 97.
104. Ibid., pp. 103–16.
105. Harold S. Colton, as cited by Fred Eggan in *Social Organization of the Western Pueblos*, p. 123.
106. Eggan, *Social Organization of the Western Pueblos*, p. 125.
107. Robert C. Euler and Henry F. Dobyns, *The Hopi People*, p. 53.

GLOSSARY OF TERMS

FOR VOLUMES I AND II

ANGLO AMERICANS Americans of European extraction.

APOCYNUM A plant related to milkweed.

ATLATL An Aztec word meaning "spear-thrower." Atlatls are short, sometimes weighted, throwing-sticks with a finger-loop handle on one end and on the other a spur, which engages a pit or cup drilled into the basal end of the arrow-like dart shaft. When the dart is thrown, the atlatl remains in the hand.

CACIQUE The supreme village or town priest under the native governmental and ceremonial organization. The Pueblo cacique is considered the primary authority in all matters. A word of Arawakan (Caribbean Indians) origin, the term was applied by Spanish officials to indigenous religious leaders.

CALICHE A crust or succession of crusts of calcium carbonate that forms within or on top of the soil of arid or semi-arid regions.

CELT A prehistoric tool of stone or bronze resembling a chisel or ax.

CHONGO The hairstyle created by forming an elongated, vertical bob of hair on the back of the head. The hair is pulled together, folded, and then wrapped with yarn.

CIBOLA The early Spanish name for the Zuñi district.

CIST An oval or circular pit, often slab-lined, used primarily for storage. Cists also served a secondary purpose as depositories for the dead.

CLAN Clans are unilineal descent groups traced through the mother's side. They are exogamous units, and among the western Pueblos each clan controls its share of the land, ceremonial associations, and ceremonies.

COMPOUND WALLS Building walls consisting of more than one course placed side by side—a double or triple wall.

CONTIGUOUS WALLS Building walls in which there are no broken joints. All portions run together and overlap.

CORRUGATED POTTERY Pottery with alternate ridges and depressions formed on the exterior surface by a coiling-and-pinching technique.

COURSED MASONRY Masonry constructed of successive rows of stones beginning with an approximately level bed.

CROSS-BEDDED Describes stratified rock that contains irregular laminations oblique to the main beds.

DEFLECTOR An upright stone slab placed on the floor between the fireplace and ventilator shaft in a pithouse or kiva. Its purpose is to deflect the inrushing air away from the fire.

DIFFUSION The spread of elements of culture from one society to another in a chain-reaction form.

ENDOGAMOUS A rule of marriage that requires its members to marry within the group.

EXOGAMOUS A rule of marriage that requires its members to marry outside the group.

EXTENDED CORPSE A burial in which the body was stretched out full length in the grave—as opposed to a flexed burial.

FETISH A relatively small object usually of stone or bone, most often carved but sometimes natural in form, ordinarily resembling a bird or animal, and believed by the Indians to have specific powers to be used for accomplishing prescribed ends. For example, an animal fetish would be used either to help the hunter find that animal or to bring the animal close to the hunter. A ritual fetish placed on an altar would invoke certain needed powers during a ceremony.

FIRE DRILLS A set consisting of a round, pointed drill stick and a hearth stick. The fire maker placed the point of the stick on the hearth and spun the stick between his hands to generate friction. Used hearth sticks are easily recognized by the small cup-shaped depressions formed in them by the spinning drill.

FISCALES Members of the secular council as set up by the Spanish. They now serve as councilors for the governor, although they once functioned as church wardens.

FLESHER A scraper usually made of bone. It was used for cleaning hides, preparing various vegetal materials for food, and for certain other household needs.

FLEXED CORPSE A method of burial used to conserve space. The legs of the corpse were drawn up until the knees almost touched the chin, the feet were also bent, and sometimes the arms were folded as well, so that a fetal position was assumed.

HESHI A semiprecious stone, used by the modern Pueblo Indians for making what they refer to as a heshi necklace. The necklace stones are fashioned like a flat-surfaced button but are smaller, with a single hole drilled in the center for the string to pass through. Ancient Anasazi used heshi stone for various kinds of personal ornamentation.

HISTORIC A term generally applied to the era of recorded history. In the case of the Pueblos, it begins with the coming of the Spanish.

HORNO An oven shaped like the top half of a beehive. It is made of stone and adobe, and has a vent opening at the top and a side doorway through which the items to be baked are passed on a spatulate-formed wooden shovel.

IMPERSONATOR In Anasazi and Pueblo usage one who impersonates a god or spirit power by wearing the mask and costume traditionally associated with the god or spirit.

INCISED In pottery, the term applies to lines grooved into soft clay with a sharp tool.

IN SITU An object still in place in its original site.

JACAL A type of construction in which walls are made of a mat of upright poles lined with branches and reeds, then heavily plastered over with mud or clay.

KATCINA A spirit being and the masked (or rarely unmasked) human who impersonates the spirit in a ceremony. Some Katcinas have always existed, others are deceased humans who return in season to bring blessings needed for human survival. There are also Katcina dolls made for teaching aids for children.

KELEHOYA A novice being initiated into a Hopi society. The word means "little chicken hawk."

KIHUS Rectangular surface ceremonial rooms with some or all of the features common to kivas.

KILLED POTTERY Pottery buried with a deceased owner in which a hole has been punched or drilled in the bottom of the vessel in order to release its soul or spirit, since the vessel is considered a part of the owner.

KISI A small cottonwood shelter used during a dance. In particular, the Hopi use one during the Snake Dance.

KIVA Pueblo ceremonial chamber. As a rule, it is wholly or partly underground, or else designed to give the effect of a subterranean room. It is circular or rectangular. Religious rites are performed here. But it is also used by the men as a "clubroom" and a workroom for their crafts.

KOSHARE/KOSSA Secret societies common to the Rio Grande Keres and Tewa pueblos. The Keresan name is Koshare. The Tewa refer to them as Kossa. Both are associated with weather control, fertility, and the supervision of ceremonies.

KOSHARE The name used at Hano for the ritual clown.

KOYEMSHI The Hopi and Zuñi name for their sacred clowns.

KWERANA/KWIRANA The secret society of the Keres and Tewa pueblos complementary to the Koshares. The Keresan name is Kwerana, the Tewa is Kwirana. They are associated with weather control, fertility, and the supervision of ceremonies.

LAMBDOID FLATTENING Flattening of the back part of the skull. In the case of the Anasazi, this was usually caused by the use of a straight wooden cradleboard.

MACAW A type of parrot with exceptionally long and colorful tail feathers which have always been prized by the Anasazi and Pueblos for use in religious ceremonies.

MANO An oval or oblong handstone used for grinding corn and other foodstuffs on a metate.

MAUL A large stone, sometimes with a hand groove, used for pounding seeds and similar items.

MEALING BIN A rectangular box made of stone or wood that contained stones used in the manner of metates for grinding meal. The ground meal was then stored in jars or pits.

METATE The grinding stone on which the mano is used.

MOIETY A dual division of the village or Pueblo.

OLLA A pottery jar with a flared neck, used for carrying or storing water and other foodstuffs.

PAHO A prayer stick. There are many different kinds and shapes, but they are usually 6 to 12 inches long, made of cottonwood sticks, and decorated with paint, corn husks, and feathers.

PETROGLYPH A rock drawing pecked into the wall surface by using another and harder rock as a pecking tool.

PICTOGRAPH A drawing painted on a rock surface.

PI-GUMME OVEN An earth oven very similar to ones used by the Hopi to bake sweet-corn mush wrapped in corn husks.

PIKI Hopi term for "paper bread." This bread is made from a cornmeal batter, colored gray with wood ashes, dexterously spread very thinly with the hand over a heated slab of stone. After baking it is rolled up like a scroll, and in time becomes so crisp that it crackles like paper.

PILASTER A square masonry column set on top of a kiva bench, upon which the ends of the roof beams are rested.

PITHOUSE A neatly excavated earthen pit ranging from 10 to 20 feet in diameter and 2 to 5 feet deep, over which walls and a roof of beams, poles, brush, and mud were constructed to form a dwelling enclosure.

PLAZA A public square.

POLYCHROME POTTERY Painted pottery with three or more colors.

PROTOKIVA The forerunner of the kiva. It was a subterranean chamber with several features common to later Pueblo ceremonial structures.

RAMADA A canopy-like shelter made of brush, used for outdoor cooking and craftwork of various kinds. Its sides were usually left open to let breezes pass through while it protected the occupants from the hot sunshine.

RHOMBUS A long, thin, sometimes pointed, stick tied near its center on the end of a cord. The stick is swung like a propeller and makes a sound like thunder. As such, the using of one is a prayer for rain.

SHERD (OR SHARD) A fragment of a broken pottery vessel.

SIPAPU A small round hole of shallow depth dug in a pithouse or kiva floor midway between the firepit and the wall. It symbolizes the mythical place of emergence through which the Anasazi ancestors passed in their journey from the Underworld, or place of creation in the inner earth, to the surface of the world. It is also the opening through which the souls of the dead return to the Underworld, and at specified times of the year Katcinas come and return through the sipapu as they bring blessings to the Pueblo people.

SLASH-AND-BURN AGRICULTURE The farming technique whereby fields are cleared, burned, and planted over and over until yield decreases. Then the fields are allowed to lie fallow for several years until they regain fertility.

SLIP A coating of especially fine clay applied to a vessel before firing to give a smooth finish.

SPALL A chip or flake removed from a larger piece of stone. Spalling is the technique of filling in the gaps between large wall stones with the small chips of stone.

TABLITA A headdress consisting of an upright flat board of varying size which is usually carved and painted, and has feathers attached. Some tablitas are complete in themselves, and others are attached to masks.

TALUS A term that usually refers to rocks that separate from the cave roofs and fall to the cave floor to form the slopes in front of cliff dwellings.

TENIENTE Lieutenant governor in the secular council.

TIPONI A fetish made up of an ear of corn, feathers, corn seeds, vegetable seeds, piñon seeds, and a variety of outer strings. Each society has its own.

TUHUPBI Gourd smoothers.

TUMPLINE A narrow woven carrying strap passed over the forehead while carrying a burden on the back.

TUSAYAN The early Spanish name for the area occupied by the Hopi.

TWILLING A system of weaving in which the woof thread is carried over one and under two or more warp threads in such a way that it produces diagonal lines or ribs on the surface of the fabric or basket.

TWINING A system of weaving in which splints or threads are intertwined and wrapped around a foundation of radiating rods or threads.

UNILINEAL The reckoning of kinship relations through a single line of descent, either the mother's or the father's side.

VIGAS Ceiling beams which project beyond the exterior wall of a building for a distance of several feet.

WHIP The ailment for which a secret society holds the "whip" or power to cure by using its specific ritual in connection with the patient.

WUYE The clan ancestors. The nonhuman partner related to each clan. It consists of an animal, plant, or a natural or supernatural phenomenon. This gives the clan its name, its whip, and its protection in return for certain related services.

BIBLIOGRAPHY

FOR VOLUMES I AND II

Aberle, S. D.
  1948   The Pueblo Indians of New Mexico: Their Land, Economy and Civil Organization. *American Anthropologist,* Vol. 50, No. 4, Pt. 2, Oct.
Adair, John
  1944   *The Navajo and Pueblo Silversmiths.* University of Oklahoma Press, Norman.
Alexander, Hartley Burr
  1953   *The World's Rim.* University of Nebraska Press, Lincoln.
Alexander, Hubert G.
       The Excavation of Jemez Cave. *El Palacio,* Vol. 38, Nos. 18–19–20.
Ambler, J. Richard
  1977   *The Anasazi.* Museum of Northern Arizona, Flagstaff.
Amsden, Charles Avery
  1949   *Prehistoric Southwesterners from Basketmaker to Pueblo.* Southwest Museum, Los Angeles.
Anderson, Douglas and Barbara
  1976   *Chaco Canyon.* Popular Series No. 17. Southwest Parks and Monuments Association, Globe, Ariz.
Anderson, Keith M.
  1969   Tsegi Phase Technology. Doctoral dissertation, University of Washington, Seattle. University Microfilms, Ann Arbor.
Anton, Ferdinand
  1968   *Pre-Columbian Art: And, Later Indian Tribal Arts,* by Frederick J. Dockstader. Harry N. Abrams, New York.
Arizona Highways
  1951   Vol. 27, No. 5.
  1953   Vol. 29, No. 7.
  1972   Vol. 48, No. 1.
  1973   Vol. 49, No. 6.
  1974   Vol. 50, No. 2.
  1975   Vol. 51, No. 7.
  1978   Vol. 54, No. 3.
Atkinson, Mary Jourdan
  1963   *Indians of the Southwest.* 4th ed. Naylor Company, San Antonio.
Austin, Mary
  1924   The Days of Our Ancients. *Survey Magazine,* pp. 33–38. Oct. 1.
Bahnimptewa, Cliff
  1971   *Dancing Kachinas.* Heard Museum, Phoenix.
Baldwin, Gordon C.
  1938   Excavations at Kinishba Pueblo, Arizona. *American Antiquity,* Vol. 4, pp. 11–21.
  1939   Material Culture of Kinishba. *American Antiquity,* Vol. 4, pp. 314–27.
Bandelier, Adolph F. A.
  1910   *Documentary History of the Rio Grande Pueblos of New Mexico.* Papers of the School of American Archaeology No. 13. Santa Fe.
  1966   *The Southwestern Journals of Adolph F. Bandelier,* 1880–1882. Charles H. Lange and Carroll L. Riley, eds. University of New Mexico Press, Albuquerque.
Baxter, Sylvester
  1882   The Father of the Pueblos. *Harper's New Monthly Magazine,* Vol. 65, pp. 72–91.
Beck, Peggy V., and Walters, A. L.
  1977   *The Sacred Ways of Knowledge, Sources of Life.* Navajo Community College, Tsaile, Ariz. Navajo Nation.
Beck, Warren A., and Haase, Ynez D.
  1969   *Historical Atlas of New Mexico.* University of Oklahoma Press, Norman.
Bedinger, Margery
  1973   *Indian Silver.* University of New Mexico Press, Albuquerque.
Billingsley, M. W.
  1971   *Behind the Scenes in Hopi Land.* Privately printed.
Bohrer, Vorsila L.
  1968   Paleoecology of an Archaeological Site Near Snowflake, Arizona. Unpublished Ph.D. dissertation, Department of Botany, University of Arizona, Tucson.

Bourke, John G.
 1884   *The Snake-Dance of the Moquis of Arizona.* Charles Scribner's Sons, New York.
Branson, Oscar T.
 1976   *Fetishes and Carvings of the Southwest.* Treasure Chest Publications, Santa Fe.
Brew, John O.
        The First Two Seasons at Awatovi. *American Antiquity,* Vol. 3, pp. 122–37.
Bunting, Bainbridge
 1976   *Early Architecture in New Mexico.* University of New Mexico Press, Albuquerque.
Bunting, Bainbridge; Booth, Jean Lee; and Sims, William R., Jr.
 1964   *Taos Adobes.* Publication No. 2, Fort Burgwin Research Center. Museum of New Mexico Press,
        Santa Fe.
Bunzel, Ruth L.
 1929   *The Pueblo Potter.* Columbia University Contributions to Anthropology, Vol. 8. Columbia Uni-
        versity Press, New York.
 1932a Introduction to Zuñi Ceremonialism. Smithsonian Institution, Bureau of American Ethnology,
        47th Annual Report, pp. 467–544. Washington, D.C.
 1932b Zuñi Katcinas. Smithsonian Institution, Bureau of American Ethnology, 47th Annual Report,
        1929–1930, pp. 837–1086. Washington, D.C.
Burroughs, Carroll A.
 1959   Searching for Cliff Dweller's Secrets. *National Geographic Magazine,* Vol. 116, No. 5.
Bushnell, G. H. S.
 1968   *The First Americans.* McGraw-Hill Book Company, New York.
Buttree, Julia M.
 1930   *The Rhythm of the Redman.* Ronald Press Company, New York.
Capps, Walter Holden (editor)
 1976   *Seeing with a Native Eye.* Harper & Row, New York.
Clemmer, Richard O.
 1978   *Continuities of Hopi Culture Change.* Acoma Books, Ramona, Calif.
Coe, Michael D.
 1962   *Mexico.* Frederick A. Praeger, New York.
Coe, William R.
 1975   Resurrecting the Grandeur of Tikal. *National Geographic Magazine,* Vol. 148, No. 6, p. 792–98.
Collier, John
 1949   *On the Gleaming Way.* Sage Books, Denver.
Colton, Harold S.
 1939   *Prehistoric Culture Units and Their Relationships in Northern Arizona.* Museum of Northern Ari-
        zona, Bulletin 17. Flagstaff.
 1959   *Hopi Kachina Dolls.* University of New Mexico Press, Albuquerque.
 1960   *Black Sand.* University of New Mexico Press, Albuquerque.
Cosgrove, Cornelius Burton
 1947   *Caves of the Upper Gila and Hueco Areas in New Mexico and Texas.* Papers of the Peabody Museum
        of American Archeology and Ethnology, Vol. 24, No. 2. Harvard University, Cambridge, Mass.
Crane, Leo
 1925   *Indians of the Enchanted Desert.* Little, Brown & Company, Boston.
Curtis, Natalie (editor)
 1907   *The Indians' Book.* Harper and Brothers Publishers, New York.
Cushing, Frank Hamilton
 1882   My Adventures in Zuñi. *Century Magazine,* Vol. 25, No. 19, pp. 191–207; Vol. 25, No. 47, pp.
        500–11; Vol. 26, No. 4, pp. 28–47.
 1883   Zuñi Fetishes. Smithsonian Institution, Bureau of American Ethnology, 2nd Annual Report,
        1880–1881. Washington, D.C.
 1974   *Zuñi Breadstuff.* Indian Notes and Monographs Vol. 8. Reprint edition, Museum of the Ameri-
        can Indian, Heye Foundation, New York. (Originally published 1920.)
Davies, Nigel
 1979   *Voyagers to the New World.* William Morrow & Co., New York.
DeHarport, David L.
 1959   An Archaeological Survey of Canyon de Chelly, Northeastern Arizona: A Puebloan Community
        Through Time. Unpublished Ph.D. Dissertation in Anthropology, Harvard University, Cam-
        bridge, Mass.
Dennis, Wayne
 1965   *The Hopi Child.* University of Virginia Institute for Research in the Social Sciences, Monograph
        26, 1940. Science Editions. John Wiley & Sons, New York.

Densmore, Frances
   1938   *Music of Santo Domingo Pueblo, New Mexico.* Southwest Museum Papers No. 12. Southwest Museum, Los Angeles.
Dickson, D. Bruce
   1975   Settlement Pattern Stability and Change in the Middle Northern Rio Grande Region, New Mexico: A Test of Some Hypotheses. *American Antiquity,* Vol. 40, No. 2, pp. 159–71.
Di Peso, Charles C.
   1979   Prehistory: O'otam. Smithsonian Institution, Handbook of North American Indians, Vol. 9, Southwest, pp. 91–99. Washington, D.C.
Ditzler, Robert E.
   1967   *The Indian People of Arizona.* Vantage Press, New York.
Dockstader, Frederick J.
   1954   *The Kachina and the White Man.* Bulletin 35, Cranbrook Institute of Science. Bloomfield Hills, Mich.
Dorsey, George A.
   1899   The Hopi Indians of Arizona. *Popular Science Monthly,* Vol. 55, pp. 732–50.
   1903   *Indians of the Southwest.* Passenger Dept., Atchison, Topeka & Santa Fe Railway System.
Dorsey, George A., and Voth, Henry R.
   1901   *The Oraibi Soyal Ceremony.* Publications of the Field Columbian Museum Anthropological Series, Vol. 3, No. 1, pp. 1–59. Chicago.
   1902   *The Mishongnove Ceremonies of the Snake and Antelope Fraternities.* Publications of the Field Columbian Museum Anthropological Series, Vol. 3, No. 3, pp. 159–261. Chicago.
Douglas, Frederic H.
   1953   Material Culture Notes for the Denver Art Museum. No. 22. Denver Art Museum, Denver.
Dozier, Edward P.
   1957   Rio Grande Ceremonial Patterns. *New Mexico Quarterly,* Vol. 27, pp. 27–34.
   1966   *Hano, a Tewa Indian Community in Arizona.* Holt, Rinehart and Winston, New York.
   1970   *The Pueblo Indians of North America.* Holt, Rinehart and Winston, New York.
Dumarest, Father Noel
   1919   *Notes on Cochiti, New Mexico.* Memoirs of the American Anthropological Association, Vol. 6, No. 3. Lancaster, Pa.
Dutton, Bertha P.
   1963a *Friendly People: The Zuñi Indians.* Museum of New Mexico Press, Santa Fe.
   1963b *Sun Father's Way: The Kiva Murals of Kuaua, a Pueblo Ruin, Coronado State Monument, New Mexico.* University of New Mexico Press, Albuquerque.
   1970   *Let's Explore Indian Villages Past and Present.* Museum of New Mexico Press, Santa Fe.
   1970   *Navaho Weaving Today.* Museum of New Mexico Press, Santa Fe.
   1975   *Indians of the American Southwest.* Prentice-Hall, Englewood Cliffs, N.J.
Earle, Edwin, and Kennard, Edward A.
   1971   *Hopi Kachinas.* Museum of the American Indian, Heye Foundation, New York.
Eddy, Frank W.
   1961   *Excavations at Los Pinos Phase Sites in the Navajo Reservoir District.* Museum of New Mexico Papers No. 4. Museum of New Mexico Press, Santa Fe.
   1964   *Metates & Manos.* Popular Series Pamphlet No. 1. Museum of New Mexico Press, Santa Fe.
Eggan, Fred R.
   1950   *Social Organization of the Western Pueblos.* Chicago University Publications in Anthropology, Social Anthropology Series. University of Chicago Press, Chicago. Reprinted 1970.
Ekstrom, M. A. and J. O.
   1973   *How to Read and Write Hopi.* Hopi Action Program, Oraibi, Ariz.
Ellis, Florence H.
   1950   Big Kivas, Little Kivas, and Moiety Houses in Historical Reconstruction. *Southwest Journal of Anthropology,* Vol. 6, pp. 286–301.
Ellis, Florence H., and Brody, J. J.
   1964   Ceramic Stratigraphy and Tribal History at Taos Pueblo. *American Antiquity,* Vol. 29, pp. 316–27.
Ellis, Florence H., and Hammack, Laurens
   1968   The Inner Sanctum of Feather Cave, a Mogollon Sun and Earth Shrine Linking Mexico and the Southwest. *American Antiquity,* Vol. 33, No. 1, pp. 25–44.
Erdoes, Richard
   1976   *The Rain Dance People.* Alfred A. Knopf, New York.
Euler, Robert C., and Dobyns, Henry F.
   1971   *The Hopi People.* Indian Tribal Series, Phoenix.

Farb, Peter
    1968   *Man's Rise to Civilization.* E. P. Dutton & Co., New York.
Fell, Barry
    1976   *America B.C.* Pocket Books, New York.
Fergusson, Erna
    1971   *New Mexico: A Pageant of Three Peoples.* Alfred A. Knopf, New York.
Fewkes, Jesse Walter
    1891a   A Few Summer Ceremonials at Zuni Pueblo. *A Journal of American Ethnology and Archaeology,* Vol. 1, pp. 1–62. Houghton, Mifflin Company, Riverside Press, Cambridge, Mass.
    1891b   Reconnoissance of Ruins in or near the Zuni Reservation. *A Journal of American Ethnology and Archaeology,* Vol. 1, pp. 93–133. Houghton, Mifflin Company, Riverside Press, Cambridge, Mass.
    1892a   A Few Summer Ceremonials at the Tusayan Pueblos. *A Journal of American Ethnology and Archaeology,* Vol. 2, pp. 1–160. Houghton, Mifflin Company, Riverside Press, Cambridge, Mass.
    1892b   The Mam-zrau-ti: A Tusayan Ceremony. *The American Anthropologist,* Vol. 5, pp. 217–46.
    1892c   A Few Tusayan Pictographs. *The American Anthropologist,* Vol. 5, pp. 9–26.
    1892d   A Report on the Present Condition of a Ruin in Arizona Called Casa Grande. *A Journal of American Ethnology and Archaeology,* Vol. 2, pp. 179–93. Houghton, Mifflin Company, Riverside Press, Cambridge, Mass.
    1893a   A-WA-TO-BI: An Archaeological Verification of a Tusayan Legend. *The American Anthropologist,* Vol. 6, pp. 363–75.
    1893b   Central American Ceremony Which Suggests the Snake Dance of the Tusayan Villagers. *The American Anthropologist,* Vol. 6, pp. 285–306.
    1894   The Walpi Flute Observance: A Study of Primitive Dramatization. *The Journal of American Folk-Lore,* Vol. 7, No. 27, pp. 265–88.
    1895   The Oraibi Flute Altar. *The Journal of American Folk-Lore.* Vol. 7, No. 31, pp. 265–84.
    1896a   Preliminary Account of an Expedition to the Cliff Villages of the Red Rock Country, and the Tusayan Ruins of Sikyatki and Awatobi, Arizona, in 1895. Smithsonian Institution, Bureau of American Ethnology Report, 1895, pp. 557–88. Washington, D.C.
    1896b   The Tusayan Ritual: A Study of the Influence of Environment on Aboriginal Cults. Smithsonian Institution, Bureau of American Ethnology Report, 1895, pp. 683–700. Washington, D.C.
    1896c   The Miconinovi Flute Altars. *The Journal of American Folk-Lore,* Vol. 9, No. 35, pp. 241–56.
    1896d   *The Prehistoric Culture of Tusayan. The American Anthropologist,* o.s., Vol. 9, No. 5. Washington, D.C.
    1897a   The Sacrificial Element in Hopi Worship. *The Journal of American Folk-Lore,* Vol. 10, No. 36, pp. 187–201.
    1897b   Tusayan Snake Ceremonies. Smithsonian Institution, Bureau of American Ethnology, 16th Annual Report, 1894–1895, pp. 267–311. Washington, D.C.
    1898a   The Growth of the Hopi Ritual. *The Journal of American Folk-Lore,* Vol. 11, No. 42, pp. 174–94.
    1898b   Preliminary Account of an Expedition to the Pueblo Ruins Near Winslow, Arizona in 1896. Smithsonian Institution, Bureau of American Ethnology Report, 1896, pp. 517–41. Washington, D.C.
    1898c   Archeological Expedition to Arizona in 1895. Smithsonian Institution, Bureau of American Ethnology, 17th Annual Report, 1895–1896, pp. 519–744. Washington, D.C.
    1899   Hopi Basket Dances. *The Journal of American Folk-Lore,* Vol. 12, No. 45, pp. 81–96.
    1900a   The Lesser New-Fire Ceremony at Walpi. *The American Anthropologist,* Vol. 2, No. 1.
    1900b   A Theatrical Performance at Walpi. Washington Academy of Sciences, Proceedings, Vol. 2, No. 33. Washington, D.C.
    1901   The Owakulti Altar at Sichomovi Pueblo. *The American Anthropologist,* Vol. 3, No. 2.
    1902   Sky-God Personations in Hopi Worship. *The Journal of American Folk-Lore,* Vol. 15, No. 56, pp. 14–32.
    1903   Hopi Katcinas Drawn by Native Artists. Smithsonian Institution, Bureau of American Ethnology, 21st Annual Report, 1899–1900. Washington, D.C.
    1904   Two Summers' Work in Pueblo Ruins. Smithsonian Institution, Bureau of American Ethnology, 22nd Annual Report, 1900–1901, Part 1, pp. 3–195. Washington, D.C.
    1911a   *Preliminary Report on a Visit to the Navaho National Monument: Arizona.* Smithsonian Institution, Bureau of American Ethnology Bulletin No. 50. Washington, D.C.
    1911b   *Antiquities of the Mesa Verde National Park: Cliff Palace.* Smithsonian Institution, Bureau of American Ethnology Bulletin No. 51. Washington, D.C.
    1915   Prehistoric Remains in Arizona, New Mexico, and Colorado. Smithsonian Miscellaneous Collections, Vol. 66, No. 3, pp. 82–98. Washington, D.C.
    1916   Prehistoric Remains in New Mexico, Colorado, and Utah. Smithsonian Miscellaneous Collections, Vol. 66, No. 17, pp. 76–92. Washington, D.C.

1917a *Archeological Investigations in New Mexico, Colorado, and Utah.* Smithsonian Miscellaneous Collections, Vol. 68, No. 1. Washington, D.C.

1917b A Prehistoric Mesa Verde Pueblo and Its People. Smithsonian Institution, Bureau of American Ethnology, Annual Report, 1916, pp. 461–88. Washington, D.C.

1919a *Prehistoric Villages, Castles and Towers of Southwestern Colorado.* Smithsonian Institution, Bureau of American Ethnology Bulletin No. 70. Washington, D.C.

1919b Designs on Prehistoric Hopi Pottery. Smithsonian Institution, Bureau of American Ethnology, 33rd Annual Report, 1911–1912, pp. 207–84. Washington, D.C.

1919c Archeological Field-Work in Southwestern Colorado and Utah. Smithsonian Explorations, 1918, Smithsonian Miscellaneous Collections, Vol. 70, No. 2, pp. 68–80. Washington, D.C.

1920a Sun Worship of the Hopi Indians. Smithsonian Institution, Bureau of American Ethnology Report, 1918, pp. 493–526. Washington, D.C.

1920b *Field-Work on the Mesa Verde National Park.* Smithsonian Miscellaneous Collections, Vol. 72, No. 1. Washington, D.C.

1921a Excavating Cliff Dwellings in Mesa Verde. *Scientific American Monthly*, Jan. 1921, pp. 9–13.

1921b Field-Work on Mesa Verde National Park. *Smithsonian Explorations, 1920*, Smithsonian Miscellaneous Collections, Vol. 72, No. 6, pp. 75–102. Washington, D.C.

1922a Fire Worship of the Hopi Indians. Smithsonian Institution, Bureau of American Ethnology, Annual Report, 1920, pp. 589–610. Washington, D.C.

1922b Ancestor Worship of the Hopi Indians. Smithsonian Institution, Bureau of American Ethnology, Annual Report, 1921, pp. 485–506. Washington, D.C.

1922c Archeological Field-Work on the Mesa Verde National Park. *Smithsonian Explorations*, Smithsonian Miscellaneous Collections, Vol. 72, No. 15, pp. 64–83. Washington, D.C.

1923 Archeological Field-Work on the Mesa Verde National Park, Colorado. *Smithsonian Explorations, 1922*, Smithsonian Miscellaneous Collections, Vol. 74, No. 5, pp. 90–115. Washington, D.C.

1924 The Use of Idols in Hopi Worship. Smithsonian Institution, Bureau of American Ethnology, Annual Report, 1922, pp. 377–97. Washington, D.C.

1925 The Hovenweep National Monument. Smithsonian Institution, Bureau of American Ethnology, Annual Report, 1923, pp. 456–80. Washington, D.C.

1926 *An Archeological Collection from Young's Canyon, Near Flagstaff, Arizona.* Smithsonian Miscellaneous Collections, Vol. 77, No. 10. Washington, D.C.

1927a The Kacina Altars in Hopi Worship. Smithsonian Institution, Bureau of American Ethnology, Annual Report, 1926, pp. 469–87. Washington, D.C.

1927b Archeological Field-Work in Arizona. *Smithsonian Explorations, 1926*, Smithsonian Miscellaneous Collections, Vol. 78, No. 7, pp. 207–32. Washington, D.C.

Fewkes, Jesse Walter, and Owens, J. G.

1892 The Lä-lä-kōn-ta: A Tusayan Dance. *The American Anthropologist*, Vol. 5, No. 2, pp. 105–30.

Fewkes, Jesse Walter, and Stephen, Alexander M.

1892 The Nä-ác-nai-ya: A Tusayan Initiation Ceremony. *The Journal of American Folk-Lore*, Vol. 5, No. 18, pp. 189–221.

1893 The Pá-lü-lü-koñ-ti: A Tusayan Ceremony. *The Journal of American Folk-Lore*, Vol. 6, No. 23, pp. 169–84.

Fleming, Henry Craig, M.D.

1924 *Medical Observations on the Zuñi Indians.* Contributions from the Museum of the American Indian, Heye Foundation, Vol. 7, No. 2. Museum of the American Indian, New York.

Folsom, Franklin

1973 *Red Power on the Rio Grande.* Follett Publishing Company, Chicago.

Forrest, Earle R.

1961 *The Snake Dance of the Hopi Indians.* Westernlore Press, Los Angeles.

1921 The Mesa Dwellers of the Painted Desert. *Travel Magazine*, Vol. 37, Aug., pp. 3–8.

1923 The Snake Dance in the Painted Desert. *Travel Magazine*, Vol. 40, Jan., pp. 16–20.

Fox, Nancy

1978 *Pueblo Weaving and Textile Arts.* A Museum of New Mexico Press Guidebook, No. 3. Museum of New Mexico Press, Santa Fe.

Frazier, Kendrick

1980 The Anasazi Sun Dagger. *Science 80*, Vol. 1, No. 1, pp. 56–67.

Fundaburk, Emma Lila, and Foreman, Mary Douglass

1957 *Sun Circles and Human Hands.* Emma Lila Fundaburk, Luverne, Ala.

Gilman, Benjamin Ives

1891 Zuni Melodies. *A Journal of American Ethnology and Archaeology*, Vol. 1, pp. 63–91. Houghton, Mifflin Company, Riverside Press, Cambridge, Mass.

Gladwin, Harold S.

1945 *The Chaco Branch Excavations at White Mound and in the Red Mesa Valley.* Medallion Papers No. 33. Gila Pueblo, Globe, Ariz.

1957   *A History of the Ancient Southwest.* Bond Wheelwright Company, Portland, Maine.

Goddard, Pliny Earle
  1928   *Pottery of the Southwestern Indians.* American Museum of Natural History, New York.
  1931   *Indians of the Southwest.* Handbook Series No. 2. American Museum of Natural History, New York.

Goldfrank, Esther Schiff
  1927   *The Social and Ceremonial Organization of Cochiti.* Memoirs of the American Anthropological Association, No. 33.
  1967   *The Artist of "Isleta Paintings" in Pueblo Society.* Smithsonian Press, Washington, D.C.

Gonzales, Clara
  1966   *The Shalakos Are Coming.* Reprint from *El Palacio.* Museum of New Mexico, Santa Fe.

Gordon, Dudley
  1972   An Early Fiesta at Laguna. *The Masterkey,* Vol. 46, No. 1. Southwest Museum, Los Angeles.

Grant, Blanche C.
  1925   *Taos Indians.* Privately printed, Taos, N. Mex.

Grant, Campbell
  1978   *Canyon de Chelly: Its People and Rock Art.* University of Arizona Press, Tucson.

Graybill, Florence Curtis, and Boesen, Victor
  1976   *Edward Sheriff Curtis: Visions of a Vanishing Race.* Thomas Y. Crowell, New York.

Gumerman, George J.
  1970   *Black Mesa: Survey and Excavation in Northeastern Arizona.* Prescott College Press, Prescott, Ariz.

Gumerman, George J., and Skinner, S. Alan
  1960   Synthesis of the Prehistory of the Central Little Colorado Valley. *American Antiquity,* Vol. 33, No. 2, pp. 185–99.

Gumerman, George J.; Westfall, Deborah; and Weed, Carol S.
  1972   *Black Mesa: Archaeological Investigations on Black Mesa: The 1969–1970 Seasons.* Prescott College Press, Prescott, Ariz.

Hack, John T.
  1942   *The Changing Physical Environment of the Hopi Indians of Arizona.* Papers of the Peabody Museum of American Archeology and Ethnology, Vol. 35, No. 1, Reports of the Awatovi Expedition, No. 1. Harvard University, Cambridge, Mass.

Haeberlin, H. K.
  1916   *The Idea of Fertilization in the Culture of the Pueblo Indians.* Memoirs of the American Anthropological Association, Vol. 3, No. 1.

Hall, Alice J., and Spier, Peter
  1975   A Traveler's Tale of Ancient Tikal. *National Geographic Magazine,* Vol. 148, No. 6, pp. 799–811.

Hall, Edward Twitchell, Jr.
  1944   *Early Stockaded Settlements in the Governador, New Mexico: A marginal Anasazi Development from Basket Maker III to Pueblo I Times.* Columbia University Press, New York.

Hargrave, Lyndon L.
  1931   Excavations at Kin Tiel and Kokopnyama. Smithsonian Miscellaneous Collections, Vol. 82, No. 11, pp. 80–120. Washington, D.C.

Harlow, Francis H.
  1970   *Historic Pueblo Indian Pottery.* Museum of New Mexico Press, Santa Fe.

Harlow, Francis H., and Young, John V.
  1965   *Contemporary Pueblo Indian Pottery.* Museum of New Mexico Press, Santa Fe.

Harrington, John Peabody
  1916   The Ethnogeography of the Tewa Indians. Smithsonian Institution, Bureau of American Ethnology, 29th Annual Report, 1907–1908, pp. 29–636. Washington, D.C.

Hart, E. Richard
  1973   *The Zuñis: Experiences and Descriptions.* Pueblo of Zuñi.

Harvey, Byron, III
  1970   *Ritual in Pueblo Art.* Museum of the American Indian, Heye Foundation, New York.

Harvey, Byron, III (editor)
  1967   *The Henry R. Voth Collection at Grand Canyon, Arizona.* From a catalogue prepared for the Fred Harvey Company in 1912. Arequipa Press, Phoenix.

Hassrick, Royal B.
  1960   *Indian Art of the Americas.* Denver Art Museum, Denver.

Haury, Emil W.
  1945   *The Excavation of Los Muertos and Neighboring Ruins in the Salt River Valley, Southern Arizona.* Papers of the Peabody Museum of American Archeology and Ethnology, Vol. 24, No. 1. Harvard University, Cambridge, Mass.

1962 The Greater American Southwest. In Robert J. Braidwood and Gordon R. Willey, eds., *Courses Toward Urban Life*, pp. 106–31. Viking Fund Publications in Anthropology, No. 32. Wenner-Gren Foundation for Anthropological Research Inc., New York.

1976 *The Hohokam*. University of Arizona Press, Tucson.

Haury, Emil W., and Hargrave, Lyndon L.

1931 *Recently Dated Pueblo Ruins in Arizona*. Smithsonian Miscellaneous Collections, Vol. 82, No. 11. Washington, D.C.

Hawkes, Jacquetta

1976 *The Atlas of Early Man*. St. Martins Press, New York.

Hayes, Alden C., and Lancaster, James A.

1975 *Badger House Community*. U.S. Department of the Interior, National Park Service, Washington, D.C.

Hegemann, Elizabeth Compton

1963 *Navaho Trading Days*. University of New Mexico Press, Albuquerque.

Helfritz, Hans

1970 *Mexican Cities of the Gods*. Praeger Publishers, New York.

Henderson, Palmer

1893 The Cliff Dwellers. *The Literary Northwest*, Vol. 3, May, pp. 79–86.

Herold, Laurance C., and Luebben, Ralph A.

1968 *Taos Archaeology*. Fort Burgwin Research Center, Publication 7. Taos, N. Mex.

Hewett, Edgar Lee

1936 *Chaco Canyon and Its Monuments*. Handbooks of Archaeological History, No. 2. University of New Mexico Press, Albuquerque.

Hewett, Edgar L., and Bandelier, Adolph F. A.

1937 *Indians of the Rio Grande Valley*. University of New Mexico and School of American Research. University of New Mexico Press, Albuquerque.

Highwater, Jamake

1976 *Song from the Earth*. New York Graphic Society, Boston.

1977 *Ritual of the Wind*. Viking Press, New York.

Hill, James N., and Hevly, Richard H.

1968 Pollen at Broken K Pueblo: Some New Interpretations. *American Antiquity*, Vol. 33, No. 2, pp. 200–10.

Hodge, Frederick W.

1898 Ascent of the Enchanted Mesa. *The Century Magazine*, Vol. 56, May, pp. 15–25.

1918 Excavations at Hawikuh, New Mexico. Smithsonian Explorations, 1917, Smithsonian Miscellaneous Collections, Vol. 68, pp. 61–72. Washington, D.C.

Hofmann, Charles

1967 *American Indians Sing*. John Day Company, New York.

Hofmann, Charles (editor)

1968 *Frances Densmore and American Indian Music*. Contributions from the Museum of the American Indian, Heye Foundation, Vol. 23. Heye Foundation, New York.

Holien, Elaine Baran

Kachinas. *El Palacio*, No. 76, No. 4. Museum of New Mexico, Santa Fe.

Holmes, William Henry

1899 *Ancient Ruins of Southwestern Colorado*. 10th Annual Report, U.S. Geological and Geographic Survey of the Territories (Hayden Survey) for 1876. Washington, D.C.

Hough, Walter

1903 Archaeological Field Work in Northeastern Arizona, Expedition of 1901, Museum-Gates Expedition. Report of the U.S. National Museum of 1901, pp. 279–358. Washington, D.C.

1915 *The Hopi Indians*. Torch Press, Cedar Rapids, Iowa.

1917 Archeological Investigations in New Mexico. Smithsonian Explorations, 1916, Smithsonian Miscellaneous Collections, Vol. 66, No. 17, pp. 99–111. Washington, D.C.

1920 Explorations of a Pit House Village at Luna, New Mexico. Proceedings of the U.S. National Museum, Vol. 55, pp. 409–31. Washington, D.C.

1929 Explorations in a Great Secret Cave in Eastern Arizona. *Art and Archeology*, Vol. 28, Oct., pp. 117–25.

Hunter, C. Bruce

1974 *A Guide to Ancient Maya Ruins*. University of Oklahoma Press, Norman.

Ickes, Anna Wilmarth

1933 *Mesa Land*. Houghton Mifflin Company, Riverside Press, Cambridge, Mass.

Irwin-Williams, Cynthia

1973 *The Oshara Tradition: Origins of Anasazi Culture*. Eastern New Mexico University, Contributions in Anthropology, Vol. 5, No. 1. Portales.

Ivers, Louise Harris
    1977   Early Photographs of Indian Pueblos in New Mexico. *The Masterkey*, Vol. 51, No. 3. Southwest Museum, Los Angeles.
Jackson, William H.
    1876   *Ancient Ruins of Southwestern Colorado.* Report of U.S. Geological and Geographic Survey of the Territories (Hayden Survey) for 1874. Washington, D.C.
James, George Wharton
    1919   *The Indians of the Painted Desert Region.* Little, Brown & Company, Boston.
    1974   *Indian Blankets & Their Makers.* Dover Publications, Inc. (Originally published 1914, by A. C. McClurg & Company, Chicago.)
James, H. L.
    1970   *Acoma, the People of the White Rock.* Rio Grande Press, Glorieta, N. Mex.
James, Harry C.
    1974   *Pages from Hopi History.* University of Arizona Press, Tucson.
Jarrett, Walter
    1978   Acoma, New Mexico Sky City. *Mankind Magazine*, Vol. 3, No. 6.
Jeancon, J. A.
    1923   *Excavations in the Chama Valley, New Mexico.* Smithsonian Institution, Bureau of American Ethnology Bulletin No. 81. Washington, D.C.
Jennings, Jesse D.
    1956   The American Southwest: A Problem in Cultural Isolations. In Robert Wauchope, ed., *Seminars in Cultural Isolation*, pp. 59–127. Memoirs of the Society of American Archaeology, No. 11. Salt Lake City.
    1966   *Glen Canyon: A Summary.* University of Utah Anthropology Papers, No. 81 (Glen Canyon Series No. 31). Salt Lake City.
    1968   *Prehistory of North America.* McGraw-Hill Book Co., New York.
Jernigan, E. Wesley
    1978   *Jewelry of the Prehistoric Southwest.* School of American Research, Santa Fe. University of New Mexico Press, Albuquerque.
Jett, Stephen C., and Bohn, Dave
    1977   *House of Three Turkeys: Anasazi Redoubt.* Capra Press, Santa Barbara.
Jones, Louis Thomas
    1967   *Indian Cultures of the Southwest.* Naylor Company, San Antonio.
Jones, Oakah L., Jr.
    1966   *Pueblo Warriors and Spanish Conquest.* University of Oklahoma Press, Norman.
Judd, Neil M.
    1916   Archeological Reconnoissance in Western Utah. Smithsonian Miscellaneous Collections, Vol. 66, No. 3., pp. 64–71. Washington, D.C.
    1917   Archeological Reconnoissance in Western Utah. Smithsonian Miscellaneous Collections, Vol. 66, No. 17, pp. 103–8. Washington, D.C.
    1919   Archeological Investigations at Paragonah, Utah. Smithsonian Miscellaneous Collections, Vol. 70, No. 3, pp. 1–37. Washington, D.C.
    1922   Archeological Investigations at Pueblo Bonito, New Mexico. Smithsonian Miscellaneous Collections, Vol. 72, No. 15, pp. 106–17. Washington, D.C.
    1923   Pueblo Bonito, the Ancient. *National Geographic Magazine*, Vol. 44, pp. 99–108.
    1924   Two Chaco Canyon Pit Houses. Smithsonian Institution, Bureau of American Ethnology, Annual Report, 1922, pp. 399–413. Washington, D.C.
    1925a   Everyday Life in Pueblo Bonito. *National Geographic Magazine*, Vol. 48, pp. 227–62.
    1925b   Archeological Investigations at Pueblo Bonito, New Mexico. Smithsonian Miscellaneous Collections, Vol. 77, No. 2, pp. 83–91. Washington, D.C.
    1926   Archeological Observations North of the Rio Colorado. Smithsonian Institution, Bureau of American Ethnology Bulletin No. 82. Washington, D.C.
    1927   Archeological Investigations at Pueblo Bonito and Pueblo Del Arroyo, New Mexico. Smithsonian Miscellaneous Collections, Vol. 78, No. 1, pp. 80–88.
    1940   *Progress in the Southwest.* Smithsonian Miscellaneous Collections, Vol. 100. Washington, D.C.
    1954   *The Material Culture of Pueblo Bonito.* Smithsonian Miscellaneous Collections, Vol. 124. Washington, D.C.
    1959   *Pueblo del Arroyo, Chaco Canyon, New Mexico.* Smithsonian Miscellaneous Collections, Vol. 138, No. 1. Washington, D.C.
    1964   *The Architecture of Pueblo Bonito.* Smithsonian Miscellaneous Collections, Vol. 147, No. 1. Washington, D.C.

Keegan, Marcia
    1972   *The Taos Indians and Their Sacred Blue Lake.* Julian Messner, New York.

Kidder, Alfred Vincent
    1924   *An Introduction to the Study of Southwestern Archaeology.* Yale University Press, New Haven & London.
    1932   *The Artifacts of Pecos.* Robert S. Peabody Foundation for Archaeology, Phillips Academy, Andover, Mass. Published for Phillips Academy by Yale University Press, New Haven.
    1958   *Pecos, New Mexico: Archaeological Notes.* Papers of the Robert S. Peabody Foundation for Archaeology, Vol. 5. Phillips Academy, Andover, Mass.

Kidder, Alfred Vincent, and Guernsey, Samuel J.
    1919   *Archeological Explorations in Northeastern Arizona.* Smithsonian Institution, Bureau of American Ethnology Bulletin No. 65. Washington, D.C.

King, Dale S. (editor)
    1945   *Arizona's National Monuments.* Southwestern Monuments Association. Popular Series, No. 2. Santa Fe.

King, Patrick
    1975   *Pueblo Indian Religious Architecture.* Patrick King, Salt Lake City.

Kirk, Ruth F.
    1943   *Introduction to Zuñi Fetishism.* Papers of the School of America Research, Archaeological Institute of America, Santa Fe, N. Mex.

Kurath, Gertrude Prokosch, with Garcia, Antonio
    1970   *Music and Dance of the Tewa Pueblos.* Museum of New Mexico, Research Records No. 8. Museum of New Mexico Press, Santa Fe.

Lange, Charles H.
    1968   *Cochiti: A New Mexico Pueblo, Past and Present.* Southern Illinois University Press, Carbondale.

Lange, Charles H., and Riley, Carroll L. (editors)
    1966   *The Southwestern Journals of Adolph F. Bandelier, 1880–1882.* University of New Mexico Press, Albuquerque.

Laski, Vera
    1959   *Seeking Life.* Memoirs of the American Folklore Society, Vol. 50.

Leighton, Dorothea C., and Adair, John
    1966   *People of the Middle Place.* Behavior Science Monographs. Human Relations Area Files Press, New Haven.

Lindsay, A. J., Jr.
    1969   The Tsegi Phase of Kayenta Cultural Tradition in Northeastern Arizona. Unpublished doctoral dissertation. University of Arizona, Tucson.

Lister, Florence C. and Robert H.
    1968   *Earl Morris & Southwestern Archaeology.* University of New Mexico Press, Albuquerque.
    1969   *The Earl H. Morris Memorial Pottery Collection.* Series in Anthropology No. 16. University of Colorado Press, Boulder.

Lister, Robert H. and Florence C.
    1978   *Anasazi Pottery.* Maxwell Museum of Anthropology, University of New Mexico. University of New Mexico Press, Albuquerque.

Litto, Gertrude
    1976   *South American Folk Pottery.* Watson-Guptill Publications, New York.

Lockett, Hattie Greene
    1933   *The Unwritten Literature of the Hopi.* University of Arizona Bulletin, Vol. 4, No. 4. Social Science Bulletin No. 2. University of Arizona, Tucson.

Longacre, William A. (editor)
    1970   *Reconstructing Prehistoric Pueblo Societies.* A School of American Research Book. University of New Mexico Press, Albuquerque.

Lummis, Charles F.
    1892   The Indian Who Is Not Poor. *Scribner's,* Vol. 12, pp. 361–71.
    1925   *Mesa, Cañon and Pueblo.* Century Company, New York & London.

Lyon, Luke
    1977   Michelangelo of the West. *New Mexico Magazine,* Vol. 55, No. 6, pp. 20–25.

McCluney, Eugene B.
    1975   The Eastern Pueblos, in Donald E. Worcester, ed., *Forked Tongues and Broken Treaties,* pp. 425–48. Caxton Printers, Caldwell, Idaho.

McIntyre, Loren
    1973   The Lost Empire of the Incas. *National Geographic Magazine,* Vol. 144, No. 6, pp. 729–87.

Mails, Thomas E.
    1972   *The Mystic Warriors of the Plains.* Doubleday & Company, Garden City, N.Y.

1974   *The People Called Apache.* Prentice-Hall, Englewood Cliffs, N.J.

1978   *Sundancing at Rosebud and Pine Ridge.* The Center for Western Studies of Augustana College, Sioux Falls, S. Dak.

Marriott, Alice

1949   *These Are the People.* Laboratory of Anthropology, Santa Fe.

Martin, Paul S.

1936   *Lowry Ruin in Southwestern Colorado.* Field Museum of Natural History Anthropological Series, Vol. 23, No. 1. Chicago.

1940   *The SU Site: Excavations at a Mogollon Village, Western New Mexico, 1939.* Field Museum of Natural History Anthropological Series, Vol. 32, No. 1. Chicago.

Martin, Paul S.; Lloyd, Carl; and Spoehr, Alexander

1938   *Archaeological Work in the Ackmen-Lowry Area, Southwestern Colorado, 1937.* Field Museum of Natural History Anthropological Series, Vol. 23, No. 2. Chicago.

Martin, Paul S.; Longacre, William A.; and Hill, James N.

1967   *Chapters in the Prehistory of Eastern Arizona, III.* Fieldiana: Anthropology, Vol. 57. Field Museum of Natural History, Chicago.

Martin, Paul S., and Plog, Fred

1973   *The Archaeology of Arizona.* American Museum of Natural History. Doubleday & Company/Natural History Press, Garden City, N.Y.

Martin, Paul S.; Rinaldo, John B.; and Antevs, Ernst

1949   *Cochise and Mogollon Sites: Pine Lawn Valley, Western New Mexico.* Fieldiana: Anthropology, Vol. 38, No. 1. Chicago Natural History Museum, Chicago.

Martin, Paul S.; Rinaldo, John B.; and Bluhm, Elaine

1954   *Caves of the Reserve Area.* Fieldiana: Anthropology, Vol. 42. Chicago Natural History Museum, Chicago.

Martin, Paul S., et al.

1962   *Chapters in the Prehistory of Eastern Arizona, I.* Fieldiana: Anthropology, Vol. 53. Chicago Natural History Museum, Chicago.

Maxwell, James A. (editor)

1978   *America's Fascinating Indian Heritage.* Reader's Digest Association, Pleasantville, N.Y.

Mera, Harry Percival

1975   *Pueblo Indian Embroidery.* William Gannon, Santa Fe.

Metcalf, Willard L.

1924   Zuñi: Leaves from a Sketch Book. *Survey Magazine,* Vol. 53, pp. 29–32.

Meyer, Karl E.

1973   Teotihuacan. *Newsweek.*

Mindeleff, Cosmos

1897   The Cliff Ruins of Canyon de Chelly, Arizona. Smithsonian Institution, Bureau of American Ethnology, 16th Annual Report, 1894–1895, pp. 73–198. Washington, D.C.

1898   Navaho Houses. Smithsonian Institution, Bureau of American Ethnology, 17th Annual Report, 1895–1896, pp. 469–517. Washington, D.C.

Mindeleff, Victor

1891   A Study of Pueblo Architecture: Tusayan and Cibola. Smithsonian Institution, Bureau of American Ethnology, 8th Annual Report, 1886–1887, pp. 3–228. Washington, D.C.

Monsen, Frederick

1907a   Pueblos of the Painted Desert: How the Hopi Build Their Community Dwelling on the Cliffs. *Craftsman,* Vol. 12, Apr., pp. 16–33.

1907b   The Primitive Folk of the Desert: Splendid Physical Development That Yet Shows Many of the Characteristics of an Earlier Race Than Our Own. *Craftsman,* Vol. 12, May, pp. 164–78.

1907c   Festivals of the Hopi: Religion the Inspiration, and Dancing an Expression in All Their National Ceremonies. *Craftsman,* Vol. 12, June, pp. 269–85.

Montgomery, H.

1894   Prehistoric Man in Utah. *The Archaeologist,* Vol. 2.

Mooney, James

1895   Recent Archeologic Find in Arizona. *The American Anthropologist,* Vol. 6, pp. 283–84.

Morgan, L. H.

1881   Houses and House-life of the American Aborigines. Contributions to North American Ethnology, Vol. 4.

Mori, Joyce and John

1972   Modern Hopi Coiled Basketry. *The Masterkey,* Vol. 46, No. 1, pp. 4–17. Southwest Museum, Los Angeles.

Morley, Sylvanus G.
  1956   *The Ancient Maya.* 3rd rev. ed. Stanford University Press, Stanford.
Morley, Sylvanus, and Kidder, Alfred V.
  1917   The Archaeology of McElmo Canyon, Colorado. *El Palacio,* Vol. 4, No. 4. Museum of New
          Mexico, Santa Fe.
Morris, Ann Axtell
  1978   *Digging in the Southwest.* rev. ed. Peregrine Smith, Santa Barbara & Salt Lake City.
Morris, Earl H.
  1919   Preliminary Account of the Antiquities of the Region Between the Mancos and La Plata Rivers
          in Southwestern Colorado. Smithsonian Institution, Bureau of American Ethnology, 33rd An-
          nual Report, 1911–1912, pp. 155–206. Washington, D.C.
  1925   Exploring in the Canyon of Death. *National Geographic Magazine,* Vol. 48, No. 3, pp. 263–300.
  1927   *The Beginnings of Pottery Making in the San Juan Area: Unfired Prototypes and the Wares of the Earliest
          Ceramic Period.* Anthropological Papers of the American Museum of Natural History, Vol. 28,
          Part 2. New York.
  1939   Archaeological Studies in the La Plata District: Southwestern Colorado and Northwestern New
          Mexico. Carnegie Institution of Washington, Publication 519. Washington, D.C.
Moseley, Michael E., and Mackey, Carol J.
  1973   Chan Chan, Peru's Ancient City of Kings. *National Geographic Magazine,* Vol. 143, No. 3, pp.
          318–55.
Moskowitz, Ira, and Collier, John
  1949   *Patterns and Ceremonials of the Indians of the Southwest.* E. P. Dutton & Co., New York.
Muench, David, and Pike, Donald G.
  1974   *Anasazi: Ancient People of the Rock.* American West Publishing Company, Palo Alto, Calif.
Nagata, Shuichi
  1970   *Modern Transformations of Moenkopi Pueblo.* University of Illinois Studies in Anthropology No. 6.
          University of Illinois Press, Urbana.
Neeley, James A., and Olson, Alan P.
  1977   *Archaeological Reconnaissance of Monument Valley in Northeastern Arizona.* Museum of Northern
          Arizona, MNA Research Paper No. 3. Flagstaff.
Nequatewa, Edmund
  1936   *Truth of a Hopi.* Museum of Northern Arizona, Bulletin No. 8. Flagstaff.
Nettl, Bruno
  1954   *North American Indian Musical Styles.* Memoirs of the American Folklore Society, Vol. 45.
Newberry, J. S.
  1876   *Report of the Exploring Expedition from Santa Fe, New Mexico, to the Junction of the Grand and Green
          Rivers of the Great Colorado of the West, in 1859.* U.S. Engineering Department, Washington, D.C.
Newman, Stanley
  1965   *Zuni Grammar.* University of New Mexico Publications in Anthropology, No. 14. University of
          New Mexico Press, Albuquerque.
Nordenskiöld, Gustaf
  1893   *The Cliff Dwellers of the Mesa Verde, Southwestern Colorado: Their Pottery and Implements.* English
          translation by D. Lloyd Morgan. P. A. Norstedt and Soner, Stockholm and Chicago.
Nusbaum, Deric
  1926   *Deric in Mesa Verde.* G. P. Putnam's Sons, New York & London.
O'Kane, Walter Collins
  1950   *Sun in the Sky.* Civilization of the American Indian Series, Vol. 30. University of Oklahoma
          Press, Norman.
Oliver, Marion L.
  1911   The Snake Dance. *National Geographic Magazine,* Vol. 22, No. 2, pp. 107–37.
Ortiz, Alfonso
  1969   *The Tewa World: Space, Time, Being, and Becoming in a Pueblo Society.* University of Chicago
          Press, Chicago.
Ortiz, Alfonso (editor)
  1972   *New Perspectives on the Pueblos.* A School of American Research Book. University of New Mexico
          Press, Albuquerque.
  1979   *The Southwest.* The Handbook of North American Indians, Vol. 9. Smithsonian Institution,
          Washington, D.C.
Owens, J. G.
  1892   Natal Ceremonies of the Hopi Indians. *A Journal of American Ethnology and Archaeology,* Vol. 2,
          pp. 161–75. Houghton Mifflin Company, Riverside Press, Cambridge, Mass.
Pagden, A. R. (editor)
  1975   *The Maya: Diego de Landa's Account of the Affairs of Yucatán.* J. Philip O'Hara, Chicago.

Parsons, Elsie Clews
    1922   *Winter and Summer Dance Series in Zuñi in 1918.* University of California Publications in Ameri-
            can Archaeology and Ethnology, Vol. 17, No. 3, pp. 171–216. University of California Press,
            Berkeley.
    1925   Introduction and Notes to Crow-wing, *A Pueblo Indian Journal, 1920–1921.* Memoirs of the
            American Anthropological Association, No. 32.
    1926   *Tewa Tales.* Memoirs of the American Folk-Lore Society, Vol. 19.
    1929   *The Social Organization of the Tewa of New Mexico.* Memoirs of the American Anthropological
            Association, No. 36.
    1930   Spanish Elements in the Kachina Cult of the Pueblos. International Congress of Americanists,
            23rd Session, Proceedings, pp. 582–603.
    1933   *Hopi and Zuñi Ceremonialism.* Memoirs of the American Anthropological Association, No. 39.
    1936   *Taos Pueblo.* General Series in Anthropology, No. 2. George Banta Publishing Company, Me-
            nasha, Wis.
    1939a   *Pueblo Indian Religion.* Vol. 1, Part 1. University of Chicago Press, Chicago.
    1939b   *Pueblo Indian Religion.* Vol. 1, Part 2. University of Chicago Press, Chicago.
    1939c   *Pueblo Indian Religion.* Vol. 2, Part 1. University of Chicago Press, Chicago.
    1939d   *Pueblo Indian Religion.* Vol. 2, Part 2. University of Chicago Press, Chicago.
    1962   *Isleta Paintings.* Esther S. Goldfrank, ed. Smithsonian Institution, Washington, D.C.
    1974   *The Pueblo of Isleta.* University of Albuquerque, Calvin Horn Publishers, Albuquerque.
Peckham, Stewart
    1965   *Prehistoric Weapons in the Southwest.* Museum of New Mexico Press, Popular Series Pamphlet
            No. 3. Santa Fe.
Pendleton, Mary
    1974   *Navajo and Hopi Weaving Techniques.* Collier Books, New York.
Pepper, George H.
    1920   *Pueblo Bonito.* Anthropological Papers of the American Museum of Natural History, Vol. 27.
            New York.
Powell, Mayor J. W.
    1972   *The Hopi Villages.* Filter Press, Palmer Lake, Colo.
Prudden, T. Mitchell
    1896   A Summer Among Cliff Dwellings. *Harpers New Monthly Magazine,* Vol. 93, No. 556,
            pp. 545–61.
    1903   The Prehistoric Ruins of the San Juan Watershed of Utah, Arizona, Colorado, and New Mexico.
            The American Anthropologist, n.s. 5, No. 2, pp. 224–88.
Qoyawayma, Polingaysi
    1964   *No Turning Back.* University of New Mexico Press, Albuquerque.
Quam, Alvina (translator)
    1972   *The Zunis: Self-Portrayals.* University of New Mexico Press, Albuquerque.
Radlauer, Ruth S.
    1977   *Mesa Verde National Park.* Children's Press, Chicago.
Reno, Phillip
    1963   *Taos Pueblo.* Swallow Press, Chicago.
Ritzenthaler, Robert E., and Johnson, Leo
    1979   The Artistry of Sumner W. Matteson. *American Indian Art Magazine,* Vol. 5, No. 1, pp. 60–67.
Roberts, Frank H. H., Jr.
    1929   *Shabik'eshchee Village, a Late Basket Maker Site in the Chaco Canyon, New Mexico.* Smithsonian
            Institution, Bureau of American Ethnology Bulletin No. 92. Washington, D.C.
    1930   *Early Pueblo Ruins in the Piedra District, Southwestern Colorado.* Smithsonian Institution, Bureau
            of American Ethnology Bulletin No. 96. Washington, D.C.
    1931   *The Ruins at Kiatuthlanna, Eastern Arizona.* Smithsonian Institution, Bureau of American Ethnol-
            ogy Bulletin No. 100. Washington, D.C.
    1932   *The Village of the Great Kivas on the Zuñi Reservation, New Mexico.* Smithsonian Institution, Bureau
            of American Ethnology Bulletin No. 111. Washington, D.C.
    1939   *Archeological Remains in the Whitewater District, Eastern Arizona.* Smithsonian Institution, Bureau
            of American Ethnology Bulletin No. 121. Washington, D.C.
    1940   Archeological Remains in the Whitewater District, Eastern Arizona. Smithsonian Institution,
            Bureau of American Ethnology Bulletin No. 126. With appendix by T. D. Stewart, "Skeletal
            Remains from the Whitewater District, Eastern Arizona." Washington, D.C.
Roberts, John M.
    1956   *Zuni Daily Life.* Note Book No. 3, Laboratory of Anthropology, University of Nebraska, Lincoln.
Rodeck, Hugo G.
    1976   Mimbres Painted Pottery. *American Indian Art,* Autumn, pp. 44–53.

Roediger, Virginia More
1961 *Ceremonial Costumes of the Pueblo Indians.* University of California Press, Berkeley and Los Angeles.
Rohn, Arthur H.
1971 *Mug House.* Archeological Research Series No. 7-D, National Park Service, U.S. Department of the Interior, Washington, D.C.
1977 *Cultural Change and Continuity on Chapin Mesa.* Regents Press of Kansas, Lawrence.
Sanders, William T., and Marino, Joseph
1970 *New World Prehistory.* Prentice-Hall, Englewood Cliffs, N.J.
Sanders, William T., and Price, Barbara J.
1968 *Mesoamerica: The Evolution of a Civilization.* Random House, New York.
Sando, Joe S.
1976 *The Pueblo Indians.* Indian Historian Press, San Francisco.
Saunders, Charles Francis
1973 *The Indians of the Terraced Houses.* Rio Grande Press, Glorieta, N. Mex. (Originally published 1912.)
Schroeder, Albert H.
Puerco Ruin Excavations, Petrified Forest National Monument, Arizona. *Plateau,* Vol. 33, No. 4, pp. 93–104. Flagstaff, Ariz.
1975 *The Hohokam, Sinagua and the Hakataya.* Occasional Paper No. 3, I.V.C. Museum Society Publication, El Centro, Calif.
1977 *Of Men and Volcanoes.* Southwest Parks and Monuments Association, Globe, Ariz.
Schroeder, Albert H. (editor)
1973 The Changing Ways of the Southwestern Indians. Rio Grande Press, Glorieta, N. Mex.
Schultz, J. W.
Why the Moquis Perform the Snake Dance. *The Pacific Monthly,* date uncertain, pp. 161–66.
Scully, Vincent
1975 Pueblo: Mountain, Village, Dance. Viking Press, New York.
Scully, Vincent, and Current, William
1971 *Pueblo Architecture of the Southwest.* Published for the Amon Carter Museum of Western Art, Fort Worth, by the University of Texas Press, Austin & London.
Sedgwick, Mrs. William T.
1926 *Acoma, the Sky City.* Harvard University Press, Cambridge, Mass.
Sergeant, Elizabeth Shepley
1928 Crisis in Sia Pueblo. *Scribner's Magazine,* Vol. 98, July, pp. 27–32.
Seton, Julia M.
1939 *The Pulse of the Pueblo.* Seton Village Press, Santa Fe.
1962 *American Indian Arts: A Way of Life.* Ronald Press Company, New York.
Sides, Dorothy Smith
1961 *Decorative Art of the Southwestern Indians.* Dover Publications, New York. (Originally published 1936).
Simmons, Marc
1974 *Witchcraft in the Southwest.* Northland Press, Flagstaff, Ariz.
Simpson, Ruth DeEtte
1953 *The Hopi Indians.* Southwest Museum Leaflets No. 25, Southwest Museum, Los Angeles.
Smith, Anne M.
1966 *New Mexico Indians.* Museum of New Mexico, Research Records No. 1, Museum of New Mexico, Santa Fe.
Smith, Watson
1952 *Kiva Mural Decorations at Awatovi and Kawaika-a, with a Survey of Other Wall Paintings in the Pueblo Southwest.* Papers of the Peabody Museum of American Archeology and Ethnology, Vol. 37, Reports of the Awatovi Expedition, No. 5. Peabody Museum, Cambridge, Mass.
1972 *Prehistoric Kivas of Antelope Mesa.* Papers of the Peabody Museum of Archeology and Ethnology, Vol. 39, No. 1. Harvard University, Cambridge, Mass.
Smith, Watson; Woodbury, Richard B.; and Woodbury, Nathalie F. S.
1966 *The Excavation of Hawikuh by Frederick Webb Hodge, Report of the Hendricks-Hodge Expedition, 1917–1923.* Contributions from the Museum of the American Indian, Heye Foundation, New York.
Snodgrass, O. T.
1975 *Realistic Art and Times of the Mimbres Indians.* O. T. Snodgrass, El Paso.
Snow, Dean
1976 The Archaeology of North America. Thames and Hudson, London.
Spinden, Herbert Joseph (editor and translator)
1976 *Songs of the Tewa.* Sunstone Press, Santa Fe.

Stephen, Alexander M.
  1929   Hopi Tales. *The Journal of American Folk-Lore,* Vol. 42, No. 163, edited by E. C. Parsons.
  1936   *Hopi Journal of Alexander M. Stephen,* edited by Elsie Clews Parsons. Columbia University Con-
           tributions to Anthropology, Vol. 23. New York.
  1940   *Hopi Indians of Arizona.* Southwest Museum Leaflets No. 14. Southwest Museum, Los Angeles.
Stevenson, James
  1891   Ceremonial of Hasjelti Dailjis and Mythical Sand Painting of the Navaho Indians. Smithsonian
           Institution, Bureau of American Ethnology, 8th Annual Report, 1886–1887, pp. 229–85. Wash-
           ington, D.C.
Stevenson, Matilda Coxe
  1894   The Sia. Smithsonian Institution, Bureau of American Ethnology, 11th Annual Report, 1889–
           1890, pp. 3–157. Washington, D.C.
  1904   *The Zuñi Indians.* Smithsonian Institution, Bureau of American Ethnology, 23rd Annual Report,
           1901–1902. Washington, D.C.
Steward, Julian H.
  1941   Archeological Reconnaissance of Southern Utah. Smithsonian Institution, Bureau of American
           Ethnology Bulletin No. 128, Anthropological Papers No. 18, pp. 275–356. Washington, D.C.
Stirling, Matthew W.
  1935   *Origin Myth of Acoma and Other Records.* Smithsonian Institution, Bureau of American Ethnology
           Bulletin No. 135. Washington, D.C.
  1940   Indian Tribes of Pueblo Land. *National Geographic Magazine,* Vol. 78, pp. 549–96.
  1955   *Indians of the Americas.* National Geographic Society, Washington, D.C.
Stuart, George E., and Stuart, Gene S.
  1969   *Discovering Man's Past in the Americas.* National Geographic Society, Washington, D.C.
Stubbs, Stanley A.
  1950   *Bird's-Eye View of the Pueblos.* Civilization of the American Indian Series, Vol 31. University of
           Oklahoma Press, Norman.
Stubbs, Stanley, and Stallings, W. S., Jr.
  1953   *The Excavation of Pindi Pueblo, New Mexico.* Monographs of the School of American Research,
           No. 18. Laboratory of Anthropology, Santa Fe.
Supplee, Charles; Anderson, Douglas; and Anderson, Barbara
  1971   *Canyon de Chelly: The Story Behind the Scenery.* KC Publications, Las Vegas.
Swanson, John R.
  1952   *The Indian Tribes of North America.* Smithsonian Institution, Bureau of American Ethnology Bul-
           letin No. 145. Washington, D.C.
Tamarin, Alfred, and Glubok, Shirley
  1975   *Ancient Indians of the Southwest.* Doubleday & Company, Garden City, N.Y.
Tanner, Clara Lee
  1968   *Southwest Indian Craft Arts.* University of Arizona Press, Tucson.
Thompson, Laura, and Joseph, Alice
  1965   *The Hopi Way.* Russell & Russell, New York.
Titiev, Mischa
  1944   *Old Oraibi: A Study of the Hopi Indians of the Third Mesa.* Papers of the Peabody Museum of
           American Archeology and Ethnology, Vol. 22, No. 1. Harvard University, Cambridge, Mass.
  1972   *The Hopi Indians of Old Oraibi.* University of Michigan Press, Ann Arbor.
Twitchell, Ralph E.
  1911   *Leading Facts of New-Mexican History.* Torch Press, Cedar Rapids, Iowa.
Tyler, Hamilton A.
  1964   *Pueblo Gods and Myths.* University of Oklahoma Press, Norman.
Udall, Louise
  1969   *Me and Mine: The Life Story of Helen Sekaquaptewa.* University of Arizona Press, Tucson.
Underhill, Lonnie E., and Littlefield, Jr., Daniel F. (editors)
  1976   *Hamlin Garland's Observations on the American Indian, 1895–1905.* University of Arizona Press,
           Tucson.
Underhill, Ruth
  1944   *Pueblo Crafts.* U.S. Department of the Interior, Bureau of American Ethnology—Division of Ed-
           ucation. Washington, D.C.
  1946   *Work a Day Life of the Pueblos.* Indian Life and Customs, No. 4, U.S. Indian Service, Phoenix
           Indian School, Phoenix.
  1953   *Red Man's America.* University of Chicago Press, Chicago.
  1976   *First Penthouse Dwellers of America.* William Gannon, Santa Fe.

Vivian, Gordon, and Reiter, Paul
    1960   The Great Kivas of Chaco Canyon and Their Relationships. Monographs of the School of American Research and the Museum of New Mexico, No. 22. Santa Fe.

Von Hagen, Victor Wolfgang
    1950   Frederick Catherwood Arch'. Oxford University Press, New York.

Voth, H. R.
    1901   *The Oraibi Powamu Ceremony.* Publications of the Field Columbian Museum Anthropological Series, Vol. 3, No. 2, pp. 60–158.
    1903a   *The Oraibi Summer Snake Ceremony.* Publications of the Field Columbian Museum Anthropological Series, Vol. 3, No. 4, pp. 262–358.
    1903b   *The Oraibi Oaqöl Ceremony.* Field Columbian Museum Anthropological Series, Vol. 6, No. 1, Publication 84.
    1912a   *The Oraibi Marau Ceremony.* Field Museum of Natural History Anthropological Series, Vol. 11, No. 1, Publication 156.
    1912b   *Brief Miscellaneous Hopi Papers.* Field Museum of Natural History Anthropological Series, Vol. 11, No. 2, Publication 157.

Waters, Frank
    1963   *Book of the Hopi.* Viking Press, New York.
    1969   *Pumpkin Seed Point.* Sage Books, Chicago.

Watson, Don
    1961   *Indians of the Mesa Verde.* Mesa Verde Museum Association, Mesa Verde National Park, Colo.

Weaver, Muriel Porter
    1972   *The Aztecs, Maya and Their Predecessors.* Seminar Press, New York.

Weaver, Thomas (editor)
    1974   *Indians of Arizona.* University of Arizona Press, Tucson.

Webb, William, and Weinstein, Robert A.
    1973   *Dwellers at the Source: Southwestern Indian Photographs of A. C. Vroman, 1895–1904.* Grossman Publishers, New York.

Weltfish, Gene
    1932   Preliminary Classification of Prehistoric Southwestern Basketry. Smithsonian Miscellaneous Collections, Vol. 87, No. 7, pp. 1–47. Washington, D.C.

Wendorf, Fred
    1954   A Reconstruction of Northern Rio Grande Prehistory. *American Anthropologist,* Vol. 56, pp. 220–27.

Wheat, Margaret M.
    1967   *Survival Arts of the Primitive Paiutes.* University of Nevada Press. Reno.

Whitaker, Kathleen
    1974a   The Zuni Shalako Festival. *The Masterkey,* Vol. 48, No. 3, pp. 84097. Southwest Museum, Los Angeles.
    1974b   The Zuni Shalako Festival. *The Masterkey,* Vol. 48, No. 4, pp. 136–47. Southwest Museum, Los Angeles.

White, Leslie A.
    1932a   *The Pueblo of San Felipe.* Memoirs of the American Anthropological Association, No. 38.
    1932b   *The Acoma Indians, People of the Sky City.* Smithsonian Institution, Bureau of American Ethnology, Annual Report, 1929–1930.
    1935   *The Pueblo of Santo Domingo, New Mexico.* Memoirs of the American Anthropological Association, No. 43.
    1942   The Pueblo of Santa Ana, New Mexico. *American Anthropologist,* Vol. 44, No. 4, Part 2.
    1943   New Material from Acoma. Smithsonian Institution, Bureau of American Ethnology Bulletin No. 136, Anthropological Papers, No. 32, pp. 301–59. Washington, D.C.
    1974   *Zia: The Sun Symbol Pueblo.* University of Albuquerque, Calvin Horn Publishers, Albuquerque. (Reprint of 1962 Bureau of American Ethnology Report.)

Willey, Gordon R.
    1966   *An Introduction to American Archaeology: Vol. 1, North and Middle America.* Prentice-Hall, Englewood Cliffs, N.J.

Winship, George Parker
    1896   The Coronado Expedition, 1540–1542. Smithsonian Institution, Bureau of American Ethnology, 14th Annual Report, 1892–1893, pp. 339–615.

Wissler, Clark
    1921   Unearthing the Secrets of the Aztec Ruin. *Harper's Monthly Magazine,* Vol. 143, No. 853, pp. 43–56.

Wormington, H. M.
 1947   *Prehistoric Indians of the Southwest.* Denver Museum of Natural History, Popular Series, No. 7. Denver.

Wormington, H. M., and Neal, Arminta
 1978   *The Story of Pueblo Pottery.* Museum Pictorial No. 2, Denver Museum of Natural History, Denver.

Wright, Barton
 1973   *Kachinas: a Hopi Artist's Documentary.* Northland Press, Flagstaff, and Heard Museum, Phoenix.
 1975a   *Kachinas: The Barry Goldwater Collection at the Heard Museum.* W. A. Krueger Company with the Heard Museum, Phoenix.
 1975b   *The Unchanging Hopi.* Northland Press, Flagstaff, Ariz.
 1976a   *Pueblo Shields: From the Fred Harvey Fine Arts Collection.* Northland Press, Flagstaff, Ariz.
 1976b   Anasazi Murals. *American Indian Art Magazine,* Vol. 1, No. 2.
 1977   *Hopi Kachinas.* Northland Press, Flagstaff, Ariz.
 1979   *Hopi Material Culture: Artifacts Gathered by H. R. Voth in the Fred Harvey Collection.* Northland Press, Flagstaff, Ariz., and Heard Museum, Phoenix.

Wright, Barton, and Roat, Evelyn
 1962   *This Is a Hopi Kachina.* Museum of Northern Arizona, North Arizona Society of Science and Art, Flagstaff.

Wright, Margaret
 1972   *Hopi Silver.* Northland Press, Flagstaff, Ariz.

Yandell, Michael D. (editor)
 1972   *Rocky Mountain and Mesa Verde National Parks.* National Parkways, Vol. 3/4. World-Wide Research and Publishing Co., Casper, Wyo.

Yava, Albert
 1978   *Big Falling Snow.* Edited by Harold Courlander. Crown Publishers, New York.

Zubrow, Ezra B. W.; Fritz, Margaret C.; and Fritz, John M. (compilers)
 1974   *New World Archaeology. Readings from Scientific American.* W. H. Freeman and Company, San Francisco.

INDEX